# Salafī Political Theology



Salafism is a theological movement whose radical wing is today affiliated with al-Qāʿida and the Islamic State, but which draws on precedents stretching back to the medieval theology of Ibn Taymiyya. This innovative study focuses on the concept of theonomy in salafī thought: the tenet that rule by God's law is an essential component of faith, and the corresponding notion that other forms of rule based on human legislation are inherently polytheistic and thereby illegitimate. It is this tenet which furnishes radical militants with their principal casus belli against ruling regimes in the Muslim world.

In this book, Daniel Lav details the intellectual grounding for modern salafī theonomy in Ibn Taymiyya's doctrine of *tawḥīd* and the writings of the early Wahhābī movement, in addition to the twentieth-century thought of Abū al-Aʿlā Mawdūdī and Sayyid Quṭb, while drawing on insights from comparative political theology to analyze this key school of thought.

Daniel Lav is a lecturer in the Department of Arabic Language and Literature at the Hebrew University of Jerusalem. His research focuses on Islamic theology, with a particular emphasis on the salafī tradition of Sunnī Islam. *Salafī Political Theology* continues the exploration of salafī intellectual history begun in his previous book, *Radical Islam and the Revival of Medieval Theology* (Cambridge, 2012).

# Salafī Political Theology

Daniel Lav
*Hebrew University of Jerusalem*

CAMBRIDGE
UNIVERSITY PRESS

CAMBRIDGE
UNIVERSITY PRESS

Shaftesbury Road, Cambridge CB2 8EA, United Kingdom

One Liberty Plaza, 20th Floor, New York, NY 10006, USA

477 Williamstown Road, Port Melbourne, VIC 3207, Australia

314–321, 3rd Floor, Plot 3, Splendor Forum, Jasola District Centre, New Delhi – 110025, India

103 Penang Road, #05-06/07, Visioncrest Commercial, Singapore 238467

Cambridge University Press is part of Cambridge University Press & Assessment, a department of the University of Cambridge.

We share the University's mission to contribute to society through the pursuit of education, learning and research at the highest international levels of excellence.

www.cambridge.org
Information on this title: www.cambridge.org/9781108495585

DOI: 10.1017/9781108850407



When citing this work, please include a reference to the DOI 10.1017/9781108850407

First published 2025

Cover image: Chronology of Ancient Nations, Or.Ms.161 f.88v, Heritage Collections, University of Edinburgh.

*A catalogue record for this publication is available from the British Library*

*A Cataloging-in-Publication data record for this book is available from the Library of Congress.*

ISBN 978-1-108-49558-5 Hardback
ISBN 978-1-108-81749-3 Paperback

# Contents


| | | |
|---|---|---|
| | *Preface* | *page* vii |
| | *Acknowledgments* | ix |
| | *Note on Transliteration* | xi |
| | Introduction | 1 |
| 1 | Monolatry in Ibn Taymiyya's Theological System | 38 |
| 2 | Monolatry in Eighteenth-Century Revivalism | 95 |
| 3 | Theonomy in Premodern Salafī Jurisprudence | 126 |
| 4 | Mawdūdī and Quṭb: The Theonomic Shift | 164 |
| 5 | Salafī Jihādī Theonomy | 240 |
| | Conclusion | 318 |
| | *Glossary* | 327 |
| | *Bibliography* | 331 |
| | *Index* | 350 |

# Preface

This is a book on the one and the many: the one God and His creation, the one sovereign and his many subjects. It is thus appropriate that the book itself be one and many.

The study began as an investigation into a characteristic doctrine of modern salafism – one especially associated with its radical wing, the salafī jihādīs – that classes human legal-political autonomy as a form of polytheism. That investigation remains the organizing axis of the book but it begot a number of preliminary investigations, both in Islamic intellectual history and others of a theoretical nature, that proved necessary in order to elucidate the doctrine in proper fashion. The modern salafī doctrine itself is treated in Chapter 5, whereas the preliminary studies leading thereto are treated in the Introduction and the first four chapters. The explanation for this structure is as follows.

It has often been thought that the aforementioned doctrine, for which I employ the term 'theonomy,' derives primarily from two twentieth-century authors whose oeuvre is usually characterized as Islamist political theory rather than theology: the Egyptian Sayyid Quṭb (d. 1966) and the Indo-Pakistani Abū al-Aʿlā Mawdūdī (d. 1979). This characterization is not truly apt even for these two figures, but it certainly misses the mark regarding the salafī doctrine of theonomy: It is *not* primarily a political one, at least as the term 'political' is commonly understood. In fact, how one delineates the relation between the theological and the political is precisely what is at stake.

For this reason the book engages its topic through the lens of comparative political theology as a complement to the main body of the research, which would be described best as Islamic intellectual history written in a traditional, philological vein. While Mawdūdī and Quṭb were historically significant to the emergence of the doctrine in the salafī milieu, the political theology of today's salafīs rests primarily on concepts drawn rather from premodern salafī theology and jurisprudential theory. The book therefore treats the relevant salafī tradition in detail, both in its premodern articulations and as reformulated in response to salient features of modernity such as secularization, democracy, and the nation-state. Special attention has been devoted to the theology of Ibn Taymiyya (d. 728/1328), the principal forefather of modern salafism, whose writings remain the touchstone of salafī orthodoxy to this day.

The result is a work that traces a long arc. While its original aim is to explore modern salafī doctrine I have approached each piece of the puzzle as a study unto itself. The book thus comprises an analysis of Ibn Taymiyya's theological system from a typological perspective; a reexamination of the relation between Ibn Taymiyya's theology and the early Wahhābī movement; a study of scriptural authority versus school authority in premodern Islamic jurisprudence; a fresh evaluation of Mawdūdī and Quṭb; and, finally, an investigation of modern salafī doctrine in relation to all the preceding.

This book is obviously not the final word on salafī political theology, nor should it be. It is an attempt to bring the topic into relief and address it in a systematic manner. Whatever benefit may be derived from the book's substantive conclusions, above all I have sought to chart a path toward thinking more profoundly about the salafī tradition and its significance. The technical analyses will be of interest primarily to scholars and students of Islamic studies, but the work as a whole, and especially the Introduction and the Conclusion, addresses a wider readership, as is appropriate to a topic that in recent years has become one of general import.

# Acknowledgments

Many have helped and supported me throughout the years since I first began this project as my doctoral dissertation at the Hebrew University of Jerusalem. First and foremost, I would like to thank my two thesis advisors, Professors Ella Landau-Tasseron and Yohanan Friedmann, both of whom are exceptional scholars, teachers, and human beings. Jan-Peter Hartung and Justyna Nedza have always lent their friendship and encouragement and shared with me valuable sources from South Asia, for which I am grateful. A number of colleagues and friends read and offered feedback on the manuscript or portions of it at various stages of the writing, alongside anonymous reviewers both for Cambridge University Press and in various other contexts, to all of whom I offer my heartful thanks. My editor at CUP, Maria Marsh, has been gracious and patient in seeing this project through to its successful conclusion, and Muhammad Ridwaan's superb copyediting has greatly improved the final text.

My doctoral research was made possible thanks to the Hebrew University of Jerusalem's President Scholarship and the Nathan Rotenstreich Scholarship. Precious time for further research and revisions was afforded me by two postdoctoral fellowships: the Yad HaNadiv Rothschild Fellowship, allowing me to spend a year at the Institute for the Transregional Study of the Contemporary Middle East, North Africa, and Central Asia at Princeton University, with special thanks due to Professor Bernard Haykel and to Joyce Slack, as well as the Department of Near Eastern Studies, its faculty, and its students who made me feel at home; and the second at the Mandel Scholion Research Center on Mount Scopus in Jerusalem, with special thanks to its academic director at the time, Professor Daniel R. Schwartz of the Department of Jewish History and Contemporary Jewry at the Hebrew University, Executive Director Keren Sagi, and of course to the Mandel family for their generosity. I owe thanks as well to the family of Bernard M. Bloomfield for their recognition and support.

Cole Bunzel has been a valuable discussion partner over the years on all matters Taymiyyan, Wahhābī, and salafī, and I have learned much as well from my conversations with Aaron Rock-Singer. Michael Ebstein is a constant friend who has enriched my thinking on Islamic theology, Ṣūfism, and mysticism, and I have benefited greatly from the expertise of my other colleagues in the Department of Arabic Language and Literature at the Hebrew University of Jerusalem, and those in the Department of Islamic and Middle Eastern Studies, where I completed my MA as well as the doctoral dissertation that led to this book.

I might never have finished my dissertation were it not for the refuge I found at Halitatea, a truly fine tea house that operated at the time on Hillel Street in Jerusalem; warm thanks to Gabriel Piamenta, Bar, Adam, Maya, Michal, and all the others.

To my parents, Michael and Iris, I owe a debt of gratitude that is beyond statement.

Any errors in the book are of course mine alone.

# Note on Transliteration

This book follows the system of transliteration of the *International Journal of Middle East Studies* for Arabic. Place names that are commonly anglicized have been given in their English forms (e.g. Medina). For the sake of consistency throughout the chapters, I have retained the Arabic transliteration conventions for Urdu letters that exist in the Arabic alphabet without regard to differences in pronunciation (thus ض = ḍ, not ẓ). The additional Urdu vowels have been written as e, o, ē, and ō. Urdu consonants not found in Arabic are transliterated as follows: پ = p, ٹ = ṫ, چ = ch, ڈ = ḋ, ڑ = ṙ, گ = g, ں = ṉ. Aspirated consonants (written with ھ in the Urdu alphabet) are noted by a superscript $^{h}$ (e.g. $b^{h}$ī), and the و following خ in words such as خود is written as a superscript $^{w}$ ($kh^{w}$ud).

# Introduction

## Theonomy and Monolatry

In August 2011 Libyan rebels overran Tripoli and deposed the Qadhdhāfī regime. Shortly thereafter a pseudonymous radical salafī scholar, Abū Hammām Bakr b. ʿAbd al-ʿAzīz al-Atharī, penned an epistle to the rebels urging them not to lay down their arms until they had established rule by the *sharīʿa*. The Libyan rebels were an eclectic mix: military defectors, tribal forces, returned exiles, and Islamists and salafīs of varying persuasions, including leaders of the Libyan Islamic Fighting Group. In the past these latter had been allied with al-Qāʿida and had shared a worldview close to the one held by Abū Hammām, but in the years preceding the Arab Spring, while languishing in Libya's prisons, they had broken with al-Qāʿida and moderated their positions.[1]

Abū Hammām warned the victorious rebels not to behave like the ancient Israelites who, after Allāh had delivered them from Egypt, asked Moses to fashion a god for them to worship, as related in the Qurʾānic narrative of the golden calf episode (7:138): "We brought Banī Isrāʾīl across the sea, and they came upon people devotedly worshipping gods they had. They said: Mūsā, make for us a god like the gods they have." In Abū Hammām's view, to establish democracy in Libya after deliverance from the previous regime would constitute a similar transgression: "Allāh saved those people [viz. the Israelites] from Firʿawn [Pharaoh], and Allāh saved these people [viz. the Libyans] from the mad Muʿammar [al-Qadhdhāfī]. Those people said after the victory: Make for us gods like they have, and these people – I mean the wicked [among them] – said: Make for us a democracy like they have!"[2] At the time he wrote these words Abū Hammām was influential but his identity unknown; we now know that he was the Bahraini scholar Turkī al-Binʿalī, who subsequently

[1] See al-Jamāʿa al-Lībiyya al-Muqātila, *Dirāsāt taṣḥīḥiyya fī mafāhīm al-jihād wa-l-ḥisba wa-l-ḥukm ʿalā al-nās*, n.p., 2010.

[2] Abū Hammām Bakr b. ʿAbd al-ʿAzīz al-Atharī, *Yā ahl al-falāḥ a-wa-qad waḍaʿtum al-silāḥ?*, 1432/2011, p. 2, www.ilmway.com/site/maqdis/MS_12156 (link no longer active).

went on to serve as the principal religious authority for the Islamic State (IS or ISIS).[3]

Later that same year the senior al-Qāʿida commander Abū Yaḥyā al-Lībī, himself a Libyan, issued a similar appeal to his countrymen. By this time the overthrow of the regime was complete, Muʿammar al-Qadhdhāfī was dead, and his son and presumptive heir Sayf al-Islām under arrest. Among the measures adopted toward instituting a new regime had been the promulgation of a draft constitution. In response to these developments Abū Yaḥyā said in a video address:

My brothers in Libya and elsewhere, we must know with certitude that our paramount issue, and the greatest of the calamities in whose hell we have been burning and over whose flame we have been turning for many long decades, does not relate [solely] to the individual persons of al-Qadhdhāfī, [Ḥusnī] Mubārak, or Zayn al-ʿĀbidīn [bin ʿAlī], or any other of the mainstays of tyranny and the pillars of Pharaohism (*al-farʿana*). Rather the chronic illness that has afflicted us lies in the criminal regimes of unbelief that these criminals imposed on our peoples, and their detaching our peoples from the rule of their Lord …

These criminal Pharaohs established injustice in place of justice and brute severity and ignominy in place of mercy, compassion, and honor. They spread corruption and enabled the corrupters, and prevented rectification and drove out the rectifiers. They imposed the laws of wayward inclinations (*sharāʾiʿ al-ahwāʾ*)[4] and drove away the law of the Lord of the earth and the heavens. They uprooted religion and obligated people to their accursed man-made law …

They dealt with the Islamic nation in the manner of the *jāhiliyya*[5] and imposed on them their man-made constitutions, which call for attributing partners to Allāh, which is absolutely the greatest sin of all. And if they granted their Lord a bit of

[3] On Turkī al-Binʿalī, see Abū Hammām Bakr b. ʿAbd al-ʿAzīz al-Atharī, *Mā al-tarjama al-ʿilmiyya li-l-shaykh Abī Hammām Bakr b. ʿAbd al-ʿAzīz al-Atharī ḥafiẓahu Allāh?*, 1432/2011, www.ilmway.com/site/maqdis/FAQ/MS_35123.html (link no longer active); Abū Usāma al-Gharīb, *al-Mukhtaṣar al-jalī bi-sīrat shaykhinā Turkī al-Binʿalī*, n.d., https://archive.org/details/almokhtasar.algali.high; Cole Bunzel, "From Paper State to Caliphate: The Ideology of the Islamic State," The Brookings Project on U.S. Relations with the Islamic World, 2015, p. 11, https://shorturl.at/HA4Uv. Al-Binʿalī was subsequently killed in a 2017 airstrike in Syria.

[4] No single English word accurately translates the range of meanings of the Arabic *hawan* (def. *hawā*, pl. *ahwāʾ*). Etymologically its basic meaning is love or attachment; in the Qurʾān it is invariably used in a pejorative sense to designate an inclination of the soul that stands in opposition to divine revelation, truth, and guidance (e.g. 53:3, 28:50, 5:77, 2:145, 13:37, 23:71, 28:50, 42:15, 47:14, 47:16, 54:3), sometimes with specific reference to matters of law, judgment, and prohibition (38:26, 6:150, 45:18, 5:48–49, 6:119). The Qurʾān even speaks of "one who takes his *hawā* as his god (*ilāh*)" (25:43, 45:23). By extension the term came to be used for heretical sects, as for example in the title of Ibn Ḥazm's heresiography *al-Faṣl fī al-milal wa-l-ahwāʾ wa-l-niḥal*.

[5] *Jāhiliyya* is the traditional term for the pre-Islamic age before Muḥammad's prophecy. The latter-day recurrence of a state of *jāhiliyya* is a common theme in the salafī tradition and in twentieth-century Islamism, as will be seen in what follows.

favor and left Him some of the religion, this was [only] in the manner of their heathen forerunners (*aslāfihim al-jāhiliyyīn*), [as Allāh described them]: "Of the crops and livestock that Allāh produced they give a portion to Allāh and say: 'this is for Allāh' – so they claim – 'and this (other portion) is for the partners' (they made for Him). What they give the partners does not reach Allāh, and what they give to Allāh reaches the partners they made for Him. In an evil manner do they judge (*sāʾa mā yaḥkumūna*)" (Qurān 6:136).

Thus you find that their constitutions – including the Libyan Interim Constitutional Declaration – stipulate that the Islamic *sharīʿa* is the principal source of legislation,[6] in exact conformity with the people of the first *jāhiliyya* who used to circumambulate the Kaʿba and pronounce the ritual acclamation: "We are at Your service, O Allāh, at Your service. We are at Your service, You have no partner, except the partner that You have. He and what is his are Yours!" They haughtily disdain to make the Islamic *sharīʿa* the sole source that invalidates all the regimes and laws that contradict it, whatever their source may be – as though the *sharīʿa* of Islam is defective and in need of completion! [Whereas] Allāh the Exalted said: "Today I have completed for you your religion, bestowed on you My full grace, and am satisfied with Islam as your religion" (Qurān 5:3).[7]

Abū Yaḥyā al-Lībī's speech touches on many themes that are central to classical Islamic political discourse: The dyads justice/injustice (*ʿadl*/*ẓulm*) and corruption/rectification (*fasād*/*iṣlāḥ*) are among the oldest in the Islamic political lexicon. Yet in addition to such common themes we also find condensed in this passage the central elements that distinguish the salafī jihādī doctrine of al-Qāʿida and the Islamic State from the broader popular currents that animated the Arab Spring.

First and foremost among these elements is the association of man-made law with polytheism. This concept distinguishes the salafī jihādīs not only from secularists and modernists but from today's Muslim Brotherhood as well, since the latter, notwithstanding its desire to Islamize society, does not hold to such a rigorous theological condemnation of human legislation and constitutions.[8] While all the participants in the uprisings against al-Qadhdhāfī, Mubārak, and Bin ʿAlī viewed their

[6] Cf. al-Majlis al-Waṭanī al-Intiqālī al-Muʾaqqat – Lībiyā, *al-Iʿlān al-dustūrī*, 3 Ramaḍān 1432 / August 3, 2011, www.wipo.int/edocs/lexdocs/laws/ar/ly/ly005ar.pdf, Article 1, p. 3.

[7] Abū Yaḥyā al-Lībī, *Lībiyā mādhā yurādu lahā?*, 2 Dhū al-Ḥijja 1432 [= October 29, 2011] (released December 5, 2011), www.shamikh1.info/vb/showthread.php?t=138186 (link no longer active).

[8] For a good example of this difference, see the radical scholar Abū al-Mundhir al-Shinqīṭī's characterization of the Egyptian constitutional crisis of late 2012, which pitted the Muslim Brotherhood-affiliated President Muḥammad Mursī against the opposition, as "a dispute between a secularist and [other] secularists over infidel laws": Abū al-Mundhir al-Shinqīṭī, *Hal yushraʿu taʾyīd Mursī fī al-qarārāt al-dustūriyya al-akhīra?*, December 3, 2012, www.ilmway.com/site/maqdis/FAQ/MS_7206.html (link no longer active).

regimes as oppressive, al-Qāʿida and other salafī jihādīs viewed them as infidel and polytheist, and subsumed all other grievances under this rubric. As Abū Yaḥyā al-Lībī explains, the problem with these regimes did not stem from the individual at their head; it was systemic, in that these forms of government arrogate Allāh's rights to humans.

To clarify this point let us focus briefly on the last portion of the above-cited passage: the comparison between modern constitutions in Muslim countries and the pre-Islamic ritual acclamation (*talbiya*). The specific *talbiya* mentioned by Abū Yaḥyā is the best known of these acclamations and is reputed to have been that of the Prophet Muḥammad's tribe, Quraysh (or of the larger Ḥums confederation in which Quraysh was a member).[9] As with other pre-Islamic *talbiyāt* pronounced during the pilgrimage its primary message was the declaration of Allāh's supremacy over the other gods worshipped alongside Him: "The Jāhiliyya tribes cannot be said to have been straightforward polytheists; they were *mushrikūn*, i.e., while accepting and admitting the existence and supreme authority of God, they associated other deities with Him."[10]

The religion of the Qurʾān broke precisely from such a high-God religion and viewed the purported monotheistic aspects of *jāhilī* religion as polytheistic in substance. The Prophet Muḥammad castigated the Arabs of the *jāhiliyya* as *mushrikūn* precisely because Allāh must be acknowledged not as the principal or supreme deity, but as the sole deity. Indeed, this concept of "to give oneself *exclusively* to God" appears to be the original meaning of the name of the new religion itself, "Islām."[11]

This dimension of Qurʾānic polemic was explored by Gerald Hawting in his *Idea of Idolatry and the Emergence of Islam*, who argued on this basis that Islam did not arise at all in polemic against Arabian polytheists but rather in a period later than the traditional dating, in a Near Eastern monotheist milieu; by this view, Islam "was concerned ... with other monotheists whose monotheism it saw as inadequate and attacked polemically as the equivalent of idolatry."[12]

9 M. J. Kister, "Labbayka, Allāhumma, Labbayka ... On a Monotheistic Aspect of a Jāhiliyya Practice," *Jerusalem Studies in Arabic and Islam* 2 (1980), pp. 33–57, at p. 36.

10 Kister, "Labbayka," p. 48. We need not be concerned here with what "straightforward polytheism" might be, though one could certainly provide examples of religions from regions other than the Near East in which there is no one high god.

11 D. Z. H. Baneth, "What Did Muḥammad Mean When He Called His Religion 'Islam'? The Original Meaning of Aslama and Its Derivatives," *Israel Oriental Studies* 1 (1971), pp. 183–190.

12 G. R. Hawting, *The Idea of Idolatry and the Emergence of Islam*, Cambridge: Cambridge University Press, 1999, p. xiii. Hawting's work builds on the earlier research of John Wansbrough; see especially *The Sectarian Milieu: Content and Composition of Islamic Salvation History*, Oxford: Oxford University Press, 1978.

Since the publication of Hawting's work further research has confirmed the traditional dating for the Qurʾān, but for our purposes it matters little whether the polemic was directed against Arabian religion in the seventh century or against rival monotheistic traditions in the eighth or ninth centuries. The point is the following: Because the Qurʾān and the *ḥadīth* waged a polemic against people (the *mushrikūn*) who themselves acknowledged the supremacy but not the exclusivity of Allāh, these sources contain ample material that could be mined by later exclusivist-minded thinkers or movements in order to castigate other self-identified Muslims as polytheists. As Hawting notes, Muḥammad b. ʿAbd al-Wahhāb, the founder of the Wahhābī movement, was able to utilize this Qurʾānic material "without any sense of strain" in support of his campaign against the Muslim cult of saints in eighteenth-century Arabia.[13]

One way to think about this exclusivist form of monotheism is what Jan Assmann has termed the "Mosaic distinction," defined as "the idea of an exclusive and emphatic Truth that sets God apart from everything that is not God and therefore must not be worshiped, and that sets religion apart from what comes to be shunned as superstition, paganism, or heresy. This idea finds its clearest expression not in the phrase 'God is one!' but [in the phrase] 'no other gods!'"[14] Presently we will define more precisely the nature of the salafī version of exclusivist monotheism promoted by Abū Yaḥyā and al-Binʿalī, but Assmann's proposal provides a good starting point. We might say that it is an Islamic variant of this 'Mosaic distinction' that Abū Yaḥyā extends to the legal-political arena: To proclaim Allāh's law, the *sharīʿa*, as the "*principal* source of legislation" is precisely to acknowledge that there exist additional legitimate sources of legislation – and this, in his view, is tantamount to acknowledging other gods.

In this study I term the doctrine underlying such applications of exclusivist monotheism to the legal-political sphere 'theonomy' (Greek: *theo*, God + *nomos*, law).[15] It is one of the principal tenets of

[13] Hawting, *Idea*, p. 64. "Sense of strain" is of course a subjective measure and this application was controversial (see Chapter 2), but it was plausible and convincing in the eyes of many.

[14] Jan Assmann, *Of God and Gods: Egypt, Israel, and the Rise of Monotheism*, Madison: University of Wisconsin Press, 2008, p. 3. While Assmann based this concept on Biblical religion and not on Arabic-Islamic sources, his characterization is remarkably apt for the Qurʾān as well. "Everything that is not God" corresponds to the Arabic *ghayr Allāh* (cf. Qurʾān 2:173, 4:82, 5:3, 6:14, 6:40, 6:46, 6:114, 6:145, 6:164, 7:140, 16:52, 16:115, 28:71–72, 35:3, 39:64, 52:43), and "no other gods" are the first words of the Muslim profession of faith, *lā ilāha*, which likewise have a Qurʾānic basis (e.g. 2:255, 3:2, 9:31, 20:14).

[15] I initially borrowed this terminology from the contemporary Christian Reconstructionist movement, which presents interesting parallels with modern salafism; see e.g. Greg L. Bahnsen, *Theonomy in Christian Ethics*, Nutley: The Craig Press, 1977. For the history of the term and a broad exploration of the concept, see Rémi Brague, *The Law*

contemporary radical salafism and is shared to varying degrees by more moderate salafī currents as well. This doctrine of theonomy should be understood as advancing two interrelated claims: (1) the institution of rule by God's law is a sine qua non of faith; and (2) other legal-political systems, and democracy in particular, are inherently polytheistic.

This book aims to trace the origins and development of modern salafī theonomic doctrine, and in particular to examine its bases in premodern salafī theology.

Modern salafīs are heir to a minoritarian Sunnī Muslim tradition that encompasses a number of tendencies and schools, primary among them the early *ahl al-ḥadīth* (the 'people of the *ḥadīth*,' often termed 'Traditionalists' in research literature) and Ḥanbalīs, the medieval Syrian scholar Taqī al-Dīn Aḥmad Ibn Taymiyya (d. 728/1328) and his circle, and the Wahhābīs. When not referring to a particular historical school my default term for this tradition will be *salafī* in keeping with current Arabic usage, despite this being something of an anachronism.[16] The assertion of filiation and continuity among the various thinkers and movements associated with this tradition is not uncontroversial and has more often been assumed than proven;[17] that a high degree of continuity

*of God: The Philosophical History of an Idea*, trans. Lydia G. Cochrane, Chicago and London: The University of Chicago Press, 2007, p. viii, n. 2, inter alia.

16 Cf. Henri Lauzière, "The Construction of *Salafiyya*: Reconsidering Salafism from the Perspective of Conceptual History," *International Journal of Middle East Studies* 42 (2010), pp. 369–389.

17 Goldziher speaks of minority schools throughout the history of Islam that resisted the accommodation of new ideas: "In the internal history of Islamic movements we witness a continual struggle of *sunna* against *bid'a*, of intransigent traditionalism against the steady extension of the borders of tradition and the breaching of its original limits. This conflict persisted throughout the history of Islam, in both its dogmatic and legal development." Ignaz Goldziher, *Introduction to Islamic Theology and Law*, trans. Andras and Ruth Hamori, Princeton: Princeton University Press, 1981, pp. 236–237. This remark serves as a prelude to Goldziher's discussion of the Ḥanbalīs, Ibn Taymiyya, and the Wahhābīs (pp. 237ff.), among whom he sees a clear filiation: "In their literary struggles against the Meccan orthodoxy – which have not halted to this day – the Wahhābīs advance against Ghazālī the doctrines of the man whom the ruling theology rejected: Ibn Taymīya" (p. 245). More recently Michael Cook has likewise underlined the Wahhābīs' debt to Ibn Taymiyya, but noted that the precise relation requires further study: "On the Origins of Wahhābism," *Journal of the Royal Asiatic Society*, Third Series 2:2 (July 1992), pp. 191–202.

For a view that calls into question the integrality of this counter-tradition in Islam, see Aziz Al-Azmeh, "Orthodoxy and Ḥanbalite Fideism," *Arabica* 35/3 (1988), pp. 253–266; Al-Azmeh argues that the Ḥanbalīs' strict conception of dogma is minimalist and has fundamentally liberal implications, and he stresses commonalities between Ḥanbalism and classical Ash'arism. Ovamir Anjum has argued that pro-democracy reformers in the orbit of the Muslim Brotherhood may understand Ibn Taymiyya better than do today's salafīs; this contention stems primarily from his reading of Ibn Taymiyya himself, which differs significantly from my own: Ovamir

does characterize them across a broad chronological scope, to the point they may be considered a single counter-tradition within Sunnī Islam, is one of the principal claims of the present book, to be substantiated in the following chapters through analysis of key terms, formulas, concepts, and arguments that are common to the tradition on the whole – with the caveat that Ibn Taymiyya differs in significant ways from the earlier tradition, and what we know today as salafī theology (as opposed to law and legal theory) derives primarily from him.

Modern salafīs draw on the resources of this premodern salafī tradition in order to contest central features of modernity. By necessity this study thus addresses, alongside the relation between the premodern and modern salafī traditions, the question of the nature of modernity itself. Theonomy is a form of heteronomy, "receiving one's law from another," and stands in opposition to autonomy, "giving oneself one's law." This opposition is a central one to the modern project, as Rémi Brague has observed:

> These opposed terms, which Kant placed at the center of moral reflection, have come to define a project: autonomy defines the ideal to be realized in an ever more radical manner; heteronomy designates the enemy that must be eliminated. In fact, the modern world, in the morality that it claims and that is its foundation, flatters itself that it has sent packing everything tainted with heteronomy, and it is pleased to understand itself as constructed on the idea of autonomy.[18]

Hence what Brague observed in his own investigation holds true here as well: Our study of modern salafī theonomy is ipso facto a study that addresses modernity, although it does so through the lens of the salafī critique and not as an independent philosophical investigation. The radical salafīs' conception of theonomy responds explicitly to the modern valorization of autonomy and does so on the basis of cultural resources from the premodern tradition.

Now let us specify further what is distinctive about salafī exclusivist monotheism, premodern and modern. For this tradition the crux of what Assmann termed the 'Mosaic distinction' is not in fact the distinction

Anjum, "Salafis and Democracy: Doctrine and Context," *The Muslim World* 106/3 (July 2016), pp. 448–473; for his characterization of the core of the Taymiyyan corpus, see p. 454; cf. Ovamir Anjum, *Politics, Law, and Community in Islamic Thought: The Taymiyyan Moment*, Cambridge: Cambridge University Press, 2014. Natana J. DeLong-Bas, in *Wahhabi Islam: From Revival and Reform to Global Jihad*, Oxford: Oxford University Press, 2004, denies the existence of any particular filiation between Ibn Taymiyya and Muḥammad b. ʿAbd al-Wahhāb; see esp. p. 53, where Ibn Taymiyya is characterized as "at most a negligible source of inspiration." This claim is erroneous. The precise relationship between Ibn Taymiyya and Ibn ʿAbd al-Wahhāb is clarified in Chapter 2.

18 Brague, *The Law of God*, p. viii.

between truth and falsehood, but rather the duty of exclusive worship and obedience to one God, and the prohibition of worship and obedience to others.[19] I will use the term 'monolatry' (Greek: *monos*, sole + *latreia*, worship) both for the practice of exclusive worship of one divinity and for the form of religion that centers it as its main feature.

It is worth pausing a moment to consider the difference between the truth-falsehood distinction and the principle of monolatry. The former is a cognitive distinction: As applied to monotheism it is a propositional attitude regarding the existence of one divinity, the nonexistence of others, attributes of the divinity, and so forth. In short, it is the domain of what we typically consider to be theology. Monolatry, in contrast, is not a cognitive position but rather a conative stance, not a propositional attitude but the directing of one's intentional and affective life to its proper object, the proper divinity.[20] It is perhaps not by chance that Aristotle mentions prayer as his sole example of non-apophantic language: "There is not truth or falsity in all sentences; a prayer is a sentence but is neither true nor false."[21]

These terms now defined we may restate the fundamental aim of this book in precise terms: It seeks to elucidate the relation between modern salafī theonomy and premodern salafī monolatry.

The book's structure follows from this aim. I first identify those medieval doctrines that have served as a basis for modern salafī theonomy; these I describe and analyze on their own terms and in their original discursive contexts. I then examine the modes by which these doctrines were perpetuated or revived up to the cusp of the modern period and subsequently reformulated in the modern period itself as theonomic doctrine proper. The book thus deals with two main issues: first, the character of the medieval salafī monolatric tradition, and second, the reasons for and manner of its modern theonomic reformulation.

In the remainder of this Introduction I will present the concept of monolatry within a broad theoretical framework. This is necessary for the

[19] In a subsequent revision to his thesis Assmann came to emphasize this facet of ancient Israelite religion as well: Jan Assmann, "Autour de l'Exode: monothéisme, difference et violence," *Revue de l'histoire des religions* 231/1 (2014), pp. 5–26.

[20] Much investigation of this topic in the field of Jewish studies was inspired by Martin Buber, *Two Types of Faith*, trans. Norman P. Goldhawk, New York, Macmillan, 1951. See e.g. Kenneth Seeskin, "Judaism and the Linguistic Interpretation of Faith," *Studies in Jewish Philosophy* 3 (1983), pp. 71–81, who distinguishes between 'faith that' and 'faith in.' The elaboration most appropriate to this book's subject matter is that of the scholar of Hellenistic Judaism Yehoshua Amir; see below.

[21] Aristotle, *Categories and De Interpretatione*, trans. J. L. Ackrill, Oxford: Clarendon Press, 1963, pp. 45–46; cf. Werner Hamacher, *Minima Philologica*, trans. Catharine Diehl and Jason Groves, New York: Fordham University Press, 2015, p. 10.

following reason: The principle of monolatry is easy to state, but in the twenty-first century its import can be difficult to grasp. This book will argue that monolatry is the central axis of salafī theology, in its original formulation in Ibn Taymiyya's writings, in the early Wahhābī movement, and among salafīs today (including and especially in its theonomic elaboration). In order to grasp the significance of this observation we need to address the topic of monolatry itself and its place in the Abrahamic religions, which I do in what follows at some length. I ask the patience of readers whose primary interest is specifically Islamic intellectual history; should they skip this portion of the Introduction they will still find much of value in the following chapters, but at some detriment to the book's general argument.

Following this discussion the Introduction will conclude with a brief overview of the contents of the following chapters and a few notes on method.

## Abrahamic Archetypes: Philosophy and Revelation, Monotheism and Monolatry

Moshe Halbertal and Avishai Margalit open their book *Idolatry* with an important insight: "different concepts of God create, when reversed, different concepts of idolatry."[22] When we wish to understand why modern salafīs conceive of human sovereignty and rule by man-made law – i.e. human autonomy – as idolatrous, we are really asking what their concept of God is, and what that concept says about the relation between the divine and human orders.

It is only natural that an investigation of this kind engage with the field of political theology, which in its broadest acceptation is the study of the manner in which conceptions of the supernatural function as a structuring element of human society. The naïve vantage point of our secular age is to assume the inherent distinctness of the religious and the political, in the sense that however the two may interact, this remains an interaction between recognizably separate spheres. By 'naïve' I mean nothing derogatory – every society has a right to its basic assumptions – but when these find their way into academic treatments of radical salafism, which explicitly contests them, the result is all too often an uncritical use of terms like 'religious' and 'political' in a manner inconsistent with the salafīs' own worldview and thus a misrepresentation of the nature of their project. The field of political theology offers explicit theoreticization of

22 Moshe Halbertal and Avishai Margalit, *Idolatry*, Cambridge, MA, and London: Harvard University Press, 1992, p. 1.

this problematic, beneficial both in itself and as a safeguard against errant presuppositions.

The point of departure for what follows is more specifically Axial theory, which overlaps with political theology as commonly understood but is not identical to it. The medieval Islamic tradition, like the Jewish and Christian ones, stood at the confluence of two originally distinct patrimonies: the monolatric heritage of the Ancient Near East (ANE), and the Greek philosophical heritage. Typologically speaking the premodern salafī heritage, and Ibn Taymiyya in particular, explicitly disaggregates the two and champions an Islamic form of monolatry. The following presentation of Axial theory is meant to provide an overarching framework within which the two patrimonies can be compared and contrasted in coherent fashion, and which will yield criteria helpful for the interpretation of Ibn Taymiyya's theological system and of salafī faith and theology on the whole.

Axial theory is a term for various lines of inquiry inaugurated or inspired by the twentieth-century German philosopher Karl Jaspers.[23] In an influential thesis Jaspers described the contemporaneous but independent formulations of a conception of transcendence in different societies in the mid-first millennium BCE as a civilization-altering development that he termed the 'Axial Age' (*Achsenzeit*).[24] Transcendence is a concept we cannot do without in a study such as ours: Theonomy, as a form of heteronomy, rests on a certain configuration of divine-human difference. This configuration stands alongside rival ones, and thus we need to make sense of the issue of transcendence on the whole, and the origins and nature of its contestation in the Islamic tradition.

Jaspers' original Axial thesis was embedded in a philosophical project: His treatment of the posited Axial Age was meant to lay the grounds for his analysis of the present and future. The term 'Axial' itself serves as a marker here: He borrowed an idea from Hegel, namely, that Jesus is the axis of human history,[25] and transposed it to a multicultural register. For

[23] Two edited volumes have been particularly influential in the field: S. N. Eisenstadt, (ed.), *The Origins and Diversity of Axial Age Civilizations*, Albany: State University of New York Press, 1986; Robert N. Bellah and Hans Joas (eds.), *The Axial Age and Its Consequences*, Cambridge, MA, and London: The Belknap Press of Harvard University Press, 2012.

[24] Karl Jaspers, *Vom Ursprung und Ziel der Geschichte*, Zürich: Artemis, 1949; Karl Jaspers, *The Origin and Goal of History*, trans. Michael Bullock, New Haven: Yale University Press, 1953.

[25] Hegel never quite used this phrasing: see e.g. Heiner Roetz, "The Axial Age Theory: A Challenge to Historicism or an Explanatory Device of Civilization Analysis? With a Look at the Normative Discourse in Axial Age China," in Bellah and Joas (eds.), *The Axial Age and Its Consequences*, pp. 248–273, at p. 250.

Jaspers the axis of human history is the Axial breakthrough itself, common to different cultures, and together they founded human civilization as we know it. This claim served in turn as the basis for a vision of communicative liberalism:

The fact of the threefold manifestation of the Axial Period [viz. in China, India, and "the West"] is in the nature of a miracle, in so far as no really adequate explanation is possible within the limits of our present knowledge. The hidden meaning of this fact, however, cannot be discovered empirically at all, as a meaning somewhere intended by someone. In enquiring after it we are really only putting our own interpretation on the facts and causing something to grow out of them for us ...

Really to visualise the facts of the Axial Period and to make them the basis of our universal conception of history is to gain possession of something *common to all mankind*, beyond all differences of creed. It is one thing to see the unity of history from one's own ground and in the light of one's own faith, another to think of it in communication with every other human ground, linking one's own consciousness to the alien consciousness. In this sense, it can be said of the centuries between 800 and 200 B.C. that they are the empirically evident axis of world history for all men.[26]

The main difficulties in Jaspers' thesis can be grouped into two critiques, one conceptual and one historical. The conceptual critique poses the question of whether there is truly any common denominator among the posited Axial revolutions in Greece, Israel, India, and China. The historical critique poses the question of what, if anything, could explain the mysterious simultaneity of the Axial revolutions – what Jaspers described in the above-cited passage as being "in the nature of a miracle." In addition, most research that follows up on Jaspers, including the present study, is more concerned with the Axial as a category of analysis than as a basis for philosophical commitment.

One development in the field that helps address these issues is the interpretation of Axial revolutions as responses to the archaic state. This interpretation partly displaces the historical question from the realm of the miracle to the better-trodden ground of archaic state-formation and the concrete historical processes of sedentarism, crop cultivation, labor specialization, surplus-based palace economies – and their sociocultural implications. This understanding of the connection between the archaic state and the Axial as a response to it has informed authors such as Jan Assmann,[27] the philosopher Marcel

[26] Jaspers, *The Origin*, pp. 18–19 (emphasis in the original).

[27] See e.g. Assmann, *Of God and Gods*, esp. pp. 76–89; Jan Assmann, *Herrschaft und Heil: Politische Theologie in Altägypten, Israel, und Europa*, München: Carl Hanser, 2000.

Gauchet,[28] and the sociologist Robert N. Bellah, whose ambitious *Religion in Human Evolution: From the Paleolithic to the Axial Age* is a sustained attempt to integrate the concept of the Axial into a comprehensive human history.[29]

As for the conceptual problem of whether the alleged Axial revolutions are similar enough to be treated as a coherent phenomenon, inquiry into their relation to the archaic state offers a path to clarify the varying conceptions of transcendence and their social ramifications by assessing them as differing responses to concrete sociohistorical formations.

Here we broach the relevance of Axial theory to the current study and its central theme: the salafī theonomic challenge to the modern nation-state, and the manner in which it echoes the response of ANE monolatry to the institution of sacral kingship. We saw a foretoken in Abū Yaḥyā al-Lībī's reference to 'Pharaohism' (*farʿana*): The Qurʾānic Firʿawn, much like the Biblical Pharaoh, does in fact represent a paradigmatic ANE god-king. This is not just a matter of general inspiration. Abū Yaḥyā's reference to Firʿawn reflects a cardinal position on the ordering and relation of the divine and human worlds, one deeply ingrained in salafī doctrine and whose archetype lies ultimately in ANE Axial monolatry.

It is a commonplace of anthropology that the basic organizing principle of human non-state societies is that of kinship. In the archaic state, by contrast, class displaced kinship as a principle of social organization, with the emergence of elites who subsisted from the extraction of surpluses from the lower orders, and vertical power relations supplanting horizontal ties based on custom and consensus. The general conception of the given changed accordingly, at least among these elites and in royal theology. While non-state societies tended to achieve social cohesion with reference to a way of being in the world coded as natural and immutable, one that transfused both the seen and the unseen, archaic state societies upheld the coercive power of the sovereign as the instantiation of justice and normative authority. Relations with the unseen became as stratified as the socio-economic order: "the upper classes claimed privileged relations with the supernatural, and rulers frequently were ascribed divine or semidivine status. Just as class had replaced both real and metaphorical kinship as a basis for organizing societies, so religious concepts replaced kinship as a medium for social and political discourse."[30]

[28] Marcel Gauchet, *Le désenchantement du monde: Une histoire politique de la religion*, Paris: Gallimard, 1985; Marcel Gauchet, *The Disenchantment of the World: A Political History of Religion*, trans. Oscar Burge, Princeton: Princeton University Press, 1997.

[29] Robert N. Bellah, *Religion in Human Evolution: From the Paleolithic to the Axial Age*, Cambridge, MA, and London: The Belknap Press of Harvard University Press, 2011.

[30] Bruce G. Trigger, *Understanding Early Civilizations*, Cambridge: Cambridge University Press, 2003, pp. 47–48.

At this point we can begin to sense that religion is a problematic category: Modern Western conceptions, both naïve and philosophical, are the outcome of long arcs of development from the Axial Age to the Reformation and Enlightenment, and retrospectives on the history of religion often bear a teleological imprint, an explicit or implicit narrative of progress. It is worth considering the counter-perspective proposed by Marcel Gauchet in his *Le désenchantement du monde*. Gauchet defines religion as the radical negation of humans' own instituting agency and argues that it found its purest expression in non-state societies, wherein the locus of the given order, both seen and unseen, lies in an absolute past, primary and immutable:

The essence of the religious act lies wholly in this antihistorical frame of mind. Religion in its pure state is drawn into a temporal division that puts the present in a position of absolute dependence on the mythical past, and guarantees the irrevocable allegiance of all human activities to their inaugural truth. At the same time it ratifies the non-appealable dispossession of human actors from what gives substance and meaning to their actions and gestures. The key to the inter-relationship between religion and society, as well as the secret of the nature of the religious, lies in its radical conservatism which structurally combines co-presence to the origin with disjunction from the originary moment.[31]

Gauchet traces the connection between this attitude of radical self-dispossession and the anthropologist Pierre Clastres' conception of *la société contre l'état*, society against the state. Clastres notes that we tend to define 'non-state societies,' as I have been doing up to this point (for lack of better terminology), in terms of a supposed lack: They lack writing, economic surpluses, and state organization, as though they were incapable of these achievements. As a counter-model Clastres argues that such societies are actively anti-state and deploy social mechanisms to prevent its emergence – perhaps most famously through the ritual redistribution of surpluses. Religious specialization is rudimentary, social norms are rooted in a cosmic order, and thus these are societies in which "the religious removal of the founding principle prohibits a separate legitimating and coercive authority."[32]

The Axial revolutions were not a simple revanche of this original 'society against the state' nor an attempt to return to pre-state religion, but this framework does set the stage for understanding them as varying responses to the archaic state. With this perspective in mind we can now examine the emergence and nature of the two forms of the Axial that

[31] Gauchet, *Le désenchantement*, p. 15; Gauchet, *The Disenchantment*, p. 25.

[32] Gauchet, *Le désenchantement*, p. 16; Gauchet, *The Disenchantment*, p. 26; cf. Pierre Clastres, *La Société contre l'État*, Paris: Les Éditions de Minuit, 1974.

directly concern us, Greek philosophy and ANE monolatry – the dual patrimony of the developed Abrahamic traditions, Islam among them.

While academic scholarship is certainly conscious of a difference between the salafī trend in Islam, on the one hand, and rationalist-speculative theology, on the other (the Muʿtazila, Ashʿarīs, and Māturīdīs), there has been insufficient systematic and theoretical treatment of the nature of this difference.[33] Some studies that broach the issue focus on how each trend configures the relation between rationalism and revelation as the central distinction;[34] while there is ample justification for this criterion, as we will see, it is not in itself sufficient. The differences between these two trends are profound and comprise capital differences in their substantive belief systems in addition to issues of epistemology and hermeneutics. I submit that in order to see these differences clearly we will do best to first consider the distinction between the Greek and Israelite archetypes of transcendence through a wide lens and in their original independent evolution so as to better understand the forms of their later interaction in the Islamic world.[35]

In each of the Greek and Israelite configurations of transcendence one can identify a number of discrete but interrelated premises or positions; each of these configurations might better be termed an economy of transcendence, as they are not singular ideas but rather a manner of fathoming and ordering the transcendent, the mundane, and the relations between them, and each has multiple ramifications that likewise stand in relation one to another. Here I will briefly outline the

[33] Binyamin Abrahamov has rightly noted the relative paucity of academic attention to Traditionalist theology. *Islamic Theology: Traditionalism and Rationalism*, Edinburgh: Edinburgh University Press, 1998, p. viii.

[34] For example, Abrahamov, *Islamic Theology*, pp. ix–xi; W. Montgomery Watt, *Islamic Philosophy and Theology: An Extended Survey*, 2nd ed., Edinburgh: Edinburgh University Press, 1985, p. 98: "The most distinctive feature of Ḥanbalite theology is its opposition to Kalām, that is, to rational argument in matters of dogma."

[35] In addition to the other sources cited in what follows, my approach in this section has been influenced above all by Yehoshua Amir's important article "Die Begegnung des biblischen und des philosophischen Monotheismus als Grundthema des jüdischen Hellenismus," *Evangelische Theologie* 38 (1978), pp. 2–19. This article crystallized my thinking (based on Ibn Taymiyya) regarding monolatry as the heart of revelational faith and suggested the appropriate terminology; it likewise adumbrates the contrasting tenets of philosophical and revelational monotheism that I present in what follows under five rubrics, and which I then apply in Chapter 1 to analysis of Ibn Taymiyya's system. While my approach is typological rather than genealogical, and the particular tradition I study generally seeks to disaggregate rather than harmonize, it does agree in many respects with Wolfson's argument that Philo of Alexandria should be seen as the progenitor of medieval philosophy in Judaism, Islam, and Christianity. Harry Austryn Wolfson, *Philo: Foundations of Religious Philosophy in Judaism Christianity and Islam*, Cambridge, MA: Harvard University Press, 1947, vol. 2, pp. 439–460.

background to and emergence of each of these economies, and then outline five contrasting tenets of each, and their interrelation within each economy, under the following rubrics:

(1) epistemology (philosophical vs. revelational)
(2) ontology vs. cratology (being vs. power)
(3) apophatism vs. cataphatism
(4) the mode of interaction between the transcendent and the mundane (mediated vs. unmediated)
(5) conceptual monotheism vs. monolatry, which can be analyzed both as a tenet within each economy and as the underlying rationale of each economy on the whole

The Abrahamic traditions served as a meeting ground for these two economies of transcendence. Under the umbrella of each of Judaism, Christianity, and Islam one finds a spectrum of thinkers, schools, and movements that negotiated different responses to this dual patrimony: rejection of one in favor of the other, harmonization of the two, or anything and everything in between. The categories enumerated above provide us with a basic theoretical structure on which to map this spectrum, and will thus allow us to speak more precisely to the specificity of salafism within the wider Islamic milieu.

In particular, Chapter 1 will attempt to show how these five categories in the economies of transcendence can fruitfully be applied to analysis of the theology of Ibn Taymiyya, the forefather of salafī theology as we know it today. The framework outlined in this Introduction will help bring to light the basic structure of Ibn Taymiyya's theology as an integral system constructed in defense of an Islamic version of the revelational economy of transcendence with monolatry at its core, in opposition to currents of Islam influenced to varying degrees by Greek-derived philosophical monotheism. I will remark that in this work I adopt to some degree, and by necessity, the voice as it were of Ibn Taymiyya and the salafī tradition. From their disaggregating vantage point any admixture of 'Islam' with the philosophical economy of transcendence was to be condemned, and while Ibn Taymiyya is a careful polemicist who brings out fine distinctions, he does rhetorically paint other trends such as the *kalām* tradition in broad 'Greek' strokes. This is not my own normative judgment; as for the analytic value of Ibn Taymiyya's contentions, readers are welcome to judge for themselves throughout the discussion below in Chapter 1.

The following exposition is by necessity broad in its sweep and specialists in the relevant fields might contest portions of it. It is nonetheless necessary to the current study as a propaedeutic, and I have attempted to present as faithful an exposition as possible.

Both Greek and Israelite transcendence emerged as different responses to an ancient model of sacral kingship in the archaic state. The cosmogonies and theomachies of the Near East and Archaic Greece recounted tales of order being forged from chaos through the rise of a god, such as Zeus or Marduk, to the position of divine sovereign. The point of these myths was not so much to explain the absolute origins of the cosmos, as modern physicists and astronomers attempt to do, but rather to explain the origin of the contemporary cosmic and human order. They were closely associated with ritual and were originally recited or symbolically reenacted at festivals of royalty celebrating the human sovereign. Order was not assumed to be a natural feature of the cosmos but was rather assured against the forces of chaos by the sovereignty of a chief god and that of his human analogue, through their exercise of supreme power over disparate unruly elements.[36]

Both economies of transcendence inherited from this ancient model a central preoccupation with unity and the relation between the one and the many. The divergent Greek and Israelite modes of transposing the ancient model onto different registers lie at the root of the contrasting models of transcendence they developed, and whose later interaction shaped the variegated landscape of medieval theology.

In Greece this transposition, as described by the classicist Jean-Pierre Vernant,[37] began with a very real crisis of sovereignty: the eclipse of the Mycenaean monarchy, which vanished toward the end of the twelfth century BCE in the Late Bronze Age collapse. The evanescence of the divine king and the collapse of the centralized palatial economy left a warrior aristocracy face to face with the village communities, with no clear rules as to how to reconfigure social relations. The search for an equilibrium between these social forces "gave rise in a time of troubles to moral thought and political speculation that amounted to an early form of human 'wisdom.'" The problem that prompted and exercised this human wisdom was that of how to reestablish human order and unity – that is, how to arrive at a new, post-royal formulation of the problems of power.[38]

[36] Jean-Pierre Vernant, *Les origines de la pensée grecque*, Paris: Presses Universitaires de France, 4th ed., 1981, pp. 106–115; Jean-Pierre Vernant, *The Origins of Greek Thought*, Ithaca: Cornell University Press, 1982, pp. 108–116. For a succinct characterization of this model, see B. Renaud, "De la bénédiction du roi à la bénédiction de Dieu (Ps 72)," *Biblica* 70 (1989), pp. 305–326, at pp. 314–315.

[37] The contrast between the emergence of Greek thought as described by Vernant and Israelite transcendence is briefly addressed in Yehuda Elkana, "The Emergence of Second-Order Thinking in Classical Greece," in Eisenstadt, *Origins and Diversity*, pp. 40–64, at pp. 43–44.

[38] Vernant, *Origines*, pp. 33–35; Vernant, *Origins*, pp. 38–40.

Even Athens, which alone maintained some continuity with the Mycenaean past, witnessed a breakup of sovereignty. The king was relegated to a purely priestly function, and political command (*arche*) became elective. "The emphasis was no longer on a single person who dominated social life, but on a multiplicity of functions that opposed each other and thus called for a reciprocal apportionment and delimitation."[39] A central question, which later was to find more rigorous formulation in philosophy, arose at this time in social and religious (Orphic) terms: How, in the absence of a single superhuman power, could the one emerge from the many, and the many from the one?[40]

Before this question emerged on a conceptual level as a touchstone of early Greek philosophy solutions to it began to be formulated in the new institution of the *polis*. The unity of the *polis* was founded in the likeness of its constituent elements, and reciprocal relations among them came to replace the older hierarchical relations of submission and dominance.[41] This primacy of a social *order* over the power of individuals found its first institutional expression in Sparta, where "*arche* [command, political power] in reality belonged exclusively to the law."[42] Sparta was famously closed off to intellectual endeavor, but elsewhere in Greece, where matters of *arche* now "had to be resolved at the conclusion of a debate,"[43] the same transformations that found institutional expression in Sparta would come to intellectual fruition.

The basic thrust of early Greek philosophy was in this way already implicit in the new human order founded on the ruins of divine sovereignty. The use of human reason to discover and institute order, and the replacement of concrete and personal power relations with abstract, impersonal laws and principles mediating among equal and opposing forces – these transpositions transformed the cosmogonical and theomachic myths of divine sovereignty as well. For example, Vernant has shown how Anaximander's natural philosophy, while clearly indebted to the mythological tradition, nonetheless completely transforms its schema. Kingship (*basileia*, *monarchia*), "which had established and maintained order in myth, appeared destructive of order in Anaximander's new perspective. Order was no longer hierarchical, but lay in the maintenance of equilibrium between powers that were now equal."[44]

39 Vernant, *Origines*, pp. 36–38; Vernant, *Origins*, pp. 41–43.
40 Vernant, *Origines*, p. 40; Vernant, *Origins*, p. 45.
41 Vernant, *Origines*, p. 56; Vernant, *Origins*, pp. 60–61.
42 Vernant, *Origines*, pp. 60–63; Vernant, *Origins*, pp. 65–68.
43 Vernant, *Origines*, p. 45; Vernant, *Origins*, p. 50.
44 Vernant, *Origines*, p. 123; Vernant, *Origins*, p. 123.

In Vernant's view Anaximander expresses this new vision in purer form than did the other pre-Socratics, since his 'one' was neither water (Thales) nor air (Anaximenes) nor any other of the observable elements in the physical universe.[45] Yet it would perhaps be instructive to shift the emphasis from their differences to what the pre-Socratics held in common. Both Anaximander and others already tied their conceptions of order to an ontological formulation of the question of the one and the many, and in this way sought a unity of Being in the universe.[46] This was not just a transformation from hierarchy to equilibrium within the framework of power, but also a transformation of the problem of the unity of *power* into the problem of the unity of *Being*, with Parmenides representing the apogee of this development: Instead of a primordial physical element, the One is identified with Being itself.[47] In other words, ancient Greece experienced a drawn-out deconstruction and reconstruction of the ancient model of sacral monarchy, through a process of abstraction that led from the One of supreme power to the various metaphysical formulations of the One and the many.

The Axial revolution in ancient Israel was of a decidedly different character. Instead of a slow transformation of the model of sacral kingship we see an acute rejection of it, the paradigmatic expression of which is God's humiliation of Pharaoh. Israelite society was not one in which sacral kingship was a past reality and bygone ideal: Sacral kingship was rather a feature of the large, centralized civilizations at Israel's borders, Egypt and Assyria, which threatened its independence. Whether or not one reads the 'anti-monarchical' portions of the Bible as fundamentally hostile to monarchy per se (i.e. including Israelite monarchy),[48] the Bible

45 Vernant, *Origines*, p. 122; Vernant, *Origins*, p. 122.

46 For the point that the fundamental material element (e.g. water, air) was not conceived of simply in cosmogonical terms but was also believed to continue to underlie existence after its differentiation into the many, see Aryeh Finkelberg, "On the Unity of Orphic and Milesian Thought," *The Harvard Theological Review* 79/4 (October 1986), pp. 321–335, esp. pp. 323–324.

47 "With Parmenides [philosophy] took its own path; it explored a new domain and posed problems unique to itself. The philosophers no longer inquired, as the Milesians had done, into the nature of order and how it was created and maintained, but into the nature of Being and Knowing and the relations between them." Vernant, *Origines*, pp. 132–133; Vernant, *Origins*, p. 131.

48 The Bible's view on the Israelite monarchy is a much-contested issue. Works that emphasize the anti-monarchical interpretation include Martin Buber, *Königtum Gottes*, Berlin: Schocken, 1932 (Martin Buber, *Kingship of God*, trans. Richard Scheimann, London: George Allen and Unwin, 1967); F. Crüsemann, *Der Widerstand gegen das Königtum. Die antiköniglichen Texte des Alten Testaments und der Kampf um den frühen israelitischen Staat*, WMANT 49, Neukirchen-Vluyn: Neukirchener Verlag, 1978; Jan Assmann, *Herrschaft und Heil: Politische Theologie in Altägypten, Israel, und Europa*, München: Carl Hanser, 2000, e.g. pp. 46ff. For the view that the Bible is consistently

on the whole is clearly hostile to the ANE model of sacral monarchy. Israel established in opposition to it a conception of God – one God – as the sole true king who wields the only claim to Israel's loyalty.

This was an act of transference, a transformation of "Assyrian politics into biblical theology." The God of the Bible has the features of "an Assyrian despot," and the loyalty He demands of His people is of the kind owed to ANE rulers by their subjects.[49] Israel, unlike Greece, did not dissolve the model of kingship into an abstract order; it rather projected it onto the divine realm and established the kingship of God in opposition to the sacral kingships of the neighboring states.[50]

This exclusivist monotheism was self-consciously a counter-religion, that is, a religion defined in explicit opposition to the polytheistic societies of the ANE.[51] The model of unity that it adopted in opposition to this plurality of divine forces was primarily that of kingship, and Biblical Axial theology is thus habitually expressed in political and basileomorphic terms: God is a king, He sits on a throne, He is mighty, He imposes His will on all others. The Sinai covenant between God and the people is closely analogous to treaties between Near Eastern monarchs and their vassals.[52] He differs from the polytheistic chief deities in significant ways: There is no story of His birth and rise to power, and only faint echoes of theomachy.[53] Nonetheless the same relation of creation, order, and power remains, only taken to such a limit that the difference in degree becomes a difference in kind. The product of Israelite transcendence is a person-like, omnipotent God, who was

pro-monarchy, see Yehezkel Kaufmann, *Toledot HaEmuna HaYisraelit*, Jerusalem: Bialik and Tel Aviv: Dvir, 1956, pp. 687ff. For a recent argument in favor of the view first advanced by Wellhausen (and challenged by Buber), namely, that the anti-monarchical texts are a late exilic product, see Reinhard Müller, *Königtum und Gottesherrschaft: Untersuchungen zur alttestamentlichen Monarchiekritik*, FAT II/3, Tübingen: Mohr Siebeck, 2004.

49 Assmann, *Of God and Gods*, p. 113.

50 See Eckart Otto, "Political Theology in Judah and Assyria: The Beginning of the Hebrew Bible as Literature," *Svensk Exegetisk Årsbok* 65 (2000), pp. 59–76, esp. pp. 64–65: "The Judaean authors of the deuteronomic loyalty oath did not simply shift the Assyrian paradigm of political theology from the Assyrian to the Judean king but created an entirely new one, which limited the claim to political loyalty by requiring absolute loyalty to God."

51 Jan Assmann, *Moses the Egyptian. The Memory of Egypt in Western Monotheism*, Cambridge, MA, and London: Harvard University Press, 1997, p. 7.

52 For references to literature on this topic, see Yael Ziegler, *Promises to Keep: The Oath in Biblical Narrative*, Leiden: Brill, 2008, p. 14, n. 89.

53 See on this topic Benjamin D. Sommer, *The Bodies of God and the World of Ancient Israel*, Cambridge: Cambridge University Press, 2009, pp. 165–172. Sommer's presentation of the issue is indebted to the arguments of Yehezkel Kaufmann.

understood as the fount of order and as an object of exclusive loyalty and devotion.

Thus both Greece and Israel witnessed the emergence of Axial, transcendent conceptions of the one and its relation to the many, but due to the different trajectories of their paths their respective conceptions of transcendence diverged greatly one from the other. What follows is a brief outline of this divergence in terms of the five basic rubrics mentioned above.

### *Epistemology: Philosophy vs. Revelation*

The transcendent, by definition, is not the mundane world that is the object of sense perception. If one wishes to to say anything particular about it the question arises of how one gains access to this other realm. Since Axial thought considers the transcendent to be the measure of truth, it is characterized by a distrust of sense perception, common opinion, inherited cultural tradition, and mundane ways of knowing in general. In the Bible this distrust is expressed in the true-false dichotomy of the 'Mosaic distinction' (which while secondary to monolatry remains an important feature); in philosophy, the true-false distinction can be seen in the thought of Parmenides, who was perhaps the first Greek philosopher to state a systematic opposition between the way of truth (*aletheia*) and the way of seeming or opinion (*doxa*).[54]

While the Axial concern for separation between the true and the false is common to both economies, their conceptions of the source of truth and the means of arriving at it are opposed. Philosophy proceeds by inquiry and reason on the presumption that at least some humans are able to transcend their own limitations, purify their conceptions, and thereby gain access to the truth. In the archaic period a distinction was drawn between the gods' knowledge and human knowledge: humans could only gain access to the former through poetic inspiration or through cultic practices such as divination. The pre-Socratic philosopher Xenophanes remained skeptical toward the ability of humans to transcend their inherent epistemological limitations, but he did introduce "the new notion that men acquire their knowledge through their own striving, that even though they may never arrive at complete enlightenment they always

[54] Recent scholarship has, however, tended to reassess Parmenides' *doxa*: While not being a true account of what-is, as represented by the goddess Aletheia, it holds circumscribed value for things available and relevant to mortal cognition. See e.g. Shaul Tor, "Parmenides' Epistemology and the Two Parts of His Poem," *Phronesis* 60/1 (2015), pp. 3–39, and the references therein.

have it in their power to search out better things."[55] Pre-Socratic philosophy continued to oscillate between the poles of the archaic association of truth with divinity and the "new notion" that truth was accessible through human endeavor. Socrates, then,

> breaks with the tradition ... and, as Cicero puts it, restores philosophy from the sky to its place on earth ... The distinction between human knowledge and divine knowledge, which had first been formulated in the area of sense perception, had helped to separate Being from Appearance ... The efforts to reconcile the two domains of divine and human knowledge had produced the rudimentary techniques of induction and deduction. All this was once more subjected to a final change when Socrates in his dialogues tried to rest his own proposals on the authority of human thought, and human speech, and nothing else.[56]

In ancient Israel, by contrast, the truth decidedly descended from above in an act of revelation. This was in keeping with the general thrust of Israelite transcendence, which, instead of "restoring philosophy from the sky to its place on earth," pursued a path of concentration and intensification of divine prerogative.

> Revealed knowledge always is (or presents itself as) extraterrestrial, or extramundane. It comes from another world, like "air from other planets blowing," to quote Stefan George. It is not knowledge based on thisworldly experience and accumulated in the course of centuries. Furthermore, it is knowledge that people are not encouraged to expand through their own experience ... The concept of revelation is the opposite of what can be called natural evidence.[57]

The contrast between these Axial epistemologies was elegantly illustrated by Yehoshua Amir in his examination of the interaction between the two in the Hellenistic period: Jews who looked favorably on the classical Greek philosophers argued that they must have ultimately received their wisdom from Moses (i.e. from revelation), whereas Greeks impressed by Moses' conception of God naturally assumed that he was a philosopher.[58]

### *Ontology vs. Cratology*

In the preceding category we discussed Parmenides' *aletheia*/*doxa* distinction. What he meant by *aletheia*, however, was above all 'reality.'[59]

[55] Bruno Snell, *The Discovery of the Mind: The Greek Origins of European Thought*, trans. T. G. Rosenmeyer, Cambridge, MA: Harvard University Press, 1953, pp. 138–139.

[56] Snell, *Discovery*, pp. 150–151. [57] Assmann, *Of God and Gods*, p. 91.

[58] Amir, "Begegnung," p. 11; cf. Wolfson, *Philo*, vol. 1, p. 20.

[59] John Palmer, *Parmenides and Presocratic Philosophy*, Oxford: Oxford University Press, 2009, pp. 89–93. Etymologically *aletheia* means something like "unveiledness" or "unconcealedness," a fact of much importance to Heidegger: see e.g. Martin Heidegger, "Vom Wesen der Wahrheit," in *Wegmarken* (*Gesamtausgabe* vol. 9),

In other words, his distinction was between, on the one hand, what really is, and, on the other, what-is-not (however "is" it may seem). We see here the origin of the close relation in ancient Greek philosophy between epistemology and ontology: What distinguishes the Parmenidean One from the many is quite simply that the One is and the many are not, and correspondingly, thought about the One is true and thought about the many is false.[60] Parmenides was unique in his solution but not in his concerns. Until one arrives at the Sophists, "the speculations of the pre-Socratics about the Divine displayed a decided singleness of character in their intellectual form, despite their diversity of aspects and the multiplicity of their points of departure. Their immediate goal was the knowledge of nature or of Being."[61]

In contrast the ancient mythological depiction of divine supremacy was cratological, that is, an expression of the power of one god over other gods or mortals.[62] It is true that Aristotle references the Homeric depiction of Zeus' supremacy over the other divinities – they could not drag him down from heaven, but he could suspend them from Mount Olympus – as a foreshadowing of his own concept of the power of the Unmoved Mover.[63] The latter, however, but wanly reflects mythological discourse on divine power and its anthropomorphic and basileomorphic bases. Likewise in the celebrated citation from the *Iliad* concluding Book XII of the *Metaphysics*, "the rule of many is not good, let one be ruler," the human model of sovereignty is applied to the Unmoved Mover but in a sense so far removed as to be metaphorical.[64] In Greece the mythological depiction of power was transposed onto a different register, and transcendent difference came to be expressed in terms of ontology rather than cratology. This demythologization took on an increasingly transcendent nature, from the Ionian encosmic identification of the sole

Frankfurt am Main: Vittorio Klostermann, 1976, pp. 177–202, esp. p. 188 (= Martin Heidegger, "On the Essence of Truth," trans. John Sallis, in *Pathmarks*, ed. William McNeill, New York: Cambridge University Press, 1998, pp. 136–154, esp. p. 144).

60 For a concise exposition of the correlation between epistemology and ontology, from Parmenides to Plotinus, see Eric D. Perl, *Theophany: The Neoplatonic Philosophy of Dionysius the Areopagite*, Albany: State University of New York Press, 2007, pp. 5–13.

61 Werner Jaeger, *The Theology of the Early Greek Philosophers*, Oxford: Oxford University Press, 1947, p. 172.

62 Cf. Assmann, *Of God and Gods*, p. 61, for the characterization of Egyptian cosmogony as "a power-oriented 'cratogony.' The emergence of the world is simultaneous with the emergence of power and sovereignty. Creation and dominion are merely two aspects of the same process."

63 Jaeger, *Theology*, p. 46.

64 Erik Peterson, "Monotheism as a Political Problem," in Erik Peterson, *Theological Tractates*, ed. and trans. Michael J. Hollerich, Stanford: Stanford University Press, 2011, pp. 68–105, at pp. 68ff.

ultimate principle of being with a material element, through Parmenides, and up to a kind of hypercosmism wherein the divine or transcendent is itself conceived of as beyond being, while bestowing being on all that is.[65]

In ancient Israel the basileomorphic model of divinity retained and even intensified the axis of power. The one and the many both existed in equal measure, but the one (God) had power over the many (creation). Israelite Axiality did not depart from the world of myth through a denaturing of the divine: The Bible's depictions of God's unique might are sufficiently similar to those used for the polytheistic principal deities that there exists substantial debate as to whether they are at all expressions of monotheism. At least according to the school of scholars who answer this question in the affirmative the difference between the Bible's monotheism and polytheistic henotheism is that the power it ascribes to God is truly absolute.[66] God, in His role as Creator, is of course the source of being as well (or at least of the current order of being, as the Biblical concept of creation is not ex nihilo); but the Biblical creation story is not concerned primarily with being but with power relations, though differing from ancient cosmogony in that God Himself has no history, is above and in control of the laws of generation, and thus in Him is concentrated perduring power over all.

We can give a concise sign of the ontological/cratological divide by returning to the terminology used to distinguish between the one and the many. As mentioned above, for Parmenides "truth" is being itself – that which truly is; and falsehood is then, necessarily, nonbeing. In contrast, the Bible's standard term for the 'many' it seeks to deny – the gods of the nations – is *ʾelīl* (sg.)/*ʾelīlīm* (pl.). This word, while perhaps a disparaging diminutive formed from the word for a/the god (*ʾēl/ʾelōhīm*), is also related to a Semitic root that signifies weakness and insignificance. There may also be an etymological connection to the concept of "nothing,"[67] but the context of the polemics in which the term is used makes it clear that even be this the case, the concept of nothing or nonexistence is

[65] On hypercosmism, see Assmann, *Of God and Gods*, pp. 72–73. It is represented in Plato's concept of the Good and in its later Neoplatonic development: cf. Perl, *Theophany*, pp. 5–13. In light of this depiction, we can perhaps interpret the criticism directed against the Ionian physicalists in Plato's *Phaedo*, 99c, namely, that they think that they have discovered "a new Atlas," as meaning that they were not yet free of encosmic mythological thought.

[66] "What is crucial for identifying monotheism is some indication that the expression of uniqueness is to be taken literally, some sign that the god being extolled is not limited by any other forces." Sommer, *Bodies of God*, p. 161.

[67] Horst Dietrich Preuss, "*ʾelîl*," in G. Johannes Botterweck and Helmer Ringgren (eds.), *Theological Dictionary of the Old Testament*, trans. John T. Willis, Grand Rapids: William B. Eerdmans, 1977, vol. 1, pp. 285–287.

not clearly differentiated from the concept of powerlessness, and it is this latter that is the main element: the *ʾelīlīm* do not see or hear, nor do they have power to act against the true God.

In later Judaism there does exist a long tradition of ontological interpretation of the tetragrammaton YHWH, as in Hebrew it reads naturally as the third-person imperfect of the standard verb for being, and as seemingly suggested by the episode of the burning bush (Exodus 3:14). Yet it is not certain that this was the original meaning of the theonym. Both internal Biblical and Egyptian evidence suggests that the name as well as the cult of YHWH were Midianite in origin, that is, from northwestern Arabia – a theory known as the Kenite hypothesis.[68] Quite apart from this hypothesis S. D. Goitein suggested a derivation of the name from the root *h-w-y*, roughly analogous in meaning to the same root in Arabic[69] and to Hebrew *q-n-ʾ*, the latter frequently associated with the tetragrammaton in the Bible and denoting love, exclusive devotion, and jealousy.[70] Thus this theonym, rather than challenging the scheme here proposed, would tend to support it, backdating monolatry to the Midianite prehistory of Biblical religion: "the tetragrammaton YHWH does not express God's characteristic of Creator and is not connected to His being the source of all, the source of existence. The Midianite milieu in which the name YHW or YHWH originated did not know the [Hebrew] verb *haya, hava*. For them [the Midianites] the special characteristic of the God YHW is not connected to His activity as a Creator God, but rather to the claim to exclusive relation He demands from His believers."[71]

The debate as to whether the Bible is monotheistic or not – i.e. whether it denies the *existence* of the other gods – is to some degree a function of the preponderance of Greek notions of the one and the many in our own conceptions, themselves due to the lasting imprint of medieval religious traditions on modern thought. The Bible itself is concerned primarily with denying the power of the other gods and their right to be worshipped, not their ontological density; whether they 'exist' or not in some other sense is a subsidiary issue.

[68] The hypothesis was first proposed in the nineteenth century but the extra-Biblical evidence for it is more recent: see e.g. Israel Knohl, "Jacob-El in the Land of Esau and the Roots of Biblical Religion," *Vetus Testamentum* 67/3 (2017), pp. 481–484.

[69] On which see above, n. 4., though the Qurʾān employs it only in a negative sense and never in relation to Allāh.

[70] S. D. Goitein, "YHWH the Passionate: The Monotheistic Meaning and Origin of the Name YHWH," *Vetus Testamentum* 6/1 (1956), pp. 1–9.

[71] Israel Knohl, *Eich Nolad HaTanach* [How the Bible was born], Modi'in: Kinneret, Zmora-Bitan, Dvir, 2018, p. 190 (identification of the theonym with monolatry), p. 191 (the quotation).

### *Apophatism vs. Cataphatism*

The fulcrum of the Greek investigation of the One is abstraction: a transcending of the apparent multiplicity and impermanence of the phenomena. Xenophanes expressed the superiority of one single god with the words "One god is the highest among gods and men / In neither his form nor his thought is he like unto mortals," and elsewhere he attacked anthropomorphic representations of gods, including those contained in Homer and Hesiod, as mere social projections that were unbecoming of true divinity.[72] Later philosophers and commentators who continued to profess respect for these canonical texts developed instead methods of allegorical exegesis that eliminated the personhood of the ancient gods and associated them with natural cosmic forces.[73] The Platonic Good and the Aristotelian Unmoved Mover are ontologically simple philosophical postulates (or "beyond being" entirely) that could be assimilated to the God of revelation only via a thorough philosophization of the Abrahamic traditions.

The Hebrew Bible quite simply does not pose this problematic,[74] and the misconception to the contrary reflects the continued impact of the philosophizing tendencies of medieval religion on modern scholarship.[75] It is true that the cataphatic descriptions of divinity in the Bible are often contextually linked with God's power: For example, Genesis 1:26 tells us that humans are given rule over other living things because they were created in God's 'form' and 'shape,' thus seeming to suggest that God's 'form' and 'shape' themselves are related to His rule over creation. Yet the idea that the plastic descriptions of divinity are mere allegories for this content is one that is foreign to the logic of revelation. There is a clear, essential linkage in the Biblical economy of transcendence between cataphatism and the cratological emphasis, just as there is a clear,

72 Jaeger, *Theology*, pp. 42–48.

73 See e.g. David Dawson, *Allegorical Readers and Cultural Revision in Ancient Alexandria*, Berkeley: University of California Press, 1992, pp. 23–51.

74 Kaufmann, *Toledot Ha-Emunah Ha-Yisraelit*, p. 229. Yehoshua Amir notes that the 'problem of anthropomorphism' (i.e. the idea that the anthropomorphic descriptions of God were problematic) first arose in Judaism only in the Hellenistic milieu, with Aristobulos, who applied to the Bible the kind of rationalizing exegesis that the Greeks employed with respect to their archaic poetry. Amir, "Begegnung," pp. 12–13. See also Daniel Boyarin, "The Eye in the Torah: Ocular Desire in Midrashic Hermeneutic," *Critical Inquiry* 16 (1990), pp. 532–550, at p. 533: "*only* under Hellenic influence do Jewish cultures exhibit any anxiety about the corporeality or visibility of God; the biblical and Rabbinic religions were quite free of such influences and anxieties." Cited in Wesley Williams, "A Body unlike Bodies: Transcendent Anthropomorphism in Ancient Semitic Tradition and Early Islam," *Journal of the American Oriental Society* 129/1 (2009), pp. 19–44, at p. 20, n. 6 cont.

75 See Sommer, *Bodies of God*, pp. 1–10, for a survey and discussion of this topic.

essential linkage in philosophical monotheism between apophatism and the ontological emphasis. The plastic depictions of divinity in the texts of revelation do not stand in opposition to their 'allegorical' meanings but rather serve as the basis for them.[76]

### *Mediation vs. Unmediatedness*

The Axial revolution, in both its forms here discussed, contains within itself an inherent tension between, on the one hand, the delineation of absolute difference between the transcendent and the mundane, and, on the other, an attempt to rebridge the Axial gap thus opened. The Axial revolution, in its quest for the different and transcendent, remains after all a human revolution, and some explanation must be found for how humans are able to relate to the transcendent, what it means to them, and what sociocultural ramifications it entails.

The Greek philosophical trend of abstraction of the divine and its apophatic thrust rendered the possibility of direct divine intervention in the world more distant. The closing of this gap thus requires some kind of continuum and intermediate stages that bridge between the divine world and the mundane one, a conception fully elaborated in Neoplatonic theories of emanation.[77] In contrast, the proximity of the Biblical conception of God to the ancient mythological representations allows Him to continue to interact directly with the mundane world: He speaks, hears, and even enters the battlefield. The term used by Yehoshua Amir for this feature of revelational monotheism (as opposed to philosophical monotheism) is *Unmittelbarkeit*[78] – 'directness' or 'immediacy,' or, etymologically related to the latter, 'unmediatedness.'

This insight resolves the perplexing question of why the Bible forbids iconographic representations, not just of false gods, but also of the true God, whereas it poses no objection to the linguistic anthropomorphism in which it so freely indulges. If the rationale behind the prohibition of images was that they are erroneous representations of divinity, one would expect linguistic anthropomorphism to be problematic as well. The issue

[76] Halbertal and Margalit, *Idolatry*, pp. 10–11, 36.

[77] I cannot concur with the following statement of Halbertal and Margalit: "Hierarchical and organic conceptions of the world of divinity stand in opposition to the picture of simple unity of the philosophers" (*Idolatry*, p. 4). It could be argued that it is precisely the philosophical search for the "simple unity" of God that requires such a hierarchy in order to rebridge the gap with the mundane. This is at least how the issue appears from the perspective of the revelational economy: cf. Chapter 1, in the discussion of Ibn Taymiyya's critique of Ibn Sīnā's *al-Risāla al-aḍḥawiyya*.

[78] Amir, "Begegnung," p. 4.

is not conceptual, but rather relational. It is fundamental to the Biblical conception of God that His interaction with the world be real and direct; the offer of devotion through the intermediary of an iconographic representation was considered idolatrous because it was construed as a violation of this principle of unmediatedness.[79]

### *Conceptual Monotheism vs. Monolatry*

In this Introduction we have already addressed the difference between a concept of God and a relationship with God. The philosophical economy of transcendence is the origin of our concept of theology as thinking and speaking about God. The word 'theology' (*theologia*) appears to have been coined by Plato:

> He introduced it in the *Republic*, where he wanted to set up certain philosophical standards and criteria for poetry. In his ideal state the poets must avoid the errors of Homer, Hesiod, and the poetic tradition in general, and rise in their representation of the gods to the level of philosophical truth. The mythical deities of early Greek poetry were tinged with all kinds of human weakness; but such an idea of the gods was irreconcilable with Plato's and Socrates' rational conception of the divine. Thus, when Plato set forth … 'outlines of theology' in the *Republic*, the creation of that new word sprang from the conflict between the mythical tradition and the natural (rational) approach to the problem of God.[80]

This kind of theology, often called "natural theology," emerged from the basic Greek dynamic of transcendence: the path of abstraction and rationalization. The thrust of this theology was not the rejection of false gods, but rather the rejection of incorrect or inappropriate conceptualizations of the divine, viewed as the product of a primitive stage of thought that needed to be brought into harmony with reason. The primary aim of this quest is to arrive at correct *ideas* about God or the gods.

The heart of revelational monotheism, in contrast, is not an idea of God, but rather a relationship with God, and the core of this relationship is exclusive obedience. This feature of revelational monotheism derives from its origin as a transcendent projection of sacral monarchy, from which it borrowed the basic elements of command, loyalty, and allegiance – all rendered possible only on the basis of cataphatism and unmediatedness. "Indeed, the anthropomorphic description of God, so scathingly attacked by the mediaeval philosophers, is in fact the core of the biblical concept of God, as only by being a paradigmatic personality

[79] Amir, "Begegnung," pp. 7–8; Assmann, *Of God and Gods*, p. 87. But cf. Halbertal and Margalit, *Idolatry*, pp. 50–66.
[80] Jaeger, *Theology*, p. 4.

can He command people to follow Him."[81] The exclusivity of God's claim to obedience is also clearly connected to the cratological model, in which God holds uncontested power over all. The central aspect of the Axial in ancient Israel is, then, the exclusiveness of the relation with this God; and just as His distinguishing trait is His power over all rather than His ontological difference, so the distinguishing feature of Biblical religion is not denial of the ontological density of other 'gods' but rather *monolatry* – the rejection of worship of other gods and exclusive submission and devotion to the one God.[82]

This is a distinction of capital importance, and one that provides the basic framework for everything that follows in this book. In Biblical scholarship the term 'monolatry' is generally reserved for a pre-monotheistic stage of Israelite religion in which other gods were still believed to exist and have power, but in which worship was restricted to one of them. Alternatively, it can be used to denote exclusivity of worship without relation to exclusivity of belief (i.e. there could be either monotheistic or polytheistic monolatry).[83] Under either of these definitions, monotheism – as a concept – is accorded pride of place, and monolatry in and of itself is conceived as either falling short of it or as ancillary to it. I adopt here, however, the argument of Yehoshua Amir that monolatry is to be considered "not just, as is customary, as a preliminary stage, but rather as the true religious core of Biblical monotheism."[84] Idolatry is so vigorously condemned in the Bible not (or at least not primarily) because it is a conceptual error, but rather because it is considered an act of disloyalty and betrayal.[85]

Each of the two archetypes described above, philosophical transcendence and revelational transcendence, presents a relatively stable world of meaning. The internal variations within each type offer different solutions to a problem, or varying degrees of insistence on one aspect of the economy, but the central questions and basic configuration are for the most part consistent. The same cannot be said of the three major Abrahamic traditions. Each was (and is) a meeting-place of the two

[81] Benjamin Uffenheimer, "Myth and Reality in Ancient Israel," in Eisenstadt, *Origins*, pp. 135–168, at p. 152. See also Halbertal and Margalit, *Idolatry*, pp. 10–11: "it is anthropomorphism that gives meaning to the sin of idolatry"; and p. 21: "A personal, anthropomorphic God is essential in order for it to be possible to speak of the sin of idolatry."

[82] See Buber, *Königtum Gottes*, pp. 89ff.; Buber, *The Kingship of God*, pp. 108ff.

[83] Sommer, *Bodies of God*, p. 147.

[84] Amir, "Begegnung," p. 4: "möchte ich die Monolatrie nicht nur, wie üblich, als eine Vorstufe, sondern geradezu als den eigentlichen religiösen Kern des biblischen Monotheismus bezeichnen."

[85] Halbertal and Margalit, *Idolatry*, pp. 21ff.

economies and was formed through a constant negotiation of their relation one to another.

An important feature of this meeting of the two economies is contestation and instability. Features of transcendence that made perfect sense in their original economy become problematic when attempts are made to reconcile them. For example, the original revelational economy does not consider the existence of internal complexity in God to be problematic; to the contrary, God's being endowed with attributes was, as noted, an essential and constitutive feature of Biblical transcendence. The philosophical economy, however, in its search for the ontological uniqueness and simplicity of the One, views positive attributes as a violation of transcendence. In early Islamic theology the Muʿtazila – notwithstanding the obscurity of their precise debt to Late Antique philosophy[86] – clearly attempted to reconcile the God of revelation and the demand for ontological simplicity. The debate over the divine attributes in medieval Islam can thus be analyzed through the prism of the two economies and the strategies employed in relation to them.

This is only one example. In Chapter 1 the typology outlined above will be applied systematically to an analysis of Ibn Taymiyya's theology, and it will be argued that Ibn Taymiyya was a consistent defender of the revelational economy against the philosophical one. Above all, Ibn Taymiyya insisted on the primacy of monolatry over conceptual monotheism. His formulation of monolatry as an explicit theological doctrine was to prove tremendously influential on salafī thought, and in essence laid the principal ground for the subsequent developments treated in this study, up to and including present-day salafī theonomy.

## Outline of the Present Work

Chapter 1 is devoted to an analysis of Ibn Taymiyya's theology in light of the typology developed above. Clearly there can be no question of

[86] Richard M. Frank, a scholar keener than most to emphasize the indigenous Arab-Muslim nature of the Muʿtazila (in contrast with the *falāsifa*), nonetheless agrees that "in a real and basic sense the fundamental questions are Greek, for the tradition of their explicit conception and formulation as theroretical questions is Greek in origin." Richard MacDonough Frank, *Beings and Their Attributes: The Teaching of the Basrian School of the Muʿtazila in the Classical Period*, Albany: State University of New York Press, 1978, p. 1. For possible philosophical antecedents, see e.g. Shlomo Pines, *Studies in Islamic Atomism*, trans. Michael Schwarz, ed. Tzvi Langermann, Jerusalem: Magnes Press, The Hebrew University of Jerusalem, 1997, pp. 108–141 (who also addresses possible Indian influences at length); Josef van Ess, *The Flowering of Muslim Theology*, trans. Jane Marie Todd, Cambridge, MA, and London: Harvard University Press, 2006, pp. 79–115; Josef van Ess, *Theology and Society in the Second and Third Centuries of the Hijra*, vol. 4, trans. Gwendolin Goldbloom, Leiden and Boston: Brill, 2019, pp. 514–534.

providing a complete survey of the voluminous Taymiyyan corpus in these terms. My aim rather is to provide a general exposition of Ibn Taymiyya's theology as an integral system. The chapter will focus on the central place accorded in the system to monolatry, which in Ibn Taymiyya's terminology is called *tawḥīd al-ulūhiyya*, and which he consistently describes as the true heart of Islam. He argues that nearly everyone, whether Muslim or unbeliever, already acknowledges God's objective existence and knows Him as the Creator of the world; this aspect of divinity he terms *rubūbiyya*, and acknowledgment of it *tawḥīd al-rubūbiyya*. He accuses a great many of his contemporaries, such as Ashʿarī theologians and Ṣūfī mystics, of focusing on *rubūbiyya* to the exclusion of *ulūhiyya* – in other words, on conceptual monotheism to the exclusion of monolatry – and thus as failing to uphold the heart of Islam, that which differentiates Muslims from unbelievers. The chapter examines the different discursive and polemical contexts in which Ibn Taymiyya formulates his distinctive positions on each of the five topics adumbrated in this Introduction and examines their coherence as a theological system centered on monolatry.

Chapter 2 builds on this analysis in order to clarify the relation between Ibn Taymiyya's theology and the early Wahhābī movement, through a comparison between the writings of its founder, Muḥammad b. ʿAbd al-Wahhāb (d. 1206/1792), and those of Ibn Taymiyya. The chapter demonstrates that Ibn ʿAbd al-Wahhāb adopted the concept of *tawḥīd al-ulūhiyya* and made of it the centerpiece and raison d'être of his movement. While the connection between the two thinkers has been known to academic researchers since Goldziher, most did not correctly identify *tawḥīd al-ulūhiyya* as the definitive borrowing that served as the casus belli for the Wahhābī war on the Muslim cult of saints. Furthermore, a trend in the scholarship starting in the 1970s has tended to downplay the importance of Ibn Taymiyya's influence on Ibn ʿAbd al-Wahhāb altogether; for these reasons a reexamination of the issue was in order. In addition, the chapter demonstrates that Ibn ʿAbd al-Wahhāb's Yemeni contemporary Muḥammad b. Ismāʿīl al-Ṣanʿānī (d. 1182/1769), commonly known as Ibn al-Amīr, likewise embraced Ibn Taymiyya's doctrine of *tawḥīd al-ulūhiyya*; this suggests that a general reexamination of eighteenth-century revivalist currents may be required so as to distinguish between a general concern for orthopraxy and truly doctrinaire monolatry of Taymiyyan inspiration.

Chapter 3 remains in the premodern period but shifts focus from Taymiyyan theology to a precedent for modern theonomy from the field of jurisprudential theory (*uṣūl al-fiqh*). The chapter examines polemic against the theory and practice of *taqlīd*, that is, adherence to the legal precedents of an individual jurist or law school in place of direct derivation of judgments from revelation (the Qurʾān and the *sunna*). The authors of these polemical writings, who were broadly affiliated with what we would call today the salafī jurisprudential tradition (Ḥanbalīs and others generally affiliated with the *ahl al-ḥadīth*), characterized categorical forms of *taqlīd* as polytheism (*shirk*). Their underlying argument was that adherence to law in matters of prohibition and permission is a form of worship, and thus adherence to human precedent, in place of deriving legal determinations from the divinely revealed sources, is tantamount to worship of humans in place of Allāh. The chapter traces this polemic from the fifth/eleventh-century authors Abū Bakr al-Bayhaqī and Ibn ʿAbd al-Barr, through Ibn Taymiyya and his foremost student Ibn Qayyim al-Jawziyya (d. 751/1350), up to eighteenth- and nineteenth-century authors such as Ibn ʿAbd al-Wahhāb, Muḥammad al-Shawkānī, and scholars from the Indian Ahl-i Ḥadīth. In addition, the chapter argues that an influential academic article on *taqlīd* and *ijtihād* by Wael Hallaq mischaracterized both the nature of the polemic and the affiliation of anti-*taqlīd* scholars: Hallaq projected onto them a modernist concern for creative development of the law, whereas the basis for premodern opposition to *taqlīd* was rather a salafī concern for the exclusivity of legal obedience to Allāh.

Chapter 4 examines the theonomic doctrine of two influential twentieth-century authors, the Indo-Pakistani Abū al-Aʿlā Mawdūdī and the Egyptian Sayyid Quṭb. Neither of these authors was affiliated with the salafī tradition, and they are often thought to represent a specifically modern and political form of Islamism: Mawdūdī was the founder of the Jamāʿat-i Islāmī organization, and Quṭb was a prominent ideologue of the Muslim Brotherhood in Egypt. Nonetheless, this chapter's examination of their theonomic doctrine of *ḥākimiyya* shows it to bear significant structural parallels to the salafī theological and jurisprudential precedents discussed in the first three chapters. Much like Ibn Taymiyya and Ibn ʿAbd al-Wahhāb, Mawdūdī and Quṭb consistently distinguish between two aspects of divinity, one relating to Allāh's objective nature as the supreme wielder of power over the cosmos, and another relating to His normative authority in relation to human life. The major distinction between their doctrine of *ḥākimiyya* and Taymiyyan *tawḥīd al-ulūhiyya* lies in Mawdūdī and Quṭb's conceptualization of the latter aspect of divinity: In their system, the primary demand that it makes on humans is not ritual worship but legal-political obedience. The chapter presents evidence that Mawdūdī's use of a fundamentally monolatric basis to define Islam itself as theonomy was influenced by salafī precedents; in addition, the chapter demonstrates that Quṭb's debt to Mawdūdī was greater than is often acknowledged, and that in the writings of his late period he adopted the *ḥākimiyya* doctrine in full from Mawdūdī, to a degree not fully appreciated in the literature to date. Building on this analysis the chapter argues that Mawdūdī and Quṭb's modernity lies not so much in a depature from traditional Islamic conceptions per se but rather in their reconfiguration of ones formerly identified with the premodern salafī tendency in response to secularization processes in the Muslim world, and specifically the modern nation-state's claim to ultimate legal-political supremacy.

Finally, Chapter 5, dealing primarily with the period between the 1970s and the 1990s, examines the emergence of theonomy as a central preoccupation in modern salafī theology. The chapter opens with an analysis of Muslim Brotherhood Supreme Guide Ḥasan al-Huḍaybī's arguments on the topic of *ḥākimiyya*. Despite apparent surface agreement, the analysis of al-Huḍaybī's writings shows that he in fact rejected the central bases on which Mawdūdī and Quṭb erected theonomy as a true criterion of faith. In contrast with this rejection on the part of the mainstream Muslim Brotherhood, the chapter demonstrates that theonomy took root in the widespread milieu of thinkers and movements that combined Quṭbist thought with the salafī tradition. In parallel, circles of quietist salafīs produced their own theonomic doctrine based on the premodern salafī precedents discussed in the first three chapters and applied it to issues such as parliamentary elections and democratic participation. Salafī jihādī authors built on these earlier forays but elaborated a more uncompromising doctrine that embedded theonomy closely in the Taymiyyan configuration of *tawḥīd*. On this basis the salafī jihādīs argued that theonomy lies at the very heart of Islam and they accordingly condemned even instrumental compromises with democracy as acts of unbelief. Insisting on the apostasy of the ruling regimes, they enthusiastically embraced armed jihād as the proper means to establish rule by Allāh's law.

## Notes on Method

This book was written in the dual perspective of the intellectual history of Islam and comparative political theology. Here I will address each of these perspectives in turn before concluding the Introduction with some broader remarks on the nature of this present study, what it purports to explain, and equally important, what it does not.

As regards intellectual history, the study traces a number of interrelated issues in Islamic theology and jurisprudence over a wide span of time through close readings of the relevant texts. The initial identification of authors and themes was dictated by my primary aim in the study, namely, to explain the intellectual precedents and the historical development of the doctrine of theonomy in modern-day salafī thought. To this end the modern literature, selections of which are analyzed in Chapter 5, provided the indications for where to look in the premodern sources. The guiding principle underlying this approach is that modern salafī literature is best understood in light of the literature that its authors themselves read and cite. Salafism is, among other things, a learned textual tradition that poses a constant demand for theological justification of one's positions in the terms of the tradition.[87] I thus followed first of all the paths of inquiry that the literature itself suggested, and for the most part this approach has proven fruitful. (Mawdūdī and Quṭb are an exception as their historical impact is not fully reflected in present-day salafī texts; see Chapter 5.)

I then approached the relevant literature, both premodern and modern, on its own terms, in the classic approach of Islamic studies. Some precisions are in order as to what it means to approach literature on its own terms. It has been important, first and foremost, to avoid presentist bias, that is, the back-projection of later conceptions onto earlier authors in an anachronistic fashion – especially as traditional Islamic scholarship is conservative in the sense that it often seeks to ascribe even that which is clearly novel to earlier authoritative figures.[88]

In the salafī school, notwithstanding the rhetorical elevation of the Qurʾān and the *sunna* as the sole authoritative sources, there exists considerable pressure to demonstrate conformity between one's own ideas and Ibn Taymiyya's doctrines. The role of the academic scholar is to approach such claims with skepticism. While I ultimately argue that premodern doctrines do in fact lay the ground for modern salafī theonomy I have treated this as a claim to be proven, and my conclusions are not identical to the claims of modern salafīs themselves. Their doctrine of

[87] See e.g. ʿAlī al-Ḥalabī's account of what he was doing at the moment his teacher Shaykh Muḥammad Nāṣir al-Dīn al-Albānī died in Jordan (meant in part to explain and justify his absence). He was participating in a study session in Riyadh between the evening and night prayers and, in response to a question posed by one of the participants, sought to establish the orthodoxy of al-Albānī's theological positions by arguing that they are in agreement with Ibn Taymiyya and Ibn Qayyim al-Jawziyya. ʿAlī b. Ḥasan al-Ḥalabī al-Atharī, "Maʿa shaykhinā nāṣir al-sunna wa-l-dīn fī shuhūr ḥayātihi al-akhīra," in Nūr al-Dīn Ṭālib (ed.), *Maqālāt al-Albānī*, Riyadh: Dār Aṭlas, 1421/2000, pp. 207–213, at p. 212.

[88] Cf. Bertrand Russell's observation regarding the Scholastics: "When they were original, they tried to conceal the fact." *History of Western Philosophy and Its Connection with Political and Social Circumstances from the Earliest Times to the Present Day*, London: George Allen and Unwin, 1946, p. 451.

theonomy is one that is unique in historical terms and which responds to challenges that are specific to the modern age. It is only through close attention to each author's writings and his contemporary discursive contexts that one can map the diachronic continuities and discontinuities that shape this intellectual history.

Opposite the tendency of modern salafīs to assert a smooth continuity with their early and medieval forebears, much current academic literature promotes the contrary view, namely, that modern radical authors are ignorant and their claims to continuity unfounded.[89] My own study found modern salafīs, including radical ones, generally to be astute readers of Ibn Taymiyya and the salafī tradition, but methodologically I have attempted to neutralize any bias toward one position or the other.

The relevance of political theology has already been explored in this Introduction. From the methodological standpoint it provides the best overall perspective for the study. The doctrine of theonomy lies at the seam of what we consider to be the religious and the political, and we simply cannot apply these terms to the analysis of our sources without explicit theoretization, especially as they tend to configure these elements in a manner that contests our own native understanding. Political theology reminds us that there is no one natural configuration of the relation between divine and mundane authority and that the issue requires case-sensitive analysis within a comparative and typological perspective. Theonomy's contention that divine legal sovereignty is the only legitimate basis for political rule invites us to rethink configurations of the theological and the political. That said, my object of study is specifically salafī theonomy and not the concept of theonomy in general, nor do I address at any length other Muslim or non-Muslim critiques of secularization and democracy that do not share salafī premises. This study correspondingly remains anchored in its sources, with the wider perspectives simply meant to help elucidate them – though in the Conclusion I do circle back to topics in political theology outlined in this Introduction in order to further clarify the place of salafī theonomy in comparison with other political theologies of the modern era.

Finally I would like to address the question of what this study seeks to explain and what it does not. Most monographs on modern Islamic radicalism weave a cohesive narrative comprised both of analysis of

[89] Much of the literature in this vein relates specifically to the relation (or lack thereof) between modern radicalism and Ibn Taymiyya. Examples include Mona Hassan, "Modern Interpretations and Misinterpretations of a Medieval Scholar: Apprehending the Political Thought of Ibn Taymiyya," in Yossef Rapoport and Shahab Ahmed (eds.), *Ibn Taymiyya and His Times*, Karachi: Oxford University Press, 2010, pp. 338–366; Yayha Michot, *Ibn Taymiyya against Extremisms*, Beirut: Dar Albouraq, 1433/2012.

ideology, as it is usually called, and various forms of social-historical description (biography and/or social, political, or institutional history). The present study diverges from this pattern. It seeks to highlight continuities and evolution across a broad arc of history, its chronological and theoretical scope are correspondingly capacious, and this naturally comes at the expense of much else.

This choice does not in itself constitute an a priori position on the relevance or aptness of other approaches. There is no inherent contradiction between the existence of ideational continuities over the long term and a given thinker being motivated to partake in them due to considerations relating to immediate circumstances. This study simply emphasizes the former perspective, and in consequence the external social developments that it does take into account are primarily large-scale ones of general import, those whose relevance is unquestionable in light of the sources themselves. In particular, Chapters 4 and 5 argue that the modern theonomic discourse emerged largely in response to the secularization of legal-political systems in the Middle East over the course of the nineteenth and twentieth centuries.

On the whole, however, this book does not purport to identify 'causes' of modern salafī radicalism. For one thing, whether this book is about real-world action at all is a question of perspective. I argue that a defining feature of salafism as a counter-tradition is its privileging of praxis over theory, monolatry over 'mere' monotheism – and monolatry is not an idea but rather a kind of Gestalt, the ground for an entire socioreligious construction of the world, encompassing not only propositional attitudes and discursive propositions but also imaginal realities and affective dispositions. On the other hand, salafism, even when viewed as a social phenomenon, places great emphasis on education and textual study, and my particular object of inquiry lies precisely in the realm of the discursive proposition, to wit, various formulations of monolatry and theonomy in learned Islamic discourse. This is speech about action, a discourse that theoretizes action, and not action itself. I have sought to understand a language, to render it intelligible to others, and to suggest a framework for understanding its significance.

This is not the place for a general discursus on causation and history, but I will offer a few thoughts on how this book can inform future studies on topics of a more concrete social-historical order.

When a human undertakes an intentional act 'for a reason' we normally understand that reason as an answer to the question 'why did they do it?' The explanatory power of this 'for a reason' is baked into the very concept of intentional action and appears to be a fundamental category of human understanding. Natural languages code for objective-oriented action in various ways, and legal systems weigh intentionality as an element of the act.

Yet what seems a given at the level of the individual appears problematic at broader levels of social organization. It is difficult enough to determine an individual's aim in performing a given act let alone find ways to aggregate countless individual aims and actions, correlated in this way or that, into an explanation of group behavior. Thus when social-historical research speaks of causes it often tends to mean by the term something more 'objective': a fluctuation in oil prices, the repression experienced by the Egyptian Muslim Brothers under ʿAbd al-Nāṣir, a change in one variable that impacts other variables.

In other words, the attempt to arrive at metrics and causal analysis (as widely understood) often seeks to sidestep the inherently intentional and creative nature of human action. As Talcott Parsons writes:

> The positivistic reaction against philosophy has, in its effect on the social sciences, manifested a strong tendency to obscure the fact that man is essentially an active, creative, evaluating creature. Any attempt to explain his behavior in terms of ends, purposes, ideals, has been under suspicion as a form of "teleology" which was thought to be incompatible with the methodological requirements of positive science. One must, on the contrary, explain in terms of "causes" and "conditions," not of ends.[90]

This same suspicion is often (perhaps especially) harbored against the humanistic disciplines – in our context theology, philology, Islamic studies. By these lights, a humanistic 'qualitative' study is subjective and impressionistic, not explanatory and scientific. Yet the intentional and subjective nature of human action is to this author's mind a social fact, as close to a universal axiom of human behavior as we can determine. As such, we cannot do without ends and all that goes into the human conceptualization of ends.

As Cornelius Castoriadis has noted, Western thought has not bequeathed us an ontology of the social-historical. Above all it has elided the role of human imagination and creativity and the inherent instability and unpredictability they entail. As with the ontology of particular existents, the thorniest problem is that of change over time, and for human societies this is a problem that an overly deterministic conception of causation cannot resolve:

> The non-causal ... comes into play as behavior that is not simply 'unpredictable' but rather *creative* (on the level of individuals, groups, classes, or entire societies).

[90] Talcott Parsons, "The Place of Ultimate Values in Sociological Theory," *International Journal of Ethics* 45/3 (April 1935), pp. 282–316, at p. 282.

It comes into play not as a simple deviation from an existing type, but as the *establishing* of a new type of behavior, the *instituting* of a new social rule, the *invention* of a new object or a new form. In short, it comes into play as an arising or producing that is not susceptible to deduction on the basis of the precedent situation ... It has already been remarked that the living being is more than a simple mechanism because it can offer new responses to new situations. The historical being, however, is more than the simply living being because it can offer new responses to the 'same' situations and can create new situations. History cannot be thought on the basis of a determinist scheme (nor for that matter a simple 'dialectical' one) because it is the domain of *creation*.[91]

There are certainly regions of human life that display regularities and these are more susceptible to causal analysis. The Axial thesis, however, while sensitive to social-historical circumstance, is fundamentally at odds with the idea that human society and its fundamental tectonics are *determined* by observable factors in the realm of the seen. For this reason any elaboration of the social dimensions of 'Axial' cultural content, such as our monolatry-theonomy nexus, would require us to take seriously what Castoriadis termed "the imaginary institution of society."

In sum, this study seeks to explain only what it explicitly seeks to explain. It is my hope that it will prove a worthy contribution both to the growing literature on modern salafism and to the study of comparative political theology in the modern age.

[91] Cornelius Castoriadis, *L'institution imaginaire de la société*, Paris: Seuil, 1975, p. 65.

# 1 Monolatry in Ibn Taymiyya's Theological System

In the Introduction I briefly outlined the doctrine of theonomy as it has been elaborated by contemporary Islamic radicals, defining it as comprising two interrelated claims: (1) the institution of rule by God's law is a sine qua non of monotheistic/monolatric faith; and (2) other legal-political systems, and democracy in particular, are inherently polytheistic. My task here, and for the rest of this study, will be to trace the historical evolution of this concept of theonomy.

The reason why I have begun this task with a chapter on Ibn Taymiyya is not that he elaborated an explicit theonomic doctrine akin to the modern one. Modern salafīs generally view their war on the political polytheism of democracy and man-made legislation as a newly arisen front in the general salafī war on polytheism,[1] and thus the precedents they adduce from premodern thinkers are not often political ones, but rather theological and jurisprudential. The question that I pose here is not where one may find direct precedents for modern salafīs' concern with political polytheism, but rather what kind of conception of faith – what kind of theology – is a necessary condition for the emergence of modern salafī theonomy.

It is not fortuitous that in our day the dogmatic espousal of a strict theonomic doctrine is primarily the province of the salafī jihādī school, which sees itself as the rightful heir to Ibn Taymiyya and to the salafī tradition as a whole. I will argue in the coming chapters that modern salafī theonomy is deeply indebted to a central and distinctive feature of Ibn Taymiyya's theology: the precedence he accorded to monolatry over conceptual monotheism, and his consequent insistence that the essence of Islam is servitude and obedience to Allāh and His law. Our description of the historical evolution of salafī theonomy will thus need to begin from an investigation into Ibn Taymiyya's doctrine of monolatry and its place in his theology.

[1] See e.g. Abū Muḥammad ʿĀṣim al-Maqdisī, *Kashf al-niqāb ʿan sharīʿat al-ghāb*, [written 1408/1988,] pp. 2–3, www.ilmway.com/site/maqdis/MS_38438.html (link no longer active).

This chapter approaches the thought of Ibn Taymiyya in relation to the general theoretical framework outlined in the Introduction. It will attempt to show that Ibn Taymiyya was, first and foremost, a sophisticated defender of the revelational economy of transcendence against the philosophical one. Ibn Taymiyya's theological writings will be analyzed here in relation to each of the five basic topics discussed in the Introduction: epistemology, cratology vs. ontology, cataphatism vs. apophatism, the mode of interaction between the transcendent and the mundane (unmediated vs. mediated), and finally and most importantly, monolatry vs. conceptual monotheism.

The aforementioned topics are tightly interwoven in Ibn Taymiyya's writings. I would argue that his well-known tendency to seemingly digress from one topic to another is generally due, in fact, precisely to the systematic nature of his theology. These apparent digressions usually reveal themselves to be variations on a theme, a mapping of a question's place within the system alongside and as an aid to its resolution. The separate treatment of these topics in what follows is thus somewhat artificial, a flaw I will attempt to remedy through a demonstration of how the different aspects of the system stand in relation one to another.

It should be noted that the systematicity of Ibn Taymiyya's theology is not universally acknowledged. Certainly he is not systematic in the typical *kalām* or philosophical sense, despite his considerable acumen in the rational sciences. It does make sense to discuss what Ovamir Anjum has called Ibn Taymiyya's "deconstructive project,"[2] and I myself consider his system to be in a sense an anti-system, one that by design destabilizes merely human reifications in order to open onto the divine. This deconstructive or anti-systemic element will come to light at points throughout the present chapter. Nonetheless, I concur with Sophia Vasalou's observation that "it would be a mistake to exaggerate the fragmentation and negative character of Ibn Taymiyya's thought … certain general plots recur with unfailing regularity … his writing keeps gravitating toward a set of thematic clusters and these with distinct internal relations to one another."[3] Thus my specific argument – namely, that Ibn Taymiyya's system exemplifies and means to defend a revelational archetype of monotheism against the philosophical one – should help to elucidate as well the overall question of what Ibn Taymiyya's unusual system is, how it is constructed, and what it means.

In Ibn Taymiyya's thought, the first four topics – epistemology, cratology vs. ontology, cataphatism vs. apophatism, and the mode of

[2] Anjum, *Politics*, p. 183.

[3] Sophia Vasalou, *Ibn Taymiyya's Theological Ethics*, New York: Oxford University Press, 2016, p. 19.

interaction between the transcendent and the mundane (unmediated vs. mediated) – fall under a general rubric known as *tawḥīd al-rubūbiyya* (sometimes translated as "Unicity of Lordship"), whereas monolatry is referred to as *tawḥīd al-ulūhiyya* (sometimes translated as "Unicity of Godship"). Although at times the issue of cataphatism is set off as a third form of *tawḥīd*, called *tawḥīd al-asmāʾ wa-l-ṣifāt* ("Unicity of the Names and the Attributes"), the fundamental distinction in Ibn Taymiyya's theology is between Allāh's two aspects of *rubūbiyya* and *ulūhiyya*. *Rubūbiyya* refers to Allah's objective nature, both in itself and in relation to the world, whereas *ulūhiyya* refers to Allāh as an object of worship and devotion.

What Ibn Taymiyya believes to be the correct positions on each of the first four topics collectively make up proper *tawḥīd al-rubūbiyya*. What is required for each of them is first and foremost a proper propositional attitude. Yet even the 'correct' positions on these issues only make up one part of *tawḥīd*, and the lesser part at that; they are collectively what we can term roughly as 'monotheism.' They need to be complemented by *tawḥīd al-ulūhiyya*, that is, exclusivity of worship of Allāh or 'monolatry.' In what follows, the issue of the interrelation between these two aspects of divinity will be a major concern. In particular we will see that Ibn Taymiyya ascribes priority to *tawḥīd al-ulūhiyya* over *tawḥīd al-rubūbiyya* – that is, to monolatry over conceptual monotheism – and makes it the linchpin of the entire system. This will then serve as the basis in later chapters for an investigation of how, in the modern era, the monolatric emphasis came increasingly to be interpreted in terms of theonomy.

## Epistemology

The question of whether God exists, or of how to prove that God exists, is not a natural component of the revelational economy. Its concern is rather for the exclusivity and quality of belief and devotion to the one God, whose existence is not in question. This generalization appears to hold true for early Islam as well; in the words of Majid Fakhry, "prior to the rise of the Muʿtazilah, who initiated the whole current of scholastic theology (kalām) in Islam, of course, the question of the demonstrability of God's existence, like the remaining questions of rational theology, could hardly arise."[4] By Ibn Taymiyya's time, however, proof of Allāh's existence was a much-debated topic in theology, and was considered by

[4] Majid Fakhry, "The Classical Islamic Arguments for the Existence of God," *The Muslim World* 47/2, 1957, pp. 133–145, at p. 135.

various currents of rationalist theology a necessary prerequisite for faith in Allāh and in His revelation. The establishment of such a proof necessarily depended on the resolution of more general epistemological problems: what premises can be considered known by necessity (i.e. what premises can be considered self-evident) and how one can reason from such premises to arrive at a logically necessary conclusion.[5]

Ibn Taymiyya's writings on this question can be characterized as an attempt to explain, in rational discursive fashion, why the question should not arise at all. This issue is illustrative of Ibn Taymiyya's unique position as a philosophically sophisticated defender of the revelational economy. To attempt to remain insulated from philosophical influence and maintain a simple faith in Allāh remained an ideal. However, once philosophical and theological speculation had become widespread in the Islamic milieu, the effective defense of the revelational economy that Ibn Taymiyya sought to mount would require an engagement with the arguments of his adversaries and the elaboration of an alternative explanation of how it is that we have knowledge of Allāh.

For Ibn Taymiyya, unlike the *kalām* theologians he opposed, the question of how we know the existence of Allāh is not a special case of the general question of how we know what we know. The relation is precisely the inverse: Knowledge of Allāh is the basis for knowledge in general: "Allāh, may He be praised, in that He is the First, who created all beings, and the Last, the telos of all occurrences, is the comprehensive foundation, and thus knowledge of Him is the foundation of all knowledge and encompasses it."[6]

Thus, generally speaking, Ibn Taymiyya's answer to the question both of how we know Allāh and how we know what we know is that what we know is from Allāh, and not from ourselves.[7] This principle is premised

5 This holds true whether or not these premises were explicitly constituted as a separate and preliminary object of inquiry; on this development, see Fakhry, "Classical Islamic Arguments," p. 134. On the issue in general, see e.g. Herbert A. Davidson, *Proofs for Eternity, Creation, and the Existence of God in Medieval Islamic and Jewish Philosophy*, New York and Oxford: Oxford University Press, 1987; Ayman Shihadeh, "The Existence of God," in Tim Winter (ed.), *The Cambridge Companion to Classical Islamic Theology*, New York: Cambridge University Press, 2008, pp. 197–217; Wilferd Madelung, "Abū l-Ḥuṣayn al-Baṣrī's Proof for the Existence of God," in James E. Montgomery (ed.), *Arabic Theology, Arabic Philosophy: From the Many to the One: Essays in Celebration of Richard M. Frank*, Leuven: Peeters, 2006, pp. 273–280.

6 *Allāh subḥānahu lammā kāna huwa al-awwal alladhī khalaqa al-kā'ināt wa-l-ākhir alladhī ilayhi taṣīru al-ḥādithāt fa-huwa al-aṣl al-jāmi' fa-l-'ilm bihi aṣl kull 'ilm wa-jāmi'uhu.* Taqī al-Dīn b. Taymiyya, *Majmū'at al-fatāwā*, al-Manṣūra: Dār al-Wafā', 1426/2005, vol. 2, p. 16.

7 Such an approach obviously invites charges of circularity. For responses to this charge, see Ibn Taymiyya, *Majmū'at al-fatāwā*, vol. 2, pp. 48ff.

on the foundational distinction between the Creator and the created, the Lord and those subject to Him: "The servant (*al-ʿabd*), in that he is created and subject to the Lord … his knowledge and action derive from (*ʿāda ilā*) his Creator." Ibn Taymiyya explains that Allāh is the foundation (*aṣl*) and that humans and their knowledge are the derivative (*farʿ*), and thus the proper order is to derive the derivative from the foundation. This conception is placed in explicit contrast to the "path of philosophy [and] speculative theology" (*al-ṭarīqa al-falsafiyya al-kalāmiyya*), whose adherents "started from themselves, and made themselves the foundation from which things are to be derived … and thus they discussed (*takallamū fī*) their attainment of knowledge and said that it is at times through the senses, at times through reason, and at times through both."[8]

Given that for Ibn Taymiyya knowledge in general begins from knowledge of Allāh, the stakes at issue in epistemology are of inherent theological and normative import. He frequently returns to this basic differentiation between two contrasting epistemological paths, one beginning from Allāh and the other from humans, as a general explanation for the difference between right belief and heresy. The main locus of this contrast is Ibn Taymiyya's critique of the use of *qiyās* in theology. The word *qiyās* in this context can refer either to a formal Aristotelian syllogism or to other forms of analogical reasoning. As we will see presently, Ibn Taymiyya argues that the use of *qiyās* in attaining knowledge of Allāh is not only of limited effectiveness, but also leads to polytheism (*shirk*), for the simple reason that *qiyās* is based on a similitude or common denominator between the two terms of comparison, thereby placing Allāh and creation on the same plane.

This fundamental and structural opposition to philosophical epistemology is certainly central to Ibn Taymiyya's thought. It ought not be confused, however, with a blind fideism that demands unthinking acceptance of revelation devoid of any correspondence to the assent of reason.[9] Rather, Ibn Taymiyya's epistemology is built on his conception of a natural congruence between divinely implanted human nature – the

[8] Ibn Taymiyya, *Majmūʿat al-fatāwā*, vol. 2, p. 19.

[9] See on this Ibn Taymiyya's refutation of Ibn Rushd's characterization of the so-called *ḥashwiyya* as holding that knowledge of Allāh derives from revelation to the exclusion of reason: Ibn Rushd, *al-Kashf ʿan manāhij al-adilla fī ʿaqāʾid al-milla*, Beirut: Markaz Dirāsāt al-Waḥda al-ʿArabiyya, 1998, pp. 101–102; Ibn Taymiyya, *Bayān talbīs al-jahmiyya fī taʾsīs bidaʿihim al-kalāmiyya*, Medina: Mujammaʿ al-Malik Fahd, 1426[/2005], vol. 2, pp. 131–132. Aziz Al-Azmeh's statement that the Ḥanbalīs relied on the "dogmatic utterance," which he characterizes as "a technical one, not native to the human understanding nor innate to it," and his relegation of the concept of the *fiṭra* to part of a "dialectical repertory" is inaccurate, at least as regards Ibn Taymiyya. Al-Azmeh, "Orthodoxy and Ḥanbalite Fideism," pp. 257–258.

*fiṭra*[10] – and Allāh's "signs" – *āyāt*. There are three important features to the kind of knowledge that this epistemology yields: (1) it is specific; (2) it is direct; (3) it leads to action.

### *Specificity*

Ibn Taymiyya's emphasis on knowledge of particulars needs to be accentuated, as it is fundamental to Ibn Taymiyya's formulation of cataphatic theology as well (on which see below). Aristotle, in chapter 24 of Book I of the *Posterior Analytics*, had argued for the primacy of universal over particular demonstration. In Aristotle himself this method of abstraction, seen as a condition for the attainment of certain knowledge, stands in tension with his granting of ontological priority, *pace* Plato, to individual substances over universals.[11] This tension carried over to Muslim Peripatetics who, even when upholding Aristotelian ontology against Muslim Neoplatonists, continued to treat universals as prior in their logic.

In contrast, Ibn Taymiyya regularly insists that just as the particular is prior in ontology, so it is prior in epistemology. A good example of Ibn Taymiyya's insistence on this disjuncture between the universal, as treated in Aristotelian logic, and particular being, which for him is the primary object of knowledge, is the following passage from his *Mukhtaṣar naṣīḥat ahl al-īmān fī al-radd ʿalā manṭiq al-yūnān*:

> Universal, general propositions are not found in extramental existence (*fī al-khārij*) in universal and general form (*kulliyyatan ʿāmmatan*). They are only universal in the mind, not in [extramental] particulars. As for extramental existents, they are particular things. Each existent has an essence (*ḥaqīqa*) that is particular to it and by which it is differentiated from everything else, and which nothing else shares with it.
>
> Thus it is impossible to deduce through a syllogism (*bi-l-qiyās*) the specificity of a particular existent. They [sc. the logicians] admit this and say that the syllogism does not indicate (*dalla ʿalā*) the particular thing. They may express this as: [the syllogism] does not indicate the partial (*al-juzʾī*), but rather the universal (*al-*

10 See Livnat Holtzman, "Human Choice, Divine Guidance, and the *Fiṭra* Tradition: The Use of Hadith in Theological Treatises by Ibn Taymiyya and Ibn Qayyim al-Jawziyya," in Rapoport and Ahmed (eds.), *Ibn Taymiyya and His Times*, pp. 163–188; Jon Hoover, *Ibn Taymiyya's Theodicy of Perpetual Optimism*, Leiden and Boston: Brill, 2007, pp. 39–44.

11 Edward Booth, *Aristotelian Aporetic Ontology in Islamic and Christian Thinkers*, Cambridge: Cambridge University Press, 1983, pp. 2ff. Chapter 24 of Book I of the *Posterior Analytics* specifically denies that the use of a universal in logic implies its ontological existence "simply because it has a single denotation." Aristotle, *Posterior Analytics and Topica*, ed. Hugh Tredennick and E. S. Forster, London and Cambridge, MA: Loeb Classical Library, 1960, p. 141.

> *kullī*). Thus the syllogism does not yield knowledge of any particular existent (*amr mawjūd bi-ʿaynihi*). And every existent is a particular existent. Thus [the syllogism] does not yield knowledge of any of the essences of existents. It only yields abstract, universal things that are conceived in the mind, not real-world existence in the particulars.[12]

This argument is important to Ibn Taymiyya not so much in itself as in its application to the theological question of how we know Allāh, as can be seen from the continuation of the passage:

> The syllogistic proofs mentioned by the speculative [theologians or philosophers] (*al-nuẓẓār*), and which they call proofs that affirm the existence of the Creator, may He be praised – none of these indicate (*yadullu ʿalā*) His particularity, but only an abstract thing, the conceptualization of which does not preclude association (*al-sharika*) in it. If one says: something is originated, and every originated thing must necessarily have an originator, this only relates to an abstract, universal originator, the conceptualization of which does not preclude association in it. Its specificity is known only through another knowledge, which makes it Allāh in [people's] hearts.
>
> They [sc. the theologians and philosophers] admit this, since the conclusion [of a syllogism] goes no further than the premises, and the premises necessarily contain a universal proposition, and the universal does not indicate (*yadullu ʿalā*) the particular (*al-muʿayyan*).

For Ibn Taymiyya, to know Allāh is to know Him as particular and unique. The fact that he uses the word *sharika* to voice his concern with precluding association in one's conception of Allāh – that is, with developing a conception that precludes the possibility of commonality between Him and created beings – alludes, through etymological resonance with the word *shirk*, to the theological stakes at issue in this epistemological question. In a passage in *Bayān talbīs al-jahmiyya* this connection between formal logical proof of Allāh and polytheism is rendered more explicit:

> Allāh the Exalted has the highest likeness [*li-llāh al-mathal al-aʿlā*; cf. Qurʾān 16:60]. Thus it is impermissible for Him to be placed in an analogy of comparison (*qiyās tamthīl*) in which the foundation (*aṣl*) and the derivative (*farʿ*) are equated; and likewise He is not to be placed in a categorical syllogism (*qiyās shumūl*) in which the same judgment applies to [both] terms. This is because Allāh, may He be praised, is not alike to any other, nor can anything be equated with Him whatsoever. The employment of this kind of *qiyās* is tantamount to comparing Allāh to others (*ḍarb al-amthāl li-llāh*), and this is *shirk*.[13]

[12] Ibn Taymiyya, *Majmūʿat al-fatāwā*, vol. 9, p. 126.
[13] Ibn Taymiyya, *Bayān talbīs al-jahmiyya*, vol. 2, p. 347.

In the same vein, Ibn Taymiyya writes that those philosophers or speculative theologians (*ahl al-naẓar wa-l-qiyās*) who base their faith on syllogistic proofs believe there to be a common denominator between Allāh and others (as this is an inherent premise of their methodology), and are thereby guilty of associationist polytheism (*ṣārū mushrikīn bihi*). This is the case even when what they affirm of Allāh is true as far as it goes, since they fall short of understanding Allāh in such a way as to preclude commonality between Him and others.[14]

Ibn Taymiyya does not rule out the use of *qiyās* entirely with regard to Allāh, but he contends that the only permissible form is the a fortiori argument. Every perfection in created beings is to be attributed to Allāh a fortiori, and likewise imperfections in created beings are to be denied of Allāh.[15] The a fortiori argument, which Ibn Taymiyya argues appears in the Qurʾān itself,[16] does place Allāh in relation to other terms of comparison; since we ourselves are created, contingent beings, we cannot help but conceive of Allāh through appropriate (*mutawāṭiʾa*) terms and descriptions that contain both commonality and differentiation with created beings in such manner as to rule out partnership. Prophets and (to a lesser extent) gnostics can attain a more direct and profound knowledge of Allāh's specific characteristics (*khuṣūṣiyyāt*) as they truly are,[17] but this knowledge complements rather than contradicts the more general and approximate knowledge of Allāh available to all.

Ibn Taymiyya's insistence that universals are hysterogenic[18] – that is, they exist solely in the mind as an abstraction from our experience of particulars – is a recurring theme in his critique of other theological and mystical systems;[19] here we will only touch on the issue briefly where

14 Ibn Taymiyya, *Majmūʿat al-fatāwā*, vol. 2, p. 43. I am not aware of precedents for Ibn Taymiyya's specific arguments associating *qiyās* with *shirk* but he did not invent the theme. The Successor Muḥammad b. Sīrīn is reported to have said: "The first one to draw an analogy was Iblīs, and the sun and the moon were only worshipped due to the drawing of analogies" (*awwal man qāsa Iblīs wa-mā ʿubidat al-shams wa-l-qamar illā bi-l-maqāyīs*). Cited in Ibn Taymiyya, *Bayān talbīs al-jahmiyya*, vol. 1, p. 454.

15 See Hoover, *Ibn Taymiyya's Theodicy*, pp. 56ff.

16 Hoover, *Ibn Taymiyya's Theodicy*, pp. 59–62.

17 Ibn Taymiyya, *Majmūʿat al-fatāwā*, vol. 2, pp. 47–48.

18 Literally "later in origin" or "later-born." For the origin of the term, see Christoph Helmig, "Proclus' Criticism of Aristotle's Theory of Abstraction and Concept Formation in *Analytica Posteriora* II 19," in Frans A. J. de Haas, Mariska Leunissen, and Marije Martijn (eds.), *Interpreting Aristotle's* Posterior Analytics *in Late Antiquity and Beyond*, Leiden: Brill, 2010, pp. 27–54, at p. 29.

19 Ideally Ibn Taymiyya's doctrine on universals should be compared to those of his predecessors and contemporaries. I am not aware of another thinker for whom the issue was so pivotal in theology, but Ibn Taymiyya was not the only one to adopt some form of nominalism or conceptualism. It has been argued that al-Ghazālī stood at the beginning of this development in the Muslim world, which as in Latin scholasticism

relevant, as in the following section ("Cratology"). At present we will now describe Ibn Taymiyya's alternative epistemological approach, which centers on the concept of the *āya* and the *fiṭra*.

In the continuation of the passage cited above from *Mukhtaṣar naṣīḥat ahl al-īmān*, Ibn Taymiyya writes that in contrast with the path of *qiyās*, which does not lead one to knowledge of the particular (i.e. Allāh's specificity), stand

> the signs (*āyāt*) that Allāh mentions in the Qur'ān, such as what He said (Qur'ān 2:164): "Indeed, in the creation of the heavens and the earth, [in the alternation of night and day, in the ships that sail in the sea, bringing what is of benefit to people, in the water that Allāh brings down from the heavens and by which He revives the earth after its death, in Allāh's disseminating all kind of living being in the revived land, in the directing of the winds and the clouds that are subject [to Him] twixt the heavens and the earth, [in all these] are signs (*āyāt*) to people with understanding]" and other [such signs] which indicate the particular, like the sun, which is a sign of daytime.

> Indicative proof (*dalīl*) is a more inclusive category than *qiyās*, since an indicative proof might be from a particular to a particular, as for example [the location of] the Ka'ba is proven from the indication (*yustadallu bi-*) of the stars and other heavenly bodies. The signs indicate the Creator Himself (*nafs al-khāliq*), may He be praised, and not a common denominator between Himself and others, for everything other than Him is in need of Him Himself (*muftaqir ilayhi nafsihi*) [i.e. and not an abstract conception of Him], and thus the necessary conclusion from their existence is the existence of the Creator Himself in His specificity (*'ayn al-khāliq nafsihi*).[20]

We see again in this passage the intimate connection in Ibn Taymiyya's thought between, on the one hand, the general epistemological issue of how one acquires knowledge, and, on the other, the theological issue of how one arrives at true knowledge of Allāh. In his view knowledge of

represented a turn away from the Neoplatonized Aristotle: Frank Griffel, *Al-Ghazālī's Philosophical Theology*, Oxford: Oxford University Press, 2009, p. 97, also pp. 163–167, 176–178. The general topic still awaits systematic study. For the Avicennan background, see Michael Marmura, "Quiddity and Universality in Avicenna," in Parviz Morewedge (ed.), *Neoplatonism and Islamic Thought*, Albany: State University of New York, 1992, pp. 77–87; Michael Marmura, "Avicenna's Critique of Platonists in Book VII, Chapter 2 of the *Metaphysics* of His *Healing*," in Montgomery (ed.), *Arabic Theology*, pp. 355–369. Ibn Taymiyya seems to read a doctrine of hysterogenic universals into Aḥmad b. Ḥanbal's contention, contra the Jahmites, that "those versed in the rational sciences (*ahl al-'aql*) know that a thing that is not like [other] things is not a thing." Ibn Taymiyya understands this statement as countering the Jahmites' reluctance to describe Allāh as a "thing" (*shay'*) by insisting that the similarity in "thingness" between Allāh and creation is purely nominal. Ibn Taymiyya, *Dar' ta'āruḍ al-'aql wa-l-naql aw muwāfaqat ṣaḥīḥ al-manqūl li-ṣarīḥ al-ma'qūl*, Riyadh: Dār al-Kunūz al-Adabiyya, 1411/1991, vol. 5, pp. 178–179.

20 Ibn Taymiyya, *Majmū'at al-fatāwā*, vol. 9, p. 126.

Allāh is precisely knowledge of His specificity, and analogy and syllogism are incapable of leading one to knowledge of Allāh as an *individuum*. The sign (*āya*) is specific, in contrast with analogy and syllogism, which work through the general.

### *Directness*

The sign (*āya*) in Ibn Taymiyya's conception is also direct: Since it does not pass through a general common denominator, it is "from a particular to a particular." The directness of the indication or pointer (*dalīl*) is the second of its critical features. In a certain sense Ibn Taymiyya's emphasis on the *āya* as a sign found in the natural or human world and which leads to knowledge of Allāh sounds similar to the Muʿtazila's emphasis on reflection on nature and speculation as a prerequisite to attainment of knowledge of Allāh. The crucial difference between the two paths lies in the directness and existential immediacy of the *āya*.

This difference will perhaps be best illuminated through the concept of "creature-feeling" (Kreaturgefühl) elaborated by the scholar of comparative religion Rudolf Otto. Otto's concept was at once a development and critique of the religious epistemology of the liberal Protestant theologian Friedrich Schleiermacher. This latter thinker, like other Enlightenment-era Protestant thinkers, was concerned with preserving an authentic place for religion in the face of the seeming incommensurability of orthodoxy and reason. His solution was to ground religion in the realm of feeling, somewhat akin to aesthetic sensibility, and in particular in the human's consciousness of his own dependence (Abhängigkeit) on something greater. Once this absolute, natural grounds for religion had been isolated one could then learn about divinity by inference from one's own subjective state.[21] In his critique of Schleiermacher, Otto, who was likewise interested in identifying absolute, natural grounds for religion, built on this concept of dependence. He contended, however, that this experience is qualitatively distinct from the mundane experience of dependence and rebaptized it as "creature-feeling" (Kreaturgefühl), which he defined as "the emotion of a creature, submerged and overwhelmed by its own nothingness in contrast to that which is supreme above all creatures."[22] More important for our purposes, however, is

[21] See Walter H. Capps, *Religious Studies: The Making of a Discipline*, Minneapolis: Fortress Press, 1995, pp. 13ff.

[22] Rudolf Otto, *The Idea of the Holy*, 2nd ed., trans. John W. Harvey, London: Oxford University Press, 1950, p. 10; Rudolf Otto, *Das Heilige*, Gotha: Leopold Klotz, 1929, p. 10.

Otto's description of the immediacy with which creature-feeling flows from the objective reality that gave rise to it:

> According to him [Schleiermacher] the religious emotion would be directly and primarily a sort of *self*-consciousness, a feeling concerning oneself in a special, determined relation, viz. one's dependence. Thus, according to Schleiermacher, I can only come upon the very fact of God as the result of an inference, that is, by reasoning to a cause beyond myself to account for my 'feeling of dependence.' But this is entirely opposed to the psychological facts of the case. Rather, the 'creature-feeling' is itself a first subjective concomitant and effect of another feeling-element, which casts it like a shadow, but which in itself indubitably has immediate and primary reference to an object outside the self.[23]

The "immediate and primary reference to an object outside the self" is quite close to Ibn Taymiyya's description of the pointing process by which a human, upon considering one of Allāh's signs (*āyāt*), has knowledge of Allāh. Likewise, as we saw in the passage from *Mukhtaṣar naṣīḥat ahl al-īmān*, the operation of the *āya* brings such knowledge through the basic creaturely condition of lack or being-in-need (*iftiqār*), akin to the psychological experience of Abhängigkeit or Kreaturgefühl. The pious quality of this knowledge is underlined by Ibn Taymiyya through a *ḥadīth* that he cites in this context: The Companion Jubayr b. Muṭʿim, upon hearing the verse (Qurʾān 52:35) "Or were they created without there being anything (that created them),[24] or are they the creators?" said: "When I heard it I felt my heart splitting open."[25] Ibn Taymiyya's interest in this *ḥadīth* is clearly due to the contrast he finds therein to the path of the *kalām* theologians. The verse asks the unbelievers a rhetorical question that parallels the cosmological proof of the *kalām* theologians, namely, that a created being must necessarily have a creator. The verse, however, dispenses with the need for a formal proof, instead speaking directly and immediately to the basic human knowledge implanted in the *fiṭra*: "Their knowledge regarding their own status [sc. that they are created] is known in and of itself in the *fiṭra* and there is no need for it to be deduced [by saying]: every existent (*kāʾin*) is originated, or every contingent being does not exist of its own accord."[26] The knowledge that results from this creature-feeling is thus characterized as more direct than that derived from

[23] Otto, *Idea*, p. 10; Otto, *Das Heilige*, pp. 10–11.
[24] The translation here is in accordance with Ibn Taymiyya's understanding of the verse, as he glosses *am khuliqū min ghayr shayʾin* as *a-ūjidū min ghayr mubdiʾin*.
[25] Ibn Taymiyya, *Majmūʿat al-fatāwā*, vol. 2, p. 13.
[26] Ibn Taymiyya, *Majmūʿat al-fatāwā*, vol. 2, p. 13. Here as elsewhere Ibn Taymiyya directs his critique to both the traditional *kalām* cosmological proof, which focuses on the concept of origination (*ḥudūth*), and to Ibn Sīnā's ontological proof, which focuses on the concept of contingency (*imkān*). Cf. below in the "Cratology" section.

*kalām* arguments; in addition, the *ḥadīth* is used to emphasize the experiential impact of this immediate form of knowledge.

In fact, while Ibn Taymiyya likes to situate his own path as intermediate between that of the rational theologians and the Ṣūfīs, combining the advantages of each while sidestepping their pitfalls,[27] on the question of epistemology he is clearly closer to the Ṣūfī conception of experiential and pious knowledge of Allāh than he is to the logical proofs of the philosophers and *kalām* theologians. He frequently cites in approbation (notwithstanding a certain reserve in this regard) the responses of two Ṣūfī shaykhs against *kalām* theologians on the topic of knowledge of Allāh. One is a statement attributed to Ismāʿīl al-Kūrānī, who said to ʿIzz al-Dīn b. ʿAbd al-Salām: "You say that Allāh is known by a proof, and we say that He made Himself known to us and thus we know Him." The other is the statement of Najm al-Dīn Kubrā, who, when asked by Fakhr al-Dīn al-Rāzī how apodictic knowledge (*ʿilm al-yaqīn*) is attained, said: "It is experiential cognitions (*wāridāt*) that come to souls such that the souls are incapable of rejecting them … for us [viz. the Ṣūfīs] certain knowledge is found necessarily, and not through speculation."[28]

The response attributed here to the Ṣūfī Najm al-Dīn Kubrā is a clever appropriation of the *kalām* theologians' own categories of knowledge. The phrase "that come to souls such that the souls are incapable of rejecting them" (*taridu ʿalā al-nufūs taʿjizu al-nufūs ʿan raddihā*) is in fact a *kalām* definition of necessary or immediate (*ḍarūrī*) knowledge,[29] that is, knowledge that is self-evident and that serves as a basis for further propositions. In *kalām* theology knowledge of God was not considered necessary knowledge of this type but was rather attained through reasoning based on necessary knowledge. In this anecdote Najm al-Dīn Kubrā has simply applied the formula to the Ṣūfīs' "experiential cognitions" (*wāridāt*), in essence arguing that they meet the *kalām*'s criteria for necessary knowledge and thus are not in need of any further proof. It is clear, then, why Ibn Taymiyya is interested in citing this anecdote as support for his claim that knowledge of Allāh is necessary and immediate, in contrast with the *kalām* proofs of Allāh's existence.

[27] This is the general framework in which he presents his own doctrine in the *Qāʿida awwaliyya*, printed in Ibn Taymiyya, *Majmūʿat al-fatāwā*, vol. 2, pp. 7–15.

[28] Ibn Taymiyya, *Majmūʿat al-fatāwā*, vol. 2, pp. 18, 53; vol. 4, p. 31, has the latter episode in more detail.

[29] This particular definition of *ʿilm ḍarūrī* appears to be taken from Mānkdīm's commentary on the Muʿtazilī al-Qāḍī ʿAbd al-Jabbār's *Sharḥ al-uṣūl al-khamṣa*. See Mohd Radhi Ibrahim, "Immediate Knowledge according to al-Qāḍī ʿAbd al-Jabbār," *Arabic Sciences and Philosophy* 23 (2013), pp. 101–115, at p. 102. On the issue in general, see also Binyamin Abrahamov, "Necessary Knowledge in Islamic Theology," *British Journal of Middle Eastern Studies* 20/1 (1993), pp. 20–32.

Ibn Taymiyya's basic religious epistemology is quite close to Otto's. The context in which he elaborated the concept of the *āya* was likewise similar to that in which Schleiermacher and Otto were writing: opposition to those who wished to grant priority to philosophical reasoning over direct religious knowledge and experience. In contrast with the two latter thinkers, however, Ibn Taymiyya did not attempt to save religious epistemology by carving out a space for it distinct from the rational. His contention was that religious epistemology is the basis for, and in concert with, true rationality.[30] We find in his doctrine, then, an attempt to encompass a unity of rational knowledge and affective piety oriented to direct cognition of the specific and particular reality of Allāh.

### *Knowledge and Action*

There remains one final aspect of Ibn Taymiyya's religious epistemology that requires emphasis: its connection to action. The movement of the heart that accompanies the attainment of pious, direct awareness of Allāh (as opposed to mere speculative knowledge of His existence) leads one to exclusive devotion to and action for Him. Thus, when Ibn Taymiyya argues that his path of knowledge of Allāh through His signs combines certitude of knowledge with experiential depth, one of the points that he emphasizes is that, while neither the epistemological path of the *kalām* theologians nor that of the heterodox Ṣūfīs are entirely invalid, they do not, in themselves, lead to the performance of obligations and avoidance of the forbidden and thus do not lead to salvation.[31] This topic will be explored more fully below in our discussion of monolatry (*tawḥīd al-ulūhiyya*) in Ibn Taymiyya's economy of transcendence.

## Cratology

This category in the economies of transcendence stems from the question: What is the central axis on which the difference between Allāh and not-Allāh pivots? It is inherent to the Axial project to attempt to

[30] This is evident in the fact that Ibn Taymiyya did not restrict his focus on the *āya* to the question of knowledge of Allāh but expanded it into a more general epistemological doctrine that he employed in his legal methodology as well. On this application, see Baber Johansen, "Signs as Evidence: The Doctrine of Ibn Taymiyya (1263-1328) and Ibn Qayyim al-Jawziyya (d. 1351) on Proof," *Islamic Law and Society* 9/2 (2002), pp. 168–193, esp. pp. 186ff.

[31] Ibn Taymiyya, *Majmūʿat al-fatāwā*, vol. 2, p. 51; see also p. 33, where he states that the Qurʾān's internal logic yields both knowledge (*ʿilm*) and action (*ʿamal*), whereas the logicians' *qiyās* yields only intellectual assent (*taṣdīq*) in matters of fact without relation to action. This theme is clearly related to Ibn Taymiyya's theology of faith; see below in the section "On the Origins of the Concept of *Tawḥīd al-ulūhiyya*."

maximize the opposition between the transcendent and the mundane, but the configurations of this opposition differ between the philosophical and the revelational economies. In the Introduction a basic contrast was described between the philosophical emphasis on ontology as the main axis of transcendent difference and the revelational emphasis on divine power. In this section I will attempt to show that Ibn Taymiyya consistently upholds the cratological conception in opposition to Islamic variants of ontological transcendence.

If one assumes that the most fundamental fact about the universe is being and conceives of being itself as an object of inquiry – that is, metaphysics – then it is only natural to construct the opposition between Allāh and not-Allāh as some kind of opposition in their manner of being. The most radical formulation of this is to be found in Neoplatonism, which systematized Plato's characterization, in the *Republic*, of the Good as "beyond being" and worked out the implications of this conception for the nature of the One, both in itself and in its relation to the many. Neoplatonism had a tremendous influence on Islamic thought, in particular on the Ismāʿīlīs, Islamic philosophers, and Ṣūfī monists.[32] The radical formulation of the One as "beyond being" is reflected in Jahm b. Ṣafwān's position that it cannot be said of Allāh that He is a being (*shayʾ*),[33] but was generally tempered by subsequent Islamic Neoplatonists. In the Arabic Plotinus tradition (which postdates Jahm) we find that Plotinus' citation of Plato in *Enneads* V.2, "The One is all things and not one of them,"[34] was emended in the so-called "*Theology of Aristotle*," Mīmar X, to: "The pure One is the *cause* of all beings, and is not *like* any of the beings" (*al-wāḥid al-maḥḍ huwa ʿillat al-ashyāʾ kullihā wa-laysa ka-shayʾ min al-ashyāʾ*).[35] Such emendations nothwithstanding, the fact remains that the basic construction of transcendence on the ontological axis was fully assimilated into the Islamic currents influenced by Greek thought.

The most influential Islamic formulation of ontological transcendence in Ibn Taymiyya's time was Ibn Sīnā's doctrine that Allāh is the sole

[32] The interrelation among these groups and their doctrines is now receiving increased attention. See Michael Ebstein, *Mysticism and Philosophy in al-Andalus: Ibn Masarra, Ibn al-ʿArabī and the Ismāʿīlī Tradition*, Leiden and Boston: Brill, 2014.

[33] Richard M. Frank, "The Neoplatonism of Jahm b. Ṣafwān," *Le Muséon* 78 (1965), pp. 395–424, at pp. 398–402.

[34] Plotin, *Traités 7-21*, trans. and ed. L. Brisso et al., Paris: Flammarion, 2003, p. 217, cf. Plato, *Parmenides* 160b2–3.

[35] ʿAbd al-Raḥmān Badawī, *Aflūṭīn ʿinda al-ʿarab*, Cairo: Maktabat al-Nahḍa al-Miṣriyya, 1955, p. 134 (emphasis added); Peter S. Adamson, "The Arabic Plotinus: A Study of the 'Theology of Aristotle' and Related Texts," PhD diss., University of Notre Dame, 2000, p. 183; see also p. 205, on the phrase *anniyya faqaṭ*: "striking here is the affirmation, *contra* Plotinus, that God is not utterly beyond being"; cf. also p. 192.

necessary existent (*wājib al-wujūd*), while all other existents, when considered in and of themselves, are possible or contingent (*mumkin al-wujūd*).[36] It is clear that for Ibn Sīnā this is the fundamental difference between Allāh and others, since he understands the study of being qua being – that is, metaphysics – to be the highest science,[37] and the necessary/contingent distinction to be the fundamental principle in the classification of being.[38] Another variant, current among Ṣūfī monists, was that Allāh is absolute or pure existence (*al-wujūd al-muṭlaq*), while other entities are somethings that have existence.[39] Our purpose here is not to investigate these formulations in their own right, but merely to underline the fact (perhaps taken for granted by specialists in these areas) that all of them view the issue of the relation and difference between Allāh and creation primarily in ontological terms.

In contrast with these ontological foci, the revelational economy maintains that the primary mode of relation between the one and the many is cratological: The one differs from the many in that it holds absolute power over them. It is true that in this economy as well all beings have existence through being created by God, whereas God is uncreated, and this is in a certain sense an ontological distinction. However, in the revelational economy, as in the Ancient Near Eastern cosmogonies, creation is not primarily an account of existence itself but rather an expression of the power relations between God and other existents. In Ibn Taymiyya's critique of Muslim ontological monotheism we will see that he subscribes to this cratological view.

Ibn Taymiyya does not object to the formula that Allāh is the sole existent whose existence is necessary in itself (*wājib al-wujūd bi-dhātihi*); he objects only to the overemphasis placed on this differentiation since he does not believe it to be the principal one between Allāh and not-Allāh. As a dry formulation it is one of those conclusions reached by logical proof that, while accurate, does not reveal the specificity of Allāh, and is likened to the meat of a lean camel on a craggy mountain – difficult to

[36] See Alexander Treiger, "Avicenna's Notion of Transcendental Modulation of Existence (*taškīk al-wujūd, analogia entis*) and Its Greek and Arabic Sources," in Felicitas Opwis and David Reisman (eds.), *Islamic Philosophy, Science, Culture, and Religion: Studies in Honor of Dimitri Gutas*, Leiden and Boston: Brill, 2012, pp. 327–363; Robert Wisnovsky, *Avicenna's Metaphysics in Context*, Ithaca: Cornell University Press, 2003.

[37] See Amos Bertolacci, *The Reception of Aristotle's* Metaphysics *in Avicenna's* Kitāb al-Shifāʾ*: A Milestone of Western Metaphysical Thought*, Leiden and Boston: Brill, 2006, pp. 265–266.

[38] Ibn Sīnā, *Kitāb al-shifāʾ/Ilāhiyyāt (1)*, ed. G. Qanawātī and S. Zāyid, Cairo, 1960, p. 37.

[39] See e.g. William Chittick, "Ṣadr al-Dīn Qūnawī on the Oneness of Being," *International Philosophical Quarterly* 21 (1981), pp. 171–184. For Ibn Taymiyya's criticism of al-Qūnawī's doctrine, see *Majmūʿat al-fatāwā*, vol. 2, pp. 102ff. (discussed below).

reach and not much worth the effort.[40] For Ibn Taymiyya, Allāh is indeed necessarily existent, but to reduce His essential nature (*ḥaqīqa*) solely to this aspect is a gross error, and falls as short of correct characterization of Him as if one were to say that the essential nature of all other existents is simply that their existence is contingent.[41]

The same cannot be said, however, for the formula that Allāh is absolute existence (*al-wujūd al-muṭlaq*). In what follows I will discuss further the meaning of the term *muṭlaq*; for the time being it can be taken to mean something close to *per se* or as such. Ibn Taymiyya objects to this formula, philosophically on the basis of his doctrine of hysterogenic universals, and theologically due to the formula's monist implications and its obliteration (in his view) of any true distinction between Allāh and not-Allāh.

An extensive discussion of the formula is to be found in Ibn Taymiyya's critique of al-Ṣadr al-Qūnawī, a prominent disciple of Muḥyī al-Dīn b. al-ʿArabī.[42] The basic principle of al-Qūnawī's doctrine is the identification of Allāh with pure existence, that is, existence qua existence, as such, free of any delimitation, particularization, or entification (*taʿyīn, taʿayyun*). When existence is entified through a succession of progressive hypostases it becomes creation. Thus both Allāh and creation are existence, with the difference between them being the differentiation between existence in its absolute and particularized forms. However, since nothing existent is outside of existence, the system is ultimately a monist one: William Chittick notes that for al-Qūnawī, "in all levels and at all stages, Being is Being and nothing else,"[43] or in Ibn Taymiyya's words: "He [al-Qūnawī] stated explicitly that nothing exists save the pure existence that flows in the particular existents."[44]

If one puts aside for the moment al-Qūnawī's ultimate monism, his system, which displays strong Neoplatonic influence, assigns ontological priority to universals (e.g. 'human,' as opposed to individual humans), as these are higher in the chain of being than particulars and thus closer to existence as such. As previously noted in the "Epistemology" section

[40] Ibn Taymiyya, *Majmūʿat al-fatāwā*, vol. 2, p. 20.
[41] Ibn Taymiyya, *Majmūʿat al-fatāwā*, vol. 2, p. 61.
[42] Ibn Taymiyya differentiates between various Ṣūfī monist (*ittiḥādī*) doctrines, including those of Ibn al-ʿArabī and al-Qūnawī, both in his exposition of them and in his normative evaluation. For the sake of simplicity my comments here will be restricted to the critique of al-Qūnawī. It may be noted that, according to Chittick, "Qūnawī's presentation of Ibn al-ʿArabī's teachings provides the basis for most later interpretations of the master": Chittick, "Ṣadr al-Dīn Qūnawī," p. 172.
[43] Chittick, "Ṣadr al-Dīn Qūnawī," p. 183.
[44] *Fa-qad ṣaraḥa bi-annahu mā thamma siwā al-wujūd al-muṭlaq al-sārī fī al-mawjūdāt al-muʿayyana.* Ibn Taymiyya, *Majmūʿat al-fatāwā*, vol. 2, p. 102.

above, Ibn Taymiyya holds the contrary position and argues that universals are hysterogenic – that is to say, their existence is purely a posterior mental one born of the mind's recognition of commonalities among concrete, particular extramental existents. For this reason, Ibn Taymiyya argues that al-Qūnawī's conception of Allāh as absolute existence (*al-wujūd al-muṭlaq*), that is, existence as such when not particularized or entified in any particular existent, denies Allāh any concrete extramental existence at all.

In slightly more detail the argument runs as follows. Ibn Taymiyya distinguishes between two kinds of absoluteness (*iṭlāq*). One kind is that which is defined in opposition to specification or particularization and is called "absolute on the condition of absoluteness" (*muṭlaq bi-sharṭ al-iṭlāq*), whereas the other is simply the thing considered in itself, without regard to its specification or particularization, and is called "absolute not conditioned on absoluteness" (*muṭlaq lā bi-sharṭ al-iṭlāq*). This second kind of "absolute" is close to the meaning of *muṭlaq* as "without qualification": the verb *aṭlaqa* can mean to use a word or expression (especially a polyvalent one) without qualifying or specifying its meaning, and thus the second kind of "absolute" really means freedom from any qualification, including the qualification of absoluteness in the first sense (i.e. as defined in opposition to the particular). Since for Ibn Taymiyya universals are purely hysterogenic, he argues that the first kind of "absolute" has no extramental existence at all. The second kind of "absolute" can be said to exist in the real world, but only as entified in particular existents and never separately from them. Thus "water" taken in the first sense of absolute exists only in the mind and not in extramental reality, whereas "water" in the second sense of absolute does exist in all the real-world existents that are water of one kind or another (e.g. rose water) but does not exist outside the mind in itself, i.e. there is no real-world instance of "water" without any further qualification.

For this reason, Ibn Taymiyya holds that "absolute existence" (*al-wujūd al-muṭlaq*), depending on which kind of absolute is meant, either (a) has no extramental existence at all, or (b) has no separate extramental existence. Al-Qūnawī's doctrine, then, is either (a) denial of Allāh's existence altogether, or (b) denial of any separate existence to Allāh – that is, He would have extramental existence only insofar as He is entified in the various particular existents that have "existence," rendering Him purely immanent. The first option is self-evidently untenable, and the second is untenable for Ibn Taymiyya due to his own theological commitment to a transcendentally separate Allāh distinct from His creation[45]

[45] Ibn Taymiyya, *Majmūʿat al-fatāwā*, vol. 2, pp. 101–106.

(see the section "Unmediatedness" below). Due to his own view on the ontological priority of the particular over the universal, Ibn Taymiyya contends that what was for al-Qūnawī the purest articulation of Allāh's transcendence is in fact the obliteration of any transcendental distance whatsoever between Allāh and creation.

In addition to critiques of specific ontotheological doctrines such as those of Ibn Sīnā and al-Qūnawī, Ibn Taymiyya also outlines more general critiques of the ontological focus. For example, in the course of a discussion of Ibn al-ʿArabī and his followers, he ascribes the origin of their doctrine of the unity of existence to the 'Sabians' (viz. the pagan philosophers) who were not adherents of *tawḥīd* but instead acknowledged absolute existence (*al-wujūd al-muṭlaq*). This emphasis on existence itself is the reason why the Aristotelian school considered the most noble of sciences to be metaphysics, which the later (i.e. Islamic) philosophers termed the 'divine science.' "And the subject of this science ... is absolute existence and its concomitants."[46] In Ibn Taymiyya's view, it is this incorrect turn to ontology that lies at the root of philosophical deviation from a true understanding of Allāh: "As for taking knowledge of Allāh, which is the highest and noblest of sciences, and placing it [in this context] and making of it one among the parts of what is the highest science to them, that is, speculation on existence and its concomitants ... this is the origin of the rationalist heresy (*al-ḍalāl al-qiyāsī*)."[47]

Here we find a fine example of Ibn Taymiyya's penchant for categorical generalizations in theological polemic. Ibn al-ʿArabī is worlds apart from Aristotle, as Ibn Taymiyya himself was fully aware: In another passage he writes that the closest precedent he had found for the Ṣūfī monist school was the view of Parmenides that "existence is one," and notes that Aristotle had opposed this view.[48] Yet for Ibn Taymiyya the fundamental orientation that is common to Ibn al-ʿArabī, Aristotle, and even the *kalām* theologians[49] is the preoccupation with existence as such, and from his vantage point on the other side of the cratological/ontological divide he thus groups them in the same general camp.

[46] Ibn Taymiyya, *Majmūʿat al-fatāwā*, vol. 2, p. 58.

[47] Ibn Taymiyya, *Majmūʿat al-fatāwā*, vol. 2, p. 59.

[48] Ibn Taymiyya, *Majmūʿat al-fatāwā*, vol. 2, p. 107. The text does not explicitly name Parmenides but the reference is clear from the "existence is one" formula. Cf. *Physics* I 2–3 in Aristotle, *Physics Books I and II*, trans. William Charlton, Oxford: Clarendon Press, 1970, pp. 1–7.

[49] Cf. Ibn Taymiyya's characterization of the *kalāmiyyūn*'s focus on ontology in *Majmūʿat al-fatāwā*, vol. 2, p. 31: *ghālib naẓarihim wa-qawlihim fī al-thubūt wa-l-intifāʾ wa-l-wujūd wa-l-ʿadam wa-l-qaḍāyā al-taṣdīqiyya fa-ghāyatuhum mujarrad al-taṣdīq wa-l-ʿilm wa-l-khabar.*

Ibn Taymiyya's subsequent detailed critique of the priority accorded to metaphysics begins with the following:

> Allāh, may He be praised, is the highest and the greatest. For this reason, the watchword of the most perfect of religions is *Allāh akbar*, in [the Muslims'] prayers, their call to prayer, and their festivals ... Allāh is the highest, and He is the greatest. And knowledge is in accordance with the object of knowledge, and thus cognition and knowledge of Him [viz. and not of existence per se] must be the greatest and highest of sciences.[50]

The most important fact of existence for Ibn Taymiyya is not existence itself, but rather that there exists one being who is supreme over the others. The words just cited are followed by a sentence that colors the ontological distinction that Ibn Taymiyya does himself acknowledge in cratological hues: "Allāh, may He be praised, is God [*al-Ḥaqq*, literally 'the True (Being)'] who is existent in and of Himself, and all that is not Him is His creation, subject to a Lord and subdued under His power."[51] The prioritization of existence as such obscures the true characteristic of transcendent difference in Ibn Taymiyya's view, namely, the power differential between the Lord and His subjects. This is not just an isolated passage; in many of his attacks on ontotheology he inflects the ontological distinction into the domain of lordship and power. In another passage, directed against the Ṣūfī monists' and Qarmaṭīs'[52] equation of Allāh with absolute existence, Ibn Taymiyya states that their doctrines are implicit in (*lāzim li-*) the view of the philosophers and the Muʿtazila, before rejoining with a cratologized version of the ontological distinction: "But as for creation having existence only from the Creator, may He be praised, this is true. And (*thumma*) He is the Creator of all beings, their Lord, and their Owner. Nothing is, save by His power, will, and creation, and He is the Creator of all things, may He be praised and exalted."[53]

Let us examine one final and somewhat more involved example of Ibn Taymiyya's subsuming of ontology to cratology. This example is to be found in his critique of both sides in the dispute between the Islamic philosophers and the Ashʿarīs on the question of whether the celestial bodies are eternal or created. Ibn Sīnā held that the celestial bodies are eternal but are perpetually caused by God. They are characterized as contingent existents, meaning that when viewed in and of themselves there is no logical necessity that they exist, and they could just as well not

[50] Ibn Taymiyya, *Majmūʿat al-fatāwā*, vol. 2, pp. 59–60.
[51] Ibn Taymiyya, *Majmūʿat al-fatāwā*, vol. 2, p. 60.
[52] *al-qarāmiṭa al-bāṭiniyya*: a pejorative epithet for the Ismāʿīlīs and other esoteric Shīʿī sects.
[53] Ibn Taymiyya, *Majmūʿat al-fatāwā*, vol. 2, pp. 22–23.

exist. God causes their existence not in the sense of a temporal act of creation but through a perpetual ontological relation that makes the celestial bodies "necessary of existence through another" (*wājib al-wujūd bi-ghayrihi*).[54] This view that the celestial bodies (or any part of the cosmos) are eternal was an anathema to the *kalām* theologians. In fact, the "initial issue" in rational theology was not whether God exists, as this was a nearly universally held tenet, but rather "whether the world is eternal or had a beginning."[55] In both Muʿtazilī and Ashʿarī *kalām*, the standard proof that the world was created was based on the principle that whatever cannot be free of generated accidents is itself generated;[56] and since *kalām* atomist physical theory stipulates that necessary concomitants of physical bodies such as composition and motion are generated, the bodies themselves are likewise generated.[57]

Ibn Taymiyya's critique of both the philosophers' and the *kalām* theologians' arguments rests inter alia on a proposition that is superficially similar to the *kalām* argument but which contains an important difference. This proposition is: An entity in which are present generated things *that are generated by another* is itself generated.[58] For Ibn Taymiyya it is the presence in the entity specifically of such generated things as are generated by another (and not generated things per se) that proves (a) that the other who generates these things controls and subjugates the entity (*mutaṣarrif fīhi qāhir lahu*); and, consequently (b) that the entity itself is not existent in its own right and is not autarkic, and thus cannot but be generated and created.

On these grounds, Ibn Taymiyya argues that the causal relationship described by Ibn Sīnā between the celestial bodies and God contradicts his attribution of eternity to the celestial bodies, as their dependence on and subjugation to God necessitates their being created entities. The same grounds, however, serve as a critique of the *kalām* theologians on two points. First, the *kalām* theologians held that the created entities' dependence on and need for God in order to be characterizes only the moment of their generation (*ḥāl ḥudūthihi faqaṭ*), whereas for Ibn Taymiyya the determinative factor is the entities' subjugation to another

[54] See Wisnovsky, *Avicenna's Metaphysics*, pp. 254–255; Davidson, *Proofs for Eternity*, pp. 289–293; Ayman Shihadeh, *Doubts on Avicenna: A Study and Edition of Sharaf al-Dīn al-Masʿūdī's Commentary on the* Ishārāt, Leiden and Boston: Brill, 2016, pp. 86ff.

[55] Davidson, *Proofs for Eternity*, p. 1.

[56] See e.g. Ibn Mattawayh, *al-Tadhkira fī aḥkām al-jawāhir wa-l-aʿrāḍ*, Cairo: Dār al-Thaqāfa, 1975, p. 91 ("*fī anna mā lam yakhlu min al-muḥdath fa-huwa muḥdath*").

[57] Davidson, *Proofs for Eternity*, pp. 134–143.

[58] *Mā lam yakhlu min ḥawādith yuḥdithuhā fīhi ghayruhu fa-huwa ḥadīth*; *mā qāmat bihi ḥawādith min ghayrihi fa-huwa ḥādith*. Ibn Taymiyya, *Majmūʿat al-fatāwā*, vol. 6, p. 199 (emphasis added).

power, and this dictates that their relation to God be (as it was for Ibn Sīnā) one of perpetual need and dependence. Second, Ibn Taymiyya's insistence that it is specifically the presence of generated things generated by another that renders an object subjugated and thereby created has an important ramification. It leaves him free to argue that the presence of generated things or events in an entity does not necessitate that that entity itself be generated when it is the entity itself that generates them. The implications of this distinction with respect to God's nature will be further explored in the following section ("Cataphatism"); for our present purposes, what merits note is simply that for Ibn Taymiyya the state of being created is a corollary of the state of being under the power of another, and it is this latter factor that is determinant in his arguments. He thus sums up the priority of the power relation in a statement that he attributes to the Companions, but which sounds suspiciously like a consciously cratologized reformulation of the *kalām* theologians' proof of creation: "the occurrence of generated things in the cosmos shows that it is subject to a Lord ... and whatever is subject to a Lord is [itself] generated."[59]

Let us now sum up the issues of epistemology and cratology vs. ontology before moving on to the next topics. For Ibn Taymiyya, knowledge of existence as such is in no way knowledge of Allāh in His specificity; it is only knowledge of a mentally constructed common denominator between Him and others, as gained through *qiyās*. This knowledge, like that of any other universal, is for Ibn Taymiyya purely hysterogenic. It cannot be higher than knowledge of what things actually are: the essential nature (*ḥaqīqa*) of Allāh and the essential nature of others, which tell us what makes Him specifically different. And since Allāh is something specific, He is not to be equated with 'necessary existence,' let alone 'absolute existence.' Allāh is a specific, particular being, who, as Lord, holds absolute power over all that is not Him.

## Cataphatism

The issue of Allāh's attributes is one of the most famous and controversial ones in Islam.[60] The origin of the dispute is a complex issue, but here

[59] *Wa-li-hādhā kāna al-ṣaḥāba yadhkurūna anna ḥudūth al-ḥawādith fī al-ʿālam yadullu annahu marbūb ... wa-l-marbūb muḥdath.* Ibn Taymiyya, *Majmūʿat al-fatāwā*, vol. 6, pp. 198–200.

[60] On the issue in general, see e.g. Daniel Gimaret, *Dieu à l'image de l'homme: les anthropomorphismes de la sunna et leur interpretation par les théologiens*, Paris: Cerf, 1997; Williams, "A Body unlike Bodies," and p. 29, n. 70, for further references; Livnat Holtzman, *Anthropomorphism in Islam: The Challenge of Traditionalism (700–1350)*, Edinburgh: Edinburgh University Press, 2018.

as elsewhere in Islamic theology the basic framework for understanding it is that of the meeting and interaction of the Near Eastern revelational and Greek philosophical variants of monotheism. For example, in the eyes of the Traditionalists who affirmed a literal reading of Allāh's attributes as described in the Qurʾān and the *sunna*,[61] the paradigmatic originator of apophatic heresy (*taʿṭīl*) in Islam was the radical Umayyad-era theologian Jahm b. Ṣafwān – and Jahm's system has been shown to be Neoplatonic in character.[62]

The Ḥanbalīs and *ahl al-ḥadīth*, in this matter as in others, were traditionally reluctant to defend their position in non-Scriptural terms. The best way to understand their position is simply to say that they were not particularly bothered by the questions with which the Muʿtazila and the philosophers were preoccupied. The Allāh described in the Qurʾān and the *ḥadīth* is plausible in and of Himself; the nature of His existence becomes problematic only in the prism of an ontological monotheism that construes Allāh's unity as a freedom from internal complexity and which thus requires a complex theoretical apparatus in order to reconcile Allāh's unity thus construed with His various powers.

Ibn Taymiyya, while more philosophically sophisticated and engaged than his forerunners, remains true to their project. His basic approach is simply to disentangle the Allāh of revelation from the Allāh of the philosophers and to use the tools of philosophy and *kalām* to show that apophatism derives from the particular ontological focus of the philosophical economy, which is neither logically necessary nor reconcilable with the cratological Allāh of revelation. We can see the connection between this issue and ontology in Ibn Taymiyya's frequent insistence that a God without attributes not only fails to exist and function as described in revelation, but is in fact altogether nonexistent.[63] Ibn Qayyim al-Jawziyya's *al-Ṣawāʿiq al-mursala*, an exhaustive defense of Scriptural, cataphatic monotheism, describes apophatism and the

[61] See Wesley Williams, "Aspects of the Creed of Ahmad Ibn Hanbal: A Study of Anthropomorphism in Early Islamic Discourse," *International Journal of Middle East Studies* 34 (2002), pp. 441–463; Binyamin Abrahamov, "The *Bi-lā Kayfa* Doctrine and Its Foundations in Islamic Theology," *Arabica* 42/3 (1995), pp. 366–379.

[62] See Frank, "The Neoplatonism of Jahm b. Ṣafwān." Frank likewise remarks that "there can be little doubt" that Aḥmad b. Ḥanbal and Ibn Taymiyya clearly understood the implications of Jahm's doctrine: p. 395, n. 2.

[63] Ibn Taymiyya, *Dar*ʾ, vol. 5, p. 46 ("*wa-ammā dhāt mujarrada ʿan hādhihi al-ṣifāt aw ṣifāt mujarrada ʿanhā fa-lā wujūda lahā*"), vol. 5, p. 163 ("*mā lā ṣifata lahu lā wujūda lahu fī al-wujūd*"); Ibn Taymiyya, *Bayān talbīs al-jahmiyya*, vol. 1, p. 6 ("*wa-l-muʿaṭṭil yaʿbudu ʿadaman*), p. 220 (*fa-athbatū mā lā yakūnu mawjūdan illā fī al-adhhān lā fī al-aʿyān*), vol. 2, p. 341 (*mā lā yumkinu maʿrifatuhu bi-shayʾin min al-ḥawāss fa-innamā yakūnu maʿdūman lā mawjūdan*), vol. 5, p. 433 (*nafy mubāyanatihi li-l-ghayr yūjibu ʿadam qiyāmihi bi-nafsihi*).

concomitant belief that the literal meaning of revelation contradicts reason as deriving from one ultimate source of error: the principle that there can be no internal multiplicity in the One. The author provides a multitude of arguments from both revelation and reason on this topic, but at root he is simply saying to the deniers of attributes that they have imported a problematic from an entirely different economy, and that this problematic wreaks destruction on the entire economy of revelation and is tantamount to outright denial of Allāh.[64]

Ibn Taymiyya's conception of Allāh as a complex entity possessed of attributes separates out the question of divine ontological unity, as construed by the philosophers and *kalām* theologians, from the question of divine multiplicity in the sense of acknowledgment of a multiplicity of divinities, and limits the definition of polytheism to the latter.[65] For the Muʿtazila these issues were closely related and they were wont to compare Traditionalist affirmation of the divine attributes to the Christian trinity, Manichean dualism, and so forth;[66] for Ibn Taymiyya, however, these are simply unrelated issues. Allāh is a single entity that has distinctive characteristics; since ontological simplicity is not a requirement for his monotheism, there is no equivalence between affirmation of this complexity and acknowledgment of a multiplicity of deities.[67]

The issue of Allāh's attributes is likewise intertwined with the topic of epistemology as well as cratology vs. ontology. Both the epistemological approach and the ontological emphasis of *kalām* theology had important implications for the debate over the status of Allāh's attributes and were connected with the adoption of (at least) a partially apophatic stance on the issue. It is for this reason that Ibn Taymiyya, who rhetorically equated any allegorical approach to the attributes with full-blown apophatism, referred to Ashʿarīs such as Fakhr al-Dīn al-Rāzī as Jahmites – as in the title of Ibn Taymiyya's *Bayān talbīs al-jahmiyya*, which was written in refutation of al-Rāzī's *Asās al-taqdīs*.[68]

Ibn Taymiyya often discusses the relation among these topics in his treatment of the *kalām* proof for the existence of Allāh based on the

[64] Ibn Qayyim al-Jawziyya, *al-Ṣawāʿiq al-mursala ʿalā al-jahmiyya wa-l-muʿaṭṭila maʿa takmilatihi min mukhtaṣar al-ṣawāʿiq al-mursala*, Sidon and Beirut: al-Maktaba al-ʿAṣriyya, 1428/2007, pp. 417ff.

[65] See e.g. Ibn Taymiyya's rejoinder to Ibn Sīnā in *Darʾ*, vol. 5, p. 52.

[66] Thus Abū al-Ḥusayn al-Baṣrī, cited in Ibn Taymiyya, *Darʾ*, vol. 5, pp. 37–38. For a criticism of al-Ashʿarī along similar lines, see al-Shaykh al-Mufīd, *Awāʾil al-maqālāt fī al-madhāhib wa-l-mukhtārāt*, ed. M. Muḥaqqiq, Tehran, 1983, 11.20–12.8, cited in Wisnovsky, *Avicenna's Metaphysics in Context*, p. 232, n. 17.

[67] See e.g. *Darʾ*, vol. 5, pp. 46, 52.

[68] For al-Rāzī's views, see Binyamin Abrahamov, "Faḫr al-Dīn al-Rāzī on the Knowability of God's Essence and Attributes," *Arabica* 49 (2002), pp. 204–230.

generated nature of the cosmos, which we touched on above at the end of the "Cratology" section. It will be recalled that for the *kalām* theologians (including the Ashʿarīs), the presence in an object of generated accidents proves the generated nature of the object itself. This proof (or a variant of it) was considered fundamental to all of religious belief: The *mutakallimūn* held that without it, one could not establish that Allāh alone is the sole eternal being and the sole Creator, and that all else is thus dependent on His will.[69] Ibn Taymiyya, in addition to his criticisms of the proof itself, objected to according such a role to a rational proof that is not mentioned anywhere in the revealed texts. Moreover, he argued that the proof is responsible for the *kalām* theologians' adoption of varying degrees of apophatism. The basic rule was that the theologians had to deny the presence in Allāh of whatever they considered to be the kind of accident that proved an object's generated nature. If motion is considered such, Allāh could not be characterized by motion, and could neither place Himself above the throne after the six days of creation nor descend from it at any time; and if the theologians considered a body (*jism*) to necessarily be a substrate for the accident of composition, then Allāh could not be a body and must not have any of those features that suggest corporeality, Scriptural evidence notwithstanding.

Ibn Taymiyya employs a number of rational arguments against these conclusions in order to show that they are not a necessary demand of reason; for our purposes, however, the essential point is the connection this dispute shows among the various elements of the competing economies of transcendence. Ibn Taymiyya advances a series of interrelated claims: The epistemological basis for *kalām* is in error, since it holds that revelation is not a self-sufficient source of knowledge and needs to be grounded in rational proof; the rational proof adopted by the *kalām* theologians is indebted to philosophical preoccupation with issues of ontology; and a corollary of this rational proof is the denial of Allāh's attributes, in contravention of the description of Allāh revealed to humans by Allāh Himself and the Prophet.[70]

The affirmation of Allāh's attributes is not only unobjectionable in Ibn Taymiyya's view but also required. This could be viewed as deriving simply from his epistemological premises: If revelation is the font of truth then one is required to affirm its contents, and the literal reading of the

[69] Cf. Davidson, *Proofs for Eternity*, pp. 1–3.

[70] Ibn Taymiyya discusses the connection between the proof of creation and denial of the attributes in numerous passages. See e.g. *Darʾ*, vol. 2, pp. 149ff., 302ff., *Bayān talbīs al-jahmiyya*, vol. 1, pp. 219–223, 372–374, 440–446, *Majmūʿat al-fatāwā*, vol. 2, pp. 20, 27ff., 44, vol. 6, pp. 143–144.

Qur'ān is that Allāh sits, descends, has a hand, and so forth. But the cataphatic conception of Allāh also plays an active role in the larger theological system, in the prominence Ibn Taymiyya accorded to the concept expressed by the term *khaṣā'iṣ* (or *khuṣūṣiyyāt*), by which he refers both to the particular and unique features of Allāh's being and to His exclusive domains of power, authority, and rights – and in particular, His right to be worshipped,[71] which is the fifth topic in our treatment of Ibn Taymiyya's system (see the section "Monolatry and the Meaning of *Ilāh*" below).

This conception of Allāh as a specific being differentiated from others by His attributes comes into especially clear relief in Ibn Taymiyya's polemics against Ibn al-ʿArabī and the *waḥdat al-wujūd* school. These latter are not easily classified in terms of apophatism or cataphatism, since their ontological monotheism is expanded into a monism that encompasses the entire world in all its particulars as facets of divinity.[72] In this monist schema true monotheism is to affirm of Allāh everything in the full plenitude of existence, and thus to affirm of Him only a limited set of particular characteristics is imperfect *tawḥīd* (as is denial of His attributes).[73] This conception is the polar opposite of Ibn Taymiyya's in that it effaces the difference between Allāh and creation, whereas for Ibn Taymiyya it is recognition and respect for Allāh's specificity and exclusivity that is the very basis of monotheism. This opposition can be seen, for example, in a statement that Ibn Taymiyya attributes to the Ṣūfī monists: "the Christians disbelieved solely through their restriction [viz. of divinity] (*takhṣīṣ*)," that is, they are unbelievers because they only affirm that Jesus is God (Qur'ān 5:17), whereas in truth – according to the Ṣūfī monists – all creation is God.[74] For Ibn Taymiyya, *takhṣīṣ* – that is, the

[71] Hoover, *Ibn Taymiyya's Theodicy*, p. 67, points out the connection in Ibn Taymiyya's writings between Allāh's attributes and His right to be worshipped. For terms from the root *kh-ṣ-ṣ*, see in relation to the attributes: *Majmūʿat al-fatāwā*, vol. 2, pp. 47–48; and in relation to Allāh's exclusive right to worship: *Fī wujūb ikhtiṣāṣ al-khāliq bi-l-ʿibāda wa-l-tawakkul ʿalayhi* in *Majmūʿat al-fatāwā*, vol. 1, pp. 32ff., and p. 216, on created beings' not having a right to Allāh's *khaṣā'iṣ*.

[72] This is, for example, the theme of the Nūḥ chapter in Ibn al-ʿArabī's *Fuṣūs al-ḥikam*: Muḥyī al-Dīn Ibn ʿArabī, *Fuṣūṣ al-ḥikam*, ed. Abū al-ʿAlā ʿAfīfī, Beirut: Dār al-Kitāb al-ʿArabī, 1400/1980, pp. 68–74.

[73] Jon Hoover has observed that there exists an unexpected similarity between Ibn Taymiyya and Ibn al-ʿArabī on the question of the divine attributes, as the doctrines of both combine affirmation of the attributes and denial of comparability with creation. Hoover, *Ibn Taymiyya's Theodicy*, p. 47. Although the two thinkers develop this formulation in radically different directions it is perhaps worth exploring whether they drew on a common font of early Ṣūfī teachings on the attributes.

[74] Ibn Taymiyya, *Majmūʿat al-fatāwā*, vol. 2, p. 82. I have not been able to locate this statement in Ṣūfī writings, but the theme is common enough; it parallels, for example,

restriction of attributes, powers, realms of authority, and rights to Allāh alone, and by which He is differentiated from His creation – is the very heart of *tawḥīd*.

Ibn Taymiyya considered this monist doctrine altogether beyond the pale, but as we have seen, his conception of Allāh's cataphatic specificity placed him at loggerheads with the more sober *kalām* theologians as well. Likewise, in keeping with Halbertal and Margalit's statement that "different concepts of God create, when reversed, different concepts of idolatry,"[75] the apophatic and cataphatic conceptions of *tawḥīd* yield radically differing definitions of *shirk*. In the former, *shirk* is primarily the belief in some form of internal complexity in God, whereas for the latter it is failure to affirm Allāh's exclusive attributes or respect His exclusive rights.

## Unmediatedness

As noted in the Introduction a central feature of revelational monotheism, in opposition to philosophical monotheism, is an emphasis on the directness and immediacy of God's relations with the mundane world. Yehoshua Amir referred in this context to the "Unmittelbarkeit" (unmediatedness) of God's relation with the world and argued that it is the principle underlying the Biblical prohibition of images.[76] In the Qur᾽ān the principle of unmediatedness appears in two complementary aspects. Regarding Allāh it is expressed in the directness with which He interacts with the world; and regarding humans, in the prohibition of appealing to intermediaries in their worship of Allāh.[77] The first of these aspects is the topic of the present section; the second will be treated in the following section on monolatry and the meaning of *ilāh* in Ibn Taymiyya's system.

With this topic we move from emphasis on the difference between Allāh and creation – the Axial gap, if you will – to the concurrent and seemingly paradoxical insistence on the directness with which Allāh bridges this gap. In his introduction to a recent survey volume on

Ibn al-ʿArabī's treatment of why Nūḥ's people refused to desist from worship of the gods Wadd, Suwāʿ, Yaghūth, Yaʿūq, and Nasr: Ibn ʿArabī, *Fuṣūṣ*, p. 72.

[75] Halbertal and Margalit, *Idolatry*, p. 1.

[76] Amir, "Begegnung," pp. 4, 7; cf. Assmann, *Herrschaft und Heil*, pp. 260, 262.

[77] These two topics correspond roughly to the subject matter of two articles by Patricia Crone on the Qur᾽ān's depiction of the interaction between the Prophet and the *mushrikūn*: "Angels versus Humans as Messengers of God: The View of the Qur᾽ānic Pagans," in Philippa Townsend and Moulie Vidas (eds.), *Revelation, Literature, and Community in Late Antiquity*, Tübingen: Mohr Siebeck, 2011, pp. 315–336; "The Religion of the Qur᾽ānic Pagans: God and the Lesser Deities," *Arabica* 57 (2010), pp. 151–200.

Islamic theology, Tim Winter writes that regarding the "fundamental tension between transcendence and immanence" in Islam it could be said, "at the risk of very crude generalization, that the Qurʾan's theology of transcendence was explored by the *kalām* folk, and its theology of immanence by the Sufis, which is why, perhaps, we should seek for Islam's greatest theologians among those who emphasized the symbiosis of the two disciplines."[78] Ibn Taymiyya is perhaps one of these greatest theologians of Islam, but his reconciliation between Allāh's transcendence and unmediated proximity does not quite fall under Winter's description. His version of transcendence is not that of *kalām*, and it is probably best not to employ the term "immanence" to characterize any aspect of his thought, since he denies that Allāh in His selfhood is immanent to the world in any way. Rather, his reconciliation of Allāh's transcendence and proximity is of the kind we described in the ideal type of revelational monotheism, in which it is precisely the conception of a concrete and spatially transcendent God endowed with attributes that permits Him to interact with the mundane world directly and exercise His power without intermediaries.

The treatise in which Ibn Taymiyya deals in most concentrated fashion with this topic is probably his *Fī al-jamʿ bayna ʿulūw al-rabb ʿazza wa-jalla wa-bayna qurbihi min dāʿīhi wa-ʿābidīhi* ("On the Reconciliation between the Lord's Transcendence and His Proximity to Those Who Pray to and Worship Him").[79] This brief treatise is built on the framework of the Qurʾānic data, which describe Allāh both as spatially transcendent (*ʿulūw, istiwāʾ, fawqiyya*) and as proximate to His creation (*maʿiyya, qurb*). After surveying relevant verses, Ibn Taymiyya enumerates three errant schools, each of which offer a wrong solution to the reconciliation of these two aspects of divinity and thus hold to a wrong configuration of Allāh's transcendence and proximity, before contrasting them with the true solution of the *salaf*.

The first of the errant schools Ibn Taymiyya lists is the Jahmite apophatists who deny Allāh's ubiety: He is neither in the world nor outside it, neither above it nor below it. Ibn Taymiyya argues that, unlike the other errant schools, the Jahmites have no textual evidence whatsoever for this view and thus they treat all the relevant texts with either allegorical interpretation (*taʾwīl*) or demurral regarding their meaning (*tafwīḍ*). While Ibn Taymiyya does not elaborate on this point, one can see in the "neither/nor" formulations he ascribes to the Jahmites a fine example of

[78] Winter (ed.), *Islamic Theology*, p. 6.
[79] Ibn Taymiyya, *Majmūʿat al-fatāwā*, vol. 5, pp. 140–157.

apophatic theology, according to which nothing whatsoever can be truly predicated of God.[80]

The second view is that of the Najjāriyya,[81] some Jahmites, and Ṣūfīs of the Ibn al-ʿArabī school, who hold either the immanentist doctrine (*ḥulūl*) stating that Allāh is Himself omnipresent (*innahu bi-dhātihi fī kull makān*), the monist doctrine described in the previous section, or something intermediate between the two. Ibn Taymiyya clearly lumps together adherents of quite different schools in this category, the common denominator among them being that they base their views on the "proximity" texts and interpret the "transcendence" texts allegorically.[82]

Ibn Taymiyya characterizes the third school as those who maintain at one and the same time that Allāh is both above the throne and omnipresent (*huwa fawqa al-ʿarsh wa-huwa fī kull makān*). The list of those who adhere to this doctrine or a variant of it is likewise eclectic, but Ibn Taymiyya seems most concerned with the Ṣūfīs who espoused it, including the Ḥanbalī Ṣūfī al-Anṣārī al-Harawī, whom Ibn Taymiyya generally respects but regularly faults for adopting some Ṣūfī heterodoxies, such as *ḥulūl* immanentism (which is how Ibn Taymiyya classifies the statement "He is omnipresent").[83] This school, while further from contravening the texts of revelation than the preceding two, is still faulted for (1) professing a self-contradictory doctrine; and (2) erroneously believing that the texts of revelation describe Allāh as omnipresent.

It is worth noting what is not said in this brief survey: Ibn Taymiyya does not fault anyone for maintaining transcendence to an excessive degree in a manner that excludes proximity. On most topics Ibn Taymiyya attempts to portray his own Traditionalist doctrine as a golden mean between opposing heterodoxies, even when the contemporary map of Islamic beliefs clearly places him to one side of the mainstream: On the question of faith he presents himself as intermediate between the Murjiʾa

80 Ibn Taymiyya, *Majmūʿat al-fatāwā*, vol. 5, pp. 140–141.
81 So called after Ḥusayn b. Muḥammad al-Najjār (d. 220/835). Al-Ashʿarī classifies him as a Murjiʾite: Abū al-Ḥasan ʿAlī b. Ismāʿīl al-Ashʿarī, *Maqālāt al-islāmiyyīn wa-ikhtilāf al-muṣallīn*, Beirut: al-Maktaba al-ʿAṣriyya, 1411/1990, vol. 1, p. 216.
82 Ibn Taymiyya, *Majmūʿat al-fatāwā*, vol. 5, p. 141.
83 Ibn Taymiyya, *Majmūʿat al-fatāwā*, vol. 5, p. 142. Ibn Qayyim al-Jawziyya's *Madārij al-sālikīn*, a commentary on al-Harawī's *Manāzil al-sāʾirīn*, expands on Ibn Taymiyya's reservations toward his Ḥanbalī Ṣūfī predecessor; see Ovamir Anjum, "Sufism without Mysticism? Ibn Qayyim al-Ǧawziyya's Objectives in *Madāriǧ al-Sālikīn*," in "A Scholar in the Shadow: Essays in the Legal and Theological Thought of Ibn Qayyim al-Ǧawziyya," ed. Caterina Bori and Livnat Holtzman, special issue, *Oriente Moderno* 90/1 (2010), pp. 153–180. The position was not necessarily a Ṣūfī one: cf. Jon Hoover, "Ibn Taymiyya's Use of Ibn Rushd to Refute the Incorporealism of Fakhr al-Dīn al-Rāzī," in Abdelkader Al Ghouz (ed.), *Islamic Philosophy from the 12th to the 14th Century*, Göttingen: Bonn University Press, 2018, pp. 469–491.

and the Khārijites; on the question of attributes intermediate between the apophatists and those who assimilate Allāh to His creation, and so forth. On the question of transcendence and immanence, however, Ibn Taymiyya apparently cannot produce an example of a school that emphasizes Allāh's transcendence to a fault. (The 'Jahmite' conception, while clearly rigorous, is not regarded by him as an expression of true transcendence.)

This orientation receives positive expression in Ibn Taymiyya's exposition of the *salaf*'s view and in his criticism of the other schools. The tendency throughout is to stress Allāh's transcendence at the expense of His immanence. The compensation for this Axial distance lies in the cataphatic depiction of Allāh, which allows for the directness of His knowledge, action, and intervention in the mundane world. This combination of insistence on transcendent distance together with proximity through Allāh's powers and volitional action (rather than the proximity of His selfhood) is summed up in the doctrine Ibn Taymiyya ascribes to the *salaf*, who are said to adhere to the totality of the texts from the Qur'ān and the *sunna*, and who profess that

> Allāh the Exalted is above His heavens, on (*'alā*) His Throne, separate from (*bā'in min*) His creation, and they are separate from Him. And He is likewise with (*ma'a*) humans (*al-'ibād*) in general through His knowledge, and with His prophets and righteous ones through His aid, support, and provision. And He is likewise proximate and answers [prayer] (*qarīb mujīb*).[84]

The description of Allāh as *bā'in* – separate – from His creation is a rare instance in which non-Qur'ānic terminology was adopted into statements of Ḥanbalī doctrine, presumably due to the need to formulate a clear principle of difference and transcendence in opposition to the competing philosophical and 'Jahmite' configurations of transcendence (which of course the Traditionalists refused to recognize as such).

When Ibn Taymiyya faults al-Anṣārī al-Harawī for adopting a doctrine that is, in his view, a form of immanentism (*ḥulūl*), he cites as a counterpoint a definition of *tawḥīd* from another Ḥanbalī Ṣūfī, Junayd, who defined it as "to separate the originated from the pre-eternal" (*ifrād al-ḥudūth 'an al-qidam*). Ibn Taymiyya then expands on this definition: "The upholder of *tawḥīd* (*al-muwaḥḥid*) must differentiate (*tamyīz*) between the pre-eternal Creator and the created originated beings and must not intermix

[84] *Fa-innahum athbatū … anna llāha ta'ālā fawqa samāwātihi wa-annahu 'alā 'arshihi bā'in min khalqihi wa-hum minhu bā'inūn wa-huwa ayḍan ma'a al-'ibād 'umūman bi-'ilmihi wa-ma'a anbiyā'ihi wa-awliyā'ihi bi-l-naṣr wa-l-ta'yīd wa-l-kifāya wa-huwa ayḍan qarīb mujīb.* Ibn Taymiyya, *Majmū'at al-fatāwā*, vol. 5, p. 143.

one with the other."[85] The central axis of Ibn Taymiyya's conception, then, is separation, differentiation, and distinction between Allāh and created beings.

Naturally enough, this axis manifests itself as well in Ibn Taymiyya's restrictive interpretation of the expressions relating to Allāh's proximity in the Qurʾān and the *ḥadīth*, which aims to rule out any suggestion that Allāh is Himself omnipresent. He divides the texts that state that Allāh is "with" (*maʿa*) created beings into two categories, general (*maʿiyya ʿāmma*) and particular (*maʿiyya khāṣṣa*). As for the general, Allāh is "with" His creatures through His knowledge;[86] this is what is meant in the verses in which Allāh's "withness" (*maʿiyya*) appears to apply indiscriminately to all, as in Qurʾān 57:4, "and He is with you (pl.) wherever you may be."[87] In other words, the expression refers to Allāh's omniscience rather than His omnipresence, "and this does not necessitate His selfhood being intermixed with theirs."[88] The expression is like those relating to Allāh's hearing, seeing, writing, and so forth, in which the simple meaning is to be considered true, as is the cratological implication that Allāh knows and will reward good behavior and will punish bad behavior.[89] The particular kind of "with" (*maʿa*), in contrast, relates specifically to the prophets and the saints (*awliyāʾ*), as in Qurʾān 16:128: "Allāh is with the pious and those who do good."[90] In this case Ibn Taymiyya interprets "with" as meaning that Allāh provides them aid and support.[91]

Ibn Taymiyya's more extended discussion relates to the expressions of proximity (*qurb*) in relation to Allāh. Ibn Taymiyya distinguishes between texts in which the expression is used in the singular, such as Qurʾān 2:186 ("I am close"), and those in which the expression is used in the plural, such as Qurʾān 50:16 ("We are closer to [a human being] than his

85 *Lā budda li-l-muwaḥḥid min al-tamyīz bayna al-qadīm al-khāliq wa-l-muḥdath al-makhlūq fa-lā yakhtaliṭu aḥadahumā bi-l-ākhar.* Ibn Taymiyya, *Majmūʿat al-fatāwā*, vol. 5, p. 142.

86 Ibn Taymiyya, *Majmūʿat al-fatāwā*, vol. 5, pp. 140, 143.

87 Ibn Taymiyya, *Majmūʿat al-fatāwā*, vol. 5, p. 140. Since the aim in this section is simply to explain Ibn Taymiyya's configuration of transcendence I will not here delve into his exegetical principles and whether his understanding of the verses truly lives up to the Traditionalist ethos of adherence to the literal meaning of the texts. It is worth noting, however, that in this case the full verse tends to support Ibn Taymiyya's interpretation, in that it is itself a Throne verse, whose literal thrust is thus one of spatial transcendence, and likewise in that it repeatedly emphasizes Allāh's knowledge of events in the heavens and on earth as well as of human activities.

88 *wa-lā yalzamu min hādhā an takūna dhātuhu mukhṭalitatan bi-dhawātihim.* Ibn Taymiyya, *Majmūʿat al-fatāwā*, vol. 5, p. 143.

89 Ibn Taymiyya, *Majmūʿat al-fatāwā*, vol. 5, p. 143.

90 Ibn Taymiyya, *Majmūʿat al-fatāwā*, vol. 5, p. 140.

91 Ibn Taymiyya, *Majmūʿat al-fatāwā*, vol. 5, p. 143.

jugular vein"). The plural appears to be the more problematic usage. Ibn Taymiyya maintains that it is the royal "we," which in proper Arabic usage (*kalām al-ʿarab*) is used of a king whose agents do nothing of their own accord; all the more so is it appropriate for Allāh to speak thus, since not only are His agents, the angels, entirely subject to His command, but He created them, their actions, and their power (*qudra*), and He is autarkic and has no need of them (*wa-huwa ghanī ʿanhum*).[92] In this sense, proximity (*qurb*), like the general use of "with" (*maʿa*), refers to knowledge, as both Allāh and the angels know humans' thoughts; with regard to the angels it can also mean the proximity of the angels' selves (*dhawāt*), but Ibn Taymiyya is careful to exclude this interpretation with respect to Allāh and to restrict His proximity in this usage to His knowledge.[93]

Ibn Taymiyya maintains that expressions of proximity in the singular are used with respect to Allāh solely in connection with His answering prayer. He notes that this is the context in which Qurʾān 2:186 speaks of proximity: "When My servants ask you concerning Me, surely I am close: I answer the prayer of the supplicant." He cites as well a *ḥadīth*, likewise on the topic of prayer, in which an expression of proximity is used of Allāh in the singular: "Restrain yourselves (*irbaʿū ʿalā anfusikum*), for you are not praying to one who is deaf or absent: Rather you are praying to one who is hearing and close. The one to whom you are praying is closer to each and every one of you than the neck of his riding camel." We find the same connection in the following *ḥadīth*: "The servant is closest to his Lord when he is prostrate [i.e. in prayer]" and in Qurʾān 96:19: "prostrate yourself and draw close."[94]

Yet precisely in prostration it is prescribed that one should say: "Praised be my Lord the most High" (*subḥāna rabbī al-aʿlā*). Ibn Taymiyya explains this as follows: Prostration is the greatest expression of humility and self-abasement. The worshipper in this state has nothing in and of himself and is as absolute nothingness, and it is thus appropriate precisely in this state to refer to Allāh as the most High. This is the essence of the entire relation between the Lord and His servants, and the more one lives up to it the closer one comes to Allāh:

> There is nothing [i.e. no relation] between the Lord and the servant other than pure servitude (*maḥḍ al-ʿubūdiyya*). The more the servant consummates it, the closer he comes to the Lord, because He, may He be praised, is righteous, magnanimous, and does good, and [thus] gives the servant what befits him.

92 Ibn Taymiyya, *Majmūʿat al-fatāwā*, vol. 5, p. 144.
93 Ibn Taymiyya, *Majmūʿat al-fatāwā*, vol. 5, p. 145.
94 Ibn Taymiyya, *Majmūʿat al-fatāwā*, vol. 5, p. 144.

The greater is [the servant's] need for Him, he is less in need, and the greater his humility, the greater his honor.[95]

Ibn Taymiyya strongly emphasizes that Allāh's proximity is restricted to these meanings, of which the most important is clearly His proximity to His servants in the servitude relation, and he argues, contra the immanentists (*ḥulūliyya*), that there is nothing in the Qurʾān or *sunna* that refers to the proximity of Allāh's self (*dhāt*) to all created beings in every state.[96] In other words, the basic relation of Allāh to the mundane world is one of transcendence and power (including omniscience) rather than omnipresence; His proximity is for the most part an expression of the directness or unmediatedness of the Lord-servant relationship, which is the only channel of access by which humans can come close to their Lord. This brings us to our final category, monolatry.

## Monolatry and the Meaning of *Ilāh*

So far we have separated out four general topics in Ibn Taymiyya's system: the epistemological, the cratological, the cataphatic, and unmediatedness. Taken together these can be considered one of the two aspects of *tawḥīd* that Ibn Taymiyya considers obligatory, and fall under the general rubric of *tawḥīd al-rubūbiyya*. It is striking, given the acerbity of Ibn Taymiyya's polemic on these issues, that he nonetheless regularly affirms the following point: *Tawḥīd al-rubūbiyya* is something held in common by all the schools in Islam, with the sole exception of the Ṣūfī monists and other *bāṭinī*s (adherents of esoteric Shīʿī sects). What he means of course is not that there is agreement on the particulars, but rather that all these schools profess the belief in one God who is Creator and wields ultimate power over creation. Even more striking is Ibn Taymiyya's claim that *tawḥīd al-rubūbiyya* is the common belief not only of the various schools of Islam, but also of the other monotheistic traditions, and even of the *mushrikūn*. For example, he writes that *tawḥīd al-rubūbiyya* "is something the foundation of which no one contests. They only contest some of its details (*baʿḍ tafāṣīlihi*), such as the disputes of the Zoroastrians, the dualists, the materialists, the *qadariyya*, and the likes of them among the philosophers (*mutafalsifa*) and the Muʿtazila."[97]

It goes without saying, then, that for Ibn Taymiyya profession of *tawḥīd al-rubūbiyya* is not sufficient for one to be considered a Muslim.

[95] Ibn Taymiyya, *Majmūʿat al-fatāwā*, vol. 5, pp. 146–147.
[96] Ibn Taymiyya, *Majmūʿat al-fatāwā*, vol. 5, p. 149.
[97] Ibn Taymiyya, *Majmūʿat al-fatāwā*, vol. 2, p. 29.

For all the importance of the disputes on *rubūbiyya* issues heretofore described, the capital distinction between proper *tawḥīd* and faulty *tawḥīd* does not lie therein – a fact reflected perhaps in Ibn Taymiyya's reluctance to consider error in these matters as grounds for *takfīr*.[98] Put simply, the measure of true *tawḥīd* is not so much monotheism – that is, *belief* in Allāh as the one God – but rather monolatry, that is, exclusive servitude to this one God. In Ibn Taymiyya's terminology, this required monolatry is termed *tawḥīd al-ulūhiyya* (or *al-ilāhiyya*), a concept that stands at the heart of the Taymiyyan system and constitutes its most central and controversial feature.

To understand both the terminology and the concept of *tawḥīd al-ulūhiyya* we need to start from Ibn Taymiyya's writings on the meaning of the word *ilāh*. One becomes a Muslim by pronouncing the declaration of faith (*shahāda*): the testimony that there is no god but Allāh and that Muḥammad is Allāh's Messenger. Observant Muslims repeat the *shahāda* daily in prayer, and a number of Prophetic *ḥadīth*s predicate salvation on this declaration. The word conventionally translated as "god" in this declaration is '*ilāh*': *lā ilāha illā llāh*.

Ibn Taymiyya defines *ilāh* more specifically within a general schema that distinguishes between two fundamental aspects of divinity, *ulūhiyya* and *rubūbiyya*. These are abstract nouns derived respectively from the terms *ilāh* and *rabb*. *Ulūhiyya* refers to divinity as an object of worship or servitude (*ʿibāda*, *ʿubūdiyya*), whereas *rubūbiyya* refers to Allāh as Creator and Master of all. *Ilāh* is thus defined as "that which is deified (*yuʾallahu*) and worshipped through love, repentance, exaltation, and reverence."[99] It is this aspect of divinity that expresses the telos of human existence:

> Allāh created creation for comprehensive worship of Him (*li-ʿibādatihi al-jāmiʿa*), for knowledge of Him, and for repentance to Him, for love of Him, and unadulterated devotion to Him. Through remembrance of Him hearts find rest, and through the vision of Him in the next world eyes are gladdened. Nothing He bestows on them in the next world is as dear to them as to regard Him, and nothing He bestows on them in this world is greater than faith in Him. Their need for Him in the aspect of their worship of Him and their deification [of Him] is like – nay, greater than – their need for Him in the aspect of His creation of them and His *rubūbiyya* over them, for that is the goal for which they have been intended.[100]

According to Ibn Taymiyya, this is the reason why the declaration of *tawḥīd* states "*lā ilāha illā llāh*" – there is no *ilāh* but Allāh. In another

[98] See e.g. Ibn Taymiyya, *Majmūʿat al-fatāwā*, vol. 5, pp. 156–157, *Darʾ*, vol. 2, p. 315.
[99] Ibn Taymiyya, *Majmūʿat al-fatāwā*, vol. 1, p. 21.
[100] Ibn Taymiyya, *Majmūʿat al-fatāwā*, vol. 1, p. 22.

passage he spells this out explicitly, in a discussion of the conditions for becoming a Muslim and the immunity of blood and property that comes with this status:

This [the *shahāda*] includes acknowledgment (*iqrār*) of Him and worship of Him alone, for an *ilāh* is something worshipped (*maʿbūd*). [The Prophet] did not say [I will fight people until they profess:] There is no *rabb* but Allāh, because the term *ilāh* is more indicative of the intended meaning of worship of Him, and it was for this sake that creation was created, and this is what they were commanded.[101]

Ibn Taymiyya continues (in the previous passage): "And as for *tawḥīd al-rubūbiyya*, which all people have acknowledged (*aqarra bihi al-khalq*) and which has been investigated (*qarrarahu*) by the speculative theologians, it alone is not sufficient, and [the fact that they affirm only this aspect of divinity] is rather to their discredit."[102] At times Ibn Taymiyya is exceedingly harsh in his insistence that profession of *tawḥīd al-rubūbiyya* alone is no merit:

The path of *kalām* yields only affirmation [of Allāh] (*iqrār*) and acknowledgment of His existence. When this is obtained without servitude and turning-to-[Allāh] it is a curse and damnation to the one who obtains it, as is recounted in the *ḥadīth*: "He who receives the harshest punishment on the Day of Resurrection is a scholar to whom Allāh has granted no benefit from his knowledge." [Such a one is] like the accursed Iblīs [Satan], for Iblīs acknowledges his Lord and affirms His existence, but as he does not worship Him he is the head of the damned, and all of the damned [are so] due to their following him.[103]

In other words, Ibn Taymiyya's doctrine of *tawḥīd* emphasizes monolatry over monotheism. For him *tawḥīd* is not just a matter of holding the correct propositional attitude regarding Allāh but is also and primarily a matter of directing one's worship to Him in the proper manner. This privileging of monolatry over conceptual monotheism should be regarded as the bedrock of his theological system.

As noted in the Introduction, Yehoshua Amir argued that monolatry is to be considered "not just, as is customary, as a preliminary stage, but rather as the true religious core of Biblical monotheism."[104] Ibn Taymiyya's *tawḥīd al-ulūhiyya* is monolatry in the sense in which Amir employs the term: not just one that happens to be monotheistic, but a monolatry that constitutes the very core of *tawḥīd* and is the decisive

[101] Ibn Taymiyya, *Majmūʿat al-fatāwā*, vol. 2, p. 15. The text has "Allāh" instead of "*ilāh*" (*fa-inna sma llāh adall ʿalā maqṣūd al-ʿibāda lahu*) but this is presumably a corruption in the text, as the point of the passage is to explain why the *shahāda* is *lā ilāha* rather than *lā rabba*.

[102] Ibn Taymiyya, *Majmūʿat al-fatāwā*, vol. 1, p. 22.

[103] Ibn Taymiyya, *Majmūʿat al-fatāwā*, vol. 2, p. 14.

[104] Amir, "Begegnung," p. 4.

factor that distinguishes Muslims from non-Muslims, and especially as the dividing line between true Muslims and others who consider themselves to be so but who are actually guilty of *shirk*. In many passages he intentionally conflates pagans from the *jāhiliyya*, Christians, antinomian Ṣūfīs, and extremist Shīʿīs. The common denominator among them is acknowledgment of *tawḥīd al-rubūbiyya* together with failure to uphold *tawḥīd al-ulūhiyya*;[105] they are monotheists, but not monolatrists. Thus extremist Shīʿīs are accused of ascribing *ulūhiyya* to their imāms, ignorant Ṣūfīs do the same with regard to the prophets and righteous individuals, and both are similar in this respect to the Christians (who ascribe both *ulūhiyya* and *rubūbiyya* to the prophet ʿĪsā/Jesus).[106]

The achievement of *tawḥīd al-ulūhiyya* requires exclusive devotion to and worship of Allāh. *Shirk* (polytheism) occurs whenever one accords to created beings any of those things to which Allāh has an exclusive right, whether in the realm of *ulūhiyya* (devotion and worship) or in the realm of *rubūbiyya*.[107] Thus in order to understand what this *tawḥīd* entails we need to examine how Ibn Taymiyya conceives of Allāh's status in relation to the mundane world and His prerogatives in relation to humans. The basic principle here is the same one of separation, transcendence, and difference that we encountered in various topics relating to *tawḥīd al-rubūbiyya*. In a passage in which Ibn Taymiyya enunciates this doctrine of Allāh's exclusive rights, he cites a *ḥadīth* in which the Prophet says that the greatest of sins is "for you to make a *nidd* for Allāh, when it is He who created you." *Nidd* is one of the terms used in the Qurʾān for the false gods that are associated with Allāh (e.g. Qurʾān 2:22 and 39:8, both cited in this same passage), but the basic meaning of the term, as Ibn Taymiyya takes care to point out, is "equivalent" or "equal" (*wa-l-nidd al-mithl*).[108] *Shirk* is then a confusion between Allāh and creation, and *tawḥīd* requires the maintenance of their proper separation and respect for Allāh's prerogatives – a concept for which (as previously noted) Ibn Taymiyya sometimes uses the term *khaṣāʾiṣ*,[109] and for the act of respecting these prerogatives, *ikhtiṣāṣ*.[110]

The connection between maintenance of Allāh's transcendence and difference and *tawḥīd al-ulūhiyya* is illustrated well in a *ḥadīth* that Ibn

105 Ibn Taymiyya, *Majmūʿat al-fatāwā*, vol. 1, pp. 52, 67–68, 75, 82.
106 Ibn Taymiyya, *Majmūʿat al-fatāwā*, vol. 1, p. 52.
107 *Fa-man jaʿala lillāh niddan min khalqihi fīmā yastaḥiqquhu ʿazza wa-jalla min al-ilāhiyya wa-l-rubūbiyya fa-qad kafara bi-ijmāʿ al-umma*; Ibn Taymiyya, *Majmūʿat al-fatāwā*, vol. 1, p. 69.
108 Ibn Taymiyya, *Majmūʿat al-fatāwā*, vol. 1, p. 69.
109 For example, Ibn Taymiyya, *Majmūʿat al-fatāwā*, vol. 1, p. 216.
110 For example, the chapter heading "*Fī wujūb ikhtiṣāṣ al-khāliq bi-l-ʿibāda wa-l-tawakkul ʿalayhi*": Ibn Taymiyya, *Majmūʿat al-fatāwā*, vol. 1, p. 32.

Taymiyya cites repeatedly regarding the issue of *istishfāʿ*, a term denoting a request from another to plead on one's behalf: "A man said to the Prophet: 'We ask Allāh to plead with you on our behalf, and we ask you to plead with Allāh on our behalf.' The Prophet replied: 'Allāh is too great for that (*shaʾn Allāh aʿẓam min dhālika*). He is not to be asked to plead with anyone from among His creation.'"[111] It is not clear how many people would fall into this error of thinking that Allāh could plead before a human, but Ibn Taymiyya extends this principle to the more common question of who has the right and ability to plead before Allāh on another's behalf, writing that Allāh is "too exalted (*aʿlā shaʾnan*) for anyone to plead for another before Him without His permission."[112] In this He is differentiated from created beings, since "a created being pleads for another before a created being without his permission, and [in so doing] is a partner to him in the attainment of the request; but Allāh the Exalted has no partner."[113]

It is on this basis that Ibn Taymiyya forbids many Ṣūfī cultic practices that were widespread in his day. In addition to the aforementioned *istishfāʿ*, which was often directed to the Prophet, other prophets, and deceased Ṣūfī masters, the same basic principle is invoked to forbid most forms of *tawassul* (usually meaning appeal to Allāh while invoking an intermediary) and *istighātha* (appeal to a created being for help in a matter beyond his or her natural capacity to perform).[114] In addition, Ibn Taymiyya's insistence on respect for Allāh's prerogatives extends beyond these cultic practices to affective acts of the heart: It is *shirk* to direct toward the Prophet, a shaykh, or other created beings any of the feelings or emotions that must be directed exclusively toward Allāh, such as fear, reliance, and hope.[115] Not all of these are necessarily the kind of 'greater *shirk*' (*shirk akbar*) that renders one an apostate:[116] In these theological writings Ibn Taymiyya does not always bother to delineate such jurisprudential distinctions, since his purpose is simply to propound the basic obligations of humans toward Allāh and the principles underlying them.

111 Ibn Taymiyya, *Majmūʿat al-fatāwā*, vol. 1, pp. 80, 173, 221.
112 Ibn Taymiyya, *Majmūʿat al-fatāwā*, vol. 1, p. 222.
113 Ibn Taymiyya, *Majmūʿat al-fatāwā*, vol. 1, p. 224.
114 Ibn Taymiyya, *Majmūʿat al-fatāwā*, vol. 1, pp. 78–87, 120, 147–149, 163, 200–202, 229, 238, 246.
115 Ibn Taymiyya, *Majmūʿat al-fatāwā*, vol. 1, pp. 42, 54, 71–72, 206–207, 214.
116 This is evident, for example, in his mention of "one who worships someone other than Allāh and relies on him – even if he [sc. the worshipper] is a Muslim; for *shirk* in this nation is more inconspicuous than the creeping of an ant" (*wa-immā an yaʿbuda ghayra llāh wa-yastaʿīnahu wa-in kāna musliman fa-l-shirk fī hādhihi al-umma akhfā min dabīb al-naml*). Ibn Taymiyya, *Majmūʿat al-fatāwā*, vol. 1, p. 30.

In keeping with the theme of umediatedness, Ibn Taymiyya at times emphasizes Allāh's proximity in order to underscore His transcendence. The rationale behind this relates to one of the fundamental challenges inherent in monotheism. Overemphasis on God's ontological difference in an attempt to preserve His transcendence – typically expressed in a denial of attributes – is precisely what invites appeal to lesser divinities (whether called gods, angels, or anything else); the revelational economy, with the monolatric emphasis at its core, requires that God be distinct and different but not in such a way as to become detached from direct relation to human experience.[117] Thus, in a passage in which Ibn Taymiyya asserts that "one who affirms intermediaries between Allāh and His creation like the intermediaries between kings and [their] subjects is a polytheist (*mushrik*) – indeed, this [viz. the use of intermediaries to reach Allāh] is the [very] religion of the polytheist idol worshippers," he cites Qurʾān 2:186 – the same verse discussed above in the context of unmediatedness – as evidence for the directness of Allāh's reign: "When My servants ask you [O Prophet] about Me, I am close, and I answer the prayer of the supplicant when he calls on Me; so let them accept My call and believe in Me, that they might walk in the right way."[118] The human need for a proximate deity is in this way paradoxically related to Allāh's transcendence and difference: It is with an earthly king of flesh and blood that one may need to appeal to intermediaries, but Allāh, due precisely to His difference from humans, manages His affairs directly, and thus there is no need and no license to approach Him indirectly through intermediaries. In response to the argument of the *mushrikūn* that God is too great and glorious for humans to approach Him without any interposed intermediaries and chamberlains, Ibn Taymiyya replies in an equally basileomorphic register that for a King (i.e. God) who is able to hear and respond to His subjects' needs without intermediaries or chamberlains it is rather a mark of His perfection to do so.[119]

We find a similar theme in a passage interpolated from a fatwā Ibn Taymiyya wrote in Egypt in 711/1311-1312 on monolatry and the polytheism of turning to intermediaries. In this fatwā Ibn Taymiyya states: "The religion of Islam is based on two foundations: that Allāh alone be worshipped and that nothing be associated with Him, and that He be

[117] See on this topic Halbertal and Margalit, *Idolatry*, pp. 21ff., on the centrality of the personalistic and anthropomorphic God to the Bible's ban on idolatry, in contrast with the Maimonidean conceptions of divinity and idolatry (on which see pp. 109ff.).

[118] *Wa-idhā saʾalaka ʿibādī ʿannī fa-innī qarībun ujību daʿwat al-dāʿī idhā daʿānī fa-l-yastajībū lī wa-l-yuʾminū bī laʿallahum yarshudūna*. Ibn Taymiyya, *Majmūʿat al-fatāwā*, vol. 1, p. 102.

[119] Ibn Taymiyya, *Majmūʿat al-fatāwā*, vol. 6, pp. 77–78.

worshipped in the manner He prescribed on the tongue of His Prophet." He follows this statement with a brief explanation of the meaning of *ilāh* and the assertion that the meaning of the *shahāda* is precisely the monolatric definition of Islam he has just given. It is in this context that, shortly thereafter, Ibn Taymiyya cites the aforementioned Qurʾān 2:186, the "restrain yourselves (*irbaʿū ʿalā anfusikum*)" *ḥadīth* (likewise discussed above), and a second *ḥadīth* that further underscores Allāh's proximity: "When any of you goes to pray, he should not spit in front of him, for Allāh is in front of him."[120] Typically, Ibn Taymiyya follows this directly with a declaration of Allāh's transcendence, again underscoring the fact that he views these seemingly contradictory aspects of Allāh's relation to the world as congruent and mutually reinforcing:

> And He, may He be praised, is above His heavens on His throne, separate from His creation. Nothing of His selfhood is in His creations, and nothing of His creations is in His selfhood. And He, may He be praised, is self-sufficient and independent of the throne and His other creations, and is not in need of anything from His creations. Rather, it is He who, in His omnipotence, carries the throne and the carriers of the throne.[121]

In this way the unmediated nature of Allāh's relation to the mundane, which is itself premised in Ibn Taymiyya's economy on the cratological and cataphatic emphases, serves in turn as a premise for monolatry and the contention that *tawḥīd al-ulūhiyya* is the defining core of Islam.

In light of the above we need to modify our understanding of Ibn Taymiyya's claim that all sects (apart from the Ṣūfī monists and the *bāṭinīs*) are united in professing *tawḥīd al-rubūbiyya* – that is, they acknowledge a Lord and Creator and differ only in the "details" of this doctrine (*baʿḍ tafāṣīlihi*),[122] whereas the difference between true faith and the sects lies in the matter of *tawḥīd al-ulūhiyya*. This manner of phrasing the issue is polemical and is meant to underscore the importance of *tawḥīd al-ulūhiyya*. It should not be taken, however, to mean that the differences in *tawḥīd al-rubūbiyya* are unimportant, as the "details" phraseology would seem to suggest. There exists a tight interrelation between, on the one hand, Ibn Taymiyya's particular configuration of transcendence in matters of *rubūbiyya* and, on the other, the centrality of *tawḥīd al-ulūhiyya* in his system.

[120] Ibn Taymiyya, *Majmūʿat al-fatāwā*, vol. 1, p. 252.
[121] *Wa-huwa subḥānahu fawqa samāwātihi ʿalā ʿarshihi bāʾinun min khalqihi laysa fī makhlūqātihi shayʾun min dhātihi wa-lā fī dhātihi shayʾun min makhlūqātihi wa-huwa subḥānahu ghanī ʿan al-ʿarsh wa-ʿan sāʾir al-makhlūqāt lā yaftaqiru ilā shayʾin min makhlūqātihi bal huwa al-ḥāmil bi-qudratihi al-ʿarsh wa-ḥamalat al-ʿarsh.* Ibn Taymiyya, *Majmūʿat al-fatāwā*, vol. 1, p. 253.
[122] Ibn Taymiyya, *Majmūʿat al-fatāwā*, vol. 2, p. 29.

Let us give one final example of this interrelation, to be found in Ibn Taymiyya's critique of Ibn Sīnā's *al-Risāla al-aḍḥawiyya fī al-maʿād*. The central topic Ibn Taymiyya takes issue with in Ibn Sīnā's treatise is that of Allāh's attributes, but in fact the interrelation between all five topics in the economies of transcendence can be seen through this discussion.[123]

Already in the lead-in to his detailed refutation of Ibn Sīnā, Ibn Taymiyya raises the topic of epistemology by paraphrasing the twelfth-century Ashʿarī theologian and doxographer Abū al-Fatḥ al-Shahrastānī as follows: "the foundation of all the kinds of heterodoxy is the according of priority to *raʾy* over the revealed texts and the choosing of errant inclination over divine law."[124] In other words, the measure of truth is revelation, and systems built on what many humans consider to be reason are to be decried as mere opinion (*raʾy*). As it happens, Ibn Sīnā himself portrays revelation and philosophical reason as coming into conflict; he, however, champions the latter. Ibn Sīnā considers revelation a sort of conventional prop for the masses (*al-ʿāmma*) that does not and cannot teach true *tawḥīd*, as this true *tawḥīd* lies at such a height of philosophical abstraction and sophistication as to be impossible to convey to the multitude.[125] In other words, for Ibn Sīnā, the measure of truth is reason; revelation does not disclose truth but merely establishes social convention.

This true *tawḥīd* is described by Ibn Sīnā as follows:

> Affirmation of the Creator as one, sanctified in His being free of any quantity, quality, place, time, position, or alteration,[126] such that one comes to the point of belief in Him as a single essence that can have no partner in species, nor have any existential [division into] part, whether in quantity or of accident, and cannot be either exterior to the world or within it, nor any 'where' such that one could point to its being here or there.[127]

[123] On this lengthy critique, taken from *Darʾ taʿāruḍ al-ʿaql wa-l-naql*, see Yahya Michot, "A Mamlūk Theologian's Commentary on Avicenna's *Risāla Aḍḥawiyya*, Being a Translation of a Part of the *Darʾ al-Taʿāruḍ* of Ibn Taymiyya, with Introduction, Annotation, and Appendices, Part I," *Journal of Islamic Studies* 14/2 (2003), pp. 149–203.

[124] Ibn Taymiyya, *Darʾ*, vol. 5, p. 7.

[125] Cf. Assmann, *Herrschaft*, pp. 17–18, on the concept of the truth deficit ("Wahrheitsdefizit") of exoteric religion in the eyes of philosophical monotheism (or in Assmann's terminology, natural theology or cosmotheism).

[126] These terms appear to be taken from Aristotle's categories; cf. Soheil M. Afnan, *Philosophical Terminology in Arabic and Persian*, Leiden: Brill, 1964, p. 90.

[127] *Iqrār bi-l-ṣāniʿ muwaḥḥadan muqaddasan ʿan al-kam wa-l-kayf wa-l-ayn wa-matā wa-l-waḍʿ wa-l-taghayyur ḥattā yaṣīra al-iʿtiqād bihi annahu dhāt wāḥida lā yumkinu an yakūna lahā sharīk fī al-nawʿ aw yakūna lahā juzʾ wujūdī kammī aw maʿnawī wa-lā yumkinu an yakūna khārijatan ʿan al-ʿālam wa-lā dākhilatan fīhi wa-lā ḥayth taṣiḥḥu al-ishāra ilayhi annahu hunā aw hunāk*. Ibn Taymiyya, *Darʾ*, vol. 5, p. 11.

This kind of *tawḥīd* is typical of the philosophical economy of transcendence, which is concerned primarily with the apophatic characterization of the ontic nature of the One as free from attribute, and which Ibn Taymiyya decries as negationism (*taʿṭīl*). Indeed, for Ibn Taymiyya and other cataphatists, one who worships such a God worships nonexistence.[128] Ibn Sīnā, for his part, states that such an appreciation is precisely why true *tawḥīd* cannot possibly be transmitted to the masses: Had the true Arabs of the past or the rude Hebrews been given such a *tawḥīd* they would have hurried to denounce it as faith in a nonexistent.[129]

Thus we see a clear connection in Ibn Sīnā among topics one, two, and three of the economy (philosophical epistemology, ontological focus, and apophatism). Ibn Taymiyya, in his response, connects these to the final two topics as well, and argues that Ibn Sīnā's formulation of transcendence would obstruct the directness of the Allāh-creation relation and would thereby preclude monolatry:

> As for what Ibn Sīnā said: "Is He one in essence with a multiplicity of attributes, or capable of being multiple (*qābil li-kathratin*)? Exalted be He above that in any form whatsoever." We say to him: The divine Book is full of affirmation of attributes of Allāh the Exalted, such as knowledge, ability, mercy, and so forth, and no two thinking individuals have ever disputed that the texts do not indicate denial of the attributes …
>
> As for his saying "or capable of being multiple," this is a misleading phrase (*lafẓ mumawwih*). If he meant by this a multiplicity of gods (*kathrat al-āliha*) – and he did not mean this – then it is known that Allāh, praised be He, explained more than once that God is one God, and the Qurʾān is full of denial of multiplicity of gods and denial of all manner of *shirk*. But if he meant the multiplicity of His attributes, which is indicated by His names and His signs [or: verses], then [Ibn Sīnā's] saying of the Lord "exalted be He above that" is like the polytheists' exaltation of Him such that He cannot be supplicated or worshipped without an intermediary, and their exaltation of Him such that He cannot send a human prophet. And [Ibn Sīnā's] purification of Him from His attributes is like the polytheists' purification of Him of being one God who has a human prophet.[130]

Ibn Taymiyya's equation here of philosophical monotheism with the *shirk* of the pre-Islamic Arabs is a function of his own monolatric emphasis. For him, Ibn Sīnā's God, in addition to being a mental construct that can have no real-world existence, lacks the cataphatic features that make unmediatedness and monolatry possible. Likewise, these opposing conceptions of *tawḥīd* yield opposing conceptions of

[128] *Al-muʿaṭṭil aʿmā wa-l-mushabbih aʿshā wa-l-muʿaṭṭil yaʿbudu ʿadaman wa-l-mushabbih yaʿbudu ṣanaman.* Ibn Taymiyya, *Bayān talbīs al-jahmiyya*, vol. 1, p. 6.

[129] Ibn Taymiyya, *Darʾ*, vol. 5, p. 11.

[130] Ibn Taymiyya, *Darʾ*, vol. 5, pp. 50–52.

*shirk*. For Ibn Sīnā, *shirk* is the affirmation of internal multiplicity in Allāh. In contrast, for Ibn Taymiyya, *shirk* is primarily appeal to intermediaries in worship, and he thus argues that *shirk* is a natural consequence of Ibn Sīnā's distant and abstract conception of *tawḥīd*. Both Ibn Sīnā and the Qur'ānic *mushrikūn* had a conception of transcendence, but their configuration of it excluded what is, for Ibn Taymiyya, true monotheism and monolatry, and thus in his view guaranteed the persistence of polytheism.

This example, taken together with the others we have seen of the interrelation of the various aspects of Ibn Taymiyya's system, suggests that while *tawḥīd al-ulūhiyya* is certainly for him the linchpin of Islam, his rhetorical denigration of the importance of *tawḥīd al-rubūbiyya* should be taken with a grain of salt. Doctrinal differences in matters of *rubūbiyya* are important to him as well, both in and of themselves and also (and especially) because a 'wrong' configuration of *tawḥīd al-rubūbiyya* can practically rule out the attainment of *tawḥīd al-ulūhiyya*.

## On the Origins of the Concept of *Tawḥīd al-ulūhiyya*

We have seen how the concept of *tawḥīd al-ulūhiyya* plays a decisive role in Ibn Taymiyya's understanding of Islam and what it is to be a Muslim. One question that has scarcely been asked in the scholarly literature is how Ibn Taymiyya came to formulate this concept and whether there is any precedent for it.[131] This issue has been raised polemically by opponents of the doctrine, who, in addition to arguing that it was wrong on the merits, could also argue that it was unprecedented – a serious charge, given Ibn Taymiyya's self-presentation and reputation as a champion of salafī creed.[132] This question, then, highlights Ibn Taymiyya's paradoxical stature as a systematizer of salafī doctrine, which up to his time had consciously resisted systematization.

While further research into this question will be necessary before firm conclusions can be drawn, it is possible at this point to at least indicate some leads that might shed light on the genesis of the doctrine. We will

[131] While not posing the question in quite this way, many of the discussions in Hoover, *Ibn Taymiyya's Theodicy*, are helpful in formulating possible answers. Specific references will be provided in what follows. For a modern Wahhābī attempt to locate precedent for Ibn Taymiyya's two-part *tawḥīd*, see now Cole M. Bunzel, *Wahhābism: The History of a Militant Islamic Movement*, Princeton and Oxford: Princeton University Press, 2023, p. 128, n. 5.

[132] For a twentieth-century example, see Yūsuf al-Dijwī (d. 1946), "Tawḥīd al-ulūhiyya wa-tawḥīd al-rubūbiyya," in *Maqālāt wa-fatāwā*, Cairo: al-Hay'a al-ʿĀmma li-Shu'ūn al-Maṭābiʿ al-Amīriyya, 1401/1981, vol. 1, pp. 248–272, esp. p. 249; reprinted from *Majallat al-azhar* 4/4, Rabīʿ I, and 4/5, Rabīʿ II, 1352 [= 1933].

now turn our attention to (1) a terminological precedent relating to *ilāh*; (2) a doctrinal precedent in the theology of faith (*īmān*); and two specific modes of elaboration of the doctrine of *tawḥīd al-ulūhiyya*: (3) as intra-Ṣūfī polemic; and (4) as a transvaluation of Aristotelian etiology as interpreted in Islamic philosophy.

### Ilāh *in the Exegetical Tradition*

Ibn Taymiyya's relational definition of *ilāh* as "an object of worship" is far from unique. One finds something like it in the standard lexicons. Al-Jawharī's *Ṣiḥāḥ*, written toward the end of the fourth/tenth century, gives *alaha* as a verb meaning "to worship" (*ʿabada ʿibādatan*), and interprets the name Allāh as derived from the word *ilāh*, itself analyzed as a passive participle (*fiʿāl bi-maʿnā mafʿūl*) with the meaning of "worshipped" (*maʾlūh ayy maʿbūd*). Al-Jawharī then glosses the plural *āliha* as "idols" (*aṣnām*) and explains that the appellation is in accordance with the pagans' belief that worship is due to the idols, and not in accordance with the reality of the idols[133] – in other words they are not true gods but are called *āliha* because of humans' conception that worship is due to them. Similar entries are found in the later works *Lisān al-ʿarab*[134] and *Tāj al-ʿarūs*,[135] and while this was not the only interpretation of the word it appears to have been the historically prevalent one.[136] In this sense Ibn Taymiyya's *tawḥīd al-ulūhiyya* could be considered, to a certain extent, to be the working out of the theological implications, in application to Allāh, of the widespread relational definition of the term *ilāh*.

Why both Ibn Taymiyya and the lexicographers chose to interpret *ilāh* in this way is less evident, but it may derive in part from the exegetical tradition. Al-Jawharī refers to an alternate reading of Qurʾān 7:127 attributed to Ibn ʿAbbās, according to which Firʿawn's people did not ask him whether he would allow the Israelites to "abandon you and your gods (*wa-ālihataka*)," but rather asked him whether he would allow the Israelites to "abandon you and worship of you (*wa-ilāhataka*),"[137] with

[133] Ismāʿīl b. Ḥammād al-Jawharī, *al-Ṣiḥāḥ*, Beirut: Dār al-ʿIlm li-l-Malāyīn, 1399/1979, vol. 6, pp. 2223–2224.

[134] Ibn Manẓūr al-Ifrīqī al-Miṣrī, *Lisān al-ʿarab*, Beirut: Dār Ṣādir/Dār Bayrūt, 1375/1956, vol. 13, pp. 466–471.

[135] Murtaḍā al-Zabīdī, *Tāj al-ʿarūs fī jawāhir al-qāmūs*, Beirut: Dār al-Fikr, 1414/1994, vol. 19, pp. 6–9.

[136] The lexicographical tradition on *ʾ-l-h* is rather inventive. In point of fact *il/el* is a common Semitic root for a divinity, and *ilāh* is identical to the Hebrew *eloah*. Cf. D. B. Macdonald, "Ilāh," in C. E. Bosworth et al. (eds.), *The Encyclopedia of Islam*, 2nd ed., vol. 3, pp. 1093–1094.

[137] al-Jawharī, *al-Ṣiḥāḥ*, vol. 6, p. 2223.

*ilāha* understood as a verbal noun. This reading appears intended to bring the verse in line with the general Qurʾānic depiction of Firʿawn as himself being the god of the Egyptians: Thus Ibn ʿAbbās is reported to have justified his reading with the words "Firʿawn was worshipped, and did not worship." This tradition is reported by al-Ṭabarī in his *tafsīr* on verse 7:127,[138] who likewise mentions it and similar statements attributed to Ibn ʿAbbās in his own comments on the *basmala*, where he argues that the meaning of *ulūhiyya* is worship (*ʿibāda*), and the meaning of *ilāh* "one who is worshipped" (*al-maʿbūd*).[139]

Another impetus for the adoption of the relational definition of *ilāh* in Qurʾānic exegesis was the pair of theologically problematic verses 6:3 and 43:84. Qurʾān 6:3 reads: "And He is Allāh in the heavens and on earth; He knows what you conceal and what you reveal, and He knows what you earn" (*wa-huwa Allāh fī al-samāwāt wa-fī al-arḍ yaʿlamu sirrakum wa-jahrakum wa-yaʿlamu mā taksibūna*). This verse was one of the three *mutashābih* (ambiguous) Qurʾānic verses that, according to Aḥmad b. Ḥanbal, Jahm b. Ṣafwān used to rely on to substantiate his views.[140] The appeal of the verse to Jahm was clearly its immanentist implications, and thus Ibn Ḥanbal, in an attempt to deny the implication that Allāh is omnipresent, interpreted the verse as meaning that Allāh is *ilāh* in the heavens and *ilāh* on earth, in the sense that Allāh is omniscient and thus knows all that is in the heavens and on earth.[141] This resolution, while similar to (and perhaps an inspiration for) the manner in which Ibn Taymiyya denied Allāh's omnipresence, does not itself bring us any closer to the relational meaning of *ilāh* as "worshipped"; in Ibn Taymiyya's categorization, Allāh's omniscience falls under the aspect of *rubūbiyya* rather than of *ulūhiyya*. It is an example, however, of the tendency to interpret Qurʾān 6:3, contra the Jahmites, in light of the similarly worded Qurʾān 43:84, "And it is He who is *ilāh* in heaven and

[138] Abū Jaʿfar al-Ṭabarī, *Jāmiʿ al-bayān ʿan taʾwīl āy al-qurʾān*, ed. Maḥmūd Muḥammad Shākir and Aḥmad Muḥammad Shākir, Egypt: Dār al-Maʿārif, 1957, vol. 13, p. 39 (no. 14966).

[139] al-Ṭabarī, *Jāmiʿ al-bayān*, vol. 1, pp. 122ff.

[140] Aḥmad Ibn Ḥanbal, *al-Radd ʿalā al-jahmiyya wa-l-zanādiqa*, Riyadh: Dār al-Thabāt, 1424[/2003], pp. 95–97, 143–150. The authenticity of this treatise is a matter of controversy. Ibn Taymiyya cited it frequently as Ibn Ḥanbal's, but al-Dhahabī believed the attribution dubious. For a survey of the issue, see Saud Saleh AlSarhan, "Early Muslim Traditionalism: A Critical Study of the Works and Political Theology of Aḥmad Ibn Ḥanbal," PhD diss., University of Exeter, 2011, pp. 48–53, who concludes that the long recension, which is the widespread version of the treatise, is inauthentic. A similar conclusion is reached by Andrew McLaren: "Ibn Ḥanbal's Refutation of the Jahmiyya: A Textual History," *Journal of the American Oriental Society* 140/4 (2020), pp. 901–926.

[141] Ibn Ḥanbal, *al-Radd*, p. 149.

*ilāh* on earth, and He is Wise and Knowing" (*wa-huwa alladhī fī al-samāʾ ilāh wa-fī al-arḍ ilāh wa-huwa al-ḥakīm al-ʿalīm*); and the interpretation of *ilāh* in 43:84 and/or "Allāh" in 6:3 as "worshipped" is widespread in the exegetical tradition, where it is often attributed to the early exegetes Mujāhid b. Jabr and Qatāda b. Diʿāma.[142] The anti-Jahmite thrust of this exegesis (whether in its origin or in its application) is further suggested by its adduction in al-Bukhārī's *Khalq afʿāl al-ʿibād* amidst other statements in condemnation of the Jahmites and negationists,[143] and Ibn Kathīr, who himself favors this exegesis on Qurʾān 6:3, writes that whatever their differences all the exegetes agree that the interpretation of the "early Jahmites" (*al-jahmiyya al-uwal*) that Allāh is omnipresent is to be condemned.[144]

### *The Dispute on the Theology of Faith (*Īmān*)*

While Ibn Taymiyya's terminology of *tawḥīd al-ulūhiyya* and its systematic differentiation from *tawḥīd al-rubūbiyya* were new, they are related to his writings on a classic topic of intra-Muslim polemic: the nature and definition of faith (*īmān*). To present this issue somewhat schematically, the early dispute on the nature and definition of faith was marked by two extremes, both of which are considered heretical in Sunnism. The Khārijites included acts in the definition of faith and thus held any grave sin of commission or omission to be apostasy; the Murjiʾites, in contrast, excluded acts from the definition of faith, and thus held that no Muslim falls into apostasy due to an act so long as he professes correct belief. Sunni orthodoxy on this issue, while universally held to be a median position between these two poles, was never well-defined. Ibn Taymiyya, in his writings on the topic, argued that the Ashʿarīs and the Māturīdīs had essentially adopted the Murjiʾite position, in that they considered the

142 For example, Abū Jaʿfar al-Naḥḥās, *Maʿānī al-qurʾān al-karīm*, ed. Muḥammad ʿAlī al-Ṣābūnī, Mecca: Jāmiʿat Umm al-Qurā, 1409/1988, vol. 2, pp. 399–400; Abū al-Faraj Ibn Muḥammad al-Jawzī, *Zād al-masīr fī ʿilm al-tafsīr*, Beirut: Dār al-Fikr, 1407/1987, vol. 7, pp. 108–109.

143 Muḥammad b. Ismāʿīl al-Bukhārī, *Khalq afʿāl al-ʿibād wa-l-radd ʿalā al-jahmiyya wa-aṣḥāb al-taʿṭīl*, Beirut: Muʾassasat al-Risāla, 1411/1990, p. 20.

144 Ibn Kathīr al-Dimashqī, *Tafsīr al-qurʾān al-ʿaẓīm*, Beirut: Dār al-Kutub al-ʿIlmiyya, 1419/1998, vol. 3, p. 215. Ibn Kathīr (d. 774/1373), while himself a Shāfiʿī in jurisprudence, was a supporter of Ibn Taymiyya, and the latter's influence can be seen to some degree in his *tafsīr*. See Walid A. Saleh, "Ibn Taymiyya and the Rise of Radical Hermeneutics: An Analysis of *An Introduction to the Foundations of Qurʾānic Exegesis*," in Rapoport and Ahmed (eds.), *Ibn Taymiyya and His Times*, pp. 123–162, at p. 153. As noted, however, the relational interpretation of this verse contra the Jahmites predates Ibn Taymiyya, and thus Ibn Kathīr's adoption of it is not necessarily in itself evidence of the influence of Ibn Taymiyya's discussions of the term *ilāh*.

condition for faith to be simply *taṣdīq*, defined as factual belief in the existence of Allāh and the veracity of the Prophet Muḥammad and revelation. In contrast with this position, Ibn Taymiyya forcefully insisted that acts are an equal component of faith together with belief in the heart and profession of the tongue.[145]

This conception of the centrality of acts to faith naturally feeds into Ibn Taymiyya's foregrounding of monolatry as expressed in his doctrine of *tawḥīd al-ulūhiyya*. For example, we have already mentioned Ibn Taymiyya's adduction of Iblīs as emblematic of *tawḥīd al-rubūbiyya* without *tawḥīd al-ulūhiyya*.[146] It is certainly no coincidence that a parallel is to be found between this argument and the portrayal of Iblīs in Ibn Taymiyya's writings on the theology of faith. In these latter writings, Ibn Taymiyya argues that Iblīs did not deny Allāh or any other factual component of faith. He understands Iblīs' *kufr* as a *kufr* of disobedience in deed, and not one of factual disbelief, and thus Iblīs serves him as a standard proof that acts (*ʿamal*) can negate one's faith (*īmān*), and consequently are to be considered an essential component thereof.[147] These arguments, one drawn from Ibn Taymiyya's "new" theological system and the other drawn from his defense of Traditionalist orthodoxy on a classic dispute, are in fact one and the same: Conceptual belief in Allāh without submission and obedience to Him is not faith and is not Islam. In this sense *tawḥīd al-ulūhiyya* can be considered a discursive theological formulation of the monolatric emphasis already present in the Traditionalist school, as expressed in its doctrine on the status of acts in faith.

### *Intra-Ṣūfī Polemic*

Ibn Taymiyya's emphasis on *tawḥīd al-ulūhiyya* is often formulated as a critique of Ṣūfī fatalism and passivity, which he characterizes as a function of exclusive focus on the aspect of *rubūbiyya* to the exclusion of *ulūhiyya*. Ibn Taymiyya's formulations of the issue in a Ṣūfī register are characterized by the distinctive terminological dyad of *ḥaqīqa kawniyya* (cosmic or ontological reality) vs. *ḥaqīqa sharʿiyya* or *ḥaqīqa dīniyya* (normative or religious reality), itself a subset of an overarching *kawnī* vs. *sharʿī/dīnī* distinction that mirrors the *rubūbiyya/ulūhiyya* one.[148]

145 On Ibn Taymiyya's polemic on this issue, see Daniel Lav, *Radical Islam and the Revival of Medieval Theology*, New York: Cambridge University Press, 2012, pp. 30–40.

146 Ibn Taymiyya, *Majmūʿat al-fatāwā*, vol. 2, p. 14.

147 See Ibn Taymiyya, *Majmūʿat al-fatāwā*, vol. 7, pp. 121, 193, 312, 327; discussed in Lav, *Radical Islam*, pp. 36–37.

148 On this topic, see Hoover, *Ibn Taymiyya's Theodicy*, pp. 122ff.; Arjan Post, *The Journeys of a Taymiyyan Sufi: Sufism through the Eyes of ʿImād al-Dīn Aḥmad al-Wāsiṭī (d. 711/1311)*, Leiden and Boston: Brill, 2020, pp. 260–262.

*Ḥaqīqa* has a number of meanings in Arabic. In *kalām* usage, for example, it can mean a thing's essence (as opposed to its existence). Ibn Taymiyya here is clearly using the term in its Ṣūfī acceptation, in which *ḥaqīqa* means something like "the ultimate (ideal) divine reality of the universe."[149] Ibn Taymiyya's differentiation between *ḥaqīqa kawniyya* and *ḥaqīqa sharʿiyya/dīniyya* is in essence a critique of heterodox Ṣūfism that is analogous to his critique of *kalām* theology through the differentiation between *tawḥīd al-rubūbiyya* and *tawḥīd al-ulūhiyya*. The *ḥaqīqa kawniyya* (cosmic or ontological reality), which corresponds to *rubūbiyya*, refers to Allāh in His capacity as Creator and Master of the cosmos:

> When the secret of *rubūbiyya* becomes manifest to the servant – that sovereignty (*mulk*) and governance (*tadbīr*) are entirely in the hands of Allāh the Exalted ... every benefit, harm, movement, rest, contraction (*qabḍ*), expansion (*basṭ*), raising, and lowering that he sees, he sees Allāh the Exalted, may He be praised, as its actor, creator, contractor, expander, raiser, and lowerer. This vision (*shuhūd*) is the secret of the cosmic words (*al-kalimāt al-kawniyyāt*), and it is the knowledge of the attribute of *rubūbiyya*.[150]

In itself this cosmic aspect of Allāh is true and needs to be affirmed, but of course for Ibn Taymiyya it is not sufficient in itself. In his *Risālat al-ʿubūdiyya*, after touching on the now-familiar argument that the *mushrikūn* affirmed this aspect of Allāh while worshipping others apart from Allāh, Ibn Taymiyya writes: "Many who speak of the *ḥaqīqa* [viz. Ṣūfīs] and witness it witness only this *ḥaqīqa*, which is the *ḥaqīqa kawniyya*, the witnessing and knowledge of which is common to the believer and the unbeliever, the pious and the impious. In fact, Iblīs acknowledges this *ḥaqīqa*, as do those condemned to hellfire."[151]

In Ibn Taymiyya's further condemnation of the Ṣūfī who acknowledges solely the *ḥaqīqa kawniyya*, we find an explicit equation between the *ḥaqīqa dīniyya* and Allāh's aspect of *ulūhiyya*:

> One who stops at this *ḥaqīqa* (viz. *al-ḥaqīqa al-kawniyya*) and the witnessing of it, and does not perform what Allāh commanded in accordance with *al-ḥaqīqa al-dīniyya*, which is worship of Him that relates to His *ulūhiyya* and obedience to His command and the command of His Prophet, is of the ilk of Iblīs [who

149 Louis Massignon, *Essay on the Origins of the Technical Language of Islamic Mysticism*, trans. Benjamin Clark, Notre Dame: University of Notre Dame Press, 1997, p. 28. Massignon sees this usage of the term as late and "bad," but it was the one prevalent in the Ṣūfism of Ibn Taymiyya's day.

150 Ibn Taymiyya, *Majmūʿat al-fatāwā*, vol. 1, p. 70.

151 Ibn Taymiyya, *Risālat al-ʿubūdiyya*, in Yāsir Burhāmī, *al-Kawāshif al-muḍiyya ʿan laʾāliʾ risālat al-ʿubūdiyya*, Alexandria: Dār al-Īmān, n.d., p. 23 (= *Majmūʿat al-fatāwā*, vol. 10, p. 95).

acknowledged Allāh but did not obey Him] and those condemned to hellfire. And if, together with this, he thinks himself to be among the elite of Allāh's saints and of the people of gnosis (*ma'rifa*) and realization (*taḥqīq*) who are exempted from *shar'ī* command and prohibition, then he is among the worst of the people of unbelief and heresy.[152]

The adduction of Iblīs as an example reinforces the identification between the *ḥaqīqa kawniyya* (in the Ṣūfī register), *taṣdīq* (in the theology of faith), and *rubūbiyya*, as distinguished from the *ḥaqīqa shar'iyya/dīniyya*, *'amal*, and *ulūhiyya*. The use of Iblīs as a negative example connects between Ibn Taymiyya's writings on the nature of *tawḥīd*, his intra-Ṣūfī polemic, and his writings on the nature of faith, and suggests that these are in essence all the same issue.

It is worth focusing our attention on the term *taḥqīq*, which is a second-form verbal noun from the root *ḥ-q-q* and means in the Ṣūfī context something like attainment or realization of the ultimate divine reality (*ḥaqīqa*).[153] Ibn Taymiyya alludes, in the last passage cited, to Ṣūfīs who believe *taḥqīq* to be realization solely of the *ḥaqīqa kawniyya*, the cosmic or ontological reality, to the exclusion of the normative command and prohibition expressed in the *ḥaqīqa dīniyya*. Ibn Taymiyya himself, in contrast, frequently uses the term *taḥqīq* precisely for achievement or realization of *tawḥīd al-ulūhiyya* – that is, of the *ḥaqīqa dīniyya*, with the result that in Ibn Taymiyya's writings "*taḥqīq al-tawḥīd*" or "*taḥqīq al-shahāda*" frequently denotes monolatry in particular, that is, exclusive obedience to and worship of Allāh, and avoidance of worship of not-Allāh.[154] The use of *taḥqīq*

[152] Ibn Taymiyya, *Risālat al-'ubūdiyya*, p. 24 (= *Majmū'at al-fatāwā*, vol. 10, p. 95).

[153] Cf. Michael Cooperson, *Classical Arabic Biography: The Heirs of the Prophets in the Age of Al-Ma'mūn*, Cambridge: Cambridge University Press, 2004, p. 156: "Mysticism is a mode of cognition that treats the objects of belief as objects of experience: what the Sufis called *taḥqīq* or 'realization.'" Cited in Anjum, "Sufism without Mysticism?," p. 165.

[154] Cf. Ibn Taymiyya, *Majmū'at al-fatāwā*, vol. 1, p. 96, on the inability of others to harm or benefit without Allāh's permission, and the impermissibility of asking them to do so: *fa-ta'ayyana anna al-amr kullahu 'ā'idun ilā taḥqīq al-tawḥīd*; vol. 1, p. 103, on obedience being owed to Allāh and the Prophet, whereas fear, hope, and so forth must be felt exclusively with regard to Allāh and none other: *wa-qad kāna al-nabī ṣallā Allāh 'alayhi wa-sallama yuḥaqqiqu hādhā al-tawḥīd li-ummatihi wa-yaḥsimu mawādd al-shirk idh hādhā taḥqīq qawlinā lā ilāha illā llāh*; vol. 1, p. 213, on the prohibition of worshipping at the Prophet's grave and otherwise blurring the distinction between him and Allāh: *wa-hādhā taḥqīq al-tawḥīd ma'a annahu ṣallā Allāh 'alayhi wa-sallama akram al-khalq 'alā llāh wa-a'lāhum manzilatan 'inda llāh*; vol. 1, p. 218, where the language of *taḥqīq* is applied to the profession of faith: *wa-dīn al-islām mabnī 'alā aṣlayni wa-humā taḥqīq shahādat an lā ilāha illā llāh wa-anna Muḥammadan rasūl Allāh*; similarly in vol. 1, p. 231 (interpolation from a fatwā delivered in Egypt in 711/1311 – cf. vol. 1, p. 219), where, after discussing the need for strict differentiation between the Prophet and Allāh, Ibn Taymiyya writes that the two principles of exclusive worship of Allāh alone, and worship of Him only in the ways that He prescribed, are *taḥqīq shahādat an lā ilāha illā llāh wa-anna Muḥammadan rasūl Allāh*; and vol. 1, p. 251 (likewise from the Egyptian fatwā):

in this sense appears to be a conscious reappropriation of the term, indicating how intra-Ṣūfī polemic and Ibn Taymiyya's own conception of orthodox Ṣūfism contributed to the formulation of the doctrine of *tawḥīd al-ulūhiyya* and its technical vocabulary.

A final example of this influence can be found in Ibn Taymiyya's tendency to employ a "Ṣūfī" resolution in response to an inherent tension between *rubūbiyya* and *ulūhiyya*, or between the cosmic/ontological reality and the religious/normative one. Within the Taymiyyan system, the demand for exclusivity of devotion and obedience to Allāh, mandated by the aspect of *ulūhiyya*, is predicated on the cratological conception of Allāh as omnipotent Lord: The telos of humans is simply to serve the true Lord as He commanded. Yet Allāh's omnipotence, mandated by the aspect of *rubūbiyya*, and the configuration of humans' relation to Him primarily through the figure of Kreaturgefühl and powerlessness, necessarily emphasizes the concept of *al-qaḍāʾ wa l-qadar*: the irrefragability of divine will and divine power, including Allāh's power over human action, in the form of predetermination. Thus one of the inherent tensions of the Taymiyyan system can be stated as follows: How can Allāh's creation of human acts (*khalq al-afʿāl*) and absolute power over humans be reconciled with the demand for humans' obedience and devotion, which would seem to rest on the premise that they possess independent will and ability?

It must be emphasized that this tension is internal to the Taymiyyan system. Ibn Taymiyya's general methodology in theological issues, as we have seen, is to disentangle separate economies, point to the foreign origins of philosophical concepts, and then offer a rational, discursive explanation of the internal logic of the revelational economy. Here, however, this is not possible: Both in the Qurʾānic data themselves and in the construction of the Taymiyyan system, the human obligation at the center of *tawḥīd al-ulūhiyya* and the divine power at the center of *tawḥīd al-rubūbiyya* stand in natural tension. The status of the human act is in other ways as well a unique topic in Ibn Taymiyya's theology, and a technical examination of it would take us too far afield for present purposes;[155] my intention here is simply to point to a particular Ṣūfī resolution of the issue that Ibn Taymiyya at times employs.

*wa-ammā al-dākhilūna fī al-islām idhā lam yuḥaqqiqū al-tawḥīd wa-ttibāʿ al-rasūl bal daʿaw al-shuyūkh al-ghāʾibīn wa-staghāthū bihim*, and in the continuation of the passage a parallel to infra, p. 218, on the *shahāda*, but with *ḥaqīqa* in place of *taḥqīq*: *wa-dīn al-islām mabnī ʿalā aṣlayni … wa-hādhāni humā ḥaqīqat qawlinā ashhadu an lā ilāha illā llāh wa-ashhadu anna Muḥammadan ʿabduhu wa-rasūluhu.*

155 For treatments of Ibn Taymiyya's doctrine on the human act and related issues, see Hoover, *Ibn Taymiyya's Theodicy*, pp. 136–176, and the works cited therein, esp. Daniel

The Ṣūfīs who stop at realization of *al-ḥaqīqa al-kawniyya* are faulted not for reaching an inaccurate realization, but only an incomplete one. The witnessing of Allāh's *rubūbiyya* and the *ḥaqīqa kawniyya* is itself true, but so is the normative reality of command and prohibition, and the issue arises of how to reconcile the two perspectives of divine omnipotence and human responsibility. While not explicitly acknowledging the existence of any paradox or failure of discursive explanation, Ibn Taymiyya nonetheless repeatedly turns to an aporetic statement attributed to the Ḥanbalī Ṣūfī ʿAbd al-Qādir al-Jīlānī, who, contrasting himself with those who passively submit to Allāh's predetermining will, said: "As for me, an aperture has opened up for me in it [viz. Allāh's will], and I have struggled against God's preordinations through God and for the sake of God. The worthy man (*al-rajul*) is he who struggles against *qadar*, not he who falls in line with *qadar*."[156]

Thus, in addition to the specifically Ṣūfī formulation of the *rubūbiyya/ulūhiyya* distinction surveyed above, we see here that Ibn Taymiyya likewise has recourse to a respected Ḥanbalī Ṣūfī predecessor in order to explain how to simultaneously affirm both aspects of divinity in full without falling into either denial of *qadar* or passivity and antinomianism. It is noteworthy that the same Ṣūfī formulations of the issue are in evidence in Ibn Taymiyya's commentary on ʿAbd al-Qādir al-Jīlānī's *Futūḥ al-ghayb*.[157] Further study would be required before Ibn Taymiyya's precise debt to Ḥanbalī Ṣūfism could be properly assessed,[158] but in light of the above it seems certain that it was at least a contributing influence on his formulation of the *rubūbiyya/ulūhiyya* distinction.

Gimaret, "Théories de l'acte humain dans l'école Ḥanbalite," *Bulletin d'études orientales* 29 (1977), pp. 157–178. For more on the relation between Ibn Taymiyya's doctrine on the human act and its relation to *tawḥīd al-ulūhiyya*, see Daniel Lav, "Ashʿarism, Causality, and the Cult of Saints," *Jerusalem Studies in Arabic and Islam* 50 (2021), pp. 255–312. On the topic in general in Sunnī theology, Daniel Gimaret, *Théories de l'acte humain en théologie musulmane*, Paris: J. Vrin, 1980.

156 Ibn Taymiyya, *Risālat al-ʿubūdiyya*, in Burhāmī, *al-Kawāshif al-muḍiyya*, pp. 26–27 (= Ibn Taymiyya, *Majmūʿat al-fatāwā*, vol. 10, p. 96, cited also in vol. 8, p. 185).

157 Ibn Taymiyya, *Risālat sharḥ kalimāt min futūḥ al-ghayb*, in *Jāmiʿ al-rasāʾil*, vol. 2, pp. 71–189, at p. 109. And see Thomas F. Michel, "Ibn Taymiyya's *Sharḥ* on the *Futūḥ al-ghayb* of ʿAbd al-Qādir al-Jīlānī," *Hamdard Islamicus* 4/2 (Summer 1981), pp. 3–12.

158 On this topic, see also George Makdisi, "The Hanbali School and Sufism," *Boletin de la Asociación Española de Orientalistas* XV (1979), pp. 115–126; George Makdisi, "Ibn Taimīya: A Ṣūfī of the Qādiriya Order," *American Journal of Arabic Studies* 1 (1974), pp. 118–129 (both reprinted in George Makdisi, *Religion, Law, and Learning in Classical Islam*, Hampshire: Variorum, 1991); E. Geoffroy, "Le traité de soufisme d'un disciple d'Ibn Taymiyya: Aḥmad ʿImād al-dīn al-Wāsiṭī," *Studia Islamica* 82 (1995), pp. 83–101; Post, *Journeys of a Taymiyyan Sufi*.

### *Transvaluation of Aristotelian Etiology*

While the preceding three elements certainly contributed to Ibn Taymiyya's doctrine of *tawḥīd al-ulūhiyya*, it appears that the most important model for Ibn Taymiyya's elaboration of his theology through the systematic *ilāh*/*rabb* distinction was, surprisingly, Islamic philosophical discourse on causation, perfection, and well-being.[159] The basic terms of reference in these discussions were taken from Aristotle, and in particular his enumeration of four kinds of causes: material, formal, efficient, and final. Not all these are what we normally think of as a cause in everyday language. The material cause is that out of which something is (e.g. a statue's material cause might be bronze), and the formal cause is the thing's form or shape. It is the other two that are of interest to us here. The efficient cause is close to what we naturally think of as a cause; Aristotle defines it as "the primary source of change or rest." The final cause is defined as "the end, that for the sake of which a thing is done."[160]

There are any number of Arabic-language writings, including the translations of Aristotle, in which Ibn Taymiyya would have encountered discussions of causality in these terms. His primary point of reference, however, appears to be Ibn Sīnā who, influenced by the late antique Neoplatonic tradition, spoke of God as both the efficient cause and the final cause of the cosmos.[161] In Ibn Sīnā's writings these two aspects of divinity correlate with the overarching Neoplatonic framework of procession and reversion. Procession refers to the process of existentiation of the cosmos that starts from an overabundance of being in God and flows

[159] This section follows up on the comments of Jon Hoover, who has already noted Ibn Taymiyya's use of the philosophical (and particularly Avicennan) terminology of causation, his application of it to *ulūhiyya* and *rubūbiyya*, and its role in establishing the primacy of *ulūhiyya*. See Hoover, *Ibn Taymiyya's Theodicy*, pp. 28–29, 121.

[160] Andrea Falcon, "Aristotle on Causality," in Edward N. Zalta (ed.), *The Stanford Encyclopedia of Philosophy (Winter 2012 Edition)*, http://plato.stanford.edu/archives/win2012/entries/aristotle-causality/.

[161] Ibn Taymiyya was aware that Neoplatonic influence accounted for differences in doctrine between Ibn Sīnā and Aristotle, who had described the Unmoved Mover solely as a final cause (and specifically, as a final cause of planetary motion). See Ibn Taymiyya, *Majmūʿat al-fatāwā*, vol. 6, p. 200, for a reference to the influence of Proclus on Ibn Sīnā's depiction of God as efficient cause. While Robert Wisnovsky has produced ample evidence documenting Ibn Sīnā's interest in describing divinity as both an efficient and a final cause, it should be noted that in this passage Ibn Taymiyya states that Ibn Sīnā focused (contra Aristotle) on its being an efficient cause; this suggests that his understanding of Ibn Sīnā may have been closer to that of Naṣīr al-Dīn al-Ṭūsī (cf. Wisnovsky, *Avicenna's Metaphysics*, p. 187). How Ibn Taymiyya read Ibn Sīnā on this matter deserves further inquiry, especially as it would shed light on his intention in incorporating the etiological framework into his own doctrine of *tawḥīd*.

down from Him through a chain of progressively less perfect beings, whereas reversion refers to each being's striving for its own perfection and its desire to reascend the chain of being. When viewed from the perspective of procession, God appears as the ultimate efficient cause of a being's existence; when viewed from the perspective of reversion, God appears as the final cause of a being's essence, perfection, or well-being.[162]

Ibn Taymiyya, of course, was not a Neoplatonist and did not adopt the framework of procession and reversion. Nonetheless, many elements of Ibn Sīnā's system do seem to have influenced the doctrine of *tawḥīd al-ulūhiyya*, especially the identification of God as the agent (*fāʿil*) or efficient cause (*ʿilla fāʿiliyya*) of beings with respect to their existence, and as the telos (*ghāya*) or final cause (*ʿilla ghāʾiyya*) of beings with respect to their well-being or perfection. Stated colloquially, Ibn Taymiyya adopted from Ibn Sīnā the idea that as efficient cause God is the source of existence, or the "how" of existence, and as final cause He is the point of existence, or the "why" of existence.

Discussions of efficient and final causation are strewn throughout Ibn Taymiyya's writings; it seems that despite the philosophical origins of the terminology, it was rendered more palatable by the use of parallel concepts in Arabic grammar, Qurʾānic exegesis, and jurisprudence.[163] Discussion of Allāh in particular as efficient cause and final cause likewise arises in Ibn Taymiyya's writings in various contexts;[164] here we will focus on his systematic exposition of this framework in the *Faṣl fī al-tawḥīd*, printed in volume six of the *Jāmiʿ al-masāʾil*.[165]

The *Faṣl fī al-tawḥīd* is structured as an explanation of Qurʾān 21:22: "Had there been in the heavens and earth gods (*āliha*) other than Allāh both would have fallen into a state of corruption." Ibn Taymiyya argues against the use of this verse in *kalām* writings as proof that the world cannot have two Lords (*rabbāni*), an argument known as the Proof from Mutual Obstruction (*dalīl al-tamānuʿ*). Naturally Ibn Taymiyya agrees that the world can have only one Lord (*rabb*), but he interprets this verse in particular as yielding the more significant conclusion that it can likewise have only one *ilāh*. Given that the other gods who are denied

[162] See Wisnovsky, *Avicenna's Metaphysics*, esp. pp. 181ff.
[163] See Ibn Taymiyya, *Majmūʿat al-fatāwā*, vol. 6, pp. 253–254: "this is called the final cause (*al-ʿilla al-ghāʾiyya*), which the jurisprudents call *ḥikmat al-ḥukm*," vol. 6, p. 300; Ibn Taymiyya, *Jāmiʿ al-masāʾil*, Mecca: Dār ʿĀlam al-Fawāʾid, 1422[/2001–2002], vol. 6, p. 60, for a discussion of the use of the letter *lām* to mean "*kay*" and efficient and final causation in relation to Qurʾān 7:179.
[164] See e.g. Ibn Taymiyya, *Majmūʿat al-fatāwā*, vol. 2, p. 29, vol. 14, p. 171.
[165] Ibn Taymiyya, *Jāmiʿ al-masāʾil*, vol. 6, pp. 87–129.

in the verse are referred to as *āliha*, the plural of *ilāh*, Ibn Taymiyya's argument revolves around an extended discussion of the difference between the two aspects of *rubūbiyya* and *ulūhiyya*.

In the opening words of the *Faṣl fī al-tawḥīd* we find an identification of *rubūbiyya* and *ulūhiyya* with, respectively, efficient and final causation: "In what preceded this I wrote principles relating to *tawḥīd al-rubūbiyya* and *tawḥīd al-ulūhiyya*, and regarding how just as it is impossible for creation to have two *rabb*s, so it is impossible for it to have two *ilāh*s, and I spoke of the efficient and final causes."[166] Ibn Taymiyya then launches into a discussion of unicity in causation, with implicit reference to a standard *kalām* argument, ubiquitous in proofs of creation, that an infinite regress of originated beings or events is an impossibility. Ibn Taymiyya affirms that it is impossible for an efficient cause to be its own cause, or for two efficient causes each to be the cause of the other. An efficient cause is temporally prior to its effect, and thus in order for an efficient cause to be its own cause it would have to be prior to itself; likewise, in order for two efficient causes to reciprocally cause one another, each would have to be prior to the other: A would be prior to B, but B must also be prior to A, so A would have to be prior-to-prior-to-itself, and so forth.

This is more or less standard fare; Ibn Taymiyya's real purpose in raising the issue of infinite regress of efficient causation is to argue that a similar logic applies to final causation as well. Since a final cause is an aim or a goal for the sake of which one acts, its realization must be temporally posterior to its effect. For an effect to be its own final cause, it would then have to be posterior to itself, and in order for two final causes to reciprocally cause one another, each would have to be posterior to the other and to itself, and so forth. In either case we encounter circularity or infinite regress. Thus, just as no effect can have more than one true efficient cause, which must be exterior to it, so no effect can have more than one true final cause, which also must be exterior to it.[167]

Following some further precisions on this topic Ibn Taymiyya returns to Qurʾān 21:22, "Had there been in the heavens and earth gods (*āliha*) other than Allāh both would have fallen into a state of corruption." As noted, this verse was frequently used in *kalām* writings as Scriptural support for the Proof from Mutual Obstruction. Variations aside, the basic idea is that were there two Lords, neither could enjoy fullness of power or be completely autarkic in his control of the cosmos, since the other would have equal power and could obstruct his will or

166 Ibn Taymiyya, *Jāmiʿ al-masāʾil*, vol. 6, p. 87.
167 Ibn Taymiyya, *Jāmiʿ al-masāʾil*, vol. 6, p. 87.

actions.[168] Ibn Taymiyya's discussion of the rational proof itself is not of particular interest to us here; after all, according to him, it demonstrates only *tawḥīd al-rubūbiyya*, which as we have seen he considers to be a matter of near consensus among Muslims and non-Muslims alike. What is of interest is Ibn Taymiyya's argument, *pace* the *kalām* theologians, that verse 21:22 is not an affirmation of *tawḥīd al-rubūbiyya* but rather of *tawḥīd al-ulūhiyya*.[169]

The rest of the *Faṣl* fleshes out the topic of *tawḥīd al-ulūhiyya* in the framework of causality. "I say that just as it is impossible for there to be two *rabb*s, each of them being the causal agent of a thing (*fāʿil al-shayʾ*), so it is impossible for there to be two *ilāh*s, each of them being the thing's object of worship (*maʿbūd al-shayʾ*). This is as I said previously, that it is impossible for each of two things to be the efficient cause of the other (*fāʿilan li-l-ākhar wa-ʿillatan lahu*), and it is impossible for each of them to be the aim (*al-maqṣūd*) of the other and its final cause (*al-ʿilla al-ghāʾiyya lahu*)."[170] It is clear here that the aspect of *rabb* is equated with the efficient cause, and the aspect of *ilāh* with the final cause.

Ibn Taymiyya continues with the following contention: Just as nothing in creation is its own *rabb* and efficient cause (*rabban li-nafsihi fāʿilan*), so nothing in creation is in itself the aim of its own existence (*maqṣūdan li-nafsihi hiya al-ghāya al-maṭlūba min wujūdihi*). Just as all created beings have a *rabb* who is other than them and who made them and originated them, so they all must have an *ilāh* who is other than themselves.[171]

This conception of Allāh as final cause in addition to efficient cause dictates that, just as He alone is the absolute origin of things' existence, so He alone is the sole absolute "for-the-sake-of-which" of existence. Just as He is necessary (of existence) in Himself, so He and He alone is loved in and of Himself and for Himself (*li-nafsihi*),[172] and all that He loves is thus a derivative consequence of His own self-love.[173]

As mentioned earlier, Ibn Sīnā had followed in the footsteps of late antique Neoplatonism, which associated, on the one hand, the efficient cause with existence (Gk. *to einai*) and, on the other, the final cause with

[168] See e.g. Abū al-Ḥasan al-Ashʿarī, *Risāla ilā ahl al-thaghr*, 2nd ed., ed. ʿAbdallāh Shākir Muḥammad al-Junaydī, Medina: Maktabat al-ʿUlūm wa-l-Ḥikam, 1422/2002, pp. 156–157; and further references in Muḥammad b. ʿAbd al-Raḥmān Abū Sayf al-Jihnī, "al-Tamānuʿ al-dāll ʿalā al-tawḥīd fī kitāb Allāh wa-naqd masālik al-mutakallimīn," *Majallat Jāmiʿat Umm al-Qurā li-ʿUlūm al-Sharīʿa wa-l-Dirāsāt al-Islāmiyya* 45 (Dhū al-Qaʿda 1429 AH), pp. 105–132, at pp. 115–117.

[169] Ibn Taymiyya, *Jāmiʿ al-masāʾil*, vol. 6, p. 98.

[170] Ibn Taymiyya, *Jāmiʿ al-masāʾil*, vol. 6, p. 99.

[171] Ibn Taymiyya, *Jāmiʿ al-masāʾil*, vol. 6, p. 99.

[172] Ibn Taymiyya, *Jāmiʿ al-masāʾil*, vol. 6, p. 100.

[173] Ibn Taymiyya, *Jāmiʿ al-masāʾil*, vol. 6, p. 105.

well-being (Gk. *to eu einai*). Echoes of this pairing are clear in Ibn Taymiyya's *Faṣl fī al-tawḥīd*: "If [Allāh] is the *rabb* and sovereign of all things, with no thing having *existence* (*wujūd*) save for His power and will, so He is the *ilāh* of all creation, and there is no *ilāh* but He, and creation has no *well-being* (*ṣalāḥ*) save in His being their object of worship that is the primary intention in all their movements."[174]

The parallels between Ibn Taymiyya's *rubūbiyya*/*ulūhiyya* distinction and Ibn Sīnā's Neoplatonic scheme of divine causality are too conspicuous to be mere coincidence. It is clear that this is an intentional borrowing. The case before us, however, is not one of simple influence. On the one hand, Ibn Taymiyya borrowed the philosophers' terminology in order to critique the *kalām* theologians and their emphasis on *rubūbiyya* to the degree of neglect of *ulūhiyya*, as in their alleged misapplication of Qur'ān 21:22. As we have seen, this claim is one of the most constant themes in Ibn Taymiyya's writings on *tawḥīd al-ulūhiyya* and in his critique of *kalām* in general. Likewise, Ibn Sīnā's assignation of primacy to final causation over efficient causation[175] may well have influenced the manner in which Ibn Taymiyya insisted on the priority of *ulūhiyya*, as for example in a passage in which Ibn Taymiyya first states this priority in the formal language of causation – "the final cause is more perfect (*akmal*) than the efficient cause, as it is what made the agent the agent" – and then follows with the more distinctive Taymiyyan formulation: "His being creation's *ilāh* that is worshipped is more perfect (*akmal*) than the aspect of His being a *rabb* who aids them."[176] On the other hand, the interpretation that Ibn Taymiyya gives to Allāh's being the final cause and telos of existence differs from that of the philosophers, and in essence the manner in which he repurposes their framework ultimately turns it against them in defense of the monolatric emphasis of his own revelational monotheism.

This can be seen, for example, in his *Faṣl fī ḥaqq Allāh ʿalā ʿibādihi*, which likewise expounds on the aspect of *ulūhiyya* in terms of final causality. This essay is structured around Qur'ān 51:56, "I only created the jinn and humans in order that they worship Me," and the immediately following verses.[177] Here Ibn Taymiyya, like the philosophers, describes Allāh as the final cause, but unlike them he defines the manner in which this final causality is expressed in relation to created beings as being that of servitude: "Allāh created the jinn and the humans, and the

[174] Ibn Taymiyya, *Jāmiʿ al-masāʾil*, vol. 6, p. 109 (emphasis added).
[175] See Wisnovsky, *Avicenna's Metaphysics*, pp. 175, 179, 187.
[176] Ibn Taymiyya, *Jāmiʿ al-masāʾil*, vol. 6, p. 119.
[177] Ibn Taymiyya, *Jāmiʿ al-masāʾil*, vol. 6, p. 45.

telos (*ghāya*) that is beloved for them, through which they reach perfection (*yakmulūna*), achieve well-being (*yaṣluḥūna*), attain honor, and through which God loves them, is for them to worship Him."[178] Likewise, in the *Faṣl fī al-tawḥīd*, it is asserted that the well-being of angels, jinn, and humans is only achieved when Allāh is their *ilāh* and the object of their worship and all their movements, in love and humility.[179]

In fact, Ibn Taymiyya concludes the *Faṣl fī al-tawḥīd* with a critique of the philosophers which in itself might appear out of place unless one understands that he has just finished expounding the essentials of his own theological doctrine in language borrowed from them, and for this reason needs to clarify the opposition between his own system and theirs:

> This foundation [viz. self-perfection through servitude to Allāh] is firmly settled for [those of] the people of the religions [who are] followers of the religion of Ibrāhīm, the people of the *ḥanīf* [religion]. For others it is not. Even the philosophers of divinity (*al-mutafalsifa al-ilāhiyyūn*) and their followers among the people of religion, notwithstanding their claim to have mastered the certain sciences and true wisdom, and who said: the happiness of souls is their perfection (*kamāluhā*) in knowledge and action – they are [in fact] the people who are the farthest from this, since for them the telos (*ghāya*) of the happiness of souls is solely the attainment of knowledge, and true knowledge of universals (*kulliyyāt*), which have no extramental existence qua universals; and the existence that they affirm for the Necessarily Existent is of this type.[180]

Here Ibn Taymiyya returns to his habitual critique of merely conceptual monotheism, which he denounces in the name of his own monolatric doctrine.

He argues, in essence, that for all that the philosophers speak of the final cause of existence and of human perfection, they remain circumscribed within the speculative, philosophical realm of intellection. For Ibn Taymiyya the final cause, or *ilāh*, is a real, concrete being that loves and hates, and must be loved and feared with the whole of one's being in complete servitude. In addition, despite the parallelism in the formal proofs regarding the unicity of the *rabb* as efficient cause and the unicity of the *ilāh* as the final cause, there exists one important difference: While it is impossible for something to be its own *rabb*, it is not impossible for it to be its own *ilāh*, but rather forbidden. Created beings are capable of taking other than Allāh as their *ilāh*, and indeed much of the Qurʾān is concerned with rebuking those who do so as polytheists. The entire point

[178] Ibn Taymiyya, *Jāmiʿ al-masāʾil*, vol. 6, p. 62.
[179] Ibn Taymiyya, *Jāmiʿ al-masāʾil*, vol. 6, p. 122.
[180] Ibn Taymiyya, *Jāmiʿ al-masāʾil*, vol. 6, p. 123.

of the aspect of *ulūhiyya* is that it superposes a normative dimension of meaning onto the dimension of plain existence. Thus, according to Ibn Taymiyya, it is because Qur'ān 21:22 relates to *ulūhiyya* rather than *rubūbiyya* that it states that the presence of other *ilāh*s would entail the "corruption" of heaven and earth, rather than their nonexistence.[181] The topic of the verse is well-being or proper being, and not (*pace* the *kalām* theologians) the bare fact of being.

The normative import of Allāh's *ulūhiyya*/final causation can be seen again when, toward the end of the *Faṣl fī al-tawḥīd*, Ibn Taymiyya cites Qur'ān 8:39, "And fight them until there is no more strife (*fitna*) and religion is entirely for Allāh," and then explains: "if religion is not for Allāh, and the movements of humans are for other than Allāh, then there is strife and corruption; and well-being is for the movements to be for Allāh, and corruption is for them to be for other than Allāh."[182] This is true well-being, even if it entails bloodshed and killing, because it serves the true final cause. Elsewhere, when Ibn Taymiyya discusses Allāh's final causality in a theodicean vein, he explains how an apparent evil can be good when understood to serve the final cause through an example that could easily have been taken from the writings of a modern radical:

> If it were said Muḥammad and his nation (*umma*) spill blood and spread corruption on earth, that would be condemnation of them, and would be falsehood. And if it were said: they wage jihād for the sake of Allāh so that Allāh's word be supreme and religion be entirely for Allāh, and they kill whoever obstructs them in that, that would be praise of them, and it would be true.[183]

While many modern-day radicals who hold to Ibn Taymiyya's doctrine of *tawḥīd al-ulūhiyya* as salafī orthodoxy would be reluctant to admit the role that philosophy played in its original formulation, in content Ibn Taymiyya remained true to the devotional, monolatric emphasis of the revelational economy of transcendence.

## Conclusion

Ibn Taymiyya was a sophisticated defender of the form of religion we have termed the revelational economy, which he inherited from earlier Ḥanbalīs and Traditionalists but which he developed with original arguments and whose elements he integrated into a coherent and discursively elaborated theological system. The linchpin of this system was the

[181] Ibn Taymiyya, *Jāmiʿ al-masāʾil*, vol. 6, p. 126.
[182] Ibn Taymiyya, *Jāmiʿ al-masāʾil*, vol. 6, p. 127.
[183] Ibn Taymiyya, *Majmūʿat al-fatāwā*, vol. 14, p. 171.

doctrine of *tawḥīd al-ulūhiyya*, which stated that Islam is defined primarily by exclusivity of worship of Allāh rather than belief in Allāh's objective qualities. This principle runs like a thread through Ibn Taymiyya's arguments in defense of other aspects of his system: revelational epistemology, opposition to the ontological turn of the philosophers and *kalām* theologians, affirmation of the divine attributes, and defense of a physically transcendent divinity whose mode of interaction with the mundane world is unmediated. While I have suggested possible precedents for the doctrine of *tawḥīd al-ulūhiyya* in the theology of faith and in the Ḥanbalī Ṣūfī tradition, the doctrine on the whole is strikingly original and appears to have emerged largely out of Ibn Taymiyya's engagement with (and against) philosophy. The doctrine was also revolutionary: It argued that the predominant schools of Sunnī Islam were unaware of the true nature of Islam and that many widely employed cultic practices were substantially equivalent to the form of *shirk* for which the Qurʾān condemned the *mushrikūn*. Ibn Taymiyya's polemics were often abstruse and their radical implications embedded in layers of scholastic dispute. Centuries would pass before others streamlined the doctrine of *tawḥīd al-ulūhiyya* and converted it into a rallying cry for a real-world battle against polytheism.

# 2 Monolatry in Eighteenth-Century Revivalism

In the Introduction I argued that one of the contributions of Axial theory to the analysis of human society and religion is that it allows us to address conceptions of transcendence as an active factor in the reshaping of human life. The Wahhābī movement that arose in the mid-eighteenth century in central Arabia is a paradigmatic example thereof. The rapid expansion of this movement, both through conquest and through the dissemination of its ideas beyond the Arabian Peninsula, sent waves through the Islamic world that continue to reverberate to this day.[1]

Ibn Taymiyya's doctrine of *tawḥīd al-ulūhiyya* was the core organizing principle and the raison d'être of the early Wahhābī mission and the central point of contention between it and its opponents. In this chapter we will see that the mission was premised on the following interrelated tenets, all of them taken from Ibn Taymiyya's doctrine (as described in Chapter 1):

- The cosmos was created for the sake of worship of Allāh.
- The prophets were sent to bring humans to exclusive worship of Allāh (*tawḥīd al-ulūhiyya*, i.e. monolatry).
- The unbelievers to whom the prophets were sent already acknowledged Allāh's existence and His cosmic aspect as Creator and Sustainer (*tawḥīd al-rubūbiyya*, i.e. monotheism).
- The dividing line between the religion of the prophets (Islam) and those of the unbelievers is thus worship of one God to the exclusion of others, and not belief in one God to the exclusion of others.
- *Lā ilāha illā llāh*, which differentiates Muslims from unbelievers and expresses the essence of Islam, means specifically that there is no object (worthy) of worship apart from Allāh, and is a statement of *tawḥīd al-ulūhiyya* and not of *tawḥīd al-rubūbiyya*.

[1] The best general histories of the Wahhābī movement are David Commins, *The Wahhabi Mission and Saudi Arabia*, London and New York, I. B. Tauris, 2006; and Cole Bunzel, *Wahhābism*. For references to additional publications on the topic, see the literature survey below.

- The prevalent form of *shirk*, which is the negation of Islam, is precisely the worship of others as intermediaries with Allāh alongside acknowledgment of His *rubūbiyya*.
- Those who pronounce *lā ilāha illā llāh* with their tongues and believe in Allāh's *rubūbiyya*, but worship others as intermediaries with Allāh, are *mushrikūn* and not Muslims.

In the subsequent history of the Saudi-Wahhābī polity we certainly encounter other social and political facts that significantly mute this original impetus – for example, the persistent tension between theological imperatives and raison d'état[2] – but at its origin the movement was focused on a constitutive transcendent vision that saw monolatry as the telos of human existence, the message of revelation, and the central criterion for faith. As a result, the movement regarded features of the prevalent form of Islam at the time, and in particular the widespread cult of saints, as manifestations of polylatry that it was its duty to eradicate.

## The Question of the Origins of Wahhābism

The observation that Ibn ʿAbd al-Wahhāb was deeply influenced by Ibn Taymiyya is not new. The connection between the Wahhābī movement and Ibn Taymiyya has long been noted in the academic literature and its nature debated. Ignaz Goldziher asserted that the Wahhābīs were championing the doctrine of Ibn Taymiyya in opposition to the prevailing

[2] See Abdulaziz H. Al-Fahad, "From Exclusivism to Accommodation: Doctrinal and Legal Evolution of Wahhabism," *New York University Law Review* 79/2 (May 2004), pp. 485–519; Nabil Mouline, *The Clerics of Islam: Religious Authority and Political Power in Saudi Arabia*, trans. Ethan S. Rundell, New Haven and London: Yale University Press, 2014. Likewise, this chapter addresses only Wahhābī doctrine, and not the historical question of the rise of the first Saudi state, for which question one would have to assess the interplay of ideational and sociohistorical factors. Various theses have been proposed regarding the latter, such as population growth, detribalization of the settled population in the oases, and developments in firearms technology. See e.g. Uwaidah M. Al-Juhany, *Najd before the Salafi Reform Movement: Social, Political and Religious Conditions during the Three Centuries Preceding the Rise of the Saudi State*, Reading, UK: Ithaca Press, 2002; Michael Cook, "The Expansion of the First Saudi State: The Case of Washm," in C. E. Bosworth, Charles Issawi, Roger Savory, and A. L. Udovitch (eds.), *The Islamic World: Essays in Honor of Bernard Lewis*, Princeton: The Darwin Press, 1989, pp. 661–700; Abdulaziz H. Al-Fahad, "The *ʿImama* vs. the *ʿIqal*: *Hadari*-Bedouin Conflict and the Formation of the Saudi State," in Madawi Al-Rasheed and Robert Vitalis (eds.), *Counter-Narratives: History, Contemporary Society, and Politics in Saudi Arabia and Yemen*, New York: Palgrave Macmillan, 2004, pp. 35–75; Leor Halevi, "Arabians for Guns: Wahhabi Matchlocks, World Trade, and the Rise of the First Saudi State," *Journal of the Royal Asiatic Society*, Series 3, 33/2 (2023), pp. 401–442. For an evaluation of some of these theses, see Bunzel, *Wahhābism*, pp. 191–192.

scholarly currents of their time.[3] However, he viewed the Wahhābī war on the cult of saints through the general lens of Ḥanbalī condemnation of *bid'a*, rather than the specifically Taymiyyan doctrine of *tawḥīd al-ulūhiyya*,[4] and this rather misses the central point of the Wahhābī mission. An article by Richard Hartmann from the 1920s noted that one of the *'aqīda*s (creeds) penned by Ibn 'Abd al-Wahhāb is highly derivative of Ibn Taymiyya's *al-'Aqīda al-wāsiṭiyya*,[5] but Hartmann perpetuated Goldziher's misplaced emphasis when he wrote that the "marrow" (*das Wesentlichste*) of Ibn 'Abd al-Wahhāb's mission, and the reason for his characterization of the cult of saints as polytheism, was the war on *bid'a*.[6] Louis Massignon, in a brief article a few years earlier, had called Wahhābism "l'application politique pratique du néo-ḥanbalisme d'Ibn Taymiyah,"[7] but his subsequent characterization of Wahhābī beliefs likewise does not mention *tawḥīd al-ulūhiyya*, or anything else that might distinguish Ibn Taymiyya or the Wahhābīs from the more general Ḥanbalī ethos of opposition to *bid'a*.[8]

Henri Laoust, on the other hand, was aware of the doctrine of *tawḥīd al-ulūhiyya* as an important element of Muḥammad b. 'Abd al-Wahhāb's thought, and he noted the close connection between it and the doctrine of the same name in Ibn Taymiyya's writings.[9] Nonetheless, Laoust's survey of the relation between these two thinkers still dwells far longer on other issues of *'aqīda* that were less central to both thinkers'

[3] Goldziher, *Introduction to Islamic Theology and Law*, p. 241: "It was the influence of Ibn Taymīya's teachings that called forth, around the middle of the eighteenth century, one of the recent religious movements in Islam: that of the Wahhābīs."

[4] Goldziher, *Introduction to Islamic Theology and Law*, pp. 236–245; and likewise in his "Review of Walter M. Patton's *Aḥmed ibn Ḥanbal and the Miḥna*," *Zeitschrift der Deutschen Morgenländischen Gesellschaft* 53 (1899), pp. 155–160. Goldziher was apparently not aware of the specific features of Ibn Taymiyya's doctrine that distinguished him from the general run of Ḥanbalism; this is understandable given the state of research at the time, and he notes in his review of Patton (p. 156) that Ibn Taymiyya's theology was in need of more serious study.

[5] Richard Hartmann, "Die Wahhābiten," *Zeitschrift der Deutschen Morgenländischen Gesellschaft* 78 (1924), pp. 176–213, at p. 186.

[6] Hartmann, "Die Wahhābiten," p. 187. At no point in his article does Hartmann mention *tawḥīd al-ulūhiyya* or any of its characteristic features.

[7] Louis Massignon, "Les vraies origines dogmatiques du Wahhabisme," *Revue du monde musulman* 36 (1918–1919), pp. 320–328, at p. 324.

[8] Massignon, "Les vraies origines," pp. 324–325: "Le ḥanbalisme strict d'Ibn 'Abd al-Wahhâb, cette predication d'un retour à l'Islam primitive, à la constitution démocratique de la société, à la simplicité du culte, dégagé des subtilités des glossateurs et des dévotions adventices, la suppression du luxe somptuaire, de la musique et des oeuvres d'art, toutes innovations (*bida'*) admises par al-Ghazâlî ... et blâmées par son adversaire, Ibn Taymiyah."

[9] Henri Laoust, *Essai sur les doctrines sociales et politiques de Takī-d-Dīn Aḥmad b. Taimīya*, Cairo: L'institut Français d'archéologie orientale, 1939, pp. 531–533.

systems.[10] Furthermore, *tawḥīd al-ulūhiyya* receives only a brief allusion in his main discussion of Wahhābī *takfīr* and the Wahhābīs' war on the cult of saints.[11] It is not clear that Laoust understood the true import of *tawḥīd al-ulūhiyya* or its role in redefining the criteria for faith, since he characterized it more as a moral concern than a truly theological one.[12] Laoust's appraisal thus seems to reflect the common bias toward conceptual monotheism, the same bias that Ibn Taymiyya – and Ibn ʿAbd al-Wahhāb in his wake – fought to overturn. As for the relation between monolatry and ethics, this is an issue that Ibn ʿAbd al-Wahhāb addresses at the very outset of his early treatise *Kitāb al-tawḥīd*. The first chapter, whose theme is the priority of monolatry (see below), cites Qurʾānic passages (17:23ff., 4:36ff., 6:151ff.) that open with the prohibition of worshipping other entities and then continue with interpersonal moral injunctions.[13] His aim in citing these passages is to tie 'horizontal' ethical obligations to the 'vertical' imperative of monolatry, with the former subsidiary to the latter and deriving therefrom.

While all the aforementioned studies contributed insights into Wahhābī doctrine and its relation to Ibn Taymiyya, none accorded the doctrine of *tawḥīd al-ulūhiyya* the place it ought to have received as the borrowing that definitively shaped the Wahhābī movement. To my knowledge the only older study that did so was a doctoral thesis by the Dutch scholar Roelof Willem van Diffelen, published in 1927 under the title *De leer der Wahhabieten*.[14] The work begins with a short introduction,

10 Laoust, *Essai*, pp. 514–524. While Laoust argues that there exist (more or less minor) divergences in emphasis between the two thinkers on a number of issues, his general evaluation is that Ibn ʿAbd al-Wahhāb's doctrine was highly derivative of Ibn Taymiyya's, and he is dismissive of the later thinker's abilities. See his characterization of Ibn ʿAbd al-Wahhāb's work as composed of "petits catéchismes, le plus souvent fort brefs et monotones, sans ampleur dialectique, ni réelle vivacité polémique. Sans originalité non plus, et d'un style mediocre, ils résument, en l'étriquant, la pensée d'Ibn Taimīya, sans la moindre compromission d'opportunisme" (p. 513).

11 Laoust, *Essai*, p. 525, mentions "les deux forms de *tauḥīd*" in connection with the Wahhābīs' tendency to be expansive in *takfīr* and capacious in their definition of *shirk*. Shortly thereafter, however (p. 526), he explains the intransigence of the early Wahhābī movement on these matters (in contrast with the relative moderation of later periods) as having been "pour les besoins de sa politique."

12 Laoust, *Essai*, p. 531. Prior to this treatment in his chapter on the Wahhābīs, Laoust's sole mention of the doctrine of *tawḥīd al-ulūhiyya* comes on p. 472, at the very end of the section of the book dealing with Ibn Taymiyya himself, under the rubric of "ethics." He is, however, correct in describing Ibn Taymiyya's theology as one that promotes action in the sense of *ʿibāda* (p. 177).

13 ʿAbd al-ʿAzīz b. Zayd al-Rūmī et al. (eds.), *Muʾallafāt al-shaykh al-imām Muḥammad b. ʿAbd al-Wahhāb*, n.p.: Jāmiʿat al-Imām Muḥammad b. Suʿūd al-Islāmiyya, n.d., vol. 1, pp. 7–8.

14 Roelof Willem van Diffelen, *De leer der Wahhabieten*, Leiden: Brill, 1927.

in which van Diffelen discusses the influence of Ibn Taymiyya on the Wahhābīs and states what the central focus should be when considering this influence: Muḥammad b. ʿAbd al-Wahhāb and his followers adopted Ibn Taymiyya's conception of *tawḥīd* and put it into practice,[15] and this *tawḥīd* doctrine constituted the core of Wahhābī teaching and the major difference between them and their opponents.[16]

In his first chapter, on "the Wahhābīs and monotheism," van Diffelen expands on this central issue. Ibn ʿAbd al-Wahhāb's belief that his own period was similar to that of the *jāhiliyya*, and that many of his ostensible coreligionists were actually idolaters, was closely tied to his differentiation between *tawḥīd al-rubūbiyya* and *tawḥīd al-ulūhiyya*, and especially to his claim that the Qurʾānic *mushrikūn* upheld *tawḥīd al-rubūbiyya* (i.e. they acknowledged Allāh as sole Creator, Sustainer, etc.) and were fought by the Prophet solely because they fell short of *tawḥīd al-ulūhiyya* (worship of Allāh to the exclusion of others). Thus just as the Prophet was sent to call people to exclusivity of worship and to fight those who resisted, so the Wahhābīs attempted to do so as well.[17] Van Diffelen then notes that this distinction between *tawḥīd al-rubūbiyya* and *tawḥīd al-ulūhiyya* was already present in the writings of Ibn Taymiyya and Ibn Qayyim al-Jawziyya, and he even calls attention to their use of the parallel terminological dyad of *ḥaqīqa kawniyya* and *ḥaqīqa dīniyya*.[18]

Van Diffelen thus made two major advances. On the synchronic level he identified *tawḥīd al-ulūhiyya* as the central axis of Wahhābī doctrine and as the heart of the conflict between the Wahhābīs and their opponents; and on the diachronic level he correctly observed that *tawḥīd al-ulūhiyya* was a doctrine taken over from Ibn Taymiyya.

Van Diffelen's study does not seem to have made much of an impact. This is partly due to the fact that in the 1970s new trends emerged in academic scholarship on eighteenth-century revivalist movements that served to divert attention away from the issue of Ibn ʿAbd al-Wahhāb's debt to Ibn Taymiyya. These new approaches have much to offer for the study of eighteenth-century Islamic revivalism in general but represent a wrong turn in our attempt to understand the early Wahhābīs.

In 1975, John Voll published an article that sought to resituate the Wahhābī movement as one among a number of eighteenth-century revivalist movements, all of them interconnected through student-teacher relationships to a circle of scholars in Medina, and more specifically to the figure of the *ḥadīth* scholar and Naqshbandī Ṣūfī Muḥammad

[15] Van Diffelen, *Leer*, p. 4. [16] Van Diffelen, *Leer*, pp. 5–6.
[17] Van Diffelen, *Leer*, pp. 7–11. [18] Van Diffelen, *Leer*, p. 11.

Ḥayāt al-Sindī.[19] This was a bold reorientation away from the question of Taymiyyan influence in favor of a more synchronic perspective:

> In terms of Islamic fundamentalism, many attempts have been made to show how the Wahhābīs influenced other revivalist movements, but less has been done in analyzing the context out of which Wahhābism itself grew. It certainly is possible to note the potential fundamentalism of the Ḥanbalī tradition, especially as defined by Ibn Taymiyya. It is, however, not at all clear that the spirit of Ibn Taymiyya was the dominant one among the Ḥanbalīs of the eastern Arab world in the eighteenth century. It was a part of Muḥammad ibn ʿAbd al-Wahhāb's inspiration, but one might also see inspiration for vigorous reform coming from the study of *ḥadīth* as presented by Muḥammad Ḥayyā. Through this teacher, Ibn ʿAbd al-Wahhāb certainly must have had an introduction to a broader world of religious scholarship within which ideas of reform were developing.[20]

Whether or not Ibn Taymiyya set the tone for other eighteenth-century Ḥanbalīs is something of a red herring, since the relevant question is the degree of his influence on one particular eighteenth-century Ḥanbalī and his followers. As for Voll's suggestion of an alternative source of inspiration for the Wahhābī movement in the teachings of Muḥammad Ḥayāt al-Sindī, we are faced with the difficulty that there exists little to no affinity between the doctrines of al-Sindī and Ibn ʿAbd al-Wahhāb. Voll cites Henri Laoust's suggestion that there was influence on the matter of rejection of imitation of earlier authorities and embrace of *ijtihād*.[21] This is speculative: one can admit it as a possibility, and al-Sindī did author a tract on this topic,[22] but to my knowledge Ibn ʿAbd al-Wahhāb never cites him as an influence or authority thereon.[23] More important, however, is the fact that these questions of jurisprudential methodology were not at all central to the Wahhābī movement, whose core is a theological doctrine of *tawḥīd*, with the Wahhābī war on *shirk* as its practical expression. For this central issue of condemnation of the cult of saints and tomb-centered worship, the evidence of influence is all but nonexistent. Voll's claim that al-Sindī did transmit such teachings to Ibn ʿAbd al-Wahhāb[24] is drawn from George Rentz's 1948 doctoral thesis on

[19] John Voll, "Muḥammad Ḥayyā al-Sindī and Muḥammad Ibn ʿAbd al-Wahhāb: An Analysis of an Intellectual Group in Eighteenth-Century Madīna," *Bulletin of the School of Oriental and African Studies* 38/1 (1975), pp. 32–39.

[20] Voll, "Muḥammad Ḥayyā al-Sindī," pp. 38–39.

[21] Voll, "Muḥammad Ḥayyā al-Sindī," p. 32.

[22] Muḥammad Ḥayyāt al-Sindī, *Tuḥfat al-anām fī al-ʿamal bi-ḥadīth al-nabī ʿalayhī al-ṣalāt wa-l-salām*, Beirut: Dār Ibn Ḥazm, 1414/1993.

[23] For more on Ibn ʿAbd al-Wahhāb's views on jurisprudential *taqlīd* and *ijtihād*, see Chapter 3.

[24] Voll, "Muḥammad Ḥayyā al-Sindī," p. 32.

the early Wahhābī movement,[25] which itself bases this claim on a single passage of a Wahhābī chronicle. Even this slight evidence is not especially reliable as some versions of the text identify Ibn ʿAbd al-Wahhāb as the speaker in this passage rather than al-Sindī.[26]

Voll himself revised his argument in an article published more than a decade later.[27] He still attributed significance to the scholarly community in Mecca and Medina as a common point of contact for revivalists such as Muḥammad b. ʿAbd al-Wahhāb, Shāh Walī Allāh of Delhi, and others,[28] and contended that "there is enough interaction among revivalists in the eighteenth century so that one cannot reject interpretations which involve an awareness that the revivalist movements of the eighteenth century did not emerge in isolation. In fact, this study concludes that any attempt to understand revivalist movements exclusively (or even

[25] George S. Rentz, "Muḥammad ibn ʿAbd al-Wahhāb (1703/04-1792) and the Beginnings of Unitarian Empire in Arabia," PhD diss., University of California, 1948, pp. 27–28. I have used a subsequent edition, published as *The Birth of the Islamic Reform Movement in Saudi Arabia: Muḥammad Ibn ʿAbd al-Wahhāb (1703/4-1792) and the Beginnings of Unitarian Empire in Arabia*, London: Arabian Publishing, 2004, where the passage in question appears on p. 32.

[26] Rentz writes as follows: "One day when Ibn ʿAbd al-Wahhāb was standing beside the chamber that contains the Prophet's tomb in the great mosque of Medina, a throng of people gathered about, praying to the Prophet and beseeching him to aid them. Muḥammad Ḥayāh chanced along and joined his pupil, who asked him what he had to say about the behavior of the throng. The teacher replied that what the people were doing was futile and vain, an answer in full accord with Unitarian [viz. Wahhābī] doctrine as understood by the young man of Najd: prayers such as these should be directed to God alone and to no other, not even the Prophet, noble as he had been." In the edition I consulted of Rentz's source, the Wahhābī chronicle *ʿUnwān al-majd fī taʾrīkh najd*, the account is as follows: "*wa-ḥukiya anna al-shaykha Muḥammad waqafa yawman ʿinda al-ḥujra al-nabawiyya ʿinda unās yadʿūna wa-yastaghīthūna ʿinda qabr al-nabī ṣallā llāh ʿalayhi wa-sallama fa-rāʾahu Muḥammad Ḥayāt fa-atā ilā al-shaykh wa-qāla mā taqūlu qāla inna hāʾulāʾi mutabbar mā hum fīhi wa-bāṭil mā kānū yaʿmalūna* (ʿUthmān b. ʿAbdallāh Ibn Bishr, *ʿUnwān al-majd fī taʾrīkh najd*, 4th ed., Riyadh: Dārat al-Malik ʿAbd al-ʿAzīz, 1402/1982). There is no reason to suppose that the subject of the sentence should change before the question is asked, and the plain reading of this account is that it was Muḥammad Ḥayāt al-Sindī who saw Ibn ʿAbd al-Wahhāb, came to him, and asked him his view, and that the reply is thus Ibn ʿAbd al-Wahhāb's and not al-Sindī's. Michael Cook has noted that in a British Library manuscript Ibn ʿAbd al-Wahhāb is identified as the speaker, but the Beirut print edition that he consulted has the speaker as al-Sindī: Cook, "On the Origins," p. 192. The language of the reply is a Qurʾānic verse relating to the Israelites (7:139), a verse that Ibn ʿAbd al-Wahhāb often cites (as part of the *dhāt anwāṭ ḥadīth*) in relation to his own contemporaries; cf. e.g. ʿAbd al-Raḥmān b. Muḥammad b. Qāsim al-ʿĀṣimī al-Najdī (ed.), *al-Durar al-saniyya fī al-ajwiba al-najdiyya*, 6th ed., n.p., 1418/1996, vol. 2, p. 26.

[27] John O. Voll, "Linking Groups in the Networks of Eighteenth-Century Revivalist Scholars: The Mizjaji Family in Yemen," in Nehemia Levtzion and John O. Voll (eds.), *Eighteenth-Century Renewal and Reform in Islam*, Syracuse: Syracuse University Press, 1987, pp. 69–92.

[28] Voll, "Linking Groups," p. 70.

primarily) in local terms will miss major dimensions of their significance."[29] In this article, however, Voll took pains to specify that the existence of scholarly networks does not imply any uniformity of doctrine, and that the common denominator among the revivalist figures is rather one of "mood or tone": dissatisfaction with the contemporary situation, hope for improvement, and emphasis on the need for human effort to effect change.[30] Since another of the common features in the network was the combination of stress on *ḥadīth* study together with a Ṣūfī *ṭarīqa* affiliation, Voll now suggested that the Wahhābīs were a "critical exception" to the general case,[31] though he continued to maintain that the more general spirit of revivalism may have influenced Ibn ʿAbd al-Wahhāb, just as the Wahhābīs may have influenced other movements that did not agree with all aspects of their teachings.[32]

In sum, Voll's approach provides a welcome perspective on eighteenth-century Islamic scholarship and its connection to revivalist thinkers and movements, but on the question of Wahhābī origins it does not offer us much, and in fact his thesis is more robust if we substract the Wahhābīs from it and consider them a case apart. There is overwhelming evidence for Ibn ʿAbd al-Wahhāb having derived his doctrine from Ibn Taymiyya, as we will see, whereas the proposed connection to Voll's networks remains at a very general level of potential inspiration.

The popularity of Voll's approach, however, seems to have knocked Ibn Taymiyya off the radar of many subsequent scholars of Wahhābism. A work of much merit in other respects, Esther Peskes' *Muḥammad b. ʿAbdalwahhāb (1703-92) im Widerstreit*[33] is a case in point. In her introduction Peskes criticizes earlier generations of authors on Wahhābism (Goldziher, Hartmann, van Diffelen, Margoliouth, and Laoust) for their preoccupation with Ibn Taymiyya, and (unjustly) claims that neither van Diffelen nor Laoust took the trouble to examine in depth the writings of Ibn ʿAbd al-Wahhāb himself. While she concedes that it is evident from his writings that Ibn Taymiyya did indeed influence Muḥammad b. ʿAbd al-Wahhāb, she argues that the tendency to focus on this influence was rooted in a general and unfounded belief on the part of the aforementioned authors that the eighteenth century was a period of decline and stagnation in the Islamic world, and thus that anything of interest in a thinker from this period must necessarily be

[29] Voll, "Linking Groups," p. 71.
[30] Voll, "Linking Groups," p. 81.
[31] Voll, "Linking Groups," p. 86.
[32] Voll, "Linking Groups," p. 87.
[33] Esther Peskes, *Muḥammad b. ʿAbdalwahhāb (1703-92) im Widerstreit: Untersuchungen zur Rekonstruktion der Frühgeschichte der Wahhābīya*, Beirut: Franz Steiner, 1993 (henceforth: *Widerstreit*).

derivative of an earlier thinker such as Ibn Taymiyya. Citing studies such as Voll's, Peskes argues that the time has come to reexamine Ibn ʿAbd al-Wahhāb's thought and the origins of Wahhābism in light of their contemporary environment rather than through the prism of Ibn Taymiyya.[34]

*Pace* Peskes, I would argue that the general grand-historical views of the earlier scholars, even were they as she describes, are irrelevant to the issue at hand. The question that she contests them on is a discrete one: What relation exists between the doctrines of Ibn Taymiyya and Ibn ʿAbd al-Wahhāb, and to what extent can this influence be seen to account for the views and actions of the latter? Peskes appears to have taken an a priori stance on this question, despite the solid work already done on it by van Diffelen in particular. And while she criticizes scholars such as van Diffelen and Laoust for allegedly not paying sufficient attention to Ibn ʿAbd al-Wahhāb's writings,[35] she herself used nothing by Ibn Taymiyya apart from *al-ʿAqīda al-wāsiṭiyya*, which I believe she misinterprets as well (see below).

As it happens, Peskes, even more than van Diffelen, does an excellent job of according *tawḥīd al-ulūhiyya* its proper place at the center of Ibn ʿAbd al-Wahhāb's doctrine and of identifying it as the Streitpunkt between the Wahhābīs and their opponents.[36] It is precisely this correct emphasis that should lead to the conclusion that Ibn ʿAbd al-Wahhāb's debt to Ibn Taymiyya was of capital importance. Instead, Peskes merely remarks in a footnote (referring to van Diffelen) that Ibn Taymiyya also had a doctrine distinguishing between *tawḥīd al-rubūbiyya* and *tawḥīd al-ulūhiyya*, but then downplays this fact by noting that Ḥanbalī contemporaries of Ibn ʿAbd al-Wahhāb vehemently denied that the conclusions the latter drew from this two-part *tawḥīd* were identical to Ibn Taymiyya's.[37] And while Peskes at least broached the issue, other analyses of eighteenth-century revivalism that touch on Ibn ʿAbd al-Wahhāb's *rubūbiyya/ulūhiyya* distinction ignore the Ibn Taymiyya connection altogether.[38]

[34] Peskes, *Widerstreit*, pp. 2–5.

[35] Peskes, *Widerstreit*, p. 3, seems to imply that van Diffelen used only the *Kitāb al-tawḥīd*, alongside numerous works of Ibn Taymiyya, and states that Laoust did not cite Ibn ʿAbd al-Wahhāb at all. Neither of these assertions is true.

[36] Peskes, *Widerstreit*, pp. 15–27, esp. pp. 21–24.

[37] Peskes, *Widerstreit*, p. 21, n. 33, p. 22, n. 33 cont.

[38] Ahmad Dallal, "The Origins and Objectives of Islamic Revivalist Thought, 1750-1850," *Journal of the American Oriental Society* 113/3 (1993), pp. 341–359, esp. pp. 350–351; DeLong-Bas, *Wahhabi Islam*, p. 57, and cf. p. 53 for the claim that Ibn Taymiyya was "at most a negligible source of inspiration." Studies that do clearly assert the derivation of Wahhābī *tawḥīd al-ulūhiyya* from Ibn Taymiyya include Bernard Haykel, *Revival and Reform in Islam: The Legacy of Muhammad al-Shawkānī*, Cambridge: Cambridge University Press, 2003, pp. 135–136; and now in great detail in Bunzel, *Wahhābism*, esp. pp. 92–190.

A counterweight to this trend is Michael Cook's article "On the Origins of Wahhābism." While not expressly framed as a refutation of Voll's thesis, Cook argues that the relevant sources do not convincingly identify any contemporary teacher as a plausible source for Ibn ʿAbd al-Wahhāb's doctrine.[39] Cook then turns to the possibility of a literary source, and based on a survey of explicit references to earlier scholars in Ibn ʿAbd al-Wahhāb's writings, as well as corroborative evidence from early polemics, he concludes that "the upshot is to confirm what in essence we already knew: the dependence of the Shaykh on the two great Ḥanbalite scholars of eighth/fourteenth-century Damascus," Ibn Taymiyya and Ibn Qayyim al-Jawziyya.[40] Cook does not specify the precise nature of this connection in terms of doctrine: He writes that "while generally aware of the purport of the Shaykh's doctrine of *shirk*, and of the hostility it encountered, I am unable to identify the precise respects in which it differed from the views of his predecessors and contemporaries. I have not found the existing secondary literature helpful on this score."[41] Cook characterizes his article as "a first approach" and, after presenting the evidence for Ibn ʿAbd al-Wahhāb's dependence on Ibn Taymiyya and Ibn Qayyim al-Jawziyya, notes that this topic ought to be treated in comprehensive fashion in a dissertation.[42]

More recently Cole Bunzel has published the best account to date of the relation between the two scholars' doctrines.[43] The present chapter seeks to further document and explain this connection, with a narrow focus on the topic of monolatry, and thereby to specify what it was in Ibn ʿAbd al-Wahhāb's doctrine on *tawḥīd* and *shirk* that distinguished him so sharply from his contemporaries.

In what follows I will address Ibn ʿAbd al-Wahhāb's writings relating to *tawḥīd al-ulūhiyya* and, building on Chapter 1, point out their Taymiyyan basis. This will be followed by a discussion of two additional issues: first, the topic of *bidʿa*, which, as mentioned, earlier scholars erroneously assumed to be Ibn ʿAbd al-Wahhāb's primary concern and the focal point of his war on the cult of saints; and second, the topic of *taqlīd* and *ijtihād*, which recent scholarship has suggested represents a point of similarity between Ibn ʿAbd al-Wahhāb and the scholarly circles in Medina. Finally, I will briefly discuss a treatise on monolatry authored by a contemporary of Ibn ʿAbd al-Wahhāb, the Yemeni scholar Muḥammad b. Ismāʿīl al-Ṣanʿānī, and will demonstrate that it likewise was deeply indebted to the doctrine of *tawḥīd al-ulūhiyya*.

[39] Cook, "On the Origins," pp. 197–198.
[40] Cook, "On the Origins," pp. 199–200.
[41] Cook, "On the Origins," p. 191, n. 2.
[42] Cook, "On the Origins," p. 198, n. 68.
[43] Bunzel, *Wahhābism*, esp. pp. 92–190.

## The Streitpunkt

Van Diffelen's attempt to establish a single axis on which revolved the conflict between the Wahhābīs and their opponents, and to which the other topics of dispute are subsidiary, was not an a priori bias on his part. It is a clearly visible emphasis in Muḥammad b. ʿAbd al-Wahhāb's writings themselves, itself inherited from Ibn Taymiyya, though brought further into relief in Ibn ʿAbd al-Wahhāb's stripped-down presentation. Through the real-world political and military confrontation that it engendered in eighteenth-century Arabia *tawḥīd al-ulūhiyya* became a true Streitpunkt in the full sense of the word.

We already saw the Taymiyyan basis for this emphasis in Chapter 1. Undergirding Ibn Taymiyya's at times intricate discourses on *tawḥīd al-ulūhiyya* lie a few simple arguments: Exclusivity of worship is the telos of existence; for its sake the prophets were sent; the *mushrikūn* of the *jāhiliyya* acknowledged *tawḥīd al-rubūbiyya* and were considered polytheists because they did not fulfill *tawḥīd al-ulūhiyya*; and many self-described Muslims likewise fail to fulfill *tawḥīd al-ulūhiyya* and thus fall into *shirk*.

Of the basic Taymiyyan motifs, it is above all the point that exclusivity of worship – *tawḥīd al-ulūhiyya* – constituted the point of contention between the Prophet and the *mushrikūn* that is central to Ibn ʿAbd al-Wahhāb's writings. He never tires of arguing that *tawḥīd al-ulūhiyya* is likewise what he calls people to and what separates him and his followers from their opponents. This Streitpunkt argument can be viewed as the converse of Halbertal and Margalit's dictum mentioned in the Introduction, namely, that "different concepts of God create, when reversed, different concepts of idolatry."[44] For Ibn ʿAbd al-Wahhāb, if one identifies the precise nature of the *shirk* that is denounced in the Qurʾān then one will know the true meaning of *tawḥīd*.

This is apparent already in the first chapter of *Kitāb al-tawḥīd*. The earliest of Ibn ʿAbd al-Wahhāb's writings, the work is composed in a style approaching that of the classical *ahl al-ḥadīth* treatises and consists primarily of Qurʾānic verses and *ḥadīth*s. Ibn ʿAbd al-Wahhāb's laconic commentary is, with few exceptions, restricted to brief remarks labeled *masāʾil* at the end of each chapter, though much can be learned of his views from the choice of textual sources and their arrangement as well.

The first verse cited in chapter 1 of the *Kitāb al-tawḥīd* is the same one that Ibn Taymiyya frequently relied on to express the idea that *tawḥīd al-ulūhiyya* is the telos of existence (51:56): "I only created the jinn and

[44] Halbertal and Margalit, *Idolatry*, p. 1.

humans in order that they worship Me."[45] The second verse cited (16:36) states that prophets were sent to every nation to order them to worship Allāh and to turn away from the *ṭāghūt*. If we consider the *masāʾil* at the end of the chapter, the first states simply: *al-ḥikma fī khalq al-jinn wa-l-ins*. *Ḥikma*, whose standard translation is 'wisdom,' is probably intended here in its Taymiyyan meaning of 'purpose' (related to final causation)[46]: Ibn ʿAbd al-Wahhāb is stressing the point that Qurʾān 51:56 describes the purpose of creation as worship of Allāh. The second of the *masāʾil* is terse but already broaches the Streitpunkt issue. It reads: "Worship (*ʿibāda*) is *tawḥīd*, because that was the point of conflict (*li-anna al-khuṣūmata fīhi*)."[47] This is presumably a commentary on the second verse (16:36) and is meant as a reference to the opposition with which the prophets were met when they commanded worship of Allāh alone. The reasoning can be reconstructed as something like the following: *Tawḥīd* is what separates the prophets' religion from that of their opponents; what the prophets commanded was exclusive *ʿibāda*, and this was what led others to oppose them; therefore *ʿibāda* is *tawḥīd*.

In another epistle we find likewise a citation of Qurʾān 51:56 and then language nearly identical to that in *Kitāb al-tawḥīd*: "Worship (*ʿibāda*) is *tawḥīd*, because that was the point of conflict between the prophets and the nations," followed by a citation of Qurʾān 16:36. Here, however, this is followed by further elaboration of the kinds of *tawḥīd*, an explanation that the *mushrikūn* of the Prophet's time already acknowledged *tawḥīd al-rubūbiyya*, and the statement that "it was over *tawḥīd al-ulūhiyya* that conflict arose, in the past and in the present" (*wa-l-aṣl al-thānī wa-huwa tawḥīd al-ulūhiyya fa-huwa alladhī waqaʿa fīhi al-nizāʿ fī qadīm al-dahr wa-ḥadīthihi*).[48] This parallel passage, with its more explicit language, confirms that the terse opening of *Kitāb al-tawḥīd* is indeed an exposition of *tawḥīd al-ulūhiyya*. It likewise intimates that the same Streitpunkt was operative in Ibn ʿAbd al-Wahhāb's own day as in the time of the prophets.

This latter point is stated more explicitly in a few other passages. For example, in an epistle dealing with exclusivity of worship – including and especially supplication – Ibn ʿAbd al-Wahhāb writes: "this is what is [disputed] between us and the others" (*fa-hādhā alladhī baynanā wa-bayna al-nās*).[49] Elsewhere he insists that everything that has been said

[45] al-Rūmī et al. (eds.), *Muʾallafāt*, vol. 1, p. 7.

[46] Ibn ʿAbd al-Wahhāb was certainly aware of the dispute over whether Allāh acts for a purpose. In *Durar*, vol. 1, p. 179, his critique of Ashʿarī voluntarism clearly uses the term *ḥikma* in this sense: *wa-mā ẓannū annahu khilāf al-ḥikma qālū lā yafʿalu li-ḥikma bal li-mashīʾa*.

[47] al-Rūmī et al. (eds.), *Muʾallafāt*, vol. 1, p. 8.

[48] *Durar*, vol. 2, pp. 66–67.

[49] *Durar*, vol. 2, p. 130.

about him is a lie except for the fact that he calls people to *tawḥīd* and forbids them *shirk*.[50] In a response to a scholar from Medina he writes that the cause of the dispute between him and others is not any matter in the *sharīʿa* (viz. *furūʿ*), and that the reason others oppose him is the same reason why people opposed the prophets, namely, his insistence that devotion to not-Allāh is *shirk*.[51] Finally, in another epistle, Ibn ʿAbd al-Wahhāb states that the point of conflict between the Prophet Muḥammad and his people was exclusivity of worship, and cites a number of Qurʾānic verses (including 51:56 and 16:36) to emphasize that this was the mission of the prophets and is the telos of existence. He then states, in an apparent reference to his own day: "the only thing that we denounced them for and pronounced *takfīr* on them for is *al-shirk billāh*, for example, supplication of a prophet."[52] In light of this we can understand why Ibn ʿAbd al-Wahhāb insists that what is at stake between his camp and that of his opponents is no normal controversy, but the very heart of religion: "This *fitna* that is occurring is not about issues of *furūʿ*, over which scholars to this day disagree without this being a matter for condemnation. Rather this [*fitna*] is about the testimony *lā ilāha illā llāh*, and rejection (*kufr*) of the *ṭāghūt*."[53]

## The Meaning of *Lā ilāha illā llāh*

In Chapter 1 we saw that for Ibn Taymiyya the meaning of the Muslim profession of faith, *lā ilāha illā llāh*, hinged on the meaning of the word *ilāh*, and thus in essence on the entire theological framework of the *rubūbiyya*/*ulūhiyya* distinction. In Ibn Taymiyya's view *ilāh* means an object of worship, and thus *lā ilāha illā llāh* is a statement not of belief in one God (in the *rubūbiyya* sense) but rather a commitment to not devote worship to anyone but Allāh.

Muḥammad Ibn ʿAbd al-Wahhāb follows Ibn Taymiyya in this matter and thereby arrived at opinions far removed from those prevalent in his contemporary milieu. He himself, in a statement that shocked some of his contemporaries,[54] testified in an early epistle:

> By Allāh, He apart from whom there is no *ilāh*, I had studied religion (*ṭalabtu al-ʿilm*), and those who knew me then believed that I possessed knowledge. But at that time I did not know the meaning of *lā ilāha illā llāh*, and I did not know the religion of Islam, before this beneficence that Allāh granted [me]. Likewise none of my teachers (*mashāyikhī*) knew it. Any of the scholars in al-ʿĀriḍ [Ibn

[50] *Durar*, vol. 1, pp. 72, 81. [51] *Durar*, vol. 1, pp. 58–59. [52] *Durar*, vol. 1, p. 144.
[53] *Durar*, vol. 2, p. 62.
[54] Huṣayn b. Ghannām, *Taʾrīkh najd*, Beirut and Cairo: Dār al-Shurūq, 1415/1994, p. 271.

ʿAbd al-Wahhāb's native region] who claims that he knew the meaning of *lā ilāha illā llāh* or knew the meaning of Islam before this time, or claims that one of his teachers knew it, is lying.[55]

This passage led his contemporary opponents to ask incredulously whence Ibn ʿAbd al-Wahhāb learned his views if not from his teachers,[56] and has also featured in modern academic discussion of the inspiration for Wahhābī doctrine.[57]

In this passage Ibn ʿAbd al-Wahhāb characterizes his divergence from the views accepted in the local scholarly tradition as a matter of understanding the meaning of *lā ilāha illā llāh*. This was not a mere turn of phrase: Ibn ʿAbd al-Wahhāb himself writes that knowledge of the meaning of *ilāh* is the foundation of religion and the differentiator (*al-fāriqa*) between Muslims and unbelievers.[58] This newfound interpretation of *ilāh* and of *lā ilāha illā llāh*, which turned out to be of great historical moment, was simply Ibn Taymiyya's, as we will now see.

Ibn ʿAbd al-Wahhāb's discussions of the meaning of *ilāh* can be schematically divided into two types (though these are often intermingled in his writings): explanations of the word's meaning, and polemical 'translations' that seek to exemplify the true sense of *ilāh* by referencing contemporary expressions that he claims are equivalent to it in meaning.

Among the straightforward definitions of *ilāh* we find Ibn Taymiyya's tautological definition *alladhī tuʾallihuhu al-qulūb*[59] and close variants, at times cited explicitly from Ibn Taymiyya,[60] at times in Ibn ʿAbd al-Wahhāb's own voice.[61] More frequent is the definition of *ilāh* as *maʿbūd*, an object of worship.[62] As noted in Chapter 1, this is a standard lexicographical definition, but the emphasis on this meaning of *ilāh* as a

55 Ibn Ghannām, *Taʾrīkh najd*, p. 310. 56 Ibn Ghannām, *Taʾrīkh najd*, p. 271.

57 Cook, "On the Origins," pp. 201–202. Cook cites the passage as corroborating evidence that Ibn ʿAbd al-Wahhāb derived his views from reading Ibn Taymiyya and Ibn Qayyim al-Jawziyya rather than from any contemporary teacher.

58 *Durar*, vol. 1, p. 111.

59 A standard commentary on *Kitāb al-tawḥīd* actually names Ibn Qayyim al-Jawziyya as the source for this particular wording: ʿAbd al-Raḥmān b. Ḥasan Āl al-Shaykh, *Fatḥ al-majīd bi-sharḥ kitāb al-tawḥīd*, Alexandria and Cairo: Dār al-ʿAqīda, 1427/2006, p. 39; but Ibn Taymiyya used it as well (see below, n. 60); and for a similar formulation, cf. Ibn Taymiyya, *Majmūʿat al-fatāwā*, vol. 1, p. 21.

60 Ibn Ghannām, *Taʾrīkh najd*, p. 278 (the passage cited here is condensed from Ibn Taymiyya, *Iqtiḍāʾ al-ṣirāṭ al-mustaqīm li-mukhālafat aṣḥāb al-jaḥīm*, Riyadh: Maktabat al-Rushd, 1411/1991, vol. 2, pp. 854–855), cf. p. 280: *wa-taʾammal kalām al-shaykh fī maʿnā al-ilāh alladhī tuʾallihuhu al-qulūb*.

61 Ibn Ghannām, *Taʾrīkh najd*, p. 369.

62 *Durar*, vol. 1, pp. 112, 130, 138, vol. 2, pp. 103, 127, cf. vol. 2, p. 73, *alladhī yuqṣadu li-l-ʿibāda*. In the context of supplication (which Ibn ʿAbd al-Wahhāb considers a form of worship), Ibn Ghannām, *Taʾrīkh najd*, p. 341.

basis for monolatric doctrine is characteristically Taymiyyan. In one epistle Ibn ʿAbd al-Wahhāb takes issue with the Ashʿarī view (which he attributes to al-Ashʿarī himself) that the meaning of *ilāh* is *al-qādir* (powerful, capable), and that *ulūhiyya* is *qudra*.[63] This criticism as well is a reprise of Ibn Taymiyya, who saw in this Ashʿarī interpretation a reduction of the profession of faith to a mere profession of *tawḥīd al-rubūbiyya*.[64]

In addition to these straightforward definitions, Ibn ʿAbd al-Wahhāb also provides us with 'translations' relevant to the contemporary polemical context. A typical example is:

> *Ilāh* in their [viz. the Qurʾānic *mushrikūn*'s] language is what is called in our language a possessor of *sirr* [for the meaning of this term see below], and what the Ṣūfīs (*al-fuqarāʾ*) call their shaykh, meaning thereby that he is supplicated and harms and benefits. They acknowledge Allāh's exclusivity in [the areas of] creation and provision, but that is not the meaning of *ilāh*; rather an *ilāh* is one that is turned to [viz. in devotion], supplicated, and hoped from.[65]

Another passage offers a similar 'translation': "It is known that languages differ. The object of worship among the Arabs [viz. of the *jāhiliyya*] was [called] *ilāh*,[66] which is what the commoners among us call *sayyid*, shaykh, and possessor of *sirr*." For this somewhat obscure expression *alladhī fīhi sirr* Ibn ʿAbd al-Wahhāb provides the following explanation: "The ancient Arabs called *ulūhiyya* what the commoners among us call *sirr*, because *sirr* in their usage is power to harm and benefit, and [its possessor] being worthy of being supplicated, hoped from, feared, and depended upon."[67]

The aim of these translations is to strip away what Ibn ʿAbd al-Wahhāb views as mere linguistic variation in order to show that the *ilāh*s of the *jāhiliyya* were precisely the same kind as those 'worshipped' in his own day by people who considered themselves Muslims. It is clear that Ibn

[63] *Durar*, vol. 1, pp. 112–114; cf. Abū Manṣūr ʿAbd al-Qādir al-Baghdādī, *Kitāb uṣul al-dīn*, Istanbul: Maṭbaʿat al-Dawla, 1346/1928, p. 123, for an ascription of the gloss to al-Ashʿarī.

[64] See e.g. Ibn Taymiyya, *Iqtiḍāʾ*, vol. 2, pp. 854–855; ʿAbd al-Raḥmān b. Ṣāliḥ b. Ṣāliḥ al-Maḥmūd, *Mawqif Ibn Taymiyya min al-ashāʿira*, Riyadh: Maktabat al-Rushd, 1415/1995, pp. 946, 973ff.

[65] Ibn Ghannām, *Taʾrīkh najd*, p. 244 (= *Durar*, vol. 2, p. 41).

[66] Read *al-ilāh* for *wa-l-ilāh*.

[67] Ibn Ghannām, *Taʾrīkh najd*, p. 287. The common meaning of *sirr* is 'secret.' I have not found any literature on the term's meaning in the cult of saints as described by Ibn ʿAbd al-Wahhāb. I can only conjecture that it may derive from the usage of *sirr* in Ṣūfism to denote a subtle spiritual faculty at times associated with union with the divine. See Shigeru Kamada, "A Study of the Term *Sirr* (Secret) in Sufi *Laṭāʾif* Theories," *Orient* 19 (1983), pp. 7–28.

ʿAbd al-Wahhāb's treatment of this issue runs within the overarching *rubūbiyya/ulūhiyya* framework, as evidenced by his reference to the Ṣūfīs' acknowledgment of Allāh's exclusivity in matters of creation and provision. In principle the power to harm and benefit ought to likewise fall on the *rubūbiyya* side of the equation; Ibn ʿAbd al-Wahhāb frequently mentions it among the aspects of *rubūbiyya* that the Qurʾānic *mushrikūn* acknowledged.[68] The mention of it here in the context of the meaning of *ilāh* thus presents some difficulty, but it appears that the point is not the content of this belief in itself, but rather its role in spurring individuals to attitudes and acts of devotion directed to the object of 'worship,' and it is these latter that truly make of it an *ilāh* (which, it will be recalled, means for him precisely 'an object of worship').[69]

As for the related issue of the meaning of *lā ilāha illā llāh*, we saw above Ibn ʿAbd al-Wahhāb's claim that it was not known in his region prior to his own preaching. Indeed, he writes that most people do not have any idea that the *shahāda* has a precise meaning at all, and when they do attribute to it some meaning they erroneously believe it to be a statement of the exclusivity of Allāh in *rubūbiyya*.[70] For his part, Ibn ʿAbd al-Wahhāb never tires of insisting that it is a statement of monolatry and not monotheism, *tawḥīd al-ulūhiyya* and not *tawḥīd al-rubūbiyya*. This contention follows logically (as it did for Ibn Taymiyya) from his interpretation of the term *ilāh*:

> If it is said "There is no *khāliq* (Creator) but Allāh," then that is known, no one creates the creation but Allāh ... Likewise [the meaning of] "No one provides provision but Allāh" [is known]. Likewise if it is said *lā ilāha illā llāh* [then this means something specific]. So reflect on this, may Allāh have mercy on you, and inquire about the meaning of *ilāh*, just as you inquire about the meaning of *al-khāliq* (Creator) and *al-rāziq* (Provider). Know that the meaning of *ilāh* is an object of worship.[71]

In another passage Ibn ʿAbd al-Wahhāb returns to this argument that one must know the precise meaning of *ilāh*, just as one knows that Allāh's other names, such as *al-khāliq* (Creator), *al-rāziq* (Provider), and *al-mudabbir* (Master) have a specific and known content. To say *lā ilāha illā llāh* and to know its meaning is *tawḥīd al-ulūhiyya*, just as knowledge

[68] For example, *Durar*, vol. 1, p. 59, vol. 2, pp. 33, 37–38, 76–77, 83, 87, 147.

[69] It is also likely that Ibn ʿAbd al-Wahhāb does not mean that these Ṣūfīs attribute to their shaykhs an inherent power to harm and benefit, but merely powers of intercession and intermediation with Allāh; this is suggested by a parallel passage: *Durar*, vol. 2, p. 117. For Ibn ʿAbd al-Wahhāb this was a distinction without a difference as he holds the polylatry of the Qurʾānic *mushrikūn* to have been of this same type: see e.g. *Durar*, vol. 2, pp. 41, 118–119.

[70] *Durar*, vol. 2, pp. 129, 153–154, cf. p. 56.

[71] *Durar*, vol. 2, p. 103.

and belief in the content of these other names is *tawḥīd al-rubūbiyya*.[72] It was the former that Ibn ʿAbd al-Wahhāb viewed as lacking among his contemporaries, and in particular among the scholars: "Most people, though they know this religion, hear the scholars in Sudayr and Washm, and others, saying: 'we uphold *tawḥīd* of Allāh, we know that no one but Allāh can benefit or harm, and that the righteous (*ṣāliḥūn*) neither benefit nor harm.' You then know that [these scholars] know only the *tawḥīd* of the unbelievers, *tawḥīd al-rubūbiyya*."[73]

Given that *ilāh* means an object of worship, what is being denied in the *shahāda* is that there is any rightful object of worship apart from Allāh: "its meaning is that there is no true object of worship (*maʿbūd bi-l-ḥaqq*) apart from Allāh." It is denial and affirmation: "*lā ilāha* denies all that is worshipped apart from Allāh, and *illā llāh* affirms worship to Allāh alone without partner in worship of Him, just as He has no partner in His sovereignty (*mulk*)."[74] In more detail, Ibn ʿAbd al-Wahhāb writes that the central message of the Prophet Muḥammad's mission was

> to make religion exclusive to Allāh (*ikhlāṣ al-dīn lillāh*) by worshipping Him alone without partner, and the prohibition of *shirk* – that none but Him be supplicated ... that none but Him be prostrated before or bowed to, that none but Him be supplicated to ward off harm or bring benefit, that none be vowed to but Him, that none be sworn by but Him, that none be sacrificed to but Him, and that worship is not worthy (*lā taṣluḥ*) but to Him alone, without partner. And this is the meaning of the words *lā ilāha illā llāh*.[75]

This last passage is a fine example of how Ibn ʿAbd al-Wahhāb's condemnation of contemporary ritual polylatry was directly dependent on his understanding of the *shahāda* in terms of monolatry. We find an additional example in a response he authored to one of his earliest opponents, Sulaymān b. Muḥammad b. Suḥaym.[76] Among Ibn Suḥaym's criticisms of Ibn ʿAbd al-Wahhāb was that he pronounced *takfīr* on someone who slaughtered a sacrifice, pronouncing Allāh's name over it as one should, but with intention that the sacrifice ward off the jinn (viz. a vow was made over it to the jinn). According to Ibn Suḥaym, this contravenes the opinion of the *ʿulamāʾ*, who merely said that the meat from such a sacrifice is forbidden to eat, and made no mention of the act being *kufr*.[77] Ibn ʿAbd al-Wahhāb's response was that the scholars' statement that it is *ḥarām* is not necessarily exclusive of it being

[72] *Durar*, vol. 2, pp. 125–126. [73] *Durar*, vol. 2, p. 77.
[74] *Durar*, vol. 1, p. 130, cf. likewise p. 153. [75] *Durar*, vol. 2, p. 40.
[76] On Ibn Suḥaym and his exchange with Ibn ʿAbd al-Wahhāb, see Bunzel, *Wahhābism*, pp. 58–62.
[77] Ibn Ghannām, *Taʾrīkh najd*, p. 272.

*kufr* as well, and to prove that it is, he adduces a late Ḥanbalī manual of *fiqh*, al-Ḥajjāwī's *Iqnāʿ* (presumably because it is a source acknowledged as authoritiative by Ibn Suḥaym, himself a Ḥanbalī).[78] The proof is as follows: The *Iqnāʿ* states explicitly that vows are a form of worship; and since it is known that *lā ilāha illā llāh* means one must not worship anyone but Allāh, a vow to anyone but Allāh must necessarily be *shirk*.[79] In truth, the Ḥanbalī *fiqh* manual mentioned in this passage only provides part of the argument, and the true heart of Ibn ʿAbd al-Wahhāb's reasoning is an application of Ibn Taymiyya's understanding of the *shahāda* as a statement of monolatry.[80]

## The Insufficiency of Mere Verbal Enunciation of *Lā ilāha illā llāh*

Muḥammad b. ʿAbd al-Wahhāb stresses the notion that one must realize and implement the meaning of *lā ilāha illā llāh* (as described above), and that mere verbal enunciation of the words does not count for anything. Since to pronounce the *shahāda* is to obligate oneself to monolatry, the verbal testimony is rendered invalid if one fails to restrict one's devotion to Allāh: "someone who worships Allāh night and day and then supplicates a prophet or *walī* at his graveside has taken two *ilāh*s, and has not

78 For this technique of argumentation, cf. *Durar*, vol. 1, p. 73: Ibn ʿAbd al-Wahhāb writes that since his opponents reject his arguments from the Qurʾān, *ḥadīth*, and early scholars on methodological grounds, saying that they are obligated to follow the opinions of the later scholars, "I say to them: I contest the Ḥanafī with the words of the later scholars of the Ḥanafī school, and [likewise] the Mālikī, the Shāfiʿī, and the Ḥanbalī – I contest each one using the writings of their later scholars whom they rely on." As for Ibn ʿAbd al-Wahhāb's own opinion on al-Ḥajjāwī's *Iqnāʿ*, he writes disapprovingly that it is "mostly contrary to the *madhhab* [school] and *naṣṣ* [texts] of Aḥmad [b. Ḥanbal]." *Durar*, vol. 1, p. 45.

79 Ibn Ghannām, *Taʾrīkh najd*, pp. 303–304.

80 Muḥammad b. ʿAbd al-Wahhāb's brother Sulaymān argued in his anti-Wahhābī polemic that Ibn Taymiyya himself did not consider slaughter to not-Allāh as grounds for *takfīr*: Sulaymān b. ʿAbd al-Wahhāb, *al-Ṣawāʿiq al-ilāhiyya fī al-radd ʿalā al-wahhābiyya*, Istanbul, 1399/1979, p. 8. Muḥammad b. ʿAbd al-Wahhāb characterizes Ibn Taymiyya's view as being that the slaughter is forbidden on two grounds, *uhilla li-ghayr Allāh* and *dhabīḥat murtadd*: *Durar*, vol. 2, p. 47. Cf. Ibn Taymiyya, *Iqtiḍāʾ*, vol. 2, pp. 565–566. Ibn Taymiyya writes that the slaughter is forbidden when the sacrifice was made to saints or to celestial bodies, even if the slaughterer pronounced the *basmala* over the animal. He then adds that "if these [slaughterers] are apostates, then their slaughter is in no way permitted, but rather two prohibitions are combined in their slaughter." It is not entirely clear whether the sacrifice to not-Allāh is itself the cause of apostasy in the second scenario, as Muḥammad b. ʿAbd al-Wahhāb seemed to claim. Ibn Taymiyya's phrasing appears to suggest that at least some who perform this act are not necessarily apostates. This, however, is not the same as saying that the act itself is never grounds for *takfīr*, and thus Sulaymān b. ʿAbd al-Wahhāb's characterization of the passage does not appear to me entirely accurate either.

testified *lā ilāha illā llāh.*"[81] As noted, this understanding of the *shahāda* follows naturally from the meaning of *ilāh* as an object of worship, as we can see in this statement that Ibn ʿAbd al-Wahhāb cites from Ibn Taymiyya against the Islamic philosophers:

> Even if they were to uphold *tawḥīd* of Allāh in words and speech by describing Him as His prophets described Him, they would then have *tawḥīd* without acts (*ʿamal*), and that does not suffice for salvation. [In order to be saved,] one must worship Allāh alone without partner and take Him as *ilāh*, and that is the meaning of the words *lā ilāha illā llāh.*[82]

The underlying concept here is that actions can belie one's words: Anyone who turns to a tomb, tree, celestial body, angel, or prophet with a request to bring benefit or ward off harm "has taken it as an *ilāh* apart from Allāh, and denies (*mukadhdhib*) *lā ilāha illā llāh.*" Ibn ʿAbd al-Wahhāb means literally that such an individual has negated his own profession of faith, since he writes that he is to be asked to repent, and if he does not, he is to be killed (viz. as an apostate).[83] Polylatric actions can thus be denial (*takdhīb*) of one's profession of faith; in another passage he likewise writes that they can constitute *jaḥd* (lit. 'rejection,' 'denial') of the *shahāda.*[84] *Takdhīb* and *jaḥd* are terms normally used to denote what must issue from an individual for him to be considered an apostate: Thus for example in al-Ṭaḥāwī's popular *ʿaqīda*: "no one exits faith except by rejecting (*juḥūd*) that which brought him into it."[85] This condition is more commonly understood as demanding an express verbal rejection of faith or of a tenet of faith (including commandments, e.g. *zakāt*) before a judgment of apostasy can be rendered, but it is eminently logical that Ibn ʿAbd al-Wahhāb would view polylatric actions as fulfilling this same function. If faith and *tawḥīd* were just belief in Allāh (i.e. *tawḥīd al-rubūbiyya*) this would not make sense, but since for him *tawḥīd* is first and foremost a commitment to exclusivity of worship (i.e. *tawḥīd al-ulūhiyya*), polylatric devotion can be considered *takdhīb* or *jaḥd* of "that which brought him into it."[86]

[81] Ibn Ghannām, *Taʾrīkh najd*, p. 341.
[82] Ibn Taymiyya, *Majmūʿat al-fatāwā*, vol. 9, p. 22; Ibn Ghannām, *Taʾrīkh najd*, p. 373. Ibn ʿAbd al-Wahhāb's text differs slightly from the printed edition of the *fatāwā* and he characterizes the statement as being directed against the *mutakallimūn*, whereas the context in the original passage indicates that it was directed rather against the *falāsifa*.
[83] *Durar*, vol. 2, p. 87. [84] Ibn Ghannām, *Taʾrīkh najd*, pp. 341–342.
[85] ʿAlī b. ʿAlī b. Muḥammad b. Abī al-ʿIzz, *Sharḥ al-ṭaḥāwiyya fī al-ʿaqīda al-salafiyya*, Riyadh: Maktabat al-Riyāḍ al-Ḥadītha, n.d., p. 277.
[86] Indeed in Ibn ʿAbd al-Wahhāb's writings, *tawḥīd* when unspecified by a qualifier means *tawḥīd al-ulūhiyya*. See e.g. *Durar*, vol. 1, p. 126: *wa-aʿẓam mā amara llāhu bihi al-tawḥīd wa-huwa ifrād Allāh bi-l-ʿibāda.*

Here we see how the doctrine of *tawḥīd al-ulūhiyya* is the essential element in Ibn ʿAbd al-Wahhāb's propensity for *takfīr* of his contemporaries and belligerent action against them. Mere verbal profession of *lā ilāha illā llāh* does not suffice to guarantee the inviolability of one's life and property, and in his view many of his contemporaries' actions belied their verbal profession and rendered their blood and property licit. In a colorful elaboration of this point he writes the following regarding those who say the words of the profession of faith but do not act in accordance with its meaning, a group whom he declares are *mushrikūn*:

> *lā ilāha illā llāh* is a fortress, but they have aimed the mangonels of denial at it and shot the rocks of demolition, and the enemy entered among them, wrested away from them the meaning, and left them with the form … they wrested away the meaning of *lā ilāha illā llāh*, and what was left to them was the prattle of the tongue and the clatter of the letters. This is mention of the fortress without the fortress [itself]. And just as the mention of fire does not burn, the mention of water does not drown, the mention of bread does not sate, and the mention of a sword does not cut, so mention of the fortress does not protect [one's blood and property].[87]

In addition to the connection traced here to the issue of *tawḥīd al-ulūhiyya*, Ibn ʿAbd al-Wahhāb's view on the insufficiency of mere verbal enunciation of the *shahāda* is likewise related to the topic of the theology of faith and whether acts (*ʿamal*) are a necessary component of *īmān*. As we saw in Chapter 1, the two issues of *tawḥīd al-ulūhiyya* and the theology of faith are related one to another in Ibn Taymiyya's writings. Ibn ʿAbd al-Wahhāb does not often use the terminology of the classical debate on faith when expounding on *tawḥīd al-ulūhiyya*, but it does crop up. He naturally affirms the salafī position that faith (*īmān*) is composed of belief, speech, and acts, and increases and decreases,[88] but beyond that he also uses terminology that attests to a more distinctive Taymiyyan imprint: For example, he employs the Taymiyyan terminology of *murjiʾat al-fuqahāʾ* to describe Abū Ḥanīfa and his followers (i.e. pre-Māturīdī Ḥanafīs). He also adopts Ibn Taymiyya's claim that Murjiʾite influence lies behind the judicial opinion that one who does not pray, but acknowledges that prayer is obligatory, is not an apostate and should only be killed as a *ḥadd* punishment.[89]

[87] *Durar*, vol. 2, p. 113.

[88] See *Durar* vol. 1, pp. 96, 97, 187; cf. p. 36, where he approvingly notes the agreement of his Shāfiʿī contemporary ʿAbdallāh b. Muḥammad b. ʿAbd al-Laṭīf with al-Bukhārī's definition of faith contra "*madhhab aʾimmatikum al-mutakallimīn*," viz. the Ashʿarī school.

[89] *Durar*, vol. 1, p. 111. On Ibn Taymiyya's terminology of *murjiʾat al-fuqahāʾ*, see Lav, *Radical Islam*, pp. 31–32; on Ibn Taymiyya's argument regarding capital punishment for failure to pray, see pp. 38–39. For another parallel, see Ibn ʿAbd al-Wahhāb's adduction of Iblīs and Firʿawn as proof that *kufr* can occur despite the presence of *taṣdīq/maʿrifa*: *Durar*, vol. 1, p. 121, vol. 2, pp. 71, 125; cf. Lav, *Radical Islam*, pp. 36–37.

One particular framework that Ibn ʿAbd al-Wahhāb employs at times to present the *rubūbiyya/ulūhiyya* distinction implicitly relates it to the theology of faith, and specifically to the role of acts in faith. This framework addresses the issue through the prism of "Allāh's acts" and "the servant's acts." Ibn ʿAbd al-Wahhāb writes that there is no dispute, neither among unbelievers nor Muslims, regarding Allāh's acts: Everyone agrees that His acts are creation, provision (*rizq*), harm, benefit, and so forth. The distinction between unbelievers and Muslims is that the latter accomplish *tawḥīd* of Allāh both in His acts and in their own acts, that is, in their worship (*ʿibāda*), whereas the former accomplish *tawḥīd* of Allāh only in His acts, but commit *shirk* in their own acts (i.e. by directing *ʿibāda* to others as well).[90] Likewise, he writes that both believers and *munāfiqūn* say the *shahāda* verbally, but the difference is that believers say it while knowing its meaning in their hearts, and with acts of the limbs in accordance with it, whereas *munāfiqūn* say it without understanding its meaning and without action in accordance with it.[91]

Thus while the theology of faith per se and its attendant terminology play only a minor role in Ibn ʿAbd al-Wahhāb's writings, the general theme of the centrality of acts in faith was certainly present, and we know as well that Ibn ʿAbd al-Wahhāb was familiar with Ibn Taymiyya's writings on this topic. I therefore cannot agree with Esther Peskes, who has argued that the two scholars diverged on this issue. Peskes notes the Allāh's acts/servant's acts framework, and accurately describes *tawḥīd al-ulūhiyya* in Ibn ʿAbd al-Wahhāb's writings as "das active Element, mit dem der Gläubige durch sein eigenes Handeln, durch den Dienst an Gott allein, das Bekenntnis zur Einheit Gottes in die Tat umsetzt";[92] she argues, however, that this emphasis on acts as a necessary component of faith differed from the doctrine of Ibn Taymiyya, who, in line with the "consensus" of Sunnī *ʿulamāʾ* and in contrast with Ibn ʿAbd al-Wahhāb, supposedly viewed verbal profession of the *shahāda* as the sole dividing line between faith and unbelief.[93] She bases this assertion on Ibn Taymiyya's statement in *al-ʿAqīda al-wāsiṭiyya* that unlike the *khawārij*, the *ahl al-sunna wa-l-jamāʿa* do not declare anyone an unbeliever due to sin (*maʿāṣī, kabāʾir*). This statement, however, is formulaic, and only means that the specific categories of acts known as *maʿāṣī* and *kabāʾir* are not apostasy. It does not rule out acts per se (of commission or omission)

[90] *Durar*, vol. 1, p. 62, cf. p. 168 (dealing only with the *ulūhiyya* half) and vol. 2, p. 67 (*al-aṣl al-awwal tawḥīd al-rubūbiyya … wa-huwa tawḥīd Allāh bi-fiʿlihi … wa-l-aṣl al-thānī wa-huwa tawḥīd al-ulūhiyya … wa-huwa tawḥīd Allāh bi-afʿāl al-ʿibād*).
[91] *Durar*, vol. 2, p. 46. [92] Peskes, *Widerstreit*, pp. 22–23.
[93] Peskes, *Widerstreit*, p. 21, n. 32.

as a potential cause of apostasy, a position that Ibn Taymiyya explicitly denounces as Murjiʾite.[94] One can in fact adduce similar statements from Ibn ʿAbd al-Wahhāb as well, such as "I do not pronounce *takfīr* on anyone among the Muslims for sin (*bi-dhanb*)."[95]

## *Shirk* and *Bidʿa*

In summary, we can say that Ibn ʿAbd al-Wahhāb's condemnation of popular 'polylatric' devotion as *shirk*, and of his contemporaries as *mushrikūn*, was firmly grounded in his adoption of Ibn Taymiyya's doctrine of *tawḥīd al-ulūhiyya*. This is a much more specific intellectual architecture than simple opposition to *bidʿa* (illicit innovation in religion), which Goldziher believed to be the motive force behind the Wahhābī condemnation of the cult of saints. These two issues are in fact regularly separated out in Ibn ʿAbd al-Wahhāb's writings. For example, he takes up the Taymiyyan formulation[96] (without explicit attribution) that "these two principles are the essence (*jummāʿ*) of the religion: [1] that we not worship anyone but Allāh, and [2] that we not worship Him through innovations (*bidaʿ*), but rather through what He decreed." Ibn ʿAbd al-Wahhāb goes on to say that the first of these principles is the meaning of the first part of the *shahāda*, the commitment to monolatry; the second principle, that the worship of Allāh must be solely through what He decreed, and with avoidance of *bidʿa*, is the meaning of the second part of the *shahāda*, "and Muḥammad is the Messenger of Allāh," which entails obedience to the law that the Prophet brought.[97]

It is true in a general sense that the cult of saints and worship of not-Allāh could be considered an innovation in religion, as in Ibn ʿAbd al-Wahhāb's view it represents a departure from the Islam of the Prophet and the *salaf*; on occasion he even refers to it as such.[98] Nonetheless the vast majority of his polemic against what he viewed as *shirk* hinges on the first half of the *shahāda*, the meaning of *ilāh*, and the *rubūbiyya/ulūhiyya* opposition. The issue of *bidʿa* is normally presented (as in the above-cited passage) as a subsidiary one to the main Streitpunkt, and refers not to polylatry, but to incorrect forms of monolatry: "One who supplicates

[94] Ibn Taymiyya, *Majmūʿat al-fatāwā*, vol. 7, p. 375; Lav, *Radical Islam*, pp. 38–39.
[95] *Durar*, vol. 1, p. 32: *wa-lā ukaffiru aḥadan min al-muslimīn bi-dhanb wa-lā ukhrijuhu min dāʾirat al-islām*.
[96] Cf. Ibn Taymmiyya, *Majmūʿat al-fatāwā*, vol. 1, pp. 63, 140, 218, 231, 248, 251, 260.
[97] *Durar*, vol. 2, p. 82.
[98] For example, *Durar*, vol. 1, p. 87, where he describes it as *min ḥawādith al-umūr*; and vol. 2, p. 83: *wa-l-shirk bidʿa wa-l-mubtadiʿ yaʾūlu ilā al-shirk*.

not-Allāh has committed *shirk*, and one who supplicates Allāh [in a way] He has not permitted has innovated."[99]

## *Taqlīd* and Monolatry

The topic of *taqlīd* will be treated at length in Chapter 3, which will trace a line of premodern salafī polemic against jurisprudential *taqlīd* that equated it with *shirk*. Ibn ʿAbd al-Wahhāb did condemn *taqlīd* in these terms, but the topic most frequently arises in his writings as an adjunct issue to his condemnation of ritual polylatry. This is a different aspect of the topic: *taqlīd* not as *shirk* in its own right, but as a methodological impediment to recognizing and avoiding ritual *shirk*.

This distinction is important because Ibn ʿAbd al-Wahhāb's project is sometimes conflated in the research literature with other contemporary reformist trends in the Muslim world that sought to promote jurisprudential *ijtihād*.[100] These latter trends were part of an urbane scholarly discourse that is itself an important element of the wider picture of eighteenth-century Islam, but is distinct from Ibn ʿAbd al-Wahhāb's central preoccupation with monolatry. Chapter 3 will argue that even his engagement with the issue of *taqlīd* in the jurisprudential context falls under this central preoccupation; here, however, we will limit our discussion to his treatment of the issue of *taqlīd* in connection with ritual monolatry.

Ibn ʿAbd al-Wahhāb's basic methodological premise in his argumentation is that the Qurʾān's fundamental message of monolatry is clear and requires no special expertise to understand. As he puts it, the greater part of the Qurʾān is devoted to explaining, in different ways, "the making of religion exclusive to Allāh, without partner, and explanation of its opposite, which is *shirk* … in language that the most doltish of commoners can understand."[101] In this passage, as elsewhere, Ibn ʿAbd al-Wahhāb (in contrast with Ibn Taymiyya) does not expound much on the epistemological priority of the Qurʾān as a topic in its own right; he emphasizes it

99 *Durar*, vol. 2, p. 83: *fa-man daʿā ilā ghayr Allāh fa-qad ashraka wa-man daʿā llāha bi-ghayr idhnihi fa-qad ibtadaʿa.*

100 For example, Basheer M. Nafi, "A Teacher of Ibn ʿAbd al-Wahhāb: Muḥammad Ḥayāt al-Sindī and the Revival of *Aṣḥāb al-Ḥadīth*'s Methodology," *Islamic Law and Society* 13/2 (2006), pp. 208–241. Nafi's characterization of *tawḥīd al-ulūhiyya* as being about "holding Him [Allāh] as the master and the ultimate sovereign of life" (p. 218) misses the point of the *rubūbiyya*/*ulūhiyya* distinction, and he likewise makes no mention of exclusivity of worship in his characterization of the "main themes" of the Wahhābī movement as being "its emphasis on the Qurʾān and the Sunna; its attack on divisions between the *madhhab*s and on imitation (*taqlīd*); and its rejection of Ibn ʿArabī's doctrine of *waḥdat al-wujūd*" (p. 222).

101 *Durar*, vol. 1, p. 172: *al-aṣl al-awwal ikhlāṣ al-dīn lillāh waḥdahu lā sharīka lahu wa-bayān ḍiddihi alladhī huwa al-shirk billāh wa-kawn akthar al-qurʾān fī bayān hādhā al-aṣl min wujūh shattā bi-kalām yafhamuhu ablad al-ʿāmma.*

rather for the simple reason that, in his view, the Qurʾān contains the divine imperative of monolatry in clear terms. Ibn ʿAbd al-Wahhāb then goes on to assert that over time Satan (Shayṭān) convinced the majority of the *umma* to view exclusivity of worship (*ikhlāṣ*) as denigration of the righteous (*ṣāliḥūn*), and *shirk* – viz. supplication of them – as love for the righteous.[102] Further on in the passage we then find explicit mention of *ijtihād*: Satan's spurious argument (*shubha*) is that one must leave aside the Qurʾān and the *sunna* unless one is a *mujtahid muṭlaq* who fulfills such-and-such conditions – conditions that, Ibn ʿAbd al-Wahhāb argues, it is not clear that even Abū Bakr and ʿUmar fulfilled.[103] People wrongly think that the Qurʾān is difficult to understand,[104] whereas in Ibn ʿAbd al-Wahhāb's view its basic message is as plain as day, but is consistently violated due to its being shielded from sight by the practice of *taqlīd*.

Let us consider another passage that clarifies further how the *taqlīd* issue arises in Ibn ʿAbd al-Wahhāb's writings as a subordinate one to the monolatry polemic. The passage is from an open epistle in which Ibn ʿAbd al-Wahhāb sets forth the principal purpose of his mission. He asserts that he calls people to exclusivity of worship (*ikhlāṣ al-dīn lillāh*) and forbids them supplication of the prophets and the righteous and other forms of ritual polylatry. His elaboration of this theme contains all the elements we surveyed above: the distinction between *tawḥīd al-ulūhiyya* and *tawḥīd al-rubūbiyya*; the point that the *mushrikūn* acknowledged the latter, and that their *shirk* in worship consisted of appeal to intermediaries and intercessors with Allāh; the mission of the prophets was solely to propagate *tawḥīd al-ulūhiyya*; explanation of *ulūhiyya* in terms of the meaning of *ilāh*; the point that one must uphold the meaning of *lā ilāha illā llāh* and not just profess it verbally; and emphasis of the Streitpunkt: "The upshot is that everything that has been said about me, apart from calling people to *tawḥīd* and forbidding them *shirk*, is false."[105] He then writes that one of the most astounding things he heard from his opponents is that when he explained to them Qurʾānic verses that show that the *mushrikūn* acknowledged Allāh's *rubūbiyya* aspect and only supplicated their objects of worship as intercessors with Allāh – with the point clearly being that this same *shirk* is found among his contemporaries – they answered: "We and those like us are not allowed to act [directly] on the Qurʾān, nor on the words of the Prophet, nor on the words of the early scholars, and we only obey what the later scholars said."[106]

[102] *Durar*, vol. 1, p. 172. [103] *Durar*, vol. 1, p. 174. [104] *Durar*, vol. 1, p. 175.
[105] *Durar*, vol. 1, pp. 64–72.
[106] *Durar*, vol. 1, pp. 72–73; and cf. p. 82 for nearly identical language.

In other words, the *taqlīd/ijtihād* issue was generally not raised by Ibn ʿAbd al-Wahhāb himself but arose rather out of his opponents' attempts to refute, on methodological grounds, his arguments for monolatry. We do not have to rely on Ibn ʿAbd al-Wahhāb's testimony on this score, as it is corroborated by extant anti-Wahhābī polemic as well: For example, his brother Sulaymān opens his anti-Wahhābī treatise with the argument that Muḥammad b. ʿAbd al-Wahhāb does not fulfill the conditions for *ijtihād*.[107] Perhaps in response to such arguments Ibn ʿAbd al-Wahhāb points out that the Qurʾān depicts the *mushrikūn* as using a similar defense of their practices, and he states that *taqlīd* is the most important principle on which the *kuffār*, "early and late," base their religion.[108]

None of this is to say that Ibn ʿAbd al-Wahhāb was entirely uninterested in the issue of excessive *madhhab* partisanship or other 'normal' features of the *taqlīd/ijtihād* debate. We find, for example, condemnation of "*al-taʿaṣṣub li-l-madhhab*" in his *Masāʾil al-jāhiliyya*, a work that lists characteristics of the original *jāhiliyya* with the polemical purpose of implying that they have recurred in his own day.[109] It appears, however, as *masʾala* number fifty-five, long after the central topic of ritual monolatry and any number of other issues.

## Ibn al-Amīr's *Taṭhīr al-iʿtiqād ʿan adrān al-ilḥād*

Muḥammad b. Ismāʿīl al-Ṣanʿānī (d. 1182/1769) was a Yemeni contemporary of Muḥammad b. ʿAbd al-Wahhāb. Commonly known as Ibn al-Amīr, he was an important figure in a lineage of Yemeni *ḥadīth* scholars who could broadly be classified as salafī.[110] This Yemeni salafī tradition predated the rise of the Wahhābīs, and when Ibn al-Amīr first heard of Ibn ʿAbd al-Wahhāb's activities in Najd he authored a poem in praise of him, though he later retracted his support.[111]

To my knowledge, no detailed study has been devoted to Ibn al-Amīr's major work on issues of monolatry, *Taṭhīr al-iʿtiqād ʿan adrān al-ilḥād*. As this work cites Ibn al-Amīr's own poem in praise of Ibn ʿAbd al-Wahhāb[112] it must have been written at some point between the writing

107 Ibn ʿAbd al-Wahhāb, *al-Ṣawāʿiq al-ilāhiyya*, pp. 3ff. 108 *Durar*, vol. 2, pp. 133–134.
109 *Durar*, vol. 2, p. 140 (= al-Rūmī et al. (eds.), *Muʾallafāt*, vol. 1, p. 344).
110 See Haykel, *Revival and Reform*, p. 10.
111 Cook, "On the Origins," pp. 200–201; Haykel, *Revival and Reform*, pp. 128–129; Bunzel, *Wahhābism*, pp. 80–84.
112 Muḥammad b. Ismāʿīl b. Ṣalāḥ al-Yamanī al-Ṣanʿānī, *Taṭhīr al-iʿtiqād ʿan adrān al-ilḥād*, ed. Nāṣir b. ʿĀʾiḍ b. Ḥasan, with *sharḥ* by ʿAlī b. Muḥammad b. Sinān Āl Sinān, Mecca: Maṭābiʿ al-Waḥīd, 1425[/2004], p. 112.

of this poem and his subsequent retraction, that is, between 1163/1749-1750 and 1170/1756-1757.[113] An analysis of *Taṭhīr al-iʿtiqād* will show that Ibn al-Amīr's affinity with the Wahhābī movement went far beyond general similarities. His own conception of *tawḥīd* is very clearly adopted from Ibn Taymiyya, and his opposition to widespread ritual practices in his day and characterization of them as *shirk* is, like it was for Ibn ʿAbd al-Wahhāb, premised on the doctrine of *tawḥīd al-ulūhiyya.* It is not clear that Ibn al-Amīr adopted this doctrine by way of the Wahhābīs. Given that Ibn ʿAbd al-Wahhāb's own doctrine is so clearly drawn from Ibn Taymiyya, Ibn al-Amīr could well have already held similar views, as perhaps suggested in his poem in praise of Ibn ʿAbd al-Wahhāb: "I was gladdened by what I heard of his path / a path I had thought I was alone in" (*la-qad sarranī mā jāʾanī min ṭarīqihi / wa-kuntu arā hādhihi al-ṭarīqa lī waḥdī*).[114] For present purposes we will leave this question open. Likewise, I will not address here the question of the later disagreement between the two scholars, and will focus simply on pointing out the Taymiyyan basis of *Taṭhīr al-iʿtiqād.*

The work can be divided into two basic parts: The first lays out Ibn al-Amīr's doctrine on *tawḥīd* and *shirk,*[115] and the second applies these concepts to a condemnation of practices current in his day and discussion of the related issues of *takfīr* and belligerency, primarily through the device of responses to hypothetical questions and objections.[116]

That the entire work is premised on the doctrine of *tawḥīd al-ulūhiyya* is already evident in its opening pages. In the *ḥamdala* we read: "Praise be to Allāh, who does not accept *tawḥīd* of His *rubūbiyya* from humans until they render to Him exclusive *tawḥīd al-ʿibāda.*"[117] Ibn al-Amīr then explains that he was obligated to write the treatise in order to fulfill his duty to condemn tomb-centered devotion and other practices that were widespread in his day. This is followed by five foundational principles (*uṣūl*) and three chapters in which the theoretical grounds for this condemnation are established.

[113] For the dating, see Cook, "On the Origins," pp. 200–201.

[114] Muḥammad b. Ismāʿīl al-Amīr al-Ḥusaynī al-Ṣanʿānī, *Dīwān al-Amīr al-Ṣanʿānī*, Cairo: Maṭbaʿat al-Madanī, 1384/1964, p. 130.

[115] al-Ṣanʿānī, *Taṭhīr al-iʿtiqād*, pp. 67–112.

[116] al-Ṣanʿānī, *Taṭhīr al-iʿtiqād*, pp. 113–179.

[117] al-Ṣanʿānī, *Taṭhīr al-iʿtiqād*, p. 67. Ibn al-Amīr has a slight preference for the term *tawḥīd al-ʿibāda* over *ilāhiyya* or *ulūhiyya*, but he uses them all interchangeably. This is natural enough, since *ilāh* is understood as meaning an object of worship, and *tawḥīd al-ulūhiyya* as exclusivity of worship. Ibn ʿAbd al-Wahhāb frequently employs similar language. For example, *Durar*, vol. 1, p. 143, on the mission of the prophets: *wa-aʿẓam mā amarū bihi tawḥīd Allāh bi-ʿibādatihi.*

The exposition is similar to what we have seen in our preceding analyses of Ibn Taymiyya's and Ibn ʿAbd al-Wahhāb's writings. In the five foundational principles we are told that *tawḥīd* is of two kinds, *tawḥīd al-rubūbiyya* and *tawḥīd al-ʿibāda*. The Qurʾānic *mushrikūn* already acknowledged *tawḥīd al-rubūbiyya*, that is, they acknowledged Allāh in His aspect of Creator and Sustainer, and the prophets' mission was thus to reaffirm this and to call the *mushrikūn* to the second kind of *tawḥīd*, that is, *tawḥīd al-ʿibāda*. This is why Qurʾānic verses such as 35:3, 16:17, 14:10, 6:14, 31:11, and 46:4 have the prophets addressing the *mushrikūn* through rhetorical questions that presume their prior knowledge of Allāh. Likewise, Ibn al-Amīr argues that the term *sharīk* (partner) itself already attests to this acknowledgment of Allāh on the part of the *mushrikūn*, and demonstrates that the *mushrikūn*'s objects of worship were not taken to the exclusion of Allāh, but were believed to bring the worshipper closer to Allāh and to act as intercessors with Him. When the prophets called on their peoples to embrace the second kind of *tawḥīd*, they instructed them to say *lā ilāha illā llāh* and to believe in its meaning, which Ibn al-Amīr defines as "acknowledgment of the exclusivity of Allāh in *ilāhiyya* and worship, and denial and disavowal of what is worshipped apart from Him" (*ifrād Allāh taʿālā bi-l-ilāhiyya wa-l-ʿibāda wa-l-nafy li-mā yuʿbadu min dūnihi wa-l-barāʾa minhu*). Ibn al-Amīr, like Ibn ʿAbd al-Wahhāb, stresses that what is required in order to become a believer (*muʾmin*) is not just verbal enunciation of the *shahāda*, but implementation of its meaning.[118]

The only one of Ibn al-Amīr's foundational principles that does not directly relate to the nature of *tawḥīd* is the first, namely, the principle that everything in the Qurʾān is true.[119] This premise, while seemingly uncontroversial – and polemically presented as such – is meant to justify Ibn al-Amīr's direct adduction of the Qurʾān throughout the treatise as grounding for his theological claims. As we noted in the case of Ibn ʿAbd al-Wahhāb, this was by no means uncontroversial in the eighteenth-century scholarly milieu, and later in the treatise Ibn al-Amīr explicitly addresses the objection that his views are in contravention of a supposed scholarly consensus (*ijmāʿ*).[120]

The exposition of these foundational principles is followed by three chapters that expand on the themes already introduced. One of these is very brief and enumerates the different kinds of worship (*ʿibāda*) as those relating to belief (*iʿtiqād*), those relating to speech, those relating to the

[118] al-Ṣanʿānī, *Taṭhīr al-iʿtiqād*, pp. 78–91.
[119] al-Ṣanʿānī, *Taṭhīr al-iʿtiqād*, pp. 75–77.
[120] al-Ṣanʿānī, *Taṭhīr al-iʿtiqād*, pp. 151–159.

body, and those relating to one's money or property.[121] Given that the doctrine of *tawḥīd al-ulūhiyya* emphasizes that worship is constitutive of the idols (because an *ilāh* is anything taken as an object of worship), defining the meaning and forms of worship is of great importance, as such acts even when directed toward the righteous are considered *shirk*. Just as ʿĪsā (Jesus) was a true prophet but became an idol to Christians through their worship of him, so the cult of saints is at times directed to truly righteous individuals who nonetheless become idols to their worshippers through their worship of them.[122] It is unknown to me whether there is any special import to Ibn al-Amīr's classification of worship as presented in this chapter, but elsewhere he regularly provides lists of practices that parallel those of Ibn ʿAbd al-Wahhāb and which typically include supplication, vows, appealing for aid, sacrifice, and so forth.[123]

The themes of the next two chapters are monolatric in the Taymiyyan sense: respectively, that the prophets were sent to call people to exclusivity of worship, rather than to acknowledgment of Allāh as Creator, since the *mushrikūn* already acknowledged this;[124] and that the *mushrikūn*'s acknowledgment of Allāh's *rubūbiyya* was of no benefit to them, since they did not uphold exclusivity of worship.[125] This provides the groundwork for the treatise's long final chapter, which applies the monolatric framework to a condemnation of practices current in Ibn al-Amīr's own day as *shirk*.

The final chapter begins with a statement of the purpose of the entire treatise. Ibn al-Amīr writes that once one understands the preceding points, one understands that anyone who believes in the ability of a tree, stone, tomb, angel, jinn, or living or dead individual to harm or benefit, bring one closer to Allāh, or intercede with Allāh, such a person has committed *shirk*, akin to what the *mushrikūn* believed regarding their idols – and all the more so one who vows his property or child to a living or dead individual, requesting thereby what should only be asked of Allāh, such as healing the ill – "for that is the very same *shirk* as that of the idol-worshipping *mushrikūn*, then and now" (*fa-inna hādha huwa al-shirk bi-ʿaynihi alladhī kāna wa-yakūnu ʿalayhi al-mushrikūn ʿubbād*

121 al-Ṣanʿānī, *Taṭhīr al-iʿtiqād*, pp. 92–93.
122 al-Ṣanʿānī, *Taṭhīr al-iʿtiqād*, p. 99: *wa-man faʿala shayʾan min dhālika li-makhlūq min ḥayy aw mayyit aw jamād aw ghayr dhālika fa-qad ashraka fī al-ʿibāda wa-ṣāra man tufʿal lahu hādhihi al-umūr ilāhan li-ʿābidīhi sawāʾun kāna malakan aw nabiyyan aw waliyyan aw shajaran aw qabran aw jinniyyan aw ḥayyan aw mayyitan.*
123 For example, al-Ṣanʿānī, *Taṭhīr al-iʿtiqād*, p. 138: *min duʿāʾihim wa-nidāʾihim wa-l-tawassul bihim wa-l-istighātha wa-l-istiʿāna wa-l-ḥilf wa-l-nudhūr wa-ghayr dhālika.*
124 al-Ṣanʿānī, *Taṭhīr al-iʿtiqād*, pp. 94–99.
125 al-Ṣanʿānī, *Taṭhīr al-iʿtiqād*, pp. 100–103.

*al-aṣnām*).[126] The only distinction between the tomb-centered worship of his own day and the *shirk* of the Arabs of the *jāhiliyya* lies in the names by which they refer to their idols, as the polytheists of his own day do not call them a *ṣanam* or a *wathan* (two classical words for 'idol') but rather a *walī* (saint), *qabr* (tomb), or *mashhad* (mausoleum). As we saw with Ibn ʿAbd al-Wahhāb's contemporary 'translations' of *ilāh*, Ibn al-Amīr views this as a distinction without a difference, since calling something by a different name does not change its meaning: These objects of worship remain idols (*ṣanam*, *wathan*), since those who worship them act with them as the *mushrikūn* did with their idols (*idh hum muʿāmilūna lahā muʿāmalat al-mushrikīn li-l-aṣnām*).[127] Here again we see that in Ibn al-Amīr's monolatric doctrine, as in those of Ibn Taymiyya and Ibn ʿAbd al-Wahhāb, the class of idols is not a closed set, but includes rather anything apart from Allāh to which worship (in a broad sense) is directed. This expository portion of the treatise concludes with a citation of Ibn al-Amīr's own poem in praise of Ibn ʿAbd al-Wahhāb (*al-abyāt al-najdiyya*),[128] a fact that perhaps points to the latter's role in inspiring the composition of *Taṭhīr al-iʿtiqād*.

The remainder of the treatise is devoted to refutation of various hypothetical objections and questions, with Ibn al-Amīr's answers often recapitulating and expanding on the themes announced in the expository portion of the treatise. For example, on the issue of the insufficiency of verbal enunciation of the *shahāda*, Ibn al-Amīr has the hypothetical questioner object that his contemporaries and the *mushrikūn* are not the same, since the former have said *lā ilāha illā llāh* (the profession of faith), and this profession grants immunity, as in the *ḥadīth* "I was commanded to fight people until they say *lā ilāha illā llāh*, and if they say it then their blood and property are immune to violation by me except by right." Likewise, the hypothetical objectioner argues that the Prophet reproached the Companion Usāma b. Zayd for having killed someone after he said *lā ilāha illā llāh*, and likewise that people in his day, in addition to pronouncing the *shahāda*, also perform the other pillars of Islam (prayer, fasting, the *zakāt* tithe, and pilgrimage), in contrast with the *mushrikūn*. In reply, Ibn al-Amīr writes that the "I was commanded to fight" *ḥadīth* contains the stipulation "except by right" (*illā bi-ḥaqqihā*), which means: granting of *ilāhiyya* and *ʿubūdiyya* exclusively to Allāh, and those who practice tomb-centered devotion (the "*qubūriyyūn*") do not grant Him exclusive *ulūhiyya* and

[126] al-Ṣanʿānī, *Taṭhīr al-iʿtiqād*, pp. 104–107.
[127] al-Ṣanʿānī, *Taṭhīr al-iʿtiqād*, pp. 107–109.
[128] al-Ṣanʿānī, *Taṭhīr al-iʿtiqād*, p. 112.

worship.[129] Thus their verbal statement of the profession of faith (*kalimat al-shahāda*) is of no avail, since it is only efficacious together with adherence to its meaning. A similar theme is sounded in Ibn al-Amīr's answer to the *qubūriyyūn*'s protest that they do not commit *shirk*: Their words are of no avail, since their actions belie their speech (*li-anna fiʿlahum akdhaba qawlahum*), and there is thus no difference between them and idol-worshipping *mushrikūn*.[130]

This brief summary of the contents of *Taṭhīr al-iʿtiqād* should be sufficient to demonstrate the similarities between Ibn al-Amīr's conception of monolatry and that of Ibn ʿAbd al-Wahhāb. Their condemnations of contemporary ritual practice as polylatric rested on the same foundations: the distinction between *tawḥīd al-rubūbiyya* and *tawḥīd al-ulūhiyya*; the comparison, on this basis, between the Qurʾānic *mushrikūn* and their contemporaries; the idea that worship is constitutive of the idol; the interpretation of the *shahāda* in terms of monolatry; and the emphasis on the need to understand and implement the meaning of the *shahāda* as opposed to mere verbal profession. Further analysis of *Taṭhīr al-iʿtiqād* might well indicate differences of nuance that foreshadowed the later rift between the two scholars, but the fundamental commonalities are striking. This Yemeni treatise demonstrates that adoption of Ibn Taymiyya's doctrine of *tawḥīd al-ulūhiyya*, and its application to contemporary practice, was not limited to the Wahhābī movement, and was a major component in the views of at least one additional prominent eighteenth-century revivalist. This finding suggests that it might be fruitful to reexamine the issue of eighteenth-century revivalism from a closer doctrinal perspective in order to differentiate cases of genunine adoption of Taymiyyan monolatry from the more general revivalist concern for orthopraxy.

## Conclusion

Chapter 1 introduced the doctrine of *tawḥīd al-ulūhiyya* through the writings of its formulator, Ibn Taymiyya. There it was argued that this doctrine, whose central contention is that Islam is first and foremost monolatry rather than 'mere' monotheism, was the linchpin of Ibn Taymiyya's theological system. It was also noted that this was a

[129] Ibn al-Amīr apparently understands the suffix *-hā* as a feminine singular referring to the statement *lā ilāha illā llāh*, i.e. one's blood and property is immune to attack except on grounds relating to the statement *lā ilāha illā llāh*. This is one of the common glosses of the stipulation: See M. J. Kister, "*…Illā bi-ḥaqqihi…* A Study of an Early *Ḥadīth*," *Jerusalem Studies in Arabic and Islam* 5 (1984), pp. 33–52, at pp. 48–49.

[130] al-Ṣanʿānī, *Taṭhīr al-iʿtiqād*, p. 116.

distinctive doctrine that set Ibn Taymiyya apart from the mainstream of Islamic religious thought in his day, as could be seen in the fact that the various formulations of the doctrine served as polemic against the *kalām* theologians (including the Ashʿarīs) and the majority of Ṣūfīs. As a natural corollary of the doctrine he certainly condemned the cult of saints as a violation of monolatry (and this condemnation was controversial already in his own day), but this was only one branch of an elaborate intellectual structure. Likewise, while Ibn Taymiyya was an influential public figure, he never attempted to establish a separate political or military power to enforce his vision, and the socially disruptive potential of his doctrine remained for the most part latent.

More than four centuries after the death of Ibn Taymiyya a provincial scholar in central Arabia fell under the spell of the doctrine of *tawḥīd al-ulūhiyya* and made it the central plank of a mission that was at one and the same time religious, political, and military. In the fractious conditions of eighteenth-century Arabia monolatry became a socially disruptive force that was promoted and contested not only with words but also with the sword. There was no historical necessity that this should have been the case: At any number of early junctures the mission of Muḥammad b. ʿAbd al-Wahhāb could have been cut short, and had it been we might never have heard of him at all. Typologically speaking, however, the Wahhābī movement brought to expression a belligerent propensity that is inherent in monolatry itself. The Egyptologist Jan Assmann has argued that such belligerency against the "pagan within" – an "extrasystemic other" within one's own society – is a native characteristic of what he terms exclusivist monotheism, and what we have been terming monolatry.[131] Chapters 4 and 5 will examine further disruptive transmutations of this monolatric thrust in the modern era. Chapter 3, however, will remain in the premodern period and will discuss a facet of Islamic monolatry that touches on the legal sphere rather than the ritual, and which thus foreshadows the theonomic variant of monolatry that would emerge in its own right in the twentieth century.

[131] Assmann, *Of God and Gods*, pp. 29–33. Assmann prefers the terminology of exclusivism to 'monolatry' (p. 4), but his characterization of the phenomenon is essentially identical to what I here term monolatry, and he avoids the term simply because in most Biblical scholarship it denotes a proto-monotheist stage of religion.

# 3 Theonomy in Premodern Salafī Jurisprudence

This chapter will trace a kind of jurisprudential corollary to the premodern salafī emphasis on exclusivity of worship, a corollary found in polemical writings against the practice of *taqlīd*. *Taqlīd* is normally defined as blind acceptance of a legal authority's ruling without knowing or investigating the proofs on which it rests. While the issue is still a controversial one in the academic literature, there is rough agreement on the point that the theory and practice of *taqlīd* gained preeminence over the course of time, and that this development contributed to the consecration of the four Sunnī legal schools – the Mālikīs, the Ḥanafīs, the Shāfiʿīs, and the Ḥanbalīs – as the sole orthodox ones.

Numerous jurists of a more or less salafī orientation, from the fifth/eleventh century and up to the modern era, polemicized against *taqlīd* by arguing that it is tantamount to polytheism (*shirk*). A constant in these polemics is the use of a particular prooftext: Qurʾān 9:31 and an associated exegetical *ḥadīth* that explicitly ties acceptance of non-divine legislation to polytheism. The authors surveyed in this chapter applied these prooftexts to the question of jurisprudential *taqlīd* and argued that blind adherence to a particular legal school or to the views of a particular imām, rather than to the original sources of law (the Qurʾān and the *ḥadīth*), is *shirk* – a form of worship directed to others apart from Allāh.

The primary purpose of the present chapter's analysis of this polemic is to prepare the ground for discussion, in Chapters 4 and 5, of the manner in which it served as a precedent for the characterization of parliamentary legislation as polytheism in modern theonomy. In addition, by calling attention to the salafī orientation of premodern anti-*taqlīd* polemic and the salience of the theme of *shirk* therein I hope to correct some errors that have arisen in academic study of the *ijtihād*/*taqlīd* issue.

A number of prooftexts from the Qurʾān and the *ḥadīth* characterize law-giving as an exclusive prerogative of Allāh (and of the Prophet insofar as he is Allāh's messenger). Examples include the three verses 6:57, 12:40, and 12:67 that state that "rule is Allāh's alone" (*in al-ḥukmu illā lillāh*). A number of verses likewise obligate believers to exclusive adherence to Allāh's law and warn against following the laws of others. Qurʾān 5:50 reads: "Is it the rule (*ḥukm*) of the *jāhiliyya* that you seek? Whose rule is better than Allāh's for a God-fearing people?," and in a similar vein we find in 4:60: "Have you not seen those who claim to believe in what was revealed to you [O Prophet] and what was revealed to those before you; they wish to appeal in judgment (*yataḥākamū*) to the *ṭāghūt*, though they were commanded to reject it, but the Shayṭān seeks to lead them grievously astray." At times an even more explicit connection is drawn between the validity of one's faith and acceptance of Allāh's law, as in Qurʾān 4:65: "Nay, by your Lord, they do not believe until they refer to your judgment (*yuḥakkimūka*) that which is in dispute among them, and then find no opposition in their hearts to your ruling and submit to it entirely"; and likewise 5:44: "and those who do not rule (*yaḥkum*) by what Allāh revealed, they are the unbelievers." The key terms in these verses are drawn from the root *ḥ-k-m*, in the sense of law or a judicial ruling. In another verse (42:21) we find a derivative of the root *sh-r-ʿ* in the sense of "law-giving" tied to polytheism: "Or do they have [i.e. take for themselves] partners [to Allāh in divinity] (*shurakāʾ*) who have legislated (*sharaʿū*) for them in religion that for which Allāh has not given permission?"

Texts such as these are the basis for the tenet that acceptance of and submission to the law of Allāh and the Prophet is a necessary component of faith. As a general belief this tenet is shared far more widely than the specific premodern salafī tradition treated here, much as the tenet that only Allāh may be worshipped, discussed in the previous chapters, is as a general belief shared far more widely – indeed one could well say universally. Yet just as Ibn Taymiyya and Ibn ʿAbd al-Wahhāb developed the latter tenet in a radical direction, decrying widely accepted ritual practices in the Muslim world as *shirk*, so the premodern salafī legal tradition sharpened the opposition between divine and human law, castigating widely accepted judicial approaches as an infringement of Allāh's law-giving prerogative. The subsequent chapters of this book will demonstrate how this specific salafī legacy, both theological and jurisprudential, grounds modern radical theonomy as a trend distinct from other movements which may share some of its concerns, but not its patrimony nor its radical conclusions. At present we turn to our analysis of anti-*taqlīd* polemic, with special focus on Qurʾān 9:31, the exegetical *ḥadīth* thereon, and the manner in which the premodern salafī tradition employed them as a theonomic argument in intra-Muslim debates in jurisprudence.

## Anti-*taqlīd* Polemic

The association of obedience to human law with polytheism has not received sufficient notice in academic literature on the *ijtihād*/*taqlīd* dispute, despite significant evidence in the pertinent sources that it was a central issue. Wael Hallaq, in his influential article "Was the Gate of Ijtihad Closed?," associated *ijtihād* with creativity, open-mindedness, and capacious use of *qiyās* (legal analogy), and in consequence associated the fundamentalist literalism of the early Ḥanbalīs and *ahl al-ḥadīth* with *taqlīd* and opposition to *ijtihād*.[1] In fact the opposite is true: as we will see, strident opposition to *taqlīd* was a hallmark of Ḥanbalī and other *ahl al-ḥadīth*-leaning scholars, and was of a piece with their salafī jurisprudential methodology and their staunch opposition to *ra'y*. And conversely, as Rudolph Peters has observed, "*ijtihād* is structurally related to fundamentalism."[2]

Indeed, it could be said that condemnation of *taqlīd* was often simply an additional expression of the salafī theological concern for exclusivity of worship and obedience. This association of *taqlīd* and *ra'y* with *shirk* was already expressed in a statement attributed to Aḥmad b. Ḥanbal, as follows: "I wonder at people who know the *isnād* [viz. of a Prophetic *ḥadīth*] and know it to be sound, and [nonetheless] adopt the *ra'y* of Sufyān [viz. al-Thawrī]. Allāh the Exalted said [Qur'ān 24:63]: 'Let those who shrink from his [the Prophet's] command beware lest *fitna* befall them, or grievous punishment.' Do you know what *fitna* is? It is *shirk*."[3]

1 Wael B. Hallaq, "Was the Gate of Ijtihad Closed?," *International Journal of Middle East Studies* 16/1 (March 1984), pp. 3–41. These points have already been addressed in brief but insightful comments in Christopher Melchert, *The Formation of the Sunni Schools of Law, 9th–10th Centuries C.E.*, Leiden: Brill, 1997, pp. 16–18. Despite framing his article as an argument against Schacht, Hallaq's characterization of the nature and purpose of *ijtihād* is fundamentally in line with Schacht's, as already noted in Haykel, *Revival and Reform in Islam*, p. 80. At the close of the present chapter I will return to Hallaq's views in some more detail.

2 Rudolph Peters, "Ijtihād and Taqlīd in 18th and 19th Century Islam," *Die Welt des Islams*, New Series, 20/3–4 (1980), pp. 131–145, esp. pp. 131–132.

3 Reported (in slightly different variants) by al-Faḍl b. Ziyād and Abū Ṭālib, by way of Ibn Taymiyya, as cited in ʿAbd al-Raḥmān b. Ḥasan Āl al-Shaykh, *Fatḥ al-majīd sharḥ kitāb al-tawḥīd*, Muʾassasat Qurṭuba, n.d., pp. 556–557. One variant is likewise reported in Ibn Baṭṭa al-ʿUkbarī, *al-Ibāna ʿan sharīʿat al-firqa al-nājiyya wa-mujānabat al-firaq al-madhmūma*, 2nd ed., Riyadh: Dār al-Rāya, 1415/1994, vol. 1, p. 260. *Fitna* is a complex concept, which is why I have left it untranslated. Its basic meaning is to tempt or seduce; in Islamic usage it can mean temptation by Satan, whence the additional meanings of tribulation, strife, or discord. The gloss of *fitna* as *shirk* is common in exegesis of Qurʾān 8:39; see e.g. al-Ṭabarī, *Jāmiʿ al-bayān*, vol. 13, pp. 537ff.

With this in mind it is not surprising that the renewed wave of condemnation of *taqlīd*, from the eighteenth century on, was spearheaded by fundamentalist scholars and movements inspired at least in part by the Ḥanbalīs and the *ahl al-ḥadīth*, such as Muḥammad al-Shawkānī in Yemen and the Indian Ahl-i Ḥadīth, who took their very name from the early school.

Before going on to examine these polemics in detail it is worth making the following cautionary observation. While I hope to demonstrate that the theme of *shirk* was ubiquitous in anti-*taqlīd* polemic, it is rare to find statements that specify that the *shirk* associated with *taqlīd* can in certain circumstances rise to the level of actual apostasy (as opposed to *shirk aṣghar*/*kufr aṣghar*, that is, "minor" forms of polytheism or unbelief that do not negate one's status as a Muslim). The one unambiguous statement of this nature that I have encountered is from Ibn Taymiyya, as follows: "Whoever requires *taqlīd* of one imām in particular (*bi-ʿaynihi*) should be asked to repent. If he repents [he is spared], and if not, he is to be killed. And one who says 'One should [practice *taqlīd* of one imām in particular]' is ignorant and deviant."[4] The stipulation of *bi-ʿaynihi* is an important one that we will see recur in numerous polemics to follow.

## *Qurʾān 9:31 and the "Taking of Lords in Place of Allāh"*

The most commonly cited prooftext in which the connection between obedience to human authority and polytheism is set forth is an exegetical *ḥadīth* on Qurʾān 9:31. The verse, originally a denunciation of Jews and Christians, reads: "They took their rabbis and priests as lords other than Allāh, and likewise Jesus son of Maryam, though they were commanded to worship one God alone, and there is no god but He; gloried be He above what they associate (with Him)." The *ḥadīth* normally mentioned or alluded to in connection with this verse is as follows:

> ʿAdī b. Ḥātim said: I came to the Prophet of Allāh, Allāh's blessing and peace be upon him, wearing a golden crucifix on my neck. He said: ʿAdī, cast that idol off your neck! ʿAdī said: so I cast it off, and came to where he was as he was reading from *sūrat barāʾa* [the "disavowal chapter," another name for chapter 9 of the Qurʾān]. He read the verse "They took their rabbis and priests as lords in place of Allāh." (ʿAdī) said: I said: O Prophet of Allāh, we [sc. the Christians] do not worship them! He (the Prophet) said: Do they not forbid what Allāh permitted,

[4] *Wa-man awjaba taqlīd imām bi-ʿaynihi ustutība fa-in tāba wa-illā qutila wa-in qāla yanbaghī kāna jāhilan ḍāllan.* ʿAlāʾ al-Dīn Abū al-Ḥasan ʿAlī b. ʿAbbās al-Baʿlī, *al-Ikhtiyārāt al-fiqhiyya min fatāwā Shaykh al-Islām Ibn Taymiyya*, ed. Muḥammad Ḥāmid al-Fiqī, Beirut: Dār al-Maʿrifa, n.d., p. 333.

and you forbid it; and do they not permit what Allāh forbade, and you permit it? (ʿAdī) said: I said: Indeed! He (the Prophet) said: That is worship of them.[5]

This accusation is a familiar one with regard to the Jews: It was a staple of Sadducee and (later) Karaite polemic that the rabbis contravened revelation with their oral law. The Qurʾānic context may suggest this interpretation as well, as two verses earlier, in *āyat al-jizya* (9:29), the scriptuaries are described as "those who do not forbid what Allāh and His Prophet forbade" (among other transgressions). Regarding the Christians it is possible that the Qurʾānic verse and/or its exegesis allude to Matthew 16:19, in which Jesus, after telling Peter that he is the rock upon whom he will build his church, adds: "I shall give unto thee the keys of the kingdom of heaven: and whatsoever thou shalt bind on earth shall be bound in heaven: and whatsoever thou shalt loose on earth shall be loosed in heaven."[6]

It is not certain, however, that this exegesis was ever solely, or even primarily, directed against the Jews and Christians. Here we will briefly survey evidence suggesting that it may have originated in Umayyad-era intra-Islamic polemic.

The version of the tradition cited above, and similar ones that relate this exegesis on the authority of the Prophet, have Kufan *isnād*s, the common portion of which runs: ʿAbd al-Salām b. Ḥarb (d. 187/802) – Ghuṭayf b. Aʿyan – Muṣʿab b. Saʿd – ʿAdī b. Ḥātim.[7] Ghuṭayf was not always classified as a reliable transmitter,[8] and of the six canonical

[5] *ʿAn ʿAdī b. Ḥātim qāla ataytu rasūl Allāh ṣallā Allāh ʿalayhi wa-sallama wa-fī ʿunuqī ṣalībun min dhahab fa-qāla yā ʿAdī iṭraḥ hādhā al-wathan min ʿunuqika qāla fa-ṭaraḥtuhu wa-ntahaytu ilayhi wa-huwa yaqraʾu fī sūrat barāʾa fa-qaraʾa hādhihi al-āya ittakhadhū aḥbārahum wa-ruhbānahum arbāban min dūni llāh fa-qāla qultu yā rasūl Allāh innā lasnā naʿbuduhum fa-qāla a-laysa yuḥarrimūna mā aḥalla Allāh fa-tuḥarrimūnahu wa-yuḥillūna mā ḥarrama Allāh fa-tuḥillūnahu qāla qultu balā qāla fa-tilka ʿibādatuhum*. al-Ṭabarī, *Jāmiʿ al-bayān*, vol. 14, p. 210; and see there for variants.

[6] This hypothesis has been raised by at least one Muslim exegete, the thirteenth–fourteenth century Ḥanbalī Najm al-Dīn al-Ṭūfī: Sulaymān b. ʿAbd al-Qawī al-Ṭūfī, *al-Ishārāt al-ilāhiyya ilā al-mabāḥith al-uṣūliyya*, Cairo: Dār al-Fārūq al-Ḥadītha, 1423/2002, vol. 2, p. 274. Whatever the specific intent of this verse, Christianity was frequently associated with straying from revealed law in the early centuries of Islam. For example, it is reported that al-Shāfiʿī, who waged battle against the regional schools in order to establish the primacy of Prophetic *ḥadīth* in jurisprudence, was once asked whether he ruled in accordance with a certain *ḥadīth*. He replied with the rhetorical question: "Do you see a *zunnār* on my waist?" The *zunnār* was the kind of belt worn by Christians; al-Shāfiʿī was saying that it would be a Christian trait to not rule in accordance with the *ḥadīth*. Abū Ismāʿīl ʿAbdallāh b. Muḥammad al-Anṣārī al-Harawī, *Dhamm al-kalām wa-ahlihi*, Medina: Maktabat al-ʿUlūm wa-l-Ḥikam, 1418/1988, vol. 3, pp. 12–14.

[7] al-Ṭabarī, *Jāmiʿ al-bayān*, vol. 14, pp. 209–211.

[8] Cf. Aḥmad b. ʿAlī b. Ḥajar Shihāb al-Dīn al-ʿAsqalānī, *Tahdhīb al-tahdhīb*, Beirut: Muʾassasat al-Risāla, 1416/1996, vol. 3, p. 377.

collections the tradition appears only in al-Tirmidhī, who labels it an isolated (*gharīb*) tradition and notes that Ghuṭayf was not known as a transmitter of traditions (*laysa bi-maʿrūf fī al-ḥadīth*).[9] Al-Bukhārī knew the tradition and related it in his *Taʾrīkh*, but not in his authoritative *Ṣaḥīḥ*.[10]

There exist as well alternate, non-Prophetic versions of a similar exegesis of Qurʾān 9:31, which are likewise of Kufan provenance. The portion of the *isnād* common to most of them is: Ḥabīb b. Abī Thābit – Abū al-Bakhtarī – Ḥudhayfa (sc. b. al-Yamān), though in one version the Companion Ḥudhayfa is omitted (Jarīr and Ibn Fuḍayl – ʿAṭāʾ – Abū al-Bakhtarī) and the exegesis attributed directly to the Successor Abū al-Bakhtarī, who was Ḥudhayfa's *mawlā* (non-Arab tribal client).[11] In the academic study of *ḥadīth* it has been theorized (and fairly widely accepted) that traditions were historically first circulated in the name of Successors and subsequently in the name of Companions, with the attribution of traditions to the Prophet being an even later development.[12] Of our two separate Kufan chains of transmission, it would be reasonable to ascribe priority to the non-Prophetic version, and in particular to the isolated version in al-Ṭabarī's *Tafsīr* that brings the exegesis of verse 9:31 directly in the name of the Successor Abū al-Bakhtarī. Another argument for the primacy of this version is that it is shorter and simply answers the exegetical difficulty in the verse, to wit, how the Christians and Jews can be said to worship their rabbis and priests. It reads:

"They took their rabbis and priests as lords other than Allāh." [Abū al-Bakhtarī] said: They [the rabbis and priests] hastened to prohibit that which Allāh

[9] Abū ʿĪsā Muḥammad b. ʿĪsā al-Tirmidhī, *al-Jāmiʿ al-kabīr*, Beirut: Dār al-Gharb al-Islāmī, 1996, vol. 5, p. 173.

[10] Ismāʿīl b. Ibrāhīm al-Bukhārī, *Kitāb al-taʾrīkh al-kabīr*, n.p., n.d., vol. 4, p. 106. Cf. also Sulaymān b. Aḥmad al-Ṭabarānī, *al-Tafsīr al-kabīr*, Irbid: Dār al-Kitāb al-Thaqāfī, 2008, vol. 3, pp. 306–307.

[11] al-Ṭabarī, *Jāmiʿ al-bayān*, vol. 14, pp. 211–213 (the version omitting Ḥudhayfa is no. 16637); ʿAbd al-Razzāq al-Ṣanʿānī, *Tafsīr al-qurʾān*, Riyadh: Maktabat al-Rushd, n.d., vol. 2, p. 272; Abū Bakr al-Bayhaqī, *al-Madkhal ilā al-sunan al-kubrā*, n.p.: Dār al-Khulafāʾ li-l-Kitāb al-Islāmī, n.d., pp. 209–210 (mentions both the Prophetic and non-Prophetic versions); Abū Bakr al-Bayhaqī, *al-Sunan al-kubrā*, Beirut: Dār al-Maʿrifa, n. d., vol. 10, p. 116 (both Prophetic and non-Prophetic versions); ʿAbd al-Raḥmān al-Suyūṭī, *al-Durr al-manthūr fī al-tafsīr bi-l-maʾthūr*, Beirut: Dār al-Fikr, 1403/1983, vol. 4, pp. 173–174 (both Prophetic and non-Prophetic versions). For the relation between Ḥudhayfa and Abū al-Bakhtarī, see Redwan Sayed, *Die Revolte des Ibn al-Ašʿaṯ und die Koranleser: Ein Beitrag zur Religions- und Sozialgeschichte der frühen Umayyadenzeit*, Freiburg: Klaus Schwarz, 1977, p. 360, citing Khalīfa b. Khayyāṭ's *Taʾrīkh*.

[12] See Joseph Schacht, *The Origins of Muhammadan Jurisprudence*, Oxford: Clarendon Press, 1950, pp. 30, 33.

permitted, and they hastened to permit that which Allāh forbade. [The Jews and Christians] obeyed them in this. Allāh deemed obedience of them to be worship of them. And if [the rabbis and priests] had said [to the Jews and Christians] "worship us" they would not have done so.[13]

The story of the encounter between ʿAdī b. Ḥātim and the Prophet appears to be a topos, and a later embellishment of the basic exegesis – especially given that ʿAdī may have served as a stock figure for transmission of such anti-Christian or anti-scriptuary traditions: He is one of the transmitters of the well-known exegesis of Qurʾān 1:7 that glosses *al-maghḍūb ʿalayhim* (those who have incurred Allāh's wrath) as the Jews and *al-ḍāllīn* (those who have gone astray) as the Christians.[14]

This Abū al-Bakhtarī (Saʿīd b. Fayrūz al-Ṭāʾī[15]), whom we have identified as a possible originator of the Qurʾān 9:31 exegesis, is a figure of some interest. He played a role in the revolt of Ibn al-Ashʿath (81–83/700–702), and is mentioned as a prominent member of the batallion of rebel 'Qurʾān-readers' (*katībat al-qurrāʾ*), whom he stoically encouraged to soldier on after the death of their commander before falling in battle himself.[16] The potential significance of this connection lies in the fact that it was a staple of rebel polemic to accuse the Umayyad governor al-Ḥajjāj of "permitting the forbidden" – the same action that our tradition castigates as idolatry. Ibn al-Ashʿath had his followers swear to wage jihād against the "permitters" (sc. of the forbidden; *jihād al-muḥillīn*),[17] and Abū al-Bakhtarī's fellow Kufan Qurʾān-reader Ibn Abī Laylā enjoined the batallion to fight "these permitters [sc. of the forbidden] and innovators" (*fa-qātilū hāʾulāʾi al-muḥillīn al-muḥdithīn al-mubtadiʿīn*).[18]

[13] *ʿAn Abī al-Bakhtarī ittakhadhū aḥbārahum wa-ruhbānahum arbāban min dūni llāh qāla nṭalaqū ilā ḥalāl Allāh fa-jaʿalūhu ḥarāman wa-nṭalaqū ilā ḥarām Allāh fa-jaʿalūhu ḥalālan fa-aṭāʿūhum fī dhālika fa-jaʿala llāh ṭāʿatahum ʿibadatahum wa-law qālū lahum uʿbudūnā lam yafʿalū.* al-Ṭabarī, *Jāmiʿ al-bayān*, vol. 14, pp. 211–212.

[14] al-Tirmidhī, *al-Jāmiʿ al-kabīr*, vol. 5, pp. 69–71. I should add that these considerations relate only to ascribing priority to the Ḥudhayfa/Abū al-Bakhtarī version over the ʿAdī b. Ḥātim/Prophetic transmission, and within the former to Abū al-Bakhtarī. I make no attempt to assess the plausibility of the *isnād*s, and my focus on Abū al-Bakhtarī is for thematic reasons, to be explained presently. Clearly these considerations will be unconvincing to those who categorically date the origins of traditions to a period later than that of the Successors.

[15] Cf. al-ʿAsqalānī, *Tahdhīb al-tahdhīb*, vol. 2, p. 38.

[16] Abū Jaʿfar al-Ṭabarī, *Taʾrīkh al-umam wa-l-mulūk*, Beirut: Dār al-Kutub al-ʿIlmiyya, 1422/2001, vol. 3, pp. 631, 635, 636, 638, 640; Martin Hinds (trans.), *The History of al-Ṭabarī*, Albany: SUNY Press, 1990, vol. 23, pp. 25–26, 36–38, 42, 48.

[17] al-Ṭabarī, *Taʾrīkh*, vol. 3, p. 624; Hinds, *History*, vol. 23, p. 8, renders the phrase as "struggle against those who violate that which is sacred."

[18] al-Ṭabarī, *Taʾrīkh*, vol. 3, p. 635; Hinds, *History*, vol. 23, p. 36: "so fight these innovators, who deem licit that which is illicit."

It is true that such rhetoric was not entirely confined to the rebels: When the governor of Khurāsān, al-Muhallab b. Abī Ṣufra, attempted to dissuade Ibn al-Ashʿath from rebellion he wrote that the rebel commander would be endangering his soul by "shedding blood and permitting the forbidden" (*fa-lā tuʿarriḍhā lillāh fī safk dam wa-lā istiḥlāl muḥarram*).[19] Much as with the accusation of "abandoning the Prophet's *sunna*" that featured regularly in Umayyad-era revolts,[20] the accusation of "permitting the forbidden" probably did not have much precise content in the first century AH, apart perhaps from its connotation of permitting the spilling of inviolable blood. It was basically a way to say that one's enemy had deviated from correct faith and practice. In summary, the exegetical tradition on Qurʾān 9:31 possibly originated from the milieu of the *qurrāʾ* of this period and had something like the following sense: just as the rabbis and priests were the wrong leaders because they employed human judgment instead of adhering to divine law, so the Umayyads as well.

### *Al-Bayhaqī and Ibn ʿAbd al-Barr*

However the theme of "permitting the forbidden" was understood in Umayyad-era theopolitical disputes, it reappeared in following centuries among the arsenal of arguments deployed against *taqlīd* of the law schools, and it is in this context that we find the widespread dissemination of the *ḥadīth* on Qurʾān 9:31, particularly in its Prophetic version. It features as a central theme in the condemnations of *taqlīd* authored by two roughly contemporaneous scholars in the first half of the fifth/eleventh century, the Khurāsānian Shāfiʿī Abū Bakr al-Bayhaqī and the Andalusian Mālikī Yūsuf Ibn ʿAbd al-Barr, as well as in the writings of their contemporary, the Ẓāhirī Ibn Ḥazm (to whom I will return later).

Al-Bayhaqī (d. 458/1066) narrates a number of versions of the 9:31 exegesis in his *al-Madkhal ilā al-sunan al-kubrā* under the chapter title *Bāb tark al-ḥukm bi-taqlīd amthālihi min ahl al-ʿilm ḥattā yaʿlama mithla ʿilmihim* (roughly: "One Should Not Follow the Ruling of Other Scholars until One's Degree of Learning Is Comparable to Theirs"). This chapter has six components. (1) Citation of Qurʾān 17:36, "Follow not that of

[19] al-Ṭabarī, *Taʾrīkh*, vol. 3, p. 624; Hinds, *History*, vol. 23, p. 9: "by shedding blood or by deeming licit that which is not."

[20] See Patricia Crone and Martin Hinds, *God's Caliph: Religious Authority in the First Centuries of Islam*, Cambridge: Cambridge University Press, 1986, pp. 63–64. For reflections in the same vein on the meaning of *ḥudūd* in early Islam, cf. Gerald R. Hawting, "The Significance of the Slogan *lā ḥukma illā lillāh...*," *Bulletin of the School of Oriental and African Studies* 41 (1978), pp. 453–463.

which you have no knowledge (*ʿilm*)." (2) Narration of a statement from al-Shāfiʿī that knowledge (*ʿilm*) of the *sharīʿa* consists of two elements, adherence (*ittibāʿ*) and deduction (*istinbāṭ*). Adherence is adherence to the Qurʾān; if the answer is not found there then to the *sunna*; and if the answer is not found there then to the consensus of the *salaf*. If none of these provide an answer, then one must deduce the *sharīʿa* through *qiyās* (legal analogy) based on a precedent found in the Qurʾān, the *sunna*, or the consensus of the *salaf*, in that order. One may not deduce an opinion through other than *qiyās*, and if qualified interpreters of the *sharīʿa* differ in their deductions then each is required to follow his own *ijtihād*, and not to relinquish it in favor of the opinion of another. (3) Narration of the tradition in which the Prophet, when sending Muʿādh b. Jabal as his representative to Yemen, asks him on what basis he plans to judge if called upon to do so. The answer given by Muʿādh, and which the Prophet approves, is that he will judge by the Qurʾān, and then by the *sunna* of the Prophet, and failing that, he will conduct unflagging *ijtihād* (*ajtahidu raʾyī wa-lā ālū*). (4) Narration of a number of versions of the Qurʾān 9:31 exegesis. (5) Abū Yūsuf's admonition that "no one is permitted to say as we say until he knows on what basis we said it." (6) An aphorism related in the name of al-Shāfiʿī: "One who seeks knowledge (*ʿilm*) without [its] proof is like one who gathers wood by night, and carries a bundle of firewood in which, unbeknownst to him, lies a viper that will bite him."[21]

Likewise, in *al-Sunan al-kubrā* itself, al-Bayhaqī narrates the 9:31 exegesis in a chapter titled *Bāb mā yaqḍī bihi al-qāḍī wa-yuftī bihi al-muftī fa-innahu ghayr jāʾiz lahu an yuqallida aḥadan min ahli dahrihi wa-lā an yaḥkuma aw yuftiya bi-l-istiḥsān* ("The Basis on Which Qāḍīs and Muftīs should Rule, and the Impermissibility of Their Practicing *Taqlīd* of Their Contemporaries or of Ruling by *Istiḥsān*"[22]). This chapter consists mainly of traditions from the Prophet, Abū Bakr and ʿUmar, and other Companions that enjoin one to rule by the Qurʾān, then the *sunna*, and then *ijmāʿ*, and only in the absence of these to employ individual *ijtihād*. The final three traditions in the chapter turn to the topic of *taqlīd* and *istiḥsān*, as announced in the chapter title (though the

21 al-Bayhaqī, *al-Madkhal*, pp. 207–211.

22 *Istiḥsān* means roughly 'juristic preference.' In the usage of its dectractors it signifies a preference without any sound basis in textual sources or in analogy. Thus al-Shāfiʿī is reported to have said "the practitioner of *istiḥsān* legislates." Defenders of the practice argued that that it was a general term for a variety of acceptable procedures and did not mean unsupported personal preference. Aron Zysow, *The Economy of Certainty: An Introduction to the Typology of Islamic Legal Theory*, Atlanta: Lockwood, 2013, pp. 240ff.

latter topic is only broached implicitly). First we hear that ʿUmar scolded a secretary of his who wrote the phrase "what Allāh showed to the Commander of the Faithful ʿUmar" (*mā arā llāhu amīr al-muʾminīn ʿUmar*) and told him to write instead "what ʿUmar saw as right (*mā raʾā ʿUmar*), and if it is correct it is from Allāh, and if it is error then it is from ʿUmar." In other words, even the pious caliph ʿUmar was not gifted with divine inspiration, and his own opinions were merely human ones.[23] This is followed by a warning from Ibn Masʿūd not to practice *taqlīd* in religion (*a-lā lā yuqallidanna rajulun rajulan dīnahu*), since one can thereby fall into unbelief if the object of one's *taqlīd* has fallen into unbelief. Finally, al-Bayhaqī brings two versions of the 9:31 exegesis (ʿAdī b. Ḥātim and Ḥudhayfa). Al-Bayhaqī's point in adducing the exegesis is clearly to say that the practice of *taqlīd* is similar to the Jews' and Christians' taking of their religious authorities as "lords in place of Allāh."[24]

Notable is al-Bayhaqī's choice to place this entire chapter of the *Sunan* (unlike the parallel chapter in the *Madkhal*) in a political context. He does so by opening with al-Shāfiʿī's exegesis of Qurʾān 4:59, "[O you who believe, obey Allāh, obey the Prophet, and those in authority among you;] when you have a dispute over a matter, refer it to Allāh and to the Prophet, if you be believers in Allāh and the Last Day; that is best and most fitting in the end." Al-Shāfiʿī glosses "when you have a dispute" in the following manner: "that is – and Allāh knows best – they and their amīrs whom they were commanded to obey."[25] Al-Shāfiʿī's exegesis is presumably based on the common interpretation of "those in authority" (*ūlū al-amr*) as the amīrs (*umarāʾ*). In other words: Obey Allāh, the Prophet, and the political leaders, but obedience to the latter is subject to the constraints of the Qurʾān and the *sunna*. Likewise, al-Bayhaqī mentions the 9:31 exegesis in his *Shuʿab al-īmān* in a chapter that deals primarily with how one is to relate to iniquitous rulers, and here he chooses to cite a rather tame version (attributed to Ḥudhayfa), that the Jews' and Christians' "taking of lords" was obedience to the rabbis and priests in sin (*fī al-maʿāṣī*).[26] This framing of the theme, together with the adduction of al-Shāfiʿī's exegesis of Qurʾān 4:59 in the opening of the chapter in the *Sunan*, adds another dimension to the issue. Al-Bayhaqī was certainly warning against *taqlīd* in the pure jurisprudential sense – that is, acceptance of another scholar's opinion without proof – but he

[23] This is the normative view in classical Sunnī scholarship. On earlier traditions that considered ʿUmar as a legislator in his own right, see Avraham Hakim, "ʿUmar b. al-Ḫaṭṭāb: L'autorité religieuse et morale," *Arabica* 55/1 (2008), pp. 1–34.
[24] al-Bayhaqī, *al-Sunan al-kubrā*, vol. 10, pp. 113–116.
[25] al-Bayhaqī, *al-Sunan al-kubrā*, vol. 10, p. 113.
[26] al-Bayhaqī, *Shuʿab al-īmān*, Beirut: Dār al-Kutub al-ʿIlmiyya, 1421/2000, vol. 7, p. 45.

was also subtly warning the qāḍī and the muftī that they must adhere to the Qur'ān and the *sunna* rather than "taking as lords" the political leaders who had appointed them.

A more influential use of the 9:31 exegesis in condemnation of *taqlīd* was that of the Andalusian reformist Mālikī scholar Ibn ʿAbd al-Barr (d. 463/1071). In the chapter of his *Jāmiʿ bayān al-ʿilm wa-faḍlihi* on the topic of *taqlīd* – a chapter that served as a template for much later anti-*taqlīd* literature – Ibn ʿAbd al-Barr opens his argument by citing Qur'ān 9:31 and the ʿAdī b. Ḥātim *ḥadīth*. Thus our tradition serves as the centerpiece of a true *locus classicus* of anti-*taqlīd* polemic, and Ibn ʿAbd al-Barr likewise notes that this and other verses had already been employed by scholars before him in a similar manner ("*wa-qad iḥtajja al-ʿulamāʾ bi-hādhihi al-āyāt fī ibṭāl al-taqlīd*").

It should be noted, however, that Ibn ʿAbd al-Barr himself attempts to limit the tradition's implication of a *taqlīd*-as-polytheism equation in the following manner. After citing the tradition and other prooftexts of a similar nature, he writes:

> The *ʿulamāʾ* have adduced these verses as proof to invalidate *taqlīd*. The fact that those people [i.e. the people denounced in the Qur'ānic verses] were unbelievers did not prevent [the *ʿulamāʾ*] from adducing them [in condemnation of *taqlīd* of Muslim authorities], because the similarity does not lie in the one being an unbeliever and the other a believer, but rather the similarity lies in the fact that both are instances of *taqlīd* of someone without that person having presented proof. Thus one may practice *taqlīd* of someone and thereby commit unbelief, practice *taqlīd* of another and thereby commit sin, or practice *taqlīd* of still another in a lesser matter and thereby commit error. In this way each incurs blame for practicing *taqlīd* without proof, because all of this is *taqlīd*, each case being similar, even though the sins [in each case] differ.[27]

We learn from this passage that Ibn ʿAbd al-Barr is not truly condemning *taqlīd* per se as polytheism but is merely exploiting the association between the two in the sources as a polemical trope. In his view, *taqlīd* is blameworthy insofar as it constitutes an abdication of one's responsibility to independently verify the rulings of another, as thereby one forfeits any possibility of defense against adopting wrong judgment and practice.

### *Ibn Taymiyya and Ibn Qayyim al-Jawziyya*

Other scholars made more vigorous use of Qur'ān 9:31 and of ʿAdī b. Ḥātim. As an example we will now consider a fatwā by Ibn

[27] Ibn ʿAbd al-Barr, *Jāmiʿ*, vol. 2, p. 110.

Taymiyya on the question of *taqlīd* in which he associates the practice more clearly with polytheism.

The fatwā was written in response to a question "regarding an individual who learned *fiqh* according to one of the four legal schools and became well-versed in it, and afterwards occupied himself with *ḥadīth*, and saw sound *ḥadīth*s regarding which he did not know of anything that abrogated them, limited their application, or opposed them, and that [his] legal school contravened. Is he allowed to act in accordance with that legal school, or does he have to turn to action in accordance with the *ḥadīth*s, and to contravene his legal school?"

This question is the clearest kind of test case regarding the issue of *taqlīd* and *ijtihād*. Much of the academic literature on the topic focuses on the question of the technical ability or inability of later scholars to conduct independent assessments of the law (which was indeed an important component of the debate). Here, however, the question concerns a competent scholar who is fluent in his own school of law and realizes that it contravenes the *ḥadīth* in some matter. (It is worth noting that the questioner asks only whether he is *permitted* to continue to follow his legal school; it apparently did not occur to him to ask whether it might be obligatory.) This kind of test case is a clear echo of the dispute between the original *ahl al-ḥadīth* and the ancient schools; it is also where we are most likely to find the legislation-as-polytheism theme as an expression of the conflict between divine and human law.

Ibn Taymiyya's response begins with the following general outlines: It is known from the Qur'ān, the *sunna*, and the consensus that it is obligatory to obey Allāh and the Prophet, and that it is not obligatory to follow any specific person (*bi-ʿaynihi*) apart from the Prophet in all that he commands or forbids. All four eponyms of the legal schools forbade others to practice categorical *taqlīd* of them. One who is incapable of knowing proofs is exempt from the obligation of *ijtihād*, but everyone must learn as much of these proofs as they are able. As for one who is capable of deriving proofs (*istidlāl*), Ibn Taymiyya notes that some scholars absolutely forbid him *taqlīd* whereas others give him blanket permission. Ibn Taymiyya's own preferred view is that he is allowed to practice *taqlīd* in case of need (*ḥāja*) – for example, if he is pressed for time. *Ijtihād* is divisible, that is, in order to engage in *ijtihād* on a given question one does not have to be expert in all fields, but only in the field relevant to the question at hand; this presumably further reduces the scope of permissible *taqlīd*.

Now Ibn Taymiyya comes to the specific question of the *mustaftī*. He supposes something that was not explicit in the question, namely, that the view supported by the *ḥadīth* was already adopted by one of the other eponyms – presumably based on his assumption that the questioner has some competence in jurisprudence but is not a fully independent *mujtahid*. He rules that in this case, the scholar described in the question should follow the view that is supported by the *ḥadīth* and that was adopted by the other eponym, rather than the view of his own legal school.

Ibn Taymiyya then addresses three hypothetical objections. The first argues that indeed someone fully capable of *ijtihād* would have to adopt this course, but the *ijtihād* of the person in question is lacking, and there might be other arguments of which he is unaware, and which would outweigh the prooftext. Ibn Taymiyya's response is that one is only required to investigate to the extent of one's ability, and if after having done so in this question the weight of evidence appears to support the view of the other school, then one should adopt that view. If afterwards it becomes clear to him that the truth is elsewhere, he should again change views, and this is praiseworthy, whereas remaining with a view that appears contrary to the evidence, or changing views arbitrarily, is blameworthy.

The second hypothetical objection that Ibn Taymiyya alludes to is the argument that if the eponym knew the *ḥadīth*, or even related it himself, and then ruled against it, he must have had a reason for doing so even if we do not know what that reason was. Ibn Taymiyya answers that the eponyms are to be forgiven for those occasions on which they overruled a *ḥadīth*, but these excuses are not valid for someone who knows the truth in the matter. For example, one who sincerely believes that "the practice of one of the cities" (viz. Mālik b. Anas regarding the practice of Medina) takes precedence over a *ḥadīth* is excused for believing so, but one to whom it is clear that a sound *ḥadīth* takes precedence over (Medinan) practice cannot be excused for failing to adopt it. In this passage Ibn Taymiyya refers to an earlier work in which he had expounded this principle, *Rafʿ al-malām ʿan al-aʾimma al-aʿlām*. The ostensible aim of this work was to refute the idea that any of the eponyms should be blamed for intentionally ruling against the *ḥadīth*, based on the principle that a *mujtahid* who errs is still rewarded for his efforts. On closer examination, however, the treatise appears to severely limit the scope for *taqlīd* of a legal school, since Ibn Taymiyya makes clear that he views *uṣūl* such as adherence to Medinan practice as erroneous, and he views the exculpatory consideration (*ʿudhr*) as applying to the eponyms themselves but not necessarily to those who follow their views.[28]

[28] Ibn Taymiyya, *Rafʿ al-malām ʿan al-aʾimma al-aʿlām*, Riyadh: al-Riʾāsa al-ʿĀmma li-Idārāt al-Buḥūth al-ʿIlmiyya wa-l-Iftāʾ wa-l-Daʿwa wa-l-Irshād, 1413[/1992] (= Ibn Taymiyya, *Majmūʿat al-fatāwā*, vol. 20, pp. 129–162); see e.g. pp. 33–37 (= *Majmūʿat al-fatāwā*, vol. 20, pp. 138–139).

The third hypothetical objector says to the questioner: "Are you more knowledgeable, or Imām So-and-so?" Ibn Taymiyya parries this objection by saying that the eponym in question was opposed on this issue by others who were more or less his equal, and alludes to Qurʾān 4:59: "O you who believe, obey Allāh and obey the Prophet and those in authority among you, and if you have a dispute in a matter refer it to Allāh and to the Prophet if you be believers in Allāh and the Last Day; that is best and most fitting in the end." In other words, since the matter is disputed among the eponyms (or other early authorities), one ought to refer it back to the Qurʾān and the *sunna*.

It is in the follow-up to this third objection that Ibn Taymiyya directly broaches the conflict between the authority of revelation and adherence to merely human opinion. First he mentions someone who disputed Ibn ʿAbbās' transmission from the Prophet permitting *mutʿa*, which in this case refers not to temporary marriage but to the practice of exiting *iḥrām* (ritual purity) between the *ʿumra* rites and the *ḥajj*.[29] This interlocutor says to Ibn ʿAbbās: "Abū Bakr and ʿUmar said [such and such prohibiting the practice]," to which Ibn ʿAbbās replies: "You are close to having a rock fall on you from the sky! I say: 'The Prophet (Allāh's blessing and peace be upon him) said,' and you say: 'Abū Bakr and ʿUmar said'?" Likewise, Ibn ʿUmar argues in this same matter: "Does the command of the Prophet (Allāh's blessing and peace be upon him) have more right to be followed, or the command of ʿUmar?" In other words, the *ḥadīth* trumps the merely human views of Abū Bakr and ʿUmar, notwithstanding the fact that among the non-prophets involved in this debate Abū Bakr and ʿUmar were of higher status than Ibn ʿAbbās and Ibn ʿUmar.

Finally, Ibn Taymiyya caps off his fatwā with the following:

> If this gate [viz. the gate of *taqlīd*] were opened, then it would be obligatory to turn away from the command of Allāh and the Prophet. The status of each imām among his followers would be like that of the Prophet (Allāh's blessing and peace be upon him) among his *umma*. This is a switching (*tabdīl*) of religion similar to that for which Allāh blamed the Christians: "They took their rabbis and priests as lords in place of Allāh, and likewise Jesus son of Maryam, though they were

[29] *Mutʿa* (or *tamattuʿ*) in this meaning appears to have been a classic test-case for the primacy of Prophetic tradition over the views of Companions: Al-Shāfiʿī already mentioned it as an example of Medinese preference for the decisions of ʿUmar over traditions from the Prophet. See Schacht, *Origins of Muhammadan Jurisprudence*, p. 25. Likewise, Ibn ʿAbd al-Barr (though himself ostensibly a Mālikī) mentions the same issue in a chapter on the primacy of Prophetic *sunna* over the views of the *ʿulamāʾ*: *Jāmiʿ*, vol. 2, pp. 195–196; cf. Ibn Ḥazm, *al-Iḥkām fī uṣūl al-aḥkām*, Cairo: Dār al-Ḥadīth, 1404/1984, vol. 6, pp. 247, 249. For the issue in general, see Arthur Gribetz, *Strange Bedfellows:* Mutʿat al-nisāʾ *and* Mutʿat al-ḥajj*: A Study Based on Sunnī and Shīʿī Sources of* Tafsīr, Ḥadīth, *and* Fiqh, Berlin: Klaus Schwarz, 1994.

commanded to worship one God alone, and there is no god but He; gloried be He above what they associate (with Him)."[30]

Thus unlike Ibn ʿAbd al-Barr, Ibn Taymiyya does not view *taqlīd* as merely opening the door to substantive error. It is the relation itself that a *muqallid* adopts toward his imām that constitutes a "taking of lords in place of Allāh," and which is tantamount to replacing Islam with some other religion. And while Ibn Taymiyya's fatwā relates to the issue of jurisprudential *taqlīd*, he – like al-Bayhaqī before him – subtly relates it as well to the question of obedience in a political context. The very first tradition cited in the fatwā, used to bolster the assertion that no one apart from Allāh and the Prophet is owed total obedience, is Abū Bakr's statement as caliph: "Obey me insofar as I obey Allāh, and if I sin against Allāh then obedience to me is not incumbent upon you."[31]

Much more than Ibn Taymiyya himself, it was his student Ibn Qayyim al-Jawziyya who polemicized extensively against *taqlīd*, and he is (along with Ibn ʿAbd al-Barr) one of the scholars cited most frequently by later authors on the topic.[32] The main book in which Ibn al-Qayyim dealt with these issues was his somewhat unusual work on legal matters, *Iʿlām al-muwaqqiʿīn ʿan rabb al-ʿālamīn*. Particularly influential was the long passage in which Ibn al-Qayyim conducts a hypothetical debate between a *muqallid* and a "*ṣāḥib ḥujja*,"[33] which is closely preceded by his citation of Ibn ʿAbd al-Barr's chapter on *taqlīd*, including Qurʾān 9:31 and the exegetical tradition.[34] Again we see anti-*taqlīd* polemic framed as an assertion of the exclusive priority of Allāh's law over that of humans.

### *Revivalist Anti-*taqlīd *Polemic: Eighteenth to Twentieth Centuries*

I will now turn to an examination of anti-*taqlīd* polemic among fundamentalist revivalist movements and thinkers, from the Arabian Wahhābīs to the Indian Ahl-i Ḥadīth. The intervening period was one in which opinion in favor of *taqlīd* had clearly strengthened, and while proponents

[30] Ibn Taymiyya, *Majmūʿat al-fatāwā*, vol. 20, pp. 117–120.
[31] Ibn Taymiyya, *Majmūʿat al-fatāwā*, vol. 20, p. 117.
[32] For a partial English translation of Ibn al-Qayyim's writings on this topic and a discussion of their influence on the Indian Ahl-i Ḥadīth, see Abdul-Rahman Mustafa, *On Taqlīd: Ibn al Qayyim's Critique of Authority in Islamic Law*, New York: Oxford University Press, 2013.
[33] That is, one capable of presenting proofs: Ibn Qayyim al-Jawziyya, *Iʿlām al-muwaqqiʿīn ʿan rabb al-ʿālamīn*, 2nd ed., Beirut: Dār al-Kutub al-ʿIlmiyya, 1414/1993, vol. 2, pp. 140ff.
[34] Ibn Qayyim al-Jawziyya, *Iʿlām*, vol. 2, pp. 131ff.

of *ijtihād* were not lacking[35] I am unaware of any major new contributions to the anti-*taqlīd* polemic prior to the eighteenth century.

The association between *taqlīd* and *shirk* comes through clearly in Muḥammad b. ʿAbd al-Wahhāb's *Kitāb al-tawḥīd*. Unlike the other works surveyed here the topic of this work was not at all jurisprudential methodology: *Kitāb al-tawḥīd* is a work of theology devoted to expounding *tawḥīd* – in particular *tawḥīd al-ulūhiyya*, as we saw in Chapter 2 – and warning against various forms of *shirk*. For this reason, the very inclusion of a chapter in condemnation of *taqlīd* within the work already frames the issue in terms of *shirk* and *tawḥīd*. It is only natural that the ʿAdī b. Ḥātim *ḥadīth* is one of the prooftexts cited in this brief chapter,[36] and in fact is alluded to in its title, which reads: "One Who Obeys the Scholars (*ʿUlamāʾ*) and the Amīrs (*Umarāʾ*) in Forbidding What Allāh Has Permitted or in Permitting What Allāh Has Forbidden Has Taken Them as Lords in Place of Allāh."[37] Also noteworthy in this *tabwīb* is the mention of *umarāʾ* – political leaders – though nothing in the chapter itself clarifies what kind of political polytheism Ibn ʿAbd al-Wahhāb had in mind.[38]

The chapter in *Kitāb al-tawḥīd* is skeletal in nature but Ibn ʿAbd al-Wahhāb's indebtedness to the line of anti-*taqlīd* polemic we have surveyed is evident from his other writings as well. We find a similar use of Qurʾān 9:31 and its exegesis in an undated epistle he addressed to one of his former teachers, the Shāfiʿī qāḍī ʿAbdallāh b. Muḥammad b. ʿAbd al-Laṭīf from the al-Aḥsāʾ region of the Arabian Peninsula.[39] This epistle[40] was written in response to criticism of Ibn ʿAbd al-Wahhāb to which his erstwhile teacher was apparently party – a fact that seems to have pained Ibn ʿAbd al-Wahhāb considerably since in the past the two had enjoyed good relations. In particular he mentions favorably marginalia that ʿAbdallāh b. Muḥammad had written on al-Bukhārī in which

35 See Hallaq, "Gate," pp. 27ff.

36 Ibn ʿAbd al-Wahhāb's use of the ʿAdī b. Ḥātim tradition was already noted in Peskes, *Widerstreit*, pp. 33ff., 37ff.

37 ʿAbd al-Raḥmān b. Ḥasan, *Fatḥ al-majīd*, pp. 553–554.

38 Ibn ʿAbd al-Wahhāb's grandson ʿAbd al-Raḥmān b. Ḥasan writes that the *tabwīb* alludes to Qurʾān 33:67, in which the unbelievers roasting in hellfire say: "we were but obeying our chiefs and our dignitaries (*sādatanā wa-kubarāʾanā*) and they led us astray." Be that as it may, this does not do much to explain Ibn ʿAbd al-Wahhāb's inclusion of political authorities as targets in a polemic traditionally addressed against religious authorities. ʿAbd al-Raḥmān b. Ḥasan, *Qurrat ʿuyūn al-muwaḥḥidīn*, Riyadh: Maktabat al-Rushd, n.d., p. 186.

39 Ibn ʿAbd al-Wahhāb studied with him in al-Aḥsāʾ after leaving Basra. See ʿAbdallāh b. ʿAbd al-Raḥmān b. Ṣāliḥ Āl Bassām, *ʿUlamāʾ najd khilāla thamāniyat qurūn*, 2nd ed., Riyadh: Dār al-ʿĀṣima, 1419[/1998], vol. 1, pp. 133–134.

40 *Durar*, vol. 1, pp. 35–55.

he endorsed the latter's view on the nature of faith in opposition to that of the Ashʿarī school.[41]

The precise nature of the criticism to which Ibn ʿAbd al-Wahhāb was responding is not specified in the text. There is mention of the sixteenth-century Shāfiʿī Ibn Ḥajar al-Haytamī, a scholar who had penned well-known condemnations of Ibn Taymiyya and Ibn Qayyim al-Jawziyya,[42] but Ibn ʿAbd al-Wahhāb does not appear to be answering these critiques. At a later point the epistle does address some theological issues that were in dispute between Ibn Taymiyya and al-Haytamī, such as Allāh's attributes,[43] but the main portion of the epistle deals instead with *taqlīd* and it is solely in this context that al-Haytamī is mentioned in his role as a legal authority who was an object of *taqlīd* for later Shāfiʿīs.

For example, after Ibn ʿAbd al-Wahhāb argues that one must follow the views of other eponyms against al-Shāfiʿī if the *ḥadīth* supports their view, he adds: "That was an argument according to your premise, but it is known that in reality the one you follow is Ibn Ḥajar [i.e. and not al-Shāfiʿī], and you do not pay any heed to those who contravened him – whether prophet, Companion, Successor, or even al-Shāfiʿī himself."[44] Likewise, after Ibn ʿAbd al-Wahhāb asserts that most later scholars contravened the path of the *salaf*, he adds that the best of the later scholars, "such as Ibn al-Qayyim, the *ḥāfiẓ* al-Dhahabī, the *ḥāfiẓ* al-ʿImād Ibn Kathīr, and the *ḥāfiẓ* Ibn Rajab, harshly condemned the [scholars] of their times, who were, by consensus, better than [the later] Ibn Ḥajar and the author of the *Iqnāʿ*."[45] "The *Iqnāʿ*" is a reference to al-Ḥajjāwī's manual of Ḥanbalī *fiqh*, which Ibn ʿAbd al-Wahhāb subsequently asserts is "mostly contrary to the *madhhab* (legal school) and *naṣṣ* (texts) of Aḥmad [b. Ḥanbal himself]."[46] Then, in reference to Ibn Ḥajar al-Haytamī's work of Shāfiʿī *fiqh Tuḥfat al-muḥtāj*, he asks: "Is the obligation incumbent on every Muslim to seek knowledge of what Allāh revealed to His Prophet ... or is it incumbent on him to follow, for example, the *Tuḥfa*?"[47]

Ibn ʿAbd al-Wahhāb's argument against his critics in this epistle is thus centered on the theme that one must follow the views of the Qurʾān and

41 *Wa-akhrajta lī karārīs min al-Bukhārī katabtahā wa-naqalta ʿalā hawāmishihā min al-shurūḥ wa-qulta fī masʾalat al-īmān allatī dhakara al-Bukhārī fī awwal al-ṣaḥīḥ hādhā huwa al-ḥaqq alladhī adīnu llāha bihi fa-aʿjabanī hādhā al-kalām li-annahu khilāf madhhab aʾimmatikum al-mutakallimīn*. *Durar*, vol. 1, p. 36.

42 See Khaled El-Rouayheb, "From Ibn Ḥajar al-Haytamī (d. 1566) to Khayr al-Dīn al-Ālūsī (d. 1899): Changing Views of Ibn Taymiyya among non-Ḥanbalī Sunni Scholars," in Rapoport and Ahmed (eds.), *Ibn Taymiyya and His Times*, pp. 269–318, esp. pp. 271–275; Lav, "Ashʿarism," pp. 274–276.

43 *Durar*, vol. 1, p. 50. 44 *Durar*, vol. 1, p. 44. 45 *Durar*, vol. 1, p. 38.

46 *Durar*, vol. 1, p. 45 (already cited supra, Chapter 2). 47 *Durar*, vol. 1, p. 39.

the *sunna* as understood by the *salaf* rather than adhering to the views of the later scholars. Ibn ʿAbd al-Wahhab cites a number of *ḥadīth*s that foretell that Muslims will follow in the path of the Jews and Christians and the *sunan* of those that came before them, and argues that latter-day Muslims, just like the scriptuaries condemened in Qurʾān 2:79, "have written a book with their own hands and said 'this is from Allāh,' and abandoned the Book of Allāh and its implementation."[48] When he summarizes the heart of the question as being whether one must follow the revealed texts or works like al-Haytamī's *Tuḥfa*, he argues that "the most knowledgeable among the later scholars, such as Ibn al-Qayyim" vociferously condemned *taqlīd* as an alteration of Allāh's religion (*taghyīr li-dīni llāh*). Ibn ʿAbd al-Wahhāb then writes that the proponents of *taqlīd* are precisely analogous to the Jews and Christians as described in Qurʾān 9:31 and the ʿAdī b. Ḥātim *ḥadīth* – i.e. that obedience to their scholars is tantamount to taking them as lords. He does not enter into detailed argumentation against *taqlīd*, but simply refers ʿAbdallāh b. Muḥammad to Ibn al-Qayyim's *Iʿlām al-muwaqqiʿīn* – which was apparently not well known in the region, since Ibn ʿAbd al-Wahhāb takes the trouble to tell him precisely where in al-Aḥsāʾ it may be found.[49]

As noted in Chapter 2 it is atypical for Ibn ʿAbd al-Wahhāb to engage with the *fiqh* debate to this extent, as he most frequently addressed the *taqlīd* issue in an incidental manner as it arose in connection with his principal focus on ritual monolatry. Toward the end of the epistle Ibn ʿAbd al-Wahhāb does chastise ʿAbdallāh for his failure to condemn "idol worship" in his region,[50] but the bulk of the epistle is devoted to *taqlīd* in the properly jurisprudential sense. In summary, Ibn ʿAbd al-Wahhāb was concerned with the *taqlīd*/*ijtihād* debate, but *pace* much of the secondary literature it was not one of his central focuses. When he did join the debate his argumentation adhered to the classic lines of salafī anti-*taqlīd* polemic, which served to link his condemnation of *taqlīd* to his emphasis on *tawḥīd al-ulūhiyya* as another front in the battle against *shirk*.[51]

We likewise find the ʿAdī b. Ḥātim *ḥadīth* cited in relation to *taqlīd* in the writings of another major figure in eighteenth-century Islamic revivalism, Ibn ʿAbd al-Wahhāb's Indian contemporary Shāh

[48] *Durar*, vol. 1, pp. 38–39. [49] *Durar*, vol. 1, pp. 39–40.
[50] *Durar*, vol. 1, pp. pp. 53–54.
[51] The better-known Wahhābī anti-*taqlīd* polemic is Ibn Muʿammar (ʿUmar b. Nāṣir b. ʿUthmān), *Risālat al-ijtihād wa-l-taqlīd*, in Muḥammad Rashīd Riḍā (ed.), *Majmūʿat al-rasāʾil wa-l-masāʾil al-najdiyya*, Egypt: Maṭbaʿat al-Manār, 1344[/1925], vol. 2. This treatise is heavily reliant on Ibn Taymiyya and Ibn Qayyim al-Jawziyya, and cites at length the same fatwā by the former discussed earlier in this chapter, including the concluding portion that applies Qurʾān 9:31 to the issue of *taqlīd* (pp. 11–14).

Walī Allāh (d. 1176/1762). In his *'Iqd al-jīd fī aḥkām al-ijtihād wa-l-taqlīd*, Walī Allāh writes:

Regarding an unlearned individual (*'āmmī*) who practices *taqlīd* toward one of the jurisprudents in particular (*bi-'aynihi*), believing that someone like him cannot err and that what he says is absolutely correct, and saying in his heart that he will not abandon *taqlīd* of him even if the proof goes against him – that is what al-Tirmidhī related from 'Adī b. Ḥātim: "I heard the Prophet of Allāh reading 'they have taken their rabbis and priests as lords in place of Allāh,' and then he said: 'They did not worship them, but they held to be permitted whatever they permitted to them, and forbade whatever they forbade them.'"[52]

Walī Allāh was no anti-*taqlīd* radical,[53] but we see that regarding this extreme case – obedience to an imām *bi-'aynihi* – he is no less willing than others to characterize *taqlīd* as *shirk*. Likewise, in his enumeration of forms of *shirk* in *Ḥujjat Allāh al-bāligha*, Walī Allāh cites verse 9:31 and the 'Adī b. Ḥātim tradition, and then explains why this obedience to the rabbis and priests is *shirk*: It is because *shirk* is to ascribe Allāh's attributes to humans, and the authority to permit and forbid is one of Allāh's attributes.[54]

Starting in the late eighteenth/early nineteenth century a number of scholars began to engage in more radical and categorical anti-*taqlīd* polemic. Place of pride in this development belongs to the Yemeni scholar Muḥammad al-Shawkānī (d. 1834), and in particular to his tract *al-Qawl al-mufīd fī adillat al-ijtihād wa-l-taqlīd*.[55]

Al-Shawkānī describes his initial turn against *taqlīd* as stemming from his own independent inclination, at the very outset of his studies,[56] but his mature works reveal a clear debt to the earlier polemicists we have surveyed. What is unique in al-Shawkānī is the intensity of his condemnation of *taqlīd* and the degree of explicitness with which he spells out the equation of *taqlīd* with polytheism (*shirk*). For example, we find the following statement in his *Adab al-ṭalab wa-muntahā al-arab*:

No one ... should claim that the servitude that Allāh commanded His subjects does not apply to him (*laysa li-wāḥidin ... an yadda'iya annahu ghayr muta'abbid bi-mā ta'abbada Allāh bihi 'ibādahu*) or that he stands outside of legal obligation (*taklīf*) or

[52] Shāh Walī Allāh Aḥmad b. 'Abd al-Raḥīm al-Fārūqī al-Dihlawī, *'Iqd al-jīd fī aḥkām al-ijtihād wa-l-taqlīd*, Sharjah: Dār al-Fatḥ, 1415/1995, pp. 45–46; and identical language in his *Ḥujjat Allāh al-bāligha*, Beirut: Dār al-Jīl, 1426/2005, vol. 1, p. 265.

[53] Cf. al-Dihlawī, *'Iqd al-Jīd*, p. 40, and *Ḥujjat Allāh al-bāligha*, vol. 1, p. 263.

[54] al-Dihlawī, *Ḥujjat Allāh al-bāligha*, vol. 1, p. 121; on the general principle that attribution of Allāh's attributes to humans is *shirk*: p. 119.

[55] Here I will only address al-Shawkānī's writings in relation to the *taqlīd*-as-polytheism theme; for a broader analysis of al-Shawkānī's views on *ijtihād* and *taqlīd* and of his activities in their historical context, see Haykel, *Revival and Reform*, pp. 76–108.

[56] Muḥammad b. 'Alī al-Shawkānī, *Adab al-ṭalab wa-muntahā al-arab*, Ṣan'ā': Maktabat al-Irshād, 1419/1998, pp. 88–89.

that he is not judged by the laws of the *shar*ʿ and that what Allāh demanded from the rest of people is not demanded of him. All the more so should no one [claim] to rise to the level of legislation (*tashrī*ʿ), the fixing of *sharʿī* laws, and obliging the servants of Allāh, glorified be He, to follow his own opinion (*raʾy*) that he promulgates.

This is a matter that is for Allāh alone, glorified be He, and not for anyone aside from Him among humans, whoever they may be – except for that which He entrusted to the prophets … And even the prophets themselves are subject to the servitude that Allāh commanded them, legally obligated to what Allāh imposed on them, and they need to fulfill what Allāh demanded of them … Their message is restricted to what Allāh the Exalted commanded them to transmit, and they do not legislate to His servants other than what He commanded them to pass on. They have nothing to do with this apart from mere transmission from Allāh and mediation between Him and His servants in what He legislated for them and subjected them to in servitude …

So what then regarding servants of Allāh apart from them, those who are not prophets and whom Allāh did not make free from error, such as the Companions, the Successors, and those that followed them, such as the imāms of the legal schools and other bearers of knowledge? One who claims that any of these can innovate in Allāh's *shar*ʿ what was not in it, or that he can impose a form of worship (*taʿabbud*) on the servants of Allāh that is outside of what is found in the *shar*ʿ – that individual has grossly calumniated Allāh, has put words in the mouth of Allāh the Exalted that He did not say … This is a rank that is only for Allāh, a grade not achieved by anyone but Him, and no one but Him [may] claim it. One who claims it for someone other than Him, whether explicitly or implicitly (*taṣrīḥan aw talwīḥan*), has entered himself into one of the gates of polytheism (*shirk*).[57]

In this passage (in contrast with Ibn ʿAbd al-Barr's view) it is the very act of taking someone as an authority apart from Allāh that is considered *shirk*. We still find some caution in that al-Shawkānī, somewhat like Walī Allāh before him, seems to condition this *shirk* not on the sole act of *taqlīd*, but rather on the beliefs that motivate it. It is not specified precisely what kind of speech (or action?) would be required to qualify as implicit ("*talwīḥan*") attribution of legislative authority to humans, but it appears to be something beyond simple *taqlīd*. This we know from a later passage in the same work, in which al-Shawkānī writes that unlike those who practice popular religion (grave visitation, etc.), the earlier practitioners of *taqlīd*, while blameworthy, still "did not confuse the meaning of *lā ilāha illā llāh*, did not play around with *tawḥīd*, and did not enter into the gates of polytheism, the straits of denial (*juḥūd*),[58] and the tribulations of the *jāhiliyya* and its beliefs."[59]

[57] al-Shawkānī, *Adab al-ṭalab*, pp. 84–85.
[58] *Juḥūd* (also *jaḥd*) means rejection or denial; as a technical term, it means the kind of rejection or denial of faith, or a tenet thereof, that is tantamount to apostasy.
[59] al-Shawkānī, *Adab al-ṭalab*, p. 204.

*Adab al-ṭalab* is primarily hortatory in nature; the basis for these views was set out at greater length in al-Shawkānī's *al-Qawl al-mufīd*, in which we also encounter his use of Qurʾān 9:31 and the ʿAdī b. Ḥātim exegesis. The first mention occurs when al-Shawkānī differentiates between a *mujtahid* who was unable to reach a conclusion on a certain issue and for this reason practiced *taqlīd*, and someone who practices *taqlīd* of another on every issue without asking for proofs from the Qurʾān and the *sunna*. Al-Shawkānī writes that this latter practice is precisely what the Qurʾān described as "taking rabbis and priests as lords" (*fa-innā hādhā huwa ʿayn ittikhādh al-aḥbār wa-l-ruhbān arbāban*).[60]

The primary use of this prooftext in *al-Qawl al-mufīd* occurs midway through the tract. Al-Shawkānī compares the Sunnī practitioners of *taqlīd* unfavorably with the early Hādawī Zaydīs, in that the former imposed on themselves *taqlīd* of one [authority] in particular (*taqlīd al-muʿayyan*) and claimed that the gate of *ijtihād* closed after the development of the schools.[61] Al-Shawkānī terms this view "the wellspring of illicit innovations" (*umm al-bidaʿ*) and writes: "as though this *sharīʿa* that is among us from the Qurʾān and the Prophet's *sunna* has been abrogated, with the abrogator being the *taqlīd* that they innovated in Allāh's religion." Al-Shawkānī writes that the practitioners of *taqlīd* do not explicitly state this "infidel statement and *jāhilī* saying," but deceptively turn instead to the ostensibly more palatable statement that "the gate of *ijtihād* is closed." But al-Shawkānī writes that this too is a calumny against Allāh –

> as though what He legislated for them in His book and on the tongue of His Prophet (Allāh's blessing and peace be upon him) is not an absolute law, but only a restricted and temporary law [in force] until an end point, that is, the establishment of these schools, and after their appearance there is no more Qurʾān and no *sunna*, and someone arose to legislate for this nation a new *sharīʿa* and to innovate for them a new religion.

It is in this context that al-Shawkānī cites our verse, Qurʾān 9:31.[62] He clearly means to say thereby that just as the Jews and Christians strayed from Allāh's revelation by "taking their rabbis and priests as lords in place of Allāh," so too the practitioners of *taqlīd* did the same by taking the eponyms of the law schools as lords in place of Allāh.

60 Muḥammad b. ʿAlī al-Shawkānī, *al-Rasāʾil al-salafiyya fī iḥyāʾ sunnat khayr al-bariyya*, 2nd ed., Beirut: Dār al-Kitāb al-ʿArabī, 1414/1994, p. 196.

61 al-Shawkānī, *al-Rasāʾil*, p. 221. The Hādawīs are the Yemeni Zaydī Shīʿī sect founded by the imām al-Hādī ilā al-Ḥaqq Yaḥyā b. al-Ḥusayn (d. 298/911). On al-Shawkānī's conflicts with the Hādawīs, see Haykel, *Revival and Reform*, pp. 139–184.

62 al-Shawkānī, *al-Rasāʾil*, pp. 222–223.

Al-Shawkānī then turns his attention to the later Hādawī Zaydīs (that is, his Yemeni contemporaries), writing that unlike their predecessors, they outstripped the Sunnī practitioners of *taqlīd* in their fierce condemnation of opponents of *taqlīd*, since they perceived such opposition to be a derogation of the status of ʿAlī b. Abī Ṭālib. Al-Shawkānī does not mince words: He calls these people "*taqlīd*-practicing devils" (*shayāṭīn al-muqallida, abālīs al-muqallida*), "a terminal disease," and a "fatal poison." In reference to these Zaydīs al-Shawkānī cites a few versions of the exegetical tradition on Qurʾān 9:31 from al-Bayhaqī and Ibn ʿAbd al-Barr.[63] He then cites a few additional Qurʾānic verses in which the unbelievers use *taqlīd* as an excuse for their unbelief; al-Shawkānī writes explicitly that although these verses were revealed regarding the *kuffār* they apply as well to the *muqallidūn*, since the cause for which the verse condemned the *kuffār* is present in the latter as well (*li-ittiḥād al-ʿilla*).[64]

Al-Shawkānī's more trenchant style of anti-*taqlīd* polemic was characteristic as well of the Indian Ahl-i Ḥadīth, a salafī movement that emerged in South Asia in the nineteenth century. The first major anti-*taqlīd* tract of the Indian Ahl-i Ḥadīth proper – as opposed to those Indian scholars they viewed as their predecessors, such as Walī Allāh and Shāh Ismāʿīl (d. 1831) – was the Urdu-language *Miʿyār al-ḥaqq*, authored by one of the movement's founders, Nadhīr Ḥusayn Dihlawī (d. 1902). The circumstances of its writing underline the continuity between the Ahl-i Ḥadīth and their intellectual forebears in India.

*Miʿyār al-ḥaqq* was written in refutation of a treatise titled *Tanwīr al-ḥaqq* and in defense of the book criticized by this latter work, Shāh Ismāʿīl Shahīd's *Tanwīr al-ʿaynayn fī ithbāt rafʿ al-yadayn.*[65] After an initial chapter devoted to the proper status to be accorded to Abū Ḥanīfa the treatise turns to a general discussion of *taqlīd*. The portion of interest to us here is Nadhīr Ḥusayn's division of the kinds of *taqlīd* practiced by a nonexpert (*lā-ʿilmī*) into four categories: obligatory (*wājib*), permitted (*mubāḥ*), forbidden and heterodox innovation (*ḥarām o bidʿat*), and polytheism (*shirk*).[66] Nadhīr Ḥusayn gives the following example for this

[63] al-Shawkānī, *al-Rasāʾil*, pp. 223–225. [64] al-Shawkānī, *al-Rasāʾil*, pp. 225–226.

[65] Nadhīr Ḥusayn Dihlawī, *Miʿyār al-ḥaqq fī tanqīd tanwīr al-ḥaqq*, Lahore/Faisalabad, Maktabah-yi Islāmiyya, 2007, pp. 25–28. The author writes that while the Urdu treatise *Tanwīr al-ḥaqq* was circulated under the name of the scholar Muḥammad Quṭb al-Dīn, it was in fact based on materials collected in Arabic by Nadhīr Ḥusayn's own former student, Muḥammad Shāh Punjābī, whom he accuses of having split off (*iʿtazala*) from him in the same manner that Wāṣil b. ʿAṭāʾ, the early Muʿtazilī, split off from Ḥasan al-Baṣrī.

[66] Nadhīr Ḥusayn, *Miʿyār al-ḥaqq*, pp. 80–81. This division applies only to the nonexpert; the author holds that *taqlīd* is never permissible for an *ʿālim*: see pp. 73–74 (the chapter titled "*ʿĀlim ke liʾē taqlīd jāʾiz nahīṉ*").

fourth category: A nonexpert *muqallid* follows the ruling of a *mujtahid*, and then, after learning of a sound *ḥadīth* that contradicts the ruling, and which is not abrogated and not opposed by another *ḥadīth*, he without good reason says that the *ḥadīth* is not to be accepted or that it should be interpreted in accordance with the ruling of the imām.[67]

The section that follows, in which Nadhīr Ḥusayn elaborates on this polytheistic kind of *taqlīd*, is centered entirely on Qurʾān 9:31 and the ʿAdī b. Ḥātim *ḥadīth*. He first cites a passage on this verse which connects it directly to the issue of *taqlīd*; Ḥusayn cites it from al-Ḥasan b. Muḥammad al-Nīsābūrī's *tafsīr*, *Gharāʾib al-qurʾān wa-raghāʾib al-furqān*, but al-Nīsābūrī's entire passage is in fact taken from *Mafātīḥ al-ghayb* by Fakhr al-Dīn al-Rāzī. In this passage al-Rāzī writes that most of the Qurʾānic exegetes explained that "taking them as lords" meant that they "obeyed them in their commands and prohibitions," and then cites the ʿAdī b. Ḥātim tradition. After citing another tradition of similar import, al-Rāzī writes:

> Our shaykh and master (*mawlā*), the seal of the true scholars and the *mujtahidūn*, may Allāh be pleased with him,[68] said: "I saw a group of those who practice *taqlīd* of the jurisprudents. I read out to them many Qurʾānic verses on some issues in which their legal school contradicted these verses. They did not accept these verses and did not pay them heed. They remained looking at me like someone who is astonished, as though to say: 'How can one act on the plain meaning of these verses when the transmission from our forerunners is contrary to them?' If you were to consider this with the attention it deserves you would see that this malady flows in the veins of most people in the world."

Al-Rāzī then explains why the obedience to the rabbis and priests described in the verse is *kufr* and not just sin (*fisq*): "The sinner, though he accepts Satan's call, does not venerate him, but rather curses him and belittles him, whereas [the Jews and Christians] accepted the opinion (*qawl*) of the rabbis and priests and venerated them – that is the difference."[69]

Nadhīr Ḥusayn then moves on to cite statements by a number of Indian scholars on this issue. After adducing the passage from Shāh

[67] Nadhīr Ḥusayn, *Miʿyār al-ḥaqq*, p. 81.

[68] It is not entirely clear to whom this refers. The salafī jihādī author ʿUmar ʿAbd al-Raḥmān (formerly the chief religious authority for the Egyptian al-Jamāʿa al-Islāmiyya), in his discussion of this passage in his doctoral thesis from al-Azhar, is uncertain whether the scholar meant is al-Rāzī's father, ʿUmar Ḍiyāʾ al-Dīn, or whether it is al-Baghawī. ʿUmar ʿAbd al-Raḥmān, *Mawqif al-qurʾān min khuṣūmihi*, Cairo: Dār Miṣr al-Maḥrūsa, 2006, p. 312, n. 28.

[69] Fakhr al-Dīn al-Rāzī, *Tafsīr al-Fakhr al-Rāzī al-mushtahir bi-l-tafsīr al-kabīr wa-mafātīḥ al-ghayb*, Beirut: Dār al-Fikr, 1401/1981, vol. 16, pp. 38–39; al-Ḥasan b. Muḥammad al-Qummī al-Nīsābūrī, *Tafsīr gharāʾib al-qurʾān wa-raghāʾib al-furqān*, Beirut: Dār al-Kutub al-ʿIlmiyya, 1416/1996, vol. 3, p. 457; Nadhīr Ḥusayn, *Miʿyār al-ḥaqq*, p. 82.

Walī Allāh that we have already examined, he cites the *tafsīr* written by Walī Allāh's son Shāh ʿAbd al-ʿAzīz on Qurʾān 2:22 ("and do not knowingly make for Allāh partners"). ʿAbd al-ʿAzīz writes that in the same way that worship (*ʿibādat*) of not-Allāh is *shirk* and *kufr*, so absolute *taqlīd* of another in a ruling that is in clear contravention of Allāh's law is *kufr*, just as Allāh related regarding the rabbis and priests in Qurʾān 9:31.[70]

The next passage cited is from the tract *Tanwīr al-ʿaynayn fī ithbāt rafʿ al-yadayn* by Walī Allāh's grandson (and ʿAbd al-ʿAzīz's nephew), Shāh Ismāʿīl – the tract in defense of which Nadhīr Ḥusayn wrote *Miʿyār al-ḥaqq* in the first place. The context of the passage cited is a polemic against what Shāh Ismāʿīl characterizes as the "terminal disease" of exaggeration in *taqlīd*,[71] by which he means adherence to Ḥanafī rulings in the face of clear evidence from the *ḥadīth* that proves them incorrect. The first portion of Shāh Ismāʿīl's treatise had dealt with the textual evidence in favor of raising one's hands before and after prostration in prayer. The salience of this issue, which was to become a clear marker of the divide between the Ahl-i Ḥadīth and Ḥanafīs in the Indian subcontinent, lay in the fact that the Ḥanafī practice of not raising one's hands at these points in prayer is based on *ḥadīth* that are generally classified as weak, whereas other *ḥadīth* classified as sound support the practice. The question thus proved an exemplary litmus test for the issue of the permissibility of *taqlīd* of one's school in the face of contrary textual evidence.

After his survey of the evidence from the *ḥadīth* Shāh Ismāʿīl moves on to meta-objections raised by Ḥanafīs to the practice of raising one's hands. They apparently did not object to adherents of other schools following this practice but argued that a Ḥanafī may not do so. The reasoning is as follows: The individual who reached the conclusion in favor of raising one's hands must be either a *mujtahid* or a *muqallid*. If he claims to be a *mujtahid*, he is lying, because such people in these days are "rarer than red sulphur" (*aʿazz min al-kibrīt al-aḥmar*). And if he is a *muqallid*, then he is not allowed to stray from the teachings of his school on this question.[72] Shāh Ismāʿīl answers with the following arguments: First, the *mujtahid* who is "rarer than red sulphur" is the *mujtahid muṭlaq* (i.e. one who does not affiliate with any of the four schools of law), but there is nothing wrong with (for example) a Ḥanafī exercising *ijtihād* on a particular issue and concluding that the view of another school is the correct one, as indeed many prominent Ḥanafīs have done in the

70 Nadhīr Ḥusayn, *Miʿyār al-ḥaqq*, p. 84.

71 Mawlānā Ḥājjī Muḥammad Ismāʿīl, *Tanwīr al-ʿaynayn fī ithbāt rafʿ al-yadayn*, n.p.: Maṭbaʿ Raḥmānī, 1256/[1840–1841], p. 99.

72 Ismāʿīl, *Tanwīr al-ʿaynayn*, pp. 91ff.

past.[73] It is in response to the exaggerators in *taqlīd*,[74] those who argue that adherence to the Ḥanafī school prohibits such *ijtihād*, that Shāh Ismāʿīl writes the passage cited by Nadhīr Ḥusayn, which reads as follows:

Would that I knew (*layta shiʿrī*)! How can it be permitted to adhere to *taqlīd* of one individual in particular (*muʿayyan*) in a case where it is possible to refer to explicit transmissions from the Prophet, Allāh's blessing and peace be upon him, which indicate the opposite of the opinion of the imām who is the object of *taqlīd*? If an individual does not abandon the opinion of his imām [in such a case] then there is some measure of polytheism in him (*fīhi shāʾiba min al-shirk*), as indicated by the *ḥadīth* related by al-Tirmidhī from ʿAdī b. Ḥātim.[75]

After citing the ʿAdī b. Ḥātim *ḥadīth*, Shāh Ismāʿīl then argues that it is not a blanket condemnation of *taqlīd*, since were it so then every non-expert (*ʿāmmī*) would be obligated to perform *ijtihād*; but he likewise writes that it does not refer to the extreme case of explicit rejection of texts that contradict the opinion of one's imām. He avers rather that the *ḥadīth* applies to one who (falsely) interprets away evidence so as to make it accord with the opinion of one's imām (*taʾwīl al-dalāʾil al-sharʿiyya ilā qawl aʾimmatihim*), and thus we learn that one who does so with regard to evidence from the Qurʾān and the *sunna* is tainted with "Christianity" and has a portion in polytheism (*shawb min al-naṣrāniyya wa-ḥaẓẓ min al-shirk*). Shāh Ismāʿīl then notes his amazement that instead of fearing this *shirk* into which they have fallen, those who are overly zealous toward their school attempt to prevent others from escaping this polytheism.[76]

The final source cited by Nadhīr Ḥusayn in this section is the Qurʾānic exegesis authored by Qāḍī Thanāʾ Allāh Pānīpattī (d. 1810), who was influenced by Walī Allāh and possibly studied with him directly.[77] In his commentary on Qurʾān 3:64 Pānīpattī cites our verse and the ʿAdī b. Ḥātim tradition, and adds:

From here it is clear that if someone learns of a sound *ḥadīth* that goes back to the Prophet, without there being a contrary *ḥadīth* or one that abrogates it, and if there is a fatwā for example from Abū Ḥanīfa, may Allāh's mercy be upon him, that contravenes it, and if one of the four eponyms has ruled in accordance with this *ḥadīth*, then it is incumbent on this person to follow the established *ḥadīth*. And let not his petrifaction (*jumūd*) in his legal school keep him from this, otherwise he falls under [Qurʾān 3:64] "taking some among us as lords in place of Allāh."[78]

[73] Ismāʿīl, *Tanwīr al-ʿaynayn*, pp. 93ff. [74] Ismāʿīl, *Tanwīr al-ʿaynayn*, pp. 99ff.
[75] Ismāʿīl, *Tanwīr al-ʿaynayn*, p. 110.
[76] Ismāʿīl, *Tanwīr al-ʿaynayn*, pp. 112–114; Nadhīr Ḥusayn, *Miʿyār al-ḥaqq*, pp. 84–85.
[77] See Martin Riexinger, *Sanāʾullāh Amritsarī (1868-1948) und die Ahl-i-Ḥadīs im Punjab unter britischer Herrschaft*, Würzburg: Ergon, 2004, p. 83. Riexinger already noted the fact that Pānīpattī is cited here by Nadhīr Ḥusayn (p. 83, n. 98).
[78] Nadhīr Ḥusayn, *Miʿyār al-ḥaqq*, p. 86.

Finally, we find Qur'ān 9:31 and the 'Adī b. Ḥātim tradition in the anti-*taqlīd* polemics of a subsequent Indian Ahl-i Ḥadīth scholar, Muḥammad Ṣiddīq Ḥasan Khān. After citing the passage from Fakhr al-Dīn al-Rāzī's *tafsīr*, he copies (without attribution) the following comments by al-Shawkānī on the verse:

In this verse is [a matter] that cries out to anyone with a heart or who has [ears] to listen. It is a prooftext regarding *taqlīd* in Allāh's religion and preference for the words of predecessors (*aslāf*) over what is found in the precious Qur'ān and the pure *sunna*. For the obedience of the adherent of a legal school to a scholar of this nation whose view he imitates and whose *sunna* he follows, despite this scholar's contravention of the content of the texts, what Allāh's proofs and demonstrations uphold, and what His [revealed] books and prophets spoke – this is like the Jews' and Christians' taking of their rabbis and priests as lords in place of Allāh. This is because it was stated definitively that [the Jews and Christians] did not worship them, but rather obeyed them, forbade what they forbade and permitted what they permitted, and this is the deed committed by the practitioners of *taqlīd* in this nation. Their deed is more similar to [that of the Jews and Christians] than is the similarity between two eggs, two dates, or as water to water.

O servants of Allāh, O followers of [the Prophet] Muḥammad b. 'Abdallāh! What are you thinking? You have put the Qur'ān and the *sunna* aside and turned to men – men whom, like yourselves, Allāh has subjected to the Qur'ān and the *sunna*, and from whom He has demanded action in accordance with what they indicate. You have acted in accordance with their opinions, which were not established on the basis of truth and which had no support in the religion. The texts of the Qur'ān and the *sunna* call out in the most eloquent voice and exclaim as loud as can be the opposite view, yet you lend them deaf ears, hardened hearts, diseased understanding, broken intellects, weak minds, and ailing thoughts. It is as though you recited [the verse]:

I am but from the Ghaziyya tribe – if it errs / I err, and if it takes the right course, so do I.[79]

May Allāh guide you and me: Replace books that your dead predecessors wrote for you with the Book of Allāh, who created them and you, to whom they and you are subjected, the one they and you worship; and replace the sayings of those you call your imāms and the *ra'y* that they brought you with the sayings of your imām and theirs, your role model and theirs, the original imām, Muḥammad b. 'Abdallāh, may Allāh's blessing and peace be upon him.[80]

[79] This verse by the poet Durayd b. al-Ṣimma is often cited as exemplary of the *jāhilī* ethos of tribal solidarity. It is used here to imply that the blind allegiance of practitioners of *taqlīd* to their legal schools is akin to that of the *jāhiliyya* Arabs to their tribes. The poem is in Ḥabīb b. Aws Abū Tamām, *Diwan al-ḥamasa*, Beirut: Dar al-Qalam, n.d., vol. 1, p. 337; on the poem in the tribal context, see Reynold A. Nicholson, *A Literary History of the Arabs*, New York: Scribner, 1907, p. 83. I owe thanks to my colleague Iyas Nasser for sharing with me his knowledge of this verse.

[80] Ṣiddīq b. Ḥasan al-Qannawjī, *Fatḥ al-bayān fī maqāṣid al-qur'ān*, Sidon and Beirut: al-Maktaba al-'Aṣriyya, 1416/1996, vol. 5, pp. 284ff.; and likewise in Ṣiddīq b. Ḥasan al-Qannawjī, *al-Dīn al-khāliṣ*, Beirut: Dār al-Kutub al-'Ilmiyya, 1415/1995, vol. 4,

## The Nature of the *Ijtihād/Taqlīd* Dispute

All the preceding suggests that the central issue in premodern condemnation of *taqlīd* was the opposition between merely human opinion and divinely revealed law. The theoretical supremacy of the latter was of course universally acknowledged, but the authors surveyed felt that the spread of *taqlīd* had in practice led to the enthronement of *raʾy* and obedience to human law – that is, the "taking of lords in place of Allāh." It is this condemnation of *taqlīd*, based largely on Qurʾān 9:31 and its exegetical *ḥadīth*, that served as a precedent for the condemnation of parliamentary legislation as polytheistic in modern theonomic doctrine. The transition is natural enough, as the scholarly tradition described in this chapter already applied the central theme of exclusivity of worship to the legal sphere and erected a sharp opposition between divine and human law.

Before leaving the premodern polemic, however, we ought to pause to rectify some misconceptions that have been introduced into academic literature on *taqlīd* and *ijtihād* in recent decades. Those familiar with Wael Hallaq's influential article "Was the Gate of Ijtihad Closed?" will likely have noticed already that our characterization of the pro- and anti-*taqlīd* factions is nearly diametrically opposed to his. The premodern anti-*taqlīd* polemics provided a powerful precedent for modern salafīs precisely because, *pace* Hallaq, they were of a 'salafī' nature and served to connect between typically salafī theological and jurisprudential concerns. This point will thus require some further clarification before proceeding.

Hallaq wrote his article in order to contest the claim of Joseph Schacht and others that a consensus had been reached circa 300 AH (or later in the opinion of some) that the "gate of *ijtihād*" had been closed and *taqlīd* universally recognized as an obligation. Hallaq argues that this view is "entirely baseless and inaccurate" and that *ijtihād* was so central a tenet that "all groups and individuals who opposed it were finally excluded from Sunnism." He acknowledges that the matter was a subject of controversy but argues that the very fact of the controversy demonstrates that *ijtihād* always had its proponents, thus precluding the formation of any consensus requiring *taqlīd*.[81]

pp. 81ff.; Muḥammad b. ʿAlī b. Muḥammad al-Shawkānī, *Fatḥ al-qadīr al-jāmiʿ bayna fannay al-riwāya wa-l-dirāya min ʿilm al-tafsīr*, Beirut: Dār al-Maʿrifa, 1428/2007, pp. 567–568.

[81] Hallaq, "Gate," p. 4. I should note here that my critique will focus on this one article by Hallaq in particular, which was unusually influential and thus deserves separate treatment. Hallaq's later writings emphasize a more positive role for *taqlīd* in the formation of mature Islamic jurisprudence and stable judicial institutions. See Wael

Schacht's depiction was certainly too categorical and stood in need of correction. Despite the polemical tone of his article, however, Hallaq does not go far enough in his attempt at rectification and in fact concedes some of the basic outlines of Schacht's depiction. This is evident from his characterization of the procedure of *ijtihād*, which he describes as follows: It is the use of *qiyās* (juristic analogy) regarding an unprecedented case, to be employed only after failure to find a judgment "in the works of renowned jurists." Even then, the *mujtahid* is to turn to the primary sources only in the absence of any similar case that could serve as precedent.[82] This is not substantially different from Schacht's characterization of the "closing of the door of *ijtihād*" (cited at the outset of Hallaq's article) as the doctrine that "all future activity would have to be confined to the explanation, application, and, at the most, interpretation of the doctrine as it had been laid down once and for all."[83] Hallaq too, in essence, claims that *taqlīd* was mandated wherever possible; his *mujtahid* would depart from this prescription only in new cases for which no precedent whatsoever presented itself.

The anti-*taqlīd* literature we have surveyed here, however, shows that the scope of the polemic was by no means limited to the issue of new and unprecedented cases. (It is also not clear how one could practice *taqlīd* at all in a truly unprecedented case.) This has been clear throughout the writings I have surveyed. Ibn Taymiyya's fatwā, for example, addresses an apparent conflict between revealed texts and human opinion and mandates departure from the view of one's own legal school, even on ostensibly long-settled questions, when this is what the revealed texts demand.[84]

Equally problematic is Hallaq's mischaracterization of the school affiliations of the pro- and anti-*taqlīd* camps, which derives from his conception of the nature of the issue on the whole. Nearly every reconstruction of the origins of Islamic jurisprudence, whether traditional Muslim or academic-critical, describes an early tension between two camps, the *ahl al-ra'y* and the *ahl al-ḥadīth*, with the former consisting of jurists who tended to capacious use of *qiyās* and creative jurisprudence – or, put less

B. Hallaq, *Authority, Continuity and Change in Islamic Law*, Cambridge: Cambridge University Press, 2004, esp. pp. 86–120 (and for a mention and defense of "Gate": p. 56, n. 143). This less judgmental and more analytical attitude toward *taqlīd* has been a general feature of recent literature; see e.g. Mohammad Fadel, "The Social Logic of *Taqlīd* and The Rise of the *Mukhtaṣar*," *Islamic Law and Society* 3/2 (1996), pp. 193–233.

82 Hallaq, "Gate," p. 4. 83 Hallaq, "Gate," p. 3.

84 Hallaq does discuss the issue of *mujtahid*s who are classified as *muṭlaq* or *mustaqill*, but his emphasis throughout is on "the potential and ability of the legal system to provide solutions to all newly arising problems"; "Gate," pp. 18–19; see likewise p. 11: "although the activity of deriving solutions for new problems continued indefinitely."

favorably, casuistry – whereas the latter consisted of scholars who emphasized strict adherence to Prophetic traditions – or, put less favorably, narrow-minded literalism. Hallaq unreservedly assigns the pro-*ijtihād* position to the *ahl al-ra'y* and describes the opponents of *ijtihād* and proponents of *taqlīd* in the third to fifth centuries AH as coming from the ranks of the *ahl al-ḥadīth*. This description is clearly founded on Hallaq's identification of *ijtihād* with *qiyās* ("a principle that constituted the backbone of ijtihad").[85] According to Hallaq, the moderates among the Ḥanbalīs and *ahl al-ḥadīth* - those willing to coexist with the *ahl al-ra'y* "who employed qiyas" – came to temper their pro-*taqlīd* positions, whereas extremists, such as Dāwūd al-Ẓāhirī, rejected *qiyās* and were thus eventually written out of Sunnism.[86]

Hallaq does recognize that in later times it was the Ḥanbalīs and a faction of Shāfiʿīs who occupied the pro-*ijtihād* position, as against the Ḥanafīs, Mālikīs, and other Shāfiʿīs,[87] and (in apparent contradiction with his prior characterization) he likewise notes that the Ḥanbalī Ibn ʿAqīl cited Ibn Ḥanbal's opposition to *taqlīd*.[88] Likewise, most if not all of the anti-*taqlīd* authors Hallaq mentions for the eighteenth to nineteenth centuries – including Ibn ʿAbd al-Wahhāb and al-Shawkānī – clearly belong to the *ahl al-ḥadīth* camp. Yet nowhere in his article does Hallaq offer an explanation for these developments, which, in his scheme of things, would have to be considered a major realignment. As it happens, this was no realignment at all, but rather a perpetuation of the original pattern. A number of precisions will show Hallaq's characterization of the original positions of the various camps to be erroneous.

First, there is no positive correlation between rejection of *qiyās* and support of *taqlīd* – in fact there is a negative correlation between the two. Hallaq rightly notes that Dāwūd b. ʿAlī's treatise against *qiyās* generated significant opposition, but he gives short thrift to Dāwūd's parallel condemnation of *taqlīd*, noting only that "Dawud disapproved of taqlid and

85 Hallaq, "Gate," p. 7.

86 Hallaq, "Gate," p. 8. Hallaq writes further on that "in order to survive within Sunnism, Hanbalism had to go through a process of moderation and change from an extreme theological group to a peculiarly moderate law school" (p. 10). This is an issue that deserves serious consideration and a parsing of different tendencies within Ḥanbalism, and his characterization may well hold for many in the school. As for Ibn Taymiyya, Al-Matroudi's comparison of Aḥmad b. Ḥanbal's and Ibn Taymiyya's principles of jurisprudence led him to conclude that the principles of the two scholars "were, to a considerable degree, identical." Abdul Hakim I. Al-Matroudi, *The Ḥanbalī School of Law and Ibn Taymiyyah: Conflict or Conciliation*, London and New York: Routledge, 2006, p. 48. More to the point, however, we have seen that it was precisely their "extreme theology" (and not moderation of the same) that led many Ḥanbalīs and other like-minded scholars to oppose *taqlīd*.

87 Hallaq, "Gate," p. 22.

88 Hallaq, "Gate," p. 17.

claimed that one need not follow a human authority if he can use the legal sources." He likewise does not explain how such an attitude could fit his characterization of the relation between the two issues. Dāwūd did not just disapprove of *taqlīd*, but wrote an independent treatise in condemnation of it,[89] just as he wrote against *qiyās*. Nor was his stance anomalous among the Ẓāhirīs. Hallaq fails to mention that Ibn Ḥazm, for example, was one of the fiercest anti-*taqlīd* polemicists in the history of Muslim jurisprudence. It is worth examining in some detail Ibn Ḥazm's polemics on this matter in his *al-Iḥkām fī uṣūl al-aḥkām*, as they attest to the ferocity of anti-*taqlīd* sentiment precisely among the anti-*qiyās* faction of jurisprudents. Both positions, opposition to *taqlīd* and opposition to *qiyās*, stemmed from the same zealous concern for fidelity to the texts of revelation.

The targets of Ibn Ḥazm's anti-*taqlīd* polemic are predominantly Ḥanafīs and Mālikīs, and to a slightly lesser extent Shāfiʿīs as well. The absence of Ḥanbalīs from the list is telling and indicates that Ibn Ḥazm did not generally consider them to be proponents of *taqlīd*. An independent chapter is devoted to refuting "Those Who Say That No One May Opt [for a Different Legal Opinion] after Abū Ḥanīfa." The chapter title notwithstanding, Ibn Ḥazm's argument is directed against Mālikī *taqlīd* as well, whereas Ibn Ḥanbal, al-Shāfiʿī, Isḥāq b. Rāwayhi, Dāwūd b. ʿAlī, and others are mentioned as examples of scholars who postdated Abū Ḥanīfa and Mālik but whose views were more correct due to their knowledge of and adherence to traditions.[90]

The chapter "*Fī ibṭāl al-taqlīd*" is mostly devoted to refuting specific arguments in favor of *taqlīd*; these were presumably put forth by Ḥanafīs, Mālikīs, and Shāfiʿīs, since it is these schools that are repeatedly condemned in Ibn Ḥazm's refutations. The first argument-refutation pair is a typical example: In response to the claim that Ibn Masʿūd practiced *taqlīd* of ʿUmar b. al-Khaṭṭāb, thus validating the practice, Ibn Ḥazm first argues that the claim itself is not true, and then adds:

> It is truly astounding that they prove their position through the lie that Ibn Masʿūd used to practice *taqlīd* of ʿUmar, when they [themselves] are not in favor of *taqlīd* of all the views of ʿUmar, nor of Ibn Masʿūd, but rather practice *taqlīd* of people whom Ibn Masʿūd did not [practice *taqlīd* of], people whom Ibn Masʿūd never saw, such as Abū Ḥanīfa, Mālik, and al-Shāfiʿī![91]

This same grouping of Ḥanafīs, Mālikīs, and Shāfiʿīs as practitioners and proponents of *taqlīd* recurs constantly in this chapter[92] and those

[89] Ignaz Goldziher (trans. Wolfgang Behn), *The Ẓāhirīs*, Leiden: Brill, 2008, pp. 30–31.
[90] Ibn Ḥazm, *al-Iḥkām*, vol. 4, pp. 604–609.
[91] Ibn Ḥazm, *al-Iḥkām*, vol. 6, pp. 228–229.
[92] Ibn Ḥazm, *al-Iḥkām*, vol. 6, pp. 233, 235, 236, 237, 243, 250, 252, 255, 270.

following it, titled "*Mā qālahu Allāh ta'ālā fī ibṭāl al-taqlīd*"[93] and "*Fī su'āl al-ruwāt 'an aqwāl al-'ulamā'*";[94] the subsequent chapter, titled "*Hal yajūzu taqlīd ahl al-madīna,*" is naturally directed primarily against the Mālikīs, though even here we find a mention of the same tripartite grouping.[95] In contrast, *taqlīd* of dyed-in-the-wool *ahl al-ḥadīth* scholars such as Aḥmad b. Ḥanbal or Dāwūd b. 'Alī is only mentioned very occasionally in passing.[96] Likewise, the ultimate theological basis for Ibn Ḥazm's condemnation of *taqlīd* was identical to that found in the Ḥanbalīs, conservative Shāfi'īs, and the later fundamentalist and revivalist literature, as evinced for example by his numerous citations of the 9:31 exegesis in condemnation of *taqlīd.*[97]

Thus I cannot concur with Hallaq's statement that

> throughout the third, fourth, and fifth Islamic centuries, ijtihad, the only channel of legal development, was rejected by various elements. Among these were extreme legal and theopolitical groups (or sects) that called for taqlid or condemned the principle of qiyas – a principle that constituted the backbone of ijtihad. These groups came mainly from the lines of the 'people of hadith,' or Traditionalists, who were primarily concerned with the study of transmitted sources and their literal interpretation, while denying human reason any right to be exercised in ijtihad or in the process of legal reasoning.[98]

Ibn Ḥazm certainly fits the bill with regard to literalism, but this simply does not equate to support for *taqlīd* and rejection of *ijtihād.* If one's concern is for creative legal development then it is fair to characterize the Traditionalists as generally opposed, but textual literalism is not the same as *taqlīd* of earlier legal authorities, and *qiyās* "constituted the backbone of ijtihad" only for those of the *ahl al-ra'y* who construed it so.[99]

As for textual literalism and *taqlīd,* Ibn Ḥazm clearly distinguishes between adherence to the texts of revelation (the Qur'ān and the *ḥadīth*), on the one hand, and adherence to the views of post-Prophetic

93 Ibn Ḥazm, *al-Iḥkām,* vol. 6, pp. 281, 282, 283, 291, 294.

94 Ibn Ḥazm, *al-Iḥkām,* vol. 6, pp. 295, 305. This and the two previous footnotes list only those places where the three schools (and only they) are mentioned together. Numerous other passages attack one or two among the three; likewise, a very few passages mention them together with practitioners of *taqlīd* of other figures, on which see below.

95 Ibn Ḥazm, *al-Iḥkām,* vol. 6, p. 314. The argument presented in this passage is that Mālik, Abū Ḥanīfa, and al-Shāfi'ī themselves did not practice *taqlīd* of anyone, nor did they permit others to practice *taqlīd* of them or of other scholars. This is also true of Ibn Ḥanbal, and thus the omission of him from the list indicates that Ibn Ḥazm felt that only Mālikīs, Ḥanafīs, and Shāfi'īs (but not Ḥanbalīs) needed to be reprimanded on this score.

96 Ibn Ḥazm, *al-Iḥkām,* vol. 6, pp. 272–273, 297.

97 Ibn Ḥazm, *al-Iḥkām,* vol. 6, pp. 283, 290–291, 293, 317–318.

98 Hallaq, "Gate," pp. 7–8.

99 As noted above, these points were already raised in Melchert, *Sunni Schools,* pp. 16–18.

authorities, on the other. For example, he explains this central distinction between *taqlīd* and "*ittibāʿ*" – the latter designating proper adherence to the revealed texts – in response to an argument advanced by some proponents of *taqlīd*. The proponents had adduced the Qurʾān's description (4:125) of those who are best in religion as those who "follow (*wa-ittabaʿa*) the religion of Ibrāhīm" as textual support for the practice of *taqlīd*. Ibn Ḥazm responds:

> This is impudence itself! Because something that Allāh commands is not *taqlīd*, but is rather an evidence of necessary validity (*burhān ḍarūrī*). *Taqlīd* is rather the following of someone whom Allāh did not command us to follow (*bi-ittibāʿihi*).
>
> The *taqlīd* that is contested between us is the acceptance of the opinion of an individual other than the Prophet, someone whom our Lord did not command us to follow (*bi-ittibāʿihi*), without any [textual] proof (*dalīl*) that would validate his opinion as correct, solely on the basis of "so-and-so said." It is this that is null and void.

Ibn Ḥazm goes on to write that the proponents of this sort of *taqlīd*, not finding any true support for their position, apply the label of *taqlīd* to valid practices such as adherence to traditions (specifically: *khabar al-wāḥid*)[100] or to *ijmāʿ* (consensus) – presumably so as to validate their own practice of blameworthy *taqlīd* under the same appellation.[101]

Likewise, we find this passage further on:

> Some have confused matters and called adherence to what the Prophet said and to what the scholars of the Islamic nation have agreed upon "*taqlīd*." This is the practice of the sophists and those who seek to obscure and corrupt knowledge, to invalidate truths, and to sow confusion ... But know this: Acceptance of sound transmission from the Prophet, what the text and literal meaning of the Qurʾān mandates, and the consensus of the Islamic nation is not *taqlīd*, and no one is allowed to call this *taqlīd* ... because *taqlīd*, in truth, is solely the acceptance of what someone other than the Prophet said without proof.[102]

Thus for Ibn Ḥazm there is certainly no connection between textual literalism and *taqlīd*; association between the two is rather described as a dishonest strategy designed to validate practice of the latter.

It could be argued that Ibn Ḥazm, being a Ẓāhirī and thus outside of the Sunnī mainstream, need not be taken into consideration on this score. In fact, however, his conceptualization of the issue is very much

[100] The *khabar al-wāḥid* ("unit-report") is any transmission of *ḥadīth* that falls short of the conditions for *tawātur*, that is, concurrent transmission of a kind that excludes any possibility of collusion. The precise status of unit-reports is a matter of controversy; Ibn Ḥazm defended them as yielding certain knowledge. See Zysow, *Economy of Certainty*, pp. 8, 32.

[101] Ibn Ḥazm, *al-Iḥkām*, vol. 6, p. 234.

[102] Ibn Ḥazm, *al-Iḥkām*, vol. 6, pp. 268–269.

in line with that of many Sunnī scholars (including some cited by Hallaq as representatives of pro-*ijtihād* views) such as Ibn ʿAbd al-Barr, Ibn Qayyim al-Jawziyya, and, for a later period, Muḥammad al-Shawkānī.[103]

Ibn ʿAbd al-Barr writes: "Abū ʿAbdallāh b. Khuwayz Mandād al-Baṣrī al-Mālikī[104] said:

> The legal meaning of *taqlīd* is recourse to the opinion of one who provides no proof for it. This is forbidden in the *sharīʿa*. And *ittibāʿ* is [recourse to] that for which there is sound proof … When you follow the opinion of someone whose opinion is not incumbent on you by force of a [textual] proof (*dalīl*), you are practicing *taqlīd* of that individual, and *taqlīd* in Allāh's religion is not correct. And one whose opinion you must follow due to a [textual] proof, you are practicing *ittibāʿ* of that individual. *Ittibāʿ* is permitted in religion, and *taqlīd* is forbidden.[105]

Ibn Qayyim al-Jawziyya likewise copies this same passage (by way of Ibn ʿAbd al-Barr) in his *Iʿlām al-muwaqqiʿīn*.[106]

As for al-Shawkānī, the distinction between adherence to transmitted textual evidence (*riwāya*) and adherence to human opinion (*raʾy*) is one of the central themes in *al-Qawl al-mufīd*. For example, al-Shawkānī writes:

> acceptance of transmitted textual evidence (*riwāya*) is not *taqlīd*, for acceptance of *riwāya* is acceptance of proof, whereas *taqlīd* is just the acceptance of opinion (*raʾy*). There is a difference between acceptance of *riwāya* and acceptance of *raʾy*, for acceptance of *riwāya* has nothing whatsoever to do with *taqlīd*; in fact, it is the opposite of the mark (*rasm*) of one who practices *taqlīd*.[107]

This gets at the very heart of the issue: For al-Shawkānī at least, "textual literalism" is not *taqlīd*, but its very negation.

Al-Shawkānī continues, in a vein reminiscent of Ibn Ḥazm, by accusing proponents of *taqlīd* of intentional distortion in this matter: "Remember this well, for the permitters of *taqlīd* frequently seek to confuse the issue. They say, for example, that the *mujtahid* is [in fact] practicing *taqlīd* of the one who related the *sunna* to him." Other matters to which the term *taqlīd* has been wrongly applied, according to al-Shawkānī, include acceptance of a woman's testimony regarding her own ritual purity, the testimony of the *muʾadhdhin* that the time for prayer has arrived, a blind man's acceptance of guidance as to the direction of prayer, and so forth.[108] Al-Shawkānī argues that all of these

103 Hallaq, "Gate," pp. 12 (mention of Ibn ʿAbd al-Barr), 32–33 (mention of al-Shawkānī).

104 On this figure, see Miklos Muranyi, "Aus dem *Kitāb Aḥkām al-Qurʾān* des Mālikiten Ibn Ḫawāz Mandād," *Der Islam* 91/2 (2014), pp. 360–373.

105 Ibn ʿAbd al-Barr, *Jāmiʿ*, vol. 2, p. 117.

106 Ibn Qayyim al-Jawziyya, *Iʿlām*, vol. 2, p. 137.

107 al-Shawkānī, *al-Rasāʾil*, p. 204.

108 Cf. Ibn Ḥazm, *al-Iḥkām*, vol. 6, p. 234, on the time and direction of prayer as false examples of *taqlīd*; cf. vol. 6, p. 256, for another example in a similar vein.

cases are acceptance of *riwāya*, that is, of the transmission of a proof (*dalīl*); they are not the acceptance of another's opinion (*ra'y*), and thus are not *taqlīd*. Al-Shawkānī concludes: "The difference between *riwāya* and *ra'y* is clearer than the sun. One who is confused as to the difference between them should not occupy himself in fields of knowledge, for he has the understanding of a beast, though he be in the skin of a human." He then follows with the same quotation from Abū ʿAbdallāh b. Khuwayz on *taqlīd* and *ittibāʿ* cited by Ibn ʿAbd al-Barr and Ibn Qayyim al-Jawziyya.[109] There could be no clearer rejection of the equation between textual literalism and *taqlīd*: Textual literalism is adherence to proof, and *taqlīd* is adherence to human opinion without proof.

Hallaq's association of *ijtihād* and *qiyās* is likewise problematic, though not to the same degree. In contrast with anti-*taqlīd* polemic, which was truly characteristic of the *ahl al-ḥadīth* tendency,[110] promotion of *ijtihād* was a wider phenomenon and each school defined it in accordance with its own legal principles (*uṣūl*). For Ibn Ḥazm it indeed had nothing to do with *qiyās*, but for others there was a robust connection between the two, and one can find scholars and schools falling all along the spectrum between these two poles.

Ibn Ḥazm defines *ijtihād* as follows: "The facets of *ijtihād* are limited to those whose proofs I have explained: the Qur'ān and a tradition with a sound chain of transmission composed of reliable transmitters reaching back to the Prophet. These may either relate explicitly to the matter, or provide a proof (*dalīl*) from the text that is unambiguous." Any other manner of *ijtihād* is unacceptable in Ibn Ḥazm's view,[111] and, as with *taqlīd*, he argues that others have completely distorted the meaning of the term by applying it to other jurisprudential methodologies.[112] One might question what scope is left in such a schema for *ijtihād*: Ibn Ḥazm himself states that, in principle, for every question there necessarily exists a text that provides the answer,[113] which would seem to preclude any scope for

[109] al-Shawkānī, *al-Rasāʾil*, pp. 204–205.

[110] In a later work Hallaq asserts that writings in condemnation of *taqlīd* "were common to all times and to all legal schools" (*Authority*, p. 87). This is perhaps technically true, but only because the fault line between the salafī tendency and more traditional jurisprudence often ran through the schools rather than between them: Ibn ʿAbd al-Barr was not a typical eleventh-century Mālikī and Ibn ʿAbd al-Wahhāb was not a typical eighteenth-century Ḥanbalī. Hallaq's observation that such condemnations are less typical of the Ḥanafī school (*Authority*, p. 87, n. 4) is accurate and bears out this contention, as the Ḥanafīs were the most closely identified with the *ahl al-ra'y*. In addition, it probably would be fruitful to distinguish between the kind of salafī *shirk*-themed polemic surveyed in this chapter and milder forms of disapprobation of *taqlīd*, which were more widespread.

[111] Ibn Ḥazm, *al-Iḥkām*, vol. 8, p. 589. [112] Ibn Ḥazm, *al-Iḥkām*, vol. 5, pp. 161ff.

[113] Ibn Ḥazm, *al-Iḥkām*, vol. 8, p. 597 inter alia.

inquiry. However, he recognizes that in practice it is not always easy to identify the relevant text, authenticate the tradition, understand which text limits the application of the other, and so forth.

Ibn Ḥazm's conception of *ijtihād* differs considerably from the one we find, for example, in the writings of Abū Bakr al-Bayhaqī and other Shāfiʿīs. The difference could be summed up in the question of whether or not there exist cases for which no clear textual answer exists, with Ibn Ḥazm denying this possibility and the Shāfiʿīs affirming it. As we saw in al-Bayhaqī's writings on *taqlīd* and *ijtihād*, those Shāfiʿīs who remained close to the *ahl al-ḥadīth* ardently maintained the primacy of textual evidence over *raʾy*, but they did promote a *qiyās*-based *ijtihād* where no direct textual evidence was to be found.[114]

Emblematic of this parting of ways with the Ẓāhirīs are the two schools' contrasting approaches to the Muʿādh b. Jabal tradition. In this tradition, the Prophet, before sending Muʿādh to Yemen, asks him how he will judge. Muʿādh answers that first he will seek an answer in the Qurʾān, and failing that, in the *sunna*; if no answer is to be found in these, then he will conduct unflagging *ijtihād* (*ajtahidu raʾyī wa-lā ālū*). As noted, this tradition figured prominently in al-Bayhaqī's *Madkhal* as a basis for al-Shāfiʿī's jurisprudential methodology. It likewise features in some other non-Ẓāhirī anti-*taqlīd* polemic.[115] Ibn Ḥazm, of course, cannot concur with the content of this *ḥadīth*, since he holds that there are no questions for which a textual answer is absent, and thus there is no need and no permission for the kind of *ijtihād* Muʿādh was said to employ. (He judged the *ḥadīth* to be inauthentic, and as such it posed him no problem.)[116]

Hallaq's depiction of the nature of *ijtihād* is thus not wrong per se, but not entirely correct either. It is most apt for the conception of *ijtihād* among the early *ahl al-raʾy*, and those of them in later generations who continued to practice it. It holds to some degree for the Shāfiʿīs as well. In contrast – and without minimizing the important differences that existed between Ibn Ḥazm and others – the representatives of the *ahl al-ḥadīth* tendency all understood *ijtihād* primarily as an effort to remain loyal to the texts of revelation rather than succumbing to human *raʾy*. While Hallaq is right to note the acceptance of *qiyās* on the part of many

114 An attempt to find common ground between these positions can be recognized in the view of the Ḥanbalī Ibn Qayyim al-Jawziyya. He (like Ibn Ḥazm) holds that a textual answer always exists to all questions but notes that a scholar may not always be aware of it. Since (*pace* Ibn Ḥazm) he maintains, for theological reasons, that sound *qiyās* always agrees with the textual evidence, he holds it permissible to employ *qiyās* when one cannot find the relevant text. Ibn Qayyim al-Jawziyya, *Iʿlām*, vol. 1, p. 254.

115 For example, Ibn ʿAbd al-Barr, *Iʿlām*, vol. 2, pp. 55–56.

116 Ibn Ḥazm, *al-Iḥkām*, vol. 5, pp. 122–123.

Ḥanbalīs and like-minded scholars, in contrast with the Ẓāhirīs, the dominant theme in their writings on both *taqlīd* and *ijtihād* remained condemnation of unbridled *qiyās* and pure *ra'y* (of which *taqlīd* is a subset), and not, as Hallaq argues, the promotion of *qiyās*.

This comes through clearly in all the anti-*taqlīd* literature that has been surveyed here. Let us take Ibn ʿAbd al-Barr as a test case. After mentioning his rejection of *taqlīd*, Hallaq writes:

> Ibn ʿAbd al-Barr, for example, is well aware of the fact that *furūʿ* and new cases are endless and the only way for a jurist to encompass all branches of law, including the cases which may or may not have been previously solved, is to master the science of *usul*. It is significant that he mentions that Islamic law must and can deal with new issues. It is through *qiyas* and *ijtihad*, he argues, that Shariʿa can cope with the needs of Islamic society.

Here Hallaq calques a modernist conception of the issue onto Ibn ʿAbd al-Barr, whose primary concern was in fact simply to ensure adherence to the texts of revelation rather than to the views of fallible humans.[117]

This is evident, in addition to the adduction of the ʿAdī b. Ḥātim tradition at the outset of the chapter on *taqlīd*, in numerous additional passages in the *Jāmiʿ*. In a chapter written in condemnation of *ra'y* we find Ibn ʿAbd al-Barr citing ʿUmar b. al-Khaṭṭāb's description of the *ahl al-ra'y* as "the enemies of traditions" (*aʿdā' al-sunan*) as well as the Prophet's statement that the worst of the seventy-some heretical sects are "people who draw analogies in religion on the basis of their *ra'y* (*qawm yaqīsūna al-dīn bi-ra'yihim*), thereby forbidding what Allāh permitted and permitting what Allāh forbade."[118] Likewise, Ibn ʿAbd al-Barr's description of the kind of *ra'y* condemned in these traditions, brought in the name of the *jumhūr* (the majority of scholars), is a typical expression of *ahl al-ḥadīth* condemnation of the *ahl al-ra'y*: ruling based on *istiḥsān*, supposition, extracting *furūʿ* from other *furūʿ* instead of from their *uṣūl*, and so forth.[119] Later in the chapter, as though to dispel any remaining doubt as to his intention, Ibn ʿAbd al-Barr relates harsh condemnations of Abū Ḥanīfa from Mālik and Sufyān b. ʿUyayna. As is typical of *ahl al-ḥadīth*-leaning scholars in the period after the stabilization of the four-school system, he tempers these earlier

[117] On the contrast between these conceptions of the meaning of *ijtihād*, see Bernard Haykel, "On the Nature of Salafi Thought and Action," in Roel Meijer (ed.), *Global Salafism: Islam's New Religious Movement*, New York: Columbia University Press, 2009, pp. 33–57, at p. 44, n. 28.

[118] Ibn ʿAbd al-Barr, *Jāmiʿ*, vol. 2, pp. 134–135.

[119] Ibn ʿAbd al-Barr, *Jāmiʿ*, vol. 2, p. 139.

condemnations as far as the person of Abū Ḥanīfa himself is concerned, but his own leanings are nonetheless clear.[120]

## Conclusion

Let us conclude this chapter by returning to the quotation from Schacht that Hallaq cites at the outset of his article. Schacht writes that *taqlīd* was "a term which had originally denoted the kind of reference to Companions of the Prophet that had been customary in the ancient schools of law, and which now came to mean the unquestioning acceptance of the doctrines of established schools and authorities."[121] There is every indication that Schacht's statement is correct, and while to my knowledge Schacht himself never drew the logical conclusion from this observation to the nature of later anti-*taqlīd* polemic, he did here provide the correct basis. The practice of *taqlīd* was of a piece with the acceptance of post-Prophetic authority that had characterized the ancient schools; thus it was naturally the revolutionaries of the *ahl al-ḥadīth* who led the opposition to *taqlīd* of the established legal schools, just as it was they who, earlier, had opposed the ancient schools' acceptance of post-Prophetic authority. This historical continuity may be seen in the fact that it was students of al-Shāfiʿī, such as al-Muzanī and Dāwūd b. ʿAlī, who notwithstanding their significant divergences in jurisprudential methodology were both early opponents of *taqlīd*.[122] What form *ijtihād* is to take differs significantly in accordance with the *uṣūl* of the different

[120] Ibn ʿAbd al-Barr, *Jāmiʿ*, vol. 2, pp. 147–148: "The *aṣḥāb al-ḥadīth* exaggerated and overstepped the bounds in their condemnation of Abū Ḥanīfa. Their reason for this was Abū Ḥanīfa's introduction of *raʾy* and *qiyās* in preference to traditions and his taking of *raʾy* and *qiyās* into account – whereas most scholars (*akthar ahl al-ʿilm*) say that if a tradition is sound then *qiyās* and *naẓar* [in that matter] are invalid. [But in fact] these unit-reports (*akhbār al-āḥād*) that Abū Ḥanīfa rejected, he did so on the basis of a plausible interpretation (*bi-taʾwīl muḥtamal*), and in much of this others preceded him, and others who employed *raʾy* [likewise] followed him in this. In the greater part of this he was following the people of his city [Kufa], such as Ibrāhīm al-Nakhaʿī and the followers of Ibn Masʿūd. But he [i.e. Abū Ḥanīfa] and his followers exaggerated in debating hypothetical cases (*tanzīl al-nawāzil*) and answering them on the basis of their *raʾy* and their *istiḥsān*. Due to this he arrived at positions that were in great contradiction with the *salaf* ... I don't know of any scholars who are free of interpretations (*taʾwīl*) of verses or who do not follow a view (*madhhab*) with regard to the *sunna* on the basis of which they reject another *sunna*, through permissible (*sāʾigh*) interpretation or a claim of abrogation. But Abū Ḥanīfa has a lot of this, whereas others have little."

[121] Schacht, *Introduction*, pp. 70–71, cited in Hallaq, "Gate," p. 3.

[122] Al-Muzanī warns in the opening words of his *mukhtaṣar* of the *Kitāb al-umm* that al-Shāfiʿī forbade others to practice *taqlīd* of him or of others: Abū ʿAbdallāh Muḥammad b. Idrīs al-Shāfiʿī, *al-Umm*, Beirut: Dār al-Maʿrifa, 1410/1990, vol. 8, p. 1; for Dāwūd b. ʿAlī, see Goldziher, *Ẓāhirīs*, pp. 30–31.

schools; this is a topic that requires more exhaustive treatment than is possible here, and could probably be fruitfully addressed through a historical tracking of the major arguments and proofs across schools, such as the Muʿādh b. Jabal *ḥadīth*. The ultimate theological basis for vigorous condemnation of *taqlīd*, however, was the rejection of post-Prophetic legal authority. This remained consistent over time, and it was primarily a 'salafī' phenomenon.

I have devoted considerable space to this topic not solely due to its inherent importance, but also for the following reason. If one were to accept Hallaq's characterization of the issue (or any similar characterization) it would be impossible to understand how anti-*taqlīd* polemic served as an inspiration for the theonomic doctrine of modern radical salafīs and other fundamentalists.[123] In the course of Chapters 4 and 5 it will become clear that the premodern rejection of human legal autonomy, centered on Qurʾān 9:31 and the ʿAdī b. Ḥātim *ḥadīth* and expounded in anti-*taqlīd* polemic, is in fact a much-adduced precedent for modern theonomy. While it is true that the monolatric emphasis in premodern salafī theology, surveyed in Chapters 1 and 2, provides the basic template and primary inspiration for modern radical salafī doctrine, it was its jurisprudential corollary, as described in the present chapter, that prefigured the shift in theological focus from exclusivity of ritual worship to exclusivity of legal obedience.

[123] Consider, for example, the following passage from Roy Jackson: "Mawdūdī's method is 'an idiosyncratic combination of ijtihad and literalist exegesis' ... He has one foot in independent reasoning, and one foot in blind imitation: a schizophrenic ijtihad-taqlid figure" (*Mawlana Mawdudi and Political Islam: Authority and the Islamic State*, London and New York: Routledge, 2011, p. 106; he attributes the 'idiosyncratic combination' description to John Esposito, but I could not locate the reference). This mischaracterization stems from the same basic confusion between *taqlīd* and textual literalism as we found in Hallaq's article. In Chapter 4 I will address the relation between Mawdūdī's theonomy and the salafī tradition of anti-*taqlīd* polemic discussed here.

# 4 Mawdūdī and Quṭb: The Theonomic Shift

We have now completed our survey of the issues in premodern salafī monolatry that are relevant to an understanding of modern salafī theonomy. In Chapter 1 we examined Ibn Taymiyya's doctrine of *tawḥīd al-ulūhiyya* and argued that at root it is best understood as the contention that Islam is more a monolatry than a monotheism – that is, that Islam is not merely the belief in one sole God who created and controls the cosmos, but is rather the devotion of worship to that one God to the exclusion of all others. In Chapter 2 we analyzed Ibn ʿAbd al-Wahhāb's adoption and application of this doctrine of *tawḥīd al-ulūhiyya* to his contemporary environment, and its central position at the heart of the Wahhābī movement. Chapter 3 examined how this same concern for exclusivity of worship received a theonomic expression in the field of jurisprudence, through the characterization of dogmatic adherence to the legal precedents of an individual or a law school as worship of others apart from Allāh.

In principle these premodern traditions, in themselves, provide all the constitutive elements needed for the emergence of the modern salafī doctrine of theonomy. The formula is simple: Islam is worship of Allāh to the exclusion of all others; legal obedience is worship; thus legal obedience to anyone other than Allāh, such as a government based on man-made law, is polytheism. Indeed, modern salafīs, as we will see in Chapter 5, speak very much this same language and ground their thought in precisely these precedents, even as their principal preoccupation is a form of 'polytheism' – parliamentary government and human legislation – that is characteristically modern.

Nonetheless, in its historical unfolding, the displacement in application of the salafī monolatric tradition from the spheres of ritual worship and traditional jurisprudence to the legal-political sphere – what could be termed the "theonomic shift" – was not a wholly indigenous salafī development. The potential for such an application was present, but the fact that modern salafīs have exploited this potential to the full is largely due to the influence of two twentieth-century thinkers who are not normally regarded as part of the salafī tradition, but rather as the originators of a distinctly modern form of Islamism. The writings of these two thinkers, the Indo-Pakistani Abū al-Aʿlā Mawdūdī (1903–1979) and the Egyptian Sayyid Quṭb (1906–1966), are the topic of this present chapter.

Mawdūdī and Quṭb were the first modern authors to elaborate a systematic conception of Islam in which conflict between divine and human rule, and thus the issue of to whom one offers legal obedience, stood at the heart of the conflict between faith and unbelief. It was Mawdūdī who first formulated this theonomic doctrine, which in his writings often goes under the name *ḥākimiyyat.*[1] It is not clear that in Mawdūdī's writings *ḥākimiyyat* was truly a technical term for the doctrine, and Mawdūdī often used it simply as an Urdu equivalent of the English word 'sovereignty.'[2] In fact the term itself appears to be a calque from the English: an abstract noun derived from *ḥākim*, just as 'sovereignty' is derived from 'sovereign.'[3] In Quṭb's writings, however, the Arabic *ḥākimiyya* did take on something of the character of a term of art, which it has retained to this day.

Although the two men were contemporaries, born only three years apart, Quṭb's fully developed writings on the topic date from the end of his life, in the first half of the 1960s, and were (as we will see) heavily influenced by his reading of Mawdūdī. Mawdūdī's system of thought, including the central concept of *ḥākimiyyat*, had matured by the mid-1930s,[4] and his seminal *Qurʾān kī chār bunyādī iṣṭilāḥen̲* ("Four Fundamental Qurʾānic Terms"), in which he provided a systematic exposition of his system, was first published in 1941.[5] Quṭb's dependence on Mawdūdī in various aspects of his thought has of course been previously recognized;[6] the secondary aim of this chapter, in addition to

[1] But for suggestive Indian antecedents, and a comparison of Mawdūdī's conception with those of his contemporaries, see Muhammad Qasim Zaman, "The Sovereignty of God in Modern Islamic Thought," *Journal of the Royal Asiatic Society* 25/3 (July 2015), pp. 389–418.

[2] Mawdūdī at times explicitly gives the English 'sovereignty' as a gloss for *ḥākimiyyat*; e.g., Mawlānā Sayyid Abū al-Aʿlā Mawdūdī, *Qurʾān kī chār bunyādī iṣṭilāḥēn̲*, New Delhi: Markazī Maktabah-i Islāmī, 2011, p. 58 (henceforth: *Iṣṭilāḥēn̲*). Elsewhere he refers to *ḥākimiyyat* as a term taken from the field of political science: Mawlānā Sayyid Abū al-Aʿlā Mawdūdī, *Islāmī riyāsat*, Lahore: Islamic Publications (Private) Limited, 2008, p. 334.

[3] *Pace* Shahrough Akhavi, the term was not coined by Mawdūdī's Arabic translators; it is his own. Shahrough Akhavi, "The Dialectic in Contemporary Egyptian Social Thought: The Scripturalist and Modernist Discourses of Sayyid Qutb and Hasan Hanafi," *International Journal of Middle East Studies* 29 (1997), pp. 377–401, at p. 378, n. 7.

[4] Seyyed Vali Reza Nasr, *Mawdudi and the Making of Islamic Revivalism*, New York and Oxford: Oxford University Press, 1996, p. 31.

[5] Jan-Peter Hartung, *A System of Life: Mawdūdī and the Ideologisation of Islam*, London: Hurst, 2013, p. 91.

[6] Emmanuel Sivan, *Radical Islam: Medieval Theology and Modern Politics*, New Haven and London: Yale University Press, 1985; Gilles Kepel, *Muslim Extremism in Egypt: The Prophet and the Pharaoh*, Berkeley and Los Angeles: University of California Press,

examining the doctrine of *ḥākimiyya* and its theological underpinnings, will be to further specify the precise nature of Quṭb's debt to Mawdūdī.

A cardinal point that will arise from the analysis of Mawdūdī's and Quṭb's thought in this chapter is the fact that their theonomy has a thoroughly monolatric basis. In this, as in other aspects of their thought, we will see significant structural parallels between Mawdūdī and Quṭb, on the one hand, and the premodern salafī tradition, on the other. While the differences between them are not to be denied, it was these parallels that eventually allowed for the integration of their *ḥākimiyya* doctrine into the Taymiyyan belief structure of modern radical salafism. That is a process that we will examine in Chapter 5. At present we will turn our attention to the writings of Mawdūdī and Quṭb themselves.

## Abū al-Aʿlā Mawdūdī

Abū al-Aʿlā Mawdūdī was born in 1903 in Awrangabad, Deccan, in what was then British India. His family hailed from Delhi and could boast of descent both from the Chistī Ṣūfī lineage (on his father's side) and from grandees of the Mughal court (on his mother's side). Although Mawdūdī's father had briefly studied at the Aligarh Anglo-Oriental College, which represented the modernist and pro-British tendency among Indian Muslims, the family's orientation was conservative and pious. Mawdūdī was homeschooled in traditional Islamic sciences, entering school only in the eighth grade. Not long after, his father's death forced him to abandon school in order to support the family.[7]

Following in the footsteps of his older brother, Mawdūdī began a career as a journalist. Now based in Delhi, he became involved in the Indian nationalist movement, and was a supporter both of the Congress party – the officially secular but Hindu-led movement that stood at the forefront of the demand for independence from Britain – and the Khilāfat movement, a vehicle for expression of Pan-Islamic sentiment through support for the Ottoman sultan. In 1921 Mawdūdī began editing a journal of the Deobandi Jamʿiyyat ʿUlamāʾ-i Hind; in parallel, he took up religious study once again, and received an *ijāza* from his Deobandi teachers in 1926.[8]

2003, pp. 47–50; Hartung, *A System of Life*, pp. 193–214; William Shepard, "Sayyid Qutb's Doctrine of 'Jāhiliyya,'" *International Journal of Middle East Studies* 35/4 (2003), pp. 521–545, at p. 523.

7 Nasr, *Mawdudi*, pp. 9–14; Hartung, *A System of Life*, pp. 12–15.

8 Nasr, *Mawdudi*, pp. 14–19.

In the mid-1920s Mawdūdī became disenchanted with nationalism. The Khilāfat movement collapsed with Ataturk's abolition of the caliphate, and a number of episodes in India led to increasing intercommunal violence between Muslims and Hindus. In 1928 Mawdūdī ceased his work for the pro-Congress Jamʿiyyat ʿUlamāʾ-i Hind.[9] Following a process of intellectual and spiritual reexamination, Mawdūdī began to formulate his own distinctive approach to Islam and its place in life:

> There was a time when I was also a believer of traditional and hereditary religion and practiced it ... At last I paid attention to the Holy Book and the Prophet's Sunnah. I understood Islam and renewed my faith in it voluntarily. Thereafter I tried to find out and understand the Islamic system in detail. When I was satisfied in this I began to invite others to the truth.[10]

Mawdūdī went on to a long career as an Islamic activist, founding the Jamāʿat-i Islāmī organization and, following the Partition of India (1947), playing an important role in the political and religious life of Pakistan. Our present interest, however, lies in the nature of Mawdūdī's thought itself and its influence and reception in the Arabic-speaking world.

### *Approaches to Mawdūdī*

The academic literature devoted specifically to Mawdūdī is not particularly extensive. Alongside my considerable debt to the scholars to be discussed in this brief literature review, my own reading of Mawdūdī differs from theirs on certain points that bear directly on this book's overall thesis. For this reason a survey of the major studies on Mawdūdī is in order before presenting my own analysis of his writings.

The literature on Mawdūdī has focused, above all, on Mawdūdī's relation to modernity and on drawing a contrast between his system of thought and the 'traditional Islam' of the *ʿulamāʾ*. This emphasis is clearly enunciated in a work that served as the standard monograph on Mawdūdī for several decades, Seyyed Vali Reza Nasr's *Mawdudi and the Making of Islamic Revivalism*.

The chapter of Nasr's work devoted to explication of the general outlines of Mawdūdī's thought, titled "Faith and Ideology," depicts Mawdūdī's principal concern as a political one, namely, the restoration of power to Muslim society in the face of Western and Hindu ascendancy.[11] As a logical corollary of this premise, Nasr characterizes Mawdūdī's system of thought as essentially instrumental in nature.

[9] Nasr, *Mawdudi*, pp. 19–22. [10] Nasr, *Mawdudi*, p. 29. [11] Nasr, *Mawdudi*, p. 51.

By this I mean that whenever Nasr mentions a fundamental characteristic of Mawdūdī's system, he tells us how it was meant to further some real-world end. For example, Mawdūdī's "redefinition" of a Muslim was meant "to lay the foundations for the type of collective action that would preclude a secular Indian identity and would strengthen communalist feelings," and the impetus for it was "his desire to provide power and identity to Muslims by reversing the balance in relations" between Islam, Hinduism, and the West.[12] Likewise, "Mawdūdī called Muslims back to Islam but to an Islam that was rationalized and streamlined so that its social expression would be able to support a viable modern political order."[13] Or again, "The impetus for Mawdudi's exegetics was clearly sociopolitical: the Islamic revival was not intended to save individual souls, but to soothe anxieties born of social, economic, communal, and political crises before the Muslims of India."[14]

In addition to Nasr's depiction of Mawdūdī's thought as essentially political in aim and instrumental in nature, a third major theme in the chapter is the portrayal of Mawdūdī as a modernist who sought to modernize Islam,[15] this too explained in functional terms as a means to achieving a political end. In Nasr's view, the Islamic revival that Mawdūdī sought to effect was "essentially a political struggle that could succeed only if its modernizing impulse refashioned Muslim life and thought."[16]

Nasr does not define what he means by modernity and modernism in general terms, but his portrayal of Mawdūdī as a modernist appears in two different contexts. The first is Mawdūdī's embrace of modern science and technology and his belief that the principles underlying them are value-neutral.[17] The second and more significant claim is that Mawdūdī's vision of Islam itself and of Islamic society was essentially a modernizing project: Thus the "modernizing impetus of Islamic revivalism was not limited to the use of tape recorders, facsimile machines, and other instruments of the modern world, as some observers of this

[12] Nasr, *Mawdudi*, p. 51; cf. pp. 54–55, for a similarly functionalist interpretation of the Ahl-i Ḥadīth movement in India; contrast Riexinger, *Sanāʾullāh Amritsarī*, pp. 505–506, who argues that the movement cannot be described as representing any particular social class.

[13] Nasr, *Mawdudi*, p. 57. [14] Nasr, *Mawdudi*, p. 63.

[15] Nasr, *Mawdudi*, pp. 50–51, 53.

[16] Nasr, *Mawdudi*, p. 51, cf. p. 53: "Mawdudi was keen to erect exactly one such [modern] society so as to streamline Islamic culture and, hence, to concentrate the energies of Muslim faith on gaining worldly power and glory."

[17] Nasr, *Mawdudi*, p. 52. Nasr writes broadly that Mawdūdī "saw modern ideas as universal truths to be distinguished from Western ones," but from the examples he adduces it appears that he has in mind here modern science in particular.

phenomenon have contended, but encompassed values, ideas, and institutions ... [A] Muslim was a modern creature with modern social links, political aspirations, and, ultimately, cultural outlook."[18]

Nasr's depiction of Mawdūdī as a modernist in this sense does not appear to rest on the identification of characteristically modern concepts in Mawdūdī's system of thought, but rather proceeds by the *via negativa*: He identifies ideas that he regards as a departure from 'traditional' Islam and ascribes them the trait of modernity. The most important idea to which Nasr applies this argument is Mawdūdī's notion that absolute obedience and submission to God is the central element of Islam.[19] Nasr argues that this represented a complete break from the traditional understanding of Islam,[20] which, citing Seyyed Hossein Nasr, he characterizes as "essentially a way of knowledge ... Islam leads to essential knowledge which integrates a Muslim's whole being."[21] Thus Mawdūdī's "overtly and exclusively political reading was distinguished from the essentially soteriological and spiritual concerns of traditional Islam."[22]

Yet "traditional Islam" is no one single thing, and the decision to characterize it in this fashion is somewhat arbitrary. Nasr is right to note the centrality of obedience and submission in Mawdūdī's system, but rather than a modernist departure from traditional Islam, this is among the structural parallels that tie Mawdūdī to the specifically monolatric tradition in Islam and distance him from the legacy of philosophy and *kalām* theology. We will return to this point further on in the present chapter.

A major recent addition to the literature on Mawdūdī, and one that parts ways with Nasr's analysis in significant respects, is Jan-Peter Hartung's *A System of Life: Mawdūdī and the Ideologisation of Islam*. In contrast with Nasr's instrumental analysis, which suggests that Mawdūdī was first and foremost an activist, Hartung portrays Mawdūdī as a true thinker who set before himself the task of grappling with "temporally invariant core questions."[23] Likewise, in contrast with Nasr's depiction of Mawdūdī as motivated by communalist sentiment, Hartung writes:

> The Islamic state that Mawdūdī had in mind did not, like the 'Pakistan' of the AIML [All-India Muslim League], result from the communalism present in British India at that time and the ensuing political and economic resentments of Indian Muslims. His state, based on the absolute and undisputable veracity of

[18] Nasr, *Mawdudi*, pp. 50–51. [19] Nasr, *Mawdudi*, pp. 57ff.
[20] Nasr, *Mawdudi*, p. 59. [21] Nasr, *Mawdudi*, p. 66. [22] Nasr, *Mawdudi*, p. 111.
[23] Hartung, *A System of Life*, p. 64.

God's supreme sovereignty and the limited sovereignty of the believing man as crown of His creation, was necessarily a universal one.[24]

Where Hartung's analysis does largely agree with Nasr's is in his description of Mawdūdī as a "child of his time"[25] and "very much in line with the philosophical *zeitgeist*"[26] – in other words, as a thinker who worked within, or at least in relation to, modern Western categories. This is a large question and one that does not necessarily have a sole correct answer: Mawdūdī was familiar with Western (post-)Enlightenment thought in addition to traditional Islamic scholarship, such that any given idea of Mawdūdī's could theoretically derive from either fount, or from their confluence. Hartung is much more specific than Nasr when addressing the issue of Mawdūdī's modernity, outlining both a general hypothesis and numerous comparisons between specific elements in Mawdūdī's writings and various Western philosophers or intellectual currents.

Hartung's general thesis on this point may be summarized as follows: Fundamentalism is essentially a counterproject to modernity.[27] The various Enlightenment philosophies that represent modernity share certain core emphases: They rationalize the world, believe in human autonomy and promote it, and, while viewing history as a source of important lessons, they do not posit any form of normative obligation to the past.[28] In reaction to the phenomenon of modernity, the nineteenth century witnessed the birth of ideologies which, in contrast to the secular rationalism of Enlightenment thought, possessed a "quasi-religious" element. Ideologies differ from Enlightenment philosophies in that they posit an extra-human truth (e.g. dialectical materialism) that must prevail; this adherence to a truth construed as extra-human also renders these ideologies exclusivist, and mutually exclusive one of another.[29] Hartung argues that British India at the time Mawdūdī was formulating his system was a society in which Enlightenment modernity was ascendant, and thus "to cast Islam into an ideology appeared therefore [to Mawdūdī] to be a most appropriate way to relate Islam to the contemporary and heavily Western-dominated context in which he was living, while, at the same time, returning to the retrogressive method of affirming authority."[30] Thus Mawdūdī was "a child of his time"[31] and his

[24] Hartung, *A System of Life*, p. 114.
[25] Hartung, *A System of Life*, pp. 38, 70, 87.
[26] Hartung, *A System of Life*, p. 87.
[27] Hartung, *A System of Life*, p. 4. This thesis, in various forms, is widespread in the literature on fundamentalism; Hartung references in particular the German political scientist Friedemann Büttner, the sociologist Martin Riesebrodt, and Malise Ruthven.
[28] Hartung, *A System of Life*, pp. 4–5.
[29] Hartung, *A System of Life*, pp. 5–6.
[30] Hartung, *A System of Life*, p. 6.
[31] Hartung, *A System of Life*, p. 38.

project falls into the general category of the revolutionary ideologies that developed in nineteenth-century Europe, and whose impact was also felt in the colonial context. Mawdūdī, however, differed from Indian nationalists and Marxists in that his ideology, and thus his response to modernity, was constructed out of elements from the Islamic tradition: This is the "Ideologisation of Islam" to which Hartung refers in the title of his study.

That is as far as the general thesis. My own findings agree to a large extent with Hartung's description of Mawdūdī's system as a response to modernity; we will return to this topic in what follows. As for Hartung's comments on specific elements of Mawdūdī's thought and their connection to various Western thinkers, these do not always furnish convincing evidence that Western thought was his natural frame of reference. Let us consider two examples. First, when discussing Mawdūdī's contention that only prophecy yields true knowledge and true answers to life questions, in contrast with *jāhilī* systems based on sense-perception and analogical reasoning, Hartung cites the following passage from Mawdūdī's article *Islām awr jāhiliyyat*:

> Whenever you are confronted with such a situation [*ṣūrat-i ḥāl*] your first endeavour is to search for a person who claims to know a solution. Then, on the basis of circumstantial evidence [*qarā'in se*], you seek to satisfy yourself regarding whether or not such a person is trustworthy [*qābil-i i'timād*]. Then you go ahead under this guidance. When it is proven by experience [*tajriba se thābit ho jātā he*] that the information he provided has not led to any negative result whilst you acted on it, then you are convinced that this person possessed the requisite knowledge and that this information [*ma'lūmāt*] supplied by him [...] was sound [*ṣaḥīḥ*]. This is a scientific way, and if there is not any other scientific way, then this must be the only correct one for formulating one's viewpoint [*rā'y*].

Hartung comments on this passage:

> Clearly, the way in which Mawdūdī depicted the discovery of 'Islam' as the only way to provide satisfying answers to all of man's urgent questions and, moreover, a guideline to act in a contingent world reminds one strongly of an experimental design. This, along with the fact that Mawdūdī tried to sell his solution – 'Islam' – as a scientifically verified insight, is clear proof that Mawdūdī moved well within the confines of the – Western-dominated – contemporary discourse on science as the only acceptable means to generate truths.[32]

Mawdūdī certainly was concerned to portray Islam as 'scientific' in the sense that it provides certain knowledge. In itself this concern is a classic

[32] Hartung, *A System of Life*, p. 69.

one in Islamic theology, but Hartung is correct to point out that in Mawdūdī's writings it also evinces a desire to match modern Western truth-claims. The epistemological method that Mawdūdī describes in the passage, however, is not an experimental one in the modern sense. It seeks to establish the authority of an individual (the Prophet) as a source of guidance rather than to test individual hypotheses on a purely evidentiary basis. A similar argument appears in premodern apologetics precisely as a defense of the rationality of belief in the authority of prophecy, in contrast with the path of the philosophers, who argued that belief in Allāh and prophecy could only be based on epistemologically prior deductions.[33]

As a second example let us consider Hartung's discussion of Mawdūdī's approach to the Qurʾān. He rightly points out that "Mawdūdī considered it perfectly possible for man to understand at least the essence of the Qurʾān in a direct and unmediated way,"[34] and that Mawdūdī's own exegesis of the Qurʾān (the *Tafhīm al-qurʾān*) is unusual in that it does not build on the prior exegetical tradition. Hartung then compares this approach to Luther's reading of the Bible, which as a typological observation is entirely apposite. He subsequently suggests, however, that this resemblance may be due to the presence of Presbyterian missionaries in India and adds that "such optimism about the general possibility of acquiring true knowledge" was "very much in line with the philosophical *zeitgeist*."[35] All this is possible, but there are sources closer to Mawdūdī's own worldview that could have served as role models. The assertion that the Qurʾān is "easy to understand" was a commonplace of premodern salafī argumentation.[36] We encountered this argument in Ibn ʿAbd al-Wahhāb's writings in Chapter 2, and in India it was advanced, for example, in the well-known *Taqwiyat al-īmān* by Shāh Ismāʿīl Shahīd.[37]

None of this should be taken to dismiss out of hand Hartung's many and fruitful discussions of aspects of modernity in Mawdūdī and

[33] See e.g. Ibn Taymiyya, *Majmūʿat al-fatāwā*, vol. 2, pp. 48ff. And see now also Yohanan Friedmann, "Quasi-Rational and Anti-Rational Elements in Radical Muslim Thought: The Case of Abū al-Aʿlā Mawdūdī," in Yohanan Friedmann and Christoph Markschies (eds.), *Rationalization in Religions: Judaism, Christianity, and Islam*, Berlin and Boston: De Gruyter, 2019, pp. 289–300. Friedmann concludes that for Mawdūdī "rationalism is a strategy for converting people to Islam rather than a guide for human life in general" (p. 299).

[34] Hartung, *A System of Life*, p. 86.

[35] Hartung, *A System of Life*, p. 87.

[36] Jonathan A. C. Brown, "Is Islam Easy to Understand or Not? Salafis, the Democratization of Interpretation, and the Need for the Ulema," *Journal of Islamic Studies* 26/2 (2015), pp. 117–144.

[37] Brown, "Is Islam Easy?," p. 117.

comparisons between him and Western thinkers. For example, the suggestion of Hegelian influence on his conception of state would certainly be worth pursuing, especially given Mawdūdī's striking equation of the term *dīn* with the concept of 'state' in the closing pages of *Qur'ān kī chār bunyādī iṣṭilāḥen̲*[38] (to be discussed below). That said, my own reading of Mawdūdī will focus on the monolatric and theonomic basis of his thought, typological parallels between this basis and the premodern salafī tradition, and discussion of potential influence of the latter on Mawdūdī.

Another recent contribution to the literature on Mawdūdī takes quite an opposite approach. Martin Riexinger, in a brief chapter devoted to Mawdūdī in his book on Thanā' Allāh Amritsarī and the Ahl-i Ḥadīth in India, advances a number of arguments against the Mawdūdī-as-modernist thesis.[39] Riexinger compares the legal positions of Mawdūdī and Thanā' Allāh on a number of symbolically charged issues that serve as markers of modernist tendencies in Islam, such as women's status and slavery, and argues that Mawdūdī's positions were as or more conservative than those of Thanā' Allāh, who was a traditionally trained Islamic scholar (albeit not necessarily a typical one). Whereas Thanā' Allāh showed some interest in improving women's legal status, Mawdūdī showed none;[40] and while Mawdūdī held that the Qur'ān permits slavery and argued specifically against the modernist Sayyid Aḥmad Khān's attempts to show otherwise, Thanā' Allāh interpreted the Qur'ān's provisions as not constituting true slavery but rather a kind of indentured servitude for prisoners of war.[41]

Riexinger reaches similar findings in his comparison between the two on matters of Qur'ānic exegesis, concluding that in most respects Mawdūdī is the more conservative of the two.[42] Likewise, Mawdūdī explicitly attacks "bizarre" modernist *ta'wīl* (allegorical interpretation) on such questions as the existence of jinn and naturalistic interpretations of the miracles recounted in the Qur'ān.[43] Riexinger concludes from all the foregoing that the widespread distinction between 'traditional' scholars and 'modern' fundamentalists does not withstand scrutiny when one investigates their positions on concrete questions.[44] In Rieixinger's view, it is primarily Mawdūdī's journalistic style of writing, with frequent

[38] Hartung, *A System of Life*, pp. 122–124; Mawdūdī, *Iṣṭilāḥēn̲*, p. 108.
[39] Riexinger, *Sanā'ullāh Amritsarī*, pp. 549–563.
[40] Riexinger, *Sanā'ullāh Amritsarī*, p. 551.
[41] Riexinger, *Sanā'ullāh Amritsarī*, pp. 552–553.
[42] Riexinger, *Sanā'ullāh Amritsarī*, p. 556.
[43] Riexinger, *Sanā'ullāh Amritsarī*, pp. 556–558.
[44] Rieixinger, *Sanā'ullāh Amritsarī*, p. 559.

borrowings from Western political vocabulary, that feeds the impression that he is a modernist, but this impression is belied by the conservative and traditional content of Mawdūdī's positions.[45]

Riexinger succeeds in clarifying an important point, namely, that Mawdūdī can not be considered a modernist at all in the sense that we use this term for figures such as Sayyid Aḥmad Khān in India or Muḥammad ʿAbduh in the Arabic-speaking world. Riexinger's calling into question of the degree to which Mawdūdī accepted modern Western philosophy and science as the natural framework for debate is likewise a necessary corrective to Nasr's contentions on this matter.[46] It remains to be seen, however, whether the modern element in Mawdūdī is in fact solely or primarily a matter of style. While it is certainly important to take stock of concrete positions on matters of law and exegesis, as Riexinger has done, the answer to this question ultimately stands or falls on an analysis of Mawdūdī's system, that is, his core theology (or 'ideology'), which represents his distinctive contribution to Islamic thought.

In the following analysis of Mawdūdī's system I seek to demonstrate two fundamental points, using the framework developed in the preceding chapters as a basis for analysis. The first is that Mawdūdī's system is a fundamentally monolatric one. As noted above, Nasr argued that Mawdūdī's definition of Islam as absolute obedience and submission to God constituted a break from 'traditional Islam.' I argue the contrary, namely, that in fact it represents the principal point of continuity between Mawdūdī's system and (a certain) premodern Islamic tradition. It does not make sense to speak of 'traditional' Islam as though it were a unitary object; the parallel is specifically with the salafī tradition of monolatric Islam that we have discussed in previous chapters. The second point that I seek to demonstrate is that, unlike the premodern tradition, Mawdūdī adapts this monolatric template primarily as a basis for his doctrine of theonomy. In this, Mawdūdī's system can and should be regarded as not just a restatement of traditional or conservative Islamic positions, but rather (as Hartung has argued) as a thoroughgoing response to and critique of secularization and modern human autonomy.

### *The Four Terms*

Mawdūdī was a systematic thinker, one who purported to deduce a fully elaborated conception of Islam from a number of core principles.[47]

[45] Riexinger, *Sanāʾullāh Amritsarī*, p. 562.
[46] Cf. Riexinger, *Sanāʾullāh Amritsarī*, p. 549, n. 35, p. 557, n. 67.
[47] Hartung, *A System of Life*, p. 83.

He provided a succinct exposition of the foundations of his core system in the book *Qur'ān kī chār bunyādī iṣṭilāḥēn̲* ("Four Fundamental Qur'ānic Terms"; henceforth: *Iṣṭilāḥēn̲*). Our discussion of Mawdūdī will focus primarily on this work, which deserves to be treated in detail.[48] As Mawdūdī's intent in *Iṣṭilāḥēn̲* is to lay out the foundations of his system of thought, the work does not treat (or even mention) specific contemporary political issues. *Iṣṭilāḥēn̲* is a theologicial treatise – a unique one, but a theological treatise nonetheless.

The treatise presents itself as almost a work of philology. Its central methodological premise, announced by Mawdūdī in the book's introduction, is that Muslims no longer understand the original meanings of the fundamental terms of the Qur'ān, and consequently do not understand the true nature of their religion and fall into *shirk*.[49] Mawdūdī identifies four such terms as the key to understanding the Qur'ān's message: *ilāh*, *rabb*, *'ibādat*, and *dīn*. Mawdūdī uses philology as an aid to the promulgation of specific theological conclusions based on these terms, which he can then argue are not his own private conclusions but rather those of the Qur'ān itself once properly understood.

Mawdūdī mentions two reasons why latter-day Muslims no longer understand the fundamental terms of the Qur'ān. One is prosaic: With the passage of time, people have lost the "taste" of pure Arabic. The second is more significant: When people born into a society that was already Islamic encountered the fundamental terms, these no longer carried the meanings they did at the time of the revelation of the Qur'ān, that is, the meanings the terms bore in non-Islamic society.[50] At first glance this appears to be a tautology: People no longer understand the original meanings of the terms because these original meanings have been lost. It appears, however, that Mawdūdī's claim is something akin to the Streitpunkt principle that we found in Ibn 'Abd al-Wahhāb's thought. The Qur'ān was directed against the *jāhiliyya*, and one needs to understand what was at stake in the conflict with the *jāhiliyya* in order to understand what Islam is. Those born into Islam did not experience its original oppositional thrust, and in forgetting *jāhiliyya* they ceased to understand Islam. (Indeed, Mawdūdī makes abundant use of the Streitpunkt principle later in the treatise, as we will see.)

The reason why failure to understand these terms leads people into *shirk* is treated as nearly self-evident. If one does not understand what an

[48] The most extended treatment of the work to date is Hartung, *A System of Life*, pp. 91–99; my analysis concurs with Hartung's in a number of respects, notwithstanding our different points of approach.
[49] Mawdūdī, *Iṣṭilāḥēn̲*, pp. 7–10. [50] Mawdūdī, *Iṣṭilāḥēn̲*, pp. 8–9.

*ilāh* is, then one might profess *lā ilāha illā llāh* while unwittingly taking many *ilāh*s; and so forth regarding each of the terms.[51] Again, one is reminded of one of Ibn ʿAbd al-Wahhāb's central arguments: Had his contemporaries understood that an *ilāh* was precisely an intermediary, they would have known that the saints they appealed to were *ilāh*s, thereby negating their profession of faith.

Mawdūdī bases his treatise on a conception of Islam best described as monolatric, as he states in the very first paragraph of the book, in which he defines Islam through his four fundamental terms:

> The entire message (*daʿwat*) of the Qurʾān is that Allāh alone is *rabb* and *ilāh*; there is no other *ilāh* or *rabb* but He, and no one else is His partner in *ulūhiyyat* and *rubūbiyyat*; thus accept Him (*taslīm karō*) as your *ilāh* and *rabb* and deny the *ulūhiyyat* and *rubūbiyyat* of every one apart from Him; take upon yourself *ʿibādat* to Him and do not perform any kind of *ʿibādat* to anyone but Him; and to this end make your *dīn* exclusive (*khāliṣ*) and reject all other *dīn*s.[52]

At this point we have little choice but to leave the four terms *ilāh*, *rabb*, *ʿibādat*, and *dīn* untranslated in this passage, as we have not yet discussed the specification of their meaning to which the rest of the treatise is devoted. It can nonetheless be seen already that the framework into which Mawdūdī will later insert these meanings is one of monolatry, that is, exclusivity of '*ʿibādat*.' It is worth keeping in mind our discussions from previous chapters so as to stress that this is not in itself a self-evident starting point. An Islamic theological treatise could just as well open with a proof of Allāh's existence or a discussion of His nature (e.g. that He is pre-eternal, the status of His attributes, etc.); likewise, traditional *ʿaqīda* literature does not normally include any discussion of exclusivity of worship.[53] Already in this opening passage we have a foreshadowing of Mawdūdī's focus on the relational aspect of divinity, not only in the emphasis on *ʿibādat*, but also in connection with the first two terms: The Qurʾān's message is not just that Allāh *is* the sole *ilāh* and *rabb* in an objective sense, but, as Mawdūdī emphasizes, that *you* accept Allāh as *your* sole *ilāh* and *rabb*.

[51] Mawdūdī, *Iṣṭilāḥēn̲*, pp. 9–10. [52] Mawdūdī, *Iṣṭilāḥēn̲*, p. 5.

[53] For example, *al-ʿAqāʾid al-nasafiyya* by Najm al-Dīn al-Nasafī (d. 537/1142), a major *ʿaqīda* of the Māturīdī school of *kalām* that is predominant among the Ḥanafīs of South Asia, begins with the following topics: the sources of knowledge; the createdness of the world, with Allāh as its Creator; an ontological discussion of divinity and the attributes; the uncreatedness of the Qurʾān; the vision of Allāh in the afterlife; Allāh's creation of human acts. There is discussion of obedience and sin, but not of exclusivity of worship; as in the *ʿaqīda* genre in general, the aim is rather to propound the correct contents of belief. Saʿd al-Dīn al-Taftazānī, *Sharḥ al-ʿaqāʾid al-nasafiyya*, ed. Aḥmad Ḥijāzī al-Saqqā, Cairo: Maktabat al-Kulliyyāt al-Azhariyya, 1408/1988.

*The Meaning of* Ilāh The first of Mawdūdī's four fundamental terms is *ilāh*. He opens the chapter with a survey of the term's lexical signification in Arabic, noting five different meanings for the root *ʾ-l-h* based on Arabic lexicography.[54] These are bewilderment (Arabic *ḥayrān*, Urdu *sar-gashta*); finding refuge and protection from harm; turning to another in longing or desire (*shawq*); concealedness and elevation; and *ʿibāda*, which Mawdūdī glosses with the Urdu *parastish* ('worship').[55] As we saw in previous chapters, the lexicographical meaning of *ilāh* as an object of worship was central to Ibn Taymiyya's and Ibn ʿAbd al-Wahhāb's understanding of the term, and Mawdūdī as well considers the last of these meanings to be the central one. He does not, however, view the other definitions as irrelevant: He rather argues that they all feed into the central concept of worship. The idea of worship cannot occur at all until one feels some form of need or destitution (*ḥājat-mandī*) and conceives of the one worshipped as capable of fulfilling this need and extending protection. Furthermore, this conception of the one worshipped necessarily entails the idea that he is superior to the worshipper, not only in eminence, but also in power (*ṭāqat awr zōr*). As for the meanings of concealedness and bewilderment, Mawdūdī explains that no emotion of worship is aroused when the manner in which one's need is fulfilled is in accordance with a normal causal chain evident to human eyes; it arises only when the modality of the one worshipped, his power, or his manner of fulfilling the need is veiled in secrecy. When these conditions obtain, it is inevitable that a human turn to the one worshipped with longing. Thus all these definitions together make up the basis for the meaning of *ilāh* as *maʿbūd*, that is, one that is worshipped.[56]

In traditional Islamic writing it is customary to follow such a lexical survey, which gives the *lughawī* meaning of a term, with an analysis of the *sharʿī* meaning of a term, that is, the meaning it takes on in the authoritative texts of revelation. In similar fashion, Mawdūdī at this point moves on to a consideration of the meaning of *ilāh* as the term is employed in the Qurʾān. It is worth noting that the verses he discusses are those that relate specifically to "the people of the *jāhiliyya*'s conception of *ilāh*."[57] This is in keeping with his general argument in the introduction to the treatise that the proper understanding of the Qurʾān's fundamental terms

[54] Mawdūdī, *Iṣṭilāḥēn̲*, p. 11. On Mawdūdī's sources, see Hartung, *A System of Life*, p. 284, n. 156. As noted in Chapter 1, the Arabic lexicographical tradition on *ʾ-l-h* is somewhat strained, but Mawdūdī accepts it as authoritative.

[55] Mawdūdī, *Iṣṭilāḥēn̲*, p. 11. On Mawdūdī's distinction between *parastish* and other aspects of *ʿibāda*, see below.

[56] Mawdūdī, *Iṣṭilāḥēn̲*, pp. 11–13.

[57] Mawdūdī, *Iṣṭilāḥēn̲*, p. 13.

is one that refers back to the underlying *jāhilī* conceptions that the Qurʾān sought to refute.

Mawdūdī considers five clusters of verses in order to elucidate the nature of the *ilāh* in the *jāhiliyya* (and thus the meaning of *ilāh* in general), from which he draws the following points:

(1) They regarded their *ilāh*s as their allies and supporters (*pushtī-bān*) and as their protectors from harm, as for example in Qurʾān 36:74, "And they have taken *ilāh*s other than Allāh, hoping that they might be helped."[58]

(2) They supplicated these *ilāh*s with requests for aid. The *ilāh*s to whom they addressed these requests were not only supernatural beings such as angels and jinn, but also deceased humans whom they believed were capable of hearing and answering their prayers. This we learn from the Qurʾān's description of them as mortal, e.g. 16:20–22: "Those whom they call on apart from Allāh do not create a thing, and are themselves created. They are dead, not living, and do not know when they will be resurrected. Your *ilāh* is one *ilāh*." Like Ibn Taymiyya and Ibn ʿAbd al-Wahhāb,[59] Mawdūdī employs a 'natural capacity' principle to distinguish between, on the one hand, a normal and permissible kind of request, and on the other, the kind of supplication (*duʿā*) that must be directed solely to Allāh. If a man who is thirsty or sick calls to a servant to bring him water or to a doctor to treat him, he does not thereby take the servant or doctor as an *ilāh*, since the activities they undertake to fulfill the man's need follow a natural causal chain. In contrast, if he calls on a deceased *walī* (saint) for aid, he has taken that *walī* as an *ilāh*, since this supplication implies the belief that the deceased *walī* sees, hears, and wields sovereignty (*farmān-rawāʾī*) over the world of causation in a supernatural sense.[60]

(3) The Arabs of the *jāhiliyya* believed in a supreme God whom they called Allāh. The basic belief regarding the *ilāh*s was that they possessed some share in His divinity and were able to influence Him. Through their intercession (*sifārish*), benefit could be brought and harm averted, as for example in Qurʾān 10:18: "They worship apart from Allāh that which cannot harm them or benefit them, and say: these are our intercessors with Allāh." This emphasis on the

[58] Mawdūdī, *Iṣṭilāḥēn̠*, p. 13.
[59] Cf. e.g. Ibn Taymiyya, *Majmūʿat al-fatāwā*, vol. 1, p. 79; *Durar*, vol. 2, pp. 24, 37.
[60] Mawdūdī, *Iṣṭilāḥēn̠*, pp. 13–15.

notion that the *ilāh*s of the *jāhiliyya* were worshipped as intercessors is again reminiscent of Ibn Taymiyya and Ibn ʿAbd al-Wahhāb, the latter of whom even once glossed *lā ilāha illā llāh* as "negation of the intermediaries."[61] Similar also is the general principle that Mawdūdī draws from this depiction: "Thus, in accordance with their [the *jāhiliyya* Arabs'] terminology, to affirm of someone that he is an intercessor with Allāh, and out of this belief to request aid (*madad kī iltijā karnā*) of him, to perform rites of reverence and veneration before him, and to offer him vows and prayer, is to make of him an *ilāh*."[62]

(4) The Arabs of the *jāhiliyya* feared that if they caused displeasure to their *ilāh*s or neglected to revere them the *ilāh*s would visit harm upon them, as for example in Qurʾān 11:54: "We can not say but that some of our *ilāh*s have smitten you with evil."[63]

(5) Up to this point Mawdūdī has discussed *ilāh* in relation to ritual worship, with particular reference to the cult of saints, and in this matter his views are close to those of the premodern monolatric tradition. In his fifth observation Mawdūdī turns to the issue of theonomy, and here his analysis is reminiscent of the premodern theonomic tradition. The primary prooftext employed in this section is Qurʾān 9:31, which we discussed at length in Chapter 3 in the context of the *taqlīd*-as-*shirk* polemic. Mawdūdī even adduces the ʿAdī b. Ḥātim *ḥadīth*; this is especially noteworthy since it is in fact the only *ḥadīth* mentioned in all of *Iṣṭilāḥēn̲* (apart from a few mentioned in passing in the lexicographical discussions that open each chapter).

Mawdūdī writes:

In these verses another meaning of *ilāh* is encountered, one that differs entirely from the previous meanings. Here there is no conception of supernatural power. The one who is taken as an *ilāh* [in these verses] is either a human, or a human's own soul (*insān kā apnā nafs*). In this meaning he is not taken as an *ilāh* when he is supplicated or believed to hold power over benefit and harm or because his protection is sought, but rather he is taken as an *ilāh* in this meaning when his ruling is accepted as law (*us kē ḥukm kō qānūn taslīm kiyā gayā*) … and when the idea is formed that he, in his own right (*be-jāʾē kh*$^{w}$*ud*), has the authority (*ikhtiyār*) to command and forbid, without being obliged to derive authority from, and refer back to, a power (*iqtidār*) higher than himself.

[61] *Durar*, vol. 2, p. 117. [62] Mawdūdī, *Iṣṭilāḥēn̲*, pp. 15–16.
[63] Mawdūdī, *Iṣṭilāḥēn̲*, p. 17.

In the first verse [i.e. Qurʾān 9:31] there is mention of the taking of the scholars (*ʿulamāʾ*)[64] and priests (*rāhibōṉ*) as *ilāhs*.[65] We find a clear explanation of this in the *ḥadīth*. When ʿAdī b. Ḥātim (may Allāh be pleased with him) asked the Prophet (Allāh's blessing and peace be upon him) about this verse, he said that whatever your scholars and monks permit, you accept as permitted, and whatever they forbid, you accept as forbidden, without any concern for what Allāh's ruling is regarding it.[66]

Mawdūdī adduces two other verses in this section in connection with the 'legislative' kind of *ilāh*: Qurʾān 6:137, which reads: "Likewise those they hold as partners [in divinity] have made many of the *mushrikīn* look favorably upon killing their children"; and 41:21: "Or do they hold [some] to be partners [in divinity], who have legislated for them in the *dīn* that which Allāh has not permitted?" While both these verses use the term *shurakāʾ* (partners) rather than *āliha*, Mawdūdī's Urdu glosses add the words *yaʿnī shurakāʾ fī al-ulūhiyyat*; for reasons that are not entirely clear, he views these beings' 'partnership' with Allāh as partnership in Allāh's *ilāh* aspect in particular. In any event, in like manner to his comments on Qurʾān 9:31 and the ʿAdī b. Ḥātim *ḥadīth*, he writes: "These two verses are decisive [proof] that people who, without any authority from Allāh's ruling, consider some fixed custom, rule, or practice to be a valid law have [thereby] taken the legislator [viz. of this custom, rule, or practice] as a partner in *ilāhiyyat*."[67]

Just as Mawdūdī sought to find one underlying concept that tied together the various lexical meanings associated with the root *ʾ-l-h*, he now proceeds to synthesize his findings regarding the meaning of *ilāh* in the Qurʾān in order to isolate one primary idea that underlies them all. Mawdūdī argues that this underlying idea connecting the meanings of *ilāh* in the Qurʾān is that of power (*iqtidār*). The belief in the *ilāh*'s supernatural power to protect, give aid, resolve difficulties, hear prayer, and to benefit or harm is due to the attribution to the *ilāh* of some kind of power in the cosmos. Likewise, the fear that the *ilāh* will visit harm on an individual if it is displeased can only derive from the belief in the *ilāh*'s power. Regarding supplication of an *ilāh* for one's needs, in its capacity as an intermediary with Allāh, Mawdūdī argues that the cause of this

[64] The verse itself has *aḥbār*, usually interpreted as 'rabbis,' or alternatively as a class of Christian clerics. While *ʿulamāʾ* can refer to scholars of any kind, its usual meaning is Muslim scholars, and Mawdūdī's gloss likely alludes to the application of this verse to condemnation of *taqlīd*.

[65] There is some difficulty here, as the verse mentions their being taken as *arbāb* and not as *āliha*. It is possible that their status as *ilāhs* is inferred from the phrase *wa-mā umirū illā li-yaʿbudū ilāhan wāḥidan*.

[66] Mawdūdī, *Iṣṭilāḥēṉ*, pp. 17–19.

[67] Mawdūdī, *Iṣṭilāḥēṉ*, p. 19.

behavior is the belief that the *ilāh* has some share in Allāh's power. Finally, the affirmation of some individual's law as binding is likewise an acknowledgment of that individual's power. Mawdūdī concludes: "Thus the fundamental essence of *ulūhiyyat* is power" (*pas ulūhiyyat kī aṣl-i rūḥ iqtidār hay*).[68]

This is a neat and logical conclusion. It is also one in which Mawdūdī differs from the premodern monolatric tradition, notwithstanding the parallels noted above. As we saw in earlier chapters, Ibn Taymiyya and Ibn ʿAbd al-Wahhāb placed divine power – the cratological aspect – squarely on the side of *rubūbiyya*, and for this reason strenuously objected to the Ashʿarī gloss of *ilāh* as *al-qādir*. In contrast, *ilāh* denoted for them a kind of authority or right, and primarily the right to exclusive worship: It is the normative, relational aspect of divinity. This authority certainly stood in connection with divine power, and it was this connection that underlay the interrelation between *ulūhiyya* and *rubūbiyya*, but Ibn Taymiyya and Ibn ʿAbd al-Wahhāb were careful to preserve the distinction. Were it lost, one would lose the prescriptive (*sharʿī*) aspect of divinity: All human activity would fall directly under Allāh's *qadar* in a deterministic sense, just like the cosmos does, and there could thus be no meaning to human obligation (see Chapter 1).

Yet this is perhaps not so great a difference as it first appears, since in essence Mawdūdī folds the relation between power and normative authority into a single term and considers it internal to the *ilāh* aspect. To see how this is so we need to consider Mawdūdī's argumentation in the conclusion of the *ilāh* chapter of *Iṣṭilāḥēn̠*.

Mawdūdī concludes with a four-part argument, which he presents as the Qurʾān's method of deduction from premises to conclusions. First, he restates his earlier assertion regarding the relation between the term *ilāh* and power, but now with an added nuance: "*ilāhiyyat* and power (*iqtidār*) are mutually implicative (*lāzim o malzūm hayn̠*), and with respect to their essence and meaning, the two things are one."[69] In light of our comparison between Mawdūdī and premodern monolatry we could at this point insist that their being mutually implicative or one and the same thing is a difference of capital importance, but at least we can observe that Mawdūdī considers them one and the same *because* of their mutually implicative nature, and simply views the relation between them as the internal property of one single term. On this basis he begins his argument as follows:

(1) The fulfillment of needs, resolution of difficulties, provision of protection, etc. (i.e. the functions that Mawdūdī identified as essential to

[68] Mawdūdī, *Iṣṭilāḥēn̠*, p. 19. [69] Mawdūdī, *Iṣṭilāḥēn̠*, p. 27.

the nature of the *ilāh*) are not ordinary (*maʿmūlī*) matters, as they at first seem. They cannot be accomplished without control over countless causes, and in fact the fulfillment of the simplest request requires the same power as the very creation of the heavens and earth.[70]

(2) (Thus) this power is indivisible. It is impossible that the power of creation be vested in one entity, and that another be vested with the power of provision, control over health and illness, or life and death. (This is apparently understood as following from (1), since these latter powers require the same power as that responsible for creation.) "Thus it is necessarily true (*ḍarūrī hay*) that the totality of powers and authorities (*tamām iqtidārāt o ikhtiyārāt*) are under the control of one central sovereign (*farmān-rawā*)."[71]

(3) Since all power is concentrated in the hands of one sovereign, with no other having any part in it, it necessarily follows that *ulūhiyyat* is entirely exclusive (*khāṣṣ*) to this same sovereign, and no other has any power (*ṭāqat*) of providing succor, answering supplications, granting protection, etc. Not only does no other hold such powers in his own right, no one possesses powers of necessarily effective intercession with the sovereign, since to grant or not grant the intercession is entirely at the sovereign's discretion.[72]

(4) It follows from the principle of the unity of supreme power that all aspects of sovereignty (*ḥākimiyyat o farmān-rawāʾī*) are likewise concentrated in the possessor of the supreme power, and that no part of sovereignty (*ḥākimiyyat*) is transferred to another. Just as He is Creator, with no other having any part in creation, and just as He is Sustainer, with no other having any part in the provision of sustenance, and just as He controls the cosmos, and no other has any part in this, so it is certain (*yaqīnan*) that He must be the Ruler (*ḥākim*), Commander (*āmir*), and Legislator (*shāriʿ*), and that in this kind of power (*iqtidār*) as well He has no partner.

This conclusion is a central one to Mawdūdī's system: The parallel between Allāh's exclusive cosmic power (as Creator, Sustainer, etc.) and His exclusive normative authority is the basis for the entire doctrine of *ḥākimiyyat*. The passage continues in this same vein, elaborating the point: Just as no other in His dominion is a redresser of grievances, fulfiller of needs, or provider of shelter, so no other is, in his own right, a ruler, sovereign, or legislator.

70 Mawdūdī, *Iṣṭilāḥēn̠*, p. 27. 71 Mawdūdī, *Iṣṭilāḥēn̠*, p. 27.
72 Mawdūdī, *Iṣṭilāḥēn̠*, pp. 27–28.

Creation and provision of sustenance, bringing to life and putting to death, control over the sun and the moon and the alternation of night and day, predetermination (*qaḍā awr qadar*), rule and sovereignty (*ḥukm awr bād-shāhī*), command and legislation (*amr o tashrī ʿ*), all these are different facets of total power (*iqtidār*) and *ḥākimiyyat*, and this power and *ḥākimiyyat* is indivisible (*nā qābil-i taqsīm hay*).[73]

The parallelism and identification established here between Allāh's cosmic power and His normative authority entails a logical parallelism and identification between infringement of one and the other, that is to say, between different kinds of *shirk*: "If some individual, without any basis in Allāh's ruling, considers any ruling to be binding, he has committed *shirk* in just the same manner as one who supplicates another apart from Allāh."[74] Mawdūdī does not spell out the full logic of this parallel here, but if we keep in mind his preceding analysis of ritual *shirk* it becomes clear. When one supplicates an *ilāh*, one does so due to a belief in that *ilāh*'s power to fulfill the request; when one considers a ruling by someone other than Allāh (i.e. an *ilāh*) to be binding, one does so due to a belief in that *ilāh*'s authority to legislate. The parallel is thus between ascription of supernatural power to an *ilāh* and ascription of normative authority to an *ilāh*. This is why Mawdūdī's use of Qurʾān 9:31 and the ʿAdī b. Ḥātim *ḥadīth* as a basis for his fifth meaning of *ilāh* is of such importance: As in the premodern anti-*taqlīd* polemic, Mawdūdī uses them to establish an equivalence between ritual *shirk* and *shirk* of judgment and legislation.

Before moving on to the *rabb* chapter of *Iṣṭilāḥēn̲* it is worth returning briefly to the comparison between Mawdūdī and premodern monolatry. It is clear from the conclusion of the *ilāh* chapter that, notwithstanding Mawdūdī's argument for a total identification between the concept of power and that of *ilāh*, he does in fact recognize within the term a normative dimension. Mawdūdī's central parallel between cosmic power (e.g. creation, provision of sustenance) and normative 'power' (i.e. *ḥākimiyyat*) is quite similar to a central argument found in both Ibn Taymiyya's and Ibn ʿAbd al-Wahhāb's writings, namely, the argument from *rubūbiyya* to *ulūhiyya*, which they believed was the Qurʾān's own argumentation in verses such as Qurʾān 43:87. To give just one example, when Ibn ʿAbd al-Wahhāb was asked regarding the relation between *rubūbiyya* and *ulūhiyya*, he answered that *tawḥīd al-rubūbiyya* was the foundation (*aṣl*), and that people only err in *ilāhiyya* when they do not give *rubūbiyya* its full due; he then cites as a basis for this argument Qurʾān 43:87: "And if you asked them who created them, they would

[73] Mawdūdī, *Iṣṭilāḥēn̲*, p. 28. [74] Mawdūdī, *Iṣṭilāḥēn̲*, p. 28.

surely say: Allāh. How then are they deluded?"[75] What Ibn ʿAbd al-Wahhāb means by this is that the Qurʾān addressed the unbelievers' own acknowledgment of *tawḥīd al-rubūbiyya* – the objective, cosmic aspect of divinity – and argued therefrom that they should uphold *tawḥīd al-ulūhiyya* as well – the normative, relational aspect of divinity. The difference between this argument and Mawdūdī's is simply that Mawdūdī folds within the single term *ilāh* both the aspects that Ibn Taymiyya and Ibn ʿAbd al-Wahhāb referred to as *ilāh* and *rabb*, and the relation between them becomes in Mawdūdī's system an internal property of the *ilāh* aspect itself.

*The Meaning of* Rabb Mawdūdī follows a similar procedure in his discussion of the word *rabb* as he did for *ilāh*. He sees this term as well as having been distorted from its original meaning. In fact, the *rabb* chapter is far lengthier than the *ilāh* chapter, and Mawdūdī clearly sees this term as the central one on which hinges the primary dispute between Islam and unbelief, as we will see presently.

In his summary of the term *rabb* from the lexical (*lughawī*) perspective he distinguishes five meanings: (1) nourisher, provider, fosterer; (2) guardian, patron, or rectifier; (3) one who holds a central position, such that he is a gathering point for others; (4) a chief who is obeyed, a possessor of power; and (5) owner and master (*āqā*). Mawdūdī takes pains to state that it is an error to restrict the meaning of *rabb* solely to the first of these meanings, that is, to make it a synonym of *parward-gār* (provider);[76] he presumably does so because in his view the 'lordship' aspect of *rabb* is of primary significance.

Mawdūdī then goes on to survey the Qurʾān's usage of the term, providing examples for each of the five lexical uses listed above.[77] His emphasis, however – both here, and even more so in the continuation of the chapter – is clearly on meaning (4), in which *rabb* denotes power and authority over humans. Meanings (1) and (2) together are roughly the meaning of *parward-gār*, "provider," which, while a true meaning of *rabb*, Mawdūdī insisted did not exhaust the term's meaning. Meaning (3), *rabb* as possessor of a central position and as a point of reference, is not especially significant in its own right, as Mawdūdī writes that it is more or less included in meaning (4),[78] "chief" or "possessor of power."

[75] *Durar*, vol. 2, pp. 64–65.
[76] Mawdūdī, *Iṣṭilāḥēn̲*, pp. 31–33. Mawdūdī does not name the author of the definition he criticizes as wrongly restrictive, "[*al-rabb fī al-aṣl al-tarbiya wa-*]*huwa inshāʾ al-shayʾ ḥālan fa-ḥālan ilā ḥadd al-tamām*"; it is in fact from al-Rāghib al-Iṣfahānī, *al-Mufradāt fī gharīb al-qurʾān*, n.p.: Maktabat Nizār Muṣṭafā al-Bāz, n.d., p. 245.
[77] Mawdūdī, *Iṣṭilāḥēn̲*, pp. 33–37. [78] Mawdūdī, *Iṣṭilāḥēn̲*, p. 35.

Likewise, meaning (5) appears similar to (4), but from the verses adduced it seems that Mawdūdī understands it as denoting possession of or mastery over attributes and physical objects, rather than possession of powers or rights over humans: examples include (106:3) *rabb hādhā al-bayt* ("lord of this house," i.e. the Kaʿba) and (37:180) *rabb al-ʿizza* ("possessor of might").[79] Mawdūdī's discussion focuses on meaning (4), and he does not add any commentary to the verses illustrating the other meanings. In sum we are left with two basic aspects of *rabb*, the first being *parward-gār*, which refers to provision, nourishment, and guardianship; and the second being the aspect of lordship, mastery, power, and authority, especially over human subjects. This reduction of the meanings of *rabb* to two aspects, while adumbrated already in this initial discussion, becomes a major focal point for Mawdūdī later in the *rabb* chapter.

As examples of the Qurʾān's use of *rabb* in meaning (4) Mawdūdī cites two polemical verses against the Jews and Christians, Qurʾān 9:31 (which, as noted above, already figured in the *ilāh* chapter), and 3:64: "[O People of the Book, come to common ground with us: That we worship no one but Allāh,] and that we not take one another as lords beside Allāh." Both verses refer to 'lords' (*arbāb*) that are taken or might be taken apart from Allāh. According to Mawdūdī, the *arbāb* in these verses are "people (*lōg*) whose nations or groups revere them as absolute leaders and chiefs (*rahnumā o peshwā*). Their command and prohibition, rules and laws, and determinations of the permitted and the forbidden are accepted without reference to any higher authority. They are understood to possess the right (*ḥaqq-dār*) to command and prohibit in their own right (*ba-jāʾe khʷud*)."[80] Mawdūdī then cites two additional verses (12:42, 12:50) in which the prophet Yūsuf refers to Firʿawn (Pharaoh) as the Egyptians' *rabb*, "because they accepted his centrality, his supreme power (*iqtidār-i aʿlā*), and his power of command and prohibition."[81]

The idea of legislative power or authority is nowhere explicit in these verses; clearly Mawdūdī's conclusion was influenced by the ʿAdī b. Ḥātim *ḥadīth*, which he had mentioned previously in the *ilāh* chapter. Given that Qurʾān 9:31 is used in the discussion both of *ilāh* and of *rabb*, it should not surprise us that the meaning of *rabb* discussed here sounds similar to meaning (5) of *ilāh*: Both are humans to whom other humans attribute legislative authority. For Mawdūdī, then, the distinction between divine aspects does not run between the terms *rabb* and *ilāh*, but rather each of these terms contains different aspects folded within it, with considerable

79 Mawdūdī, *Iṣṭilāḥēn̲*, pp. 36–37.
80 Mawdūdī, *Iṣṭilāḥēn̲*, p. 35.
81 Mawdūdī, *Iṣṭilāḥēn̲*, pp. 35–36.

overlap between the two. This is a crucial point to keep in mind, since by this point in our study we have become accustomed to the *rabb/ilāh* distinction in the doctrines of Ibn Taymiyya and Ibn ʿAbd al-Wahhāb in which the correlation of each term with a different aspect of divinity was consistent. In what follows I will argue that Mawdūdī does in fact distinguish between two basic aspects of divinity, but in his system these do not correlate to the two different terms. His philological inquiry into the 'basic terms' is only a springboard used to uncover the purportedly original meanings of divinity that he believes were forgotten in later generations, and these meanings inhere in both terms; there is no clear *ilāh/rabb* distinction per se.

*The Streitpunkt* The remainder of the *rabb* chapter – and the longest single section in the book – is devoted to analysis of the Qurʾān's depiction of various groups of unbelievers' ideas regarding *rubūbiyyat*,[82] followed by a final section describing the Qurʾān's message (*daʿwat*) on this issue.[83] This section, which should be regarded as the heart of *Iṣṭilāḥēn̲*, hinges on what we termed in Chapter 2 the Streitpunkt principle, that is, specification of the nature of the dispute between the prophets and the unbelievers in order to isolate and define the true dividing line between Islam and unbelief.

Throughout his survey of the conflicts between the prophets and the unbelievers over the nature of divinity, Mawdūdī emphasizes the point that the unbelievers believed in Allāh as a high god who alone created the cosmos and wields ultimate power over it. This parallels the Taymiyyan theme (though not the terminology) of the *mushrikūn* acknowledging *tawḥīd al-rubūbiyya*. As for the question of what it was that the unbelievers lacked, and by dint of which lack were classified as unbelievers, Mawdūdī's answer is partly in accord with the premodern salafī tradition, but with a different inflection. The unbelievers failed to make their worship to Allāh exclusive – that is, they did not uphold ritual monolatry – but also, and more important, they took others as legislators in place of Allāh, and based their social, political, and legal order on these other divinities. This modern inflection of the issue is not itself without premodern precedent, as we saw in Chapter 3. Nonetheless, Mawdūdī's systematic exploration of this topic has the effect of shifting the Streitpunkt from monolatry to theonomy, with the same template that served premodern thinkers such as Ibn ʿAbd al-Wahhāb serving in Mawdūdī's exposition as a polemic against modern secularism.

[82] Mawdūdī, *Iṣṭilāḥēn̲*, pp. 37–72. [83] Mawdūdī, *Iṣṭilāḥēn̲*, pp. 72–80.

In order to understand this 'thenomic shift' we need to consider his analysis of the Streitpunkt in detail.

Mawdūdī proceeds chronologically, starting from the earliest nation of unbelievers mentioned in the Qur'ān, *qawm Nūḥ* (Noah's people). Mawdūdī cites Qur'ān 23:24 to prove that they did not deny Allāh's existence: When in this verse they deny that Nūḥ is a prophet, they argue that Allāh would have sent angels had He wanted to communicate with humans – thus acknowledging that they believed in Allāh.[84] Mawdūdī argues that there is no record of the unbelievers rejecting Nūḥ's statements that Allāh is their *rabb* or that He created the heavens and the earth, and he therefore concludes that they did acknowledge Allāh as Creator and even as their *rabb*, just not in all of the term's meanings. Mawdūdī argues as well that Nūḥ's people accepted Allāh as an *ilāh*, just not as the only *ilāh*. This he deduces from Nūḥ's injunction (Qur'ān 7:59) "[O people, worship Allāh,] you have no *ilāh* but Him"; had they not accepted Allāh as an *ilāh* at all, Nūḥ should have told them: "take Allāh as your *ilāh*."[85] Thus the first stage of Mawdūdī's analysis is a process of elimination: The dispute between Nūḥ and his people was not over Allāh's existence, His aspect as Creator, or acceptance of Him as a *rabb* and *ilāh*.

Mawdūdī then argues that the dispute hinged on two points. The first was Allāh's exclusivity as *ilāh*, regarding which Mawdūdī summarizes Nūḥ's message to the unbelievers as follows:

> The same one who is Lord of the worlds (*rabb al-'ālamīn*), whom you yourselves acknowledge gave existence to you and to all beings, and the same one who sustains you with necessities [of life], is in reality (*dar aṣl*) your sole *ilāh*. Apart from Him there is no *ilāh*, no other being is a fulfiller of your needs, easer of your difficulties, hearer of your supplications, or sender of aid. Thus bow your head to Him in prayer (*li-hādhā tum usī kē āgē sar niyāz j^hukā'ō*).

In opposition to this message, Nūḥ's people insisted that while Allāh is certainly *rabb al-'ālamīn*, others also had some part in the divine administration and in the fulfillment of human needs, and thus were also *ilāh*s.[86] In this passage Mawdūdī comes close to arguing in good salafī fashion that the point of dispute between Nūḥ and his people was ritual monolatry – though we see here that, just as in the *ilāh* chapter of *Iṣṭilāḥēn̲*, Mawdūdī does not treat monolatry as a truly independent variable but rather describes the unbelievers' failure to uphold monolatry as stemming from their failure to believe in Allāh's exclusivity of power.

[84] Mawdūdī, *Iṣṭilāḥēn̲*, p. 37. [85] Mawdūdī, *Iṣṭilāḥēn̲*, p. 38.
[86] Mawdūdī, *Iṣṭilāḥēn̲*, pp. 38–39.

The issue described as the second point of dispute between Nūḥ and his people was the latter's ascription of different elements of *rubūbiyyat* to different entities. According to Mawdūdī, they only accepted Allāh as their *rabb* in the meaning of Creator, Lord of heaven and earth, and Master (*mudabbir*) of beings; they did not accept Him as *rabb* in the normative sense, as sovereign, legislator, and one to whom obedience is due. In other words, Nūḥ's people divided *rubūbiyyat* into two parts, and ascribed the latter part to their chiefs and religious leaders.[87]

As noted above this distinction between two overarching aspects of *rubūbiyyat* is a central feature of Mawdūdī's treatment of the term. What was not clear from Mawdūdī's initial survey, but which is more explicit here, is that these two are what we could term Allāh's cosmic-objective and normative-relational aspects. In this way the distinction between the two aspects of *rabb* in Mawdūdī's system parallels the *rabb*/*ilāh* distinction in the writings of Ibn Taymiyya and Ibn ʿAbd al-Wahhāb, for whom *rabb* was the cosmic and objective aspect, and *ilāh* the normative and relational one. This is especially clear if we recall Ibn Taymiyya's parallel terminology for the *rabb*/*ilāh* dyad, the distinction between Allāh's cosmic or ontological will (*irāda kawniyya*) and His legislative or normative will (*irāda sharʿiyya*), in which the cosmic/normative distinction is expressed in the terminology itself. The main difference between these premodern thinkers and Mawdūdī, apart from the terminological one, is one of emphasis: Ibn Taymiyya and (especially) Ibn ʿAbd al-Wahhāb emphasized ritual monolatry as the main expression of submission to Allāh's normative aspect, which governs how humans are to relate to divinity, whereas for Mawdūdī this is expressed first and foremost through obedience to law.

Mawdūdī's depiction of the conflict between the later prophets and the unbelievers follows in much the same vein. The unbelievers of ʿĀd and Thamūd, like Nūḥ's people, are described as acknowledging Allāh's existence and accepting Him as their *ilāh* and *rabb* in the cosmic sense; the prophetic message that they rejected was (1) to make Allāh their sole *ilāh* and to worship Him alone, and (2) to accept Him as their *rabb* in the normative legislative sense.[88]

Mawdūdī argues that even Namrūd (Nimrod), a representative of the Ancient Near Eastern model of divine kingship, did not deny Allāh's existence or His cosmic *rubūbiyyat*; the only part of Allāh's divinity that he arrogated to himself was the normative aspect of *rubūbiyyat*. The discussion of Namrūd is based entirely on Qurʾān 2:258:

[87] Mawdūdī, *Iṣṭilāḥēn̲*, p. 39.
[88] Mawdūdī, *Iṣṭilāḥēn̲*, pp. 40–42.

Have you not considered he who disputed with Ibrāhīm regarding his Lord (*fī rabbihi*), because Allāh gave him kingship? When Ibrāhīm said: my Lord is He who gives life and puts to death, he said: I give life and put to death. Ibrāhīm said: Allāh causes the sun to rise from the east, so bring it from the west. Thus the unbeliever was confounded; Allāh does not guide the evildoers.[89]

Mawdūdī incorporates this elliptical disputation neatly into his Streitpunkt analysis. In accordance with his general theory (and with his preceding analysis of the views of Ibrāhīm's people),[90] he argues that it cannot be that Namrūd was denying Allāh's existence, nor was he making the absurd claim that he himself was *rabb* in the cosmic sense, that is, creator of the world, controller of the heavenly bodies, and so forth. In other words, Namrūd did not claim to be *rabb* in meanings (1) and (2) of the term. He claimed, rather, to be *rabb* in the other senses: He argued that he was the owner and master of the land over which he ruled, and thus its inhabitants were his slaves who had to obey his authority and law.

According to Mawdūdī this is what the Qurʾān means when it says that the king disputed Ibrāhīm *fī rabbihi an ātāhu llāh al-mulk*. Namrūd had heard that one of his subjects, Ibrāhīm, denied both the cosmic, supernatural *rubūbiyyat* of the heavenly bodies, and the "political and social" *rubūbiyyat* of the king, and thus Namrūd summoned him to ask who his *rabb* was. When Ibrāhīm answered that his *rabb* is the one who has power over life and death, Namrūd, on the basis of his earthly kingship, answered that it was he himself who held power over life and death. Ibrāhīm's rejoinder was that this power is inseparable from the ability to make the sun rise from where one wills – that is, that he would only attribute the *rubūbiyyat* of earthly authority to He who holds *rubūbiyyat* over the cosmos: "Ibrāhīm said to him: I acknowledge Allāh alone as *rabb*. In my view Allāh alone is *rabb* in all the senses of *rubūbiyyat*."[91]

Mawdūdī advances a similar argument regarding Firʿawn (Pharaoh), the Qurʾān's better-known exemplar of the Near Eastern god-king. The argumentation here is a bit tortuous as even Mawdūdī acknowledges that the Egyptian pharaohs did claim a connection to supernatural deities by dint of which they projected an aura of sanctity (*qudūsiyyat*), in addition to their claim to absolute sovereignty (*ḥākimiyyat-i muṭlaqa*) in earthly affairs. Nonetheless, Mawdūdī insists on the priority of *ḥākimiyyat*, arguing that the pharaohs' claim to supernatural divinity was merely a collateral effect (*maḥḍ ēk ḍimnī chīz hay*): "The basic aim was to firm up

[89] The name "Namrūd" does not appear in the Qurʾān; the identification of him with the king mentioned in verse 2:258 is standard in the exegetical literature.
[90] Mawdūdī, *Iṣṭilāḥēn*, pp. 42–45. [91] Mawdūdī, *Iṣṭilāḥēn*, pp. 46–47.

political sovereignty (*siyāsī ḥākimiyyat*), and to this end the claim to supernatural *ulūhiyyat* was employed merely as a stratagem."[92] Mawdūdī views this claim as an instrumental one, and argues that Firʿawn did not truly claim supernatural divinity for himself in senses (1) and (2) of *rabb*, that is, he did not claim to be creator and master of cosmic causality.[93] Thus "Firʿawn's basic claim was not to supernatural divinity, but to political divinity (*siyāsī khudāʾī*)," that is, meanings (3), (4), and (5) of *rabb*. Mawdūdī writes that just as with Namrūd, Firʿawn's basis for this claim was the very fact of his position of kingship, as evidenced by his response to Mūsā's (Moses') preaching (Qurʾān 43:51): "And Firʿawn proclaimed among his people: O people, is not mine sovereignty over Egypt and these rivers flowing under me? Do you not discern?"[94]

Likewise, just as Ibrāhīm's message to Namrūd was simply the affirmation that Allāh is the sole possessor of divinity in all its senses, including the normative *rubūbiyyat* of earthly authority, so Mawdūdī characterizes the message proclaimed by Mūsā:

> There is no *ilāh* or *rabb*, in any sense, apart from Allāh, Lord of the worlds. He alone is *ilāh* and *rabb* in the supernatural sense, and likewise in the political and social sense. Worship (*parastish*) is His [right] alone, and so is servitude (*bandagī*) and obedience (*iṭāʿat*), as well as adherence to [His] law [i.e. and not to another's].[95]

That this was the nature of Mūsā's message explains why Firʿawn and his ministers opposed him, as they saw Mūsā and Hārūn (Aaron) as seeking to take over their land and bring about the downfall of the country's religion and civilization.[96]

Mawdūdī makes the same argument when discussing the nature of the Jews' and Christians' unbelief as depicted in the Qurʾān. Here of course he does not have to expend as much effort in proving that these unbelievers acknowledged Allāh's existence, as this is clear from the text of the Qurʾān. Despite the Jews' and Christians' status as People of the Book (*ahl al-kitāb*), which Islamic law recognizes as a privileged category in comparison to the *mushrikūn*, Mawdūdī argues that their deviation from Allāh's religion and from the prophetic message lay in the same two points as with the other peoples: First, they failed to uphold ritual monolatry and the exclusivity of Allāh's divinity in the supernatural realm, and second, they attributed social and political *rubūbiyyat* to human leaders.

92 Mawdūdī, *Iṣṭilāḥēn̠*, pp. 58–59.
93 Mawdūdī, *Iṣṭilāḥēn̠*, p. 57.
94 Mawdūdī, *Iṣṭilāḥēn̠*, p. 59.
95 Mawdūdī, *Iṣṭilāḥēn̠*, p. 59.
96 Mawdūdī, *Iṣṭilāḥēn̠*, pp. 59–60.

As for the first of these deviations the Qur'ān describes the Jews as declaring 'Uzayr (Ezra), and the Christians the Masīḥ (Jesus), to be the son of Allāh (9:30); the Christians as having taken 'Īsā (Jesus) and Maryam (Mary) as *ilāh*s (5:116); and the People of the Book (collectively) as having taken the angels and the prophets as *rabb*s apart from Allāh (3:79–80). According to Mawdūdī such verses show that the Jews and Christians elevated prophets, saints, and angels to a divine station, took them as partners in divinity, believed them to have a share in supernatural *rubūbiyyat* and *ulūhiyyat*, and thus offered them ritual worship (*parastish*) and supplicated them.[97]

Mawdūdī's description of the Jews' and Christians' second deviation is based entirely on Qur'ān 9:31, the same verse already adduced as a central prooftext in his definitions of both *ilāh* and *rabb*. He does not mention the 'Adī b. Ḥātim tradition explicitly here, but his comments are clearly based on the *ḥadīth*'s exegesis of the verse. Mawdūdī writes that those individuals in the (Jews' and Christians') religious (*dīnī*) system whose proper role was solely to propagate the rulings contained in Allāh's law (*khodā kī sharī'at kē aḥkām batā'ēn̲*) were progressively given authority in their own right (*bā-ikhtiyār-i khʷud*) to permit and prohibit, command and forbid. Mawdūdī concludes that

> these people were afflicted with the same two momentous, fundamental deviations as Nūḥ's people, Ibrāhīm's people, 'Ād, Thamūd, the people of Madyan, and other peoples. Just like them, the [Jews and Christians] made the angels and prominent humans Allāh's partners in supernatural *rubūbiyyat*, and just like them, they accorded social (*tamaddunī*) and political (*siyāsī*) *rubūbiyyat* to humans in place of Allāh.[98]

It is worth remarking here a certain inconsistency in Mawdūdī's terminology. Earlier in *Iṣṭilāḥēn̲* the first deviation, relating to ritual monolatry and the exclusivity of Allāh's supernatural power, was analyzed primarily in relation to the term *ilāh*, whereas here Mawdūdī labels it a deviation in relation to Allāh's supernatural *rubūbiyyat* (from *rabb*). Likewise, the issue of "social and political" divinity becomes more exclusively affiliated with *rubūbiyyat* as the book progresses, even though Mawdūdī initially presented the issue, through Qur'ān 9:31 and the 'Adī b. Ḥātim *ḥadīth*, as the fifth and final meaning of *ilāh*. Once again we observe that for Mawdūdī the terms *ilāh* and *rabb* do not have one fixed meaning and do not in themselves designate different aspects of divinity. Mawdūdī's primary concern is the distinction between the 'supernatural' aspect of divinity, on the one hand (what we have termed

[97] Mawdūdī, *Iṣṭilāḥēn̲*, pp. 62–64. [98] Mawdūdī, *Iṣṭilāḥēn̲*, p. 64.

the cosmic-objective aspect), and the 'social and political' aspect, on the other (what we have termed the normative-relational aspect). These are, respectively, expressions of Allāh's exclusive power and of His right to exclusive authority. While this parallels Ibn Taymiyya's *rubūbiyya/ ulūhiyya* distinction, which likewise differentiated between cosmic-objective and normative-relational aspects, we see that in Mawdūdī's system ritual monolatry is categorized more or less as falling under the issue of power, and the normative-relational aspect of divinity mandates not so much exclusivity of worship as theonomy: a social, legal, and political order founded exclusively on Allāh's authority, as opposed to human authority.

The final conflict that Mawdūdī addresses in this section is that between the Arab *mushrikūn* and the Prophet Muḥammad, which he depicts as centering on the same two issues. The Arab *mushrikūn* not only knew of Allāh's existence, they believed that He was Creator of all things, including their own objects of worship, and accepted Him as the supreme deity. The first Qurʾānic passage that Mawdūdī cites in order to prove this, Qurʾān 23:84–90, relates Allāh's instructions to the Prophet Muḥammad on how to dispute with the *mushrikūn*:

> Say: To whom do the earth and those on it belong, if you have knowledge? They will say: To Allāh. Say: Then will you not be mindful? Say: Who is the Lord (*rabb*) of the seven heavens and Lord of the great throne? They will say: [they belong to] Allāh. Say: Then will you not fear [Him]? Say: In whose hand is dominion over all things, He who protects and against whom there is no protector, if you have knowledge? They will say: [that belongs to] Allāh. Say: How then are you deluded? No indeed, We have brought them the truth, but they are liars.[99]

After citing this passage to demonstrate that the Arab *mushrikūn* acknowledged Allāh's cosmic-objective aspect, Mawdūdī goes on to survey the Qurʾān's depiction of the *mushrikūn*'s conception of their objects of worship, referencing the verses that describe them as intermediaries and intercessors with Allāh (e.g. 39:3, 10:18).[100] On this basis Mawdūdī describes the Arab *mushrikūn* as falling into the same two deviations as the other peoples. First, in the supernatural (cosmic-objective) realm, they took other *ilāh*s and *rabb*s as partners to Allāh in *rubūbiyyat* and *ilāhiyyat*, believing that they had some purchase on governance of causal chains, and thus instead of worshipping Allāh exclusively they worshipped these others alongside Allāh.[101] As for the second deviation (in the normative-relational aspect of divinity) Mawdūdī writes:

[99] Mawdūdī, *Iṣṭilāḥē̱n*, pp. 65–66.
[100] Mawdūdī, *Iṣṭilāḥē̱n*, pp. 66–68.
[101] Mawdūdī, *Iṣṭilāḥē̱n*, pp. 68–69.

"In the matter of social (*tamaddunī*) and political (*siyāsī*) *rubūbiyyat*, their [the *mushrikūn*'s] minds were lacking completely the conception that Allāh was *rabb* in this meaning as well. They made their religious leaders, chiefs, and prominent family members *rabb* in this meaning and took their laws of life from them."[102]

As an example of this second deviation Mawdūdī cites Qur'ān 6:137 (used previously to demonstrate meaning (5) of *ilāh*): "Likewise those they hold as partners [in divinity] have made many of the *mushrikīn* look favorably upon killing their children." To Mawdūdī it is clear that the *shurakā'* (partners) in this verse are not physical idols (*but*) or supernatural deities (*devatā*) but rather human leaders. In addition, the partnership in divinity attributed to them is not governance over causality, nor were they worshipped in a ritual sense, but rather they were made partners in divinity by being granted the right to legislate in social, moral, and religious matters.[103]

The second verse Mawdūdī cites, Qur'ān 42:21, is further evidence for this contention: "Or do they have partners who have legislated for them in the *dīn* that for which Allāh has not granted permission?" Mawdūdī defers his full discussion of this verse to the final chapter of *Iṣṭilāḥēn̲* where he explores the scope of what is meant by the term *dīn*, but he states that even prior to the clarification of that issue it is clear from the verse that the Arab *mushrikūn* had leaders and chiefs who laid down rules for them, and that their acceptance of these rules as binding meant they had accepted these leaders and chiefs as partners with Allāh in divinity.[104] Incidentally, the phrase Mawdūdī uses to characterize the *mushrikūn*'s view of these rules as binding is *wājib al-taqlīd*. Given the centrality of Qur'ān 9:31 and the 'Adī b. Ḥātim *ḥadīth* to his argumentation, this phraseology suggests that he was also familiar with the use of these prooftexts to characterize jurisprudential *taqlīd* as *shirk* – a topic to which we will return at the close of our discussion of Mawdūdī.

This concludes the 'Streitpunkt' section of the book. The remainder of the *rabb* chapter is devoted to a description of the Qur'ān's message (*da'wat*), which opens with a summary of all that has preceded. In this summary Mawdūdī reduces the entire question of the nature of divinity to the two aspects we saw throughout the Streitpunkt section. He writes that none of the unbelievers denied Allāh's existence or that He was in some sense *ilāh* and *rabb*; rather "their fundamental deviation, which was common to all of them, was that they divided the five meanings of *rubūbiyyat* ... into two parts," and vested each part of divinity in different

[102] Mawdūdī, *Iṣṭilāḥēn̲*, p. 69. [103] Mawdūdī, *Iṣṭilāḥēn̲*, pp. 71–72.
[104] Mawdūdī, *Iṣṭilāḥēn̲*, p. 72.

entities. These are the same two aspects that were noted throughout the Streitpunkt section, though here reduced to two aspects of *rubūbiyyat* (i.e. without mention of *ilāh* or *ulūhiyyat*):

> [1] *Rabb* in the meaning of supernatural provision (*parwarish*) for created beings, caring for them, fulfilling their needs, and protection of them. [The unbelievers] held this kind [viz. of *rabb*] to be separate [viz. from the other kind of *rabb*]. And while they believed in Allāh as the supreme *rabb* in this meaning, they took as partners in *rubūbiyyat* angels, deities, jinn, invisible forces, stars, planets, prophets, saints, and spiritual leaders.
>
> [2] *Rabb* in the meaning of being vested with the authority of command and prohibition, possessor of supreme power, font of guidance, source of the law, head of state (*mamlakat kā ra'īs*), and center of society. [The unbelievers] held this to be a totally different aspect (*ḥaythiyyat*) [viz. from the first meaning of *rabb*]. In this sense [of *rabb*] they either believed exclusively in humans as *rabb* in place of Allāh, or else they theoretically believed in Allāh as *rabb*, but in practice bowed in obedience to the moral, social, and political *rubūbiyyat* of humans.[105]

Thus culminates Mawdūdī's line of argumentation up to this point. Mawdūdī's analysis of the terms *ilāh* and *rabb* was not meant to distinguish between them, but rather through them to arrive at his distinction between the two basic aspects of divinity, the cosmic-objective and the normative-relational. Mawdūdī originally included both supernatural power (the cosmic-objective aspect) and earthly authority (the normative-relational) as elements of *ilāh*, but throughout the Streitpunkt section we saw that *ilāh* became associated exclusively with the former, and the question of legislative authority came to be described as a *rubūbiyyat* issue. Now, in the above-cited summary, Mawdūdī describes both supernatural power and earthly authority as issues of *rubūbiyyat*. His terminology is strikingly inconsistent but his central theme is consistent to the point of monotony: Allāh is not only the sole possessor of cosmic power, for which reason He deserves exclusivity of worship, He is also the sole rightful possessor of earthly power and authority, for which reason He should enjoy a monopoly on legislation and sociopolitical obedience.

This summary leads into Mawdūdī's characterization of the message promulgated by Muḥammad and the prophets before him. It is a simple one: "There is only one *rabb* in all these meanings, and it is Allāh. *Rubūbiyyat* is indivisible (*nā qābil-i taqsīm*)."[106] Much as Ibn Taymiyya described the prophetic message as being simply that the same Allāh whose exclusive *rubūbiyya* the unbelievers acknowledged must also be

105 Mawdūdī, *Iṣṭilāḥēn̲*, p. 73. 106 Mawdūdī, *Iṣṭilāḥēn̲*, p. 73.

accorded *tawḥīd al-ulūhiyya*, so Mawdūdī describes the prophets as arguing from Allāh's role as Creator to His sole authority over earthly affairs:

> Given that He is the possessor of central power, that same God alone is both your supernatural *rabb* and your moral, social, and political *rabb* … He is the sole [rightful] object of worship (*ma'būd*) … And in like manner, He is King (*bādshāh*), sovereign (*mālik al-mulk*), He is the legislator, and it is He who is vested with authority to command and forbid.[107]

Again, the fault of the unbelievers was their separation between these two aspects: "These two aspects (*ḥaythiyyatēn̲*), which due to *jāhiliyya* you separated one from another, are in truth essential to and particular to divinity. They cannot be separated one from another, and it is not right to make created beings partners to God in either of them, in any aspect."[108]

Having reduced the entire question of divinity to that of the unity of these two aspects of *rabb*, Mawdūdī gives us one final reduction at the conclusion of the chapter. He writes that *rabb* in the Qur'ān is simply a synonym for *ḥākimiyyat* – which, lest there be any doubt as to its meaning, he glosses for the reader in English as "sovereignty."[109] The deviation of the *jāhilī* peoples, then, both those described in the Qur'ān and "up to this day,"[110] lies in their divvying up of sovereignty among different beings instead of recognizing Allāh as the sole sovereign, both of the cosmos and of human society.

*The Meaning of* 'Ibādat The first two chapters of *Iṣṭilāḥēn̲* dealt with the nature of divinity, but Mawdūdī's purpose was not so much to clarify the content of one's belief in Allāh for its own sake, but rather to understand what obligations He imposes on humanity. In the third and fourth chapters Mawdūdī expounds on this theme in more detail. The third chapter, on the term *'ibādat*, is of particular importance to our investigation as it is addresses the relation between monolatry and theonomy, between ritual worship and obedience to law.

As with the other terms Mawdūdī begins with a survey of the lexical (*lughawī*) meanings of the root *'-b-d*, this time explicitly giving his source as the Arabic lexicon *Lisān al-'arab*. The five meanings that he enumerates are (1) a slave or servant (*'abd*), in contrast with a free man (*ḥurr*); (2) humble obedience (*al-ṭā'a ma'a al-khuḍū'*); (3) worship (here the *ma'būd* gloss of *ilāh* is inverted, and *ta'allaha* is given as a gloss of *'abada*); (4) accompaniment, non-separation; and (5) hindrance.[111]

107 Mawdūdī, *Iṣṭilāḥēn̲*, pp. 73–74. 108 Mawdūdī, *Iṣṭilāḥēn̲*, p. 74.
109 Mawdūdī, *Iṣṭilāḥēn̲*, p. 79. 110 Mawdūdī, *Iṣṭilāḥēn̲*, p. 80.
111 Mawdūdī, *Iṣṭilāḥēn̲*, pp. 81–82.

Mawdūdī considers the final two meanings incidental to his aim as they are not attested in the Qurʾān,[112] and he focuses on the relations among the first three to establish a core meaning for the concept. He argues that this core meaning is to recognize another's superiority, relinquish one's autonomy, and become obedient and submissive to that other. In other words, the first meaning, that of servitude (*bandagī*, *ghulāmī*), is primary; Mawdūdī claims that this is the first meaning that would occur to an Arab, by which he means an Arab of the *jāhiliyya*.[113] From this first meaning one necessarily arrives at the related concept of obedience (*bandagī*, *iṭāʿat*), since the basic function (*aṣlī kām*) of a servant is obedience to his master. Finally, since a true servant is not just one who puts himself in his master's charge in a functional sense, but who also recognizes the supremacy of the master and is emotionally grateful for the master's favor and beneficence, he performs various rituals of reverence to the master that are collectively known as worship (*parastish*). Thus Mawdūdī enumerates three fundamental meanings of *ʿibādat* and arranges them in a logical progression of priority: (1) the servant-master relationship, from which is derived the meaning of (2) obedience, and equally essential to the concept, but last in derivation, is the notion of (3) ritual worship.[114]

Mawdūdī's broad conception of *ʿibādat*, in which ritual worship is only one manifestation of the obedience inherent to the servant-master relationship, is related to his privileging of theonomy and political sovereignty (*ḥākimiyyat*) over ritual worship as the core element of Islam. This is a significant shift in emphasis vis-à-vis the Taymiyyan monolatric tradition, though the latter did address the relation between worship and obedience: Ibn Taymiyya himself wrote that "All that Allāh orders the servant, whether as an obligatory or recommended [act] – performance of it is *ʿibāda* to Allāh";[115] and likewise he defined *ʿibāda* broadly as "a term that comprises every speech and act, interior or exterior, that Allāh loves and with which He is pleased."[116] In addition, the concept of obedience to law as *ʿibāda* was explicit in the premodern anti-*taqlīd* polemic. Nonetheless, Ibn Taymiyya, and even more so the Wahhābīs, tended to focus on ritual monolatry as the primary expression of *ʿibāda*, whereas Mawdūdī fully exploits the breadth of the concept and makes legal-political obedience its central proving ground.

[112] Mawdūdī, *Iṣṭilāḥēn̲*, p. 83. [113] Mawdūdī, *Iṣṭilāḥēn̲*, pp. 82–23.
[114] Mawdūdī, *Iṣṭilāḥēn̲*, pp. 82–83.
[115] Ibn Taymiyya, *Majmūʿat al-fatāwā*, vol. 1, p. 101.
[116] Ibn Taymiyya, *Risālat al-ʿubūdiyya*, p. 8 (= Ibn Taymiyya, *Majmūʿat al-fatāwā*, vol. 10, p. 91).

Mawdūdī goes on to survey examples of each of the three fundamental meanings of *ʿibāda* in Qurʾānic usage. When Firʿawn (Pharaoh) refers to the Israelites as *lanā ʿābidūn* (Qurʾān 23:47), he clearly meant to say that they were his servants and obedient to him, that is, meanings (1) and (2) of *ʿibāda*. Likewise, when Mūsā (Moses) reproached Firʿawn, saying "Is this the favor that you granted me, that you have enslaved (*ʿabbadta*) the Israelites?" (Qurʾān 26:22), he meant this in the first two senses of the term.

Mawdūdī argues that the term is used in the same sense in relation to Allāh in Qurʾān 2:172: "O you who believe, eat of the good things that We have provided for you and be grateful to Allāh, if it be He whom you serve (*taʿbudūna*)."[117] He describes the context of this verse as follows: The pre-Islamic Arabs obeyed restrictions on food and drink inherited from their forefathers, and when these Arabs converted to Islam, Allāh told them that if they are to serve Him (*agar tum hamārī ʿibādat kartē hō*) they need to abandon these restrictions and to eat and drink those things that He determined to be permitted (*ḥalāl*). Mawdūdī thus understands the *ʿibāda* in this verse as obedience to law and provides the following gloss: "The clear meaning of this [verse] is: If you be My slaves (*bandē*), and not slaves to your religious scholars (*pandit*)[118] and dignitaries (*buzurg*), and if you are to truly abandon obedience (*iṭāʿat o farmān-bardārī*) to them and accept obedience to Me, then follow My laws instead of theirs in matters of permission and prohibition."[119] Unsurprisingly, Mawdūdī once again cites Qurʾān 9:31 and references the ʿAdī b. Ḥātim *ḥadīth* in support of this description of legal obedience as *ʿibādat*. Further underlining the continuity with premodern intra-Islamic polemic, Mawdūdī attacks in this regard the "blind (*and$^{h}$ī*) *taqlīd*" of people who, from Mawdūdī's description, are identifiable as Ṣūfī shaykhs, those who "by way of their prayer carpets, rosaries, gowns, and wool garments deceive the servants of God and make of them devotees of themselves."[120]

The third meaning of *ʿibādat* Mawdūdī refers to is *parastish* (worship, or ritual worship). He writes that in the Qurʾān this meaning comprises two different sets of acts: (1) rites of reverence (e.g. prostration, circum-ambulation, sacrificial vows), which are considered *parastish* regardless of

117 English translations of the verse generally render the final word as 'worship,' but this would be misleading in the context of Mawdūdī's exegesis.

118 Mawdūdī uses here the term for a Hindu religious scholar, *pandit*. This is an intentional anatopism, as the Qurʾān itself was certainly not polemicizing against Hindus; the term would help drive home to Muslims living in the Hindu-majority subcontinent that to obey a human authority in legal matters is to follow another religion altogether.

119 Mawdūdī, *Iṣṭilāḥēn̲*, p. 84.

120 Mawdūdī, *Iṣṭilāḥēn̲*, p. 87.

whether the object to whom these acts are devoted is seen as an object of worship (*maʿbūd*) in itself or merely as an intermediary to and intercessor with a greater object of worship (viz. Allāh); and (2) supplication (*duʿā*). These are the typical concerns of the premodern salafī authors, and like them Mawdūdī emphasizes that the Qurʾān denounces worship of this sort directed to saints (*awliyāʾ*) and prophets,[121] even and especially when they are appealed to not as independent objects of worship but as intercessors. True to his earlier emphasis in the *ilāh* chapter, Mawdūdī describes supplication of another as stemming from a belief in that other's (supernatural) power over the world of causality (*kisī kō ʿālam-i asbāb par dhī iqtidār khayāl kar kē* ...),[122] thus making of this belief the root cause of supplication of not-Allāh.

In fact, Mawdūdī stresses acknowledgment of Allāh's unity of power as the driving force behind exclusivity of *ʿibādat* in both its forms, monolatry and theonomy.

> The Qurʾān establishes that all these kinds of objects of worship (*maʿbūd*) are false, and *ʿibādat* of them is error, whether this be servitude (*ghulāmī*), obedience (*ʿiṭāʿat*), or ritual worship (*parastish*). It says: all these objects of worship of yours, to whom you perform *ʿibādat*, are Allāh's slaves (*bandē awr ghulām*); they do not have the right to be worshipped, and you can gain nothing from worshipping them but disappointment, abjectness, and ignominy. In truth their master (*mālik*), and the master of all beings, is Allāh, and in His hands are the totality of powers (*tamām ikhtiyārāt*). Thus no one apart from Allāh alone is deserving of *ʿibādat*.[123]

After citing a number of verses that describe various objects of worship as being themselves *ʿabd* to Allāh (e.g. the prophet ʿĪsā: 4:172; the angels: 43:19)[124] and that emphasize Allāh's omnipotence, Mawdūdī writes:

> In this way, after establishing that all those to whom *ʿibādat* was devoted are slaves (*ghulām*) of Allāh and powerless (*bē-ikhtiyār*), the Qurʾān demands of all jinn and humans that *ʿibādat*, in all its meanings, be devoted to Allāh alone: servitude (*ghulāmī*) is His, obedience (*iṭāʿat*) is His, ritual worship (*parastish*) is His, and not even a scintilla of any of these kinds of *ʿibādat* [should be] for not-Allāh.[125]

This message is essentially one of monolatry, though as we have seen Mawdūdī considers theonomy to be the principal issue in true monolatry; exclusivity of ritual worship is an essential, but ultimately derivative, aspect. When in the final paragraph of the *ʿibādat* chapter Mawdūdī warns against restricting the meaning of *ʿibādat* in the Qurʾān to any

121 Mawdūdī, *Iṣṭilāḥēn̲*, p. 89.
122 Mawdūdī, *Iṣṭilāḥēn̲*, p. 87.
123 Mawdūdī, *Iṣṭilāḥēn̲*, p. 91.
124 Mawdūdī, *Iṣṭilāḥēn̲*, p. 92.
125 Mawdūdī, *Iṣṭilāḥēn̲*, p. 94.

one of its three fundamental meanings,[126] it stands to reason that he is warning primarily against its restriction to the most widespread acceptation of the term, that is, ritual worship alone. As he stated in the introduction to the treatise, the notion that *ʿibādat* is only veneration and ritual worship (*pūjā*, *parastish*) is a later corruption of the term that arose after Muslims lost touch with the concept's original and authentic scope.[127] Thus while Mawdūdī's focus on exclusivity of worship can be seen as similar to that of the salafī premodern tradition, he wields the concept as a polemic against modern secularization, the compartmentalization of religion and its relegation to the purely ritual sphere. This leads us to the final term of the treatise, *dīn*, which – in the same passage in the introduction – Mawdūdī had warned should not be reduced to the concept of 'religion.'[128]

*The Meaning of* Dīn The concluding chapter of Mawdūdī's *Iṣṭilāḥēn̲* deals with the fourth of his fundamental terms, *dīn*. As noted, Mawdūdī insisted that this word, in its true Qurʾānic meaning, does not signify 'religion'; it is rather an all-embracing concept, a complete system of life. The chapter begins, in like manner to the preceding ones, with a survey of the lexical (*lughawī*) meanings of the word *dīn*. He notes four lexical meanings: (1) coercive power and sovereignty (*ghalaba o iqtidār*, *ḥukm-rānī o farmān-rawāʾī*; the English term 'sovereignty' is likewise given as a gloss of the Urdu *quwwat-i qāhira*);[129] (2) obedience, servitude, and subjugation (*ṭāʿat*, *bandagī*, *khidmat*, *kisī kē līʾe musakhkhar honā*);[130] (3) law (*sharīʿat*, *qānūn*), a religious sect (*kēsh*, *millat*), and a path or accustomed manner (*ṭarīqa*, *rasm*, *ʿādat*); and (4) judgment, and recompense or requital for actions (*jazāʾ-i ʿamal*, *badlā*, *mukāfāt*, *fayṣala*, *muḥāsaba*).[131] According to Mawdūdī, all four of these meanings were present in the minds of the Arabs of the *jāhiliyya* but in an unorganized fashion, and the change effected in the Qurʾān's usage of the term was simply to systematize the meanings into a unified and coherent concept, as follows: (1) sovereignty (*ḥākimiyyat*) and supreme power (*iqtidār-i aʿlā*); (2) submission and obedience to this sovereignty; (3) the system of thought and action instituted by the sovereign; and (4) recompense or requital on the part of the supreme power for fidelity or infidelity to this system.[132]

Mawdūdī then provides examples of Qurʾānic verses that in his opinion illustrate the different but related meanings. Meanings (1) and (2) are

[126] Mawdūdī, *Iṣṭilāḥēn̲*, p. 98.
[127] Mawdūdī, *Iṣṭilāḥēn̲*, p. 9.
[128] Mawdūdī, *Iṣṭilāḥēn̲*, p. 9.
[129] Mawdūdī, *Iṣṭilāḥēn̲*, pp. 99–100.
[130] Mawdūdī, *Iṣṭilāḥēn̲*, p. 100.
[131] Mawdūdī, *Iṣṭilāḥēn̲*, p. 101.
[132] Mawdūdī, *Iṣṭilāḥēn̲*, p. 102.

treated together,[133] presumably due to the logical relation between them: One cannot submit to a sovereign power without there being a sovereign power. Most of the verses Mawdūdī cites employ variations of the phrase *mukhliṣan lahu al-dīn*, that is, making the *dīn* pure or exclusive to Allāh (Qurʾān 40:65, 39:11, 39:2–3, 98:5). Mawdūdī comments regarding this phrase:

The meaning of making the *dīn* exclusive (*khāliṣ*) to Allāh is that a human not submit to the sovereignty (*ḥākimiyyat, farmān-rawāʾī, ḥukm-rānī*) of anyone apart from Allāh, and to make his obedience and servitude exclusive (*khāliṣ*) to Allāh in such manner as to make no other a partner (*sharīk*) to Allāh through obedience to him in his own right, together with his obedience to Allāh.[134]

Mawdūdī's argumentation here does not stand alone, as the verses considered in themselves do little to prove the meanings of sovereignty and obedience; the argument is dependent on the preceding chapters of *Iṣṭilāḥēn*, and especially the chapter on *ʿibādat*. Mawdūdī translates all the mentions of *ʿibāda* in connection with *dīn* in Qurʾān 39:2 and 39:14–17 as *bandagī*,[135] that is, the servitude of a servant to his master. He does likewise for Qurʾān 98:5.[136] The meaning, then, is that it is the *ʿibādat* of servitude and obedience that one must devote exclusively to Allāh in order for the *dīn* to be exclusive to Him, and it follows that the *dīn* itself must be this servant-master relationship.

Mawdūdī's comment on the meaning of *mukhliṣan lahu al-dīn* already lays out the essence of his view on human government. No one apart from Allāh can be sovereign in his own right, nor may one obey any such human sovereign in his own right, since to do so is to make him a partner (*sharīk*) with Allāh – in other words, to do so is polytheism. Mawdūdī's conclusion follows naturally from his discussion of *ʿibādat*, but also from his contention that one of the two aspects of *rabb* denotes sovereignty over human affairs. The "in his own right" (*mustaqill bi-l-dhāt*) condition is an important one, since it clarifies what role Mawdūdī does leave for proper human government: If a government is based on Allāh's law and applies Allāh's judgment, then obedience to that government is obligatory, and if it is not, then obedience to it is a sin.[137] This is pure

133 Mawdūdī, *Iṣṭilāḥēn*, pp. 102–104. 134 Mawdūdī, *Iṣṭilāḥēn*, p. 104.
135 Mawdūdī, *Iṣṭilāḥēn*, p. 103. 136 Mawdūdī, *Iṣṭilāḥēn*, p. 104.
137 Mawdūdī, *Iṣṭilāḥēn*, p. 104, n. 1. As our present interest in Mawdūdī is restricted to the influence of his core system on the Arabic-speaking world and ultimately on salafism, we need not go into detail on how he himself envisioned human government operating in practice. The issue is discussed in Nasr, *Mawdudi*, pp. 87–106; Hartung, *A System of Life*, pp. 122–155; Andrew F. March, *The Caliphate of Man: Popular Sovereignty in Modern Islamic Thought*, Cambridge, MA, and London: Harvard University Press, 2019, pp. 75–113. March argues that Mawdūdī and Quṭb's conception of popular

theonomy: There is a need for human government but its role is delegatory and executive. It is Allāh who makes the laws, and thus it is He who remains the true sovereign.

If the first and second meanings of *dīn* relate to the act of submission to a higher power, the third meaning of *dīn* denotes the outcome of this submission: the divergence of humans into different paths of life, and obedience to different laws, depending on what higher power they recognize and to which they submit. Naturally the important divergence is between those who follow Allāh's *dīn* and the followers of all other *dīn*s. Thus the first verse Mawdūdī cites is (Qurʾān 10:104): "Say, O people, if you be in doubt as to my *dīn*, [know that] I do not serve (*fa-lā aʿbudu*) those whom you serve apart from Allāh, but rather I serve Allāh who causes you to die, and I was commanded to be of the believers." Here again we see the influence of the preceding discussion of the meaning of *ʿibādat*, as Mawdūdī translates it here with the terms *bandagī* and *iṭāʿat*, that is, servitude and obedience.[138] The fact that the Prophet's servitude and obedience were given to Allāh alone, as opposed to those who serve and obey others, meant that he was in a different camp – that of the believers. The importance of legislation as a function of the higher power, and thus of obedience to legislation as a criterion of adherence to a *dīn*, is underscored when Mawdūdī returns to two verses he cited previously in the *ilāh* chapter: Qurʾān 6:137, "Likewise those they hold as partners [in divinity] have made many of the *mushrikīn* look favorably upon killing their children in order to lead them to destruction and to confuse them as to their *dīn*"; and 41:21: "Or do they hold [some] to be partners [in divinity], who have legislated for them in the *dīn* that which Allāh has not permitted?"[139] This leads Mawdūdī to conclude:

> In all these verses the meaning of *dīn* is law (*qānūn*), regulations (*ḍabṭa*), *sharīʿat*, a path (*ṭarīqa*), and that system of thought and action in obedience to which a human lives his life. If the power (*iqtidār*) that is the authority for regulations and a system [of life] that are adhered to is God's power, then the human is in God's *dīn*. And if it is the power of some king, then the human is in the *dīn* of the king. If it is the power of the (Hindu) religious scholars and priests (*paṇḍit*, *prohit*), then the human is in their *dīn*. If it is the power of the family, the caste (*barādarī*), or the nation (*jumhūr-i qawm*), then the human is in their *dīn*. In short, whosoever's authority is obeyed as the final authority, and whosoever's judgments are obeyed as the last word, such that a human walks in his path – that human is a follower of his *dīn*.[140]

viceregency ("the caliphate of man") as a complement to divine sovereignty fed into later democratizing forms of Islamism (see e.g. pp. 151–152); in Chapter 5 we will examine some of the battles waged by strict salafī theonomists against such tendencies.

138 Mawdūdī, *Iṣṭilāḥēṉ*, pp. 104–105. 139 Mawdūdī, *Iṣṭilāḥēṉ*, pp. 106–107.

140 Mawdūdī, *Iṣṭilāḥēṉ*, p. 107.

This passage contains, in embryo, the core of Mawdūdī's polemic against nationalism, including (and especially) his opposition to the secular Muslim nationalism of the All-India Muslim League that led to the establishment of Pakistan. Prior to *Iṣṭilāḥēn̲* Mawdūdī had already inveighed against modern Muslims' self-conception as a 'nation' like other nations in his "Islāmī qawmiyyat kā ḥaqīqī mafhūm" ("The True Meaning of Islamic Nationalism"),[141] and his argument there assumes the definition given here of Islam as a *dīn* that precludes adherence to any rival principle of social organization on the grounds that it constitutes a different *dīn*. In "Islāmī qawmiyyat" the social implications are fleshed out at length: Islam is portrayed as a true Axial revolution that forges a new society in which obedience to Allāh is the sole organizing principle, requiring the exclusion of any nonelective basis for social order such as "blood, land, or color";[142] it is in *Iṣṭilāḥēn̲* that we see the careful and systematic deduction of the conception of Islam from which Mawdūdī draws these social implications. This passage also demonstrates that Mawdūdī's critique of nationalism is not really separate from his critiques of phenomena such as secular legislation or even Ṣūfī religious obscurantism, as in all of them it is the same issue at stake: All power and authority are concentrated in the hands of Allāh, and humans need to recognize this fact and structure their lives in submission and servitude to this one power and authority, to the exclusion of all others.

As for the fourth meaning of *dīn* – judgment, requital, and recompense – there is no need to dwell on Mawdūdī's prooftexts. All of them mention *dīn* in connection with the Day of Judgment (*yawm al-dīn*),[143] and Mawdūdī treats the connection as a self-evident one that does not require further elaboration.

It is in the final three pages of the treatise, in a subsection titled "*Dīn* Is a Comprehensive Term," that Mawdūdī's system reaches its bold conclusion. The word comprehensive (*jāmiʿ*) should be understood here in the sense of all-inclusive and total: "by *dīn* is meant a complete system of life in the totality of its creedal, theoretical, moral, and practical aspects, taken all together" (*dīn sē pūrā niẓām-i zindagī apnē tamām iʿtiqādī, naẓarī, akhlāqī awr ʿamalī pahlūōn̲ sam-ēt murād hay*).[144] According to Mawdūdī most languages have no term for such a comprehensive concept, but he writes that in modern times the term that

[141] Abū al-Aʿlā Mawdūdī, "Islāmī qawmiyyat kā ḥaqīqī mafhūm," *Tarjumān al-Qurʾān*, Ṣafar 1358/April 1939; reprinted in Abū al-Aʿlā Mawdūdī, *Tafhīmāt*, Lahore: Islamic Publications (Private) Limited, 1387/1968, vol. 1, pp. 127–145.

[142] Mawdūdī, "Islāmī qawmiyyat," p. 128.

[143] Mawdūdī, *Iṣṭilāḥēn̲*, pp. 107–108.

[144] Mawdūdī, *Iṣṭilāḥēn̲*, p. 110.

approaches it to a certain degree is 'state'; lest there be any confusion, he uses the English word in Urdu transliteration (*istēt*).[145] This striking gloss of the term *dīn* sharpens Mawdūdī's point, advanced in the introduction to *Iṣṭilāḥēn̲*[146] and reiterated here, that *dīn* does not mean "just religion" (*mujarrad "madhhab"*);[147] *dīn* encompasses, in addition to those aspects of ritual and belief that the modern world considers 'religon,' also those laws, powers, and functions that the modern world categorizes as relating to the state. Thus the Qurʾānic injunction to fight the unbelievers until there is no more *fitna* and the *dīn* be entirely Allāh's (Qurʾān 8:39) means that the believers must unflaggingly fight to topple all existing systems of life that are not based on exclusive obedience (*iṭāʿat*) and servitude (*bandagī*) to Allāh.[148]

Here, in the terms 'obedience' (*iṭāʿat*) and 'servitude' (*bandagī*) we see a connection between Mawdūdī's interpretation of *ʿibādat* and his interpretation of *dīn*: Just as the former is not just ritual worship, so the latter is not just religion. Directly preceding this Mawdūdī likewise connects his conclusion regarding *dīn* both to the discussion of *ʿibādat* and to his distinction between the two aspects of divinity. As this is a formulation that recurs in his other works, and serves as a kind of shorthand for his entire system, it is worth quoting here.

*The Argument from the Cosmic to the Normative* Commenting on the two verses "Indeed, the [only true] *dīn* in Allāh's sight is Islam" (3:19) and "Whoever seeks other than Islam as a *dīn*, it will never be accepted from him" (3:85), Mawdūdī writes:

> in Allāh's sight the only proper system of life for humans is one that is based on obedience and servitude – *islām* – to Allāh. Any other system that is based on obedience to some other supposed power will never be accepted by the Master of all beings (*mālik-i kāʾināt*), and by nature (*fiṭratan*) never can be. This is because the One by whom humans were created, to whom humans are slaves, by whom humans are supported, and in whose realm humans are in the status of subjects – He can never accept that humans pass their lives in servitude and obedience to some other power apart from Him and that they have a right to walk by the guidance of some other.[149]

The reasoning in this passage is very simple. Obedience must be granted to that same divinity who is, objectively speaking, the creator and master of the cosmos. In other words, this is an argument from the objective-cosmic aspect of divinity to the relational-normative aspect of divinity.

145 Mawdūdī, *Iṣṭilāḥēn̲*, p. 108.
146 Mawdūdī, *Iṣṭilāḥēn̲*, p. 9.
147 Mawdūdī, *Iṣṭilāḥēn̲*, p. 109.
148 Mawdūdī, *Iṣṭilāḥēn̲*, p. 111.
149 Mawdūdī, *Iṣṭilāḥēn̲*, pp. 110–111.

In Mawdūdī's view, this argument is the heart of the prophetic message, and thus of Islam itself.

This core argument recurs elsewhere in his writings on various topics. One example is the seventh and final chapter of *Khuṭbāt*, the published version of the course of lessons Mawdūdī delivered at the short-lived Dār al-Islām institute in Pathankot. The topic of this chapter is jihād, which Mawdūdī defines as the effort exerted by the believers to eradicate human rule over other humans in order to establish the exclusivity of God's rule. When he explains why rule by humans over humans is wrong, he writes:

Please consider [the following]: This earth on which you live, was it fashioned by God or by another? The people who dwell on earth, were they created by God or by another? The innumerable means of life thanks to which all humans live, were they made ready by God or by another? If the answer to all these questions be this and this alone, that the earth, the people, and all the necessities [of life] were created by God, then this means that the land is God's, the wealth is God's, and the subjects are God's.

Given that the situation is such, how then can someone else have the right to rule over God's land? How can it be right for the law in force for God's subjects to be that of someone other than God, or one made by the subjects themselves? That the land belong to one and be ruled by another, that the property belong to one and another become its owner, that the subjects be of one and sovereignty over them be given to another – how can your reason possibly agree to this?[150]

Likewise we find the very same argument in Mawdūdī's "Political Theory of Islam," this time specifically presented as the Streitpunkt between Islam and the unbelievers:

There are many verses in the Qurʾān which make it absolutely clear that the non-believers and polytheists too, who opposed the Prophets, did not deny the existence of God nor that he was the sole Creator of heavens and earth and man, nor that the whole mechanism of nature operated in accordance with His commands, nor that it is He who pours down the rain, drives the wind and controls the sun, moon, the earth and everything else …

The question arises, then what was it that gave rise to the tremendous opposition that every prophet without any exception had to face when he made this call? The Qurʾān states that the whole dispute centered round the uncompromising demand of the prophets that the non-believers should recognize as their *rabb* (Lord) and *ilāh* (Master and Law-giver) also the very Being whom they acknowledged as their Creator and that they should assign this position to none else.[151]

[150] Abū al-Aʿlā Mawdūdī, *Khuṭbāt*, New Delhi: Markazī Maktabah-i Islāmī, 2005, p. 271.
[151] Sayyid Abul Aʿlā Maudūdī, *The Islamic Law and Constitution*, 4th ed., ed. and trans. Khurshid Ahmad, Lahore: Islamic Publications (Private) Limited, 1969, pp. 122–123.

The argument in these passages is the same one made in the final pages of *Iṣṭilāḥēṉ*. Acknowledgment of God's objective-cosmic aspect – that He is the Creator, the Sustainer, etc. – necessarily demands recognition of His relational-normative aspect as well, and action in accordance with it. This is the core of Mawdūdī's doctrine of theonomy, as laid out systematically in *Iṣṭilāḥēṉ*. An even more succinct formulation is the one given earlier in *Iṣṭilāḥēṉ*, when Mawdūdī argued that the Streitpunkt between believers and unbelievers had always been their ascription of the relational-normative aspect of *rabb* to not-Allāh. The basic meaning of Islam, then, is simply that "*rubūbiyyat* is indivisible" (*nā qābil-i taqsīm*).[152]

### *Mawdūdī and Premodern Salafī Monolatry and Theonomy*

Throughout our survey of *Iṣṭilāḥēṉ* we pointed out a number of structural parallels between Mawdūdī's system and the premodern salafī monolatry of Ibn Taymiyya and Ibn ʿAbd al-Wahhāb. The distinction between the cosmic-objective and normative-relational aspects of divinity, and the argument from the former to the latter; the definition of Islam in terms of monolatry; the importance of the Streitpunkt principle – all these are points of contact between them and reveal an underlying structural commonality between Mawdūdī and this premodern tradition, despite the clear differences in style and (more significantly) in field of application. These structural parallels prepared the ground for the incorporation of *ḥākimiyya* into radical salafism later in the twentieth century – and as the latter is the primary object of our inquiry, it perhaps matters little for our purposes whether Mawdūdī himself was influenced by these premodern precedents or whether the parallels are strictly typological. The question is, however, of interest in its own right. While it is quite clear that Mawdūdī was not a Taymiyyan in any normal sense of the term, the question of Taymiyyan influence is not a mere artifact of my own arrangement of the materials. There does exist some evidence to suggest it above and beyond the aforementioned structural parallels.

This evidence is furnished by the Deobandi scholar Muḥammad Manẓūr Nuʿmānī, who was an early associate of Mawdūdī's at the Dār al-Islām in Pathankot, but split paths with him soon thereafter and became critical of his views. In his book, titled *Mawlānā Mawdūdī kē sāt$^{h}$ mērī rafāqat kī sar-guzasht awr ab mērā mawqif* ("The Story of My Association with Mawlānā Mawdūdī and My Position Today"),

[152] Mawdūdī, *Iṣṭilāḥēṉ*, p. 73.

Nuʿmānī takes issue with Mawdūdī's argument in *Iṣṭilāḥēn̲* that later Muslim society had forgotten the meaning of the Qurʾān's key terms and thus no longer understood the essence of Islam. In Nuʿmānī's view this argument, in addition to being incorrect in itself, is especially dangerous because it opens the door to heretical attacks on the faith, as it undermines the integrity and unbrokenness (*tawātur*) of the living tradition of scholarship that stretches from the Prophet and the Companions to the present day – and which, in Nuʿmānī's view, guarantees the validity of religious knowledge.[153]

Nuʿmānī's objection is typical of the response of traditional scholars when confronted with a 'salafī' challenge. In Chapter 2 we noted how Muḥammad b. ʿAbd al-Wahhāb's contemporaries were shocked by his claim that neither his teachers nor anyone else in his region knew the meaning of *lā ilāha illā llāh* before him. Nuʿmānī's reaction is a similar one: It is simply impossible that the true meaning of Islam and its fundamental concepts had not been preserved by the scholarly tradition.

The name of Ibn Taymiyya in particular arises in Nuʿmānī's account in connection with the meaning of *lā ilāha illā llāh*. Nuʿmānī recounts that one day while sitting with Mawdūdī at the Dār al-Islām in Pathankot he asked Mawdūdī if anyone before him had given *lā ilāha illā llāh* the same interpretation as he had. Mawdūdī's answer was that "there is only Shaykh al-Islām Ibn Taymiyya, who went a considerable distance in the correct way, but who turned back when he got close" (*bas shaykh al-islām Ibn Taymiyya hayn̲ jō kāfī dūr tak ṣaḥīḥ chaltē hayn̲ lēkin qarīb pahon̲ch kar muṙ jātē hayn̲*).[154]

Nuʿmānī's point in this passage is simply to emphasize how unprecedented Mawdūdī's views were, in that even the sole authority he claimed as precedent was only a partial one.[155] Nuʿmānī does not follow up on what exactly Mawdūdī meant by this statement, or why he mentioned Ibn Taymiyya in particular rather than some other authority. Generally speaking, Ibn Taymiyya does not occupy any central position in Mawdūdī's writings, certainly not in the way he does for modern salafīs. In one of his works, a kind of history of Islamic reform titled

[153] Muḥammad Manẓūr Nuʿmānī, *Mawlānā Mawdūdī kē sātʰ mērī rafāqat kī sar-guzasht awr ab mērā mawqif*, Karachi: Majlis-i Nashriyāt-i Islām, n.d., pp. 80–93.

[154] Nuʿmānī, *Mawlānā Mawdūdī*, p. 90. Nuʿmānī adds that he remembers the second half of this statement so well that he would be prepared to swear an oath that those were Mawdūdī's very words.

[155] Mawdūdī's statement *apud* Nuʿmānī is cited for the same purpose in Irfan Ahmad, "Genealogy of the Islamic State: Reflections on Maududi's Political Thought and Islamism," *Journal of the Royal Anthropological Institute* 15 (2009), pp. 145–162, at p. 156.

*Mūjaz taʾrīkh tajdīd al-islām wa-iḥyāʾihi*, Mawdūdī does include a chapter on Ibn Taymiyya that is highly laudatory, but there is no mention of Ibn Taymiyya's interpretation of *lā ilāha illā llāh*, his doctrine of *tawḥīd al-ulūhiyya*, or anything else for that matter that could not have been gleaned from biographical notices or that shows any deep familiarity with Ibn Taymiyya's writings.[156]

Yet when we consider the structural parallels we found in the course of this chapter between Mawdūdī's theonomy and Ibn Taymiyya's monolatry, Mawdūdī's statement appears in a different light than the one in which Nuʿmānī presented it, and it appears probable that Mawdūdī knew and understood the medieval scholar's basic doctrine of monolatry and its significance. Mawdūdī's and Ibn Taymiyya's interpretations of *lā ilāha illā llāh* truly are similar: They both understand it as meaning that there is no object worthy of *ʿibāda*/*ʿibādat* apart from Allāh, and not as "there is no god but Allāh" in the cosmic-objective sense. Nuʿmānī's statement simply indicates to us that around the time that Mawdūdī was authoring his seminal works he himself was aware of this similarity.

We can also offer a plausible (albeit not definite) interpretation of the second part of Mawdūdī's statement, namely, that Ibn Taymiyya turned away from the correct interpretation after having almost arrived at it. He likely meant that Ibn Taymiyya did not take the imperative of monolatry to what Mawdūdī himself viewed as its logical theonomic conclusion. The final lines of Mawdūdī's chapter on Ibn Taymiyya in *Mūjaz taʾrīkh tajdīd al-islām wa-iḥyāʾihi* seem to support this hypothesis. After praising Ibn Taymiyya for rousing the Muslims to jihād against the Mongols, he adds: "But it remains true, notwithstanding all of that, that he did not merit to launch a political movement among the Muslims through which the system of rule would be overturned, and through which the keys of rule and power would be passed from the hands of the *jāhiliyya* to the hands of Islam."[157] (It could be argued that prior to the modern-era introduction of man-made law there was no such need, but Mawdūdī claims that Mamlūk rule was, like that of the Mongols, based on the law of Chinggis Khān[158] – a view that Ibn Taymiyya himself clearly did not hold.) In other words, Mawdūdī seems to have been aware of Ibn Taymiyya's emphasis on Islam as monolatry and to have viewed it as a kind of precedent for his own views, but felt that the sociopolitical

[156] Abū al-Aʿlā Mawdūdī, *Mūjaz taʾrīkh tajdīd al-islām wa-iḥyāʾihi wa-wāqiʿ al-muslimīn wa-sabīl al-nuhūḍ bihim*, 2nd ed., trans. Muḥammad Kāẓim Sibāq, Lebanon: Dār al-Fikr al-Ḥadīth, 1386/1967, pp. 84–90. Hartung argues that despite surface appearances this work actually aims at pointing out the shortcomings in the reform projects of earlier *mujaddidūn*: Hartung, *A System of Life*, p. 78.

[157] Mawdūdī, *Mūjaz*, p. 90. [158] Mawdūdī, *Mūjaz*, p. 85, n. 1.

dimension he himself gave to the monolatric imperative was more or less unprecedented. This seems the most plausible interpretation of Mawdūdī's statement *apud* Nuʿmānī, but it must be admitted that it is thin evidence on which to base a theory of direct influence, and is probably best taken as an additional datum in support of the typological parallels that arise from analysis of Mawdūdī's writings themselves.

A related question is whether Mawdūdī might have been influenced by the premodern tradition of jurisprudential theonomy that we discussed in Chapter 3. In our analysis of *Iṣṭilāḥēn̲* we noted the salience of Qurʾān 9:31, which is mentioned in each of the treatise's four chapters, and of the exegetical ʿAdī b. Ḥātim *ḥadīth*, which is the sole *ḥadīth* mentioned in the entire treatise (apart from those used as examples of word-usage in the passages borrowed from Arabic lexicography). The verse and the *ḥadīth* were fundamental to Mawdūdī's delineation of the normative-relational aspect of divinity and to his contention that obedience to law is a form of *ʿibādat*; in other words, they lie close to the heart of his system in that they provide grounding for his interpretation of monolatry in terms of theonomy.

*Iṣṭilāḥēn̲* is not the only work in which Mawdūdī makes use of these prooftexts. He cites the ʿAdī b. Ḥātim *ḥadīth* on Qurʾān 9:31 in his *tafsīr*, *Tafhīm al-qurʾān*, and adds: "From this it is known that a human who decides the boundaries of permitted and forbidden in human life without basis in the Qurʾān in effect claims to possess divine authority, and one who accepts his right to legislate makes of him a god."[159] The *ḥadīth* also seems to have influenced his understanding of another verse, Qurʾān 3:64, which employs the language of *arbāb* in a similar context and which we saw adduced frequently in works of anti-*taqlīd* polemic alongside verse 9:31. In his 1939 article "Jihād fī sabīli llāh," in one of the many passages in which Mawdūdī expounds on the principle of divine sovereignty, he translates (3:64) "and let not any of us take any other of us as lords other than Allāh" (*wa-lā yattakhidha baʿḍunā baʿḍan arbāban min dūni llāh*) as: "and let not any of us make any other of us a possessor of command and prohibition other than Allāh" (*awr ham men̲ sē koʾī kisī kō khudā kē ba-jāʾe amr o nahy kā mālik b$^h$ī na banāʾe*).[160]

All this raises the question of whether Mawdūdī was acquainted with, and influenced by, the use of these prooftexts in anti-*taqlīd* polemic – in

159 Abū al-Aʿlā Mawdūdī, *Tafhīm al-qurʾān*, Lahore: Idārah-i Tarjumān al-Qurʾān, 1997, vol. 2, pp. 189–190.

160 Abū al-Aʿlā Mawdūdī, "Jihād fī sabīli llāh," *Tarjumān al-Qurʾān*, May 1939; reprinted in Mawdūdī, *Tafhīmāt*, vol. 1, p. 82. His translation of the same verse in his *tafsīr*, however, remains literal: Mawdūdī, *Tafhīm al-qurʾān*, vol. 1, pp. 261–262.

other words, whether his sociopolitical doctrine of theonomy was influenced by premodern jurisprudential theonomy. It is nearly certain that the answer to this question is affirmative.

Mawdūdī explicitly addresses, in various writings, the topic of jurisprudential *taqlīd* in general, and in particular the issue that had become the focal point in India for the *taqlīd* polemic, the raising of the hands before and after prostration in prayer (*rafʿ al-yadayn*; see Chapter 3). He addresses these topics primarily in the context of contemporary disputes between the Ahl-i Ḥadīth and the Ḥanafīs, and if Mawdūdī was at all familiar with the Ahl-i Ḥadīth's arguments against *taqlīd*, as it appears he was, he would certainly have encountered their use of Qurʾān 9:31 and the ʿAdī b. Ḥātim *ḥadīth*. In his book on Mawdūdī, Seyyed Vali Reza Nasr already suggested the possibility of Ahl-i Ḥadīth influence, though he situated it more on the level of their respective socioreligious agendas;[161] here I believe it possible to speak of a likely doctrinal influence.

Mawdūdī himself did not adopt the rigid anti-Ḥanafī partisanship of the Ahl-i Ḥadīth, or even express a preference for them over the Ḥanafīs. Instead, he adopted their emphasis on exclusive legal obedience to Allāh, but displaced it to the legal-political issue of *ḥākimiyya* at the level of the state. On the traditional question of jurisprudential *taqlīd* he was more forgiving, agreeing in principle with the anti-*taqlīd* position but allowing scope for well-intentioned difference of opinion on matters of *furūʿ* (substantive law). Mawdūdī, like his Arab contemporaries in the Muslim Brotherhood, based his vision of revival on the establishment of an Islamic movement that would transcend the divisions that plagued Muslim society. His project was far more doctrinally concrete than that of Ḥasan al-Bannā, but in this respect they were similar. In the Indian context this vision required sidestepping tensions between Ḥanafīs and the Ahl-i Ḥadīth.

For example, Mawdūdī was dismayed to learn, in the summer of 1945, that a *fitna* (as he called it) had erupted among some members of his Jamāʿat-i Islāmī organization over the question of *rafʿ al-yadayn* in prayer. In response, and in his capacity as head of the movement, he wrote that he considered both the Ḥanafī and the Ahl-i Ḥadīth positions to be valid and based in the *sunna*, and he decried partisanship in this issue or in any other pure *fiqh* question. All were welcome in Jamāʿat-i Islāmī, but only if they were willing to refrain from condemnation of other schools. Mawdūdī wrote that the necessary outcome of such

[161] Nasr, *Mawdudi*, pp. 54–55.

partisanship would be that *fiqh* questions would become mistaken for the foundation of religion (*aṣl-i dīn*) and each party would come to view itself as an *umma* unto itself, thus preventing Muslims from fulfilling their true purpose in life: striving to make the word of Allāh supreme (*iʿlāʾ kalimat Allāh*). Perhaps it is not by chance that the authority he chose to cite in support of his ecumenical position on *rafʿ al-yadayn* was Shāh Walī Allāh, the renowned Indian scholar whom both the Deobandis and the Ahl-i Ḥadīth claimed as their forerunner.[162]

In other words, Mawdūdī adopted the legislation-equals-*shirk* equation, but displaced it entirely from its traditional home in anti-*taqlīd* polemic and deployed it solely with regard to the question of modern legislation. For example, in the August 1934 issue of *Tarjumān al-Qurʾān* Mawdūdī fielded a question from a reader asking him to comment on a number of quotations from an unnamed scholar (presumably from the ranks of the Ahl-i Ḥadīth, or possibly from the Ahl-i Qurʾān) who condemned certain forms of *taqlīd* as polytheism. Mawdūdī responded that to truly ascribe to anyone other than Allāh the power to command and forbid (*amr o nahy*) is indeed *shirk*, but he denied that *taqlīd* in general falls into this category, since most forms of it are premised simply on the assumption that the scholars one is following have a superior understanding of Allāh's law (i.e. and not that they have the power to command or forbid in their own right).[163] In a response written ten years later to a similar question Mawdūdī repeats this argument, but appends the same stipulation that we have seen in all the major anti-*taqlīd* works (including those of moderates like Shāh Walī Allāh): To obey one's imām to such a degree that one in essence understands him to possess the power of command and prohibition, and to insist on following him even in contravention of an explicit Qurʾānic verse or *ḥadīth*, is indeed *shirk*.[164]

[162] Abū al-Aʿlā Mawdūdī, "Ikhtilāfī masāʾil par ummat-sāzī kā fitna," *Tarjumān al-Qurʾān*, July–August 1945; reprinted in Mawdūdī, *Rasāʾil o masāʾil*, Lahore: Islamic Publications (Private) Limited, 2002, vol. 1, pp. 160–169. In addition to his desire to transcend intramural divisions, Mawdūdī's more ecumenical position on such *fiqh* questions can perhaps be attributed to (or was made possible by) the fact that he did not share the Ahl-i Ḥadīth's convictions as to the epistemological certainty – and thus the authority – of the *ḥadīth* itself. For an Ahl-i Ḥadīth criticism of Mawdūdī on this issue, see Abū al-Wafāʾ Thanāʾ Allāh Amritsarī, *Khiṭāb ba Mawdūdī*, Delhi: Idārah-i Nūr al-Īmān, 1413[/1992]. I thank Jan-Peter Hartung and Justyna Nedza for providing me with this text.

[163] Abū al-Aʿlā Mawdūdī, "Ittibāʿ-i ʿulamāʾ o ṣulaḥāʾ," *Tarjumān al-Qurʾān*, August 1934; reprinted in Mawdūdī, *Rasāʾil o masāʾil*, vol. 1, pp. 32–35.

[164] Abū al-Aʿlā Mawdūdī, "Taqlīd o ʿadam-i taqlīd," *Tarjumān al-Qurʾān*, July–October 1944; reprinted in Mawdūdī, *Rasāʾil o masāʾil*, vol. 1, pp. 149–150.

It is thus clear that Mawdūdī operated in an intellectual environment where he was constantly exposed to the writings of the Ahl-i Ḥadīth. He professed admiration for the earlier scholars from this school, though he considered it later to have become filled with ignoramuses who carried on fruitless polemics with the Ḥanafīs over trivial questions.[165] It would seem logical to presume that his familiarity with the Indian incarnation of the anti-*taqlīd* polemic contributed to his focus on a legal definition of Islam in which the conflict between Allāh's law and man-made law took center stage, in the form of his theory of *ḥākimiyyat*; and while I have not found any text in which he explicitly discusses the Ahl-i Ḥadīth's use of Qur'ān 9:31 and the ʿAdī b. Ḥātim *ḥadīth*, it is hard to imagine that he was unaware of it given his familiarity with the polemic in which these served as central prooftexts.

Let us examine one final example of the relation between Mawdūdī's understanding of *ḥākimiyyat* and premodern jurisprudential theonomy. This example appears in the somewhat unlikely context of Mawdūdī's chapter on Abū Ḥanīfa's views on the caliphate in his book *Khilāfat o mulūkiyyat*.[166] The chapter begins, naturally enough for Mawdūdī, with a discussion of *ḥākimiyyat*, and Mawdūdī asserts that "when treating any given viewpoint on political leadership (*riyāsat*), the first question that arises is: to whom does this viewpoint ascribe sovereignty (*woh naẓariyya ḥākimiyyat kis kē lī'ē thābit kartā hē*)?" Mawdūdī then goes on to write that Abū Ḥanīfa's view was that God is the ruler (*ḥākim*), that the Prophet is to be obeyed in his capacity as God's representative, and that the *sharīʿat* of God and the Prophet is the supreme law, and the only law to be obeyed. It is clear that Mawdūdī offers this description as a concise synopsis of his own view on *ḥākimiyyat*; when he then wishes to demonstrate how it was Abū Ḥanīfa's as well, he writes: "Since the Imām (Abū Ḥanīfa) was essentially a legist (*qānūnī ādmī*), he expressed this content in legal language, rather than in the language of political science."[167]

The quotations that follow clarify what Mawdūdī means by Abū Ḥanīfa's "legal language": They are statements attributed to Abū Ḥanīfa in which he expresses the preeminence of the Qur'ān and the *ḥadīth* (even weak *ḥadīth*) over *ra'y* and *qiyās*. Notably, the sources for these statements are not Ḥanafī texts, but sources of a more 'salafī'

[165] Abū al-Aʿlā Mawdūdī, "Wahhābī awr wahhābiyyat," *Tarjumān al-Qur'ān*, July–October 1944; reprinted in Mawdūdī, *Rasā'il o masā'il*, vol. 1, pp. 150–151.

[166] Abū al-Aʿlā Mawdūdī, *Khilāfat o mulūkiyyat*, Lahore: Idārah-i Tarjumān al-Qur'ān, 2005, pp. 247ff.

[167] Mawdūdī, *Khilāfat*, p. 247.

orientation, such as al-Dhahabī, the Shafiʿī *ḥadīth* scholar who was close to Ibn Taymiyya's circle, and the Ẓāhirī Ibn Ḥazm.[168]

Much could be said about Mawdūdī's attempt to portray the figure of Abū Ḥanīfa as a supporter of his own doctrine of *ḥākimiyyat*, a matter of clear polemical importance in the South Asian context, and it is noteworthy that he attempted to do so via the 'salafī' theme that Abū Ḥanīfa himself (in implicit contrast to later Ḥanafīs) did not privilege *raʾy* or *qiyās* over revealed texts. What is significant for present purposes, though, is simply the equivalence that Mawdūdī establishes between 'salafī' jurisprudential methodology and *ḥākimiyyat*. In Mawdūdī's presentation, these are one and the same concept with two different expressions, one employing the language of law and jurisprudence, the other that of political science.

In summary, it appears that the general principles on which Mawdūdī based his system – both the general emphasis on monolatry, and its interpretation in terms of theonomy – were influenced to some degree by the premodern tradition. It thus seems unwarranted to characterize Mawdūdī's doctrine of absolute obedience to God as a 'modern' doctrine and as a deviation from the spirit of premodern Islam, as Seyyed Vali Reza Nasr has argued. A defining characteristic of the modern age has been the attempt to establish a mundane sovereignty of self-sufficient human autonomy without reference to a higher power – whether the sovereign in question be a dictator, a parliament, or the 'general will' of the people. This is precisely what Mawdūdī opposed: The very heart of his doctrine is an opposition between obedience to God and obedience to humans, founded on theological premises that share much with a certain strain of premodern Islamic thought, and applied to modern issues such as nationalism, the nation-state, and human legislation. What is modern about Mawdūdī is not his principles or their basis, but rather the context in which he wrote, and his attempt to reverse the modern tide through conscious reappropriation of its characteristic concepts: 'Sovereignty' (*ḥākimiyyat*) in truth belongs to God alone, and the only proper 'state' is God's *dīn*. While applied to modern problems Mawdūdī's core conception of the opposition between divine rule and human rule is not modern at all, but rather as old as monolatry itself. We will return to this topic in more detail in the conclusion to the present chapter; now we turn to an analysis of the same topics discussed above in the writings of Sayyid Quṭb.

[168] Mawdūdī, *Khilāfat*, pp. 247–248; cf. Muḥammad b. Aḥmad b. ʿUthmān al-Dhahabī, *Manāqib al-imām Abī Ḥanīfa wa-ṣāḥibayhi Abī Yūsuf wa-Muḥammad b. al-Ḥasan*, 4th ed., ed. Muḥammad Zāhid al-Kawtharī and Abū al-Wafā al-Afghānī, Hyderabad: Lajnat Iḥyāʾ al-Maʿārif al-Nuʿmāniyya, 1419[/1998], pp. 32ff.

## Sayyid Quṭb

Sayyid Quṭb was one of the most influential figures in twentieth-century Islamism. By training a schoolteacher and literatus, his life path, which took him from Egyptian nationalism to the demand to make Islam the sole basis for human life, was emblematic of a generational shift in Egypt: the waning of nationalism (whether Egyptian or pan-Arab) as a popular force, the continued spread of the Muslim Brotherhood, and, starting in the 1970s, the emergence of new and more radical Islamic groups partly inspired by Quṭb himself.

It is traditional to divide the career of Sayyid Quṭb into three phases: his early years as a nationalist and literary figure; a middle period in which he turned to Islamism, beginning in approximately 1948 and with a formal affiliation with the Muslim Brotherhood as of 1953; and a third period in which Quṭb, while still formally a leading member of the Muslim Brotherhood, developed his distinctive and more radical brand of Islamism which was to prove so influential on subsequent generations.[169]

It is the writings of this third phase that will be of interest to us here, as it was then that Quṭb's thought took a decisively theonomic turn. In particular we will focus on the works that seem to offer the best representation of Quṭb's doctrine of *ḥākimiyya* in its final form: the famous *Maʿālim fī al-ṭarīq*[170] (usually translated as "Milestones") and the posthumously published *Muqawwimāt al-taṣawwur al-islāmī* ("The Constitutive Elements of the Islamic Conception").[171] In the latter work I will focus in particular on the chapter titled "*Ulūhiyya wa-ʿubūdiyya*," which elaborates the core of Quṭb's system. Quṭb himself points to the centrality of the topic of "*ulūhiyya wa-ʿubūdiyya*" when he asserts (in *Maʿālim*) that the Meccan Qurʾān spoke of only one sole issue, "the issue of creed (*ʿaqīda*) as represented in its primary foundation: *ulūhiyya* and *ʿubūdiyya*, and the relation between them." This, in Quṭb's view, is an unchanging matter, as what is at issue therein is the very nature of human existence in the cosmos and the nature of humans' relation to their Creator; only after this first principle became firmly entrenched (viz. in Medina) did the Qurʾān turn to a detailing of its ramifications for human life.[172]

169 William Shepard places the transition to the third stage very late in Quṭb's life, at some point between 1962 and 1964. Shepard, "Sayyid Qutb's Doctrine of 'Jāhiliyya,'" p. 534.
170 Sayyid Quṭb, *Maʿālim fī al-ṭarīq*, 6th ed., Beirut and Cairo: Dār al-Shurūq, 1399/1975.
171 Sayyid Quṭb, *Muqawwimāt al-taṣawwur al-islāmī*, 5th ed., Beirut and Cairo: Dār al-Shurūq, 1418/1997.
172 Quṭb, *Maʿālim*, pp. 19–20.

The two works studied here are similar in content but different in nature. *Ma ʿālim* is primarily a programmatic work; while it does contain exposition of the central elements of Quṭb's system, and *ḥākimiyya* in particular, Quṭb does not dwell at great length on the theological underpinnings for these elements. *Ma ʿālim* was composed as a kind of guide for the group of young Muslim Brothers who came to be known, after their arrest, as the '1965 Organization.' This group specifically requested that Quṭb be their leader, and many of them at least were already familiar with his teachings.[173] Quṭb's frequent references to a 'vanguard' (*ṭalīʿa*) throughout the work should be understood as a reference to this group, or to what Quṭb believed it had the potential to become. Emphasis on praxis over abstract theory was already a major feature of Quṭb's doctrine, but in *Ma ʿālim* this tendency is further accentuated by the concrete context of the work's composition. The very title of the work gives an indication of its fundamentally programmatic nature:

> It is indispensable that the vanguard that is firmly resolved [to destroy *jāhiliyya* and revive Islam] have "signs indicating the path" (*ma ʿālim fī al-ṭarīq*), signs by which it will know the nature of its role, the essence of its task, its utmost goal (*ṣulb ghāyatihi*), and the starting point for the long journey. Likewise, it will know [by these signs] the nature of its position vis-à-vis the *jāhiliyya* that strikes its roots throughout the entire world: Where will [the vanguard] meet people and where will it part paths with them? What are its own distinctive characteristics, and what are the distinctive characteristics of the *jāhiliyya* that surrounds it? How should it address the people of this *jāhiliyya* in the language of Islam, and regarding what matters should it address them?[174]

The topic of theonomy is omnipresent in *Ma ʿālim*, but for the most part is presented in hortatory fashion as the basis for programmatic conclusions. In contrast, *Muqawwimāt* delves deeper into the theological grounding of the various aspects of Quṭb's system, first and foremost of course his doctrine of *ḥākimiyya*. Much more so than from the text of *Ma ʿālim*, it is clear from *Muqawwimāt* that Quṭb's doctrine of *ḥākimiyya*, his argumentation, and his theological grounding for the doctrine are almost entirely derivative of Mawdūdī. Quṭb's general debt to Mawdūdī, both on this topic and on other related ones, has long been recognized in the research literature;[175] our purpose here will be to point out the

[173] On the '1965 Organization' and Quṭb's role in it, see Barbara Zollner, "Prison Talk: The Muslim Brotherhood's Internal Struggle during Gamal Abdel Nasser's Persecution, 1954 to 1971," *International Journal of Middle East Studies* 39 (2007), pp. 411–433.

[174] Quṭb, *Ma ʿālim*, p. 9.

[175] See Sivan, *Radical Islam*, pp. 22–23; Kepel, *Muslim Extremism in Egypt*, pp. 47–51; Hartung, *A System of Life*, pp. 193–213.

presence of the specific features of Mawdūdī's system, as we described them in the first part of this chapter, in Quṭb's writings. To be more precise, the following discussion will seek to demonstrate that Quṭb's doctrine of *ḥākimiyya*, like Mawdūdī's, is based on the following foundations: a differentiation between two aspects of divinity, one cosmic-objective, and the other normative-relational; an argument from the cosmic-objective aspect to the normative-relational aspect;[176] the use of the Streitpunkt principle; and a basically monolatric definition of Islam, which, when paired with a widening of the meaning of *ʿibāda* to obedience to law, renders theonomy the core of the system.

### *Quṭb's Monolatric Conception of Islam*

At the opening of the "*Ulūhiyya wa-ʿubūdiyya*" chapter in *Muqawwimāt* Quṭb describes the one unitary and comprehensive principle that stands at the heart of the Islamic conception in the following words: "*ʿubūdiyya* to Allāh alone without partner, and *daynūna* [to be explained presently] to Allāh alone without rival."[177] Much like Mawdūdī's statement in the introduction to *Iṣṭilāḥēn*, we find here that in Quṭb's view Islam is less a belief system or creed than it is simply exclusivity of devotion to Allāh; similar formulas are repeated elsewhere, as when Quṭb writes that the primary goal of the revelation of the Qurʾān is "that *daynūna* and *ʿubūdiyya* be to no one but Allāh alone."[178] The pairing in these formulas of *ʿubūdiyya* and *daynūna* echoes Mawdūdī's *ʿibādat* and *dīn* and clearly shows his influence; later in the chapter Quṭb mentions the four terms (*ulūhiyya*, *rubūbiyya*, *ʿibāda*, *dīn*) with explicit reference to Mawdūdī.[179]

While Quṭb does not share Mawdūdī's pretense to philological systematicity, and his own terminology tends to be somewhat fluid, there does appear to be a distinction between *ʿubūdiyya* and *dīn*/*daynūna* in his usage. *ʿUbūdiyya* is an all-encompassing cosmic principle, the state of all beings' servitude to Allāh: "*ʿUbūdiyya* to Allāh encompasses every thing and every living being, and no thing or living being in existence stands outside of [the state of] *ʿubūdiyya* to Allāh, may He be praised. Every living being and every thing is bereft of the prerogatives of *ulūhiyya*, and

[176] Andrew March has already identified this element as the basis for Quṭb's *ḥākimiyya*: "The common Abrahamic belief in God's cosmic, creative sovereignty – what we might call divine sovereignty as fact – leads to an uncompromising insistence on God's exclusive legislative and normative sovereignty." Andrew F. March, "Genealogies of Sovereignty in Islamic Political Theology," *Social Research* 80/1 (Spring 2013), pp. 293–320, at p. 295.

[177] Quṭb, *Muqawwimāt*, p. 81. [178] Quṭb, *Muqawwimāt*, p. 119.

[179] Quṭb, *Muqawwimāt*, p. 147.

all are in the status of slaves in relation to the one singular *ulūhiyya*."[180] It is recognition of this objective cosmic dichotomy between *ʿubūdiyya* and *ulūhiyya* that stands at the foundation of Islam: "The opposition between the all-encompassing (*shāmila*) nature of the state of servitude (*ʿubūdiyya*) and the singular (*mutafarrida*) nature of *ulūhiyya* – this is the foundation of [the Islamic] conception, its anchor, its distinguishing feature, and the parting of ways between it and all other conceptions."[181] *Dīn* or *daynūna*, on the other hand, is a collective term for the specific demands that the principle of *ʿubūdiyya* presents to human society. These demands fall neatly into a consistent tripartite classification: belief (*iʿtiqād*), ritual (*shaʿāʾir*), and theonomy, which is usually designated by terms such as *ḥukm*, *ḥākimiyya*, or *taḥākum*, but also at times in a somewhat broader sense (as in Mawdūdī's writings) by *niẓām* or *niẓām al-ḥayāt*, that is, a "system of life."[182] The fulfillment of *ʿubūdiyya* in these three areas is the full meaning of *tawḥīd* and it is the meaning of *lā ilāha illā llāh*.[183] Like the other authors studied up to this point, Quṭb's understanding of *tawḥīd* and the *shahāda* is fundamentally monolatric: "Belief" is only one of the three components necessary for one's *tawḥīd* and *shahāda* to be valid, alongside ritual worship and legal obedience, and it too is subsumed under the general rubric of *ʿubūdiyya*. In order to emphasize this comprehensive meaning of *tawḥīd* and to distinguish it from other conceptions that Quṭb considers partial and deficient, he at times adds the qualifier *bi-kull madlūlātihi*, that is, *tawḥīd* in all the meanings that it encompasses.[184]

This definition of *tawḥīd* and of the *shahāda* means that one is not a Muslim until one fulfills the demand of exclusive *ʿubūdiyya* to Allāh in each of the three areas of belief, ritual, and theonomy, and one who fails to do so in any of the three areas is an unbeliever. Thus Quṭb writes, after explaining that all three areas together make up the meaning of the *shahāda*:

This is the general principle that is a necessarily known truth in religion (*maʿlūm min al-dīn bi-l-ḍarūra*),[185] and upon which rests the ruling that one is an

[180] Quṭb, *Muqawwimāt*, p. 127. [181] Quṭb, *Muqawwimāt*, p. 130.

[182] Quṭb, *Muqawwimāt*, p. 132. The distinction between *ʿubūdiyya* and *dīn*/*daynūna* is not entirely consistent, however; elsewhere (p. 147) he writes that each of Mawdūdī's four terms relates to each of the three areas of belief, ritual, and theonomy.

[183] Quṭb, *Muqawwimāt*, pp. 107, 147–148; for other mentions of the tripartite division, see pp. 112, 116, 117, 182, 184, 187.

[184] For example, Quṭb, *Muqawwimāt*, p. 183: *innamā yukāfiḥu al-islām li-taṣḥīḥ al-iʿtiqād wa-li-taṣḥīḥ al-tadayyun, yukāfiḥu min ajli al-tawḥīd al-muṭlaq al-shāmil bi-kull madlūlātihi*.

[185] The expression *maʿlūm min al-dīn bi-l-ḍarūra* is used of tenets of Islam that are held to be so evident that denial of them constitutes apostasy, as their evident nature rules out

unbeliever if he fails to render to Allāh alone – may He be praised – the totality of the exclusive rights of *ulūhiyya*, and not just some of them and not others. And these [exclusive rights of *ulūhiyya*] are the belief of the heart that *ulūhiyya* is Allāh's alone, devotion of ritual worship to Him alone, and obedience (*daynūna*) to Him alone in *ḥākimiyya*, as represented by referral in judgment (*taḥākum*) to His *sharīʿa* alone.[186]

The same tripartite scheme serves as the framework for the chapter of *Maʿālim* titled "*Lā ilāha illā llāh manhaj ḥayāt*," in which Quṭb states starkly that all contemporary societies – including ostensibly Muslim ones – are *jāhilī* because none of them devotes exclusive *ʿubūdiyya* to Allāh in all of belief, ritual worship, and legislation.[187] In order for a society to be Muslim and not *jāhilī*, it must – as the chapter title indicates – adopt the *shahāda* as its way of life, fulfilling the requirements of *ʿubūdiyya* in all three areas:

Muslim society is the society in which *ʿubūdiyya* to Allāh alone is exemplified in the beliefs and conceptions of its individuals, as well as in their rites and worship, and likewise in their collective organization (*fī niẓāmihim al-jamāʿī*) and their laws. Whenever one of these aspects disappears, Islam itself has disappeared, due to the disappearance of its first pillar – the testimony that there is no *ilāh* but Allāh and that Muḥammad is the Messenger of Allāh.[188]

True to the programmatic nature of *Maʿālim*, the chapter does not offer especially developed arguments in favor of this view. Quṭb's primary objective in the chapter is to detail, in a non-explicit but clear contrast with the classic Muslim Brotherhood model of mass activism, in what way Muslim society must be refounded from scratch through the formation of a vanguard:

Thus before one can think of establishing an Islamic system for the collective (*niẓām ijtimāʿī islāmī*), and establishing a Muslim society on the basis of this system, attention must first be focused on purifying the consciences of individuals from *ʿubūdiyya* to not-Allāh in any of its forms that we discussed previously; and these individuals who have purified their consciences from *ʿubūdiyya* to not-Allāh must gather in a Muslim association (*jamāʿa muslima*). It is from this association, whose individuals have purified their consciences from *ʿubūdiyya* to not-Allāh, in belief (*iʿtiqādan*), in [ritual] worship (*ʿibādatan*), and in law (*sharīʿatan*), that Muslim society will emerge. It will be joined by whoever wishes to live in this society in accordance with its creed, its worship, and its law, in which is exemplified *ʿubūdiyya* to Allāh alone – or in other words, in which is

the possibility of exculpatory ignorance. See e.g. Jalāl al-Dīn ʿAbd al-Raḥmān al-Suyūṭī, *al-Ashbāh wa-l-naẓāʾir fī qawāʿid wa-furūʿ fiqh al-shāfiʿiyya*, Beirut: Dār al-Kutub al-ʿIlmiyya, 1403/1983, p. 488.

186 Quṭb, *Muqawwimāt*, p. 151.

187 Quṭb, *Maʿālim*, pp. 83–96.

188 Quṭb, *Maʿālim*, p. 85.

exemplified the testimony that there is no *ilāh* but Allāh, and that Muḥammad is the Messenger of Allāh.[189]

The necessity of forming a vanguard prior to any attempt to Islamize society as a whole is clearly predicated on Quṭb's conception of what Islam is. This was not a pragmatic question of means, or at least not primarily so. It is true that the advent of the Nasserist regime in Egypt presented new challenges: As an ideological movement in its own right that wielded police-state powers to repress its rivals it certainly called into question the viability of the old Muslim Brotherhood model of mass recruitment and activism.[190] The depiction of the radicalization of Islamism in the Middle East as a reaction to the rise of the new pan-Arabist regimes is thus an internally cogent thesis, but within the logic of Quṭb's system itself his radical prescription does not flow primarily from this change of external circumstances but rather from his determination that ostensibly Muslim society was not really Muslim. The Muslim Brotherhood had a tradition of trusting in the Islamic sentiments of the masses, and thus pitting society against the state, whereas for Quṭb, with his stringent monolatric-theonomic definition of Islam, Islam was in abeyance from society itself – not just in Nasserist Egypt or Baʿthist Syria, but in all the ostensibly Muslim countries, since "all societies actually in existence in the world today fall into the category of *jāhilī* society."[191] The ostensibly Muslim societies fall into this category because they are not ruled exclusively by the *sharīʿa* and thus fail to uphold exclusivity of *ʿubūdiyya* in the area of theonomy.[192]

### *The Argument from the Cosmic to the Normative*

There is one brief chapter in *Maʿālim*, titled "*Sharīʿa kawniyya*," that deviates from the essentially programmatic nature of the book and broaches the ultimate theoretical grounding for theonomy.[193] Coming at the midpoint of the book (it is the sixth chapter out of twelve), it directly follows the chapter "*Lā ilāha illā llāh manhaj ḥayāt*" and is

[189] Quṭb, *Maʿālim*, p. 87. [190] See Sivan, *Radical Islam*, pp. 40–49.
[191] Quṭb, *Maʿālim*, pp. 88–89.
[192] Quṭb, *Maʿālim*, p. 91. This belief that the surrounding society was *jāhilī* was a principal reason why Quṭb's model for the vanguard were the Companions; see pp. 16–19. It is also what differentiates Quṭb's conception of the vanguard from the inner circle of the stratified Muslim Brotherhood, which was also a type of vanguard. On the latter, see Ella Landau-Tasseron, "Leadership and Allegiance in the Society of the Muslim Brothers," Hudson Institute Research Monographs on the Muslim World 2/5 (2010), pp. 7–8.
[193] Quṭb, *Maʿālim*, pp. 97–104.

presented as something of a continuation of the same topic in which Quṭb presents the grounding for his conclusions.

It is Quṭb himself who states, in the opening words of the "*Sharī'a kawniyya*" chapter, that he seeks therein to explain the ultimate foundation of his system. He begins with a kind of summary of the previous chapter, and then states that its conclusions derive from a cosmic principle:

When Islam establishes its belief structure, in [human] conscience and in reality, on the foundation of absolute *'ubūdiyya* to Allāh alone, and makes this *'ubūdiyya* represented equally in belief, [ritual] worship, and in law (*sharī'a*) – as this absolute *'ubūdiyya* to Allāh alone, in this form, is the meaning of *lā ilāha illā llāh* in application ... When Islam establishes its entire structure on this foundation ... it is but drawing on a foundation that is not only more comprehensive than human existence, but is more comprehensive, when properly understood (*fī taqrīrihi*), than all of existence; and it is but drawing on what is not only the way of human life alone, but what is the way of all of existence.[194]

In other words, after having described in the previous chapter the normative, prescriptive basis for human society mandated by Islam, Quṭb now states that this basis is grounded in a comprehensive cosmic reality. This cosmic reality is the fact that the cosmos in its entirety is Allāh's creation, a fact that holds necessary implications for human existence:

Allāh, who created this cosmos and created humans, and who subjected humans to His same laws to which He subjected the cosmos – He it is, may He be praised, who [likewise] laid down the *sharī'a* for humans, in order to organize the volitional aspect of their life in a manner that is in harmony with the natural aspect of their life. Thus the *sharī'a*, on this basis, is but one part of the general divine law (*al-nāmūs al-ilāhī al-'āmm*) that governs humans' nature (*fiṭra*) and the nature of general existence, and harmonizes all of it as a single whole.[195]

In other words, the normative obligation of adherence to the *sharī'a* is but a natural corollary of the objective reality of Allāh as Creator. All other parts of the cosmos are governed by, and unquestioningly obedient to, the natural laws that Allāh set in place, as are humans in all those aspects of their life that are non-volitional.[196] It is through exclusive *'ubūdiyya* to Allāh and obedience to His *sharī'a* that humans, singularly and collectively, bring their volitional lives into harmony with the rest of the cosmos and with Allāh's will:

Adherence to Allāh's *sharī'a* ... is a necessity deriving from the complete interrelation between human life and the life of the cosmos, between the

[194] Quṭb, *Ma'ālim*, p. 97. [195] Quṭb, *Ma'ālim*, p. 99.
[196] Quṭb, *Ma'ālim*, pp. 98–99.

> (natural) law (*nāmūs*) that governs human nature (*fiṭra*) and [the law] that governs this cosmos, and the necessary conformity between this general law (*nāmūs*) and the *sharīʿa* that organizes human life, which is achieved (*tataḥaqqaqu*) by humans adhering to *ʿubūdiyya* to Allāh alone, just as no human claims for himself the *ʿubūdiyya* that the cosmos devotes to Allāh alone.[197]

Quṭb thus derives the normative demand of adherence to the *sharīʿa* and comprehensive *ʿubūdiyya* – monolatry interpreted as theonomy – from the cosmic-objective aspect of Allāh's divinity, to wit, His being the sole Creator and Master of the cosmos. As we noted in the first half of the present chapter, this argument from the cosmic to the normative was already present in Mawdūdī's writings and served him frequently as a concise summation of his system.

At the end of the "*Sharīʿa kawniyya*" chapter, Quṭb cites Qurʾān 2:258 to exemplify this connection:

> Have you not considered he who disputed with Ibrāhīm regarding his Lord (*fī rabbihi*), because Allāh gave him kingship? When Ibrāhīm said: my Lord is He who gives life and puts to death, he said: I give life and put to death. Ibrāhīm said: Allāh causes the sun to rise from the east, so bring it from the west. Thus the unbeliever was confounded; Allāh does not guide the evildoers.

In itself the connection between this verse and the preceding discussion is not self-evident. Quṭb clearly has in mind Mawdūdī's exegesis of the verse, which as we saw delineates precisely the same connection between Allāh's objective and normative aspects as described by Quṭb in the "*Sharīʿa kawniyya*" chapter. That this is what Quṭb had in mind is confirmed by his treatment of this same verse in *Muqawwimāt*, which we will see in the next section.

### *The Streitpunkt*

Earlier in this chapter we discussed the long portion of Mawdūdī's *Iṣṭilāḥēn̲* that dealt with analysis of the Streitpunkt between the prophets and the various groups of unbelievers described in the Qurʾān. A similarly sustained Streitpunkt analysis and argument is to be found in Quṭb's *Muqawwimāt*, in which he maintains that the point of conflict between the prophets and the unbelievers – and thus between Islam and unbelief – was monolatry in the broad sense, with theonomy as its foremost expression. Quṭb's interpretation of these conflicts both derives from and reinforces his general contention that exclusive *ʿubūdiyya* and

[197] Quṭb, *Maʿālim*, p. 103. A similar exposition earlier in *Maʿālim* (p. 47) contains a footnote directing readers to Mawdūdī's *Mabādiʾ al-islām* for more on the topic.

*daynūna* to Allāh is "the true primary issue of creed in all the divine prophecies throughout the ages."[198] As this is the heart of prophecy and divine religion, the issue of exclusive *ʿubūdiyya* and *daynūna* must also be the crux of the "battle" (*maʿraka*) between true and false religion.[199]

Like Mawdūdī (and the premodern salafī tradition), Quṭb's analysis of the Streitpunkt builds on the distinction between the cosmic-objective and normative-relational aspects of divinity, emphasizing that the unbelievers did not deny Allāh's existence or His cosmic attributes of Creator, Sustainer, and so forth. In one formulation – which taken in isolation could easily be mistaken for Ibn ʿAbd al-Wahhāb expounding on the *mushrikūn*'s acknowledgment of *tawḥīd al-rubūbiyya* – Quṭb writes that the Arabs of Muḥammad's time "did not deny Allāh outright and did not deny that Allāh is the Creator (*khāliq*), the Sustainer (*al-rāziq*), and the Mighty (*al-qawī*) who protects, and against whom none can protect,"[200] and he then adds that the Arabs of the *jāhiliyya* only worshipped the *ilāh*s as intermediaries and intercessors with Allāh.[201] When Quṭb returns to this point in a subsequent passage, however, we begin to see how his elaboration of the theme differs from that of Ibn ʿAbd al-Wahhāb:

> The Arab *jāhiliyya* that Islam confronted for the first time in the Arabian Peninsula did not deny Allāh outright and was not oblivious to the fact that it is Allāh who is the Creator (*khāliq*), the Sustainer (*rāziq*), and the Mighty (*al-qawī*) who protects, and against whom none can protect – as we already noted. The Prophet, Allāh's blessing and peace be upon him, did not call them to belief in Allāh's existence, but rather he called them to *tawḥīd* of Allāh: He called them to the belief (*iʿtiqād*) that Allāh alone is *ilāh* and *rabb* and *al-qayyim*; he called them to worship (*ʿibāda*) of Allāh alone and ritual devotion to Him; and he called them to submit to the judgment (*taḥākum*) of the *sharīʿa* of Allāh alone and to *daynūna* to Him in *ʿubūdiyya*. And this call (*daʿwa*), complete in all these senses, is the meaning of the testimony *lā ilāha illā llāh*, which is Islam.[202]

Quṭb thus sets over and against the cosmic-objective aspect of Allāh, which even the unbelievers acknowledge, his own tripartite enumeration

198 Quṭb, *Muqawwimāt*, p. 83. 199 Quṭb, *Muqawwimāt*, p. 103.

200 The phrase *wa-huwa yujīru wa-lā yujāru ʿalayhi* is an allusion to Qurʾān 23:88; this verse is one of those used by Ibn Taymiyya, Ibn ʿAbd al-Wahhāb, and Mawdūdī to demonstrate the unbelievers' acknowledgment of Allāh's cosmic-objective aspect, and to emphasize that their unbelief related specifically to His normative aspect (*rubūbiyya* and *ulūhiyya*, respectively, for Ibn Taymiyya and Ibn ʿAbd al-Wahhāb). See Ibn Taymiyya, *Majmūʿat al-fatāwā*, vol. 1, pp. 71, 117; *Durar*, vol. 2, pp. 27–28; Mawdūdī, *Iṣṭilāḥēn*, pp. 65–66. Elsewhere Quṭb himself cites the full verse for the same purpose: *Muqawwimāt*, p. 108.

201 Quṭb, *Muqawwimāt*, p. 98.

202 Quṭb, *Muqawwimāt*, p. 107. It is not clear to me why Quṭb adds here the term *al-qayyim* to *ilāh* and *rabb*.

of belief, ritual, and legal obedience. Like Mawdūdī, he tends to group together the first two issues, belief and ritual, seeing polylatric deviation from *tawḥīd* in the ritual sense as a direct result[203] of the false belief that the lesser *ilāh*s possessed powers of necessarily efficacious intercession, and thus the ability to benefit and to harm.[204] In addition to this classic concern for ritual monolatry, Quṭb foregrounds the dispute over legal obedience, to the point of claiming that it was in truth the essential Streitpunkt (*mawḍūʿ al-ṣirāʿ al-ḥaqīqī*)[205] between Islam and *jāhiliyya*. While in principle both belief and ritual have their place within the tripartite *tawḥīd* that is the true Islam, and which is regularly contrasted to the unbelievers' mere acknowledgment of Allāh's cosmic-objective aspect, Quṭb tends at times to downplay their importance vis-à-vis *ḥākimiyya*:

> The Islamic conception, ever since it first appeared in all the divine prophecies, has never been just a creedal (*iʿtiqādī*) conception or just devotional ritual, with that being the end-all and the completion of religion (*dīn*). Rather [Islam] was a vital real-life issue, [and] this question was always posed: To whom belongs sovereignty (*mulk*) on earth? … It was over this question, and the answer to it, that the battle was waged.[206]

Just like Mawdūdī, Quṭb's implicit polemic against secularism leads him to focus on *ḥākimiyya* as the true Streitpunkt and arena for the active recognition of Allāh's normative-relational aspect, and behavior in accordance with it. The emphasis is shifted from ritual monolatry to theonomy.

Quṭb surveys the Qurʾān's depiction of the interactions between the prophets and the unbelievers in order to demonstrate that theonomy is not just now, but has always been, the essential point of conflict. The argumentation regarding some of the earlier prophets is strained, as Quṭb himself comes close to admitting,[207] but since it is axiomatic for him that the core message of all the prophets was the same[208] he reads them in light of the final revelation to Muḥammad (as he understands it). The argumentation is closely influenced by Mawdūdī, and Quṭb's discussion even contains a several-page direct quotation, with proper attribution, from the Arabic translation of *Iṣṭilāḥēn̠* dealing with Firʿawn (Pharaoh)

[203] See e.g. Quṭb, *Muqawwimāt*, p. 117: *kāna al-ʿarab … fī jāhiliyyatihim yaẓunnūna annahum yataqarrabūna ilā llāhi wa-yatazallafūna bi-tilka al-āliha … wa-kānū min thamma yataqarrabūna ilā hādhihi al-āliha al-muddaʿāt bi-l-shaʿāʾir fa-yuqaddimūna lahā al-qarābīn.*

[204] Quṭb, *Muqawwimāt*, p. 108. [205] Quṭb, *Muqawwimāt*, p. 133.

[206] Quṭb, *Muqawwimāt*, p. 134. [207] Quṭb, *Muqawwimāt*, pp. 134–135.

[208] Cf. Michael Cook, *Muhammad*, Oxford: Oxford University Press, 1983, p. 32, who notes that the Qurʾān imposes on the figures of Biblical prophets "a stereotyped conception of the monotheist messenger."

and Mūsā (Moses).[209] Even before the direct quotation, however, Mawdūdī's influence is clear in Quṭb's treatment of the disputation between Ibrāhīm and Namrūd related in Qur'ān 2:258.

As noted above, Quṭb cited Qur'ān 2:258 at the close of the "*Sharī'a kawniyya*" chapter of *Ma'ālim* without any explanation, though the context strongly suggested that Quṭb viewed it as encapsulating the argument that derives Allāh's normative authority from His cosmic-objective aspect. That argument is fleshed out in the exegesis of the verse in *Muqawwimāt*, which is identical to the one put forward by Mawdūdī in *Iṣṭilāḥēn*. The verse reads:

> Have you not considered he who disputed with Ibrāhīm regarding his Lord (*fī rabbihi*), because Allāh gave him kingship? When Ibrāhīm said: my Lord is He who gives life and puts to death, he said: I give life and put to death. Ibrāhīm said: Allāh causes the sun to rise from the east, so bring it from the west. Thus the unbeliever was confounded; Allāh does not guide the evildoers.

Quṭb writes that the king, Namrūd, claimed divinity (*rubūbiyya*) in the sense of *ḥākimiyya* over the earthly kingdom and its denizens. When Ibrāhīm said that his *rabb* is the one who gives life and puts to death, he meant that *ḥākimiyya* over the earthly kingdom belongs to the same one who holds power over life and death. The king responded that it is he who wields this power, meaning thereby that he is the ruler and the ultimate authority on matters of life and death. Quṭb interprets Ibrāhīm's response – the challenge to Namrūd to control the path of the sun – as saying: "the one who possesses authority of life and death over people is the one who possesses supreme rule in the cosmic order, and he it is who holds legal right over people's lives."[210] In other words, Quṭb understands Ibrāhīm as challenging the political order of his day on the basis of the message that lies at the heart of prophecy, namely, that divinity is not restricted to Allāh's cosmic-objective aspect, and that in fact this very aspect mandates that His normative-relational authority over human life be acknowledged as well. As in *Ma'ālim*, Quṭb writes that the continuity in Allāh's prerogatives between the two realms, the cosmic and the human, rests on the fact that human life is not isolated from the cosmos, but is rather part of it: "The only one who may claim *ḥākimiyya* in human life is the one who is able to direct the cosmos in its entirety by his power, because human life, in general and in its specifics, is dependent on [this] direction of the cosmos."[211] And since authority over human life is properly Allāh's, when a human claims it or exercises it

[209] Quṭb, *Muqawwimāt*, pp. 138–141. [210] Quṭb, *Muqawwimāt*, p. 137.
[211] Quṭb, *Muqawwimāt*, p. 138.

he is in essence claiming divinity: "If the king exercises this rule over people's lives by putting them to death or allowing them to live, when he does not possess rule over the cosmic order, then he is overstepping his specific nature as a servant [viz. of Allāh] (*ʿabd*) and is infringing on Allāh's specific nature."[212]

In summary, Quṭb was directly influenced by Mawdūdī, both in his decision to employ 'Streitpunkt analysis' as a means of clarifying the nature of Islam, and in his substantive conclusion that *ḥākimiyya* is the true Streitpunkt between Islam and *jāhiliyya*, and thus the true heart of Islam. *Maʿālim* as well contains frequent references to the Streitpunkt theme, but as with other topics, the emphasis there is less on extended analysis than on programmatic implications. For example, in chapter 2 of *Maʿālim* ("*Ṭabīʿat al-manhaj al-qurʾānī*") Quṭb tells us that the Prophet began his mission by calling people to *lā ilāha illā llāh*. He then writes (in similar fashion to Mawdūdī) that the Arabs of the *jāhiliyya* understood the meaning of *ilāh* and knew that *ulūhiyya* meant "supreme sovereignty" (*al-ḥākimiyya al-ʿulyā*); they thus understood that the words *lā ilāha illā llāh* meant "a revolt against [human] earthly rule" – and it was because they understood its meaning that they opposed this message so fiercely.[213] Quṭb then takes this brief summation of the Streitpunkt issue as a springboard for polemic against approaches to Islamic *daʿwa* less radical than his own. He argues that the Prophet, had he so wished, could have begun his mission by preaching Arab unity, social justice, or moral reform; and after rallying people to these banners and gaining their trust, could then have inculcated in them the creed of *tawḥīd*.[214] Allāh, however, knew that sound morals, justice, and other such values can only stand on a firm foundation of creed,[215] and in fact the entire *dīn* is based on the principle of the unitary nature of *ulūhiyya* (*qāʿidat al-ulūhiyya al-wāḥida*).[216] The programmatic conclusion is clear:

> Those engaged in Islamic *daʿwa* must know that when they call people to revive this *dīn*, they must first call them to embrace the creed – even if they [already] call themselves Muslims, and their birth certificates testify that they are Muslims. They must teach them that Islam is first and foremost affirmation of the creed *lā ilāha illā llāh* in its true meaning, which is to render *ḥākimiyya* to Allāh in all their matters.[217]

The fact that Quṭb employs the Streitpunkt argument to decry the use of secondary banners, even as an expedient means of outreach, epitomizes his turn away from the comparatively diffuse focus of the traditional

212 Quṭb, *Muqawwimāt*, p. 137. 213 Quṭb, *Maʿālim*, pp. 22–23.
214 Quṭb, *Maʿālim*, pp. 23–28. 215 Quṭb, *Maʿālim*, pp. 28–29.
216 Quṭb, *Maʿālim*, p. 31. 217 Quṭb, *Maʿālim*, p. 35.

Muslim Brotherhood, and in fact his turn away from his own earlier writings,[218] in favor of radical theonomy.

### *The Two Aspects of Divinity*

Sayyid Quṭb, like Mawdūdī before him, does not maintain any consistent and meaningful distinction between the terms *ilāh* and *rabb*, or between *ulūhiyya* and *rubūbiyya*, and in his writings these terminological dyads do not correspond neatly to the meaningful distinction he does draw between two aspects of divinity, those that we have termed the cosmic-objective and the normative-relational. At times Quṭb describes *ḥākimiyya* as relating to the term *ulūhiyya*: For example, in *Maʿālim*, he writes that the Arabs of the *jāhiliyya* knew that *ulūhiyya* meant "supreme sovereignty" (*al-ḥākimiyya al-ʿulyā*),[219] and he expressly states that *ulūhiyya* is a synonym for *ḥukm*.[220] Yet elsewhere he associates *ulūhiyya* with Allāh's cosmic-objective aspect, and *rubūbiyya* with His normative-relational aspect, using the terms *tawḥīd al-ulūhiyya* and *tawḥīd al-rubūbiyya* in inverse fashion from Ibn Taymiyya;[221] in this usage, what was disputed between the *jāhiliyya* and Islam was not *ulūhiyya*, but rather *rubūbiyya*, which Quṭb interprets as referring to the question of whom humans will obey, and whose law they will follow,[222] that is, the issue of *ḥākimiyya*.

At other times still, the two terms *ulūhiyya* and *rubūbiyya* appear to be essentially identical in meaning. In one of Quṭb's discussions of the meaning of the *shahāda* in *Muqawwimāt*, he writes that the testimony *lā*

[218] Quṭb appears to allude to his own *al-ʿAdāla al-ijtimāʿiyya fī al-islām* ("Social Justice in Islam"), the first Islamist book he authored, when he writes: "Allāh, may He be praised, knew that this was not the path. He knew that social justice (*al-ʿadāla al-ijtimāʿiyya*) can only emerge in society from a comprehensive creedal conception in which all matters are referred to Allāh" (*Maʿālim*, p. 26). Quṭb revised *ʿAdāla* several times in order to bring it in line with this idea and with the general evolution of his thought. William Shepard, in his detailed study of the revisions of *ʿAdāla*, notes that "Qutb's theocentrism in the last edition is also reflected in the point, central to *Milestones*, that acceptance of the basic creed (*ʿaqīdah*) that there is no god but God is logically and temporally prior to all practical application of Islamic rules." William E. Shepard, *Sayyid Qutb and Islamic Activism: A Translation and Critical Analysis of* Social Justice in Islam, Leiden: Brill, 1996, pp. xxvii–xxviii. For disapproving allusions to other writings from Quṭb's first, pre-Islamist, phase (*al-Taṣwīr al-fannī fī al-qurʾān*, *Mashāhid al-qiyāma fī al-qurʾān*), see *Maʿālim*, p. 18.

[219] Quṭb, *Maʿālim*, p. 22.

[220] Quṭb, *Maʿālim*, pp. 59–60: *al-tamarrud al-kāmil ʿalā kull waḍʿ fī arjāʾ al-arḍ al-ḥukm fīhi li-l-bashar bi-ṣūratin min al-ṣuwar aw bi-taʿbīr ākhar murādif al-ulūhiyya fīhi li-l-bashar fī ṣūratin min al-ṣuwar.*

[221] Quṭb, *Muqawwimāt*, p. 285.

[222] Cf. Sayyid Quṭb, *Fī ẓilāl al-qurʾān*, Cairo: Dār al-Shurūq, 1423/2003, vol. 4, p. 1846.

*ilāha illā llāh* encompasses all three parts of his tripartite definition of *tawḥīd* – belief, ritual, and *ḥākimiyya* – since the meaning of the *ulūhiyya* that one attests is Allāh's alone is *al-sulṭān ʿalā iṭlāqihi*: absolute rule and authority. He immediately follows this with the sentence "and *rubūbiyya* likewise means absolute *qiwāma*." The 'likewise' (*ka-dhālika*) indicates that these two meanings are close if not identical, and indeed the term *qiwāma* appears to be meant here in the sense of authority or rule, as in Qurʾān 4:34, "*al-rijāl qawwāmūn ʿalā al-nisāʾ*."[223] Thus both terms, *ulūhiyya* and *rubūbiyya*, have similar meanings, and both relate to the cosmic-objective aspect of Allāh; the *sulṭān* and *qiwāma* they express as relating to human life in particular are simply their natural corollaries in the normative-relational aspect of divinity, in accordance with the general principle, discussed above, that derives the normative from the cosmic: "Allāh's *sulṭān* and *qiwāma* over humans are the necessary consequence (*muqtaḍā*) of His *ulūhiyya* and *rubūbiyya* over the cosmic order in its entirety. Human life is a part of the cosmic order and is based on the cosmic order, as I already discussed."[224] The operative principle here lies in the assertion that "human life is a part of the cosmic order," an assertion that recurs frequently in Quṭb's arguments from the cosmic to the normative. For example, he writes that "whoever refuses to make Allāh's *sharīʿa* the governing law in all matters of life refuses to acknowledge the *ulūhiyya* of Allāh, may He be praised, even if [this refusal] be in [only] the one facet among others of this cosmos that is human life."[225]

The cosmic-objective and normative-relational aspects thus do not have a consistent terminological designation, but as we have seen, Quṭb does regularly refer to them in the context of his argument from the cosmic to the normative. At times Quṭb uses the language of Qurʾān 43:84 as a kind of shorthand reference to these two aspects: "And it is He who is *ilāh* in heaven and *ilāh* on earth" (*wa-huwa alladhī fī al-samāʾ ilāh wa-fī al-arḍ ilāh*). Thus he writes in *Maʿālim* that a society that recognizes Allāh's governance of the heavens, but does not recognize it on earth through application of His *sharīʿa*, is a *jāhilī* society; he then illustrates this point by citing Qurʾān 43:84.[226] In other words, such a society acknowledges Allāh as "*ilāh* in heaven," that is, Allāh's cosmic-objective aspect, but it does not recognizes Him as "*ilāh* on earth," that is, His normative-relational aspect.

[223] Cf. Quṭb, *Ẓilāl*, vol. 2, pp. 648–652. [224] Quṭb, *Muqawwimāt*, p. 148.
[225] Quṭb, *Muqawwimāt*, p. 180.
[226] Quṭb, *Maʿālim*, p. 106; cf. pp. 59–60 for a similar usage.

### *Theonomy as the Heart of Monolatry*

In addition to his treatment of *ḥākimiyya* in relation to the nature of divinity, and as the Streitpunkt of the prophetic missions, Quṭb also employs a more direct route that simply emphasizes theonomy as the principal expression of monolatry (*ʿubūdiyya*). The monolatric basis of theonomy in his system is already clear in his tripartite elaboration of *dīn*, in which he counts *ḥākimiyya* as one of the three areas in which *ʿubūdiyya* to Allāh must be fulfilled; and indeed it is the most important of these areas, one that Quṭb calls "the greatest servitude" (*al-ʿubūdiyya al-kubrā*).[227]

Unsurprisingly, given the clear influence of Mawdūdī, the key prooftexts for this argument are Qurʾān 9:31 and the ʿAdī b. Ḥātim *ḥadīth*. For example, Quṭb employs these sources in the chapter of *Maʿālim* titled "*al-Jihād fī sabīli llāh.*" In this chapter he conducts a polemic against the apologetic tendency among Muslim modernists that describes jihād in Islam as purely defensive.[228] Quṭb argues that there is no reason to be embarrassed about the doctrine of jihād, since its true nature is the struggle to liberate all humanity from subjugation to and worship of other humans; it is a "comprehensive revolution against the *ḥākimiyya* of humans." This is followed by an explanation of the issue of *ḥākimiyya*: "Rule in which final authority (*maradd al-amr*) belongs to humans, and in which the source of authority is humans – this is the ascription of divinity (*taʾlīh*) to humans, and makes some of them lords over others in place of Allāh."[229] Quṭb's phraseology here, *yajʿalu baʿḍahum li-baʿḍ arbāban min dūni llāh*," is redolent of Qurʾān 9:31, and is in fact an allusion to the similarly worded Qurʾān 3:64, which he goes on to cite.

Quṭb then adduces the ʿAdī b. Ḥātim tradition in order to reinforce this contention that theonomy is a form of monolatry: "The Prophet, Allāh's blessing and peace be upon him, already specified that 'obedience' (*ittibāʿ*) to law and to rule is the 'worship' (*ʿibāda*) by which the Jews and Christians became 'polytheists' (*mushrikūn*) who contravened the order they were commanded, to worship Allāh alone." Quṭb then cites the ʿAdī b. Ḥātim *ḥadīth*, and adds: "The Prophet's exegesis, Allāh's blessing and peace be upon him, of the words of Allāh, glory be to Him, is a definitive prooftext (*naṣṣ qāṭiʿ*) that shows that obedience to law and rule is worship that makes one an unbeliever (*mukhrij min al-dīn*), and it is the taking of some people as lords over others."[230]

227 Quṭb, *Maʿālim*, p. 62.
228 Quṭb, *Maʿālim*, pp. 59–60. Quṭb's line of argumentation here often parallels that of Mawdūdī in his article "Jihād fī sabīl Allāh." Cf. Hartung, *A System of Life*, pp. 209–213.
229 Quṭb, *Maʿālim*, pp. 59–60. 230 Quṭb, *Maʿālim*, pp. 62–63.

The second mention of this prooftext in *Maʿālim* comes in the "*Lā ilāha illā llāh manhaj ḥayāt*" chapter, in which (as noted earlier) Quṭb argues that all existing societies are *jāhilī* because they fail to uphold exclusive *ʿubūdiyya* to Allāh in all three required areas, namely, belief, ritual, and *ḥākimiyya*. When he explains why all Jewish and Christian societies are *jāhilī*, he explains that one of the reasons is their shortcomings in the area of *ḥākimiyya*, and it is in Quṭb's explanation of this point that he brings up the exegesis of Qurʾān 9:31:

> They are *jāhilī* societies in their regimes and their laws. None of them are founded on servitude to Allāh alone, on the affirmation that the right to *ḥākimiyya* is His alone, and on the derivation of rule (*sulṭān*) from His law. Instead, they establish human bodies that have the right to supreme *ḥākimiyya* which [in truth] belongs to none but Allāh the Exalted. In the olden days Allāh branded them as having given this right to the rabbis and priests, who legislated for them laws of their own devise, and they [the Jews and Christians] accepted from them [the rabbis and priests] what they legislated.

After citing the verse, Quṭb then explains why this was considered polytheism:

> They did not believe in the divinity of the rabbis and priests, nor did they offer them ritual worship. They only recognized their right to *ḥākimiyya*, and accepted from [the rabbis and priests] what they legislated for them, in what Allāh did not permit. A fortiori should they be branded today with polytheism and unbelief, since they have done this with people among them who are not rabbis and not priests.[231]

He then uses this theme as a basis for his argument that all ostensibly Muslim societies are in fact *jāhilī* due to their failure to uphold Allāh's *ḥākimiyya*: "[Allāh,] may He be praised, already imputed polytheism, unbelief, and deviation from exclusivity of worship to the Jews and Christians … solely because they granted to the rabbis and priests the same thing that those who call themselves 'Muslims' grant one to another."[232] In other words, Quṭb uses Qurʾān 9:31 and the ʿAdī b. Ḥātim *ḥadīth* in order to prove that obedience to law is a form of worship, and thus obedience to human law is a violation of the demands of monolatry.

### *Assessment of Influences on Quṭb*

From all the preceding it is clear that Sayyid Quṭb's doctrine of *ḥākimiyya* as elaborated in his late writings is profoundly indebted to Mawdūdī – to such an extent, in fact, that it is not clear that one should

[231] Quṭb, *Maʿālim*, p. 91. [232] Quṭb, *Maʿālim*, p. 92.

refer to it as Quṭb's doctrine at all. Not only the term *ḥākimiyya* and the idea as a general concept, but also the specific features of the doctrine were already present in Mawdūdī's writings: The distinction between two aspects of divinity, the argument from Allāh's cosmic aspect to His normative aspect, the Streitpunkt analysis, reliance on Qur'ān 9:31 and the ʿAdī b. Ḥātim *ḥadīth* as a central prooftext, and other points of analysis and exegesis that were noted as they arose. For this reason I cannot agree with Ibrahim Abu Rabiʿ's assessment that external influences, such as that of Mawdūdī, were only a "secondary" factor in the shift in Quṭb's thought, and that "the historical situation of Egypt while he was writing and his understanding of the Qur'ān were the primary influences upon his intellectual life and development."[233] We know from the references in Quṭb's own writings that he read and admired Mawdūdī's *Iṣṭilāḥēn*, which was available to him in ʿAlī Nadwī's Arabic translation (published 1955),[234] and given the striking similarities to his thought there does not seem any reason to look further in search of intellectual influences on Quṭb's elaboration of *ḥākimiyya*. There is much truth to John Calvert's assessment that "Quṭb's reception of the term reinforced an already existing tendency in his thought,"[235] and it is also true that the general idea that Allāh is ruler and the demand for implementation of the *sharīʿa* were already present in the Muslim Brotherhood (and beyond). What Quṭb received from Mawdūdī, however, was not just the term *ḥākimiyya*, but an entire doctrine – one that indeed resonated with themes in Quṭb's earlier works, but which crystallized them into a formal structure that was more radical and sharply defined.

Given this conclusion, any separate comparison of Quṭb's late doctrine to the premodern monolatric tradition would appear superfluous, as any commonalities would be the same ones already noted in our analysis of Mawdūdī. It is worth noting, however, that Quṭb is known to have become interested in this tradition late in his life. The first book listed on the study curriculum he prescribed for members of the '1965 Organization' was Ibn Taymiyya's *Risālat al-ʿubūdiyya*,[236] which

233 Ibrahim M. Abu Rabiʿ, *Intellectual Origins of Islamic Resurgence in the Modern Arab World*, Albany: State University of New York, 1996, p. 139.
234 John Calvert, *Sayyid Qutb and the Origins of Radical Islamism*, New York: Columbia University Press, 2010, p. 213; cf. p. 199 for further evidence of Quṭb's respect for Mawdūdī from the correspondence between the latter and Maryam Jameelah. William Shepard also relates that he was told by Muḥammad Quṭb, in a personal communication, that *Iṣṭilāḥēn* "was particularly appreciated by his brother [Sayyid]." Shepard, *Sayyid Qutb*, p. xxvi, n. 22 cont.
235 Calvert, *Sayyid Qutb*, p. 214.
236 Aḥmad ʿAbd al-Majīd, *al-Ikhwān wa-ʿAbd al-Nāṣir: al-qiṣṣa al-kāmila li-tanẓīm 1965*, Cairo: al-Zahrāʾ li-l-Iʿlām al-ʿArabī, 1412/1991, pp. 69–70. On the significance of the

contains the version of the *tawḥīd al-ulūhiyya* doctrine that Ibn Taymiyya elaborated as intra-Ṣūfī polemic. Considering the centrality of the concept of *ʿubūdiyya* in Quṭb's own system, it appears likely that his interest in this work by Ibn Taymiyya indicates at the least some recognition of commonalities with the medieval thinker on Quṭb's part.

## Conclusion: Mawdūdī, Quṭb, and Modernity

At the heart of Mawdūdī's and Quṭb's system is one overriding *idée fixe*: The one God who rules the cosmos must also be the sole ruler over humans, and it is humans' duty – indeed, their principal duty in life – to acknowledge Him as such and to act accordingly. This idea is certainly given modern applications, and at times even modern terminology – such as the term *ḥākimiyyat* itself in Mawdūdī's writings, where it is a calque of the term 'sovereignty' as used in Western writings in political science. The idea itself, however, is anything but new: It is akin to the one we find in Judges 8:22–23: "The men of Israel said to Gideon: Rule over us, you, your son, and your son's son, for you have saved us from the hands of the Midianites. Gideon said to them: I shall not rule over you, nor shall my son rule over you, God it is who shall rule over you." A number of scholars have long recognized that political idolatry, alongside ritual idolatry, is a major concern in the Hebrew Bible;[237] theonomy has been in the genetic code of monolatry since its inception.

Regarding the more specific question of Mawdūdī and Quṭb's relation to the medieval Islamic tradition, there can be no doubt that the main themes of medieval high theology differed from theirs, and neither shows much passion for these themes per se. Yet to portray 'traditional Islam' in a certain way, and then argue that Mawdūdī and Quṭb must be essentially modern thinkers because they deviate from this portrayal, does not appear to me to be a fruitful approach. For example, Seyyed Vali Reza Nasr writes, citing Seyyed Hossein Nasr, that "in traditional Islam, religion is 'essentially a way of knowledge … Islam leads to essential knowledge which integrates [a Muslim's] whole being.'"[238] This is perhaps an apt characterization of some currents of traditional Islam, but certainly does not fit the thought of Ibn Taymiyya and those influenced by him, for whom the heart of Islam is *ʿibāda* and who specifically decried

fact that the second book listed on the curriculum was Ibn Taymiyya's *Kitāb al-īmān*, see Lav, *Radical Islam*, pp. 57–58.

[237] See e.g. Buber, *Königtum Gottes*, pp. 3ff. (= Buber, *Kingship of God*, pp. 59ff.); Halbertal and Margalit, *Idolatry*, pp. 214–235.

[238] Nasr, *Mawdudi*, p. 66.

excessive focus on knowledge (*ʿilm*) to the exclusion of proper praxis (*ʿamal*). Specific premodern precedents for Mawdūdī's and Quṭb's focus on Islam-as-monolatry, taken both from theology and from jurisprudential theory, have been noted throughout the present chapter.

The issue of these thinkers' purported modernity intersects with a second one, namely, the thesis that Mawdūdī and Quṭb represent a 'political interpretation' of Islam, as the title of Nadwī's book written in critique of them expresses it.[239] On one level this is a truism: Both authors see the primary mission of Islam as destroying one kind of government on earth and instituting another in its place. Mawdūdī in particular greatly feeds the impression that his reading of Islam is a 'political' one through his choice of expressions in works other than *Iṣṭilāḥēṉ* that are of a more programmatic nature: Islam is cast as a revolutionary ideology, the Muslims as an "international revolutionary party," and so forth.[240] Quṭb as well often employs a kind of rhetoric of Enlightenment, discoursing even in his final works on concepts such as liberty and progress; this has led Malise Ruthven to argue that "the message of revolutionary anarchism implicit in the phrase that 'every system that permits some people to rule over others be abolished' owes more to radical European ideas going back to the Jacobins than to classical or traditional ideas about Islamic governance."[241]

Yet such rhetoric on the part of Mawdūdī and Quṭb is not in itself sufficient evidence of their supposedly modern-political worldview. The appropriation of terminology does not necessarily indicate straightforward influence: It can also be a subversive tactic used to undermine or redefine the concepts in relation to what they meant in their original context. (We saw a fine example of this technique in Chapter 1, in Ibn Taymiyya's appropriation of Neoplatonic elements from Ibn Sīnā's philosophy in his exposition of *tawḥīd al-ulūhiyya*.) What lies at the heart of Mawdūdī's and Quṭb's doctrine is not a reductive reading of Islam in political terms, but something verging on the opposite: the abolition of the sphere of autonomous human politics in favor of a theological vision

[239] Abū al-Ḥasan al-Nadwī, *al-Tafsīr al-siyāsī li-l-islām fī mirʾāt kitābāt al-ustādh Abī al-Aʿlā al-Mawdūdī wa-l-shahīd Sayyid Quṭb*, Cairo: Dār Āfāq al-Ghad, 1980. Hartung has already noted the polemical nature of this characterization and the fact that it does not do full justice to Mawdūdī's views: Hartung, *A System of Life*, p. 88.

[240] See e.g. Mawdūdī, "Jihād fī sabīli llāh," p. 77. Riexinger argues that it is above all this appropriation of Marxist-Leninist terminology that encouraged the tendency to view Mawdūdī as a modernist: *Sanāʾullāh Amritsarī*, p. 562.

[241] Malise Ruthven, *A Fury for God: The Islamist Attack on America*, London: Granta, 2002, p. 91, cited in John Gray, *Al Qaeda and What It Means to Be Modern*, New York: The New Press, 2003, p. 24.

of how this world should be ordered in relation to divinity.[242] The doctrine of *ḥākimiyya* is not really a political doctrine; it is constructed on two complementary axes, both of them theological. In relation to the nature of divinity, it rests on a parallel between Allāh's role in the natural cosmos and His role in human life; in relation to the demand of humans that they acknowledge Allāh as sole ruler, it rests on the principle of monolatry, and the opposition between monolatry and polylatry.

Much academic scholarship on Mawdūdī and Quṭb has not been interested in taking the theonomy doctrine seriously as a theological system. For example, Nasr writes that "Mawdudi considered nationalism both a cultural and a political threat. He rejected secular nationalism because he considered it 'polytheism,' a demon that would be the undoing of Muslims, and because it was a façade for the Hindu drive for power."[243] The significance of Mawdūdī's characterization of nationalism as polytheism goes far beyond its being merely a cultural or political threat. For him, nationalism is polytheism (or more precisely, polylatry) in the truest meaning of the word, because nationalism is simply a *dīn* other than the *dīn* of Islam. Thus in a passage from the "*Dīn*" chapter of *Iṣṭilāḥē̱n* that we already cited above:

> In all these verses the meaning of *dīn* is law (*qānūn*), regulations (*ḍabṭa*), *sharīʿat*, a path (*ṭarīqa*), and that system of thought and action in obedience to which a human lives his life. If the power (*iqtidār*) that is the authority for regulations and a system [of life] that are adhered to is God's power, then the human is in God's *dīn*. And if it is the power of some king, then the human is in the *dīn* of the king. If it is the power of the (Hindu) religious scholars and priests (*paṇḍit*, *prohit*), then the human is in their *dīn*. If it is the power of the family, the caste (*barādarī*), or the nation (*jumhūr-i qawm*), then the human is in their *dīn*. In short, whosoever's authority is obeyed as the final authority, and whosoever's judgments are obeyed as the last word, such that a human walks in his path – that human is a follower of his *dīn*.[244]

Likewise Quṭb writes in *Maʿālim*: "Just as Allāh does not forgive the association [of others] with Him, likewise He does not accept any path (*manhaj*) together with His path … because it is known with certitude that these are one and the same."[245] It is the demand for exclusivity of

[242] Cf. Armando Salvatore, *Islam and the Political Discourse of Modernity*, Reading, UK: Ithaca Press, 1997, p. 193, on Sayyid Quṭb: "The accomplishment of Islam on earth would bring about the end of politics."

[243] Nasr, *Mawdudi*, p. 54. [244] Mawdūdī, *Iṣṭilāḥē̱n*, p. 107.

[245] Quṭb, *Maʿālim*, p. 152: *wa-ka-mā anna llāha lā yaghfiru an yushraka bihi fa-ka-dhālika huwa lā yaqbalu manhajan maʿa manhajihi … li-anna hādhihi hiya tilka ʿalā wajh al-yaqīn*. It should be kept in mind that *manhaj* (path) is for Quṭb a wide concept that encompasses the general ordering of human life, as in the chapter of *Maʿālim* titled "*Lā*

devotion to Allāh, to be expressed through exclusive adherence to His path, that leads Quṭb to denounce nationalism and other forms of human particularism as *shirk*, a message that he finds within a particularly Axial verse in the Qur'ān (9:24) that reprimands those who love their familial relations, tribe, possessions, commerce, and dwellings more than they love Allāh, the Prophet, and jihād for the sake of Allāh.[246] Both Mawdūdī and Quṭb see true Islam not in the routinized forms that have been historically prevalent, but rather, looking back to its reputed origins, they see it as a true Axial revolution that must reorder society in light of transcendent imperatives. As Quṭb puts it, Muslim society, as opposed to *jāhilī* society, is the society that is born of a movement that "is from outside the earthly ambit and from outside the human environment."[247] Muslim society is organized solely on the basis of the transcendent creed (i.e. the principle of *'ubūdiyya* to Allāh), and thus must necessarily rupture with *jāhilī* societies, all of which are based on various forms of involuntary association, such as ethnic or territorial nationhood,[248] which represent mundane forms of allegiance as opposed to the proper transcendent allegiance to Allāh.

*Shirk* in its meaning as polylatry is entirely at home in such a conception, and there is no compelling reason why this term in the writings of Mawdūdī or Quṭb should be taken metaphorically, as a kind of stand-in for political or social concepts more familiar to the modern Western reader. We live in a world that was shaped by the Enlightenment and its 'neutralization' of the theological as a factor in political life.[249] Personal and collective piety and devotion persist, but the underlying structure of human society has been decisively secularized,[250] and thus our natural tendency upon encountering the application of theological categories to mundane human affairs is to consider them metaphors – just as, for example, we do not take Francis Bacon's enumeration of the four 'idols' in the *Novum Organum* in a true theological sense. Such modern Western 'rhetoric' of idolatry is a product of the secularizing impetus of the Enlightenment, and there is no reason to project this

*ilāha illā llāh manhaj ḥayāt*," which argues that all facets of human society need to be ordered in accordance with a proper understanding of the profession of faith: pp. 83ff.

246 Quṭb, *Ma'ālim*, p. 147.

247 *Innahā … ātiya lahum min khārij al-niṭāq al-arḍī wa-min khārij al-muḥīṭ al-basharī*. Quṭb, *Ma'ālim*, p. 117.

248 Quṭb, *Ma'ālim*, pp. 108–109, 138.

249 See Carl Schmitt, "The Age of Neutralizations and Depoliticizations," in *The Concept of the Political*, trans. George Schwab, Chicago and London: The University of Chicago Press, 2007, pp. 80–96, esp. pp. 89ff.

250 On this distinction, see Gauchet, *Le désenchantement*, pp. i–iv; Gauchet, *The Disenchantment*, pp. 1–5.

usage onto Mawdūdī and Quṭb simply because they are twentieth-century authors or because they deal with topics that our own culture does not recognize as falling within the ambit of theology.

All pre-secular societies have negotiated the relation between the political and the divine in various ways, including those societies that maintained a functional division between the political and the religious (as real-world Muslim societies historically have). In the typology elaborated by Jan Assmann of the ways in which pre-secular societies structured the relation between the political and the divine, the *ḥākimiyya* doctrine as expounded by Mawdūdī and Quṭb is a perfect fit for the category he calls 'theocracy,' defined as "the subordination of political leadership, up to the point of its abolition, in favor of sheer divine sovereignty."[251] Mawdūdī and Quṭb's interpretation of the disputation between Ibrāhīm and Namrūd is very much a reenactment of the original confrontation between this 'theocracy' model and the Ancient Near Eastern model of the god-king: Both Gideon and the Muslim Ibrāhīm say that God alone must rule. Rather than representing a 'political' reading of Islam, in the modern sense of 'political,' with religion serving merely as a veneer for a (basically secular) sociopolitical project, Mawdūdī's and Quṭb's *ḥākimiyya* is precisely a reaction against, and negation of, the secular political sphere that expanded in the Muslim world over the course of the nineteenth and twentieth centuries, especially in the arena of man-made legislation. This reaction *against* the political as an autonomous category of human existence is in the original Axial-Biblical spirit of allegiance to a transcendent sovereign in opposition to an earthly one.

Thus Quṭb's insistence that "every system that permits some people to rule over others be abolished" is not Jacobin or anarchist. To the extent there is an anarchist element it is not a modern but rather a 'Gideonite' one, deployed against an Enlightenment conception of liberty. Quṭb fully equates true human liberty with servitude to Allāh, in opposition to a human autonomy that he does not consider possible or desirable, and which he considers in fact to be servitude to other humans (or to one's own desires) that is merely wrapped in a false mantle of liberty. This Gideonite conception is, however, merged in Quṭb's thought with the Muslim political patrimony, that is, it is only a theonomic state that can prevent the rule of some humans over others. In fact Quṭb's favorite expression of the principle, the words of Ribʿī b. ʿĀmir to the Persian general Rustam in advance of the battle of Qādisiyya (c. 14–16/635–637),

[251] Jan Assmann, *Herrschaft und Heil: Politische Theologie in Altägypten, Israel, und Europa*, Munich: Carl Hanser, 2000, p. 28.

ties his theonomy to the expansionist ethos of the early Muslim polity. When Rustam asks him "What has brought you here?" Ribʿī answers: "Allāh sent us to deliver whosoever wishes from servitude to humans (*ʿibādat al-ʿibād*) to servitude to Allāh alone, from the straits of this world to abundance in this world and the next, and from the injustice of the religions to the justice of Islam."[252]

This leads us to the issue of what *is* modern in Mawdūdī and Quṭb. These two thinkers are clearly not a simple continuation of the classical Muslim tradition – not even of the premodern salafī tradition with its strong emphasis on monolatry and jurisprudential theonomy. The structural parallels with this tradition are robust, but Mawdūdī and Quṭb do represent a 'theonomic shift' in Islamic thought. In the Introduction I argued that the roots of the revelational economy of transcendence lay in a projection of the political model of Near Eastern kingship onto the divine sphere; this is the ultimate origin of the theme of exclusivity of servitude that features so prominently in the salafī monolatric tradition. What Mawdūdī and Quṭb present is a reawakening of the theme's original theopolitical import in a direct manner, in the form of a conflict between allegiance to the divine sovereign and allegiance to worldly ones. These two thinkers' novelty lies not so much in any inherent newness in their ideas, but in the foregrounding of this theopolitical content and the construction of a complete system around it. Their impetus for doing so was clearly the new and unique challenges that the modern era presents to what Assmann called the theocratic model of political theology. The modern era means many things, but the specifically theonomic focus of Mawdūdī's and Quṭb's doctrine indicates that it was the secularization of government and of the legal system that stood foremost in their minds. They were certainly troubled by other issues, such as Western geopolitical superiority, but tended to view them as secondary to, and derivative of, the root problem of *ḥākimiyya*.

Over the course of the nineteenth and twentieth centuries a number of mutually reinforcing processes pushed Muslim societies in the direction of secularization. Modernizing rulers in Egypt and the Ottoman Empire sought to regularize their countries' legal systems through progressive codification of the law and the establishment of new judicial bodies. The initiatives were motivated by a complex interaction of factors, such as the pressure of Western opinion and changes in public opinion in the domestic sphere as to the meaning of justice; these initiatives should also

[252] Quṭb, *Maʿālim*, p. 168. For the source, see al-Ṭabarī, *Taʾrīkh*, vol. 2, p. 401; Yohanan Friedmann (trans.), *The History of al-Ṭabarī*, Albany: SUNY Press, 1990, vol. 12, p. 67.

be considered as of a piece with other economic, military, and educational reforms that sought to strengthen central authority. The legal reforms began modestly, through exercise of the ruler's *siyāsa* jurisdiction[253] and codification of existing *sharʿī* rulings: To a certain degree the early stages of these reforms can be seen as a further development of long-established practice in the Ottoman Empire, which already recognized imperial law (*qānūn*) alongside the *sharīʿa*, and within the *sharīʿa* jurisdiction itself had organized the *ʿulamāʾ* into an official bureaucracy and had stipulated rules for how to follow Ḥanafī precedent. As the reforms progressed, however, they began to rely more and more on the importation of European legal codes and the adoption of non-*sharʿī* rules for court procedure, leading to a dual system in which the law and legal education and practice in most areas was no longer based on the traditional *sharīʿa* model; the traditional *sharīʿa* courts were left with jurisdiction primarily over personal status law.[254]

In other words, the advent of the modern nation-state in the Middle East went hand in hand with a transfer of jurisdiction in most areas of law away from the *sharīʿa* courts to national courts that adjudicated by Western-inspired law codes. Given the transformational nature of this change, the question should not be why this became such a contentious issue in the second half of the twentieth century, but rather why it was not so beforehand. This is what Nathan Brown calls "the puzzle of the

[253] *Siyāsa* in this context denotes the ruler's prerogative to depart in specific cases from the formal constructs of the *sharīʿa*. The nature and scope of this jurisdiction were often a matter of contention, and the issue likewise intersected with that of the proper role of the 'secular' *maẓālim* courts. For these topics in the Mamlūk period, see Jørgen S. Nielsen, *Secular Justice in an Islamic State: Maẓālim under the Baḥrī Mamlūks, 662/1264–789/1387*, Leiden: Instituut voor het Nabije Oosten, 1985; Robert Irwin, "The Privatization of 'Justice' under the Circassian Mamluks," *Mamlūk Studies Review* 6 (2002), pp. 63–70; Yossef Rapoport, "Royal Justice and Religious Law: *Siyāsah* and Shariʿah under the Mamluks," *Mamlūk Studies Review* 16 (2012), pp. 71–102.

[254] The literature on these developments is extensive. See e.g. Rudolph Peters, *Crime and Punishment in Islamic Law: Theory and Practice from the Sixteenth to the Twenty-First Century*, Cambridge: Cambridge University Press, 2005; Rudolph Peters, "Administrators and Magistrates: The Development of a Secular Judiciary in Egypt, 1842-1871," *Die Welt des Islams* 39/3 (1999), pp. 378–397; Rudolph Peters, "The Codification of Criminal Law in 19th Century Egypt: Tradition or Modernization?," in J. M. Abun-Nasr (ed.), *Law, Society, and National Identity in Africa*, Hamburg: Buske, 1991, pp. 211–225; Rudolph Peters, "'For His Correction and as a Deterrent to Others': Meḥmed ʿAlī's First Criminal Legislation (1829-1830)," *Islamic Law and Society* 6/2 (1999), pp. 164–192; Aharon Layish, "The Transformation of the Sharīʿa from Jurists' Law to Statutory Law in the Contemporary Muslim World," *Die Welt des Islams* 44/1 (2004), pp. 85–113; Guy Bechor, *The Sanhuri Code and the Emergence of Modern Arab Civil Law (1932 to 1949)*, Leiden and Boston: Brill, 2007.

political silence that greeted the substitution of Western for shariʿa-based legal models in the 19th and 20th centuries."[255]

The answer that Brown suggests provides at least a partial solution to this "puzzle." Generally speaking, the institutions that were associated with the traditional *sharīʿa* system – schools, courts, and so forth – were left intact and continued to enjoy a great degree of autonomy; the reforms consisted primarily in an ever-increasing restriction of their jurisdiction. There was little overlap with the developing parallel systems of secular law, whether in the make-up of the courts themselves or in the educational system. The *sharīʿa*, at least as it had been practiced historically, was "contained rather than endangered."[256] This explanation sits well with the fact that the most vocal protests came not from old institutions like al-Azhar, but from those with a foot in each world, such as the Islamic-oriented laity that made up the leadership of the Muslim Brotherhood – for example, the Muslim Brother ʿAbd al-Qādir ʿAwda, a judge in the national court system who was executed by the ʿAbd al-Nāṣir regime in 1954.[257] In the opening of his *al-Islām wa-awḍāʿunā al-qānūniyya*, ʿAwda makes explicit the connection between his professional position and his views on the secular law system:

> The law [in Egypt] forbids public servants, and especially judges, from expressing their views on public affairs. This is considered involvement on their part in politics. And politics, in the view of the makers of the law, is anything that touches on social, economic, and financial issues; and anything that relates to the organization of the state and its relations with individuals, groups, and [other] states; and anything relating to the form of rule; and even anything relating to the independence of states, their liberty, and their honor.
>
> The makers of the law want to make humans into instruments, and want the judge to shut his eyes and not look, to stop his ears and not hear, to hold his tongue and not speak, to renounce his humanity and not sense, feel, or think ...
>
> Can a judge remain uninvolved in an Islamic land, whose constitution stipulates that the official religion of state is Islam, but whose rulers and governments shut themselves off from Islam, and are fierce like tigers against those who serve Islam, persecute those who cooperate in piety, and protect those who cooperate in sin and aggression? [cf. Qurʾān 5:2] ...
>
> Let he who is angered be angered. There are people who will be enraged when they read these words, in defense of the idols of the contemporary age: the laws to which they are devoted, these laws that the Muslims obey in matters that anger

255 Nathan J. Brown, "Shariʿa and State in the Modern Muslim Middle East," *International Journal of Middle East Studies* 29 (1997), pp. 359–376, at p. 359.

256 Brown, "Shariʿa and State," pp. 365–368.

257 Richard P. Mitchell, *The Society of the Muslim Brothers*, London: Oxford University Press, 1969, pp. 160–161.

Allāh, and by which the Islamic governments forbid what Allāh permitted, and permit what Allāh forbade.

They will be angered because a priest from the priesthood of these idols [viz. the author] has disobeyed them and rejected them. They will be astounded: How can a judge, one of the servants of the law, attack and reject the law? They will call out to one another from all corners: Restrain this man before he smashes your idols and destroys your regime.

But how wrong they are! For this is not the idea of one individual, but rather the consciousness of a nation. This is not the appeal of the tongue, but the appeal of faith. This is the struggle for the sake of Islam. This is jihād – jihād by which we get close to Allāh …

If I were a non-Muslim judge, my tongue would sing the praises of the law (*qānūn*), like the Westerners do. If I were a Muslim judge who was ignorant of Islam, I would blindly imitate (*la-qalladtu*) the Europeans and make public my faith in the law [viz. as a religion: *wa-aẓhartu al-īmān bi-l-qānūn*]. But I am a Muslim judge who, by the grace of Allāh, knows of Islam what many [other] judges do not, and knows of the contradiction between man-made laws and Islam what few others know.[258]

While the situation described by ʿAwda was not the invention of the new regime, it was intensified by it, and it seems likely that Quṭb's adoption and popularization of Mawdūdī's 'theonomic shift' was indeed prompted by the changed realities of revolutionary Egypt. In addition to the personal and collective disappointment and hardship experienced by Quṭb on behalf of himself and the Muslim Brotherhood, the regime's reforms, such as the abolition of the *sharīʿa* courts in 1956, brought the tensions and contradictions inherent in the emergence of the modern nation-state to the fore and called for a radical reappraisal of all that had gone before. Yet while the combined effect of the revolution, the policies of the new regime, and the repression of the Muslim Brotherhood served as a prompt for the radical rethinking of fundamental issues, these conditions did not in themselves provide the form that Quṭb's system would take. As we have seen, Quṭb basically adopted the core of his final doctrine of theonomy from Mawdūdī as a complete system, one that resonated with the lines of his own thinking, but which provided clarity and systematicity.

Richard P. Mitchell, writing of the Muslim Brothers' stance on application of the *sharīʿa* up to 1954, wrote that "the intensity of feeling among Brothers on what might be called the 'social or cultural imperative' involved in the establishment of the *shariʿa* perhaps outdid the

[258] ʿAbd al-Qādir ʿAwda, *al-Islām wa-awḍāʿunā al-qānūniyya*, Cairo: al-Mukhtār al-Islāmī, 1977, pp. 7–12.

theological imperative."[259] Even ʿAwda's writings, notwithstanding strident passages like the one just cited – in which he even makes reference to secular laws as 'idols' – do not approach the radical systematicity of the *ḥākimiyya* doctrine, and his attention was focused more on particular substantive laws that contravened the *sharīʿa* than on matters of first principle.[260] In the writings from Quṭb's late period this is clearly no longer the case, and his theonomic turn led to the conclusion that not just the new regime, but the entire modern nation-state – and indeed, human legal autonomy as such – were inherently polylatric.

The theonomic shift represents, in addition to a rethinking of the basic nature of Islamic monolatry, a parsing and prioritizing of elements that in past Islamist discourse had more or less existed side by side in nonhierarchical fashion: the 'theological imperative' alongside the 'social or cultural imperative'; opposition to the importation of Western law because it was culturally inauthentic, or because it was the cause of Muslim weakness,[261] alongside opposition to it on the grounds that it was not the law of Allāh. Quṭb, following Mawdūdī, turned his attention precisely to the feature of the modern nation-state that Brown noted was responsible for the relative quiescence of the religious classes in the secularization of the legal system in prerevolutionary Egypt, namely, the fact that the *sharīʿa* had been "contained rather than endangered." In Quṭb's system, it is precisely this 'containment' that renders society *jāhilī* because it constitutes a distribution of Allāh's unique prerogatives among human *rabb*s,[262] and contradicts the fundamental principle undergirding the entire system, to wit, that Allāh alone is *ilāh* on earth as He is in heaven. It was this matter of first principle that was important to Quṭb, and it was important to him as a theological issue. As far as his legacy and influence are concerned, it was precisely this conceptualization of legal sovereignty as a theological issue that would spur the incorporation of Quṭb's ideas into radical salafism in the following decades.

259 Mitchell, *Society of the Muslim Brothers*, p. 237. Mitchell's sources include works by Quṭb, but only those of his middle period, authored in the first half of the 1950s.

260 As Mitchell notes, ʿAwda was of the opinion that most of the foreign law imported into the law code was in general agreement with the *sharīʿa*. Mitchell, *Society of the Muslim Brothers*, p. 241.

261 As per ʿAbd al-Qādir ʿAwda, *al-Islām bayna jahl abnāʾihi wa-ʿajz ʿulamāʾihi*, 5th ed., n.p.: al-Ittiḥād al-ʿĀlamī li-l-Munaẓẓamat al-Ṭullabiyya, 1405/1985, p. 5.

262 *Wa-lākinna al-maʿrakata kānat wa-sa-takūnu dāʾiman … bayna al-ʿubūdiyya lillāh waḥdahu bi-lā sharīk wa-l-daynūna lillāh waḥdahu bi-lā munāziʿ wa-bayna tawzīʿ khaṣāʾiṣ al-ulūhiyya ʿalā al-arbāb al-mutafarriqa*. Quṭb, *Muqawwimāt*, p. 103. The phrasing *al-arbāb al-mutafarriqa* alludes to the prophet Yūsuf's words in Qurʾān 12:39: "*a-arbāb mutafarriqūn khayrun am-i llāhu al-wāḥid al-qahhār*."

# 5 Salafī Jihādī Theonomy

The present chapter aims to trace the emergence of the modern salafī doctrine of theonomy, with special reference to the radical branch of modern salafism known as *al-salafiyya al-jihādiyya*. The overarching framework within which this development took place was the multifaceted interaction, over the past half-century, between the thought of Mawdūdī and Quṭb, on the one hand, and the salafī tradition, on the other. Generally speaking, the significance of Mawdūdī and Quṭb was their elevation of the issue of theonomy to a theological concern of the first order, with many following them in considering it the central theological issue of the age. At the same time, however, theonomy became progressively detached from the idiosyncracies of these thinkers' theoretical and programmatic systems and took on an increasingly salafī character. Precedents were adduced from earlier salafī and Wahhābī scholars, and discussions of modern issues such as democracy and parliamentary legislation came to be grounded in Ibn Taymiyya's *tawḥīd al-ulūhiyya*, the Wahhābī legacy of the war on the cult of saints, and premodern salafī rejection of *taqlīd* (see Chapters 1, 2, and 3, respectively). The rise of a salafī form of theonomy was a general phenomenon in the Arabic-speaking world over the course of the 1970s, 1980s, and 1990s, and was not limited to a particular country or school: It is found in Muslim Brotherhood thinkers who had absorbed salafī influence, in the Saudi religious establishment, and in independent quietist salafī circles. In this way, the issue was transformed from the influential but idiosyncratic *ḥākimiyya* of Mawdūdī and Quṭb into a legitimate (and even central) salafī doctrinal concern. Out of this ferment, the salafī jihādīs emerged as a school that wedded a radical and dogmatic doctrine of theonomy to the prosecution of armed jihād in pursuit of its application.

We have already devoted a chapter to Mawdūdī and Quṭb and the context in which they wrote; a few words are now in order regarding the modern salafī movement, and *al-salafiyya al-jihādiyya* in particular. While modern salafism on the whole is not reducible to Saudi

Wahhābism,[1] there is no denying the central role that Saudi Arabia and the Wahhābī tradition played in the perpetuation and spread of salafism. In the eighteenth century, before the advent of the Wahhābī movement, the status of Ibn Taymiyya and his teachings was marginal at best.[2] The sense of isolation felt by adherents of Ibn Taymiyya's theology is well-attested: As noted earlier (Chapter 2), Ibn ʿAbd al-Wahhāb himself, though born into a Ḥanbalī environment, wrote starkly that before the advent of his mission no one in his region knew the meaning of *lā ilāha illā llāh*[3] – by which he meant that none of them understood it as a statement of *tawḥīd al-ulūhiyya*, that is, exclusivity of worship. Likewise, his Yemeni contemporary Ibn al-Amīr, himself an adherent of the *tawḥīd al-ulūhiyya* doctrine, wrote in his poem in praise of Ibn ʿAbd al-Wahhāb: "I was gladdened by what I heard of his path / a path I had thought I was alone in."[4] It would take us too far afield to attempt a general description of the rise of salafism in the modern era, which has completely reversed this situation.[5] By the period currently under discussion, salafism was on the cusp of becoming, or was already, a major movement in the Gulf states, Jordan, and Egypt at the very least, in addition of course to Saudi Arabia.

It is by now traditional to classify modern salafism into three branches: quietist or scholastic salafīs, whose focus is on religious study, purification of creed and ritual, and nonviolent proselytization, and who have traditionally eschewed political activity; politically activist salafīs, who represent a confluence of the Muslim Brotherhood and salafī traditions (and whom I therefore propose to call 'fusionist salafīs'); and the radical salafī jihādīs, who support and engage in armed jihād to overthrow 'apostate' governments.[6] This classification is by and large an emic one, although the terminology for the different trends is somewhat fluid. In what follows I adopt this tripartite classification of modern salafism as a basis for my analysis of vectors of influence and contestation on the topic of theonomy.[7]

[1] See e.g. Laurent Bonnefoy, "How Transnational Is Salafism in Yemen?," in Meijer (ed.), *Global Salafism*, pp. 321–341.

[2] See El-Rouayheb, "From Ibn Ḥajar al-Haytamī," pp. 269–270.

[3] Ibn Ghannām, *Taʾrīkh najd*, p. 310. [4] al-Ṣanʿānī, *Dīwān*, p. 130.

[5] Relevant literature on the general history of salafism includes Meijer (ed.), *Global Salafism*; Lauzière, "The Construction of *Salafiyya*"; Henri Lauzière, *The Making of Salafism: Islamic Reform in the Twentieth Century*, New York: Columbia University Press, 2016.

[6] Quintan Wiktorowicz, "Anatomy of the Salafi Movement," *Studies in Conflict and Terrorism* 29/3 (April–May 2006), pp. 207–239, at p. 208; Haykel, "Salafi Thought," pp. 48–50. Unlike the quietists and the salafī jihādīs, no term for the third group has yet won wide acceptance in the academic literature; Wiktorowicz calls them 'politicos.'

[7] The aforementioned classification, however, has not gone unchallenged. See e.g. Justyna Nedza, "'Salafismus' – Überlegungen zur Schärfung einer Analysekategorie," in Behnam

As a general rule of thumb, the observation first made by Quintan Wiktorowicz holds true that the differences among these groups pertain first and foremost to *manhaj* – that is, the different kinds of salafīs share a common creed, but hold different views on which path or method of dealing with the world (and politics in particular) is in keeping with this creed. This generalization requires some caution: Joas Wagemakers has argued that as important a salafī jihādī figure as Abū Muḥammad al-Maqdisī shares certain commonalities with the quietist *manhaj*,[8] and it has also been argued that the salafī jihādī adoption of *takfīr* of the rulers and jihād against them cannot be divorced from creed (in particular, the application of Ibn Taymiyya's theology of faith to the issue of rule by man-made law).[9] As regards the issue of theonomy, however, Wiktorowicz's observation largely holds true: In the present chapter we will see that there exists a consideral degree of overlap in formulations of theonomic creed from each of the three branches of salafism. That said, I will argue that the salafī jihādīs, while influenced to a great degree by earlier fusionist and quietist theonomic writings, present a more consistent and intransigent version of the doctrine, and accord it a more central place in their belief structure. Above all, they characterize theonomy as a full-fledged element of Taymiyyan *tawḥīd* (especially *tawḥīd al-ulūhiyya*), and on this basis rule out instrumental compromises with democratic processes that adherents of the other two salafī branches have tended to accept. While more a difference in emphasis than in kind, this dogmatism on the part of the salafī jihādīs is clearly connected to their rejection of politics and their adoption of a jihadist *manhaj*.

The confluence of *ḥākimiyya* and *tawḥīd al-ulūhiyya* was long in the making. The 1970s and early 1980s were a period in which the two formerly separate (though structurally related) traditions, the thought of Mawdūdī and Quṭb and the salafī tradition, were fused into a new form of doctrine.[10] While the monolatric grounding of *ḥākimiyya* was already a clear feature of Mawdūdī and Quṭb's writings, it is much more so in subsequent elaborations of theonomy that ground it explicitly in the salafī theological tradition, which, needless to say, is a monolatric tradition par excellence.

T. Said and Hazim Fouad (eds.), *Salafismus: Auf der Suche nach dem wahren Islam*, Freiburg, Basel, and Vienna: Herder, 2014, pp. 80–105; Justyna Nedza, Takfīr *im militanten Salafismus: Der Staat als Feind*, Leiden and Boston: Brill, 2020, esp. pp. 3ff.

[8] Joas Wagemakers, *A Quietist Jihadi: The Ideology and Influence of Abu Muhammad al-Maqdisi*, New York: Cambridge University Press, 2012.

[9] Lav, *Radical Islam*, p. 122.

[10] Cf. Wagemakers, *A Quietist Jihadi*, pp. 34–35, 38; Lav, *Radical Islam*, pp. 168–169.

From the standpoint of a general overview this development is a relatively simple and logical one. Its historical unfolding was rather more complicated. The Islamist and salafī milieus of the past fifty years – even when we confine ourselves to the Arabic-speaking world – have been greatly variegated. The salafī jihādī doctrine of theonomy emerged in its definitive form in the writings of the school's founding scholars in the late 1980s and early 1990s, and was adopted as official dogma by jihadist organizations such as the Egyptian Jihād organization, the GIA (Groupe islamique armé, *al-jamāʿa al-islāmiyya al-musallaḥa*) in Algeria, and later al-Qāʿida and the Islamic State. The specific form this doctrine took was greatly influenced by earlier thinkers working at the intersection of Quṭbist theonomy and the salafī tradition, as well as by various controversies and polemics that arose from this ferment and which unfolded in real-world contexts such as the battlefields of Syria in the early 1980s and of Algeria in the mid-1990s.

The present chapter will survey these developments in more or less chronological order. First, I will analyze the arguments with which the mainstream Muslim Brotherhood rejected core elements of Sayyid Quṭb's theonomy; this rejection was a historic parting of ways within the Islamist movement, and meant that radical theonomy would only truly take root outside the official structures of the Muslim Brotherhood. There is considerable internal logic to this development. As we saw in Chapter 4, Mawdūdī and Quṭb's formulation of *ḥākimiyya* already bore a 'salafī' character, both in these authors' focus on Islam as exclusivity of worship and in their conceptualization, based on Qurʾān 9:31 and the ʿAdī b. Ḥātim *ḥadīth*, of legal obedience to humans as *shirk*. These emphases had little connection with the Muslim Brotherhood tradition, which historically has viewed creedal dispute as detrimental to Muslim political unity and has been ecumenical toward different schools of theology and jurisprudence (though with some general Ashʿarī affinities).[11] Thus while Mawdūdī and Quṭb themselves are not normally considered salafīs, the *ḥākimiyya* doctrine lent itself more naturally to development in the salafī milieu than in the Muslim Brotherhood.

Next, I will examine fusionist salafī writings on theonomy, and will demonstrate to what extent these authors already construed the issue in salafī terms, as well as the limits on how far the doctrine could go for those who remained in the Muslim Brotherhood's orbit. The chapter will then survey quietist salafī writings on theonomy, and will argue that, notwithstanding this tendency's well-known criticisms of Quṭb's deviations from

[11] See Lav, *Radical Islam*, pp. 49ff.

salafī orthodoxy, quietist authors were themselves elaborating a vigorous strain of theonomy on the basis of premodern and occasional twentieth-century salafī precedents. This quietist theonomy greatly influenced the salafī jihādīs' formulation of their own doctrine, even as they broke definitively with the quietists over the course of the 1980s. Salafī jihādī theonomy was thus distinguished from the earlier forays of the fusionists; there was little explicit mention of Quṭb, whereas the potential grounding offered by premodern salafism was exploited to the full. The chapter culminates in an analysis of salafī jihādī theonomy; the primary source for this discussion will be an influential work from the early 1990s, Sayyid Imām's *al-Jāmiʿ fī ṭalab al-ʿilm al-sharīf*, for reasons to be explained in due course.

It is important to note that in addition to this internal mapping of Islamic influences in the emergence of salafī jihādī theonomy, regional and global developments likewise influenced the form in which it emerged, and specifically its focus on democracy in particular as a form of polytheism. As noted in Chapter 4, reforms of the legal-political system and the substitution of man-made law for the *sharīʿa*, a historical process in Muslim societies ongoing since the nineteenth century and closely related to the emergence of the modern nation-state, provide the general context and impetus for the 'translation' of monolatry into theonomy in modern Muslim theology. The narrowing of focus to a theological critique of democracy in particular represents a separate and more recent development. Over the course of their lives Mawdūdī and Quṭb had applied the theonomic template in opposition to various movements and forms of rule, such as communism and socialism, fascism, and Arab nationalism, in addition to democracy. In contrast, salafī jihadism emerged well after the defeat of fascism in Europe, at a time when Arab nationalism had lost much of its popular appeal, the Soviet Union was teetering toward collapse, and various countries of the Middle East and North Africa were experimenting with democratic reforms. The salafī jihādīs' theological focus on opposition to democracy may appear surprising, given the widespread view of the Middle East and North Africa as lacking in true democracy. This depends, however, on one's perspective. While not ignorant of political realities, the salafī jihādīs are interested primarily in the formal bases of government, and most if not all countries in the region have constitutions that profess a version of popular sovereignty, some form of elections, parliaments endowed with a legislative function, and man-made law codes (generally based on Western models). Whether these institutions function in a democratic fashion in practice is not a matter of great concern to the salafī jihādīs, since in their view the very existence of these formally democratic features constitutes a polytheistic infringement of divine sovereignty.

On the ideological level, the conceptualization of the conflict between divine and human law thus came to be almost completely identified with a conflict between true Islam and democracy. The democratic openings in countries such as Algeria and Yemen proved tempting to a number of Islamist movements, even those that espoused *ḥākimiyya* in principle. These forays into electoral politics raised concrete questions regarding the legitimacy of forming parties, running in elections, and establishing alliances with secular factions. It was in this context that the salafī jihādīs positioned themselves as the true dogmatic exponents of theonomy who, in contrast with the backsliders and Nicodemites, did not waver in their devotion to Allāh's law as a first principle of *tawḥīd*. Their principled rejection of even instrumental uses of democratic mechanisms was not limited to polemic, but also found its expression in support for and cultivation of nascent jihadist movements such as the Algerian GIA and the Egyptian Jihād organization, who for their part explicitly embraced the doctrines and patronage of salafī jihādī scholars such as Abū Qatāda al-Filasṭīnī and Sayyid Imām al-Sharīf. All these ideational and socio-political developments crystallized in the decade between the mid-1980s and the mid-1990s to lay the foundation for salafī jihadism as we know it today: a strictly salafī movement with a dogmatic conception of theonomy as its principal theological banner and armed jihād as a means of championing it.

## Ḥasan al-Huḍaybī's Critique of *Ḥākimiyya*

In Chapter 4 we noted the specific characteristics of Sayyid Quṭb's late doctrine that distinguished it from the general run of Muslim Brotherhood thought. Quṭb's thoroughgoing monolatry, interpreted first and foremost as theonomy, placed the issue of legal obedience at the heart of Islam and as the primary criterion of belief or unbelief. Since no contemporary society upheld theonomy, Quṭb argued that the entire world, including historically Muslim countries such as Egypt, had reverted to *jāhiliyya*, and what was required was no less than the refoundation of Islam through the devoted work of a creedally pure vanguard. Quṭb never broke with the Muslim Brotherhood or its leadership over these matters, and he remained in the organization until his execution in 1966; he had even received the blessing of the Supreme Guide of the Brotherhood, Ḥasan al-Huḍaybī (d. 1973), for his leadership role in the so-called 1965 Organization.[12] After his death, however, Quṭb's doctrine

[12] ʿAbd al-Majīd, *al-Ikhwān wa-ʿAbd al-Nāṣir*, pp. 70–73.

of theonomy and its legal and programmatic implications quickly became a watershed that inaugurated an institutional separation between the traditional Brotherhood and the more radical tendencies inspired by Quṭb.

The locus classicus of Muslim Brotherhood polemic against Quṭb's late doctrine is the book *Duʿāt lā quḍāt* ("Preachers, Not Judges"), allegedly authored by the Supreme Guide al-Huḍaybī; published posthumously in 1977, it had been written years before and had circulated in Brotherhood circles. The ascription to al-Huḍaybī is controversial, but the book does represent the thinking of the senior Muslim Brotherhood leadership in their prison debates with Quṭb-inspired radicals, a project that was spearheaded by al-Huḍaybī.[13] For the sake of convenience I will refer to the book as his, with the preceding caveats in mind.

*Duʿāt lā quḍāt* does not critique Quṭb's texts themselves, and in fact never mentions Quṭb by name, presumably out of respect for a long-time associate and martyr for the cause. Al-Huḍaybī's explicit targets of criticism are Mawdūdī, on the one hand, and others who are not named, but who are obviously the radicals in the Egyptian prisons who adopted and developed Quṭb's doctrine, foremost among them Shukrī Muṣṭafā, who when later released from prison would found the Jamāʿat al-Muslimīn group (popularly known as al-Takfīr wa-l-Hijra). The nucleus of *Duʿāt lā quḍāt* was composed in response to a creedal document drawn up by the prison radicals at al-Huḍaybī's own request. The radicals' development of the theonomy doctrine consisted for the most part in drawing out jurisprudential conclusions from its general principles and declaring the rulers and large segments of society to be apostate. Al-Huḍaybī's counterarguments in *Duʿāt lā quḍāt* represent an attempt to rein in the radical tendency and reestablish the leadership's control over the Islamist movement.

As part of his attempt to refute the radicals' far-reaching conclusions, al-Huḍaybī argues that the term *ḥākimiyya* was originally coined simply as a label in order to bring to the fore a concept common to a number of Qurʾānic verses and *ḥadīth*s. The radicals, however, had then reified it into a concept in its own right, and into an *aṣl* (principle) from which to draw detailed jurisprudential conclusions, without recourse any longer to the original prooftexts and without any true understanding of the

[13] Al-Huḍaybī's general responsibility for the content of the work is widely accepted, though the text itself appears to have been largely written by a committee. See Barbara H. E. Zollner, *The Muslim Brotherhood: Hasan al-Hudaybi and Ideology*, New York: Routledge, 2009, pp. 64–71; Mathias Ghyoot, *Brothers behind Bars: A History of the Muslim Brotherhood from the Palestine War to Egypt's Prisons*, Oxford and New York: Oxford University Press, 2025, pp. 353–356.

intention of those who coined the term *ḥākimiyya* in the first place. Al-Huḍaybī's only objection to the original term and concept of *ḥākimiyya* (as he interprets it) is that it is a non-scriptural man-made term – a *muṣṭalaḥ mawḍūʿ*. Thus while he places the blame for its misuse primarily on Quṭb's radical acolytes, and implicitly exonerates Quṭb himself to a certain degree, he does treat the term *ḥākimiyya* as a kind of object lesson in the dangers of straying from scriptural terminology.[14]

While al-Huḍaybī's strategy of differentiating between Quṭb's original intention and the conclusions drawn by his followers is debatable, he does put his finger on a considerable irony: The term *ḥākimiyya*, which served as the basis for denunciation of man-made law (*al-qawānīn al-waḍʿiyya*), was itself *waḍʿī* or *mawḍūʿ* – that is, of human coinage. In essence al-Huḍaybī was arguing that fidelity to scriptural terminology and concepts was a necessary condition for fidelity to divine law, and that Quṭb's use of non-scriptural terminology – however well-intentioned – had led to undesirable consequences.

This was an important critique precisely because it bore a 'salafī' character. In fact, in the writings of Ibn Taymiyya and his circle, both man-made laws and man-made hermeneutic principles were denounced equally as *waḍʿī*. We may give as an example of the former Ibn Taymiyya's comment that the Mongols, instead of adhering to Allāh's law in judgment, judged by "*awḍāʿ lahum*,"[15] that is, laws they had invented. The designations *waḍʿī* and *qānūn waḍʿī* were more frequently applied, however, to rationalistic hermeneutical principles than to laws or law codes. In the opening of *Darʾ taʿāruḍ al-ʿaql wa-l-naql* Ibn Taymiyya refers to the hermeneutic principle established by Fakhr al-Dīn al-Rāzī and his followers, namely, that in cases in which reason and scripture oppose one another reason is to be accorded priority, as a *qānūn* that they invented (*waḍaʿūhā*);[16] and similar language recurs in the following pages regarding the invented hermeneutic *qawānīn* of others, such as al-Ghazālī and Ibn Sīnā.[17] When Ibn Kathīr – a Shāfiʿī exegete who was close to Ibn Taymiyya's circle – addresses the issue of the Mongol *yāsaq* (law code) in his commentary on Qurʾān 5:50 (*a-fa-ḥukm al-jāhiliyya yabghūna*), he writes that the verse denounces the turning away from Allāh's rule in favor of "views, wayward inclinations, and terminologies that men invent (*waḍaʿahā*) without any basis in Allāh's *sharīʿa*" (*mā siwāhu min al-ārāʾ wa-l-ahwāʾ wa-l-iṣṭilāḥāt allatī waḍaʿahā al-rijāl*

[14] Ḥasan al-Huḍaybī, *Duʿāt lā quḍāt: abḥāth fī al-ʿaqīda al-islāmiyya wa-manhaj al-daʿwa ilā llāh*, Cairo: Dār al-Ṭibāʿa wa-l-Nashr al-Islāmiyya, 1977, pp. 63–64.

[15] Ibn Taymiyya, *Majmūʿat al-fatāwā*, vol. 28, p. 276.

[16] Ibn Taymiyya, *Darʾ*, vol. 1, p. 5. [17] Ibn Taymiyya, *Darʾ*, vol. 1, pp. 5–9.

*bi-lā mustanad min sharīʿat Allāh*),[18] thus linking together hermeneutic and legal deviations. We likewise find an important terminological parallel in Ibn Qayyim al-Jawziyya's explanation of the Qurʾānic term *ṭāghūt* as both judgment by laws other than those of Allāh and man-made hermeneutical principles that distort the meaning and the application of the revealed texts (these in addition to the meaning of *ṭāghūt* as any object of worship apart from Allāh).[19]

The implicit linkage that al-Huḍaybī draws between hermeneutic and legal originalism is thus one with a solid pedigree, and it (and similar critiques) presented a challenge that salafizing radicals would attempt to meet in the coming years by replacing Quṭb's system with more established Islamic sources as a basis for theonomy. While it is true that both Mawdūdī and Quṭb had themselves raised the banner of *ad fontes*, they had done so in an idiosyncratic manner that left the bases of their doctrine open to attack.

We can see precisely what al-Huḍaybī did accept of the doctrine of *ḥākimiyya* from the opening of chapter 5 of *Duʿāt lā quḍāt*, titled "*In al-ḥukm illā lillāh*" ("Verily Judgment Is Allāh's Alone"), in a section bearing the subheading "*ʿAqīdatunā*" ("Our Creed"):

> I hold it certain and without doubt that judgment (*ḥukm*) belongs to Allāh alone, and that only He is the sole possessor of command and prohibition, to the exclusion of others. It is He, to the exclusion of others, who renders the permitted permitted and the forbidden forbidden. "Verily judgment is Allāh's alone" (*in al-ḥukm illā lillāh*: Qurʾān 12:40).
>
> And I believe in full faith that Allāh's *sharīʿa* is the truth and that what is apart from it is falsehood and oppression …
>
> And I hold it certain and without doubt that it is Allāh's *sharīʿa* that is obligatory on us, to the exclusion of other [laws]; and it is obligatory on us by dint of His command, whether a given ruler is pleased with it or not.
>
> And I believe in full faith that it is Allāh's *sharīʿa* that must be applied (*wājibat al-nafādh*), and that it is the obligation of every Muslim individual to act in accordance with it and to apply it in practice to the degree that he is able, whether the ruler applies it or acts to suspend it …
>
> And I hold it certain and without doubt that Allāh's *sharīʿa* is the only law to which it is permitted to refer in judgment … What Allāh has permitted is permitted until the Day of Resurrection, and no one, whoever they may be, can

18 Ibn Kathīr, *Tafsīr al-qurʾān al-ʿaẓīm*, vol. 3, p. 119.

19 See Yasir Qadhi, "'The Unleashed Thunderbolts' of Ibn Qayyim al-Ǧawziyyah: An Introductory Essay," in "A Scholar in the Shadow: Essays in the Legal and Theological Thought of Ibn Qayyim al-Ǧawziyya," ed. Caterina Bori and Livnat Holtzman, special issue, *Oriente Moderno* 90/1 (2010), pp. 135–149.

forbid it; and what Allāh forbade is forbidden until the Day of Resurrection, and no one, whoever they may be, can permit it.[20]

Al-Huḍaybī goes on to affirm the following propositions as well: One who believes that another has the right to permit what Allāh forbade or to forbid what Allāh permitted has apostatized, provided he has been apprised of the truth, persists in his belief despite having been reprimanded with evidence (*balaghahu al-ḥaqq wa-qāmat ʿalayhi al-ḥujja*), and is not relying for this view on a plausible interpretation of scripture (*taʾwīl*); a necessary component of faith, of *tawḥīd*, and of the profession *lā ilāha illā llāh* is the belief that Allāh is the sole possessor of command and judgment, and that one who sets some kind of limit (*ḥadd*) to His command and judgment has committed *shirk* (again, provided he has been apprised of the truth and persists in this belief despite having been reprimanded with evidence); likewise a necessary component of faith and *tawḥīd* is the belief that Allāh alone is worthy of worship (*al-maʿbūd bi-ḥaqq*); this means that He is deserving of absolute obedience (*ittibāʿ, inqiyād*), and to believe that some obedience is due to another without His permission is to make that other a partner (*nidd, sharīk*) to Allāh. Finally, al-Huḍaybī also states that the tenet that Allāh alone is worthy of worship mandates that one must carry out His orders in practice and observe His prohibitions, as "this is included in the meaning of worship" (*wa-hādhā dākhil fī maḍmūn al-ʿibāda*).[21]

As can be seen from the preceding, al-Huḍaybī agreed with the broad general principle that Allāh alone is legislator and that the exclusivity of His legislation is a matter of creed. He even voices his agreement with the crucial idea that legal obedience is a form of worship, and that attribution to another of the right to permit and forbid is apostasy. If al-Huḍaybī grants all these premises, we need at this point to ask wherein precisely lies the dispute between himself and the radicals.

To a large extent the answer to this question lies in their differing theologies of faith. As we saw in our analysis of Ibn Taymiyya's monolatry (Chapter 1), there exists a close and organic connection between, on the one hand, the priority accorded to worship over conceptual monotheism, and, on the other, the assertion that acts are a true criterion of faith and unbelief. As I have argued elsewhere, al-Huḍaybī did not accord this status to acts. Relying on the Ashʿarī theological tradition, al-Huḍaybī conditioned apostasy on express verbal statements indicative of a deviation in belief.[22] This is the governing principle, and it attenuates

[20] al-Huḍaybī, *Duʿāt*, pp. 67–68. [21] al-Huḍaybī, *Duʿāt*, pp. 68–69.
[22] See Lav, *Radical Islam*, pp. 64–72.

al-Huḍaybī's theonomy: *Belief* that another has the right to permit and forbid is apostasy, as is explicit attribution of this right to him when done out of said belief, but simple obedience to another's command and prohibition is not, as we will see presently.

For present purposes we may leave aside the technical language of the theology of faith. The same attenuation of al-Huḍaybī's commitment to theonomy is apparent in other aspects of his argumentation as well. Despite appearances, it is not the case that al-Huḍaybī accepts Quṭb's doctrine of *ḥākimiyya* in full. In fact, it could be plausibly argued that notwithstanding his surface agreement with many of its tenets, al-Huḍaybī actually rejected the essence of the doctrine as it was described in Chapter 4, namely, that the primary distinction between faith and unbelief, and the heart of Islam, is obedience to Allāh's law rather than belief in His existence and objective qualities.

The clearest evidence of this is to be found in al-Huḍaybī's treatment of two interrelated issues: the meaning of *lā ilāha illā llāh*, and his interpretation of the Streitpunkt (that is, the central point of dispute) between the prophets and the unbelievers. As for the meaning of *lā ilāha illā llāh*, al-Huḍaybī writes that it is "an utterance that one enounces in order to convey the certitude one experiences that Allāh *exists*, and that He is one, with there being no other *ilāh* apart from Him, and to affirm this."[23] This interpretation is entirely at odds with that of Mawdūdī and Quṭb, who viewed the *shahāda* not as a statement of Allāh's *existence* to the exclusion of other gods, but rather as a commitment to worship and obedience of Allāh to the exclusion of all others. Both Mawdūdī and Quṭb went to great pains to demonstrate that Allāh's existence was not a point of contention and was acknowledged by the *kuffār* themselves,[24] whereas al-Huḍaybī interprets the *shahāda* by which one becomes a Muslim as a statement regarding Allāh's existence. Al-Huḍaybī does mention the lexical definition of *ilāh* as an object of worship,[25] but he does not elaborate on the potential significance of this fact nor is it by any means central to his conception of divinity (as it was for Ibn Taymiyya and Ibn ʿAbd al-Wahhāb, and to a certain extent for Mawdūdī and Quṭb as well). It is only mentioned in passing, in connection with the dispute over whether the name Allāh is an underived proper noun or is derived from a root (with one of the candidates being *ʾ-l-h*). Ultimately al-

[23] *shahādat 'lā ilāha illā llāh' lafẓa yanṭuquhā al-marʾ li-l-ikhbār bi-mā waqaʿa fī nafsihi min tayaqqun min wujūd dhāt Allāh taʿālā wa-annahu taʿālā aḥadun lā ilāha siwāhu, iqrāran minhu bi-dhālika.* al-Huḍaybī, *Duʿāt*, p. 11 (emphasis added).

[24] See e.g. Mawdūdī, *Iṣṭilāḥēn̠*, pp. 72–73; Quṭb, *Muqawwimāt*, pp. 98, 243, 247.

[25] al-Huḍaybī, *Duʿāt*, p. 12.

Huḍaybī concludes that this entire lexical discussion is without importance and is not necessary to understanding the nature of divinity,[26] since Allāh Himself informed us that "the ability to create, exaltedness, supreme rule, the granting of protection, provision of welfare, and likewise kingship and mastery – [all these] were among the meanings [of 'Allāh'] known to many in the *jāhiliyya*."[27]

This brings us to the question of the Streitpunkt, and in this issue as well al-Huḍaybī argues a position that is entirely at odds with that of Mawdūdī and Quṭb. The meanings of 'Allāh' that al-Huḍaybī listed in the passage just cited all relate to His objective aspect; when he writes that these meanings were known to the people of the *jāhiliyya*, he does not mean by this, as Mawdūdī and Quṭb did, that they represent an incomplete understanding of divinity. To the contrary, al-Huḍaybī listed them in order to demonstrate that there is no need to investigate the lexical meanings of the names for divinity, since we already know more or less who 'Allāh' is. For al-Huḍaybī these meanings do not comprise only a cosmic-objective aspect of divinity that must be complemented by a normative-relational aspect, as Mawdūdī and Quṭb argued (see Chapter 4), but rather express the nature of Allāh as such.

This difference is further underscored when al-Huḍaybī goes on to cite as evidence for these meanings of 'Allāh' precisely the same verses that Mawdūdī and Quṭb cited as evidence that the *kuffār*'s conception of divinity was incomplete,[28] and were likewise employed by Ibn Taymiyya and Ibn ʿAbd al-Wahhāb to prove that the *kuffār* acknowledged *tawḥīd al-rubūbiyya*, and thus that this form of *tawḥīd* is not sufficient to make one a Muslim. These verses are Qurʾān 10:31, which reads: "Say [to the unbelievers]: Who gives you provision from the heavens and the earth? Or who has the power of hearing and sight? Who brings forth the living from the dead, and the dead from the living, and who regulates the affairs? They will say: Allāh"; and Qurʾān 23:84–89, which reads:

> Say: To whom do the earth and those on it belong, if you have knowledge? They will say: To Allāh. Say: Then will you not be mindful? Say: Who is the Lord (*rabb*) of the seven heavens and Lord of the great throne? They will say: [they belong to] Allāh. Say: Then will you not fear [Him]? Say: In whose hand is dominion over all things, He who protects and against whom there is no

[26] Cf. al-Huḍaybī, *Duʿāt*, p. 26, where he argues that *ilāh* and *rabb* as used in the Qurʾān are basically synonyms one of the other.

[27] *al-qudra ʿalā al-khalq wa-l-ʿuluww wa-l-tasāmī wa-l-sulṭān al-kabīr al-ʿaẓīm wa-l-ijāra wa-ijrāʾ al-rizq wa-ka-dhā al-mulk wa-l-taṣarruf kānat min al-maʿānī al-maʿrūfa bayna kathīrīn fī al-jāhiliyya li-lafẓ al-jalāla*. al-Huḍaybī, *Duʿāt*, pp. 13–14.

[28] For example, Mawdūdī, *Iṣṭilāḥēṉ*, pp. 65–66, 74.

protector, if you have knowledge? They will say: [that belongs to] Allāh. Say: How then are you deluded?[29]

Likewise, in contrast with Mawdūdī's and Quṭb's insistence that Allāh's existence and His objective aspect as Creator were not in question in the *jāhiliyya*, al-Huḍaybī points to two verses that he believes demonstrate that they were. These are Qur'ān 45:23: "And they say: there is naught but our life in this world, we die and we live, and nothing destroys us but time"; and Qur'ān 52:35–36: "Or were they created without there being anything (that created them), or are they the creators? / Or did they create the heavens and the earth? Nay, they have no certainty." The first of these verses does seem to indicate a denial of anything extra-mundane, apart from the impersonal force of time or fate (*al-dahr*), and thus serves al-Huḍaybī's purpose well. The second verse is more ambiguous: One could plausibly interpret it as al-Huḍaybī does, though we already saw (in Chapter 1) that Ibn Taymiyya understood it as a rhetorical question that appealed to the innate understanding (*fiṭra*) present in all humans that they are beings created by Allāh. In any event, it is important for al-Huḍaybī to establish that only some in the *jāhiliyya* affirmed Allāh's rule and His powers, and that others denied them.[30] In contrast with Mawdūdī and Quṭb, he considers the affirmation of Allāh's cosmic rule and His powers (what we have called His cosmic-objective aspect) to be essentially a complete depiction of divinity, and thus he needs to argue that it is that depiction itself that was at issue between the prophets who affirmed it and others in the *jāhiliyya* who denied it.

It is important to note that just as the Streitpunkt argument was a significant structural parallel between the monolatry of Ibn ʿAbd al-Wahhāb and the theonomy of Mawdūdī and Quṭb, rejection of this Streitpunkt argument is likewise a common feature to the opponents of these thinkers. To provide one example, the Tunisian Mālikī scholar Ismāʿīl al-Tamīmī, in his early nineteenth-century anti-Wahhābī polemic *al-Minaḥ al-ilāhiyya*, contested Ibn ʿAbd al-Wahhāb's depiction of the Arabs of the *jāhiliyya* as essentially monotheists whose *shirk* consisted in acts of polylatry. Al-Tamīmī quotes a passage from Ibn ʿAbd al-Wahhāb in which the latter states that the Prophet Muḥammad was sent to "a people who performed ritual devotions, performed the *ḥajj*, and invoked Allāh's name frequently, but they did not make their worship exclusive to Him, and took for themselves, apart from Him, *awliyāʾ* whose intercession they hoped for, like the angels, ʿĪsā, Maryam, and other righteous

[29] al-Huḍaybī, *Duʿāt*, p. 14. [30] al-Huḍaybī, *Duʿāt*, p. 14.

individuals."[31] Al-Tamīmī counters this idea using the same verse that al-Huḍaybī would use against Mawdūdī and Quṭb a century and a half later: "Among the Arabs were some who did not acknowledge the Creator or the resurrection. These were the *dahriyya* who said [Qur'ān 45:23]: 'there is naught but our life in this world, we die and we live, and nothing destroys us but time (*al-dahr*).'"[32] Al-Tamīmī was interested in contesting Ibn 'Abd al-Wahhāb's characterization of the Streitpunkt because he correctly understood that the point of the Streitpunkt argument was to draw a comparison between people of his own day and the Arab *mushrikūn* in the *jāhiliyya*.[33] The same is true of al-Huḍaybī, who viewed affirmation of Allāh's existence and of His objective attributes as the criterion for faith. If the true Streitpunkt were theonomy, then affirmation of Allāh's cosmic-objective aspect would not be sufficient to make one a Muslim, and the door would be open to comparisons between the old *jāhiliyya* and the new one.

This basic contention – that belief in Allāh's existence and in His objective attributes is a sufficient criterion for faith – underlies al-Huḍaybī's argumentation throughout *Du'āt*, running like a thread through his detailed refutations of the text-based arguments advanced by the radicals. Let us take just one particularly significant example, al-Huḍaybī's discussion of Qur'ān 9:31 and the 'Adī b. Ḥātim tradition.

Al-Huḍaybī mentions the 'Adī b. Ḥātim tradition a number of times in *Du'āt*. He first cites it as one of a series of prooftexts relating to the terms *dīn* and *'ibāda*.[34] His point in this passage was to argue, contra Mawdūdī, that just as there was no need for lexical analysis of the terms *ilāh* and *rabb*, so there was no need for such analysis regarding the terms *dīn* and *'ibāda*, since all that one needs to know about their meanings can be found in the Qur'ān and the *ḥadīth*. He cites it again shortly thereafter when arguing against Mawdūdī's claim that the Arabs of the Prophet's time, unlike later Muslims, understood the true meaning of these terms. Al-Huḍaybī points out that 'Adī b. Ḥātim, who certainly was an Arab of the Prophet's time, did not know that adopting the rabbis' and priests' laws was worship (*'ibāda*) of them until the Prophet taught him that it was.[35]

[31] *ba'athahu llāhu ilā qawmin yata'abbadūna wa-yaḥujjūna wa-yadhkurūna llāha kathīran illā annahum lam yufridūhu al-'ibādata bal ittakhadhū min dūnihi awliyā' rajā'an shafā'atahum ka-l-malā'ika wa-'Īsā wa-Maryam wa-ghayrihim min al-ṣāliḥīn.* Abū al-Fidā' Ismā'īl al-Tamīmī, *al-Minaḥ al-ilāhiyya fī ṭams al-ḍalāla al-wahhābiyya*, in Ḥamādī al-Radīsī [Hamadi Redissi] and Asmā' Nawīra [Asma Nouira], *al-Radd 'alā al-wahhābiyya fī al-qarn al-tāsi' 'ashar: nuṣūṣ al-gharb al-islāmī numūdhajan*, Beirut: Dār al-Ṭalī'a, 2008, p. 174.

[32] al-Tamīmī, *al-Minaḥ*, p. 175.

[33] al-Tamīmī, *al-Minaḥ*, p. 176.

[34] al-Huḍaybī, *Du'āt*, pp. 28–29.

[35] al-Huḍaybī, *Du'āt*, p. 31.

Al-Huḍaybī's main discussion of Qur'ān 9:31 and its accompanying tradition comes in chapter 8 of *Du'āt*, titled "*al-Ṭā'a wa-l-ittibā'*" ("Obedience and Following"). The chapter opens with a characterization of the radicals' position on this issue in the following words: "Some say that a Muslim apostatizes and becomes a polytheist when he obeys and follows one who does not rule by what Allāh revealed. According to what they say, obedience and following are through acts, without reference to intention and belief."[36] The radicals, according to al-Huḍaybī, held that such obedience constitutes apostasy not only when the one who obeys explicitly attributes to the one obeyed the authority to rule in contravention of or independently of Allāh's command, but also when the one who obeys does so in explicit acknowledgment that his obedience is a sin against Allāh, and even when he obeys out of a mistaken belief that the ruling is Allāh's ruling, or that the ruling is within the limits allowed by Allāh.[37] The example al-Huḍaybī cites from the radicals is the following:

> [Take the case of] a Muslim who believes that Allāh is the Creator of all that is not Him, and that He is the ruler (*al-ḥākim*) and that there is no ruler apart from Him. And this Muslim is eager to follow Allāh's commands and to avoid His prohibitions, and he performs the commandments of prayer, *zakāt*, fasting, and the pilgrimage. Then an issue arises for him regarding which he does not know what Allāh's ruling is, and he is not able to investigate the proofs and to derive rulings from them [himself]. He asks a scholar with a reputation for understanding and piety what Allāh's ruling on this issue is, and the scholar gives him an opinion which is erroneous and not in accord with Allāh's true ruling [on the matter]. Then this Muslim who asked for the opinion believes that the ruling he received from the [scholar] he trusted is Allāh's ruling, and he acts in accordance with it out of the belief that he is simply carrying out Allāh's ruling. [The radicals] say that in this action of his he has associated another with Allāh and has taken this *muftī* as his *rabb* apart from Allāh.

They bring as evidence for what they say Allāh's words [Qur'ān 9:31], "They took their rabbis and priests as lords in place of Allāh, and likewise Jesus son of Maryam," and the 'Adī b. Ḥātim *ḥadīth*. When ['Adī] said to the Prophet that they did not worship them, he responded, according to what Ibn Kathīr said in his *tafsīr* of the Qur'ān: "They indeed do, because [the rabbis and priests] forbade

[36] *Qāla al-ba'ḍ inna al-muslima yartaddu kāfiran mushrikan matā aṭā'a man lam yaḥkum bi-mā anzala llāhu ta'ālā wa-ttaba'ahu. Wa-l-ṭā'a wa-l-i'ttibā' yakūnāni – ḥasbamā qālū – bi-l-'amal dūna al-naẓar ilā al-niyya wa-l-i'tiqād.* al-Huḍaybī, *Du'āt*, p. 119.

[37] The discussion in this section of *Du'āt* deals solely with the status of those who obey non-*shar'ī* law, and I have focused on it for what it reveals of al-Huḍaybī's views on obedience as a criterion of faith. It should be noted that al-Huḍaybī opposed *takfīr* of those who actually legislate in contravention of what Allāh revealed as well. His position relied both on his arguments in the theology of faith and on an expansive application of the category of *jahl* (exculpatory ignorance). See Lav, *Radical Islam*, p. 63.

them the permitted and permitted them the forbidden, and [the Jews and Christians] followed them (*fa-ttabaʿūhum*), and that is their worship of them."

[The radicals] said that the 'following' was the action in accordance with what the priests and rabbis said, without regard to what the one who does the act believes – and this is obedience. [And they said] that the text of the verse equated between the *rubūbiyya* of obedience to the rabbis and priests through action in accordance with what they commanded [i.e. the taking of them as *arbāb*, "lords"] and the *rubūbiyya* [i.e. attribution of Lordship] of the belief that Jesus is the son of Allāh. [And they said] that this is proof that acts (*ʿamal*) and belief (*iʿtiqād*) are equal in the *sharīʿa*'s ruling, and each of them leads to commission of *shirk*.[38]

There are three things worthy of note in the position of the radicals, as characterized by al-Huḍaybī. First, their argumentation on the issue of exclusivity of obedience does not make any reference to Mawdūdī or Quṭb – this despite the fact that they were only a few years removed from Quṭb's late writings in which the issue of obedience was central, and despite al-Huḍaybī's earlier polemical characterization of the radicals as basing their jurisprudential conclusions on the (Quṭbist) concept of *ḥākimiyya*, without proper reference to prooftexts. If al-Huḍaybī's characterization in this passage is accurate, it suggests rather that the radicals, even if influenced by Quṭb, were already seeking to ground their theonomy in more traditional sources and argumentation. Second, the radicals – unlike Quṭb himself – place Qurʾān 9:31 and the ʿAdī b. Ḥātim tradition in the context of a discussion of *taqlīd*; they would surely have known of Quṭb's 'political' use of these texts in *Maʿālim* and elsewhere, but they must also have been familiar with their use in the premodern jurisprudential polemic. Third, the position attributed to the radicals is an extreme one that is not attested in the premodern anti-*taqlīd* polemic. (Whether this really was their position or a polemical mischaracterization on the part of al-Huḍaybī is difficult to know.) The hypothetical described in the passage states clearly that the *mustaftī* did not possess the requisite knowledge to derive a ruling for himself, and in such a case even the most ardent anti-*taqlīd* authors, including Ibn Ḥazm and al-Shawkānī, agreed that it is proper to seek an opinion from another who is more knowledgeable. (Although they did stipulate that one should ask him to provide the textual evidence on which his opinion is based, so that the *mustaftī* would technically be practicing *ittibāʿ* of the texts rather than *taqlīd* of a living human: see Chapter 3).

In any event, al-Huḍaybī's refutation does not just fault the radicals for taking the principle to incorrect extremes. Al-Huḍaybī denies the principle itself that 'obedience' to not-Allāh as expressed in acts can be

[38] al-Huḍaybī, *Duʿāt*, pp. 119–120.

a cause of apostasy. He argues that while the lexical meaning of *ṭāʿa* is "action in accordance with a command" (*al-ʿamal bi-l-amr*), the *sharʿī* meaning of *ṭāʿa* – that is to say, the operative meaning of this term in the texts of revelation – is "action to carry out a command together with intention and belief" (*al-ʿamal tanfīdhan li-l-amr maʿa al-niyya wa-l-iʿtiqād*).[39] Al-Huḍaybī bases this claim on the *ḥadīth* "Actions are only according to intentions, and an individual only gets what he intends. One whose emigration (*hijra*) is to Allāh and the Prophet, his emigration is to Allāh and the Prophet, and one whose emigration is to attainment in this world or a woman he intends to marry, his emigration is to what he emigrated for." Al-Huḍaybī understands this *ḥadīth* as stating a general principle applicable to all issues of obedience and disobedience: "When an individual performs acts that are commanded or forbidden in the *sharʿ*, the criterion on which the legal status of these acts depends is his intention."[40] He goes on to explain that if one's intention is to obey Allāh, then one is not considered to be obeying the *muftī* in his ruling, even if his ruling diverges in truth from Allāh's command; and conversely, if one's intention is to obey another human in everything he commands, even if it contravenes Allāh's command, then this is considered obedience to the human, regardless of whether his command happens to accord with Allāh's. It follows from this principle that if one is commanded to do something that contravenes Allāh's *sharīʿa*, and one acts in accordance with this command, but with the understanding that the one commanding does not possess the authority to replace (*tabdīl*) Allāh's *sharīʿa*, and with the understanding that his command possesses no true validity, then this action is merely sinful; it does not, of itself, constitute apostasy. The one who acts in accordance with the command is not considered to be 'following' the one commanding in the *sharʿī* sense, and he has not taken him as a lord apart from Allāh.[41]

Al-Huḍaybī then applies this general principle, namely, that intention is the operative criterion when determining the legal status of acts, to exegesis of Qurʾān 9:31 and the ʿAdī b. Ḥātim *ḥadīth*. He argues that the verse neither mentions nor alludes to acts, and speaks only of 'taking' (*ittikhādh*) others as lords apart from Allāh. According to al-Huḍaybī, this 'taking' can be effected through belief alone – that is, the belief in the

39 al-Huḍaybī, *Duʿāt*, p. 121.

40 *fa-inna al-aʿmāla al-maʾmūr bihā wa-l-manhī ʿanhā fī al-sharʿ idhā atāhā al-ʿabd fa-inna al-madāra fī ḥukmihā yatawaqqafu ʿalā niyyatihi.* al-Huḍaybī, *Duʿāt*, p. 122.

41 al-Huḍaybī, *Duʿāt*, p. 122. Al-Huḍaybī adds his usual stipulation that the general rule does not apply to specific acts that a text has specified as negating one's faith without regard to intention and belief, but as elsewhere he does not provide any examples of what such acts might be. Cf. Lav, *Radical Islam*, p. 70.

obligatory nature of obedience to another individual, without regard to whether one acts on this belief or not. As for the *ḥadīth*, al-Huḍaybī argues that the version cited by the radicals likewise does not mention action but rather states only that the Jews and Christians 'followed' the rabbis and priests (*fa-ttabaʿūhum*), and that the *sharʿī* meaning of 'following' (*ittibāʿ*) is not present without intention and belief (*niyya, iʿtiqād*). Al-Huḍaybī argues in addition that the language in other versions of the *ḥadīth* makes this point more explicit, but his argument does not really hinge on this point, since his interpretation of the *ḥadīth* follows his general convictions regarding the relation between belief and acts. Thus he concludes:

> In truth, the verse does not equate between action and belief, but rather between two beliefs whose essence is one and the same: [It equates between] the belief and the statement that ʿUzayr [Ezra] is the son of Allāh and that Jesus is the son of Allāh, and the belief and statement that the priests and rabbis possess a holiness and infallibility that mandate that one follow them, even when their command contravenes Allāh's *sharīʿa*.[42]

This conclusion should be understood as circumscribing the scope of application of al-Huḍaybī's rhetorical embrace of theonomy, and specifically of his statement that the principle that Allāh alone is worthy of worship "mandates the carrying out of Allāh's command, action in practice in accordance with what Allāh commands, and avoidance in practice of what He forbids. This is included in the meaning of worship (*wa-hādhā dākhil fī maḍmūn al-ʿibāda*) and follows from the belief that He is the [only] true object of worship."[43] Al-Huḍaybī certainly believed that it is obligatory to act in accordance with Allāh's command, but it is clear that he did not view this obligation as a true criterion of faith: One remains a Muslim as long as one believes that Allāh's law is obligatory, and one apostatizes only when one believes that the law of another is obligatory due to that individual's "holiness and infallibility." This presents a clear contrast with the doctrines of Mawdūdī and Quṭb, and cannot be considered theonomy in the true sense. Just as a true doctrine of monolatry establishes exclusivity of worship as a real criterion of faith (and in fact a criterion more important than that of conceptual belief), so

[42] al-Huḍaybī, *Duʿāt*, p. 123; and see p. 126 for the author's adduction of two brief passages from Ibn Taymiyya's *Kitāb al-īmān* in support of his position. The second of these passages, in isolation, could easily be read as conditioning the kind of legal obedience portrayed in the ʿAdī b. Ḥātim tradition on belief (*iʿtiqād*). My own view is that passages such as these ought to be interpreted in light of Ibn Taymiyya's extensive polemic in the theology of faith (and indeed in light of the doctrine of *tawḥīd al-ulūhiyya* where it intersects with the same), which generally militate against such a reading.

[43] al-Huḍaybī, *Duʿāt*, pp. 68–69.

a true monolatry-based theonomy takes legal obedience as a real criterion of faith, independent of the content of one's beliefs. In his treatment of the issue of obedience and in his reading of Qurʾān 9:31 and the ʿAdī b. Ḥātim *ḥadīth*, al-Huḍaybī makes it clear that he rejects theonomy in this sense, and that his views on legal obedience are of a piece with other facets of his thinking that we noted earlier: his interpretation of the *shahāda* as a statement of monotheism (rather than monolatry), and his contention that it was acknowledgment of Allāh's cosmic-objective aspect that constituted the Streitpunkt between the prophets and the unbelievers.

It can also be seen from the preceding how the radicals' embrace of *takfīr* of the rulers and those who obeyed them, based on Quṭb's theonomy, dictated that al-Huḍaybī's refutation, in addition to treating the *ḥākimiyya* doctrine itself, would be largely dedicated to staking out a position on the theology of faith, and in particular the status of acts in faith. Al-Huḍaybī's general argument on this score is that acts alone are never sufficient to establish a Muslim's apostasy, and that it is belief that stands as the criterion of faith or *kufr*.[44] The salience of this issue was due precisely to the fact that al-Huḍaybī agreed with some elements of Quṭb's doctrine, as is clear from the "*ʿAqīdatunā*" section of *Duʿāt*, and needed to limit its implications for *takfīr*; had he rejected the doctrine entirely the battle would have been fought on other grounds.

Yet the theology of faith, while a separate theological tradition with its own terminology, is not really a separate issue from those of monolatry and theonomy. We noted in Chapter 1 that Ibn Taymiyya's insistence on the status of acts in faith was of a piece with his *tawḥīd al-ulūhiyya*, with textual parallels between the two topics reinforcing the inherent thematic connection, namely, that a privileging of monolatry over monotheism clearly assigns more importance to acts (worship) than belief. The same can be said of Quṭb's *ḥākimiyya*: If it is to be a true theonomy, then acts of legal obedience, and not just belief, must necessarily be a true criterion of faith. Al-Huḍaybī's relatively latitudinarian position on the theology of faith, and his emphasis on belief over acts, was entirely of a piece with his rejection of Quṭbist theonomy where it truly counted.

### *A Contemporary Point of Reference: ʿUmar ʿAbd al-Raḥmān's Salafization of* Ḥākimiyya

Before leaving the milieu of early post-Quṭb Egypt let us address a final note to the topic of the 'salafization' of *ḥākimiyya*. As noted in the

[44] See Lav, *Radical Islam*, pp. 64–72.

preceding discussion, Ḥasan al-Huḍaybī's depiction of the radicals as basing their doctrine on Mawdūdī (and implicitly Quṭb) was not borne out by his own characterization of their arguments. There can be no doubt that Mawdūdī and Quṭb were responsible for raising the issue of theonomy in such force, but the movement away from their system toward a salafized form of theonomy began in the very years following Quṭb's death. For example, while both Mawdūdī and Quṭb made frequent use of Qurʾān 9:31 and the ʿAdī b. Ḥātim tradition, neither (to the best of my knowledge) connected their own usage of these texts to their usage in premodern anti-*taqlīd* polemic, though Mawdūdī – as I argued in Chapter 4 – almost certainly knew of it. This connection is made, according to al-Huḍaybī, in the radicals' prison writings.

We do not have to depend on al-Huḍaybī's testimony to confirm that attempts to salafize *ḥākimiyya* were already underway in Egypt in the early years after Quṭb's death. One example dating from 1971 shows both salafī and Quṭbist influence and clearly connects between premodern anti-*taqlīd* polemic and the condemnation of modern man-made law. This work was a doctoral thesis written at al-Azhar by ʿUmar ʿAbd al-Raḥmān,[45] who some years later was to become the *sharīʿa* authority for the Egyptian al-Jamāʿa al-Islāmiyya organization. He later served a prison sentence in the US on terrorism-related charges until his death in 2017.

In this work ʿAbd al-Raḥmān describes Qurʾān 9:31 as specifying that the scriptuaries' unbelief and polytheism inhered not only in their beliefs and statements, but also in their lived reality, because they gave the rabbis and priests "the right to legislate" (*ḥaqq al-tashrīʿ*) and obeyed them.[46] He then cites the passages from the commentaries of Fakhr al-Dīn al-Rāzī and Ṣiddīq Ḥasan Khān that we surveyed in Chapter 3, both of which employed the verse and the ʿAdī b. Ḥātim tradition in condemnation of *taqlīd*.[47] He sums up the issue with a number of conclusions

[45] Later published as ʿUmar ʿAbd al-Raḥmān, *Mawqif al-qurʾān min khuṣūmihi*, Cairo: Dār Miṣr al-Maḥrūsa, 2006. As I only have access to this published edition conclusions drawn from the book regarding Egypt in 1971 are tentative. That said, the book does not show obvious signs of revision. Kamāl Ḥabīb, in a review article for aljazeera.net, notes that Mawdūdī and Quṭb are not listed in the bibliography despite having been cited in the work itself, presumably because it was politically unfeasible to do so in Egypt in the early seventies. Kamal Ḥabīb, "Mawqif al-qurʾān min khuṣūmihi," 1 Safar 1427 / March 1, 2006, www.aljazeera.net/knowledgegate/books/2006/3/1/موقف-القرآن-من-خصومه (link no longer active).

[46] ʿAbd al-Raḥmān, *Mawqif*, p. 301. The author adds that the accusation with regard to the Jews relates to the addition of an Oral Law (the Mishnah and the Talmud) to the Torah, and with regard to the Christians it relates to their abrogation of the Torah, their claiming the right to grant or deny absolution from sin, and their claims of infallibility and authority for the Pope (p. 302).

[47] ʿAbd al-Raḥmān, *Mawqif*, pp. 303–305.

drawn from the verse, the ʿAdī b. Ḥātim *ḥadīth*, and the exegetes, of which the first is the most relevant to our inquiry – namely, that no one but Allāh has the right to legislate.

On this topic, ʿAbd al-Raḥmān writes that the verse and the *ḥadīth* make clear that "worship is obedience to laws" (*inna al-ʿibāda hiya al-ittibāʿ fī al-sharāʾiʿ*). Since the Jews and Christians did not believe in the divinity of their rabbis and priests in the dogmatic sense, nor worship them in the ritual sense, it follows that this particular verse deemed them polytheists and unbelievers "solely because they received from them [the rabbis and priests] laws which they obeyed and followed." The general principle is that "polytheism (*al-shirk billāh*) occurs in the sole granting of the right to legislate to one other than Allāh from among His servants," even when unaccompanied by polytheism in creed or ritual.[48]

This threefold categorization of polytheism as occurring in either creed, ritual, or legislation is redolent of Sayyid Quṭb. ʿAbd al-Raḥmān was clearly familiar with the salafī condemnation of *taqlīd* as polytheism, as evident for example from his quotation from Ṣiddīq Ḥasan Khān, but he had also studied Quṭb's writings.[49] Indeed, ʿAbd al-Raḥmān promptly restates his point on human legislation in Quṭbist terms (in discussion of Qurʾān 10:59–60) as follows: "prohibiting and permitting are legislation, legislation is *ḥākimiyya*, and *ḥākimiyya* is Lordship (*rubūbiyya*)."[50] He obviously felt that the salafī and Quṭbist developments of the legislation-as-polytheism equation were fully congruent one with the other.

ʿAbd al-Raḥmān expounds on this principle at some length and insists that the Qurʾān's condemnation of the scriptuaries and others from the *jāhiliyya* applies to those today who "call themselves Muslims" but who take matters of prohibition and permission into their own hands, since they view religion as pertaining solely to creed and ritual worship. He describes this undue restriction of Islam to the theological and ritual realms, to the exclusion of the legal realm, as

> the most dangerous thing that this religion is suffering in this period in history, and the most fatal of weapons with which its enemies war against it – those who eagerly affix the sign 'Islam' over situations and over people the likes of whom

[48] ʿAbd al-Raḥmān, *Mawqif*, p. 305. In the published edition the full sentence reads: *inna al-shirka billāh yataḥaqqaqu bi-mujarrad iʿṭāʾ ḥaqq al-tashrīʿ li-ghayri llāh min ʿibādihi wa-law yaṣḥabuhu shirk fī al-iʿtiqād bi-ulūhiyyatihi wa-lā taqdīm al-shaʿāʾir al-taʿabbudiyya lahu*. There is obviously a negation missing after *wa-law*, as is clear from ʿAbd al-Raḥmān's argument throughout and from the parallel with the subsequent *wa-lā*.

[49] ʿUmar ʿAbd al-Raḥmān, *Kalimat ḥaqq – murāfaʿat al-shaykh ʿUmar ʿAbd al-Raḥmān fī qaḍiyyat al-jihād*, n.d., p. 8, www.ilmway.com/site/maqdis/MS_384 (link no longer active).

[50] ʿAbd al-Raḥmān, *Mawqif*, p. 305.

Allāh the Exalted determines are polytheists who do not follow the true religion and who take lords in place of Allāh.

Pursuant to this description, ʿAbd al-Raḥmān, in a statement which in retrospect sounds like a premonition of the careers of many a salafī jihādī scholar, writes:

> If the enemies of this religion are eager to affix the sign 'Islam'[51] over those situations and people, then the obligation of the protectors of this religion is to strip away these deceiving signs and unveil what is under them, namely, polytheism, unbelief, and the taking of lords in place of Allāh; and [their obligation is] to explain to people the foundation on which the pillar of Islam's political vision is based: that all the authorities of command and legislation be stripped away from humans, as individuals and as collectives, and that no one – not even a prophet – can command or forbid without authority from Allāh.[52]

In summary, ʿUmar ʿAbd al-Raḥmān, who would go on to become an influential radical scholar, already promoted a salafized version of Quṭb's *ḥākimiyya* doctrine as early as 1971. Ḥasan al-Huḍaybī, in his polemic against the prison radicals, likewise depicted them as connecting between modern theonomy and the premodern salafī polemic against *taqlīd*. Al-Huḍaybī's own arguments against the radicals' claims, and against central portions of Mawdūdī and Quṭb's *ḥākimiyya* doctrine, were premised on a privileging of belief and intention over acts and obedience, which amounted to a severe attenuation, bordering on rejection, of both monolatry and theonomy as we have defined them throughout this study. In all these facts we can discern the germ of a major transformation: Modern theonomy was to flourish outside of, or at most on the margins of, the institutional Muslim Brotherhood. It was the salafī milieu that provided fertile ground for its subsequent development, and it would be propounded in an increasingly salafized form.

## Fusionist Salafī Theonomy

As important as developments in Egypt were, the true locus of Quṭb-salafī fusion over the course of the 1970s and 1980s was Saudi Arabia and the Gulf states (especially Kuwait), in the movement known locally as the Ṣaḥwa ("awakening"). The history of this movement has been

[51] *Lāfitat al-islām*. The language is Quṭbist: cf. e.g. Quṭb, *Maʿālim*, p. 93: *inna al-islāma lā yanẓuru ilā al-ʿunwānāt wa-l-lāfitāt wa-l-shārāt*; p. 96: *wa-l-dīn lā yuwājihu al-wāqiʿ ayyan kāna li-yuqirrahu wa-yabḥatha lahu ʿan sanad minhu wa-ʿan ḥukm sharʿī yuʿalliquhu ʿalayhi ka-l-lāfita al-mustaʿāra*.

[52] ʿAbd al-Raḥmān, *Mawqif*, pp. 306–307.

treated in depth by others[53] and will be summarized here only in its broadest outlines.

For reasons relating both to ideals of pan-Islamic unity and to intra-Arab rivalries, the Kingdom of Saudi Arabia welcomed Muslim Brothers fleeing state repression in other countries, primarily from Egypt and Syria. These Brotherhood émigrés played an important role in the development of a modern educational system in Saudi Arabia (both curricular and extracurricular), a task for which the traditional Wahhābī scholars were unprepared and which could not be entrusted to the more secular intelligentsia, who were liable to hold left-wing or Nasserist sympathies. Through Brotherhood-style organizational expansion native Saudis were recruited and a number of competing branches of the Ṣaḥwa emerged. Some were more 'Quṭbist' than others, but all of them, when compared to Brotherhood movements abroad, featured some degree of cross-fertilization with the local Wahhābī-salafī tradition. While relations between the Ṣaḥwa, the state, and the Wahhābī religious establishment were not at first especially antagonistic (at least not on the surface), the movement turned to open political agitation in the Gulf Crisis of 1990–1991 with the stationing of US troops in the Kingdom, and was then met with severe repression.

For our purposes the significant feature of the Ṣaḥwa was its role in promoting forms of Quṭb-salafī fusion, and in particular the salafization of theonomy. The phenomenon was by no means restricted to the Ṣaḥwa proper (which is why I use the term 'fusionist'); the interaction between these two currents took place throughout the Arabic-speaking world. Yet the institutional structure established by the Ṣaḥwa in the Gulf states meant that this region would play a leading role in the development. In Chapter 4 I noted parallels between the *ḥākimiyya* doctrine and classical salafī monolatry and theonomy, ones that paved the way for a further and more explicit salafization of the doctrine. In Saudi Arabia in particular, pressures of social conformity, especially in the university milieu, likewise encouraged this tendency, which is to be noted for example in the writings of the most famous of Brotherhood émigrés, Sayyid Quṭb's brother Muḥammad.[54]

[53] See especially Stéphane Lacroix, *Les islamistes saoudiens: une insurrection manquée*, Paris: Presses Universitaires de France, 2010.

[54] Stéphane Lacroix rightly notes the importance of the role Muḥammad Quṭb played, in his position at the university in Mecca eventually known as Umm al-Qurā, as interpreter of his brother's writings for the Saudi milieu. I am, however, unconvinced by his argument that Muḥammad Quṭb's early work, *Jāhiliyyat al-qarn al-ʿishrīn*, already featured an assimilation between Quṭbist and Wahhābī doctrine. The parallel in the passage cited by Lacroix, between *ʿaqīda* and the implemention of the *sharīʿa* and

### *ʿUmar Sulaymān al-Ashqar's* al-Sharīʿa al-ilāhiyya lā al-qawānīn al-jāhiliyya

A fine example of fusionist theonomy is ʿUmar Sulaymān al-Ashqar's *al-Sharīʿa al-ilāhiyya lā al-qawānīn al-jāhiliyya*, published in Kuwait in 1983.[55] Al-Ashqar was born in 1940 in the village of Barqa, near Nablus, in what was then mandatory Palestine. He moved with his family to Saudi Arabia in 1953, and after completing his secondary education and one year of university in Riyadh he enrolled in the newly established Islamic University of Medina. There he studied with major salafī scholars such as ʿAbd al-ʿAzīz b. Bāz and Muḥammad Nāṣir al-Dīn al-Albānī, and, according to the account of one of his long-time students, "took in the teachings of Muḥammad b. ʿAbd al-Wahhāb in a profound manner."[56] At the same time he took a deep interest in the Palestinian cause and identified to a large degree with the teachings of the Muslim Brotherhood, meeting with Brotherhood leaders when they visited Saudi Arabia, and in turn visiting their centers in Nablus and Amman during summer vacations.

In 1965 al-Ashqar and his close associate, the Egyptian ʿAbd al-Raḥmān ʿAbd al-Khāliq, left Saudi Arabia and settled in Kuwait, where both played a major role in the local fusionist salafī scene and in Islamist social and political activism. ʿAbd al-Khāliq, though the son of an Egyptian Muslim Brother, moved more in the salafī direction, while al-Ashqar remained closer to the Muslim Brotherhood. As a high school teacher al-Ashqar helped bring the Brotherhood style of extracurricular cultural-educational (*tarbiya*) activities to Kuwait[57] – among his student protégés was Khālid Mashʿal, later of the Palestinian Ḥamās movement – and in 1980 he took up a teaching position at Kuwait University. Over

*ḥākimiyya*, is one already present in Sayyid Quṭb's writings. Lacroix's choice to translate *ulūhiyya* as the French 'adoration' (worship) would of course be appropriate for a Wahhābī text, but Muḥammad Quṭb does not appear to be using the term in this technical sense, especially as it is directly followed by the description of Allāh as *al-khāliq al-mālik* (Creator and Master), which are *rubūbiyya* aspects in the Taymiyyan-Wahhābī system. Moreover, *Jāhiliyyat al-qarn al-ʿishrīn* was first published in 1964, well before Muḥammad Quṭb's arrival in Saudi Arabia in 1971. The example Lacroix draws from the later *Mafāhīm yanbaghī an tuṣaḥḥaḥa* appears more convincing. Lacroix, *Les islamistes saoudiens*, pp. 67–68; Muḥammad Quṭb, *Jāhiliyyat al-qarn al-ʿishrīn*, Cairo: Dār al-Shurūq, 1412/1992; for the dating of the latter: Sivan, *Radical Islam*, p. 27.

55 ʿUmar Sulaymān al-Ashqar, *al-Sharīʿa al-ilāhiyya lā al-qawānīn al-jāhiliyya*, 2nd ed., Kuwait: Dār al-Daʿwa, 1406/1986. The first edition was published in 1404/1983; the introduction is dated 2 Dhū al-Ḥijja 1403 / September 9, 1983.

56 Muḥsin Ṣāliḥ, "Qirāʾa fī al-dawr al-daʿwī wa-l-ḥarakī li-l-ʿallāma al-Ashqar," *al-Sabīl* (Jordan), August 22, 2012.

57 For a discussion on the growth of this phenomenon in Saudi Arabia, see Lacroix, *Les islamistes saoudiens*, pp. 61–64.

the course of the 1970s al-Ashqar had grown closer to the leadership of the Kuwaiti branch of the Muslim Brotherhood, which he officially joined toward the end of the decade. In the 1980s he likewise encouraged the founding of Ḥamās, a daughter movement of the Palestinian Muslim Brotherhood, and beginning in 1989 he served for a time as the head of its first Advisory Council (*majlis shūrā*). When in the wake of the First Gulf War the Palestinians were expelled from Kuwait, al-Ashqar moved to Jordan, where he lived until his death in 2012.[58]

The intersection in al-Ashqar's life between salafī influences and the Muslim Brotherhood tradition is well reflected in his *al-Sharīʿa al-ilāhiyya lā al-qawānīn al-jāhiliyya*. After an introductory section, the book consists of six parts: (1) a brief historical survey of different systems of man-made law (starting with Hammurabi); (2) a historical survey of the introduction of man-made law in Muslim lands, with a focus on the modern period; (3) a description of European ("Crusader") efforts to depose the *sharīʿa* as the legal system in force in Muslim countries; (4) a study of the modern Egyptian civil code; (5) a section discussing the Islamic view on the status of man-made law; and (6) a collection of passages from earlier Islamic scholars – all of them salafī, both premodern and modern – on the issue of man-made law.

Here we will focus primarily on the final two sections of the book, which are the most relevant to our topic, though certain aspects of the earlier sections are also of some interest – especially those that help to situate the treatise more precisely on the fusionist spectrum. Al-Ashqar's own fusionism aside, however, the treatise provided a model for later salafī writings in two major respects: the application of a salafī-based legal-theological critique to detailed analysis of man-made legal systems (for example, the Sanhūrī Code in Egypt), and the collection of theonomic precedents from earlier salafī authors. This latter feature of the treatise in effect presents an alternative lineage for theonomy to the Mawdūdī-Quṭb line, recasting it as an inherently salafī doctrine.

Al-Ashqar does not present the writing of *al-Sharīʿa al-ilāhiyya* as a response to any specific political development, but the book's dedication may relate to the Islamist uprising in Syria against the Baʿth regime in the early 1980s:

> To those who have been true to what they promised Allāh – some of them have fulfilled their vow [i.e. have been martyred], and some are still waiting, and have not changed in the least [cf. Qurʾān 33:23]; to those who do not lose heart at what afflicts them [when fighting] for the sake of Allāh [cf. Qurʾān 3:146]; to those who

58 Ṣāliḥ, "Qirāʾa."

have known the path, seen clearly, and waged jihād to raise up Allāh's word, to spread the religion of Allāh, and to implement Allāh's law, I dedicate my book.[59]

There is no specific mention here of the situation in Syria, and any number of conflicts were ongoing when these words were written in 1983: the anti-Soviet jihād in Afghanistan, the war in Lebanon, the Iran–Iraq War. But at this point in time Arab mobilization for the Afghan cause was only beginning, and it was the uprising in Syria that held the attention of Muslim Brothers and other Islamists, especially those with origins in the Levant. (We will return to this context in more detail in our discussion of another contemporary treatise, ʿAbd al-Nāṣir Jawda's *al-Ḥukm bi-mā anzala llāhu wa-takfīr al-mushrik*, which was authored in the context of the Syrian uprising.)

The portion of *al-Sharīʿa al-ilāhiyya* relevant for our purposes begins in the second chapter, in which al-Ashqar surveys the history of man-made law in Muslim lands. As noted, his focus is on the modern period: It is al-Ashqar's basic contention that the wholesale replacement of the *sharīʿa* with man-made law is a uniquely modern phenomenon that is unprecedented in the history of Islam, to be differentiated from more minor deviations in the past on the part of the Muslims, or short-lived episodes of foreign conquest in which the "enemies of Islam" tried to implement infidel law.[60] He does criticize the evolution of a *siyāsa* jurisdiction in Islam, starting with the ʿAbbāsids and progressively developing into a kind of parallel law system to the *sharīʿa* (see Chapter 4). The few pages devoted to this issue consist for the most part of citation of relevant passages from Ibn Taymiyya, with emphasis on the idea that it was the rulers' failure to fully implement the *sharīʿa* in the first place that then forced them to seek solutions outside its provisions.[61] Nonetheless, al-Ashqar writes that whether these rulers employed *siyāsa* out of ignorance or out of wayward or heretical inclinations (*hawā*), they never attempted to depose the *sharīʿa* and replace it with another system. In contrast, he argues that the Mongols' *yāsaq* was indeed similar to modern man-made law, but that its use was restricted to the ruling classes and did not persist after the Mongols' assimilation into Islamic society. Here too, the upshot of the argument is that the modern adoption of man-made law in the Islamic world is an unprecedented development.[62]

[59] al-Ashqar, *al-Sharīʿa al-ilāhiyya*, p. 5.
[60] al-Ashqar, *al-Sharīʿa al-ilāhiyya*, p. 57.
[61] al-Ashqar, *al-Sharīʿa al-ilāhiyya*, pp. 57–59.
[62] al-Ashqar, *al-Sharīʿa al-ilāhiyya*, pp. 62–63. The argument is adopted from the Egyptian salafī Aḥmad Shākir, in his comments on his abridgment of Ibn Kathīr's *tafsīr*; this same work is cited at length in chapter 6 of *al-Sharīʿa al-ilāhiyya*.

This is a standard argument in later salafī theonomic writings as well, so a few words are in order as to its importance. The argument is implicitly directed at two different kinds of opponents: ultra-radicals who backdate the decisive deviation from true Islam to a very early stage in Islamic history; and moderates who claim that this deviation never took place, and that the forms of legislation adopted in the modern era are both proper and consonant with Islamic precedent. The roots of the first tendency we saw already in Mawdūdī, who had argued that the true meaning of the *shahāda*, and thus of Islam, was theonomy, and therefore claimed that even Ibn Taymiyya, who had interpreted it as a statement of monolatry, did not get it quite right. Related to this criticism was his faulting of Ibn Taymiyya for failing to lead a revolutionary political movement to reestablish rule by the *sharīʿa*, as Mawdūdī viewed the Mamlūks' deviations from *sharīʿa* rule as hardly less egregious than those of the Mongols. This kind of ultra-radicalism, found in embryo in Mawdūdī's thought, reached full expression among some of the prison radicals in the early post-Quṭb era and especially in Shukrī Muṣṭafā's Jamāʿat al-Muslimīn, who argued that Islamic rule, and thus Islam itself, had basically ceased to exist after the period of the Rightly Guided Caliphs.

As for the moderates, they also trace an analogy between the nature of modern legislation and rule in Islamic countries and that of the premodern period, but to an opposite end. A similar analogy is likewise employed by some academic scholars in order to brand the radicals' *takfīr* of modern governments as unfounded and a distortion of Ibn Taymiyya's teachings: If the Mamlūks' deviation from rule by the *sharīʿa* was similar to that of modern governments, then the proper attitude toward modern governments would be the same one adopted by Ibn Taymiyya toward the Mamlūks – loyalty rather than revolt.[63]

Al-Ashqar's detailed treatment of the modern legal history of the Islamic world should be viewed through the prism of this overarching argument and as a means of substantiating it. He describes at some length the introduction of foreign-inspired law codes, starting with the Ottoman Penal Code of 1840[64] and then surveying further developments in the Ottoman Empire, Egypt, Iraq, Lebanon, Syria, Jordan, and even

[63] Yayha Michot, *Ibn Taymiyya against Extremisms*, p. xxvi: "It is shocking that such a 'Mongolization' of Sadat and other Muslim rulers could be conceived as faithful to the thought of the Damascene Shaykh al-Islam [Ibn Taymiyya]. He himself indeed remained always loyal vis-à-vis his own sultan, the Mamlūk al-Nāṣir Muḥammad – even though the latter was, in respect of the Sharīʿa, not much stricter than a Mongol of that time or a modern Arab-Muslim ruler."

[64] al-Ashqar, *al-Sharīʿa al-ilāhiyya*, p. 64.

India and Pakistan.[65] His most detailed treatment is reserved for the Sanhūrī Code in Egypt, which was introduced shortly before the Free Officers' revolt as a replacement for the French-derived law in place until that time, and which subsequently served as a model for modern law codes in other Arab countries. While the laws of the Sanhūrī Code were culled from diverse sources, most of them foreign, its eponymous chief author, ʿAbd al-Razzāq al-Sanhūrī, always argued that the resulting code was authentically Egyptian, and that it did not contradict the *sharīʿa.*

Regarding the philosophical basis for this code, al-Ashqar takes issue with two claims advanced by ʿAbd al-Razzāq al-Sanhūrī and other modernists. The first is the idea that, after the death of the Prophet, Allāh delegated powers of legislation to the *umma* (the Islamic nation) through the mechanism of *ijmāʿ* (consensus); al-Ashqar views this modernist interpretation of the nature of *ijmāʿ* as a blatant affront to the exclusivity of Allāh's legislative sovereignty.[66] Against similar claims enounced in a more explicitly democratic formulation, he employs the argument from cosmic-objective divinity to normative authority that was central to Mawdūdī and Quṭb's *ḥākimiyya*: "This land on which we live is part of Allāh's dominion in His wide cosmos, and the people who walk it are His creation. He is their *rabb*, their *ilāh*, and their Master, and it is His right to legislate for them, for they are but His servants and slaves."[67]

The other general claim to which al-Ashqar objects is the idea that man-made law codes of foreign inspiration or derivation are, or can be, consonant with the *sharīʿa*. Al-Sanhūrī said of his own code that the judges, when applying it, will find one of two things: either that its provisions do not contradict the principles of the *sharīʿa*, or that they are themselves the provisions of the *sharīʿa.*[68] Al-Ashqar notes that this view is not new: He describes how an al-Azhar committee appointed by Khedive Ismāʿīl Pasha had likewise claimed that the Napoleonic Code was consonant with the Mālikī school of jurisprudence.[69] (Al-Ashqar attributes this judgment more to political servility than to anything else, and does not himself delve into jurisprudential issues such as the proper application of *maṣlaḥa* on which claims such as these depend.)

In other words, al-Ashqar opposes any claim that humans have a right to legislate for themselves, or that the results of this legislation might be consonant with Allāh's *sharīʿa*. As an example of someone who rightly insisted on these matters of first principle, al-Ashqar cites none other

65 al-Ashqar, *al-Sharīʿa al-ilāhiyya*, pp. 64–77.
66 al-Ashqar, *al-Sharīʿa al-ilāhiyya*, p. 111.
67 al-Ashqar, *al-Sharīʿa al-ilāhiyya*, pp. 164–165.
68 al-Ashqar, *al-Sharīʿa al-ilāhiyya*, p. 112.
69 al-Ashqar, *al-Sharīʿa al-ilāhiyya*, p. 111.

than the late Supreme Guide of the Muslim Brotherhood, Ḥasan al-Huḍaybī. When al-Huḍaybī was summoned to present his comments on the proposed Sanhūrī Code before the Preparatory Commission, he repeatedly refused to discuss any particulars, and instead insisted on a single principle to which he already knew the Commission would not agree – namely, that all laws must be derived from the Qurʾān and the *ḥadīth*. According to al-Huḍaybī, since the Sanhūrī Code does not operate on this principle, what happens to be right or wrong in it is a matter of complete indifference.[70] Expressing this same principle in his own voice, al-Ashqar writes: "There may be, among the man-made laws, one that is better than another, but a sincere Muslim rejects them all, because they are an attack on Allāh's *ulūhiyya* and His rule."[71] The reference to al-Huḍaybī is not surprising: Al-Ashqar had always been close to the Muslim Brotherhood, and by this time had officially joined the organization in Kuwait. It is nonetheless telling that he continues to view al-Huḍaybī as a hero in the fight against man-made law several years after the official publication of *Duʿāt lā quḍāt*; this suggests that there were limits to how far even a relative radical such as al-Ashqar could go within the orbit of the Muslim Brotherhood of the 1980s (a topic to which I will return presently).

If the reference to al-Huḍaybī attests to al-Ashqar's Brotherhood affiliation, it is the final two sections of *al-Sharīʿa al-ilāhiyya* – on the Islamic view on the status of man-made law, and a collection of passages from earlier scholars on the topic – that show the extent of salafī influence on him.

At the opening of the penultimate section of the work, al-Ashqar addresses the issue of apostasy, writing that many have argued, based on a tradition attributed to the Companion Ibn ʿAbbās, that the unbelief mentioned in Qurʾānic verses such as 5:44, "Those who do not rule by what Allāh revealed, they are the unbelievers," is not true unbelief, but only "lesser unbelief" – that is, it is sin, but not apostasy.[72] Al-Huḍaybī would not be much help in countering this argument, cautious as he was on the topic of *takfīr*; instead, al-Ashqar turns to a brief but influential treatise by the former *muftī* of Saudi Arabia, Muḥammad b. Ibrāhīm Āl al-Shaykh (d. 1969), titled *Risālat taḥkīm al-qawānīn*.[73] This treatise,

[70] al-Ashqar, *al-Sharīʿa al-ilāhiyya*, pp. 138–139.
[71] al-Ashqar, *al-Sharīʿa al-ilāhiyya*, p. 146.
[72] al-Ashqar, *al-Sharīʿa al-ilāhiyya*, p. 175. For an extended discussion of this issue in debates between salafī jihādīs and Muḥammad Nāṣir al-Dīn al-Albānī, see Lav, *Radical Islam*, pp. 151–158.
[73] al-Ashqar, *al-Sharīʿa al-ilāhiyya*, pp. 175–179. For the context of this treatise, see Mouline, *Clerics of Islam*, pp. 143–145.

something of an urtext of modern salafī theonomy, was popular with Ṣaḥwa authors[74] – what better proof could there be that Quṭb's issue of *ḥākimiyya* was an authentic salafī concern than a treatise by the esteemed former *muftī* of Saudi Arabia, a descendant of Muḥammad b. ʿAbd al-Wahhāb and guardian of the Wahhābī legacy? Here we will not examine the technical aspects of Muḥammad b. Ibrāhīm's discussion of the Ibn ʿAbbās tradition; the very fact that al-Ashqar relied on it exemplifies how theonomy was constructed in the fusionist milieu. For the most part *Taḥkīm al-qawānīn* does not connect the issue of theonomy to Taymiyyan theology as explicitly as some other salafī texts do, but there is just a hint of the monolatric basis: When Muḥammad b. Ibrāhīm decries the establishment of non-*sharʿī* courts as apostasy and as a nullifier of the *shahāda*, he writes that just as one must worship only Allāh, who created humans for that very purpose, so one must submit solely to His judgment, and not to the judgment of created beings.[75]

The rest of the penultimate section continues in the vein of salafī grounding for a more uncompromising theonomy than al-Huḍaybī was willing to support. After citing Muḥammad b. Ibrāhīm, al-Ashqar writes that it is clear from the preceding that two categories of people fall into unbelief: those who legislate laws other than what Allāh revealed, and those who obey them. Regarding legislators, he mentions Qurʾān 9:31 (among other verses), and it is clear from his comments that he understands it in light of the ʿAdī b. Ḥātim tradition.[76] He follows this with supporting quotes from Ibn Taymiyya and from the twentieth-century Egyptian salafī Aḥmad Muḥammad Shākir,[77] who together with his brother Maḥmūd Muḥammad Shākir and alongside Muḥammad b. Ibrāhīm is an oft-cited precedent for salafī theonomy.[78] Regarding obedience to man-made law, al-Ashqar cites a passage from Ibn Taymiyya in condemnation of *taqlīd*, with an allusion to Qurʾān 9:31, in which he states that when this is done in the knowledge that the ruling

[74] Muḥammad Quṭb's student Safar al-Ḥawālī, for example, delivered lectures on *Risālat taḥkīm al-qawānīn*, later published in print as Safar b. ʿAbd al-Raḥmān al-Ḥawālī, *Sharḥ taḥkīm al-qawānīn*, Jedda: Maktabat Dār al-Ṣaḥāba, n.d. The original audio is available at https://audio.islamweb.net/audio/index.php?page=audioinfo&audioid=3040.

[75] al-Ashqar, *al-Sharīʿa al-ilāhiyya*, p. 178.

[76] al-Ashqar, *al-Sharīʿa al-ilāhiyya*, pp. 179–180.

[77] al-Ashqar, *al-Sharīʿa al-ilāhiyya*, pp. 180–182.

[78] See, for example, his comments on man-made law apropos Ibn Kathīr's condemnation of Mongol *yāsā* in his commentary on Qurʾān 5:50: Aḥmad Shākir, *ʿUmdat al-tafsīr ʿan al-ḥāfiẓ Ibn Kathīr*, 2nd ed., al-Manṣūra: Dār al-Wafāʾ, 1426/2005, vol. 1, pp. 696–697, n. 1; cf. Maḥmūd Muḥammad Shākir's marginalia on al-Ṭabarī's commentary on Qurʾān 5:44: al-Ṭabarī, *Jāmiʿ al-bayān*, vol. 10, pp. 348–349.

contravenes what Allāh revealed, it is an act of apostasy.[79] In conclusion, al-Ashqar writes that in no way can one say of these two categories of people that their *kufr* is short of apostasy. The kind of not ruling by what Allāh revealed that is not apostasy is the kind that is short of *tabdīl* (replacement of Allāh's laws with something else), such as straying on a particular ruling due to error or greed;[80] but this is not the case today, when modern legislation has replaced the *sharīʿa* as the law in Muslim countries.[81]

The final section of al-Ashqar's treatise presents quotations from Muslim scholars on the topic of theonomy. Here too we see al-Ashqar's attempt to provide a non-Quṭbist salafī lineage for theonomy in his choice of authorities: Ibn Taymiyya, Ibn Qayyim al-Jawziyya, Ibn Kathīr, ʿAbd al-Raḥmān b. Ḥasan (Muḥammad b. ʿAbd al-Wahhāb's grandson and the author of a standard commentary on *Kitāb al-tawḥīd*), Aḥmad Shākir, Muḥammad b. Ibrāhīm, the Mauritanian-born Wahhābī exegete Muḥammad al-Amīn al-Shinqīṭī, the leading scholar of the Saudi religious establishment (and future Grand Muftī) ʿAbd al-ʿAzīz b. Bāz, and the head of the *sharīʿa* courts in Qatar, ʿAbdallāh b. Zayd Āl Maḥmūd.[82]

It is worth considering the longest of these quotations, the one drawn from ʿAbd al-ʿAzīz b. Bāz's treatise *Wujūb taḥkīm sharʿ Allāh wa-nabdh mā khālafahu*. Even before his appointment as Grand Muftī of the Kingdom Ibn Bāz had been the central figure in the Saudi religious establishment, and as noted earlier al-Ashqar had studied with him at the University of Medina. The brief treatise addresses the obligation to apply the *sharīʿa* to two audiences: Bedouins who apply customary law, and those involved in the application of modern man-made law, from legal experts to governments.[83] The quotation from Ibn Bāz's treatise gives the clearest embedding of theonomy in salafī monolatry in all of al-Ashqar's book. Ibn Bāz describes worship as the telos of creation, explains the meaning of *ʿibāda*, and states that it mandates complete obedience to Allāh in His command and prohibition, in belief (*iʿtiqād*), in word, and in deed. One who submits to Allāh in some facets of life, but submits to created beings in others, cannot be said to worship Allāh.[84] Although there is no mention here of the *rubūbiyya*/*ulūhiyya* paradigm,

[79] al-Ashqar, *al-Sharīʿa al-ilāhiyya*, p. 183.
[80] al-Ashqar, *al-Sharīʿa al-ilāhiyya*, p. 184.
[81] al-Ashqar, *al-Sharīʿa al-ilāhiyya*, p. 189.
[82] al-Ashqar, *al-Sharīʿa al-ilāhiyya*, pp. 193–228.
[83] al-Ashqar, *al-Sharīʿa al-ilāhiyya*, pp. 217, 225. Ibn Bāz's treatise is available online at www.binbaz.org.sa/article/578.
[84] al-Ashqar, *al-Sharīʿa al-ilāhiyya*, p. 217.

the salafī-Wahhābī emphasis on exclusivity of worship is clear, and is here applied to exclusivity of legal obedience.

Ibn Bāz goes on to write that *ʿubūdiyya* to Allāh alone and referral to Him in judgment are among the meanings included in the *shahāda*;[85] for the point that legal obedience is worship just as are rites such as sacrifice and prostration, Ibn Bāz naturally cites Qurʾān 9:31 and the ʿAdī b. Ḥātim *ḥadīth*.[86] On this basis, he concludes: "Without faith is he who believes that humans' laws (*aḥkām*) and opinions are better than the law of Allāh and His Prophet, or equal or similar [in status] to it, or abandons it and puts in its place man-made laws and human systems, even if he believes that Allāh's laws are better, more perfect, and more just."[87]

*Instrumental Compromises: al-Ashqar's* Ḥukm al-mushāraka fī al-wizāra wa-l-majālis al-niyābiyya: In summary, ʿUmar Sulaymān al-Ashqar's treatise is a truly fusionist work, one that exemplifies a milieu in the early 1980s in which, in one and the same work, Ḥasan al-Huḍaybī easily rubbed shoulders with Ibn Bāz's appeal to the salafī monolatric tradition and Ibn Taymiyya's condemnation of *taqlīd*, all in condemnation of modern man-made law. The limits of such fusionism are apparent in a later work by al-Ashqar in which the pragmatic approach of the Muslim Brotherhood tempers even such ardent theonomy as al-Ashqar's. In his *Ḥukm al-mushāraka fī al-wizāra wa-l-majālis al-niyābiyya*, al-Ashqar argues that it is permitted to hold a ministerial post and to serve in parliament in countries ruled by man-made law. While this treatise was not published until some time after his move to Jordan, it reflects his thinking in the late 1980s, as it was based on the conclusions of a study group in which he participated in Kuwait before the Gulf Crisis;[88] in other words, this view on the permissibility of participation in ministries and parliaments is at most a few years removed from the writing of *al-Sharīʿa al-ilāhiyya*.

Al-Ashqar frames the question in pragmatic terms: In modern times, it is impossible to attain power and establish the Islamic state in the same fashion as the Prophet did, and the possibilities open to Islamic movements are limited to democratic means, military putsch, or armed popular revolution. He rules out the latter two, stating that the Islamic movements that opted for them paid a high price and after much

85 al-Ashqar, *al-Sharīʿa al-ilāhiyya*, p. 218.
86 al-Ashqar, *al-Sharīʿa al-ilāhiyya*, p. 219.
87 al-Ashqar, *al-Sharīʿa al-ilāhiyya*, p. 225.
88 ʿUmar Sulaymān al-Ashqar, *Ḥukm al-mushāraka fī al-wizāra wa-l-majālis al-niyābiyya*, 2nd ed., Amman: Dār al-Nafāʾis, 1429/2009, pp. 11–12.

suffering learned that their actions had been precipitous.[89] If my hypothesis was right that the principal context for the earlier treatise *al-Sharīʿa al-ilāhiyya* was the Islamist revolt in Syria, the fate of this failed revolt – and perhaps other such failures, such as those of the armed Islamist groups in Egypt – may go far in explaining why al-Ashqar turned in a relatively short period from vigorous condemnation of regimes of unbelief to permitting participation in them. He was no longer willing to dedicate books to those awaiting martyrdom and who "have not changed in the least" if their martyrdom led to nothing but decimation of the Islamist movement.

We will have more to say on the Syrian context in what follows. At present let us briefly survey the key points of *Ḥukm al-mushāraka*, limiting our interest to the question of parliamentary participation. The argument is basically two-pronged: Al-Ashqar argues that mere participation in parliament, without enacting man-made law, is not in itself apostasy;[90] the question then becomes one of weighing benefits (*maṣāliḥ*) versus detriments (*mafāsid*), and if the benefits are preponderant then participation is permitted.[91] Al-Ashqar claims that these benefits are in fact preponderant. In classic Brotherhood fashion he cites Ḥasan al-Bannā's argument that membership in parliament can serve as a powerful platform for spreading the *daʿwa*;[92] in addition, far from being participation in forbidden legislation, membership in parliament makes it possible to oppose such legislation and to propose the annulment of existing laws that contravene the *sharīʿa*.[93] As for why it is not apostasy, al-Ashqar basically argues that as long as one's intention in gaining membership in parliament is for the preceding reasons, there is simply no basis to claim that it impugns one's faith.[94] In response to a hypothetical objector who invokes the authority of Mawdūdī and Quṭb as opponents of parliamentary participation, al-Ashqar claims that there is no evidence that either of them considered membership itself in parliament (as opposed to legislation of man-made laws) to be apostasy, and he rightly notes that Mawdūdī himself came around to the view that one should participate in elections.[95] He is dismissive of arguments that membership necessarily entails implicit support for or adherence to the polytheistic functions of the parliament. For example, he argues regarding the oath of allegiance to the constitution demanded of MPs – which some argue forces them to

[89] al-Ashqar, *Ḥukm al-mushāraka*, pp. 23–25.
[90] al-Ashqar, *Ḥukm al-mushāraka*, pp. 125ff.
[91] al-Ashqar, *Ḥukm al-mushāraka*, pp. 118ff.
[92] al-Ashqar, *Ḥukm al-mushāraka*, pp. 119–120.
[93] al-Ashqar, *Ḥukm al-mushāraka*, p. 123.
[94] al-Ashqar, *Ḥukm al-mushāraka*, p. 125.
[95] al-Ashqar, *Ḥukm al-mushāraka*, pp. 127–128, 131.

endorse parliament's role as the ultimate arbiter of legislation – that one can simply add a statement to the oath that removes this difficulty[96] (presumably a statement that conditions the MP's obedience on accord with the *sharī'a* or the like).

In other words, al-Ashqar seeks to draw a clear distinction between the issue of man-made legislation, on the one hand, and participation in democratic institutions, on the other. By this view, there is no inconsistency between the strident theonomy of his *al-Sharī'a al-ilāhiyya* and the pragmatism of his *Ḥukm al-mushāraka*. Without speaking ill of Mawdūdī or Quṭb, he follows in this the classic approach of Ḥasan al-Bannā as well as later figures from the Muslim Brotherhood's moderate wing such as Sālim al-Bahnasāwī.[97] In addition to this Brotherhood tradition, al-Ashqar cites other authorities who permit membership in parliament, including a fatwā dating from 1989 by none other than 'Abd al-'Azīz b. Bāz[98] – the same authority who had provided the most explicitly theological opposition to man-made law of all those cited in *al-Sharī'a al-ilāhiyya*. We will return to the content of Ibn Bāz's fatwā later in this chapter when we consider a detailed salafī jihādī critique of it. For now, the important point to note is that this general drift toward acknowledging and embracing the benefits of democratic participation, and separating between the core issue of theonomy and questions relating to its application, was not limited to fusionists with a Muslim Brotherhood background. Just as Ibn Bāz could provide support for the equation of man-made law with polytheism, he could also be called on to permit standing for election and parliamentary activity.

### *From Fusionism to* Takfīr *of the Muslim Brotherhood: The Syrian Fighting Vanguard and 'Abd al-Nāṣir Jawda's* al-Ḥukm bi-mā anzala llāhu wa-takfīr al-mushrik

If part of al-Ashqar's reason for embracing this pragmatic outlook was the defeat of the Islamist revolt in Syria, a contemporaneous treatise, titled *al-Ḥukm bi-mā anzala llāhu wa-takfīr al-mushrik*, drew quite a different conclusion. It was written toward the end of the revolt, circa 1983, by a certain 'Abd al-Nāṣir Jawda. The author is not known to me apart from this work, but he was almost certainly affiliated with the Syrian jihadist organization known as the Fighting Vanguard (al-Ṭalī'a

96 al-Ashqar, *Ḥukm al-mushāraka*, p. 132.
97 al-Ashqar, *Ḥukm al-mushāraka*, p. 128.
98 al-Ashqar, *Ḥukm al-mushāraka*, pp. 136ff. This portion of al-Ashqar's treatise was added for the second edition.

al-Muqātila), as the book includes an introduction by this organization's commander, ʿAdnān ʿUqla.[99]

The Fighting Vanguard was a small radical organization that existed on the margins of the Syrian Muslim Brotherhood and maintained an ambiguous relationship with it. The Vanguard was founded by Marwān Ḥadīd, whose radicalism was clearly of the Quṭbist variety. Ḥadīd had met Quṭb while studying in Cairo in the early 1960s,[100] and upon his return to Syria worked toward the goal of armed confrontation with the Baʿth regime. His actions were not viewed favorably by the senior leadership of the Syrian Brotherhood, both because of their own historical commitment to nonviolence and because it was the Brotherhood that bore the brunt of the regime's retaliation for Ḥadīd's actions.[101] After receiving military training in Jordan (reportedly at a camp established by ʿAbdallāh ʿAzzām),[102] Ḥadīd launched the Fighting Vanguard in the 1970s as an organized jihadist faction. He was arrested in 1975 and died in jail soon thereafter.[103] By 1979 effective leadership of the Vanguard had passed into the hands of its final commander, ʿAdnān ʿUqla.

Marwān Ḥadīd had long favored a strategy of dragging the Muslim Brotherhood into confrontation with the regime through his actions;[104] it was ʿUqla who successfully implemented this strategy, in particular through his massacre of eighty-three ʿAlawī cadets at the Aleppo Artillery School in 1979. The harsh measures adopted by the regime against the Muslim Brotherhood in response finally drove the organization into endorsing an armed jihād[105] and soon after forming a joint command with the Fighting Vanguard.[106] What followed were three years of fighting between various Islamist forces and the Baʿthist regime, culminating in the bombardment of the Islamist stronghold of Hama in February 1982; this bombardment killed tens of thousands and definitively crushed the first attempt by Sunni Islamists to take control of the country through a popular uprising. The fighting had also brought to the

[99] The precise dating of the treatise may not be certain. In the internet version released in February 2012 by the Denmark-based al-Nūr li-l-Iʿlām al-Islāmī, ʿUqla's introduction is signed with the date 23 Jumāda II 1403 / April 7, 1983: ʿAbd al-Nāṣir Jawda, *al-Ḥukm bi-mā anzala llāhu wa-takfīr al-mushrik*, Frederiksberg, Denmark: al-Nūr li-l-Iʿlām al-Islāmī, 1433/2012, www.mediafire.com/?cwt2t6zretccqah (link no longer active), p. 15. According to a recent study of the Islamist revolt in Syria, however, ʿUqla was captured in late 1982: Raphaël Lefèvre, *Ashes of Hama: The Muslim Brotherhood in Syria*, Oxford: Oxford University Press, 2013, p. 140. I do not know how to resolve this apparent discrepancy.

[100] Lefèvre, *Ashes of Hama*, p. 98.

[101] Lefèvre, *Ashes of Hama*, p. 101.

[102] Lefèvre, *Ashes of Hama*, p. 141.

[103] Lefèvre, *Ashes of Hama*, p. 102.

[104] ʿUmar ʿAbd al-Ḥakīm [= Abū Muṣʿab al-Sūrī], *al-Thawra al-islāmiyya al-jihādiyya fī sūriyā*, n.p., n.d., vol. 1, p. 73.

[105] Lefèvre, *Ashes of Hama*, pp. 104, 109–110.

[106] See Lefèvre, *Ashes of Hama*, p. 117.

fore fissures within the Islamist movement, ones that divided even those who agreed on the use of force against the regime. It is these divergences that form the context in which ʿAbd al-Nāṣir Jawda's *al-Ḥukm bi-mā anzala llāhu* was authored.

ʿAdnān ʿUqla's introduction to the treatise specifies that it was written in response to the Syrian Muslim Brotherhood's formation of an anti-regime coalition with secular opposition parties. This coalition, known as the National Alliance for the Liberation of Syria (*al-taḥāluf al-waṭanī li-taḥrīr sūriyā*), was formed in March 1982 in the wake of the Hama massacre with the aim of establishing a democratic regime in Syria.[107] The dissemination of Jawda's treatise appears to have been part of a restructuring effort conducted by ʿAdnān ʿUqla in response to these developments. Among the measures he introduced was the establishment of a committee on creed in order to clarify the Fighting Vanguard's doctrine,[108] and it is highly probable that Jawda's treatise was part of this effort.

Despite the fact that the Islamist revolt in Syria had failed to topple the regime and had wrought destruction on the Islamist movement, ʿUqla saw in it a great benefit: It had led to a separation of the ranks, and had exposed the true face of the Syrian Muslim Brotherhood as hypocrites and enemies whose alliance with *jāhilī* groups merely aimed to establish another regime of unbelief in Syria in place of the current one.[109] ʿUqla's desire to clarify the jihadists' creed aimed to formalize this separation of the ranks, and Jawda's treatise *al-Ḥukm bi-mā anzala llāhu* was a clear step in this direction. More specifically, the treatise was probably authored in support of ʿUqla's declaration of *takfīr* against the leaders of the Syrian Brotherhood – a position that even Abū Muṣʿab al-Sūrī, the future al-Qāʿida strategist, noted with some consternation:

It should be mentioned that alongside these positive phenomena in the moves made by the [Fighting] Vanguard, a negative phenomenon became prominent, namely, their turn to extremism (*tashaddud*), in particular ʿAdnān ʿUqla and some [or: "one"] of his students ... ʿAdnān ʿUqla announced that he pronounced *takfīr* on those in the leadership of the Muslim Brotherhood and the Islamic Front who supported [the organizations' adherence to] the National Coalition (*al-taḥāluf al-waṭanī*) ... Despite the stand that some moderate [members of the Vanguard] took against this excessive tendency to proclaim *takfīr* on others, ʿAdnān [ʿUqla] continued to be convinced that this was right, and he had strong proofs in this matter that he repeated continuously; and a

[107] Jawda, *al-Ḥukm bi-mā anzala llāhu*, pp. 11, 13–14; on the National Alliance, see Lefèvre, *Ashes of Hama*, pp. 138–139.

[108] ʿAbd al-Ḥakīm, *al-Thawra al-islāmiyya*, vol. 1, p. 298.

[109] Jawda, *al-Ḥukm bi-mā anzala llāhu*, pp. 10–11.

number of members in the [Fighting] Vanguard followed his opinion on this matter.[110]

Thus while ʿAbd al-Nāṣir Jawda's treatise is not a well-known one, neither to scholars nor to later radicals, it is an important document that reflects – and perhaps itself expanded – the growing chasm between the Muslim Brotherhood and the jihadist factions. This was a development long in the making that crystallized at different times in different countries. In Syria the turning point was the 1982 Hama massacre.

While the Fighting Vanguard had been Quṭbist in outlook since its founding by Marwān Ḥadīd, Jawda's *al-Ḥukm bi-mā anzala llāhu* is basically salafī in nature, apart from a few features (to be discussed presently). It is lent a more 'fusionist' character by the context of its writing and by the additional material provided by ʿUqla, who, in addition to his introduction, bookmarked Jawda's treatise on both ends with extensive passages from Sayyid Quṭb. ʿUqla was clearly a dyed-in-the-wool Quṭbist: When he notes that it was he who added the passages at the beginning and end of the treatise, he refers to Quṭb as "the leader, the teacher, the imām, and the martyr,"[111] and his own idiom is replete with Quṭbist locutions such as "dissociation from the *jāhiliyya*" (*mufāṣalat al-jāhiliyya*)[112] and reference to *ḥākimiyya* as "the most singular characteristic of *ulūhiyya*" (*akhaṣṣ khaṣāʾiṣ al-ulūhiyya*).[113] In contrast, Jawda's treatise itself is very nearly salafī jihādī avant la lettre – which is why the prominent salafī jihādī author Abū Qatāda al-Filasṭīnī singles it out for praise, in an introduction to the internet edition, as one of the early works that set out the correct path.[114] Others have already noted the major differences between the Fighting Vanguard and the Muslim Brotherhood on the issues of democracy and alliances with secular opposition factions, and have rightly identified the root of this divergence in the Vanguard's adherence to Quṭb's principle of *ḥākimiyya*.[115] It appears, however, that the strict interpretation of the principle, and the specific form in which it was applied – which now included *takfīr* of some of the leadership of the Muslim Brotherhood itself – were due to an increasingly salafī turn in the ranks of the Vanguard, a turn that is evident from the text of *al-Ḥukm bi-mā anzala llāhu wa-takfīr al-mushrik*.

110 ʿAbd al-Ḥakīm, *al-Thawra al-islāmiyya*, vol. 1, p. 299.

111 Jawda, *al-Ḥukm bi-mā anzala llāhu*, p. 14.

112 Jawda, *al-Ḥukm bi-mā anzala llāhu*, p. 14.

113 Jawda, *al-Ḥukm bi-mā anzala llāhu*, p. 12; cf. Quṭb, *Maʿālim*, p. 80 (*al-tashrīʿ … min khaṣāʾiṣ al-ulūhiyya*), p. 91 (ostensibly Muslim societies *tuʿṭī akhaṣṣ khaṣāʾiṣ al-ulūhiyya li-ghayri llāh fa-tadīnu bi-ḥākimiyyat ghayri llāh*).

114 Jawda, *al-Ḥukm bi-mā anzala llāhu*, p. 7.

115 Lefèvre, *Ashes of Hama*, pp. 119–121.

This salafī character of Jawda's treatise is evident from the start. It opens in a Taymiyyan vein, stating that monolatry is the telos of existence and citing the Qur'ānic verse that Ibn Taymiyya typically mentions in connection with this theme: "Allāh created humans and specified what their mission is when He said (Qur'ān 51:56): 'I only created the jinn and humans in order that they worship Me.'"[116] Jawda follows this with the classic monolatric theme that the prophets only called people to exclusivity of worship: Since the Shayṭān (Satan) attempts to divert humans from this mission, Allāh sent prophets, all of whom "had only one single concern, to bring people to worship of Allāh alone without partner" (*laysa lahum illā hamm wāḥid huwa ta'bīd al-nās lillāh waḥdahu lā sharīka lahu*). As the Shayṭān's efforts did not cease after the death of the Prophet Muḥammad, later generations were also required to champion the cause in response to the specific deviations that arose at different times. After Abū Bakr and the *ridda* wars, and 'Alī's treatment of the Khārijites and those who attributed divinity to him, Jawda outlines a purely Ḥanbalī-salafī lineage of champions of the faith: Aḥmad b. Ḥanbal and his defense of the uncreatedness of the Qur'ān, Ibn Taymiyya and Ibn Qayyim al-Jawziyya's denunciation of Ṣūfī immanentism and errant cultic practices, and Muḥammad b. 'Abd al-Wahhāb, "another renewer who revived the tradition of Ibn Taymiyya and his student Ibn al-Qayyim."[117]

Jawda then goes on to write that the new deviations that have arisen in the modern period, in particular with Ataturk's destruction of the Islamic state (i.e. the replacement of the Ottoman Empire with a secular Turkish republic), are unlike those that came before. These deviations are in two issues: allegiance (*walā'*) to Allāh, the Prophet, and to the believers; and the recognition of Allāh as the supreme legal sovereign (*tawḥīd Allāh 'azza wa-jalla ka-sulṭa 'ulyā li-l-ḥukm*). It is this second issue that is the focus of the treatise: Jawda writes that in the past it was not much discussed simply because it was a self-evident tenet that no one contested, whereas today "[false] gods (*āliha*) have emerged and walk on earth claiming for themselves the right to legislate for humans," and this issue has thus become "the foundation of *shirk* and *tawḥīd* in this era."[118] Jawda asserts that some have begun to raise this issue of *shirk al-tashrī'* – the polytheism of legislation – and this could plausibly be read as an allusion to Sayyid Quṭb, but the omission of any explicit mention of Quṭb in this context is striking (though we will see presently that he does cite

116 Jawda, *al-Ḥukm bi-mā anzala llāhu*, p. 21.
117 Jawda, *al-Ḥukm bi-mā anzala llāhu*, pp. 22–23.
118 Jawda, *al-Ḥukm bi-mā anazala llāhu*, p. 24.

Mawdūdī). Jawda clearly sought to affiliate his own treatment of the issue with the precedents of Ibn Taymiyya and Ibn ʿAbd al-Wahhāb, as "a new link in the chain of struggle between the allies of [Allāh] the Merciful and the allies of Satan (*awliyāʾ al-raḥmān wa-awliyāʾ al-shayṭān*)."[119]

Jawda divides his treatise into four parts (in addition to the introduction). The first two are more theoretical or theological, and respectively address the questions "who has the right to rule and to be appealed to in judgment?" and "what is the status of this issue in the view of Islam?" Following this exposition, the remainder of the treatise addresses the jurisprudential implications following therefrom. Part 3 deals with "the ruling regarding one who appeals in judgment to [authorities] other than the Qurʾān and the Prophetic *sunna*," and part 4 with "the ruling regarding one who rules by other than what Allāh revealed."

Part 1 consists largely of two quotations. The first is a passage from the Wahhābī exegete Muḥammad al-Amīn al-Shinqīṭī's *Aḍwāʾ al-bayān* on Qurʾān 18:26, in which he writes of the prohibition of associating others in Allāh's rule.[120] The second quotation is from a text by Mawdūdī, known in Arabic as *Naẓariyyat al-islām al-siyāsiyya*. Jawda's segue from al-Shinqīṭī to Mawdūdī is extremely brief: He merely writes: "And on this basis is erected the pillar of the state [that upholds] *tawḥīd*," and then presents Mawdūdī's passage. Thus Jawda preferred al-Shinqīṭī to Mawdūdī or Quṭb for a statement of the basic principle of theonomy, but still decided to quote Mawdūdī for a more explicit elaboration of its political implications:

> This is the basis on which rests the foundation of Islam's political theory: that all powers of command and legislation be wrested from the hands of humans, individually and collectively, and that none among them be permitted to execute his command among humans and for them to obey him, and that none among them be permitted to enact a law for them, and for them to follow and obey it – for this is a matter that is Allāh's prerogative alone, and no other has any share with Him in this.[121]

The continuation of the passage is slightly more specific as to the political implications of the doctrine of *ḥākimiyya*. Mawdūdī lists the three fundamental characteristics of the Islamic state as being (1) that no individual, family, class, party, and so forth has any part in *ḥākimiyya*, which is Allāh's alone; (2) no one apart from Allāh has any part in legislation; and (3) the Islamic state is founded exclusively on the law that the

119 Jawda, *al-Ḥukm bi-mā anzala llāhu*, p. 25.
120 Jawda, *al-Ḥukm bi-mā anzala llāhu*, pp. 28–29.
121 Jawda, *al-Ḥukm bi-mā anzala llāhu*, pp. 29–30.

Prophet brought from Allāh, and the human government is only due obedience insofar as it executes this law.[122]

Jawda's own comments at the end of the section stress the idea that rule and legislation are a matter of faith (*īmān*). His argument centers on the Streitpunkt principle:

> This conception of Allāh's ruling authority is a Muslim's conception of faith in Allāh. The meaning of faith in Allāh is not faith in His existence alone, for that, in the Islamic view, is one of the self-evident matters known from natural reason (*min al-badīhiyyāt al-fiṭriyya*) that require no discussion ... The Qur'ān recorded that the *mushrikūn* acknowledged Allāh's existence ... The Muslim conception of faith in Allāh is: Allāh exists and is described by the attributes of perfection, His are the fairest names, and He alone is the true object of worship, and He alone is the legislator in this cosmos.[123]

Jawda offers the example of Fir'awn (Pharaoh) as proof that the *shirk* of the *mushrikūn* was in the matter of *ḥākimiyya*, and not in relation to the cosmic, objective attributes of divinity, such as creation or mastery over the heavenly bodies.[124] Notwithstanding Jawda's clear salafizing tendencies, this formulation of the Streitpunkt argument is still more indebted to Mawdūdī and Quṭb than to Ibn Taymiyya or Ibn 'Abd al-Wahhāb, as it focuses directly on the question of political rule and does not employ the terms *ulūhiyya* and *rubūbiyya*. One gathers that Jawda was likely someone of Quṭbist background who had begun to reformulate his expression of *ḥākimiyya* through the salafī sources he encountered, but had not yet delved profoundly into premodern salafī theology. Indeed, most (though not all) of his references are to passages by twentieth-century salafī authors that relate relatively directly to the issue of theonomy; his engagement with the premodern salafī tradition appears earnest but rudimentary.

The second section of the treatise deals with the status of the issue of *ḥākimiyya* in the view of Islam; the upshot of this section is the conclusion that appeal in judgment to a law other than Allāh's negates one's faith. Here as well the argument is pursued primarily through citation of other authors, with the main quotations being discussions of the concept of *ṭāghūt* in the Wahhābī-salafī tradition. For example, the exposition begins with a citation from al-Shinqīṭī's *Aḍwā' al-bayān* on the issue of *shirk al-ṭā'a*, that is, the "polytheism of obedience" to not-Allāh. Al-Shinqīṭī writes that the Prophet clarified this issue to 'Adī b. Ḥātim in the *ḥadīth* on Qur'ān 9:31, when he stated that obedience to the legal

[122] Jawda, *al-Ḥukm bi-mā anzala llāhu*, p. 31.
[123] Jawda, *al-Ḥukm bi-mā anzala llāhu*, p. 32.
[124] Jawda, *al-Ḥukm bi-mā anzala llāhu*, pp. 32–33.

determinations of the rabbis and priests was the taking of them as lords. He then goes on to tie this issue to that of the *ṭāghūt*: Since Qurʾān 5:60 expresses astonishment at those who claim to believe in revelation but desire to appeal in judgment to the *ṭāghūt*, this implies that their claim to be believers is a false one.[125]

There is no need to give a full summary here of the treatise, as it is more significant as a harbinger of things to come than in its own right. There are essentially two salient points. First, with the exception of the aforementioned passage from Mawdūdī – and notwithstanding the Fighting Vanguard's reputation as a faction of Quṭbist adherence – the authorities to whom Jawda appeals are almost exclusively salafī: Ibn Taymiyya,[126] Ibn Qayyim al-Jawziyya,[127] Ibn Kathīr,[128] Muḥammad b. ʿAbd al-Wahhāb,[129] his grandson ʿAbd al-Raḥmān b. Ḥasan,[130] the Indian Ahl-i Ḥadīth scholar Ṣiddīq Ḥasan Khān,[131] al-Shawkānī,[132] Aḥmad Muḥammad Shākir,[133] Maḥmūd Muḥammad Shākir,[134] the Egyptian salafī Muḥammad Ḥāmid al-Fiqī,[135] and Muḥammad al-Amīn al-Shinqīṭī.[136]

The second point is the radical juridical conclusions drawn by Jawda. All those who prepare legislation, the MPs who enact it, the ministers who implement it, the president who signs it, the judiciary, police detectives, the secret services (*al-mabāḥith*) – all these, if they do not oppose man-made legislation and are faithful to it in their work, are unbelievers. So are all individuals in the general population who are pleased with the legislation, since they have permitted (*sawwaghū*) adherence to laws other than the *sharīʿa*, even if they also affirm the latter.[137] Though not explicit in the text itself, these radical conclusions served as the basis for *takfīr* of the Syrian Muslim Brotherhood.

Thus, while Jawda's treatise bears many similarities in content to al-Ashqar's *al-Sharīʿa al-ilāhiyya*, it was in fact emblematic of a split with fusionist salafism and a premonition of the rise of the salafī jihādīs. This

125 Jawda, *al-Ḥukm bi-mā anzala llāhu*, pp. 35–36.
126 Jawda, *al-Ḥukm bi-mā anzala llāhu*, p. 48.
127 Jawda, *al-Ḥukm bi-mā anzala llāhu*, pp. 38, 59, 68, 75.
128 Jawda, *al-Ḥukm bi-mā anzala llāhu*, pp. 48–49, 59, 76–77.
129 Jawda, *al-Ḥukm bi-mā anzala llāhu*, pp. 36–38, 41, 75–76, 89–93.
130 Jawda, *al-Ḥukm bi-mā anzala llāhu*, pp. 38–40.
131 Jawda, *al-Ḥukm bi-mā anzala llāhu*, pp. 58, 59, 60–61.
132 Jawda, *al-Ḥukm bi-mā anzala llāhu*, pp. 87–88.
133 Jawda, *al-Ḥukm bi-mā anzala llāhu*, pp. 34, 43–44, 77–79.
134 Jawda, *al-Ḥukm bi-mā anzala llāhu*, pp. 69–73.
135 Jawda, *al-Ḥukm bi-mā anzala llāhu*, pp. 40–41, 81–82.
136 Jawda, *al-Ḥukm bi-mā anzala llāhu*, pp. 28–29, 35–36, 45–47, 54–56, 57–58, 60, 67.
137 Jawda, *al-Ḥukm bi-mā anzala llāhu*, p. 53.

is true not only of the substantive conclusions reached, but also in the lesson drawn from the defeat of the Islamist revolt in Syria. Whereas al-Ashqar and others took it as an object lesson in the need to adopt gradualist means of democratic participation, Jawda and ʿAdnān ʿUqla saw a great benefit in this disaster: a separation of the ranks between the true believers who remained faithful to pure theonomy and the *manhaj* of jihād, and those like the Brotherhood whose faith was weak and who, in the face of a setback, made common cause with the unbelievers.

## Quietist Salafī Theonomy

Sayyid Quṭb was a controversial figure in the quietist salafī milieu. The positions on Quṭb among independent quietists and Saudi establishment salafīs ranged from the fierce opposition of scholars such as Rabīʿ al-Madkhalī[138] to qualified appreciation on the part of others.[139] Quietist salafī opposition to Quṭb centered for the most part on his alleged deviations on classic issues of *ʿaqīda*, such as the status of Allāh's attributes. It is true that al-Madkhalī and others accused Quṭb and his followers of unbridled *takfīr* of Muslim society on the whole, but this should not be read as a rejection of theonomy itself. In fact, the principle of theonomy was rarely called into question, and the quietist salafī milieu was generally hostile to democracy, parliamentary government, and man-made law.

In parallel to the salafization project of the fusionists, who were combining Quṭbist elements and the salafī tradition, some quietist salafīs were generating their own writings on theonomy on a more purely salafī basis, and at times their conclusions provided a dogmatic counterweight to the pragmatism of many fusionists. Fusionism was after all a diverse phenomenon, and adoption of the principle of *ḥākimiyya*, qua principle, did not necessarily rule out instrumental compromises with democracy. We already saw an example in al-Ashqar's later treatise, and movements such as the Front islamique du salut (FIS) in Algeria and the Iṣlāḥ party in Yemen took to electoral politics to advance their agendas. Muḥammad Surūr, the Syrian leader and eponym of one of the major Ṣaḥwa branches (the Surūrīs) in Kuwait and Saudi Arabia, supported the FIS' electoral bid, albeit not without reserve. He wrote in his journal *al-Sunna*: "The FLN [Algeria's ruling party] and the other secular parties

[138] On al-Madkhalī's polemics against Quṭb, see Lav, *Radical Islam*, pp. 127–128.

[139] For example, the Saudi establishment scholar Bakr Abū Zayd, who reproached al-Madkhalī for being overly critical of Quṭb. See ʿAbd al-Razzāq b. Khalīfa al-Shāyijī (ed.), *Khiṭāb al-ʿallāma Bakr b. ʿAbdallāh Abū Zayd khawla kitāb duktūr Rabīʿ b. Hādī al-Madkhalī Aḍwāʾ islāmiyya ʿalā ʿaqīdat Sayyid Quṭb wa-fikrihi*, n.p.: Dār al-Tajdīd, 1417/1997.

have a united stance on the FIS, so why should we leave the FIS to face these multiple fronts on its own? Are not we, the Islamists, more worthy of being united than the communists and the secularists?" Surūr was not especially favorable toward elections: He rejected the modernists' equation of democracy and parliaments with the Islamic *shūrā* and wrote that "the tyranny of the majority is not much different than the tyranny of an individual." Yet most of his objections were of a pragmatic nature and they did not deter him from calling for support of the FIS, since "they might achieve a great deal of good, as an exception to the rule."[140] The FIS' own justification of their chosen path against the charge that they were 'democrats' made use of Quṭbist themes and terminology (e.g. "one must differentiate between taking advantage of *jāhiliyya* and calling for it").[141]

Those quietist salafīs who adopted a strict stance on theonomy and its application deployed the premodern salafī tradition in opposition to such compromises. One example of this quietist salafī theonomy is the tract *Iblāgh al-ḥaqq ilā al-khalq* by Sayyid al-Ghubāshī, who was associated with the al-Daʿwa al-Salafiyya movement in Alexandria, Egypt.[142] This is the same movement that some thirty years hence, in the wake of the Arab Spring, would itself embrace parliamentary politics and found the Nūr party. This is partly attributable to later developments among Egyptian quietist salafīs, but even at the time of its authorship *Iblāgh al-ḥaqq* may not have represented the prevailing view in al-Daʿwa al-Salafiyya, and its posterity is mostly due to its influence on early salafī jihādīs (see below). The context of its writing was the following: After the Egyptian Church called on Christians to register to vote, one or some Muslims (*baʿḍ ikhwāninā*) issued a pamphlet calling on Muslims to do the same so as not to allow the Christians to gain the upper hand.[143] *Iblāgh al-ḥaqq* was

140 Muḥammad Surūr b. Nāyif Zayn al-ʿĀbidīn, "Al-qism al-thāni, al-ḥalqa al-ūlā: al-jazāʾir min jamʿiyyat al-ʿulamāʾ ilā jabhat al-inqādh," *Majallat al-Sunna* 4 (Dhū al-Qaʿda 1410 / June 1990).

141 al-Jabha al-Islāmiyya li-l-Inqādh / al-Jaysh al-Islāmī li-l-Inqādh, *Qālū ʿannā mutaʾawwilīn fa-ajabnā mustadillīn*, n.p., n.d.

142 Al-Ghubāshī was one of the five representatives of al-Daʿwa al-Salafiyya in a televised debate with scholars from al-Azhar broadcast on Egyptian television in 1983: www.youtube.com/watch?v=o_jR9ZaTvlg. Over time he appears to have become less involved with the movement and has focused on scholarly activities and teaching at the Aḥmad b. Ḥanbal mosque in Alexandria, where he is the imām. See www.ahlalhdeeth.com/vb/showthread.php?t=155505 (link no longer active).

143 Sayyid al-Ghubāshī, *Iblāgh al-ḥaqq ilā al-khalq: risāla fī ḥukm al-mushāraka fī majlis al-shaʿb al-miṣrī*, n.d., www.ilmway.com/site/maqdis/MS_512 (link no longer active), p. 3. The author does not give any further specifics on the identity of the Muslim(s) against whose pamphlet he is arguing. Many of the arguments toward the end of the pamphlet seem to address the Muslim Brotherhood, but the phrase *baʿḍ ikhwāninā* may suggest that the pamphlet was issued by other salafīs.

written in response to the arguments presented in this pamphlet, and argues that since a parliament is an inherently polytheistic entity Muslims may not have any part in it.

After this short explanation of the reason for writing the tract, al-Ghubāshī outlines the general principle by which human legislation is considered polytheism. He opens with the words of Ibn Taymiyya at the beginning of the second portion of *al-Risāla al-tadmuriyya*. In this passage Ibn Taymiyya writes that the worship (*ʿibāda*) that one owes to Allāh requires complete obedience to Him. Islam, the true and only acceptable religion, comprises exclusive submission (*istislām*) to Allāh, "and one who submits to Him and to another is a polytheist (*mushrik*)."[144] On this connection between worship and submission to divine law, al-Ghubāshī also mentions a pithy and much-cited statement by the twentieth-century Wahhābī scholar and exegete Muḥammad al-Amīn al-Shinqīṭī, who wrote that "to attribute a partner to Allāh in His rule is akin to attributing a partner to Allāh in one's worship of Him."[145]

It is no surprise that al-Ghubāshī promptly adduces Qurʾān 9:31 and the ʿAdī b. Ḥātim tradition in support of this notion. He does so first by citing the medieval exegete al-Qurṭubī (d. 671/1273) on Qurʾān 3:64, a commentary that was clearly influenced by the ʿAdī b. Ḥātim tradition. Al-Qurṭubī writes: "'and let not any of us take any other of us as lords other than Allāh' – that is, let us not follow them in permitting anything or forbidding anything." Then, after citing 9:31, al-Qurṭubī continues: "They [the scriptuaries] made them [the rabbis and priests] as their lord (*anzalūhum manzilat rabbihim*) in accepting their prohibition and permission of things that Allāh did not prohibit and of things that Allāh did not permit."[146] Al-Ghubāshī then cites al-Bayḍāwī's gloss on the same verse, Qurʾān 3:64: "Let us not obey the rabbis in what they innovated (*aḥdathū*) in prohibition and permission, because each and every one of them is human like us," followed by explicit adduction of both Qurʾān 9:31 and the ʿAdī b. Ḥātim tradition.[147]

Based on these principles, al-Ghubāshī writes: "Know, brother, that the foundation of the issue is that these institutions [viz. parliaments]

144 al-Ghubāshī, *Iblāgh al-ḥaqq*, pp. 3–4; Ibn Taymiyya, *al-Tadmuriyya*, p. 165f.

145 al-Ghubāshī, *Iblāgh al-ḥaqq*, p. 4; Muḥammad al-Amīn al-Shinqīṭī, *Aḍwāʾ al-bayān fī īḍāḥ al-qurʾan bi-l-qurʾān*, n.p.: Dār ʿĀlam al-Fawāʾid, n.d., vol. 4, p. 83. See likewise ʿAbd al-Raḥmān b. ʿAbd al-ʿAzīz al-Sudayyis, *al-Ḥākimiyya fī tafsīr aḍwāʾ al-bayān*, Riyadh: Dār al-Ṭayyiba, 1412[/1991–1992].

146 al-Ghubāshī, *Iblāgh al-ḥaqq*, p. 4. Al-Qurṭubī does not explicitly address *taqlīd* in this passage but does add that the verse demonstrates the inadmissibility of pure *istiḥsān* without basis in a *dalīl*.

147 al-Ghubāshī, *Iblāgh al-ḥaqq*, p. 5.

were established on an unsteady precipice on the brink of *shirk*, and crumble down together with their people into hellfire ... apart from those who were ignorant [and thus not culpable], learned [their error], repented to Allāh, and rectified [their behavior]."[148] Likewise, after explaining in some detail the basis of the Egyptian constitution and the place it accords (or rather does not accord) to the *sharīʿa*, and then quoting a passage from Aḥmad Shākir in condemnation of the application of man-made law, al-Ghubāshī adds that the reader now understands from the preceding that "this parliament is founded on patent and egregious *shirk*."[149] Unlike the issue of accepting an executive post from an unbeliever, about which there can be some legitimate debate, the parliament is illegitimate in all senses and is "a fortress of paganism and *shirk*, due to its inherent attribute (*li-ṣifatihi al-lāzima*) of legislation in place of Allāh."[150]

Al-Ghubāshī was probably the most ardent of the quietist salafī authors on theonomy, but he was by no means alone. Scholars from the circle of the *ḥadīth* scholar Muḥammad Nāṣir al-Dīn al-Albānī likewise associated parliaments with *shirk* through use of Qurʾān 9:31 and the ʿAdī b. Ḥātim tradition – which is natural enough given this circle's heavy focus on opposition to *taqlīd*.[151] The use of this tradition to condemn parliamentary legislation as polytheism apparently became so widespread that some authors did not even feel the need to fully explain the proof. For example, we find an a fortiori argument from *taqlīd* as polytheism to obedience to modern law as polytheism, without explicit mention of the proof on which it rests, in a 1992 article titled "A Warning to Men against Worship of Human Idols" in the journal published by al-Albānī's circle, *al-Aṣāla*. The author, Muḥammad Mūsā Naṣr, writes:

> If the scholars considered one who obeys the *ʿulamāʾ* in their erroneous *ijtihāds* that contravened the *sharīʿa*, [even] after the error was pointed out to him, to have taken the *ʿulamāʾ* as lords, then all the more so one who obeys the *ṭawāghīt* of the land who do not institute rule by Allāh's law and who strive to extinguish Allāh's light.[152]

148 al-Ghubāshī, *Iblāgh al-ḥaqq*, p. 5.

149 al-Ghubāshī, *Iblāgh al-ḥaqq*, p. 9.

150 al-Ghubāshī, *Iblāgh al-ḥaqq*, p. 10.

151 On al-Albānī and his circle, see Stéphane Lacroix, "Between Revolution and Apoliticism: Nasir al-Din al-Albani and his Impact on the Shaping of Contemporary Salafism," in Meijer (ed.), *Global Salafism*, pp. 58–80; Lacroix, *Les islamistes saoudiens*, pp. 99–109; Jacob Olidort, "The Politics of 'Quietist' Salafism," The Brookings Project on U.S. Relations with the Islamic World, Analysis Paper no. 18, Center for Middle East Policy at Brookings, 2015; Joas Wagemakers, *Salafism in Jordan: Political Islam in a Quietist Community*, New York: Cambridge University Press, 2016.

152 Muḥammad Mūsā Naṣr, "Taḥdhīr al-bariyya min ʿibādat al-aṣnām al-bashariyya," *al-Aṣāla* 2 (15 Jumāda II 1413) [= December 1992], pp. 25–29, at p. 29.

This same issue of *al-Aṣāla* contains a joint article signed by al-Albānī himself, the Yemeni quietist scholar Muqbil b. Hādī al-Wādiʿī, and a number of others on the topics of democracy, pluralism, coalitions with secular parties, elections, and political activism.[153] Aside from the general import of these issues, the authors note a specific context at the end of the article: It was in part authored in response to a ruling by a Yemeni scholar (presumably ʿAbd al-Majīd al-Zindānī) that legitimated all of the above for the sake of his political party,[154] the Iṣlāḥ (al-Tajammuʿ al-Yamanī li-l-Iṣlāḥ);[155] special attention is devoted to refuting the ruling's justifications for the Iṣlāḥ party's alliance with the Arab Socialist Baʿth Party.[156] The authors argue that democracy, as defined by its own proponents, is popular autonomy ("rule of the people by the people"), and as such contradicts Islam, under which Allāh is the ruler. It is the regime of the *ṭāghūt*, and Allāh commanded the Muslims to reject the *ṭāghūt* and to have faith in Him. "There can be only faith in Allāh and rule by what He revealed, or faith in the *ṭāghūt* and rule by it, and everything that contradicts Allāh's law (*sharʿ*) is a *ṭāghūt*."[157] This holds true of parliaments, which the article refers to as *majālis ṭāghūtiyya*. Parliaments apply the rule of the majority, and not the rule of the Qurʾān and the *sunna*, and as such it is impermissible to accord them recognition by running in elections.[158]

It would be a mistake to reduce the quietists' characteristic avoidance of politics to a single rationale, or to generalize too broadly about this tendency that incorporated within it diverse figures and movements. Clearly a principled theonomic doctrine was one of the contributing factors, and that is the important point for our purposes. Yet the conservative ethos of the quietists led them to find ways to contain the potential implications of labeling democracy and parliaments as *shirk* or *ṭāghūt*. Nothwithstanding the radical tone of al-Ghubāshī's *Iblāgh al-ḥaqq*, in a subsequent treatise he argued for a capacious application of the category of exculpatory ignorance (*jahl*) so as to avoid declaring governments

153 Muḥammad Nāṣir al-Dīn al-Albānī, et al., "Masāʾil ʿaṣriyya fī al-siyāsa al-sharʿiyya," *al-Aṣāla* 2 (15 Jumāda II 1413), pp. 16–24.

154 al-Albānī et al., "Masāʾil," pp. 23–24.

155 I have been unable to locate the precise ruling to which the authors refer. In late 1992 the Iṣlāḥ party, founded two years previous, was preparing for national elections. See Jillian Schwedler, *Faith in Moderation: Islamist Political Parties in Jordan and Yemen*, Cambridge: Cambridge University Press, 2006, pp. 89–91. On Yemeni salafism and its opposition to the Iṣlāḥ party, see Laurent Bonnefoy, *Salafism in Yemen: Transnationalism and Religious Identity*, Oxford: Oxford University Press, 2012.

156 al-Albānī et al., "Masāʾil," pp. 19ff.; this party represented the Iraqi branch of the Baʿth in Yemen.

157 al-Albānī et al., "Masāʾil," p. 17.

158 al-Albānī et al., "Masāʾil," p. 22.

apostate.[159] Al-Albānī adopted a lenient position on the theology of faith (a 'Murji'ite' view in the eyes of his critics) to the same end.[160] As noted in connection with 'Umar Sulaymān al-Ashqar, Shaykh 'Abd al-'Azīz b. Bāz ultimately permitted running for parliament and voting in parliamentary elections on pragmatic grounds.[161] While the quietists' principled salafī elaboration of theonomy would prove influential for the development of salafī jihādī doctrine, the salafī jihādīs would refuse these means of containing its implications and would insist on drawing out more radical conclusions.

## Salafī Jihādī Theonomy

Over the course of the 1980s and early 1990s the first generation of salafī jihādī authors – some affiliated with specific militant movements, others supportive of them but writing independently – began to elaborate their own theonomic doctrine on the *shirk* of democracy and parliamentary legislation. Their doctrine was clearly indebted to the earlier forays of fusionist and quietist salafīs, but the salafī jihādī version of theonomy was to be an uncompromising one. Like many quietist salafīs they opposed the instrumental embrace of parliamentary elections on the part of the Ṣaḥwa leader Muḥammad Surūr, the Algerian FIS, and others, but they also rejected the moderating strategies of the quietists on the issue of *takfīr*. The salafī jihādīs, through a tight embedding of theonomy in the premodern salafī tradition of monolatric *tawḥīd*, insisted that the rejection of human legal-political autonomy is a core tenet of faith that brooks no compromise. In their view the ruling regimes were apostate, and the correct salafī *manhaj* was to overthrow them by force of arms and establish the rule of the *sharī'a* in their place.

### *"Differentiation of the Ranks," Militancy, and the Emergence of Salafī Jihadism*

For the first generation of salafī jihādī authors this uncompromising vision of theonomy was a key element in their self-identification as true

[159] Sayyid b. Sa'd al-Dīn al-Ghubāshī, *Sa'at raḥmat rabb al-'ālamīn li-l-juhhāl al-mukhālifīn li-l-sharī'a min al-muslimīn*, Riyadh: Dār al-Muslim, 1415/1995.

[160] See Lav, *Radical Islam*, pp. 140–159; Joas Wagemakers, "'Seceders' and 'Postponers'? An Analysis of the 'Khawarij' and 'Murji'a' Labels in Polemical Debates between Quietist and Jihadi-Salafis," in Jeevan Deol and Zaheer Kazmi (eds.), *Contextualising Jihadi Thought*, London: Hurst, 2012, pp. 145–164; Joas Wagemakers, "Contesting Religious Authority in Jordanian Salafi Networks," in Marko Milosevic and Kacper Rekawek (eds.), *Perseverance of Terrorism: Focus on Leaders*, Amsterdam: IOS Press, 2014, pp. 111–125.

[161] *Majallat Liwā' al-Islām* 11, 1409 AH, p. 7 of the supplement. I will return to this fatwā presently in connection with Sayyid Imām's critique of it.

salafīs. Many had been influenced by Quṭb in their formative period or had even been affiliated with the Ṣaḥwa. Abū Muḥammad al-Maqdisī, for example, had been a Surūrī (that is, a member of Muḥammad Surūr's *jamāʿa*) in his teenage years in Kuwait.[162] In the close-knit world of Kuwaiti Islamism and salafism he came into contact with a number of influential figures: The leading fusionist salafī and close companion of ʿUmar Sulaymān al-Ashqar, ʿAbd al-Raḥmān ʿAbd al-Khāliq, was al-Maqdisī's religious studies teacher in high school.[163] He was most influenced by Muḥammad Surūr and the Egyptian Muslim Brother Sayyid ʿĪd, a close associate of Sayyid Quṭb who had been imprisoned together with him.[164] In this environment al-Maqdisī imbibed the writings of Mawdūdī and Quṭb[165] – which is to say that he was exposed to and influenced by theonomic ideas in his formative intellectual years. From a distance of more than thirty years al-Maqdisī later offered the following appraisal of Muḥammad Surūr: He criticized the ruling regimes and looked unfavorably on affiliation with government ministries, and even pronounced a general kind of *takfīr* on them, but the details of his doctrine were not clear; for example, his position on service in the army. In addition, al-Maqdisī averred that Surūr's general disapprobation of elections and parliamentary participation was more tactical than *sharʿī*.[166]

Quietist salafism was a decisive influence in al-Maqdisī's subsequent change of course and his repudiation of his Ṣaḥwa background. The immediate influence came from veterans of al-Jamāʿa al-Salafiyya al-Muḥtasiba, the small but influential movement previously headed by Juhaymān al-ʿUtaybī (leader of the occupation of the Grand Mosque in Mecca in 1979). The JSM was a unique group that defies simple classification and has been labeled 'rejectionist,'[167] but al-Maqdisī also developed contacts with leading quietist salafīs such as al-Albānī and Ibn Bāz.[168]

162 Wagemakers, *A Quietist Jihadi*, p. 34.
163 Abū Muḥammad al-Maqdisī, *Wa-lākin kūnū rabbānniyyīn*, part 1: *al-ism wa-l-nasab wa-l-dirāsa wa-l-tadayyun wa-l-iltizām maʿa jamāʿat surūr*, 2012 [video], 28:18–28:42, http://abu-qatada.xyz/vid/visual/8901.zip (link no longer active).
164 al-Maqdisī, *Wa-lākin kūnū rabbānniyyīn*, part 1, 28:50–30:16.
165 Abū Muḥammad ʿĀṣim al-Maqdisī, *Mīzān al-iʿtidāl fī taqyīm kitāb al-mawrid al-zulāl fī al-tanbīh ʿalā akhṭāʾ al-ẓilāl*, 1422 [2001–2002], p. 5, www.ilmway.com/site/maqdis/MS_9109.html (link no longer active).
166 al-Maqdisī, *Wa-lākin kūnū rabbānniyyīn*, part 1, 30:24–32:10.
167 Thomas Hegghammer and Stéphane Lacroix, "Rejectionist Islamism in Saudi Arabia: The Story of Juhayman al-ʿUtaybi Revisited," *International Journal of Middle East Studies* 39/1 (2007), pp. 103–122. It is worth noting that Muqbil b. Hādī al-Wādiʿī, the co-author of the article cited above condemning the Iṣlāḥ party in Yemen, was himself an alumnus of Juhaymān's group (pp. 108, 111).
168 Wagemakers, *A Quietist Jihadi*, pp. 35–36; Lav, *Radical Islam*, p. 131.

One of al-Maqdisī's first mature works on theonomy, dating from the early 1980s, was in fact an adaptation of Sayyid al-Ghubāshī's *Iblāgh al-ḥaqq* to the Kuwaiti context, which al-Maqdisī then published in advance of parliamentary elections with a short introduction of his own under the title *al-Qawl al-sadīd fī bayān anna dukhūl al-majlis munāfin li-l-tawḥīd.*[169] Thus while it is true that al-Maqdisī had first encountered the issue of *ḥākimiyya* in his teenage years as a Ṣaḥwa youth from the writings of Mawdūdī and Quṭb, and notwithstanding his subsequent split with the quietists, his uncompromising version of theonomy was more in line with that of some quietist salafīs than with the fusionists.

Al-Maqdisī's background epitomizes the melting pot out of which salafī jihadism emerged. All the necessary elements were already present: not only the base elements of Quṭb's *ḥākimiyya* and classical salafī theology, but already-salafized versions of the former in fusionist writings, and forays into an indigenous version of theonomy on the part of the quietists. The distinctive feature of salafī jihadism is thus not so much originality in doctrine as a dogmatic insistence on the issue, its foregrounding as the defining issue of the age, consistency in its application, and an emphasis on "differentiation of the ranks" (*tamyīz al-ṣufūf*) – a parting of ways with all those (fusionist or quietist) who have compromised on this matter of first principle. These elements go hand in hand with the salafī jihādīs' adoption of a *manhaj* of armed jihād, an issue to which we will return presently.

The salafī jihādīs view their insistence on an intransigent version of theonomy as akin to earlier salafīs' insistence on exclusivity of worship, and themselves as the rightful heirs to this monolatric tradition. Consider the following passage by Abū Muḥammad al-Maqdisī, written in 2015, which condemns contemporary quietist salafism in terms adapted from Ibn Taymiyya's critique of *kalām* theologians:

> Some [people] weigh you solely according to the extent of your knowledge and understanding of the issue of [Allāh's] names and attributes (*bāb al-asmāʾ wa-l-ṣifāt*), or the *tawḥīd* of knowledge and affirmation, of which even Iblīs is not ignorant, or *tawḥīd al-rubūbiyya*, of which [even] the unbelievers of Quraysh were not ignorant. And according to them, this is the unblemished creed, and this is the salafī understanding and the *atharī* path, etc.
>
> And thus [in their view,] one who errs or stumbles in any of the details (*furūʿ*) of this, he is a blameworthy innovator, and their scales are not wide enough to excuse him, even if he has fulfilled (*ḥaqqaqa*) the *tawḥīd* for the sake of which all the prophets were sent [viz. *tawḥīd al-ulūhiyya*] and has waged jihād (*jāhada*) for the sake of its firmest bonds [*ʿurāhu al-wuthqā*, cf. Qurʾān 2:256 and 31:22], and

[169] al-Maqdisī's introduction in al-Ghubāshī, *Iblāgh al-ḥaqq*, p. 2.

has fought and has been killed. Whereas one who shows that he is knowledgeable [viz. of the *rubūbiyya* issues], in their opinion he is a pure salafī, and even one of the elite of the *ahl al-ḥadīth* and the leaders of the Victorious Sect[170] – and it harms him none, nor are these titles taken from him, if he destroys the firmest bonds of Islam, sullies the foundation (*aṣl*) of the message of the prophets and the quintessence of *tawḥīd al-ulūhiyya*, and is the worst of the *ṭāghūt*s. He remains in their scales the Imām of the Muslims and Amīr al-Muʾminīn, so long as he continues to set forth and know that creed![171]

This critique argues in essence that the quietist salafīs do not have their priorities straight. It is true that there is right and wrong on issues such as Allāh's attributes, but the prophets were sent for the sake of *tawḥīd al-ulūhiyya*, and that is the heart of Islam. Al-Maqdisī alludes to the examples of Iblīs and Quraysh, who were frequently adduced by Ibn Taymiyya as examples of those who professed *tawḥīd al-rubūbiyya* but fell short of *tawḥīd al-ulūhiyya* (see Chapter 1). And while this passage in particular does not specify what aspect of *tawḥīd al-ulūhiyya* the quietist salafīs fail to uphold, there is no doubt that it refers primarily to theonomy – there are not many quietist salafīs who are exacting on the matter of Allāh's attributes but forgiving toward ritual polylatry.

Another of the founders of the salafī jihādī school was the Jordanian Palestinian Abū Qatāda al-Filasṭīnī. Like al-Maqdisī he shared a concern for a differentiation of the ranks: the establishment of a pure salafī movement centered on theonomy but freed of Muslim Brotherhood influence. In his foreword to ʿAbd al-Nāṣir Jawda's *al-Ḥukm bi-mā anzala llāhu*, authored decades after the original work, Abū Qatāda writes that while many believe the jihadist uprising in Syria in the early 1980s to have been an unmitigated disaster, it was in truth a blessing, in that it unmasked the leadership of the Muslim Brotherhood and spurred the search for a salafī orientation:

The blessed jihadist movement in Syria [i.e. the Fighting Vanguard] had such merit the true extent of which is known only to Allāh the Exalted … Among the good things achieved by this blessed activity [the jihād in Syria] was that it made known to people their stations and revealed to us our true natures. It made known to us to what degree there was ignorance in us and exposed to us hidden truths about the *bidʿī* organizations [i.e. those that adopt reprehensible innovations]. Through it, and by its path, hollow leaders fell … and it became

[170] *al-ṭāʾifa al-manṣūra*. This is a reference to a number of *ḥadīth*s that describe a sect of Muslims who uphold the truth and are undeterred by those who oppose them. A more accurate but cumbersome translation of the term would be "the sect rendered victorious [by Allāh]."

[171] Abū Muḥammad al-Maqdisī, *Mīzānunā wa-mawāzīnuhum*, May 30, 2015, https://twitter.com/almaqdese0/status/604668301512278016 (link no longer active).

clear to everyone with a mind that they are like a mirage in a desert [cf. Qurʾān 24:39] that slakes not the thirst of the thirsty …

The people of guidance began an earnest and steadfast search for the truth and dedicated themselves to [the study of] books of deliverance in order to reorder their minds and to understand the divine law (*al-sharʿ*) in accordance with its true nature. This was after they perceived that there was no truth in their people and that the shaykhs in positions of leadership were like propped-up blocks of wood [an allusion to the *munāfiqūn*, the 'hypocrites' in the Qurʾān – cf. 63:4] who were not fit for the duties of this path, and perceived that the rabbis [cf. Qurʾān 9:31] had gotten their hands on a great part of *tawḥīd* in order to hide it from people's eyes. Those guided to the path … became certain after all this that it was necessary to turn the pages in search of the truth, far removed from the interpretations and readings of the later generations (*al-khalaf*), and taking guidance and discernment from the understandings of the early generations (*al-salaf*).[172]

From his exile in London in the 1990s, Abū Qatāda extended his patronage to another organization that, a decade after the Syrian Fighting Vanguard, was providing just such a radical salafī jihādī alternative to the Muslim Brotherhood style of political activism, the Algerian GIA.[173] As previously mentioned, the Islamist Front islamique du salut (FIS) had entered the elections at the beginning of the decade, and were well on their way to a landslide victory before the army canceled the elections to prevent them from taking power. This impasse set Algeria on a course for civil war, over the course of which the GIA emerged as a separate and more intransigent organization than the FIS or its military wing. Throughout the mid-1990s the GIA became increasingly extreme and was eventually disavowed by the salafī jihādī movement, but at first figures like Abū Qatāda, and many others, viewed it as the great hope for Algeria and for the movement on the whole. The series of articles he penned for the GIA's journal *al-Anṣār* was titled "*Bayna manhajayn*" ("Between Two Paths"), and in these articles he praised the GIA as a proper salafī jihad organization, in contrast with the Muslim Brotherhood-influenced FIS.

For example, in the thirtieth installment of the series, published in January 1995, Abu Qatāda responded to critics of the GIA who accused it of being an extremist Khārijite group. He wrote that such accusations were just "the exaction of revenge on the [GIA's] jihād, because it stole from them the honor of arriving at the cupola of parliament, or because the legitimate inheritance passed from the FIS to an heir – and what an excellent heir it is – called the GIA." Here the salafī jihādī concern for a differentiation of the ranks took on a decidedly factional turn, a

172 Jawda, *al-Ḥukm bi-mā anzala llāhu*, pp. 5–7.

173 Cf. Alexander Thurston, "Algeria's GIA: The First Major Armed Group to Fully Subordinate Jihadism to Salafism," *Islamic Law and Society* 24 (2017), pp. 412–436.

development presaged a decade earlier in the definitive split between the Syrian Muslim Brotherhood and the Fighting Vanguard. In other words, the emergence of salafī jihadism as a distinct theological school went hand in hand with the emergence of salafī jihādī organizations that had divorced the mainstream Islamist movements in order to carry the salafī jihādī banner into battle. The extreme animosity in this split could at times be striking, as when Abū Qatāda added:

This truth alarmed them and they began to strike out in the darkness. For our part we will have mercy on them and reveal to them something of their true nature, perhaps they will return [to the truth]. And if not, then their striking out in the darkness will kill them, and their blood will be shed with impunity. History, in accordance with Allāh's *sunna*, shows deference to no one.[174]

Later that same year history would in fact shed their blood, at the hands of the GIA.[175]

The title of Abū Qatāda's series of articles for the GIA's *al-Anṣār* journal, "Between Two Paths," points to its primary aim: to illustrate the difference between the two paths, that of the salafī jihādīs and that of the Muslim Brotherhood-style Islamists. It was intended as a kind of declaration of independence for the emerging salafī jihādī movement and a defining charter of its distinctive principles. Abū Muṣʿab al-Sūrī, veteran of the Fighting Vanguard in Syria and of the Afghan jihād, outlined the connection between the theological and the organizational developments in an article of his own in *al-Anṣār* titled "*Bayna awliyāʾ al-raḥmān wa-awliyāʾ al-fātīkān*" ("Between the Allies of God and the the Allies of the Vatican"). The title, like Abū Qatāda's "*Bayna manhajayn*," references the split in the Islamist movement: The "allies of God" are the ideologically principled jihadist movements, and in particular the GIA; the "allies of the Vatican" is a reference to the FIS leadership's endorsement of the Sant'Egidio Platform in Rome, a peace plan among Algerian factions based on democracy and national reconciliation. Abū Muṣʿab writes the following in praise of the GIA:

It has already become known that the situation of the Islamist movement has entered an important phase, after the jihadist currents passed from the stage of a phenomenon to the stage of organization and activity, and then surpassed that to the stage of authentic theoretical grounding (*taʾṣīl*) and *manhaj* ... The jihadist current has begun to put forth its own distinctive school, and its own jurisprudents, ideologues, authors, and men of letters, in order to shatter the

[174] Abū Qatāda al-Filasṭīnī, *Bayna Manhajayni* 30, *Majallat al-Anṣār* 81 (25 Shaʿbān 1415 / January 26, 1995), p. 5.

[175] See Thurston, "Algeria's GIA," pp. 426–427, on the group's assassination of two of its own commanders with an FIS background.

view … that the jihād fighters who have taken up weapons and who defend Allāh's religion everywhere today are just small bands and gangs with no ideology and no *manhaj* …

These good pages [viz. the *al-Anṣār* journal] carry the harbingers of a distinctive (*mutamayyiz*) ideology and a differentiating (*mufāṣil*) and authentically grounded *manhaj* … [in] articles like those of our brother, Shaykh Abū Qatāda al-Filasṭīnī, which trace out distinctive lines in the "Between Two Paths" series …

I have been waiting and hoping for this phenomenon, praise Allāh! I remember how the storm [of criticism] came down on us in the Afghanistan days, when a similar thing appeared in the battlefields of jihād and ideology in Peshawar, where all the schools of Islamist ideology and practice struggled one with another, and when books with a distinctive jihadist *manhaj* came out, such as [Sayyid Imām's] *al-ʿUmda fī iʿdād al-ʿudda* and [my own] *al-Tajriba al-jihādiyya fī sūriyā*.[176]

This concern for a differentiation of the ranks was omnipresent in those pivotal years and featured as the overarching theme of most of the theological and programmatic writing in the *al-Anṣār* journal. Another good example is Abū Muṣʿab al-Sūrī's serialized study and critique of the FIS: He states clearly that the aim of the series was not just analysis of the FIS itself, but rather "the main aim of this study is to bring down the [entire] school of democratic Islamic activism by bringing down [even] its most splendid, clearest, best, and strongest exemplar."[177] The main contrast in this differentiation of the ranks was between the Muslim Brotherhood and its satellite movements, on the one hand, which accepted democracy to varying degrees, and on the other hand, the radical salafī movement, with its strict theonomy and insistence on armed jihād. The FIS was the former's "splendid, clearest, best, and strongest exemplar" because it was a fusionist movement that brooked only grudging and instrumental compromises with democratic mechanisms: At least one of its leaders, ʿAlī Belḥāj, had been an ardent exponent of theonomy and opponent of democracy. Yet only a few short years after its attempt to obtain power by the ballot box even the relatively hardline FIS had fallen into the familiar pattern of negotiations with the *ṭāghūt* and alliance with secular parties. Abū Muṣʿab thus used this example to

176 ʿUmar ʿAbd al-Ḥakīm [= Abū Muṣʿab al-Sūrī], "Bayna awliyāʾ al-raḥmān wa-awliyāʾ al-fātīkān," *al-Anṣār* 88, 14 Shawwāl 1415 / March 16, 1995, pp. 13–15, at p. 13. On Sayyid Imām, see below.

177 ʿUmar ʿAbd al-Ḥakīm [= Abū Muṣʿab al-Sūrī], "Dirāsa fī fikr wa-manhaj wa-mawāqif al-jabha al-islāmiyya li-l-inqādh 16," *al-Anṣār* 112, 4 Rabīʿ II 1316 / August 31, 1995, pp. 12–14, at p. 13. For a later attack on "democratic Islamists" by the same author, see ʿUmar ʿAbd al-Ḥakīm [= Abū Muṣʿab al-Sūrī], *Daʿwat al-muqāwama al-islāmiyya al-ʿālamiyya*, n.d., pp. 1017ff. ("Masʾalat al-dīmuqrāṭiyya wa-tajārib ḥarakāt al-ṣaḥwa al-islāmiyya fīhā"), www.ilmway.com/site/maqdis/MS_11347 (link no longer active).

argue that a complete break with the Muslim Brotherhood legacy was required.

While Abū Muṣʿab al-Sūrī's enthusiasm for the emergence of the new, differentiated school is palpable, he was not really at its forefront, and was less 'differentiated' from the Muslim Brotherhood than were scholars such as Abū Qatāda, al-Maqdisī, and Sayyid Imām. It is true that his *al-Thawra al-islāmiyya al-jihādiyya fī sūriyā* was a milestone in the emergent current's denunciation of the Muslim Brotherhood – though this was a process that unfolded at different paces in different countries – but even in the Syrian context Abū Muṣʿab did not spearhead the charge. As he noted in his introduction to the book, alongside angry critics from the ranks of the Muslim Brotherhood, critics on the other side of the divide (presumably hardliners from the Fighting Vanguard or other early radical salafīs) felt that he was too forgiving of the Brotherhood and that the book in general did not make a sufficiently clean break from Brotherhood thought.[178] We already saw that Abū Muṣʿab distanced himself from ʿAdnān ʿUqla's *takfīr* of those who had signed on to the National Alliance for the Liberation of Syria, and in time he came to see Abū Qatāda as well as a 'destructive doctrinarian' whose theological purism was counterproductive.[179] None of this is to question the basic classification of Abū Muṣʿab al-Sūrī as a radical salafī and opponent of the Muslim Brotherhood – these he clearly was. He simply was more of a strategist than a dogmatic theologian, and there were others whose condemnation of the Brotherhood was more radical and systematic than his own.

### *Sayyid Imām's* al-Jāmiʿ fī ṭalab al-ʿilm al-sharīf

We saw in a passage cited above that Abū Muṣʿab al-Sūrī had mentioned Sayyid Imām's *al-ʿUmda fī iʿdād al-ʿudda* as one of the books that had set out a clear and distinct path for the emerging salafī jihadist groups amidst the ideological disarray that characterized the Arab scene in Peshawar in the 1980s. Imām – known then by the name ʿAbd al-Qādir b. ʿAbd al-ʿAzīz – was another of the founders of the salafī jihādī school, and perhaps the most influential of them in the late 1980s and early 1990s. He was the religious authority for the Egyptian Jihād organization, whose leadership had relocated to Peshawar,[180] and has also been described as

[178] ʿAbd al-Ḥakīm, *al-Thawra al-islāmiyya*, vol. 1, p. 12.

[179] Brynjar Lia, "'Destructive Doctrinarians': Abu Musʿab al-Suri's Critique of the Salafis in the Jihadi Current," in Meijer (ed.), *Global Salafism*, pp. 281–300.

[180] For biographical information on Imām and his relations with the Jihād organization and Ayman al-Ẓawāhirī, see Lav, *Radical Islam*, pp. 145–147.

the *qāḍī* of the al-Qāʿida camps.[181] Published in 1987, *al-ʿUmda* was a work on the topic of jihād written at the request of the al-Qāʿida leadership for use as a manual in the training camps in Afghanistan.[182] The majority of *al-ʿUmda* deals with the laws of jihād, relations between commanders and soldiers, and other topics that fall in the category of jurisprudence broadly defined, but it also contains much that could be described as theological or ideological. Indeed, the introduction to *al-ʿUmda* sets out precisely the relation between monolatry and theonomy that is so characteristic of the salafī jihādī school.

Imām opens this work with an exposition of Taymiyyan monolatry and an explanation of the terms *tawḥīd al-rubūbiyya* and *tawḥīd al-ulūhiyya.* He writes of the latter that it "requires compliance with the command of [Allāh], may He be praised, and with His law (*sharʿ*) that He sent with His prophets," the last of whom was Muḥammad, who brought the final, comprehensive *sharīʿa.*[183] It follows that to adopt the legal determinations (*ḥukm*) of another in preference to those of Allāh is to take that other as an *ilāh.* Sayyid Imām, like Ibn Taymiyya, defines *ilāh* as an object of worship (*maʿbūd*); and like Sayyid Quṭb he cites Qurʾān 43:84, "And it is He who is *ilāh* in heaven and *ilāh* on earth," in order to buttress the point that worldly affairs as well fall under the mandate of exclusivity of worship.[184]

Once he has explained that obedience to law falls under the ambit of *tawḥīd al-ulūhiyya*, Sayyid Imām then explains the proper aim of jihād in relation to this tenet:

> From this you understand, brother, that the invented human systems – man-made laws, democracy, socialism, communism, and so forth … are all outright unbelief (*kufr bawāḥ*). And you understand likewise that the rule

[181] al-Maqdisī, *Wa-lākin kūnū rabbānniyyīn*, part 9: *al-tadrīs fī muʿaskarāt al-qāʿida wa-l-tadarrub fīhā*, 2013 [video], 14:58–15:45, http://abu-qatada.xyz/vid/visual/9039.zip (link no longer active).

[182] On *al-ʿUmda*, see Simon Wolfgang Fuchs, *Proper Signposts for the Camp: The Reception of Classical Authorities in the Ǧihādī Manual* al-ʿUmda fī Iʿdād al-ʿUdda, Würzburg: Ergon Verlag, 2011; Simon Wolfgang Fuchs, "Do Excellent Surgeons Make Miserable Exegetes? Negotiating the Sunni Tradition in the *ǧihādī* Camps," *Die Welt des Islams* 53/2 (2013), pp. 192–237; Daniel Lav, "Jihadists and Jurisprudents: The 'Revisions' Literature of Sayyid Imam and Al-Gama'a Al-Islamiyya," in Joseph Skelly (ed.), *Political Islam from Muhammad to Ahmadinejad: Defenders, Detractors, and Definitions*, Santa Barbara: Praeger Security International, 2010, pp. 105–146. For extensive discussion of Sayyid Imām and his writings in general, see Nedza, Takfīr *im militanten Salafismus*, pp. 21–50.

[183] ʿAbd al-Qādir b. ʿAbd al-ʿAzīz [= Sayyid Imām al-Sharīf], *Risālat al-ʿumda fī iʿdād al-ʿudda li-l-jihād fī sabīl Allāh taʿālā*, n.d., p. 3, www.ilmway.com/site/maqdis/MS_636 (link no longer active).

[184] ʿAbd al-Qādir b. ʿAbd al-ʿAzīz, *al-ʿUmda*, p. 4.

(*ḥukm*) of the *ṭāghūts* that is based in many Muslim countries on these systems is a flagrant aggression against Allāh the Exalted's *ulūhiyya* over His creation on this earth … This is the enemy against whom the Muslims must rise in order to defend the *ulūhiyya* of their Lord, may He be praised … and this, in the language of the *shar*ʿ, is what is called jihād for the sake of Allāh (*fī sabīli llāh*).[185]

The theonomic jihād that is the hallmark of the salafī jihādī school is described here – in a foundational al-Qāʿida jihād manual – as an imperative deriving from the Taymiyyan doctrine of *tawḥīd al-ulūhiyya*. Imām returns to the issue of the relation between jihād and *tawḥīd* at the end of the introduction:

I had already begun to issue a series of books titled "The Call (*Daʿwa*) to *Tawḥīd*" series.[186] I made this treatise [viz. *al-ʿUmda*] an installment in this series, and it is appropriate that it should be so. How could it be otherwise? Jihād was only ordained (*shuriʿa*) in order to spread the call to *tawḥīd*, and to champion it and protect it. Did not the Prophet say: "I was commanded to fight people until they testify that there is no *ilāh* but Allāh and that Muḥammad is the Prophet of Allāh"? And he said: "I was sent with the sword before Judgment Day so that Allāh alone be worshipped without partner." *Tawḥīd* is the aim (*ghāya*), and jihād is one of the means to its realization.[187]

The scope devoted to this issue in *al-ʿUmda* itself is limited; as Imām notes, he had already authored other works devoted more specifically to the topic of *tawḥīd*. We know that he published a tract titled *Taḥqīq al-tawḥīd bi-taḥkīm sharīʿat rabb al-ʿālamīn*, whose topic was the legal status of rulers and their supporters in lands ruled by man-made law, and the legal status of those lands (i.e. whether they are the abode of war, *dār al-ḥarb*, or the abode of Islam, *dār al-islām*). Imām mentions this tract in the introduction to *al-Jāmiʿ fī ṭalab al-ʿilm al-sharīf*, noting that the same topics are covered in the latter work in less detail.[188] In any event it was *al-Jāmiʿ*, authored a few years later in the early 1990s, that was to become Sayyid Imām's most influential work and one of the most important works authored by the first generation of salafī jihādī scholars altogether. It also illustrates well the connection between traditional salafī theology and jurisprudence and modern salafī theonomy, since it encompasses

185 ʿAbd al-Qādir b. ʿAbd al-ʿAzīz, *al-ʿUmda*, p. 4.

186 In the introduction to his subsequent work, *al-Jāmiʿ*, Imām notes that this series was in fact never published. ʿAbd al-Qādir b. ʿAbd al-ʿAzīz [= Sayyid Imām al-Sharīf], *al-Jāmiʿ fī ṭalab al-ʿilm al-sharīf*, 2nd ed., n.p., 1415/1995, p. 5.

187 ʿAbd al-Qādir b. ʿAbd al-ʿAzīz, *al-ʿUmda*, p. 7. See also the section titled "Maʿālim asāsiyya fī al-jihād" (278ff.), which returns to the same themes and makes extensive use of Ibn Taymiyya's distinction between Allāh's ontological will and His legislative will, on which see Hoover, *Ibn Taymiyya's Theodicy*, pp. 122–129.

188 ʿAbd al-Qādir b. ʿAbd al-ʿAzīz, *al-Jāmiʿ*, p. 5.

sections devoted both to classical topics and to such issues as democracy, man-made law, and constitutions. For these reasons the remainder of the present chapter will be devoted to an extensive analysis of the nexus of monolatry, theonomy, and jihād in *al-Jāmiʿ* as representative of the nascent salafī jihādī movement.

The primary aim of *al-Jāmiʿ* was to provide a comprehensive basis for transforming the still-fluid radical milieu of the early 1990s into a well-educated and doctrinally sound cadre capable of assuming leadership in the Islamic world, overthrowing the apostate regimes, and instituting rule by the *sharīʿa*. It is worth bearing in mind the context of the work's composition: It was completed in Sudan, where Imām had resettled, alongside Usāma b. Lādin and Ayman al-Ẓawāhirī, after being evicted from Peshawar by the Pakistani government. This followed years during which Imām was responsible for the education of Arab volunteers in the Afghanistan-Pakistan theater. The contents of *al-Jāmiʿ* can be presumed to approximate the content of what Sayyid Imām taught in Peshawar (especially as they are consistent with the earlier *ʿUmda*) and his experience in teaching Arab volunteers who came from varying backgrounds and for varying reasons, attempting to mold them into a proper dogmatic movement. With the dispersal of the Afghan Arabs Imām no longer had a geographical base for this project and *al-Jāmiʿ* was designed to take the place of Imām's personal instruction, faute de mieux. This accounts for the hybrid nature of the work: On the one hand, *al-Jāmiʿ* is a highly structured study guide, providing introductory explanations and annotated reading lists for every topic in the Islamic sciences for beginning, intermediate, and advanced students; on the other hand, it includes numerous prolix excursus into issues of particular import for contemporary radicals, including theonomy and its ramifications.

In what follows I will survey those portions of *al-Jāmiʿ* that relate to the issue of theonomy, both in its theoretical grounding and in connection with the process of factional differentiation discussed earlier in this chapter. The survey will proceed in the following manner. First, I will address Sayyid Imām's grounding of theonomy in the classical salafī monolatry of Ibn Taymiyya's doctrine of *tawḥīd*. Second, I will examine Imām's polemic against proponents of democratic Islamism and against individuals – from Mawdūdī to ʿAbd al-ʿAzīz b. Bāz – who propounded a version of theonomy in theory but who permitted or endorsed political participation in regimes of parliamentary democracy as a pragmatic compromise. Third, I will discuss the issue of *manhaj* and Imām's contention that the theonomic imperative mandates jihād to overthrow infidel regimes that rule by man-made law.

*Theonomy and Salafī Monolatry* Numerous passages in *al-Jāmiʿ* expound on the nature of *tawḥīd* and the related issue of the meaning of the *shahāda* and its import. Imām follows Ibn Taymiyya in giving a monolatric interpretation to both. In fact, he frames all the thousand-plus pages of *al-Jāmiʿ* – a work whose title labels it as a book on the acquisition of religious knowledge – as an explication of how to uphold monolatry. In his introductory discussion of the kind of religious knowledge that is an individual obligation on all Muslims to acquire (*farḍ al-ʿayn min al-ʿilm al-sharʿī*), Imām adopts the Taymiyyan theme of monolatry as the telos of creation and writes that Allāh (Qurʾān 23:115–116) reproved those who thought that they were created without any final purpose (*ʿabathan*). He argues in good Taymiyyan fashion that everything Allāh does is for a purpose (*li-ḥikmatin*)[189] and cites Ibn Taymiyya's favored prooftext, "I only created the jinn and humans in order that they worship Me" (Qurʾān 51:56) to demonstrate that the purpose for which humans were created is in fact monolatry. Imām then explains that the content of the worship (*ʿibāda*) for the sake of which humans were created is *sharʿī* obligation, that is, what humans are required to do by the normative prescriptions of the *sharīʿa* as revealed through the prophets.[190] Thus the purpose of the acquisition of knowledge is to fulfill the mandate of monolatry for which humans were created.

Various sections of *al-Jāmiʿ* include expositions on the topic of *tawḥīd al-rubūbiyya* and *tawḥīd al-ulūhiyya*. The first treatment comes in this same portion of the work, and specifically in Sayyid Imām's explanation of the first of the five pillars (*arkān*) of Islam – the *shahāda* – and the first of the six pillars of faith, "faith in Allāh" (*al-īmān billāh*).[191] Imām writes that "faith in Allāh" is *tawḥīd*, which is divided into two parts, *tawḥīd al-rubūbiyya* and *tawḥīd al-ulūhiyya*. He defines *tawḥīd al-rubūbiyya* as

> belief that Allāh the Exalted is one, without partner, in His essence (*dhāt*), His acts, and His names and attributes ...; and the belief that Allāh the Exalted is above the heavens, sitting on the Throne, separate from creation, and He is with them [his creation] through His knowledge, His power, His omniscience, His

189 For Ibn Taymiyya's affirmation of this tenet *pace* Ashʿarī voluntarism see Hoover, *Ibn Taymiyya's Theodicy*, pp. 70ff.; and likewise above, Chapter 2 for Muḥammad b. ʿAbd al-Wahhāb's affirmation of the same in his laconic comment on Qurʾān 51:56 at the opening of his *Kitāb al-tawḥīd*: "*al-ḥikma fī khalq al-jinn wa-l-ins*."

190 ʿAbd al-Qādir b. ʿAbd al-ʿAzīz, *al-Jāmiʿ*, p. 49.

191 The five pillars of Islam are the *shahāda*, prayer, the fast, pilgrimage, and the *zakāt* tithe. The six pillars of faith are faith in Allāh, His angels, His scriptures, His prophets, Judgment Day, and faith in divine predetermination, good and bad. Both are codified in the tradition known as *ḥadīth Jibrīl*.

hearing, and His seeing; and the belief … "that there is none like unto Him, and He is the Hearing, the Seeing" (Qur'ān 42:11); and the belief that He alone is the Lord (*rabb*), Master (*mālik*), Creator (*khāliq*), Provider (*rāziq*), the one who harms and benefits, brings to life and puts to death; He it is who legislates for His creation, and none participates with Him in this; and nothing occurs in the cosmos without His permission and will, neither that which He loves and is pleased with, nor that which He loathes and abhors; and the belief that Allāh holds power over all things, and nothing is impossible for Him.[192]

Everything in this definition of *tawḥīd al-rubūbiyya* is Taymiyyan, down to the formula reconciling between Allāh's separation from His creation and His being 'with' them through (and only through) His active attributes.[193] The same can be said for the two synonyms that Imām provides for *tawḥīd al-rubūbiyya*: "the unicity of knowledge and affirmation" (*tawḥīd al-maʿrifa wa-l-ithbāt*) and "cognitive-informative unicity" (*al-tawḥīd al-ʿilmī al-khabarī*).[194] These parallel terminologies emphasize the point that the elements of *tawḥīd al-rubūbiyya* that Imām lists are all assertions regarding the nature of Allāh in which one is required to *believe* (*iʿtiqād*). This stands in contradistinction to *tawḥīd al-ulūhiyya*, which Imām here defines simply as "the worship of Allāh the Exalted alone, or the making of one's worship exclusive to Allāh the Exalted." As synonyms for *tawḥīd al-ulūhiyya* Imām gives "the unicity of worship and intention" (*tawḥīd al-ʿibāda wa-l-qaṣd*) and "volitional-conative unicity" (*al-tawḥīd al-irādī al-ṭalabī*).[195] Here again the parallel terminologies emphasize the contradistinction between the two kinds of *tawḥīd*, which Imām goes on to make explicit while also succintly explaining the interrelation between the two: "It is clear from this that *tawḥīd al-rubūbiyya* is knowledge (*ʿilm*), and *tawḥīd al-ulūhiyya* is action (*ʿamal*), and it [the latter] is the effect (*athar*) of knowledge of *tawḥīd al-rubūbiyya* on the human's actions. Both are required together in order for one's *tawḥīd* and faith to be valid."[196]

This formulation should not be understood as ascribing priority to *rubūbiyya* over *ulūhiyya*; it simply reprises Ibn Taymiyya's contention that a correct configuration of *tawḥīd al-rubūbiyya* should naturally lead to upholding *tawḥīd al-ulūhiyya* as well. Imām follows Ibn Taymiyya in

[192] ʿAbd al-Qādir b. ʿAbd al-ʿAzīz, *al-Jāmiʿ*, pp. 64–65.
[193] See Chapter 1 for my discussion of Ibn Taymiyya's *Fī al-jamʿ bayna ʿulūw al-rabb ʿazza wa-jalla wa-bayna qurbihi min dāʿīhi wa-ʿābidīhi* (in the section "Unmediatedness").
[194] ʿAbd al-Qādir b. ʿAbd al-ʿAzīz, *al-Jāmiʿ*, p. 64.
[195] ʿAbd al-Qādir b. ʿAbd al-ʿAzīz, *al-Jāmiʿ*, p. 65.
[196] ʿAbd al-Qādir b. ʿAbd al-ʿAzīz, *al-Jāmiʿ*, p. 65.

holding that the primary fault line between Muslims and unbelievers is in fact *tawḥīd al-ulūhiyya*:

> One does not become a believer through *tawḥīd al-rubūbiyya* alone, for the unbelievers whom the Prophet fought, and whose lives and property he declared licit, affirmed *tawḥīd al-rubūbiyya*: That Allāh alone without partner is the Creator, that it is He who benefits and harms, and He directs all things … This affirmation [of *tawḥīd al-rubūbiyya*] did not make them Muslims, for they made partners to Him in *ulūhiyya* by worshipping others apart from Allāh through supplication, appeal for aid, vows, sacrifice, and referral in judgment to other than Allāh the Exalted's *sharīʿa*.[197]

This of course is Ibn Taymiyya's distinctive Streitpunkt argument that was employed so extensively by Muḥammad b. ʿAbd al-Wahhāb. Likewise, Imām asserts that all the prophets were sent to their peoples to call them to *tawḥīd al-ulūhiyya* in particular, and that *tawḥīd al-ulūhiyya* was the first matter that the Prophet Muḥammad preached to the Arabs. To prove this point he adduces the Prophet's instructions to the Companion Muʿādh b. Jabal upon sending him as an emissary to Yemen. One version states: "When you come upon the scriptuaries [Jews and Christians], the first thing you call them to should be *tawḥīd* of Allāh the Exalted (*an yuwaḥḥidū llāh taʿālā*)." Imām asserts that this *tawḥīd* was *tawḥīd al-ulūhiyya* in particular, on the basis of parallel versions of the tradition in which the Prophet exhorts Muʿādh to call the scriptuaries to "worship of Allāh" or to the *shahāda*.[198] One sees here that Imām holds the meaning of the *shahāda* to be a statement of *tawḥīd al-ulūhiyya*, an equation he makes explicit elsewhere in the *Jāmiʿ* as well.[199]

This brings us to the issue of the meaning of the *shahāda*, which Imām treats in his discussion of the pillars of Islam. Much like Muḥammad b. ʿAbd al-Wahhāb (see Chapter 2) Imām insists that verbal enunciation of the *shahāda* is not sufficient to guarantee one's status as a Muslim: Fulfillment of the first pillar of Islam requires knowing the meaning of the *shahāda* and the conditions of the testimony's validity. Although one must accept another's testimony at face value and presume he is a Muslim so long as no evidence surfaces to the contrary, one who does not know its meaning is not a Muslim in Allāh's eyes and is liable to fall into actions that nullify his testimony. Imām cites al-Ghazālī on the issue of needing to understand the *shahāda*'s meaning, but his subsequent explanation of its meaning itself is distinctly Taymiyyan.

[197] ʿAbd al-Qādir b. ʿAbd al-ʿAzīz, *al-Jāmiʿ*, p. 65.
[198] ʿAbd al-Qādir b. ʿAbd al-ʿAzīz, *al-Jāmiʿ*, p. 65.
[199] ʿAbd al-Qādir b. ʿAbd al-ʿAzīz, *al-Jāmiʿ*, p. 440.

According to Imām, *lā ilāha illā llāh* comprises negation and affirmation: negation of the *ulūhiyya* of anyone apart from Allāh by abandoning worship of them, and affirmation of *ulūhiyya* to Allāh alone,

> by making Him the exclusive object of acts of worship, such as prayer, supplication (*du ʿā*ʾ), vows, sacrifice, fear, hope, and appeal in judgment. Anyone who directs any of these or other acts of worship to anyone apart from Allāh the Exalted, his action has nullified his speech, and he has not fulfilled the meaning of the *shahāda*. In fact, he is an unbeliever.[200]

It is worth noting that for Imām, understanding the meaning of the *shahāda* is a derivative rather than an inherent part of the obligation, according to the principle *mā lā yatimma al-wājib illā bihi fa-huwa wājib* ("that which is an indispensable necessity to the fulfillment of an obligation is itself an obligation").[201] The true obligation, beyond verbal enunciation of the *shahāda*, is *fulfillment* of its meaning – and, Imām explains, this is *tawḥīd al-ulūhiyya*, avoidance of *shirk*, and exclusive obedience to the Prophet (*tawḥīd al-ulūhiyya wa-ijtināb al-shirk wa-tajrīd mutābaʿat al-nabī*).[202]

Given the emphases noted in the preceding, it is not surprising that the literature Sayyid Imām recommends studying on these topics is that of the Taymiyyan, Wahhābī, and salafī traditions. In order to learn to avoid actions that nullify the *shahāda* he recommends reading Muḥammad b. ʿAbd al-Wahhāb's *Nawāqiḍ al-islām al-ʿashara* ("The Ten Nullifiers of Islam" – which, Imām writes, was culled from Ibn Taymiyya's writings).[203] On the six pillars of faith – faith in Allāh, His angels, His scriptures, His prophets, Judgment Day, and faith in divine predetermination, good and bad – Imām recommends Ibn Taymiyya's *al-ʿAqīda al-wāsiṭiyya*, and on the meaning of the *shahāda* and related topics, Ibn ʿAbd al-Wahhāb's *Kitāb al-tawḥīd* (with the commentary *Fatḥ al-majīd*), *Kashf al-shubuhāt*, and *al-Uṣūl al-thalātha*. Recommended authors on topics of creed include such modern salafīs as Aḥmad b. Ḥajar Āl Bū Ṭāmī (Raʾs al-Khayma/Qatar, d. 2002), the Egyptian Muḥammad Khalīl Harrās (d. 1975),[204] and the Syrian Muḥammad

200 ʿAbd al-Qādir b. ʿAbd al-ʿAzīz, *al-Jāmiʿ*, pp. 61–63.
201 This is a well-known legal maxim (*qāʿida fiqhiyya*); see e.g. Abū Ḥāmid al-Ghazālī, *al-Mustaṣfā min ʿilm al-uṣūl*, Medina: al-Jāmiʿa al-Islāmiyya, 1413/1993, vol. 1, pp. 231–233.
202 ʿAbd al-Qādir b. ʿAbd al-ʿAzīz, *al-Jāmiʿ*, pp. 62–63.
203 ʿAbd al-Qādir b. ʿAbd al-ʿAzīz, *al-Jāmiʿ*, p. 66.
204 Harrās headed the veteran Egyptian salafī association Anṣār al-Sunna al-Muḥammadiyya. He wrote his doctoral thesis at al-Azhar on *Ibn Taymiyya wa-naqduhu li-masālik al-mutakallimīn fī al-ilāhiyyāt wa-l-falsafa* ["Ibn Taymiyya and His Criticism of the Paths of the *Kalām* Theologians and Philosophers"] and taught both at al-Azhar and at Saudi universities. See www.ansaralsonna.com/web/play-1752.html.

b. Jamīl Zīnū (d. 2010).[205] The listing of these modern authors demonstrates that Imām did not just draw inspiration from the textual tradition of premodern salafism, but also inscribed himself within the living modern salafī milieu. By extension, the same is more or less true of the Egyptian Jihād organization and all others who learned from Imām and the other salafī jihādī scholars. While this point might appear self-evident, it is worth noting explicitly, since studies of the Egyptian Jihād organization a mere decade prior to the writing of *al-Jāmiʿ*, in the years following President Sādāt's assassination, do not classify the group as salafī, or even mention salafism for that matter.[206] The major difference between these radical individuals and groups who now identified as salafīs and the more general salafī milieu was of course the centrality of theonomy in their doctrine and their adoption of a *manhaj* of armed jihād in order to effect it. Imām was apparently not impressed with the growing body of modern theonomic literature of the kind we surveyed earlier in this chapter: He notes that works dealing with the issue of *al-ḥukm bi-ghayr mā anzala llāh* ("ruling by other than what Allāh revealed") are "rare in our days" and those that do exist contain errors.[207] Imām perhaps had in mind writings by earlier fusionists, though he does not elaborate here; in any event, his comment is illustrative of the fact that the salafī jihādīs' version of theonomy was a dogma whose precise contours were still in the process of being formulated. Whereas he had numerous works to recommend on such classic issues as *tawḥīd* and the meaning of the *shahāda*, the only work he recommends reading on *al-ḥukm bi-ghayr mā anzala llāh* is Muḥammad b. Ibrāhīm's *Taḥkīm al-qawānīn*.[208]

Imām's most systematic exposition of the relation between theonomy and classic salafī monolatry appears toward the end of the work in a section titled *Bayān taʿalluq masāʾil al-tashrīʿ wa-l-ḥukm wa-l-taḥākum bi-tawḥīdi llāh ʿazza wa-jalla* ("Explanation of the Connection between the Issues of Legislation, Rule, and Appeal in Judgment and *Tawḥīd* of Allāh").[209]

205 ʿAbd al-Qādir b. ʿAbd al-ʿAzīz, *al-Jāmiʿ*, pp. 430–431. Originally from Aleppo, Muḥammad b. Jamīl Zīnū subsequently taught in Mecca. In his autobiographical *Kayfa ihtadaytu*, Zīnū recounts that in his early education he learned *tawḥīd* from a book titled *al-Ḥuṣūn al-ḥamīdiyya*, which taught only *tawḥīd al-rabb*; it was only later that he learned that this was an error, as this was something that the Arab *mushrikūn* already acknowledged, and that it was *tawḥīd al-ilāh* that is the foundation of a Muslim's salvation. Muḥammad b. Jamīl Zīnū, *Kayfa ihtadaytu ilā al-tawḥīd wa-l-ṣirāṭ al-mustaqīm*, Riyadh: Dār al-Ṣumayʿī, 1415[/1994–1995].

206 For example, Sivan, *Radical Islam*, pp. 103–104; Kepel, *Muslim Extremism in Egypt*, pp. 191ff.

207 ʿAbd al-Qādir b. ʿAbd al-ʿAzīz, *al-Jāmiʿ*, p. 794.

208 ʿAbd al-Qādir b. ʿAbd al-ʿAzīz, *al-Jāmiʿ*, p. 433.

209 ʿAbd al-Qādir b. ʿAbd al-ʿAzīz, *al-Jāmiʿ*, pp. 798ff.

He writes at the opening of this section: "Every Muslim concerned for his religion must know that the matters of legislation (*tashrī'*), rule (*ḥukm*), and appeal in judgment (*taḥākum*) are not derivative issues of applied religious jurisprudence (*min masā'il al-aḥkām al-far'iyya fī al-dīn*), but are rather part of the foundation of faith and the heart of *tawḥīd* (*hiya dākhila fī aṣl al-īmān wa-ṣulb al-tawḥīd*)." This assertion in itself – that matters of theonomy are a core element of faith – has major implications for concrete questions of *manhaj*, as we will see presently. Here we will focus on how Imām grounds this assertion in a *rubūbiyya/ulūhiyya* analysis drawn from the Taymiyyan tradition.

Imām first reiterates the foundations of classic salafī monolatry. Allāh created creation for the sake of exclusive worship of Him without partner, as stated in Qur'ān 51:56, "I only created the jinn and humans in order that they worship Me." Knowledge and *tawḥīd* of Allāh are thus divinely implanted human nature (*fiṭra*), and likewise the prophets were all sent in order to remind humans of this and to teach them what kind of worship was obligatory on them. While the laws brought by the various prophets differed, all were sent with one single creed: The call to worship Allāh alone without partner.[210] Imām then reminds his readers that *tawḥīd* is of two kinds, *tawḥīd al-rubūbiyya* and *tawḥīd al-ulūhiyya*, before treating each one in turn and explaining its relation to theonomy. (So far we have seen theonomy expressed primarily as a corollary of *tawḥīd al-ulūhiyya*, and this will be Imām's main emphasis as well, but in his formulation of the issue in *al-Jāmi'* it is in fact grounded in both.)

Here Imām once again defines *tawḥīd al-rubūbiyya*, as follows:

> belief (*i'tiqād*) in Allāh the Exalted's unicity (*waḥdāniyya*) and His exclusivity (*tafarrudihi*) in His acts, names, and attributes, with no partner in any of this. '*Rabb*' is master (*mālik*) and one who disposes freely over others (*mutaṣarrif*). *Tawḥīd al-rubūbiyya* is also known by the names of "the unicity of knowledge and affirmation" (*tawḥīd al-ma'rifa wa-l-ithbāt*) and "cognitive-informative unicity of belief" (*al-tawḥīd al-'ilmī al-khabarī al-i'tiqādī*), because what is demanded of the servant in it is to know (*ma'rifa*) the *rabb* in His acts, names, and attributes, and to affirm what He is owed (*ithbāt mā yajibu lahu*), may He be praised, through knowledge and belief (*ma'rifatan wa-i'tiqādan*). And anyone who makes for Allāh the Exalted a partner in His essence (*dhāt*), acts, names, or attributes has made a partner (*ashraka*) for Allāh in His *rubūbiyya*, and has denied (*kafara bi-*) Allāh the Exalted ...

And among the acts of Allāh the Exalted that He reserved exclusively to Himself alone is the right to legislate for His creation by establishing laws, commands, and prohibitions for them.[211]

[210] 'Abd al-Qādir b. 'Abd al-'Azīz, *al-Jāmi'*, pp. 798–799.
[211] 'Abd al-Qādir b. 'Abd al-'Azīz, *al-Jāmi'*, p. 799.

This definition is nearly identical to the one Imām provided toward the opening of *al-Jāmiʿ* in his exposition of *rubūbiyya* and *ulūhiyya*, but here he goes on to expand on the last-mentioned point: *Tawḥīd al-rubūbiyya* is (in part) the affirmation of the exclusivity of Allāh's acts, and legislation is one of these acts. For this reason, a human who legislates for others makes of himself their *rabb*, and those who bestow on him the right to legislate, or obey him in his legislation, have taken him as a *rabb*. In order to bolster the claim that legislation is an exclusive function of Allāh in His capacity as *rabb*, Imām cites Qurʾān 9:31 and the ʿAdī b. Ḥātim *ḥadīth*, and adds the comment of the nineteenth-century Iraqi scholar Maḥmūd al-Ālūsī, in his commentary *Rūḥ al-maʿānī*: "The majority of the exegetes said: the meaning of *arbāb* [in this verse] is not that they believed them to be gods over the world (*annahum iʿtaqadū annahum ālihat al-ʿālam*), but rather the meaning is that they obeyed them in their commands and prohibitions."

Imām goes on to write that in the countries of the modern *jāhiliyya* – what are called secular countries – different groups assume the authority (*sulṭa*) to legislate for people. Principal among them are parliaments but also the heads of state who ratify laws. Both make themselves partners to Allāh in His *rubūbiyya* and establish themselves as *arbāb* in place of Allāh. In conclusion to his explanation of how theonomy relates to *rubūbiyya*, Imām cites the Wahhābī exegete Muḥammad al-Amīn al-Shinqīṭī: "Because legislation and all the laws, whether normative (*sharʿiyya*) or cosmic-deterministic (*kawniyya qadariyya*), are exclusive prerogatives of *rubūbiyya* ... anyone who adheres (*ittabaʿa*) to legislation other than Allāh's legislation has taken that legislator as a *rabb* and has made him a partner with Allāh."[212]

Imām then follows the same procedure in explaining the relation between theonomy and *tawḥīd al-ulūhiyya*. He first gives the basic definition of this kind of *tawḥīd*: "It is to make Allāh the exclusive object of worship, for an *ilāh* is an object of worship (*maʿbūd*)." This is the basic Taymiyyan definition rooted in the lexicographical tradition on *ilāh*. Equally Taymiyyan is Imām's assertion, once again, that it is *tawḥīd al-ulūhiyya* and not *tawḥīd al-rubūbiyya* that serves as the basic dividing line between believers and unbelievers:

> One who worships Allāh alone in all the forms of worship, those of the heart and in external [acts], he is the believer who upholds Allāh's unicity; and one who worships another, or who worships Him and worships another [together with Him], he is a *mushrik* unbeliever. *Tawḥīd al-ulūhiyya* is also called *tawḥīd al-ʿibāda* and volitional-intentional-conative unicity (*al-tawḥīd al-irādī al-qaṣdī*

212 ʿAbd al-Qādir b. ʿAbd al-ʿAzīz, *al-Jāmiʿ*, p. 799; al-Shinqīṭī, *Aḍwāʾ al-bayān*, vol. 7, p. 180.

*al-ṭalabī*). This is because what is asked of the human servant in this is not just knowledge of the *rabb* and affirmation of what He is owed (*mā yajibu lahu*), as in *tawḥīd al-rubūbiyya*, but rather for the servant to make his worship exclusive to his *rabb*, and likewise his will, intention, and desire.

The servant's faith is not valid until he performs both kinds of *tawḥīd* … Know that *tawḥīd al-ulūhiyya* implies (*mutaḍammin*) *tawḥīd al-rubūbiyya*, but not vice versa. Only one who believes in Allāh's unicity and His exclusivity in His essence, acts, names, and attributes – and this is *tawḥīd al-rubūbiyya* – can make worship exclusive to Allāh – and this is *tawḥīd al-ulūhiyya*. But there may be *tawḥīd al-rubūbiyya* without *tawḥīd al-ulūhiyya*. This occurs when someone knows the existence of the *rabb* and affirms His dominion, His role as Creator, and His direction [of the cosmos], but together with that either does not worship Him or associates others in his worship of Him. This was the case with the peoples to whom the prophets were sent.

Here we find a number of interrelated classic themes: the priority of *tawḥīd al-ulūhiyya* over *tawḥīd al-rubūbiyya*, the unbelievers' acknowledgment of *tawḥīd al-rubūbiyya*, and *tawḥīd al-ulūhiyya* as the message of the prophets. Imām goes on to assert that the Qurʾān itself depicts the prophets as appealing to the unbelievers' acknowledgment of *rubūbiyya* to urge them to uphold *tawḥīd al-ulūhiyya*, mentioning the same verses as do Ibn Taymiyya and Ibn ʿAbd al-Wahhāb when advancing the same claim (e.g. 10:31, 43:87, 2:21, 16:17).[213]

Imām then sums up this topic in the words of Ibn Taymiyya himself:

The meaning of *tawḥīd* is not just *tawḥīd al-rubūbiyya*, which is the belief that Allāh alone created the world, as some *kalām* theologians and Ṣūfīs think. These people think that if they establish this [i.e. Allāh's creation of the world] through proof then they have established the ultimate degree of *tawḥīd* … [Whereas in truth] one who affirms all that is due to the Exalted *rabb* in terms of His attributes, declares Him free of all the imperfections of which He is free, and affirms Him alone as Creator of all things is still not a *muwaḥḥid* so long as he has not testified that there is no *ilāh* but Allāh alone, affirms that Allāh alone is the *ilāh* to whom worship is due, and adheres to worship of Allāh alone without partner … for the Arab polytheists (*mushrikūn*) [also] affirmed that Allāh alone created all things, and were nonetheless polytheists.[214]

Imām goes on to note the connection between this distinction and jihād: The Arab polytheists' affirmation of *rubūbiyya* did not guarantee them immunity of life and property, and the Prophet fought them due to their *shirk* in *ulūhiyya*.[215]

213 ʿAbd al-Qādir b. ʿAbd al-ʿAzīz, *al-Jāmiʿ*, p. 800.
214 ʿAbd al-Qādir b. ʿAbd al-ʿAzīz, *al-Jāmiʿ*, pp. 800–801, cited in ʿAbd al-Raḥmān b. Ḥasan, *Fatḥ al-majīd*, p. 16.
215 ʿAbd al-Qādir b. ʿAbd al-ʿAzīz, *al-Jāmiʿ*, p. 801.

Up to this point Imām's survey of *tawḥīd al-ulūhiyya* is entirely in keeping with the premodern salafī tradition of Ibn Taymiyya and Muḥammad b. ʿAbd al-Wahhāb. He then explains on this basis the relation between *tawḥīd al-ulūhiyya* and theonomy, in the following simple manner: *Tawḥīd al-ulūhiyya* is the making of one's worship exclusive to Allāh (*ifrād Allāh waḥdahu bi-l-ʿibāda*); and one of the forms of worship (*ʿibādāt*) that Allāh made obligatory on His creation is to rule by His law (*sharʿ*) and to appeal to it in judgment. This is how Imām understands Qurʾān 12:40: "Judgment is Allāh's alone; He commanded that you worship none but Him" (*in al-ḥukm illā lillāh amara allā taʿbudū illā iyyāhu*). The 'worship' (*ʿibāda*) of ruling by Allāh's law is an obligation on human rulers in particular, but both rulers and ruled are obligated to refer in judgment (*al-taḥākum ilā*) to Allāh's law, and their faith is not valid if they fail to do so, as per Qurʾān 4:65: "Nay, by your Lord, they do not believe until they make you [Muḥammad] the judge in matters of dispute among themselves, and find in themselves no resistance to your decisions, and submit willingly." According to Imām, the Qurʾān's conditioning of faith on submission in judgment means that it is a form of worship that is part of the very foundation of faith (*aṣl al-īmān*).[216] As we will see, this claim has important implications for the ruling on the permissibility or impermissibility of participation in modern political systems.

Imām then sums up the relation between theonomy and the *rubūbiyya/ulūhiyya* paradigm neatly through the prism of one of this paradigm's distinctive formulations: the contrast between Allāh's acts, which are the object of *tawhid al-rubūbiyya*, and humans' acts, which are the object of *tawḥīd al-ulūhiyya*.[217] To my knowledge Imām was the first to apply this succinct formulation to the issue of theonomy:

> It is clear from the preceding that making Allāh the Exalted the exclusive legislator for creation (*ifrād Allāh taʿālā bi-l-tashrīʿ li-l-khalq*) – which is one of His acts – is part of *tawḥīd al-rubūbiyya*, and that making Him the only one by whose laws one rules and to whose laws one appeals in judgment – which are the servants' acts – is part of *tawḥīd al-ulūhiyya*. This is because *tawḥīd al-rubūbiyya* is to make Allāh exclusive in His acts (*ifrād Allāh bi-fiʿlihi*), and *tawḥīd al-ulūhiyya* is to make Allāh exclusive in the servants' acts that Allāh commanded them as worship (*ifrād Allāh bi-afʿāl al-ʿibād allatī taʿabbadahum Allāh bihā*).[218]

We saw earlier that Imām follows the premodern salafī monolatric tradition in interpreting the *shahāda* as meaning specifically that Allāh must

216 ʿAbd al-Qādir b. ʿAbd al-ʿAzīz, *al-Jāmiʿ*, p. 801.
217 Imām's formulation here is particularly reminiscent of Muḥammad b. ʿAbd al-Wahhāb; cf. *Durar*, vol. 1, pp. 62, 168, vol. 2, p. 67 (discussed in Chapter 2).
218 ʿAbd al-Qādir b. ʿAbd al-ʿAzīz, *al-Jāmiʿ*, p. 801.

be the exclusive object of worship, and in arguing that anyone who worships another apart from Allāh has thereby nullified his profession of faith. Here Imām applies this same logic to the issue of judgment by Allāh's law, which he has just argued is a form of worship:

When you understand that the point of the statement of *tawḥīd* [i.e. *lā ilāha illā llāh*] is to fulfill its meaning by making one's worship exclusive to Allāh, it becomes clear to you that one who claims to be Muslim, and prays and fasts, but rules by or appeals in judgment to a law other than Allāh's law, he is not a Muslim, because he has not made worship exclusive to Allāh and thus has not fulfilled the meaning of the statement of *tawḥīd*. Or in other words: He has said it with his tongue and nullified it by his acts.[219]

This is reminiscent of Sayyid Quṭb's insistence that *ḥākimiyya* is an essential component of *lā ilāha illā llāh*, and Imām himself adopts the language of the "modern *jāhiliyya*," but the argument is stated in explicitly salafī terms and is grounded in the *tawḥīd* doctrine inherited from Ibn Taymiyya and Muḥammad b. ʿAbd al-Wahhāb. Thus Imām continues: "This is the situation in the societies of the modern *jāhiliyya*: People pray and fast to Allāh, and together with that confer on others the right to legislate, and this is *shirk* in *rubūbiyya*; and they rule by and appeal in judgment to law other than Allāh's law, and this is *shirk* in *ulūhiyya*."[220] Imām notes that such human legal autonomy is explicitly endorsed in the Egyptian constitution: "The parliament is vested with the legislative authority" (Article 86); "Judgment (*ḥukm*) in the courts is by the [man-made] law (*qānūn*)" (Article 165); and "Crime and punishment are based solely on the law (*qānūn*)" (Article 66). Nor is Imām impressed by Article 2, which stipulates that "the principles of the Islamic *sharīʿa* are the principal source of legislation." In fact, he states that this latter article is worse unbelief than the others, since it implies that there are other sources of legislation, which is tantamount to saying "there is no principal *ilāh* but Allāh."[221]

Imām concludes his section on the relation between theonomy and *tawḥīd* with an indication of the practical implications of this theological exposition. He reiterates the point that the matters discussed therein are not just matters of applied religious jurisprudence (*min masāʾil al-aḥkām*

219 ʿAbd al-Qādir b. ʿAbd al-ʿAzīz, *al-Jāmiʿ*, p. 802.
220 ʿAbd al-Qādir b. ʿAbd al-ʿAzīz, *al-Jāmiʿ*, p. 802.
221 ʿAbd al-Qādir b. ʿAbd al-ʿAzīz, *al-Jāmiʿ*, pp. 802–803. This is the same point made two decades later by the al-Qāʿida commander Abū Yaḥyā al-Lībī; see the Introduction. Imām also points out that the constitution defines the "principles of the *sharīʿa*" as truth, justice, equality, presumption of innocence, and so forth (i.e. as something approaching the concept of natural law) and does not mandate adherence to the substantive provisions of the *sharīʿa*.

*al-far'iyya*), but rather relate to the heart of *tawḥīd* and the foundation of faith. Thus the dispute between the one who upholds them and one who abandons them is not just a dispute over what is permitted and what is forbidden: It is a dispute between faith and unbelief, Islam and *jāhiliyya*, *tawḥīd* and *shirk*, between *lā ilāha illā llāh* and there being other *ilāh*s. It follows that there are two and only two kinds of regimes: A regime in which legislation and judgment are Allāh's alone is a regime of faith, Islam, and *tawḥīd*, whereas a regime in which these are accorded to another is a regime of *kufr*, *jāhiliyya*, and *shirk*. Imām writes that it is obligatory to differentiate between these two regimes and to spread this knowledge, so that every Muslim will know that Allāh commands him to depose the infidel regimes and to establish Islamic regimes in their place.[222]

*The Critique of Democratic Islamism* This conclusion serves as a good segue into our survey of the next topic in Imām's *al-Jāmi'*, his critique of democratic Islamism. As previously noted, Imām was writing at a time when emergent organizations in a number of countries were crystallizing into a loose network of dogmatic salafī jihādī militancy. These groups stood in opposition to forms of Islamic activism that adopted pragmatic compromises with the prevailing political systems. Imām's attacks on the theoretical foundations of political pragmatism ought to be read in this context.

A central claim in *al-Jāmi'* is that the legal status of the instruments of democracy is the same as that of democracy itself, and thus any political participation in a democratic regime – for example, running for parliament, voting in parliamentary elections, or membership in political parties – is an act of apostasy. This claim is based on the arguments surveyed above that characterize theonomy as an issue of *tawḥīd*, and is directed against those who adopt instrumental compromises with democracy.

The basic characterization of democracy itself as *shirk* flows naturally from Imām's salafī theonomy. He argues that in order to understand what democracy itself is so as to render judgment on it, one has to understand it in light of those who invented the term and the institution. Against Islamic modernists who seek to see in democracy an approximation of Islamic *shūrā* (consultation), Imām adduces a linguistic-jurisprudential principle from Ibn Taymiyya and Ibn Qayyim al-Jawziyya according to which terms that are not defined either by Arabic linguistic usage (e.g. *shams* for sun, *qamar* for moon) or by the *shar'* (e.g. *ṣalāt* for prayer, *zakāt* for the tithe) must be defined by the usage (*'urf*) of

222 'Abd al-Qādir b. 'Abd al-'Azīz, *al-Jāmi'*, pp. 803–804.

those who coined the terms.[223] Since democracy is a Western term, one needs to draw its definition from its Western sources.

Imām goes on to write that the meaning of democracy in Western usage is popular sovereignty (*siyādat al-sha ʿb*); and sovereignty itself means supreme and absolute authority that is not subject to the control of any other authority. In democracy people exercise this supreme authority by choosing their rulers and by exercising their right to legislate whatever laws they like, and they normally do so by delegation, through their representatives in parliament. He cites on this score a standard Western textbook on international relations:

> Sovereignty means supreme authority which recognizes no superior and beyond which there is no legal appeal. This basic meaning has remained unchanged throughout modern times and Jean Bodin's definition made in 1576 that sovereignty is 'the supreme power over citizens and subjects unrestrained by law' has remained valid even though Bodin's sovereign absolutist ruler has now been replaced by the nation.[224]

Though aware of intellectual precedents in the writings of John Locke, Jean-Jacques Rousseau, and others, Imām follows in the footsteps of an influential book on secularism by the Saudi scholar Safar al-Ḥawālī, a leading figure in the Ṣaḥwa,[225] in considering the French Revolution as the origin of Western secular democratic regimes. He portrays the emergence of democratic popular sovereignty, as embodied in revolution-era declarations, as a revolt against the divine right of kings, and ultimately as a revolt against divine authority as such. He cites Article 6 of the 1789 Déclaration des droits de l'homme et du citoyen: "The law is the expression of the general will" (*al-qānūn huwa al-ta ʿbīr ʿan irādat al-umma*; Fr.: *La loi est l'expression de la volonté générale*) and adds: "that is, the law is not the expression of the will of the Church or of God"; and he likewise notes that the principle of popular sovereignty is codified in Article 25 of the 1793 Déclaration: "Sovereignty resides in the people" (*al-siyāda tatarakkazu fī al-sha ʿb*; Fr.: *La souveraineté réside dans le peuple*).[226]

Imām thus argues that the essence of democracy is popular sovereignty as expressed in the people's right to legislate for themselves, and this is likewise the *manāṭ al-ḥukm* for democracy – that is, the essential characteristic on which Islamic legal determinations regarding democracy are to be based. Imām then goes on to argue that the legal sovereignty that

223 ʿAbd al-Qādir b. ʿAbd al-ʿAzīz, *al-Jāmiʿ*, p. 148.

224 ʿAbd al-Qādir b. ʿAbd al-ʿAzīz, *al-Jāmiʿ*, p. 148; Joseph Frankel, *International Relations*, 2nd ed., London: Oxford University Press, 1969, p. 10.

225 On Safar al-Ḥawālī, see Lacroix, *Les islamistes saoudiens*; Lav, *Radical Islam*, pp. 86–119.

226 ʿAbd al-Qādir b. ʿAbd al-ʿAzīz, *al-Jāmiʿ*, pp. 148–149.

democracy invests in humans is an attribute (*ṣifa*) of Allāh, as expressed in verses such as Qurʾān 13:41: "Allāh judges, and none can amend His judgment." Democracy bestows divinity on humans by granting them this attribute of Allāh, and pursuant to this finding, it follows that democracy is "greater unbelief" (*kufr akbar*), namely, the kind of unbelief that negates one's faith entirely, as opposed to "lesser unbelief" (*kufr aṣghar*), a term applied to sins that do not make one an apostate. Democracy is "a religion in its own right, in which sovereignty belongs to the people, in contrast with the religion of Islam, in which sovereignty belongs to Allāh."[227]

This general characterization of democracy is of course one that Mawdūdī and Quṭb shared, and Imām does cite Mawdūdī here on the topic, but not as a supporting authority. His intention, rather, is to spear Mawdūdī on a consistency argument: "After these words, it remains for the reader to know that Mawdūdī's group, the Jamāʿat-i Islāmī in Pakistan, took democracy as its *manhaj* and participated in parliamentary elections in Pakistan – which is a secular country – both in Mawdūdī's lifetime and after his death, up to this day."[228]

Imām does not expend a great amount of effort in proving the general point that MPs fall into unbelief. Modern constitutions state that parliament is the legislative authority, and its members exercise effective sovereignty (*siyāda fiʿliyya*) on behalf of the sovereign people – and Imām already wrote that all this is polytheism.[229] The salient point in his argument about MPs, and the one to which he devotes the greater part of his attention, is his claim that even MPs who have no intention of legislating in place of Allāh, and who claim that their presence there is only for the sake of *daʿwa* and Islamic reform, have also fallen into unbelief.

Among Imām's various arguments on this point the most significant comes in the course of his refutation of a fatwā by ʿAbd al-ʿAzīz b. Bāz – the same fatwā that ʿUmar Sulaymān al-Ashqar had cited in *Ḥukm al-mushāraka* as support for the permissibility of serving in parliament. As with his critique of Mawdūdī, the argument against Ibn Bāz likewise targets a scholar who professes the correct opinion on democracy in principle, but – in Imām's view – fails to consistently rule in accordance with it in matters of practical application. As for acknowledgment of the

[227] ʿAbd al-Qādir b. ʿAbd al-ʿAzīz, *al-Jāmiʿ*, p. 149.
[228] ʿAbd al-Qādir b. ʿAbd al-ʿAzīz, *al-Jāmiʿ*, pp. 149–150. Later in the work, when criticizing Islamists who adopt the *bidʿa* of writing constitutions (even if these do not include anything that contravenes the *sharīʿa*), Imām mentions as an example the treatise *Tadwīn al-dustūr al-islāmī*, which is a work by Mawdūdī (p. 778).
[229] ʿAbd al-Qādir b. ʿAbd al-ʿAzīz, *al-Jāmiʿ*, p. 150.

principle, Imām cites Ibn Bāz's commentary on a classic work by Muḥammad b. ʿAbd al-Wahhāb outlining the ten principal 'nullifiers' of faith, the fourth of which reads: "One who believes that another's guidance is more perfect than the guidance of the Prophet, or that another's judgment is better than his judgment, like those who prefer the judgment of the *ṭāghūt*s over his judgment – he is an unbeliever." Ibn Bāz comments on this:

This includes as well everyone who believes that judgment by [a law] other than Allāh's *sharīʿa*, in transactions, criminal punishments (*ḥudūd*), or anything else, is permitted. [This is the case] even if he does not believe that [the other law] is preferable to the judgment of the *sharīʿa*, because in so doing he has made licit that about which there exists a consensus that Allāh has forbidden it; and everyone who makes licit what Allāh has forbidden, in matters that are necessarily known in religion (*maʿlūm min al-dīn bi-l-ḍarūra*) – such as fornication, wine, interest, and rule by other than Allāh's *sharīʿa* – he is an unbeliever, by the consensus of the Muslims.[230]

Sayyid Imām clearly approves of Ibn Bāz's position here, but as with the example of Mawdūdī, he cites it as a consistency argument against the Saudi scholar. The fatwā by Ibn Bāz that Imām critiques in this section of *al-Jāmiʿ* permitted running for parliament when one did so with proper intention. As noted earlier, Imām himself is completely unwilling to distinguish between the ruling on democracy itself and the ruling on democratic instruments such as parliaments:

The instruments of implementing democracy have the same legal status [as democracy itself], such as launching political parties, establishing parliaments, and participation in these parties or in parliamentary elections, as a candidate or as a voter. All this is greater unbelief on the part of the one who does it, encourages it, presents it to people in a favorable light, or is satisfied with it – even if he does not do this himself – since these are the instruments of implementing the religion (*dīn*) of the unbelievers.

Do not be dazzled into error by the great numbers who have parted paths with the religion of Islam and have entered into the religion of the unbelievers. Once they have become satisfied with democracy and its instruments, even if one of them bows in prayer a thousand times a day or recites the Qurʾān a hundred times a day, he is still an unbeliever.[231]

The fatwā by Ibn Bāz relies on the concept of *niyya* (intention) to permit running for parliament and voting for parliamentary candidates – that is, one is permitted to do so if one's intention is to use one's position in

230 ʿAbd al-Qādir b. ʿAbd al-ʿAzīz, *al-Jāmiʿ*, p. 151, citing *Majallat al-Buḥūth al-Islāmiyya* 7 (Rajab–Shawwāl 1403 [= April–July, 1983]), pp. 17–18.

231 ʿAbd al-Qādir b. ʿAbd al-ʿAzīz, *al-Jāmiʿ*, p. 433.

parliament for the sake of *da'wa* and so forth. Ibn Bāz cites on this score a *ḥadīth* that we have already encountered in this chapter in connection with Ḥasan al-Huḍaybī: "Actions are only according to intentions, and an individual only gets what he intends. One whose emigration (*hijra*) is to Allāh and the Prophet, his emigration is to Allāh and the Prophet, and one whose emigration is to attainment in this world or a woman he intends to marry, his emigration is to what he emigrated for." Ibn Bāz, after citing this *ḥadīth*, writes:

> Thus there is nothing wrong with joining parliament if the intention in so doing is to support truth and to not agree to falsehood, since there is therein a championing of truth and a joining [of the ranks] of the proselytizers for Allāh. Likewise, there is nothing wrong with obtaining a [voting] card with which one can elect righteous proselytizers and support the truth and the people of truth.[232]

Against this view, Sayyid Imām insists on the principle (cited from Abū Ḥāmid al-Ghazālī) that whereas *niyya* is an important criterion in acts of obedience and in permitted matters, it can never convert a sin into an act of obedience or make it licit. Acts that fall into the category of sin (*ma'āṣī*) can only become permitted when there is a specific textual proof that indicates this – for example, a *ḥadīth* related by Umm Kulthūm that permits lying in a state of war or for the sake of effecting reconciliation between people or between husband and wife. Furthermore, in Sayyid Imām's view – based on his grounding of theonomy in Taymiyyan *tawḥīd* – running or voting for parliament is not mere sin, but is *kufr*, which is the greatest of sins, and thus it remains *kufr* no matter what the proclaimed intention of the candidate or the voter.[233]

This dispute reaches to the heart of the role of theonomy in faith. Earlier in the present chapter I argued that Ḥasan al-Huḍaybī's reliance on this same principle of *al-a'māl bi-l-niyyāt* greatly blunted his commitment to monolatry and theonomy as a true criterion of faith, since the dividing line between faith and *kufr* in his view ultimately hinged on issues of belief rather than acts. It is true that Ibn Bāz does not go as far in this direction as did al-Huḍaybī in *Du'āt lā quḍāt*, where it was of a piece with a number of other claims; the Saudi scholar was firmly planted within the Wahhābī tradition, including its monolatric theology. That, however, is precisely the point of Sayyid Imām's critique: He argues that Ibn Bāz, by his inappropriate appeal to intention (*niyya*), undermined

232 'Abd al-Qādir b. 'Abd al-'Azīz, *al-Jāmi'*, p. 147, citing the Muslim Brotherhood periodical *Liwā' al-Islām* 11 (1409 [= 1988–1989]), p. 7 of the supplement. On *Liwā' al-Islām*, see Carrie Rosefsky Wickham, *Mobilizing Islam: Religion, Activism, and Political Change in Egypt*, New York: Columbia University Press, 2002, pp. 101–102.

233 'Abd al-Qādir b. 'Abd al-'Azīz, *al-Jāmi'*, pp. 147–148.

this very tradition and its proper application to contemporary issues. When the true polytheistic nature of democracy and its instruments is properly understood, one understands that they cannot be permitted under any circumstance, neither by intention nor by *ḍarūra* (exigent circumstance) nor *maṣlaḥa* (considerations of public utility).[234] Imām even goes so far as to compare those who enter parliament under the claim that their intention is to proselytize for Allāh's sake to the polytheists in the Qurʾān who claimed that their worship of others was for the sake of coming closer to Allāh.[235] This is a classic Wahhābī theme, simply transposed from ritual monolatry to modern theonomy, and directed against one of the leading Wahhābī scholars of the day.

The focus on Ibn Bāz was not just a function of his position but also of his influence. The original fatwā was published in 1989 in the Egyptian Muslim Brotherhood periodical *Liwāʾ al-Islām* and presumably related to debates in Egypt over the permissibility of participation in electoral politics in that country – whether in light of Quṭb's condemnations of parliaments or in light of salafī opposition such as that of Sayyid al-Ghubāshī. The influence of Ibn Bāz's position was not limited, however, to this immediate audience. Sayyid Imām writes that a number of *ʿulamāʾ* followed Ibn Bāz's ruling on this matter and permitted parliamentary participation under the pretense of exigent circumstance (*ḍarūra*). According to Imām, even some who knew better nonetheless adopted Ibn Bāz's position out of blameworthy *taqlīd*; as an example he names Safar al-Ḥawālī, the aforementioned Saudi scholar from the Ṣaḥwa movement. Imām explains that he singles him out as an example because al-Ḥawālī taught at the Faculty of *ʿAqīda* (at Umm al-Qurā University in Mecca) and knew the true meaning of *shirk* and its types, and because, in his book on secularism, he had explained the basis of democracy and its polytheistic nature.[236] This criticism is in line with Sayyid Imām's systematic critique of earlier thinkers who were in certain respects precursors of the salafī jihādī school, but who failed to press theonomic principles to what Imām considered to be their logical conclusion.

*Theonomy and Jihād* This brings us to the final point we will treat in *al-Jāmiʿ*: the connection between Imām's dogmatic formulation of theonomy and the *manhaj* of armed jihād to overthrow apostate rulers. As noted,

[234] ʿAbd al-Qādir b. ʿAbd al-ʿAzīz, *al-Jāmiʿ*, pp. 153–154, citing on the issue of *maṣlaḥa* and *ḍarūra* Ibn Taymiyya, *Majmūʿat al-fatāwā*, vol. 14, pp. 261–262, 264.

[235] ʿAbd al-Qādir b. ʿAbd al-ʿAzīz, *al-Jāmiʿ*, p. 153.

[236] ʿAbd al-Qādir b. ʿAbd al-ʿAzīz, *al-Jāmiʿ*, pp. 154–155. Cf. Safar b. ʿAbd al-Raḥmān al-Ḥawālī, *al-ʿAlmāniyya: nashʾatuhā wa-taṭawwuruhā wa-āthāruhā fī al-ḥayyāt al-islāmiyya al-muʿāṣira*, n.p.: Dār al-Hijra, n.d.

Imām insists that the instruments of democracy – forming political parties, entering parliament, and participation in parliamentary elections – are greater unbelief (*kufr akbar*), just as democracy itself is.[237] Needless to say, this position rules out the many pragmatic compromises that numerous Islamist movements, especially those related to or influenced by the Muslim Brotherhood, had adopted in various countries, and the means available to Imām to realize his ideal of theonomy are correspondingly narrow. Imām recognizes this issue but is not particularly exercised by it.

For example, consider Imām's response to the Kuwaiti fusionist salafī ʿAbd al-Raḥmān ʿAbd al-Khāliq (al-Ashqar's close associate and Abū Muḥammad al-Maqdisī's high school teacher), when the latter argued that forbidding the formation of Islamic political parties unduly restricts and weakens the *daʿwa*. Imām of course argues that there is nothing Islamic about these political parties, since as an instrument of democracy they fall under the general ruling of *kufr*, but in addition to this matter of principle he also addresses the issue of *manhaj*. Imām argues that the strength of *daʿwa* lies not in numbers or in direct influence but rather in its purity, and specifically, in establishing separation and differentiation from the unbelievers. When *daʿwa* is of this kind it attracts those who are sincere and devout rather than opportunists. For Imām, the limited appeal of true *daʿwa* is not a bug but a feature. It was the normative path of the Prophet, and is the only means to properly differentiate the ranks between adherents of Islam and unbelievers:

As for the Muslims' path of effecting change, it is known. It is not the path of polytheistic democracy, but rather the path of the Prophet, blessing and peace be upon him, and it starts with *daʿwa*: public *daʿwa* in the mosques and other gathering places, and individual *daʿwa* everywhere possible, night and day, openly and in secret, beginning with one's closest relations, openly proclaiming the truth, and informing those who have fallen into unbelief that they are unbelievers and that we wash our hands of them and their unbelief …

Among these unbelievers are those who rule by man-made law, such as judges and their ilk; those who take part in the implementation of democracy such as the leaders and members of political parties, members of parliament, and those who elect them; likewise, the soldiers who defend with their lives these infidel regimes, and those who defend them with their tongues and their pens – all these are unbelievers, and they must be told that they are. Perhaps they will repent, or some of them.

This continues until there is separation of the ranks (*tamyīz al-ṣufūf*) … and until a powerful group of Muslims takes shape that is capable of changing the ruling infidel regimes and of ruling by Islam, if Allāh brings them to power.[238]

237 ʿAbd al-Qādir b. ʿAbd al-ʿAzīz, *al-Jāmiʿ*, p. 783.
238 ʿAbd al-Qādir b. ʿAbd al-ʿAzīz, *al-Jāmiʿ*, p. 784.

This is not a *manhaj* that automatically rejects all forms of gradualism. The notion that the salafī jihādīs, or a subset of them, have promoted a *manhaj* of armed jihād alone is a mischaracterization. Another founding scholar of the salafī jihādī school, the Syrian Abū Baṣīr al-Ṭarṭūsī, at one point even tried to subsume Muḥammad Nāṣir al-Dīn al-Albānī's quietist project of "purification and education" (*al-taṣfiya wa-l-tarbiya*) into the salafī jihādī *manhaj* itself, as one of the elements of 'preparation' (*iʿdād*) for armed jihād.[239] The overriding concern is not to reject all kinds of gradualism per se, but rather to reject at all costs the siren song of pragmatic compromise with democracy – a call to which neither Quṭbists nor quietist salafīs were totally immune. The strict theonomy that the salafī jihādīs adopted as their central theological concern made of this issue a clear one of *tawḥīd* and *shirk*, and they could no more brook compromise on it than could the eighteenth-century Wahhābīs on issues of ritual monolatry such as the invocation of saints.[240]

Ultimately – and notwithstanding the importance of *daʿwa* in its broad sense – this refusal to compromise did necessarily mandate jihād as the ultimate means of achieving *tawḥīd*. It is the mutual implication of theonomic *tawḥīd* and theonomic jihād, already outlined in the introduction to Sayyid Imām's *al-ʿUmda*, that is the hallmark of the salafī jihādī school. The linkage between the two is ubiquitous in the writings of the first generation of salafī jihādīs in the 1980s and 1990s.[241] Apart from the inherent ideational connection between them in the salafī jihādī worldview, there is also the practical matter of force of arms being the only means of change left on the table once normal political means have been categorically eliminated on theological grounds. This dogmatism may preclude pragmatism, but it does not necessarily preclude realism. For

239 ʿAbd al-Munʿim Muṣṭafā Ḥalīma [= Abū Baṣīr al-Ṭarṭūsī], *Ḥukm al-islām fī al-dīmuqrāṭiyya wa-l-taʿaddudiyya al-ḥizbiyya*, Amman, 1993, p. 117, n. 1. This work dates from the period prior to the definitive break with al-Albānī and his circle, on which see Lav, *Radical Islam*, pp. 140–159.

240 Salafī jihādīs are frequently dismissive of those who continue to make of ritual monolatry their central focus in an age when the cult of saints has receded, and when the *shirk* of man-made legislation is ubiquitous. See e.g. al-Maqdisī, *Kashf al-niqāb*, pp. 2–3. The point is only about prioritization, however, and is not a sign of lassitude toward ritual *shirk*, which salafī jihādīs stridently oppose. For example, al-Maqdisī recounts a heated exchange between himself and ʿAbdallāh ʿAzzām when the latter instructed the Arab volunteers in Afghanistan not to confront their Afghan hosts over issues of ritual *shirk*, over the objections of al-Maqdisī. Abū Muḥammad al-Maqdisī, *Wa-lākin kūnū rabbānniyīn*, part 7: *marḥalat afghānistān*, 2012 [video], 22:25–28:00, http://abu-qatada.xyz/vid/visual/9035.zip (link no longer active).

241 For more on this topic, see Daniel Lav, "*Buʿithtu bi-l-sayf*: Jihad, Monolatry, and Theonomy in Modern Salafism," in Mustafa Baig and Robert Gleave (eds.), *Violence in Islamic Thought: from European Imperialism to the Post-Colonial Era*, Edinburgh: Edinburgh University Press, 2021, pp. 163–185.

his part, Sayyid Imām argues that political power ultimately lies where it always does, in the use of force by those willing to kill and be killed:

> Shaykh al-Islām Ibn Taymiyya mentioned in more than one place in his book *Minhāj al-sunna al-nabawwiyya* that the Imamate is established by the *bayʿa* of the possessors of force of arms (*shawka*), that is, of might (*quwwa*). Likewise, the Islamic state will only be established in our times through force of arms – that is, through might. Do not be deceived by the millions who vote for those who claim to be Islamists in parliamentary elections. If these millions were asked to bear arms and to wage jihād in order to impose the rule of Islam, they would slink away and run for shelter. What force of arms is there in these people, when the might of the armies is on the side of the infidel rulers? The state belongs to he who possesses might, and might means men, arms, and resources.[242]

## Conclusion

Some two decades after Sayyid Imām's *al-Jāmiʿ*, Jabhat al-Nuṣra, at the time the official al-Qāʿida affiliate in Syria, published a short tract setting forth its creed.[243] The document opens with the statement, derived from Ibn Taymiyya and common to all modern salafīs, that *tawḥīd* is comprised of three parts: *tawḥīd al-rubūbiyya*, *tawḥīd al-ulūhiyya*, and *tawḥīd al-asmāʾ wa-l-ṣifāt*.[244] Of these three, the greatest attention is devoted to *tawḥīd al-ulūhiyya*, but the portion of this section devoted to ritual monolatry (*tawḥīd al-nusuk*) is terse, stating only: "[This *tawḥīd* is achieved] through directing ritual worship (*al-ʿibādāt al-nusukiyya*) to Allāh alone, such as the worship of the heart and the limbs: fear and hope, sacrifices and vows, and so forth. Those who have deviated most in this arena are the Ṣūfīs; this is a broad topic that requires elaboration."[245] Far more emphasis is placed on the second topic under the rubric of *tawḥīd al-ulūhiyya*, which is given the name *tawḥīd al-ḥukm wa-l-qaḍāʾ wa-l-tashrīʿ* (the *tawḥīd* of rule, judgment, and legislation). In parentheses is added an additional name for this form of *tawḥīd*, *tawḥīd al-ḥākimiyya*. Just as in Sayyid Imām's treatise, the issue of theonomy, raised by Mawdūdī and Quṭb as *ḥākimiyya*, is here firmly embedded in the Taymiyyan conception of *tawḥīd*, with its distinctive monolatric

242 ʿAbd al-Qādir b. ʿAbd al-ʿAzīz, *al-Jāmiʿ*, p. 153.

243 Jabhat al-Nuṣra, *Nubdha ʿammā naʿtaqiduhu wa-nadīnu llāha bihi*, al-Manāra al-Bayḍāʾ, 2014, https://twitter.com/JabhtAnNusrah/status/438393864190033920 (link no longer active). I would like to thank Rafael Green, then at the MEMRI Jihad and Terrorism Threat Monitor (JTTM), for calling my attention to this document.

244 Jabhat al-Nuṣra, *Nubdha*, pp. 3–5. As noted above (Chapter 1), Ibn Taymiyya himself did not always separate out the last of these from *tawḥīd al-rubūbiyya*.

245 Jabhat al-Nuṣra, *Nubdha*, p. 3.

emphasis: "We hold the unicity of sovereignty to be a foundational part and a firm pillar of the unicity of *ulūhiyya* and the obligation of worship."

Again like Sayyid Imām, the credo draws from this premise radical theonomic conclusions:

> Thus we hold that one who legislates in place of Allāh laws that Allāh did not reveal, he has apostatized and is excluded from the Muslim community. And thus we hold that the rulers who rule by other than what Allāh revealed ... are apostates, even if they claim to be Muslims, due to their legislating in place of Allāh and their ruling by other than what Allāh revealed. And for this reason we hold that secularism, with all its various banners and in all its different schools, is patent unbelief that contradicts Islam and excludes one from the Muslim community; and we hold that democracy is the idol of this age, and the religion of America; it is an idolatrous regime, together with its parliaments, its elections, its constitutions, and all its other mechanisms.[246]

By the time Jabhat al-Nuṣra published their creed such a claim was utterly unremarkable; in fact, the portion of the passage that formulates the relation between *ḥākimiyya* and *ulūhiyya* is borrowed word for word from a well-known work by Abū Muṣʿab al-Sūrī.[247] It is beyond the scope of this chapter to provide an exhaustive account of the salafī jihādī literature on theonomy, which numbers thousands of treatises, sermons, pamphlets, and other forms of literature. If we take only a very specific subgenre, the critique of 'infidel' constitutions and law codes in a particular country, we find that such treatises have been authored on each of Kuwait,[248] Saudi Arabia,[249] Tunisia,[250] Libya,[251] Egypt,[252] Yemen,[253]

[246] Jabhat al-Nuṣra, *Nubdha*, pp. 3–4.

[247] ʿAbd al-Ḥakīm, *Daʿwat al-muqāwama*, p. 909. Al-Sūrī clearly means *ulūhiyya* in the technical Taymiyyan sense: He gives correct definitions of *tawḥīd al-rubūbiyya* and *tawḥīd al-ulūhiyya* at p. 905.

[248] al-Maqdisī, *Kashf al-niqāb*.

[249] Abū Muḥammad ʿĀṣim al-Maqdisī, *al-Kawāshif al-jaliyya fī kufr al-dawla al-suʿūdiyya*, 2nd ed., 1421/2000–2001, www.ilmway.com/site/maqdis/MS_816 (link no longer active).

[250] Abū al-Wafāʾ al-Tūnusī, *al-Qawl al-jalī fī naqd al-dustūr al-tūnusī al-kufrī*, 1430/2009, www.ilmway.com/site/maqdis/MS_10411 (link no longer active).

[251] ʿAbd al-Munʿim Muṣṭafā Ḥalīma [= Abū Baṣīr al-Ṭarṭūsī], *Mulāḥaẓāt ʿalā al-dustūr al-lībī al-muʾaqqat*, 1432/2011, www.abubaseer.bizland.com/refutation/read/F%20103.doc. While similar on many points to the other treatises, this critique is more moderate. On al-Ṭarṭūsī's relative moderation in general, see Joas Wagemakers, "Between Purity and Pragmatism? Abu Basir al-Tartusi's Nuanced Radicalism," in Rüdiger Lohlker and Tamara Abu-Hamdeh (eds.), *Jihadi Thought and Ideology*, Berlin: Logos, 2014, pp. 16–36.

[252] Aḥmad ʿAshūsh, *Iʿlām al-muslimīn bi-ḥaqīqat al-dustūr wa-l-qawānīn*, n.d. [posted 2013], https://shorturl.at/YypFB (link no longer active). Thanks are due to Aaron Zelin for making this text available.

[253] Abū Dharr al-Samharī al-Yamānī, *Maʿālim al-wathaniyya fī al-dawla al-yamaniyya*, 1431[/2010], www.ilmway.com/site/maqdis/MS_813 (link no longer active).

and Pakistan.[254] There remains much work to be done on this literature, and on the question of how the doctrine of theonomy intersects with militancy in various ways. The present chapter has simply sought to demonstrate the main features of salafī jihādī theonomy as it emerged in historical context, and to show its relation to the premodern and modern precedents discussed in previous chapters, using Sayyid Imām's *al-Jāmiʿ* as the primary reference.

In this chapter we have seen that the principal theoretical bases for salafī jihādī theonomy were already adumbrated by fusionists and quietist salafīs over the course of the 1970s and 1980s. Primarily due to the influence of Sayyid Quṭb, this period was marked by the growing salience of the issue of theonomy and by an attempt by all parties, to varying degrees, to provide a firm salafī basis for it in place of the idiosyncratic systems of Mawdūdī and Quṭb. We likewise saw that these various authors, notwithstanding their clear declarations of theonomic principle, tended to either condone instrumental compromises with democracy or to otherwise limit potentially radical implications of their doctrine, such as judgments of *takfīr* or resort to violence.

The salafī jihādī school, as represented by the treatises of its major early authors in the 1980s and 1990s, placed theonomy at the heart of its doctrine and rejected the forms of accommodation accepted by fusionist and quietist predecessors. Through a more explicit formulation of the relation between theonomy and Taymiyyan *tawḥīd*, the salafī jihādī authors argued that their rulings on democracy, parliaments, and man-made law are part and parcel of the very foundation of faith and that no compromise is possible with these forms of *shirk*. This dogmatization of the issue went hand in hand with the adoption of a *manhaj* of armed jihād and the emergence of militant organizations that sought to put the doctrine into practice. In the salafī jihādīs' self-conception, they are carrying on the struggle bequeathed to them by earlier generations to realize the aim for which humans were created: to make worship exclusive to Allāh, in the true sense of worship, including and especially legal-political obedience.

[254] Ayman al-Ẓawāhirī, *al-Ṣubḥ wa-l-qindīl: risāla ḥawla zaʿm islāmiyyat dustūr bākistān*, n.d., www.ilmway.com/site/maqdis/MS_16441 (link no longer active).

# Conclusion

This book has sought to explain the modern salafī doctrine of theonomy, according to which rule by Allāh's law is a sine qua non of faith, and parliamentary democracy and other systems based on human legislation are deemed inherently polytheistic. The greater part of this study has been devoted to investigating this doctrine from the perspective of Islamic intellectual history: How it developed, based on what precedents, and under what circumstances. The details of this development have often been intricate but the underlying pattern is quite simple. This Conclusion will first summarize our principal findings regarding the Islamic intellectual history of the salafī doctrine of theonomy, and then will address the significance of modern salafī theonomy through the lens of political theology by revisiting the framework outlined in the Introduction so as to better situate salafī theonomy in a wider comparative context.

Salafī theology, as formulated by Ibn Taymiyya in his *tawḥīd al-ulūhiyya* doctrine, centered on the conception that the essence of Islam is exclusivity of worship (monolatry) rather than conceptual belief in the existence of Allāh or in His objective aspect as Creator and Lord (*rubūbiyya*). According to this doctrine, the unbelievers depicted in the Qur'ān did not deny Allāh's existence or His principal objective attributes; their unbelief consisted rather in devoting worship to other entities alongside Allāh. In Ibn Taymiyya's writings this underlying principle was elaborated in different forms and terminologies in polemic against Ashʿarī theologians, Islamic philosophers, and antinomian Ṣūfīs, all of whom Ibn Taymiyya accused of focusing on matters of *rubūbiyya* at the expense of exclusivity of worship (*ulūhiyya*). In addition, the doctrine naturally furnished grounds for the condemnation of widespread forms of religious devotion as a reversion to the polylatry of the *mushrikūn*.

The early Wahhābī movement hoisted the banner of *tawḥīd al-ulūhiyya* as their casus belli in a real-world war against the Muslim cult of saints, which the Wahhābīs considered, in light of this doctrine, as substantially equivalent to the polylatry for which the Qur'ān condemned the unbelievers. *Tawḥīd al-ulūhiyya* was the signal doctrine of Wahhābism, and not, as argued by Goldziher and others, simple opposition to *bid'a* (illicit innovation in religion); nor was it renewal of *ijtihād* or any other of the tendencies promoted by contemporary eighteenth-century reformers. Our comparative study of writings by Ibn Taymiyya and Ibn 'Abd al-Wahhāb showed that the essentials of Wahhābī doctrine were all borrowed from Ibn Taymiyya's writings and did not derive from any contemporary source of inspiration.

Parallel to this emphasis on exclusivity of ritual devotion was the salafī tradition's insistence on exclusivity of legal obedience to Allāh. In polemics against the practice of *taqlīd*, authors from the salafī jurisprudential tradition – Ḥanbalīs and others adhering to the *ahl al-ḥadīth* ethos – attacked *taqlīd*, especially in its more categorical forms, as tantamount to worship of humans. The axis of this polemic was the following equation: Obedience to judicial determinations of prohibition and permission is a form of worship; thus obedience to Allāh's law, as determined from the Qur'ān and the *ḥadīth*, is worship of Allāh, whereas obedience to the precedents of a human jurist (e.g. Abū Ḥanīfa) is worship of that jurist. This polemic was a constant feature of salafī jurisprudential theory (*uṣūl al-fiqh*) from the fifth/eleventh-century writings of Ibn 'Abd al-Barr up to Muḥammad al-Shawkānī and the Indian Ahl-i Ḥadīth, and it represents a kind of theonomic corollary of premodern salafī monolatry. Based on a survey of this literature I argued that Wael Hallaq was mistaken in his equation of *taqlīd* with textual literalism and his assigning of the pro-*taqlīd* position to the *ahl al-ḥadīth.* In truth opposition to *taqlīd* was primarily a denunciation of what these authors considered to be merely human law, motivated by a 'salafī' theological concern for exclusivity of obedience to Allāh's law as transmitted in the texts of revelation.

In the twentieth century, Abū al-A'lā Mawdūdī and Sayyid Quṭb formulated a theological system that explicitly defined Islam as theonomy. Their doctrine of *ḥākimiyya* shared structural similarities with the salafī definition of Islam as monolatry, but they emphasized legal obedience as the primary form of worship and servitude to Allāh, thereby employing the template of monolatry as a theological critique of the secularization of legal-political systems in the modern Muslim world. Once the writings of Mawdūdī and Quṭb had raised the profile of the issue, the last quarter of the twentieth century witnessed an upswell of theonomic writings primarily in the modern salafī milieu that drew more explicitly on premodern salafī precedents. Many of these authors, however, tended to stop short of drawing the radical conclusion that the ruling regimes were apostate, and many endorsed instrumental compromises with democratic processes, notwithstanding their arguments that democracy itself is tantamount to polytheism.

In the 1980s and early 1990s the salafī jihādī school coalesced around an intransigent version of theonomy and patronage of militant groups who adopted this doctrine as their paramount casus belli. Salafī jihādī theonomy explicitly anchors contemporary issues relating to law, legislation, and parliamentary democracy in Ibn Taymiyya's conception of *tawḥīd*, and thus argues that rejection of democracy and democratic institutions is a fundamental and nonnegotiable foundation of faith, just as is rejection of the cult of saints. In technical terms this intransigence is expressed, for example, in arguments that the principles of exigent necessity (*ḍarūra*) and public benefit (*maṣlaḥa*) can never be applied to permit polytheism (*shirk*). In more general terms the intractability of salafī jihādī theonomy stems from a complete refusal to separate between political and theological issues. Just as one can brook no compromise with the ritual worship of idols, so no peace can be made with the 'worship' that is submission to the man-made law of human sovereigns. This theonomy is a radical theopolitical answer to structural secularization and to the notion of the sufficiency of immanent human autonomy.

The meaning of this wide arc of historical development becomes clearer when we address it through the lens of political theology, which helps lead us both to the ultimate roots of premodern salafī monolatry and its modern theonomic expressions. In addition to the discrete questions of Islamic intellectual history treated in the preceding chapters, the book on the whole is a contribution to the study of political theologies of the modern age. Throughout recorded history human societies have always formulated conceptions and structures of power and authority, whether personal, such as kingship, or abstract, such as law. There is no natural or universally valid division of these conceptions into the political or the religious and the boundaries between them are porous. Given that different historical societies (and different tendencies within them) have configured the relation between the transcendent and the mundane realms in various ways, it is these shifts that we must trace so as to understand a theopolitical doctrine such as theonomy.

In the Introduction we traced such shifts in the historical background relevant to the Abrahamic faiths, in the Axial patrimonies of ancient Israel and Greece. It was argued, following Yehoshua Amir, that each of these patrimonies converted the ANE model of sacral kingship to different registers, the one projecting the model onto the transcendent divinity and placing Him in opposition to human rule, the other dissolving it into problems of metaphysics. It was likewise argued that the later interaction between these originally distinct patrimonies yielded the variegated landscape of medieval theology in the Abrahamic faiths, thereby providing us with an analytic framework that could be applied to Ibn Taymiyya and to the salafī legacy on the whole. In the perspective of political theology, monolatry – the heart of salafī theology – can thus be understood as a theologization of the characteristic political concepts of servitude and allegiance associated with kingship. We can sum up the importance of this foray into the distant background to our topic in the words of Jan Assmann: "all significant concepts of theology – or perhaps we ought to say more modestly, several of the central concepts of theology – are theologized political concepts."[1]

In these words Assmann was responding to one of the most influential essays in modern political theology, the 1922 treatise titled simply *Political Theology* by the jurist and political theorist Carl Schmitt. In this work Schmitt famously asserted that "all significant concepts of the modern theory of the state are secularized theologicial concepts."[2] Here we encounter the second terminus of our study: the modern-day interpretation of salafī monolatry in terms of theonomy, which revives the more explicit political opposition between divine and human sovereignty that was characteristic of ancient Israelite Axiality. There are multiple perspectives through which one could address the meaning of this 'theonomic shift,' but for the purposes of this Conclusion an engagement with Schmitt and his dictum should suffice to help us situate modern salafī theonomy vis-à-vis other political theologies of the modern age. For true as it is that until recently the entire field of political theology was heavily focused on Christian Europe, we ought not view modern salafism as an exotic movement divorced from the concerns that engendered the field in the first place. Its study does require different areas of expertise, and likewise the divergent histories of modern Europe and the Islamic world need to be taken into account – but in the wider analysis we find simply another case of an Abrahamic religion encountering modernity and interacting with it in various ways, of which salafī theonomy is one.

Modern salafī authors' understanding of secularization is structurally akin to Schmitt's: They describe the modern conception of sovereignty, starting from Jean Bodin and up to its subsequent democratic investiture

[1] "Alle prägnanten Begriffe – vielleicht sagen wir lieber bescheidener: einige zentrale Begriffe – der Theologie sind theologisierte politische Begriffe." Assmann, *Herrschaft und Heil*, p. 29.

[2] "Alle prägnanten Begriffe der modernen Staatslehre sind säkularisierte theologische Begriffe." Carl Schmitt, *Politische Theologie: Vier Kapitel zur Lehre von der Souveränität*, Berlin: Duncker & Humblot, 2004, p. 43; Carl Schmitt, *Political Theology: Four Chapters on the Concept of Sovereignty*, trans. George Schwab, Chicago and London: University of Chicago Press, 2005, p. 36.

in 'the people,' as the transference of a divine attribute onto humans (see Chapter 5). While the salafī analysis is certainly independent of Schmitt's, it is entirely of a piece with his dictum "all significant concepts of the modern theory of the state are secularized theologicial concepts."

It was in response to this transference, as they perceived it, that the salafīs marshaled the theological resources available to them from the premodern tradition to decry the immanent human sovereignty of the modern nation-state – human autonomy – as *shirk*. While war on this kind of political polytheism was not a prominent feature of premodern salafism, modern salafīs argue that it is a natural application of their tradition's conception of divinity and its relation to the mundane world. The continuity with earlier salafī theology and jurisprudential theory is clear and has been documented throughout the preceding chapters; the differences are due less to the impact of intellectual or religious influences extraneous to the salafī tradition and more to the fundamental transformations in Muslim societies brought on by the advent of the modern age.

Radical salafī theonomy is only one theological response to modern secularization, one that is highly determined by the distinctive features of the salafī tradition. It certainly draws on certain medieval Islamic sources and conceptions, but this does not mean that 'Islam' as such rejects democracy or secularization (much as salafīs like to present the issue in this manner). Just as salafī theology was originally constructed, in Ibn Taymiyya's writings, in conscious opposition to the predominant tendencies in medieval Islam, so we have seen that the radical salafī version of theonomy was generally constructed in explicit opposition to various widespread Islamic tendencies condemned by the salafī jihādīs as 'democratic.' While there exist many other modern Muslim (not to mention non-Muslim) critiques of democracy and secularization, no other takes this particular form. Salafī theonomy taps into an ancient concern for exclusivity of obedience that has been a feature of the Abrahamic faiths since the time of the Bible, and which received exceptionally cogent expression in the theology of Ibn Taymiyya. It is this specific legacy, rather than some generic conception of Islam, that laid the grounds for the intransigent rejection of modern democracy and man-made law as a form of polytheism that must be combated by force of arms.

The specificity of this premodern legacy explains cardinal differences in contour between salafī theonomy and other violent antidemocratic movements, such as fascism for example. In order to further elucidate this point let us return to Schmitt's aforementioned dictum in context:

All significant concepts of the modern theory of the state are secularized theologicial concepts not only because of their historical development – in which they were transferred from theology to the theory of state, whereby, for example, the omnipotent God became the omnipotent lawgiver – but also because of their systematic nature, the recognition of which is necessary for a sociological consideration of these concepts. The exception in jurisprudence is analogous to the miracle in theology. Only by being aware of this analogy can we appreciate the manner in which the philosophical ideas of the state developed in the last centuries.[3]

The development outlined in this passage is the transference of transcendent sovereignty onto an immanent human political order. The central theme of Schmitt's essay is his distinction between two different conceptions of the state and its relation to law, "two types of juristic scientific thought according to whether an awareness of the normative character of the legal decision is or is not present,"[4] each of which emerged from a different theological perspective on divine sovereignty.

The first type, which Schmitt labels 'decisionist,' is represented in the passage cited above and whose preeminent representative was Thomas Hobbes. He and others sought to characterize the emergent nation-state in opposition to the medieval estates as unbound in its power and the source of all legitimate authority. The sovereign state makes the law, is the font thereof, and thus logically cannot itself be bound by it. Whence the importance of the parallel between the miracle and the state of exception as a distinguishing criterion for the decisionist model: Just as God suspends the laws of nature when He deems necessary, so the sovereign may, upon recognizing the need to declare a state of exception, suspend the legal order he has instituted – and this is the very mark and proof that he is sovereign.

The second and contrary type is that of Enlightenment rationalism, which sought to elaborate a theory in which the state is bound by a conception of law that excludes the exception:

The exception was something incommensurable to John Locke's doctrine of the constitutional state and the rationalist eighteenth century. The vivid awareness of the meaning of the exception that was reflected in the doctrine of natural law in the seventeenth century was soon lost in the eighteenth century, when a relatively lasting order was established. Emergency law was no law at all for Kant. The contemporary theory of the state reveals the interesting spectacle of the two tendencies facing one another, the rationalist tendency, which ignores the emergency, and the natural law tendency, which is interested in the emergency and emanates from an essentially different set of ideas.[5]

[3] Schmitt, *Political Theology*, p. 36. [4] Schmitt, *Political Theology*, p, 33.
[5] Schmitt, *Political Theology*, pp. 13–14.

The upshot of this Enlightenment rationalist tendency is the negation of sovereignty itself as Schmitt and the 'decisionist type' define it: "All tendencies of modern constitutional development point toward eliminating the sovereign in this sense."[6] And thus regarding Schmitt's contemporaries in the field of legal theory whom he found to be representative of the rationalist tendency: "[Hans] Kelsen solved the problem of the concept of sovereignty by negating it. The result of his deduction is that 'the concept of sovereignty must be radically repressed.'"[7] And Hugo Krabbe's "theory of the sovereignty of laws rests on the thesis that it is not the state but law that is sovereign."[8] If the decisionist model was rooted in a conception of a sovereign God who intervenes in the world through the miracle, this Enlightenment rational model transfers onto the positive law of the state a conception, derived from Enlightenment Deism, of the laws of nature as regular and immutable: "This theology and metaphysics rejected not only the transgression of the laws of nature through an exception brought about by direct intervention, as is found in the idea of a miracle, but also the sovereign's direct intervention in a valid legal order."[9]

From the preceding we can see that salafī theonomy stands in opposition to the sovereignty of the state as defined by Schmitt, and indeed to the modern nation-state to which Hobbes had ascribed omnipotence by way of transference from God to the mundane sovereign. The 'decisionist type' has a respectable pedigree and such a sovereignty is not inherently fascist, but when radicalized it certainly is a crucial element of fascism. One can even observe a certain affinity between salafī theonomy and Enlightenment rationalist legal thought in that both seek to eliminate the human sovereign in the name of the law. Yet for the salafīs this law that must be sovereign remains the divine law, not a human law: Their theonomy is a rejection of transference altogether and both the Hobbesian sovereign and the Enlightenment sovereignty of law are *ṭawāghīt*, ersatz deities who must be combatted.

Transference rests on an ontological or figurative continuum between divinity and the mundane ruler. This is an anathema to the salafīs: In their eyes it is a modern refiguration of sacral monarchy, whereas the salafīs champion what Assmann referred to as theocracy and what we have termed theonomy, "the subordination of political leadership, up to the point of its abolition, in favor of sheer divine sovereignty."[10] Their

[6] Schmitt, *Political Theology*, p. 7.
[7] Schmitt, *Political Theology*, p. 21, citing Kelsen's *Das Problem der Souveränität*.
[8] Schmitt, *Political Theology*, p. 21.
[9] Schmitt, *Political Theology*, pp. 36–37.
[10] Assmann, *Herrschaft und Heil*, p. 28.

robust conception of human political *viceregency* leads to an authoritarian rather than an anarchist expression of the principle, and it goes without saying that salafī jihādī organizations can be ruthless in wielding state repression in the name of theonomy, as attested by the brief years of Islamic State rule in Iraq and Syria. But the typological distinction remains: If decision and law-giving are the defining features of human *sovereignty* then they certainly do seek its abolition, and in fact the attempt to eradicate it is their primary formal causus belli.

This notion that it is the law of God that is truly sovereign is expressed by Ibn Qayyim al-Jawziyya in a remarkable passage in *I'lām al-muwaqqi'īn*, in which he discusses the injury to the law incurred by reliance on judicial opinion (*ra'y*) and analogy (*qiyās*) instead of the *ḥadīth*. In a string of political metaphors the author depicts this injury as an evisceration of the *sovereignty* of the *ḥadīth*:

> Among the proponents of judicial opinion and analogy, the traditions (*sunan, āthār*) sit desolate on their thrones, their laws rendered inoperative, deposed from their rule (*sulṭān*) and governance (*wilāya*). They bear the name, but to others the judgment [or rule: *ḥukm*]. They mint the coins, and to them is addressed the Friday sermon, but to others the authority to command and forbid.[11]

Here Ibn al-Qayyim employs language relating to the nominal authority of the later 'Abbāsid caliphate. The minting of coins and the mention of the caliph's name in the Friday sermon were classic symbols of rule, and only these remained while actual and effective rule passed to others, the various courtly and military factions who held the true reins of power. In Ibn al-Qayyim's metaphor it is the revealed law, the Prophetic traditions, that are truly sovereign but whose sovereignty has been usurped by errant and misguided jurists.

This conception of the sovereignty of the divine law, or the sovereignty of God expressed in His law-giving, is thus antithetic to the kind of antidemocratic movements that champion radical sovereign decisionism. For Schmitt the state is primary and the law secondary, and in consequence the characteristic of the sovereign is the decision on the state of exception to the law.[12] For the salafīs the state is secondary and derivative, its sole raison d'être being to uphold the immutable law. Human viceregency is merely executive and administrative, and the issue of the

[11] Ibn Qayyim al-Jawziyya, *I'lām al-muwaqqi'īn*, vol. 1, p. 187. The passage cited opens with *qālū*, "they say," viz. the opponents of this reliance on *ra'y* and *qiyās*, but the wording appears to be Ibn al-Qayyim's own.

[12] "The existence of the state is undoubted proof of its superiority over the validity of the legal norm." Schmitt, *Political Theology*, p. 12.

state of exception does not arise – in the ideal salafī state there is no constitution to suspend, and no authority to suspend the *sharīʿa*.

Despite the focus of salafī jihādīs on modes of action they believe will herald the Islamic state – and the state-orientation seemingly expressed in the very name of the Islamic State organization – their doctrine is profoundly anti-state in nature if what we mean by a state is something like the modern nation-state. A passage from ʿAbd al-Salām Faraj's *al-Farīḍa al-ghāʾiba* provides a nice illustration of the subsidiary nature of the state in the theonomic worldview. This treatise was a publication of the Egyptian Jihād organization in the lead-up to their assassination of President Anwar al-Sādāt, and it relied heavily on Ibn Taymiyya's Mongol fatwās to argue that the regime was apostate due to its ruling by man-made law.[13] In the treatise Faraj writes regarding the the obligation to establish an Islamic state: "Establishing Allāh's rule (*ḥukm*) on Earth is incumbent on the Muslims, turning to Allāh's law in judgment (*iḥtikām*) is incumbent on the Muslims, thus that there be an Islamic state is incumbent on the Muslims, for whatever is a necessary condition for the fulfillment of an obligation is itself obligatory."[14]

This reinforces a cardinal point we have noted throughout this study, namely, that salafī theonomy revives Israelite Axiality in erecting the divine sovereign in opposition to mundane sovereigns: "No god but God" means, among other things, no king but God. The doctrine is a rejection of the entire scope of modern structural secularization, which in the salafī theonomic worldview leads not to a legitimate and self-sufficient human autonomy, but only to worship and servitude of some humans toward others.

Our study has thus led us to the cusp of fundamental human questions regarding our own standing in the modern age by way of an examination of a particularly radical response to them, one that perhaps has assisted in bringing these questions into relief and demonstrating their historical relevance and salience. In so doing it is my hope that, alongside this book's investigations of discrete topics in salafī intellectual history, it has also furthered our understanding of radical salafī theonomy as one chapter in a general account of political theologies of the modern age.[15]

13 Johannes J. G. Jansen, *The Neglected Duty: The Creed of Sadat's Assassins and Islamic Resurgence in the Middle East*, New York and London: Macmillan, 1986.

14 Muḥammad ʿAbd al-Salām Faraj, *al-Farīḍa al-ghāʾiba*, n.p, n.d., p. 9. The principle cited here is the same legal maxim mentioned in Sayyid Imām's treatment in the *Jāmiʿ* of the meaning of the *shahāda*; see Chapter 5.

15 Cf. Lav, *Radical Islam*, p. 203.

# Glossary

| | |
|---|---|
| *ahl al-ḥadīth*: | an originalist tendency in early Islam emphasizing adherence to the literal meaning of the Qurʾān and to the Prophetic *ḥadīth* (q.v.); the rivals of the *ahl al-raʾy* (q.v.). |
| *ahl al-raʾy*: | a tendency in early Islamic jurisprudence allowing a wide scope for the use of analogy (*qiyās*, q.v.) and judicial reasoning or discretion (*raʾy*, q.v.). |
| apophatism: | negative theology; denial of the divine attributes out of a desire to affirm God's unity; cf. cataphatism (q.v.). |
| *ʿaqīda:* | creed; a treatise on creed. |
| Ashʿarī: | an adherent of the school of *kalām* (q.v.) named for Abū al-Ḥasan al-Ashʿarī (d. 324/936), predominant in the Arabic-speaking world from medieval times to the twentieth century. |
| Axial: | a conception of transcendence bearing implications for the reordering of human society. |
| *āya* (pl. *āyāt*): | a divine sign; a verse of the Qurʾān. |
| *bāṭiniyya* (sg. *bāṭinī*): | a pejorative collective term for esoteric Shīʿīs. |
| *bidʿa* (pl. *bidaʿ*): | (illicit) innovation in religion. |
| cataphatism: | affirmation of the divine attributes. The antonym of apophatism (q.v.). |
| cratological: | pertaining to power, and to divine power in particular. |
| *daʿwa*: | preaching; the call to Islam; Islamic outreach. |
| *fiqh*: | Islamic jurisprudence. |
| *fitna*: | temptation; in Islamic usage, temptation by the Shayṭān (Satan). |

| | |
|---|---|
| *fiṭra*: | divinely implanted human nature. |
| *furūʿ* (sg. *farʿ*): | substantive matters of law in Islamic jurisprudence (*fiqh*, q.v.). |
| *ḥadīth* (pl. *aḥādīth*): | a transmitted report of the Prophet Muḥammad's words or deeds. |
| *ḥajj*: | the pilgrimage to Mecca in the month of Dhū al-Ḥijja. |
| *ḥākimiyya*: | sovereignty, and specifically the sovereignty of Allāh; the doctrine of theonomy (q.v.). |
| Ḥanafī (pl. *aḥnāf*): | an adherent of the school of law named for Abū Ḥanīfa (d. 150/767). |
| Ḥanbalī (pl. *ḥanābila*): | an adherent of the school of law named for Aḥmad b. Ḥanbal (d. 241/855). |
| hysterogenic: | Greek for 'later-born,' said of universals, meaning they are extrapolated from observed commonalities among particular existents. |
| *ʿibāda*: | worship, servitude. |
| *ijmāʿ*: | scholarly consensus. |
| *ijtihād*: | the derivation of juridical rulings from the sources without adhering to precedent; cf. *taqlīd* (q.v.). |
| *ilāh*: | God or a god; in salafī theology, God in His aspect of being worthy of worship; cf. *rabb* (q.v.). |
| *īmān*: | faith. |
| *isnād*: | the chain of transmission of a *ḥadīth* (q.v.) |
| *istiḥsān*: | juristic preference. |
| *jāhiliyya*: | the state of polytheism, barbarism, and ignorance in the Arabian Peninsula prior to the advent of Islam; the concept was revived by Sayyid Quṭb, who argued that traditionally Muslim societies had reverted to *jāhiliyya*. |
| *jahl*: | a jurisprudential term for exculpatory ignorance. |
| Kaʿba: | the stone building in the Great Mosque of Mecca that serves as the Muslim direction of prayer (*qibla*, q.v.) and as the site of the pilgrimage (*ḥajj*, q.v.). |
| *kalām*: | the Islamic tradition of speculative theology. |
| *khārijī*(pl. *khawārij*): | the Khārijites, an early sect that pronounced *takfīr* (q.v.) on others for grave sins of commission or omission and rebelled against the political authorities. |
| *kufr*: | unbelief. |
| *kufr akbar*: | "major" unbelief that negates one's status as a Muslim. |
| *kufr aṣghar*: | "minor" unbelief that does not negate one's status as a Muslim. |
| *madhhab*: | a school of jurisprudence or of theology. |

Mālikī: an adherent of the school of law named for Mālik b. Anas (d. 179/795).

*manhaj*: in contemporary salafism, the path or method to be followed in real-world application of the salafī creed (*ʿaqīda*, q.v.).

Māturīdī: an adherent of the Ḥanafī (q.v.) school of *kalām* (q.v.) named for Abū Manṣūr al-Māturīdī (d. 333/944), historically predominant in Asia and the Turkish-speaking areas of the Ottoman Empire.

monolatry: (Greek: *monos*, sole + *latreia*, worship): the worship of one God alone; cf. polylatry (q.v.).

*murjiʾ*(pl. *murjiʾa*): the Murjiʾites, an early sect that declined to pass judgment on the faith or unbelief of the third and fourth caliphs, ʿUthmān and ʿAlī; a school of theology that does not count acts as a constitutive element of faith.

*mushrik*(pl. *mushrikūn*, *-īn*): a polytheist or polylatrist; one who commits 'associationism' (*shirk*, q.v.).

Muʿtazila (sg. Muʿtazilī): an early school of *kalām* (q.v.).

polylatry: the devotion of worship to more than one divinity; cf. monolatry (q.v.).

*qibla*: the direction of prayer.

*qiyās*: analogy, as employed in *fiqh* (q.v.) and *kalām* (q.v.); also a syllogism, in logic and philosophy.

*rabb*: God, literally "lord"; in salafī theology, God in His aspect as Creator, Provider, and His other objective attributes; cf. *ilāh* (q.v.).

*raʾy*: judicial reasoning or discretion; literally "view," "opinion."

*rubūbiyya*: an abstract noun formed from *rabb* (q.v.), the aspect of God in His capacity as *rabb*.

*salaf*: the righteous early Muslim generations.

Shāfiʿī: an adherent of the school of law named for Muḥammad b. Idrīs al Shāfiʿī (d. 204/820).

*shahāda*: the Muslim profession of faith.

*sharīʿa*: Islamic law.

*shirk*: the association of another together with Allāh, i.e. associationist polytheism or polylatry.

*shirk akbar*: "major" polytheism that negates one's status as a Muslim.

*shirk aṣghar*: "minor" polytheism that does not negate one's status as a Muslim.

*sunna*: the Prophetic example and path, as reported in the *ḥadīth* (q.v.).

*tafsīr*: Qur'ānic exegesis; the genre of Qur'ānic exegesis.

*ṭāghūt* (pl. *ṭawāghīt*): a Qur'ānic term for an idol or false god. In salafī theology, anyone or thing to whom worship or obedience is offered.

*takfīr*: a ruling judging another to be an unbeliever or apostate.

*talbiya*: a ritual acclamation associated with the pilgrimage to Mecca.

*taqlīd*: (blind) adherence to the juridical precedents of an individual or law school; cf. *ijtihād* (q.v.).

*tawḥīd*: in non-Taymiyyan contexts generally rendered as divine unity or 'monotheism.' In salafī usage: divine exclusivity, to acknowledge something as Allāh's alone or to devote something to Him alone; cf. *tawḥīd al-rubūbiyya* (q.v.), *tawḥīd al-ulūhiyya* (q.v.).

*tawḥīd al-rubūbiyya*: in salafī theology, the acknowledgment of Allāh as sole Creator, Sustainer, etc., viz. the sole possessor of His *rubūbiyya* (q.v.) attributes.

*tawḥīd al-ulūhiyya*: in salafī theology, the devotion of worship solely to Allāh; cf. *ulūhiyya* (q.v.).

*ta'wīl*: an interpretation of a religious text or tenet.

theonomy: (Greek: *theo*, God + *nomos*, law): rule by God's law.

Traditionalist: an adherent of the *ahl al-ḥadīth* (q.v.).

*ulūhiyya*: an abstract noun formed from *ilāh* (q.v.), the aspect of God in His capacity as *ilāh*, viz. His being worthy of worship.

*'umra*: the lesser pilgrimage to Mecca, which may be performed at any time of year.

*uṣūl al-fiqh*: jurisprudential theory, literally "the foundations of *fiqh*" (q.v.).

*waḥdat al-wujūd*: a monist Ṣūfī doctrine, literally "the unity of existence."

Wahhābī: an adherent of the movement founded by Muḥammad b. 'Abd al-Wahhāb (d. 1203/1792).

# Bibliography


ʿAbd al-Ḥakīm, ʿUmar [= Abū Muṣʿab al-Sūrī]. "Bayna awliyāʾ al-raḥmān wa-awliyāʾ al-fātīkān," *al-Anṣār* 88, 14 Shawwāl 1415 / March 16, 1995, pp. 13–15.

*Daʿwat al-muqāwama al-islāmiyya al-ʿālamiyya*. N.d. www.ilmway.com/site/maqdis/MS_11347 (link no longer active).

"Dirāsa fī fikr wa-manhaj wa-mawāqif al-jabha al-islāmiyya li-l-inqādh 16," *al-Anṣār* 112, 4 Rabīʿ II 1316 / August 31, 1995, pp. 12–14.

*al-Thawra al-islāmiyya al-jihādiyya fī sūriyā*. N.p., n.d.

ʿAbdallāh b. ʿAbd al-Raḥmān b. Ṣāliḥ Āl Bassām. *ʿUlamāʾ najd khilāla thamāniyat qurūn*, 2nd ed. Riyadh: Dār al-ʿĀsima, 1419[/1998].

ʿAbd al-Majīd, Aḥmad. *al-Ikhwān wa-ʿAbd al-Nāṣir: al-qiṣṣa al-kāmila li-tanẓīm 1965*. Cairo: al-Zahrāʾ li-l-Iʿlām al-ʿArabī, 1412/1991.

ʿAbd al-Qādir b. ʿAbd al-ʿAzīz [= Sayyid Imām al-Sharīf]. *al-Jāmiʿ fī ṭalab al-ʿilm al-sharīf*, 2nd ed. N.p., 1415/1995.

*Risālat al-ʿumda fī iʿdād al-ʿudda li-l-jihād fī sabīl Allāh taʿālā*. N.d. www.ilmway.com/site/maqdis/MS_636 (link no longer active).

ʿAbd al-Raḥmān b. Ḥasan Āl al-Shaykh. *Fatḥ al-majīd bi-sharḥ kitāb al-tawḥīd*. Alexandria and Cairo: Dār al-ʿAqīda, 1427/2006.

*Qurrat ʿuyūn al-muwaḥḥidīn*. Riyadh: Maktabat al-Rushd, n.d.

ʿAbd al-Raḥmān b. Muḥammad b. Qāsim al-ʿĀṣimī al-Najdī (ed.). *al-Durar al-saniyya fī al-ajwiba al-najdiyya*, 6th ed. N.p., 1418/1996.

ʿAbd al-Raḥmān b. Ṣāliḥ b. Ṣāliḥ al-Maḥmūd. *Mawqif Ibn Taymiyya min al-ashāʿira*. Riyadh: Maktabat al-Rushd, 1415/1995.

ʿAbd al-Raḥmān, ʿUmar. *Kalimat ḥaqq – murāfaʿat al-shaykh ʿUmar ʿAbd al-Raḥmān fī qaḍiyyat al-jihād*. N.d. www.ilmway.com/site/maqdis/MS_384 (link no longer active).

*Mawqif al-qurʾān min khuṣūmihi*. Cairo: Dār Miṣr al-Maḥrūsa, 2006.

Abrahamov, Binyamin. "The *Bi-lā Kayfa* Doctrine and Its Foundations in Islamic Theology," *Arabica* 42/3 (1995), pp. 366–379.

"Faḫr al-Dīn al-Rāzī on the Knowability of God's Essence and Attributes," *Arabica* 49 (2002), pp. 204–230.

*Islamic Theology: Traditionalism and Rationalism*. Edinburgh: Edinburgh University Press, 1998.

"Necessary Knowledge in Islamic Theology," *British Journal of Middle Eastern Studies* 20/1 (1993), pp. 20–32.

Abū Hammām Bakr b. ʿAbd al-ʿAzīz al-Atharī [= Turkī al-Binʿalī]. *Mā al-tarjama al-ʿilmiyya li-l-shaykh Abī Hammām Bakr b. ʿAbd al-ʿAzīz al-Atharī ḥafiẓahu Allāh?* 1432/2011. www.ilmway.com/site/maqdis/FAQ/MS_35123.html (link no longer active).

*Yā ahl al-falāḥ a-wa-qad waḍaʿtum al-silāḥ?* 1432/2011. www.ilmway.com/site/maqdis/MS_12156 (link no longer active).

Abū Qatāda al-Filasṭīnī. *Bayna Manhajayni* 30, *Majallat al-Anṣār* 81, 25 Shaʿbān 1415 / January 26, 1995.

Abu Rabiʿ, Ibrahim M. *Intellectual Origins of Islamic Resurgence in the Modern Arab World.* Albany: State University of New York, 1996.

Abū Tamām, Ḥabīb b. Aws. *Diwān al-ḥamāsa.* Beirut: Dār al-Qalam, n.d.

Abū Usāma al-Gharīb. *al-Mukhtaṣar al-jalī bi-sīrat shaykhinā Turkī al-Binʿalī.* N.d. https://archive.org/details/almokhtasar.algali.high.

Abū Yaḥyā al-Lībī. *Lībiyā mādhā yurādu lahā?* 2 Dhū al-Ḥijja 1432 [= October 29, 2011] (released December 5, 2011). Video. www.shamikh1.info/vb/showthread.php?t=138186 (link no longer active).

Adamson, Peter S. "The Arabic Plotinus: A Study of the 'Theology of Aristotle' and Related Texts." PhD diss., University of Notre Dame, 2000.

Afnan, Soheil M. *Philosophical Terminology in Arabic and Persian.* Leiden: Brill, 1964.

Ahmad, Irfan. "Genealogy of the Islamic State: Reflections on Maududi's Political Thought and Islamism," *Journal of the Royal Anthropological Institute* 15 (2009), pp. 145–162.

Akhavi, Shahrough. "The Dialectic in Contemporary Egyptian Social Thought: The Scripturalist and Modernist Discourses of Sayyid Qutb and Hasan Hanafi," *International Journal of Middle East Studies* 29 (1997), pp. 377–401.

al-Albānī, Muḥammad Nāṣir al-Dīn, et al. "Masāʾil ʿaṣriyya fī al-siyāsa al-sharʿiyya," *al-Aṣāla* 2 (15 Jumāda II 1413) [= December 1992], pp. 16–24.

AlSarhan, Saud Saleh. "Early Muslim Traditionalism: A Critical Study of the Works and Political Theology of Aḥmad Ibn Ḥanbal." PhD diss., University of Exeter, 2011.

Amir, Yehoshua. "Die Begegnung des biblischen und des philosophischen Monotheismus als Grundthema des jüdischen Hellenismus," *Evangelische Theologie* 38 (1978), pp. 2–19.

Amritsarī, Abū al-Wafāʾ Thanāʾ Allāh. *Khiṭāb ba Mawdūdī.* Delhi: Idārah-i Nūr al-Īmān, 1413[/1992].

Anjum, Ovamir. *Politics, Law, and Community in Islamic Thought: The Taymiyyan Moment.* Cambridge: Cambridge University Press, 2012.

"Salafis and Democracy: Doctrine and Context," *The Muslim World* 106/3 (July 2016), pp. 448–473.

"Sufism without Mysticism? Ibn Qayyim al-Ǧawziyya's Objectives in *Madāriǧ al-Sālikīn*," in "A Scholar in the Shadow: Essays in the Legal and Theological Thought of Ibn Qayyim al-Ǧawziyya," ed. Caterina Bori and Livnat Holtzman, special issue, *Oriente Moderno* 90/1 (2010), pp. 153–180.

al-Anṣārī al-Harawī, Abū Ismāʿīl ʿAbdallāh b. Muḥammad. *Dhamm al-kalām wa-ahlihi.* Medina: Maktabat al-ʿUlūm wa-l-Ḥikam, 1418/1988.

Aristotle. *Categories and De Interpretatione*, trans. J. L. Ackrill. Oxford: Clarendon Press, 1963.

*Physics Books I and II*, trans. William Charlton. Oxford: Clarendon Press, 1970.

*Posterior Analytics and Topica*, ed. Hugh Tredennick and E. S. Forster. London and Cambridge, MA: Loeb Classical Library, 1960.

al-Ashʿarī, Abū al-Ḥasan. *Maqālāt al-islāmiyyīn wa-ikhtilāf al-muṣallīn*. Beirut: al-Maktaba al-ʿAṣriyya, 1411/1990.

*Risāla ilā ahl al-thaghr*, 2nd ed., ed. ʿAbdallāh Shākir Muḥammad al-Junaydī. Medina: Maktabat al-ʿUlūm wa-l-Ḥikam, 1422/2002.

al-Ashqar, ʿUmar Sulaymān. *Ḥukm al-mushāraka fī al-wizāra wa-l-majālis al-niyābiyya*, 2nd ed. Amman: Dār al-Nafāʾis, 1429/2009.

*al-Sharīʿa al-ilāhiyya lā al-qawānīn al-jāhiliyya*, 2nd ed. Kuwait: Dār al-Daʿwa, 1406/1986.

ʿAshūsh, Aḥmad. *Iʿlām al-muslimīn bi-ḥaqīqat al-dustūr wa-l-qawānīn*. N.d. [posted 2013]. https://shorturl.at/YypFB (link no longer active).

al-ʿAsqalānī, Aḥmad b. ʿAlī b. Ḥajar Shihāb al-Dīn. *Tahdhīb al-tahdhīb*. Beirut: Muʾassasat al-Risāla, 1416/1996.

Assmann, Jan. "Autour de l'Exode: monothéisme, difference et violence," *Revue de l'histoire des religions* 231/1 (2014), pp. 5–26.

*Herrschaft und Heil: Politische Theologie in Altägypten, Israel, und Europa*. München: Carl Hanser, 2000.

*Moses the Egyptian: The Memory of Egypt in Western Monotheism*. Cambridge, MA, and London: Harvard University Press, 1997.

*Of God and Gods: Egypt, Israel, and the Rise of Monotheism*. Madison: University of Wisconsin Press, 2008.

ʿAwda, ʿAbd al-Qādir. *al-Islām bayna jahl abnāʾihi wa-ʿajz ʿulamāʾihi*, 5th ed. N.p.: al-Ittiḥād al-ʿĀlamī li-l-Munaẓẓamāt al-Ṭullābiyya, 1405/1985.

*al-Islām wa-awḍāʿunā al-qānūniyya*. Cairo: al-Mukhtār al-Islāmī, 1977.

Al-Azmeh, Aziz. "Orthodoxy and Ḥanbalite Fideism," *Arabica* 35/3 (1988), pp. 253–266.

Badawī, ʿAbd al-Raḥmān. *Aflūṭīn ʿinda al-ʿarab*. Cairo: Maktabat al-Nahḍa al-Miṣriyya, 1955.

al-Baghdādī, Abū Manṣūr ʿAbd al-Qādir. *Kitāb uṣūl al-dīn*. Istanbul: Maṭbaʿat al-Dawla, 1346/1928.

Bahnsen, Greg L. *Theonomy in Christian Ethics*. Nutley: The Craig Press, 1977.

al-Baʿlī, ʿAlāʾ al-Dīn Abū al-Ḥasan ʿAlī b. ʿAbbās. *al-Ikhtiyārāt al-fiqhiyya min fatāwā Shaykh al-Islām Ibn Taymiyya*, ed. Muḥammad Ḥāmid al-Fiqī. Beirut: Dār al-Maʿrifa, n.d.

Baneth, D. Z. H. "What Did Muḥammad Mean When He Called His Religion 'Islam'? The Original Meaning of Aslama and Its Derivatives," *Israel Oriental Studies* 1 (1971), pp. 183–190.

al-Bayhaqī, Abū Bakr. *al-Madkhal ilā al-sunan al-kubrā*. N.p.: Dār al-Khulafāʾ li-l-Kitāb al-Islāmī, n.d.

*Shuʿab al-īmān*. Beirut: Dār al-Kutub al-ʿIlmiyya, 1421/2000.

*al-Sunan al-kubrā*. Beirut: Dār al-Maʿrifa, n.d.

Bechor, Guy. *The Sanhuri Code and the Emergence of Modern Arab Civil Law (1932 to 1949)*. Leiden and Boston: Brill, 2007.

Bellah, Robert N. *Religion in Human Evolution: From the Paleolithic to the Axial Age*. Cambridge, MA, and London: The Belknap Press of Harvard University Press, 2011.

Bellah Robert N., and Hans Joas. *The Axial Age and Its Consequences*. Cambridge, MA, and London: The Belknap Press of Harvard University Press, 2012.

Bertolacci, Amos. *The Reception of Aristotle's Metaphysics in Avicenna's Kitāb al-Shifāʾ: A Milestone of Western Metaphysical Thought*. Leiden and Boston: Brill, 2006.

Bonnefoy, Laurent. "How Transnational Is Salafism in Yemen?," in Roel Meijer (ed.), *Global Salafism: Islam's New Religious Movement*. New York: Columbia University Press, 2009, pp. 321–341.

*Salafism in Yemen: Transnationalism and Religious Identity*. Oxford: Oxford University Press, 2012.

Booth, Edward. *Aristotelian Aporetic Ontology in Islamic and Christian Thinkers*. Cambridge: Cambridge University Press, 1983.

Boyarin, Daniel. "The Eye in the Torah: Ocular Desire in Midrashic Hermeneutic," *Critical Inquiry* 16 (1990), pp. 532–550.

Brague, Rémi. *The Law of God: The Philosophical History of an Idea*, trans. Lydia G. Cochrane. Chicago and London: The University of Chicago Press, 2007.

Brown, Jonathan A. C. "Is Islam Easy to Understand or Not? Salafis, the Democratization of Interpretation, and the Need for the Ulema," *Journal of Islamic Studies* 26/2 (2015), pp. 117–144.

Brown, Nathan J. "Shariʿa and State in the Modern Muslim Middle East," *International Journal of Middle East Studies* 29 (1997), pp. 359–376.

Buber, Martin. *Kingship of God*, trans. Richard Scheimann. London: George Allen and Unwin, 1967.

*Königtum Gottes*. Berlin: Schocken, 1932.

*Two Types of Faith*, trans. Norman P. Goldhawk. New York: Macmillan, 1951.

al-Bukhārī, Muḥammad b. Ismāʿīl. *Khalq afʿāl al-ʿibād wa-l-radd ʿalā al-jahmiyya wa-aṣḥāb al-taʿṭīl*. Beirut: Muʾassasat al-Risāla, 1411/1990.

*Kitāb al-taʾrīkh al-kabīr*. N.p., n.d.

Bunzel, Cole M. "From Paper State to Caliphate: The Ideology of the Islamic State," The Brookings Project on U.S. Relations with the Islamic World, 2015. https://shorturl.at/HA4Uv.

*Wahhābism: The History of a Militant Islamic Movement*. Princeton and Oxford: Princeton University Press, 2023.

Burhāmī, Yāsir. *al-Kawāshif al-muḍiyya ʿan laʾāliʾ risālat al-ʿubūdiyya*. Alexandria: Dār al-Īmān, n.d.

Calvert, John. *Sayyid Qutb and the Origins of Radical Islamism*. New York: Columbia University Press, 2010.

Capps, Walter H. *Religious Studies: The Making of a Discipline*. Minneapolis: Fortress Press, 1995.

Castoriadis, Cornelius. *L'institution imaginaire de la société*. Paris: Seuil, 1975.

Chittick, William. "Ṣadr al-Dīn Qūnawī on the Oneness of Being," *International Philosophical Quarterly* 21 (1981), pp. 171–184.

Clastres, Pierre. *La Société contre l'État*. Paris: Les Éditions de Minuit, 1974.
Commins, David. *The Wahhabi Mission and Saudi Arabia*. London and New York: I.B. Tauris, 2006.
Cook, Michael. "The Expansion of the First Saudi State: The Case of Washm," in C. E. Bosworth, Charles Issawi, Roger Savory, and A. L. Udovitch (eds.), *The Islamic World: Essays in Honor of Bernard Lewis*. Princeton: The Darwin Press, 1989, pp. 661–700.
*Muhammad*. Oxford: Oxford University Press, 1983.
"On the Origins of Wahhābism," *Journal of the Royal Asiatic Society*, Third Series 2/2 (July 1992), pp. 191–202.
Cooperson, Michael. *Classical Arabic Biography: The Heirs of the Prophets in the Age of Al-Maʾmūn*. Cambridge: Cambridge University Press, 2004.
Crone, Patricia. "Angels versus Humans as Messengers of God: The View of the Qurʾānic Pagans," in Philippa Townsend and Moulie Vidas (eds.), *Revelation, Literature, and Community in Late Antiquity*. Tübingen: Mohr Siebeck, 2011, pp. 315–336.
"The Religion of the Qurʾānic Pagans: God and the Lesser Deities," *Arabica* 57 (2010), pp. 151–200.
Crone, Patricia, and Martin Hinds. *God's Caliph: Religious Authority in the First Centuries of Islam*. Cambridge: Cambridge University Press, 1986.
Crüsemann, F. *Der Widerstand gegen das Königtum. Die antiköniglichen Texte des Alten Testaments und der Kampf um den frühen israelitischen Staat*. WMANT 49. Neukirchen-Vluyn: Neukirchener Verlag, 1978.
Dallal, Ahmad. "The Origins and Objectives of Islamic Revivalist Thought, 1750-1850," *Journal of the American Oriental Society* 113/3 (1993), pp. 341–359.
Davidson, Herbert A. *Proofs for Eternity, Creation, and the Existence of God in Medieval Islamic and Jewish Philosophy*. New York and Oxford: Oxford University Press, 1987.
Dawson, David. *Allegorical Readers and Cultural Revision in Ancient Alexandria*. Berkeley: University of California Press, 1992.
DeLong-Bas, Natana J. *Wahhabi Islam: From Revival and Reform to Global Jihad*. Oxford: Oxford University Press, 2004.
al-Dhahabī, Muḥammad b. Aḥmad b. ʿUthmān. *Manāqib al-imām Abī Ḥanīfa wa-ṣāḥibayhi Abī Yūsuf wa-Muḥammad b. al-Ḥasan*, ed. Muḥammad Zāhid al-Kawtharī and Abū al-Wafā al-Afghānī, 4th ed. Hyderabad: Lajnat Iḥyāʾ al-Maʿārif al-Nuʿmāniyya, 1419[/1998].
Diffelen, Roelof Willem van. *De leer der Wahhabieten*. Leiden: Brill, 1927.
Dihlawī, Nadhīr Ḥusayn. *Miʿyār al-ḥaqq fī tanqīd tanwīr al-ḥaqq*. Lahore/ Faisalabad: Maktabah-yi Islāmiyya, 2007.
al-Dihlawī, Shāh Walī Allāh Aḥmad b. ʿAbd al-Raḥīm al-Fārūqī. *Ḥujjat Allāh al-bāligha*. Beirut: Dār al-Jīl, 1426/2005.
*ʿIqd al-jīd fī aḥkām al-ijtihād wa-l-taqlīd*. Sharjah: Dār al-Fatḥ, 1415/1995.
al-Dijwī, Yūsuf. *Maqālāt wa-fatāwā*. Cairo: al-Hayʾa al-ʿĀmma li-Shuʾūn al-Maṭābiʿ al-Amīriyya, 1401/1981.
Ebstein, Michael. *Mysticism and Philosophy in al-Andalus: Ibn Masarra, Ibn al-ʿArabī and the Ismāʿīlī Tradition*. Leiden and Boston: Brill, 2014.

Eisenstadt, S. N. "The Axial Age Breakthroughs: Their Characteristics and Origins," in S. N. Eisenstadt (ed.), *The Origins and Diversity of Axial Age Civilizations*. Albany: State University of New York Press, 1986, pp. 1–26.

Elkana, Yehuda. "The Emergence of Second-Order Thinking in Classical Greece," in S. N. Eisenstadt (ed.), *The Origins and Diversity of Axial Age Civilizations*. Albany: State University of New York Press, 1986, pp. 40–64.

Fadel, Mohammad. "The Social Logic of *Taqlīd* and the Rise of the *Mukhtaṣar*," *Islamic Law and Society* 3/2 (1996), pp. 193–233.

Al-Fahad, Abdulaziz H. "From Exclusivism to Accommodation: Doctrinal and Legal Evolution of Wahhabism," *New York University Law Review*, 79/2 (May 2004), pp. 485–519.

"The *'Imama* vs. the *'Iqal*: *Hadari*-Bedouin Conflict and the Formation of the Saudi State," in Madawi Al-Rasheed and Robert Vitalis (eds.), *Counter-Narratives: History, Contemporary Society, and Politics in Saudi Arabia and Yemen*. New York: Palgrave Macmillan, 2004, pp. 35–75.

Fakhry, Majid. "The Classical Islamic Arguments for the Existence of God," *The Muslim World* 47/2 (1957), pp. 133–145.

Falcon, Andrea. "Aristotle on Causality," in Edward N. Zalta (ed.), *The Stanford Encyclopedia of Philosophy (Winter* 2012 *Edition)*. http://plato.stanford.edu/archives/win2012/entries/aristotle-causality/.

Finkelberg, Aryeh. "On the Unity of Orphic and Milesian Thought," *The Harvard Theological Review*, 79/4 (October 1986), pp. 321–335.

Frank, Richard M. *Beings and Their Attributes: The Teaching of the Basrian School of the Mu'tazila in the Classical Period*. Albany: State University of New York Press, 1978.

"The Neoplatonism of Jahm b. Ṣafwān," *Le Muséon* 78 (1965), pp. 395–424.

Frankel, Joseph. *International Relations*, 2nd ed. London: Oxford University Press, 1969.

Friedmann, Yohanan. "Quasi-Rational and Anti-Rational Elements in Radical Muslim Thought: The Case of Abū al-A'lā Mawdūdī," in Yohanan Friedmann and Christoph Markschies (eds.), *Rationalization in Religions: Judaism, Christianity, and Islam*. Berlin and Boston: De Gruyter, 2019, pp. 289–300.

Fuchs, Simon Wolfgang. "Do Excellent Surgeons Make Miserable Exegetes? Negotiating the Sunni Tradition in the *ǧihādī* Camps," *Die Welt des Islams* 53/2 (2013), pp. 192–237.

*Proper Signposts for the Camp: The Reception of Classical Authorities in the Ǧihādī Manual al-'Umda fī I'dād al-'Udda*. Würzburg: Ergon Verlag, 2011.

Gauchet, Marcel. *Le désenchantement du monde: Une histoire politique de la religion*. Paris: Gallimard, 1985.

*The Disenchantment of the World: A Political History of Religion*, trans. Oscar Burge. Princeton: Princeton University Press, 1997.

Geoffroy, E. "Le traité de soufisme d'un disciple d'Ibn Taymiyya: Aḥmad 'Imād al-dīn al-Wāsiṭī," *Studia Islamica* 82 (1995), pp. 83–101.

al-Ghazālī, Abū Ḥāmid. *al-Mustaṣfā min 'ilm al-uṣūl*. Medina: al-Jāmi'a al-Islāmiyya, 1413/1993.

al-Ghubāshī, Sayyid b. Saʿd al-Dīn. *Iblāgh al-ḥaqq ilā al-khalq: risāla fī ḥukm al-mushāraka fī majlis al-shaʿb al-miṣrī*. N.d. www.ilmway.com/site/maqdis/MS_512 (link no longer active).

*Saʿat raḥmat rabb al-ʿālamīn li-l-juhhāl al-mukhālifīn li-l-sharīʿa min al-muslimīn*. Riyadh: Dār al-Muslim, 1415/1995.

Ghyoot, Mathias. *Brothers behind Bars: A History of the Muslim Brotherhood from the Palestine War to Egypt's Prisons*. Oxford and New York: Oxford University Press, 2025.

Gimaret, Daniel. *Dieu à l'image de l'homme: les anthropomorphismes de la sunna et leur interpretation par les théologiens*. Paris: Cerf, 1997.

"Théories de l'acte humain dans l'école Ḥanbalite," *Bulletin d'études orientales* 29 (1977), pp. 157–178.

*Théories de l'acte humain en théologie musulmane*. Paris: J. Vrin, 1980.

Goitein, S. D. "YHWH the Passionate: The Monotheistic Meaning and Origin of the Name YHWH," *Vetus Testamentum* 6/1 (1956), pp. 1–9.

Goldziher, Ignaz. *Introduction to Islamic Theology and Law*, trans. Andras and Ruth Hamori. Princeton: Princeton University Press, 1981.

Review of Walter M. Patton's *Aḥmed ibn Ḥanbal and the Miḥna*, *Zeitschrift der Deutschen Morgenländischen Gesellschaft* 53 (1899), pp. 155–160.

*The Ẓāhirīs*, trans. Wolfgang Behn. Leiden: Brill, 2008.

Gray, John. *Al Qaeda and What It Means to Be Modern*. New York: The New Press, 2003.

Gribetz, Arthur. *Strange Bedfellows:* Mutʿat al-nisāʾ *and* Mutʿat al-ḥajj*: A Study Based on Sunnī and Shīʿī Sources of* Tafsīr, Ḥadīth*, and* Fiqh. Berlin: Klaus Schwarz, 1994.

Ḥabīb, Kamāl. "Mawqif al-qurʾān min khuṣūmihi," 1 Safar 1427 / March 1, 2006. www.aljazeera.net/knowledgegate/books/2006/3/1/موقف-القرآن-من-خصومه (link no longer active).

Hakim, Avraham. "ʿUmar b. al-Ḫaṭṭāb: L'autorité religieuse et morale," *Arabica* 55/1 (2008), pp. 1–34.

Halbertal, Moshe, and Avishai Margalit. *Idolatry*. Cambridge, MA, and London: Harvard University Press, 1992.

Halevi, Leor. "Arabians for Guns: Wahhabi Matchlocks, World Trade, and the Rise of the First Saudi State," *Journal of the Royal Asiatic Society*, Series 3, 33/2 (2023), pp. 401–442.

Ḥalīma, ʿAbd al-Munʿim Muṣṭafā [= Abū Baṣīr al-Ṭarṭūsī]. *Ḥukm al-islām fī al-dīmuqrāṭiyya wa-l-taʿaddudiyya al-ḥizbiyya*. Amman, 1993.

*Mulāḥaẓāt ʿalā al-dustūr al-lībī al-muʾaqqat*. 1432/2011. www.abubaseer.bizland.com/refutation/read/F%20103.doc.

Hallaq, Wael B. *Authority, Continuity and Change in Islamic Law*. Cambridge: Cambridge University Press, 2004.

"Was the Gate of Ijtihad Closed?," *International Journal of Middle East Studies*, 16/1 (March 1984), pp. 3–41.

Hamacher, Werner. *Minima Philologica*, trans. Catharine Diehl and Jason Groves. New York: Fordham University Press, 2015.

Hartmann, Richard. "Die Wahhābiten," *Zeitschrift der Deutschen Morgenländischen Gesellschaft* 78 (1924), pp. 176–213.

Hartung, Jan-Peter. *A System of Life: Mawdūdī and the Ideologisation of Islam*. London: Hurst, 2013.

Hassan, Mona. "Modern Interpretations and Misinterpretations of a Medieval Scholar: Apprehending the Political Thought of Ibn Taymiyya," in Yossef Rapoport and Shahab Ahmed (eds.), *Ibn Taymiyya and His Times*. Karachi: Oxford University Press, 2010, pp. 338–366.

al-Ḥawālī, Safar b. ʿAbd al-Raḥmān. *al-ʿAlmāniyya: nashʾatuhā wa-taṭawwuruhā wa-āthāruhā fī al-ḥayyāt al-islāmiyya al-muʿāṣira*. N.p.: Dār al-Hijra, n.d.

*Sharḥ taḥkīm al-qawānīn*. Jedda: Maktabat Dār al-Ṣaḥāba, n.d.

Hawting, G. R. *The Idea of Idolatry and the Emergence of Islam*. Cambridge: Cambridge University Press, 1999.

"The Significance of the Slogan *lā ḥukma illā lillāh…*," *Bulletin of the School of Oriental and African Studies* 41 (1978), pp. 453–463.

Haykel, Bernard. "On the Nature of Salafi Thought and Action," in Roel Meijer (ed.), *Global Salafism: Islam's New Religious Movement*. New York: Columbia University Press, 2009, pp. 33–57.

*Revival and Reform in Islam: The Legacy of Muhammad al-Shawkānī*. Cambridge: Cambridge University Press, 2003.

Hegghammer, Thomas, and Stéphane Lacroix. "Rejectionist Islamism in Saudi Arabia: The Story of Juhayman al-ʿUtaybi Revisited," *International Journal of Middle East Studies* 39/1 (2007), pp. 103–122.

Heidegger, Martin. *Pathmarks*, ed. William McNeill. New York: Cambridge University Press, 1998.

*Wegmarken* (Gesamtausgabe vol. 9). Frankfurt am Main: Vittorio Klostermann, 1976.

Helmig, Christoph. "Proclus' Criticism of Aristotle's Theory of Abstraction and Concept Formation in *Analytica Posteriora* II 19," in Frans A. J. de Haas, Mariska Leunissen, and Marije Martijn (eds.), *Interpreting Aristotle's Posterior Analytics in Late Antiquity and Beyond*. Leiden: Brill, 2010, pp. 27–54.

Holtzman, Livnat. *Anthropomorphism in Islam: The Traditionalist Challenge (700–1350)*. Edinburgh: Edinburgh University Press, 2018.

"Human Choice, Divine Guidance, and the *Fiṭra* Tradition: The Use of Hadith in Theological Treatises by Ibn Taymiyya and Ibn Qayyim al-Jawziyya," in Yossef Rapoport and Shahab Ahmed (eds.), *Ibn Taymiyya and His Times*. Karachi: Oxford University Press, 2010, pp. 163–188.

Hoover, Jon. *Ibn Taymiyya's Theodicy of Perpetual Optimism*. Leiden and Boston: Brill, 2007.

"Ibn Taymiyya's Use of Ibn Rushd to Refute the Incorporealism of Fakhr al-Dīn al-Rāzī," in Abdelkader Al Ghouz (ed.), *Islamic Philosophy from the 12th to the 14th Century*. Göttingen: Bonn University Press, 2018, pp. 469–491.

al-Huḍaybī, Ḥasan. *Duʿāt lā quḍāt: abḥāth fī al-ʿaqīda al-islāmiyya wa-manhaj al-daʿwa ilā llāh*. Cairo: Dār al-Ṭibāʿa wa-l-Nashr al-Islāmiyya, 1977.

Ibn ʿAbd al-Barr. *Jāmiʿ bayān al-ʿilm wa-faḍlihi*. Egypt: Idārat al-Ṭibāʿa al-Munīriyya, 1958.

Ibn ʿAbd al-Wahhāb, Sulaymān. *al-Ṣawāʿiq al-ilāhiyya fī al-radd ʿalā al-wahhābiyya*. Istanbul, 1399/1979.

Ibn Abī al-ʿIzz, ʿAlī b. ʿAlī b. Muḥammad. *Sharḥ al-ṭaḥāwiyya fī al-ʿaqīda al-salafiyya*. Riyadh: Maktabat al-Riyāḍ al-Ḥadītha, n.d.
Ibn ʿArabī, Muḥyī al-Dīn. *Fuṣūṣ al-ḥikam*, ed. Abū al-ʿAlā ʿAfīfī. Beirut: Dār al-Kitāb al-ʿArabī, 1400/1980.
Ibn Baṭṭa al-ʿUkbarī. *al-Ibāna ʿan sharīʿat al-firqa al-nājiyya wa-mujānabat al-firaq al-madhmūma*, 2nd ed. Riyadh: Dār al-Rāya, 1415/1994.
Ibn Bāz, ʿAbd al-ʿAzīz. *Wujūb taḥkīm sharʿ Allāh wa-nabdh mā khālafahu*. N.d. www.binbaz.org.sa/article/578.
Ibn Bishr, ʿUthmān b. ʿAbdallāh. *ʿUnwān al-majd fī taʾrīkh najd*, 4th ed. Riyadh: Dārat al-Malik ʿAbd al-ʿAzīz, 1402/1982.
Ibn Ghannām, Ḥuṣayn. *Taʾrīkh najd*. Beirut and Cairo: Dār al-Shurūq, 1415/1994.
Ibn Ḥanbal, Aḥmad. *al-Radd ʿalā al-jahmiyya wa-l-zanādiqa*. Riyadh: Dār al-Thabāt, 1424[/2003].
Ibn Ḥazm. *al-Iḥkām fī uṣūl al-aḥkām*. Cairo: Dār al-Ḥadīth, 1404/1984.
Ibn Kathīr al-Dimashqī. *Tafsīr al-qurʾān al-ʿaẓīm*. Beirut: Dār al-Kutub al-ʿIlmiyya, 1419/1998.
Ibn Manẓūr al-Ifrīqī al-Miṣrī. *Lisān al-ʿarab*. Beirut: Dār Ṣādir/Dār Bayrūt, 1375/1956.
Ibn Mattawayh. *al-Tadhkira fī aḥkām al-jawāhir wa-l-aʿrāḍ*. Cairo: Dār al-Thaqāfa, 1975.
Ibn Muḥammad al-Jawzī, Abū al-Faraj. *Zād al-masīr fī ʿilm al-tafsīr*. Beirut: Dār al-Fikr, 1407/1987.
Ibn Qayyim al-Jawziyya. *Iʿlām al-muwaqqiʿīn ʿan rabb al-ʿālamīn*, 2nd ed. Beirut: Dār al-Kutub al-ʿIlmiyya, 1414/1993.
*al-Ṣawāʿiq al-mursala ʿalā al-jahmiyya wa-l-muʿaṭṭila maʿa takmilatihi min mukhtaṣar al-ṣawāʿiq al-mursala*. Sidon and Beirut: al-Maktaba al-ʿAṣriyya, 1428/2007.
Ibn Rushd. *al-Kashf ʿan manāhij al-adilla fī ʿaqāʾid al-milla*. Beirut: Markaz Dirāsāt al-Waḥda al-ʿArabiyya, 1998.
Ibn Sīnā. *Kitāb al-shifāʾ/Ilāhiyyāt (1)*, ed. G. Qanawātī and S. Zāyid. Cairo, 1960.
Ibn Taymiyya. *Bayān talbīs al-jahmiyya fī taʾsīs bidaʿihim al-kalāmiyya*. Medina: Mujammaʿ al-Malik Fahd, 1426[/2005].
*Darʾ taʿāruḍ al-ʿaql wa-l-naql aw muwāfaqat ṣaḥīḥ al-manqūl li-ṣarīḥ al-maʿqūl*. Riyadh: Dār al-Kunūz al-Adabiyya, 1411/1991.
*Iqtiḍāʾ al-ṣirāṭ al-mustaqīm li-mukhālafat aṣḥāb al-jaḥīm*. Riyadh: Maktabat al-Rushd, 1411/1991.
*Jāmiʿ al-masāʾil*. Mecca: Dār ʿĀlam al-Fawāʾid, 1422[/2001–2002].
*Jāmiʿ al-rasāʾil*. Jedda: Dār al-Madanī, 1405/1984.
*Majmūʿat al-fatāwā*. Al-Manṣūra: Dār al-Wafāʾ, 1426/2005.
*Minhāj al-sunna al-nabawiyya*. Beirut: Dār al-Kutub al-ʿIlmiyya, 1420/1999.
*Rafʿ al-malām ʿan al-aʾimma al-aʿlām*. Riyadh: al-Riʾāsa al-ʿĀmma li-Idārāt al-Buḥūth al-ʿIlmiyya wa-l-Iftāʾ wa-l-Daʿwa wa-l-Irshād, 1413[/1992].
*al-Tadmuriyya*. Riyadh: Maktabat al-ʿUbaykan, 1416[/1996].
Ibrahim, Mohd Radhi. "Immediate Knowledge according to al-Qāḍī ʿAbd al-Jabbār," *Arabic Sciences and Philosophy* 23 (2013), pp. 101–115.

Irwin, Robert. "The Privatization of 'Justice' under the Circassian Mamluks," *Mamlūk Studies Review* 6 (2002), pp. 63–70.
al-Iṣfahānī, al-Rāghib. *al-Mufradāt fī gharīb al-qur'ān*. N.p.: Maktabat Nazār Muṣṭafā al-Bāz, n.d.
Ismāʿīl, Mawlānā Ḥājjī Muḥammad. *Tanwīr al-ʿaynayn fī ithbāt rafʿ al-yadayn*. N.p.: Maṭbaʿ Raḥmānī, 1256[/1840–1841].
al-Jabha al-Islāmiyya li-l-Inqādh / al-Jaysh al-Islāmī li-l-Inqādh, *Qālū ʿannā muta'awwilīn fa-ajabnā mustadillīn*. N.p., n.d.
Jabhat al-Nuṣra. *Nubdha ʿammā naʿtaqiduhu wa-nadīnu llāha bihi*. al-Manāra al-Bayḍā', 2014. https://twitter.com/JabhtAnNusrah/status/438393864190033920 (link no longer active).
Jackson, Roy. *Mawlana Mawdudi and Political Islam: Authority and the Islamic State*. London and New York: Routledge, 2011.
Jaeger, Werner. *The Theology of the Early Greek Philosophers*. Oxford: Oxford University Press, 1947.
al-Jamāʿa al-Lībiyya al-Muqātila. *Dirāsāt taṣḥīḥiyya fī mafāhīm al-jihād wa-l-ḥisba wa-l-ḥukm ʿalā al-nās*. N.p., 2010.
Jansen, Johannes J. G. *The Neglected Duty: The Creed of Sadat's Assassins and Islamic Resurgence in the Middle East*. New York and London: Macmillan, 1986.
Jaspers, Karl. *The Origin and Goal of History*, trans. Michael Bullock. New Haven: Yale University Press, 1953.
*Vom Ursprung und Ziel der Geschichte*. Zürich: Artemis, 1949.
Jawda, ʿAbd al-Nāṣir. *al-Ḥukm bi-mā anzala llāhu wa-takfīr al-mushrik*. Frederiksberg, Denmark: al-Nūr li-l-Iʿlām al-Islāmī, 1433/2012. www.mediafire.com/?cwt2t6zretccqah (link no longer active).
al-Jawharī, Ismāʿīl b. Ḥammād. *al-Ṣiḥāḥ*. Beirut: Dār al-ʿIlm li-l-Malāyīn, 1399/1979.
al-Jihnī, Muḥammad b. ʿAbd al-Raḥmān Abū Sayf. "al-Tamānuʿ al-dāll ʿalā al-tawḥīd fī kitāb Allāh wa-naqd masālik al-mutakallimīn," *Majallat Jāmiʿat Umm al-Qurā li-ʿUlūm al-Sharīʿa wa-l-Dirāsāt al-Islāmiyya* 45 (Dhū al-Qaʿda 1429 AH), pp. 105–132.
Johansen, Baber. "Signs as Evidence: The Doctrine of Ibn Taymiyya (1263-1328) and Ibn Qayyim al-Jawziyya (d. 1351) on Proof," *Islamic Law and Society* 9/2 (2002), pp. 168–193.
Al-Juhany, Uwaidah M. *Najd before the Salafi Reform Movement: Social, Political and Religious Conditions during the Three Centuries Preceding the Rise of the Saudi State*. Reading, UK: Ithaca Press, 2002.
Kamada, Shigeru. "A Study of the Term *Sirr* (Secret) in Sufi *Laṭā'if* Theories," *Orient* 19 (1983), pp. 7–28.
Kaufmann, Yehezkel. *Toledot HaEmuna HaYisraelit*. Jerusalem: Bialik; Tel Aviv: Dvir, 1956.
Kepel, Gilles. *Muslim Extremism in Egypt: The Prophet and the Pharaoh*. Berkeley and Los Angeles: University of California Press, 2003.
Kister, M. J. "...*Illā bi-ḥaqqihi*... A Study of an Early *Ḥadīth*," *Jerusalem Studies in Arabic and Islam* 5 (1984), pp. 33–52.
"Labbayka, Allāhumma, Labbayka ... On a Monotheistic Aspect of a Jāhiliyya Practice," *Jerusalem Studies in Arabic and Islam* 2 (1980), pp. 33–57.

Knohl, Israel. *Eich Nolad HaTanach* [How the Bible was born]. Modi'in: Kinneret, Zmora-Bitan, Dvir, 2018.

"Jacob-El in the Land of Esau and the Roots of Biblical Religion," *Vetus Testamentum* 67/3 (2017), pp. 481–484.

Lacroix, Stéphane. "Between Revolution and Apoliticism: Nasir al-Din al-Albani and His Impact on the Shaping of Contemporary Salafism," in Roel Meijer (ed.), *Global Salafism: Islam's New Religious Movement*. New York: Columbia University Press, 2009, pp. 58–80.

*Les islamistes saoudiens: une insurrection manquée*. Paris: Presses Universitaires de France, 2010.

Landau-Tasseron, Ella. "Leadership and Allegiance in the Society of the Muslim Brothers," Hudson Institute Research Monographs on the Muslim World 2/5 (2010).

Laoust, Henri. *Essai sur les doctrines sociales et politiques de Taḳī-d-Dīn Aḥmad b. Taimīya*. Cairo: L'institut Français d'archéologie orientale, 1939.

Lauzière, Henri. "The Construction of *Salafiyya*: Reconsidering Salafism from the Perspective of Conceptual History," *International Journal of Middle East Studies* 42 (2010), pp. 369–389.

*The Making of Salafism: Islamic Reform in the Twentieth Century*. New York: Columbia University Press, 2016.

Lav, Daniel. "Ashʿarism, Causality, and the Cult of Saints," *Jerusalem Studies in Arabic and Islam* 50 (2021), pp. 255–312.

"*Buʿithtu biʾl-sayf*: Jihad, Monolatry, and Theonomy in Modern Salafism," in Mustafa Baig and Robert Gleave (eds.), *Violence in Islamic Thought: From European Imperialism to the Post-Colonial Era*. Edinburgh: Edinburgh University Press, 2021, pp. 163–185.

"Jihadists and Jurisprudents: The 'Revisions' Literature of Sayyid Imam and Al-Gama'a Al-Islamiyya," in Joseph Skelly (ed.), *Political Islam from Muhammad to Ahmadinejad: Defenders, Detractors, and Definitions*. Santa Barbara: Praeger Security International, 2010, pp. 105–146.

*Radical Islam and the Revival of Medieval Theology*. New York: Cambridge University Press, 2012.

"Review of Joas Wagemakers, *A Quietist Jihadi: The Ideology and Influence of Abu Muhammad al-Maqdisi*," *Islam and Christian–Muslim Relations* 24/4 (2013), pp. 594–552.

Layish, Aharon. "The Transformation of the Sharīʿa from Jurists' Law to Statutory Law in the Contemporary Muslim World," *Die Welt des Islams* 44/1 (2004), pp. 85–113.

Lefèvre, Raphaël. *Ashes of Hama: The Muslim Brotherhood in Syria*. Oxford: Oxford University Press, 2013.

Lia, Brynjar. "'Destructive Doctrinarians': Abu Musʿab al-Suri's Critique of the Salafis in the Jihadi Current," in Roel Meijer (ed.), *Global Salafism: Islam's New Religious Movement*. New York: Columbia University Press, 2009, pp. 281–300.

Macdonald, D. B. "Ilāh," in C. E. Bosworth et al. (eds.), *The Encyclopedia of Islam*, 2nd ed., vol. 3, pp. 1093–1094.

Madelung, Wilferd. "Abū l-Ḥuṣayn al-Baṣrī's Proof for the Existence of God," in James E. Montgomery (ed.), *Arabic Theology, Arabic Philosophy: From the Many to the One: Essays in Celebration of Richard M. Frank*. Leuven: Peeters, 2006, pp. 273–280.

al-Majlis al-Waṭanī al-Intiqālī al-Mu'aqqat – Lībiyā. *al-I'lān al-dustūrī*, 3 Ramaḍān 1432 / August 3, 2011. www.wipo.int/edocs/lexdocs/laws/ar/ly/ly005ar.pdf.

Makdisi, George. "The Hanbali School and Sufism," *Boletin de la Asociación Española de Orientalistas XV* (1979), pp. 115–126.

"Ibn Taimīya: A Ṣūfī of the Qādiriya Order," *American Journal of Arabic Studies* 1 (1974), pp. 118–129.

*Religion, Law, and Learning in Classical Islam*. Hampshire: Variorum, 1991.

al-Maqdisī, Abū Muḥammad ('Āṣim). *Kashf al-niqāb 'an sharī'at al-ghāb* [written 1408/1988]. www.ilmway.com/site/maqdis/MS_38438.html (link no longer active).

*al-Kawāshif al-jaliyya fī kufr al-dawla al-su'ūdiyya*, 2nd ed., 1421[/2000–2001]. www.ilmway.com/site/maqdis/MS_816 (link no longer active).

*Mīzān al-i'tidāl fī taqyīm kitāb al-mawrid al-zulāl fī al-tanbīh 'alā akhṭā' al-ẓilāl*, 1422[/2001–2002]. www.ilmway.com/site/maqdis/MS_9109.html (link no longer active).

*Mīzānunā wa-mawāzīnuhum*, May 30, 2015. https://twitter.com/almaqdese0/status/604668301512278016 (link no longer active).

*Wa-lākin kūnū rabbānniyyīn*, part 1*: al-ism wa-l-nasab wa-l-dirāsa wa-l-tadayyun wa-l-iltizām ma'a jamā'at surūr*, 2012. Video. http://abu-qatada.xyz/vid/visual/8901.zip (link no longer active).

*Wa-lākin kūnū rabbānniyīn*, part 7: *marḥalat afghānistān*, 2012. Video. http://abu-qatada.xyz/vid/visual/9035.zip (link no longer active).

*Wa-lākin kūnū rabbānniyyīn*, part 9, *al-tadrīs fī mu'askarāt al-qā'ida wa-l-tadarrub fīhā*, 2013. Video. http://abu-qatada.xyz/vid/visual/9039.zip (link no longer active).

March, Andrew F. *The Caliphate of Man: Popular Sovereignty in Modern Islamic Thought*. Cambridge, MA, and London: Harvard University Press, 2019.

"Genealogies of Sovereignty in Islamic Political Theology," *Social Research* 80/1 (Spring 2013), pp. 293–320.

Marmura, Michael. "Avicenna's Critique of Platonists in Book VII, Chapter 2 of the *Metaphysics* of His *Healing*," in James E. Montgomery (ed.), *Arabic Theology, Arabic Philosophy: From the Many to the One: Essays in Celebration of Richard M. Frank*. Leuven: Peeters, 2006, pp. 355–369.

"Quiddity and Universality in Avicenna," in Parviz Morewedge (ed.), *Neoplatonism and Islamic Thought*. Albany: State University of New York, 1992, pp. 77–87.

Massignon, Louis. *Essay on the Origins of the Technical Language of Islamic Mysticism*, trans. Benjamin Clark. Notre Dame: University of Notre Dame Press, 1997.

"Les vraies origines dogmatiques du Wahhabisme," *Revue du monde musulman* 36 (1918-1919), pp. 320–328.

Al-Matroudi, Abdul Hakim I. *The Ḥanbalī School of Law and Ibn Taymiyyah: Conflict or Conciliation*. London and New York: Routledge, 2006.

Mawdūdī, Mawlānā Sayyid Abū al-Aʿlā. *The Islamic Law and Constitution*, ed. and trans. Khurshid Ahmad, 4th ed. Lahore: Islamic Publications (Private) Limited, 1969.

*Islāmī riyāsat*. Lahore: Islamic Publications (Private) Limited, 2008.

*Khilāfat o mulūkiyyat*. Lahore: Idārah-i Tarjumān al-Qurʾān, 2005.

*Khuṭbāt*. New Delhi: Markazī Maktabah-i Islāmī, 2005.

*Mūjaz taʾrīkh tajdīd al-islām wa-iḥyāʾihi wa-wāqiʿ al-muslimīn wa-sabīl al-nuhūḍ bihim*, 2nd ed., trans. Muḥammad Kāẓim Sibāq. Lebanon: Dār al-Fikr al-Ḥadīth, 1386/1967.

*Qurʾān kī chār bunyādī iṣṭilāḥēn̲*. New Delhi: Markazī Maktabah-i Islāmī, 2011.

*Rasāʾil o masāʾil*. Lahore: Islamic Publications (Private) Limited, 2002.

*Tafhīm al-qurʾān*. Lahore: Idārah-i Tarjumān al-Qurʾān, 1997.

*Tafhīmāt*. Lahore: Islamic Publications (Private) Limited, 1387/1968.

McLaren, Andrew. "Ibn Ḥanbal's Refutation of the Jahmiyya: A Textual History," *Journal of the American Oriental Society* 140/4 (2020), pp. 901–926.

Melchert, Christopher. *The Formation of the Sunni Schools of Law, 9th–10th Centuries C.E.* Leiden: Brill, 1997.

Michel, Thomas F. "Ibn Taymiyya's *Sharḥ* on the *Futūḥ al-ghayb* of ʿAbd al-Qādir al-Jīlānī," *Hamdard Islamicus* 4/2 (Summer 1981), pp. 3–12.

Michot, Yahya. *Ibn Taymiyya against Extremisms*. Beirut: Dar Albouraq, 1433/2012.

"A Mamlūk Theologian's Commentary on Avicenna's *Risāla Aḍḥawiyya*, Being a Translation of a Part of the *Darʾ al-Taʿāruḍ* of Ibn Taymiyya, with Introduction, Annotation, and Appendices, Part I," *Journal of Islamic Studies* 14/2 (2003), pp. 149–203.

Mitchell, Richard P. *The Society of the Muslim Brothers*. London: Oxford University Press, 1969.

Mouline, Nabil. *The Clerics of Islam: Religious Authority and Political Power in Saudi Arabia*, trans. Ethan S. Rundell. New Haven and London: Yale University Press, 2014.

Müller, Reinhard. *Königtum und Gottesherrschaft: Untersuchungen zur alttestamentlichen Monarchiekritik*. FAT II/3. Tübingen: Mohr Siebeck, 2004.

Muranyi, Miklos. "Aus dem *Kitāb Aḥkām al-Qurʾān* des Mālikiten Ibn Ḫawāz Mandād," *Der Islam* 91/2 (2014), pp. 360–373.

Mustafa, Abdul-Rahman. *On Taqlīd: Ibn al Qayyim's Critique of Authority in Islamic Law*. New York: Oxford University Press, 2013.

al-Nadwī, Abū al-Ḥasan. *al-Tafsīr al-siyāsī li-l-islām fī mirʾāt kitābāt al-ustādh Abī al-Aʿlā al-Mawdūdī wa-l-shahīd Sayyid Quṭb*. Cairo: Dār Āfāq al-Ghad, 1980.

Nafi, Basheer M. "A Teacher of Ibn ʿAbd al-Wahhāb: Muḥammad Ḥayāt al-Sindī and the Revival of *Aṣḥāb al-Ḥadīth*'s Methodology," *Islamic Law and Society* 13/2 (2006), pp. 208–241.

al-Naḥḥās, Abū Jaʿfar. *Maʿānī al-qurʾān al-karīm*, ed. Muḥammad ʿAlī al-Ṣābūnī. Mecca: Jāmiʿat Umm al-Qurā, 1409/1988.

Naṣr, Muḥammad Mūsā. "Taḥdhīr al-bariyya min ʿibādat al-aṣnām al-bashariyya," *al-Aṣāla* 2 (15 Jumāda II 1413) [= December 1992], pp. 25–29.

Nasr, Seyyed Vali Reza. *Mawdudi and the Making of Islamic Revivalism*. New York and Oxford: Oxford University Press, 1996.

Nedza, Justyna. "'Salafismus' – Überlegungen zur Schärfung einer Analysekategorie," in Behnam T. Said and Hazim Fouad (eds.), *Salafismus: Auf der Suche nach dem wahren Islam*, Freiburg, Basel, and Vienna: Herder, 2014, pp. 80–105.
*Takfīr im militanten Salafismus: Der Staat als Feind*. Leiden and Boston: Brill, 2020.
Nicholson, Reynold A. *A Literary History of the Arabs*. New York: Scribner, 1907.
Nielsen, Jørgen S. *Secular Justice in an Islamic State: Maẓālim under the Baḥrī Mamlūks, 662/1264 – 789/1387*. Leiden: Instituut voor het Nabije Oosten, 1985.
al-Nīsābūrī, al-Ḥasan b. Muḥammad al-Qummī. *Tafsīr gharāʾib al-qurʾān wa-raghāʾib al-furqān*. Beirut: Dār al-Kutub al-ʿIlmiyya, 1416/1996.
Nuʿmānī, Muḥammad Manẓūr. *Mawlānā Mawdūdī kē sāt$^{h}$ mērī rafāqat kī sar-guzasht awr ab mērā mawqif*. Karachi: Majlis-i Nashriyāt-i Islām, n.d.
Olidort, Jacob. "The Politics of 'Quietist' Salafism," The Brookings Project on U.S. Relations with the Islamic World, Analysis Paper no. 18, Center for Middle East Policy at Brookings, 2015.
Otto, Eckart. "Political Theology in Judah and Assyria: The Beginning of the Hebrew Bible as Literature," *Svensk Exegetisk Årsbok* 65 (2000), pp. 59–76.
Otto, Rudolf. *Das Heilige*. Gotha: Leopold Klotz, 1929.
*The Idea of the Holy*, 2nd ed., trans. John W. Harvey. London: Oxford University Press, 1950.
Palmer, John. *Parmenides and Presocratic Philosophy*. Oxford: Oxford University Press, 2009.
Parsons, Talcott. "The Place of Ultimate Values in Sociological Theory," *International Journal of Ethics* 45/3 (April 1935), pp. 282–316.
Perl, Eric D. *Theophany: The Neoplatonic Philosophy of Dionysius the Areopagite*. Albany: State University of New York Press, 2007.
Peskes, Esther. *Muḥammad b. ʿAbdalwahhāb (1703-92) im Widerstreit: Untersuchungen zur Rekonstruktion der Frühgeschichte der Wahhābīya*. Beirut: Franz Steiner, 1993.
Peters, Rudolph. "Administrators and Magistrates: The Development of a Secular Judiciary in Egypt, 1842-1871," *Die Welt des Islams* 39/3 (1999), pp. 378–397.
"The Codification of Criminal Law in 19th Century Egypt: Tradition or Modernization?," in J. M. Abun-Nasr (ed.), *Law, Society, and National Identity in Africa*, Hamburg: Buske, 1991, pp. 211–225.
*Crime and Punishment in Islamic Law: Theory and Practice from the Sixteenth to the Twenty-First Century*. Cambridge: Cambridge University Press, 2005.
"'For His Correction and as a Deterrent to Others': Meḥmed ʿAlī's First Criminal Legislation (1829-1830)," *Islamic Law and Society* 6/2 (1999), pp. 164–192.
"Ijtihād and Taqlīd in 18th and 19th Century Islam," *Die Welt des Islams*, New Series, 20/3–4 (1980), pp. 131–145.
Peterson, Erik. *Theological Tractates*, ed. and trans. Michael J. Hollerich. Stanford: Stanford University Press, 2011.

Pines, Shlomo. *Studies in Islamic Atomism*, trans. Michael Schwarz, ed. Tzvi Langermann. Jerusalem: Magnes Press, The Hebrew University of Jerusalem, 1997.

Plotin. *Traités 7-21*, trans. and ed. L. Brisso et al. Paris: Flammarion, 2003.

Post, Arjan. *The Journeys of a Taymiyyan Sufi: Sufism through the Eyes of ʿImād al-Dīn Aḥmad al-Wāsiṭī (d. 711/1311)*. Leiden and Boston: Brill, 2020.

Preuss, Horst Dietrich. "*ʾelîl*," in G. Johannes Botterweck and Helmer Ringgren (eds.), *Theological Dictionary of the Old Testament*, trans. John T. Willis. Grand Rapids: William B. Eerdmans, 1977, vol. 1, pp. 285–287.

Qadhi, Yasir. "'The Unleashed Thunderbolts' of Ibn Qayyim al-Ǧawziyyah: An Introductory Essay," in "A Scholar in the Shadow: Essays in the Legal and Theological Thought of Ibn Qayyim al-Ǧawziyya," ed. Caterina Bori and Livnat Holtzman, special issue, *Oriente Moderno* 90/1 (2010), pp. 135–149.

Quṭb, Muḥammad. *Jāhiliyyat al-qarn al-ʿishrīn*. Cairo: Dār al-Shurūq, 1412/1992.

Quṭb, Sayyid. *Fī ẓilāl al-qurʾān*. Cairo: Dār al-Shurūq, 1423/2003.

*Maʿālim fī al-ṭarīq*, 6th ed. Beirut and Cairo: Dār al-Shurūq, 1399/1975.

*Muqawwimāt al-taṣawwur al-islāmī*, 5th ed. Beirut and Cairo: Dār al-Shurūq, 1418/1997.

Rapoport, Yossef. "Royal Justice and Religious Law: *Siyāsah* and Shariʿah under the Mamluks," *Mamlūk Studies Review* 16 (2012), pp. 71–102.

al-Rāzī, Fakhr al-Dīn. *Tafsīr al-Fakhr al-Rāzī al-mushtahir bi-l-tafsīr al-kabīr wa-mafātīḥ al-ghayb*. Beirut: Dār al-Fikr, 1401/1981.

Renaud, B. "De la bénédiction du roi à la bénédiction de Dieu (Ps 72)," *Biblica* 70 (1989), pp. 305–326.

Rentz, George S. *The Birth of the Islamic Reform Movement in Saudi Arabia: Muḥammad Ibn ʿAbd al-Wahhāb (1703/4-1792) and the Beginnings of Unitarian Empire in Arabia*. London: Arabian Publishing, 2004.

Riḍā, Muḥammad Rashīd (ed.). *Majmūʿat al-rasāʾil wa-l-masāʾil al-najdiyya*. Egypt: Maṭbaʿat al-Manār, 1344[/1925].

Riexinger, Martin. *Sanāʾullāh Amritsarī (1868-1948) und die Ahl-i-Ḥadīs im Punjab unter britischer Herrschaft*. Würzburg: Ergon, 2004.

El-Rouayheb, Khaled. "From Ibn Ḥajar al-Haytamī (d. 1566) to Khayr al-Dīn al-Ālūsī (d. 1899): Changing Views of Ibn Taymiyya among non-Ḥanbalī Sunni Scholars," in Yossef Rapoport and Shahab Ahmed (eds.), *Ibn Taymiyya and His Times*. Oxford: Oxford University Press, 2010, pp. 269–318.

al-Rūmī, ʿAbd al-ʿAzīz b. Zayd et al. (eds.). *Muʾallafāt al-shaykh al-imām Muḥammad b. ʿAbd al-Wahhāb*. N.p.: Jāmiʿat al-Imām Muḥammad b. Suʿūd al-Islāmiyya, n.d.

Russell, Bertrand. *History of Western Philosophy and Its Connection with Political and Social Circumstances from the Earliest Times to the Present Day*. London: George Allen and Unwin, 1946.

Ruthven, Malise. *A Fury for God: The Islamist Attack on America*. London: Granta, 2002.

Saleh, Walid A. "Ibn Taymiyya and the Rise of Radical Hermeneutics: An Analysis of *An Introduction to the Foundations of Qurʾānic Exegesis*," in

Yossef Rapoport and Shahab Ahmed (eds.), *Ibn Taymiyya and His Times*. Karachi: Oxford University Press, 2010, pp. 123–162.

Ṣāliḥ, Muḥsin. "Qirā'a fī al-dawr al-da'wī wa-l-ḥarakī li-l-'allāma al-Ashqar," *al-Sabīl* (Jordan), August 22, 2012.

Salvatore, Armando. *Islam and the Political Discourse of Modernity*. Reading, UK: Ithaca Press, 1997.

al-Ṣan'ānī, 'Abd al-Razzāq. *Tafsīr al-qur'ān*. Riyadh: Maktabat al-Rushd, n.d.

al-Ṣan'ānī, Muḥammad b. Ismā'īl b. Ṣalāḥ al-Yamanī. *Dīwān al-Amīr al-Ṣan'ānī*. Cairo: Maṭba'at al-Madanī, 1384/1964.

*Taṭhīr al-i'tiqād 'an adrān al-ilḥād*, ed. Nāṣir b. 'Ā'iḍ b. Ḥasan, with *sharḥ* by 'Alī b. Muḥammad b. Sinān Āl Sinān. Mecca: Maṭābi' al-Waḥīd, 1425[/2004].

Sauer, Werner, and Jörg Büchli. "Truth," in Hubert Cancik and Helmuth Schneider (eds.), *Brill's New Pauly*, 2016. http://referenceworks.brillonline.com/entries/brill-s-new-pauly/truth-e12208610.

Sayed, Redwan. *Die Revolte des Ibn al-Aš'aṯ und die Koranleser: Ein Beitrag zur Religions- und Sozialgeschichte der frühen Umayyadenzeit*. Freiburg: Klaus Schwarz, 1977.

Schacht, Joseph. *The Origins of Muhammadan Jurisprudence*. Oxford: Clarendon Press, 1950.

Schmitt, Carl. *The Concept of the Political*, trans. George Schwab. Chicago and London: The University of Chicago Press, 2007.

*Political Theology: Four Chapters on the Concept of Sovereignty*, trans. George Schwab. Chicago and London: University of Chicago Press, 2005.

*Politische Theologie: Vier Kapitel zur Lehre von der Souveränität*. Berlin: Duncker & Humblot, 2004.

Schwedler, Jillian. *Faith in Moderation: Islamist Political Parties in Jordan and Yemen*. Cambridge: Cambridge University Press, 2006.

Seeskin, Kenneth. "Judaism and the Linguistic Interpretation of Faith," *Studies in Jewish Philosophy* 3 (1983), pp. 71–81.

al-Shāfi'ī, Abū 'Abdallāh Muḥammad b. Idrīs. *al-Umm*. Beirut: Dār al-Ma'rifa, 1410/1990.

Shākir, Aḥmad. *'Umdat al-tafsīr 'an al-ḥāfiẓ Ibn Kathīr*, 2nd ed. al-Manṣūra: Dār al-Wafā', 1426/2005.

al-Shawkānī, Muḥammad b. 'Alī. *Adab al-ṭalab wa-muntahā al-arab*. Ṣan'ā': Maktabat al-Irshād, 1419/1998.

*Fatḥ al-qadīr al-jāmi' bayna fannay al-riwāya wa-l-dirāya min 'ilm al-tafsīr*. Beirut: Dār al-Ma'rifa, 1428/2007.

*al-Rasā'il al-salafiyya fī iḥyā' sunnat khayr al-bariyya*, 2nd ed. Beirut: Dār al-Kitāb al-'Arabī, 1414/1994.

al-Shāyijī, 'Abd al-Razzāq b. Khalīfa (ed.). *Khiṭāb al-'allāma Bakr b. 'Abdallāh Abū Zayd khawla kitāb duktūr Rabī' b. Hādī al-Madkhalī aḍwā' islāmiyya 'alā 'aqīdat Sayyid Quṭb wa-fikrihi*. N.p.: Dār al-Tajdīd, 1417/1997.

al-Shaykh al-Mufīd. *Awā'il al-maqālāt fī al-madhāhib wa-l-mukhtārāt*, ed. M. Muḥaqqiq. Tehran, 1983.

Shepard, William. *Sayyid Qutb and Islamic Activism: A Translation and Critical Analysis of* Social Justice in Islam. Leiden: Brill, 1996.

"Sayyid Qutb's Doctrine of 'Jāhiliyya,'" *International Journal of Middle East Studies* 35/4 (2003), pp. 521–545.
Shihadeh, Ayman. *Doubts on Avicenna: A Study and Edition of Sharaf al-Dīn al-Masʿūdī's Commentary on the* Ishārāt. Leiden and Boston: Brill, 2016.
"The Existence of God," in Tim Winter (ed.), *The Cambridge Companion to Classical Islamic Theology*. New York: Cambridge University Press, 2008, pp. 197–217.
al-Shinqīṭī, Abū al-Mundhir. *Hal yushraʿu taʾyīd Mursī fī al-qarārāt al-dustūriyya al-akhīra?* December 3, 2012. www.ilmway.com/site/maqdis/FAQ/MS_7206.html (link no longer active).
al-Shinqīṭī, Muḥammad al-Amīn. *Aḍwāʾ al-bayān fī īḍāḥ al-qurʾān bi-l-qurʾān*. N.p.: Dār ʿĀlam al-Fawāʾid, n.d.
Ṣiddīq b. Ḥasan al-Qannawjī. *al-Dīn al-khāliṣ*. Beirut: Dār al-Kutub al-ʿIlmiyya, 1415/1995.
*Fatḥ al-bayān fī maqāṣid al-qurʾān*. Sidon and Beirut: al-Maktaba al-ʿAṣriyya, 1416/1996.
al-Sindī, Muḥammad Ḥayyāt. *Tuḥfat al-anām fī al-ʿamal bi-ḥadīth al-nabī ʿalayhī al-ṣalāt wa-l-salām*. Beirut: Dār Ibn Ḥazm, 1414/1993.
Sivan, Emmanuel. *Radical Islam: Medieval Theology and Modern Politics*. New Haven and London: Yale University Press, 1985.
Snell, Bruno. *The Discovery of the Mind: The Greek Origins of European Thought*, trans. T. G. Rosenmeyer. Cambridge, MA: Harvard University Press, 1953.
Sommer, Benjamin D. *The Bodies of God and the World of Ancient Israel*. Cambridge: Cambridge University Press, 2009.
al-Sudayyis, ʿAbd al-Raḥmān b. ʿAbd al-ʿAzīz. *al-Ḥākimiyya fī tafsīr aḍwāʾ al-bayān*. Riyadh: Dār al-Ṭayyiba, 1412[/1991–1992].
Surūr, Muḥammad b. Nāyif Zayn al-ʿĀbidīn. "Al-qism al-thāni, al-ḥalqa al-ūlā: al-jazāʾir min jamʿiyyat al-ʿulamāʾ ilā jabhat al-inqādh," *Majallat al-Sunna* 4 (Dhū al-Qaʿda 1410 / June 1990).
al-Suyūṭī, ʿAbd al-Raḥmān. *al-Ashbāh wa-l-naẓāʾir fī qawāʿid wa-furūʿ fiqh al-shāfiʿiyya*. Beirut: Dār al-Kutub al-ʿIlmiyya, 1403/1983.
*al-Durr al-manthūr fī al-tafsīr bi-l-maʾthūr*. Beirut: Dār al-Fikr, 1403/1983.
al-Ṭabarānī, Sulaymān b. Aḥmad. *al-Tafsīr al-kabīr*. Irbid: Dār al-Kitāb al-Thaqāfī, 2008.
al-Ṭabarī, Abū Jaʿfar. *The History of al-Ṭabarī*, ed. Ehsan Yarshater. Albany: SUNY Press, 1987–1999.
*Jāmiʿ al-bayān ʿan taʾwīl āy al-qurʾān*, ed. Maḥmūd Muḥammad Shākir and Aḥmad Muḥammad Shākir. Egypt: Dār al-Maʿārif, 1957.
*Taʾrīkh al-umam wa-l-mulūk*. Beirut: Dār al-Kutub al-ʿIlmiyya, 1422/2001.
al-Taftazānī, Saʿd al-Dīn. *Sharḥ al-ʿaqāʾid al-nasafiyya*, ed. Aḥmad Ḥijāzī al-Saqqā. Cairo: Maktabat al-Kulliyyāt al-Azhariyya, 1408/1988.
Ṭālib, Nūr al-Dīn (ed.). *Maqālāt al-Albānī*. Riyadh: Dār Aṭlas, 1421/2000.
al-Tamīmī, Abū al-Fidāʾ Ismāʿīl. *al-Minaḥ al-ilāhiyya fī ṭams al-ḍalāla al-wahhābiyya*, in Ḥamādī al-Radīsī [Hamadi Redissi] and Asmāʾ Nawīra [Asma Nouira], *al-Radd ʿalā al-wahhābiyya fī al-qarn al-tāsiʿ ʿashar: nuṣūs al-gharb al-islāmī numūdhajan*. Beirut: Dār al-Ṭalīʿa, 2008, pp. 169–270.

Thurston, Alexander. "Algeria's GIA: The First Major Armed Group to Fully Subordinate Jihadism to Salafism," *Islamic Law and Society* 24 (2017), pp. 412–436.

al-Tirmidhī, Abū ʿĪsā Muḥammad b. ʿĪsā. *al-Jāmiʿ al-kabīr*. Beirut: Dār al-Gharb al-Islāmī, 1996.

Tor, Shaul. "Parmenides' Epistemology and the Two Parts of His Poem," *Phronesis* 60/1 (2015), pp. 3–39.

Treiger, Alexander. "Avicenna's Notion of Transcendental Modulation of Existence (*taškīk al-wujūd, analogia entis*) and Its Greek and Arabic Sources," in Felicitas Opwis and David Reisman (eds.), *Islamic Philosophy, Science, Culture, and Religion: Studies in Honor of Dimitri Gutas*. Leiden and Boston: Brill, 2012, pp. 327–363.

Trigger, Bruce G. *Understanding Early Civilizations*. Cambridge: Cambridge University Press, 2003.

al-Ṭūfī, Sulaymān b. ʿAbd al-Qawī. *al-Ishārāt al-ilāhiyya ilā al-mabāḥith al-uṣūliyya*. Cairo: Dār al-Fārūq al-Ḥadītha, 1423/2002.

al-Tūnusī, Abū al-Wafāʾ. *al-Qawl al-jalī fī naqd al-dustūr al-tūnusī al-kufrī*. 1430/2009. www.ilmway.com/site/maqdis/MS_10411 (link no longer active).

Uffenheimer, Benjamin. "Myth and Reality in Ancient Israel," in S. N. Eisenstadt (ed.), *The Origins and Diversity of Axial Age Civilizations*. Albany: State University of New York Press, 1986, pp. 135–168.

ʿUmar ʿAbd al-Raḥmān. *Kalimat ḥaqq – murāfaʿat al-shaykh ʿUmar ʿAbd al-Raḥmān fī qaḍiyyat al-jihād*. N.d. www.ilmway.com/site/maqdis/MS_384 (link no longer active).

*Mawqif al-qurʾān min khuṣūmihi*. Cairo: Dār Miṣr al-Maḥrūsa, 2006.

van Ess, Josef. *The Flowering of Muslim Theology*, trans. Jane Marie Todd. Cambridge, MA, and London: Harvard University Press, 2006.

*Theology and Society in the Second and Third Centuries of the Hijra*, trans. Gwendolin Goldbloom. 4 vols. Leiden and Boston: Brill, 2017–2019.

Vasalou, Sophia. *Ibn Taymiyya's Theological Ethics*. New York: Oxford University Press, 2016.

Vernant, Jean-Pierre. *Les origines de la pensée grecque*, 4th ed. Paris: Presses Universitaires de France, 1981.

*The Origins of Greek Thought*. Ithaca: Cornell University Press, 1982.

Voll, John. "Linking Groups in the Networks of Eighteenth-Century Revivalist Scholars: The Mizjaji Family in Yemen," in Nehemia Levtzion and John O. Voll (eds.), *Eighteenth-Century Renewal and Reform in Islam*. Syracuse: Syracuse University Press, 1987, pp. 69–92.

"Muḥammad Ḥayyā al-Sindī and Muḥammad Ibn ʿAbd al-Wahhāb: An Analysis of an Intellectual Group in Eighteenth-Century Madīna," *Bulletin of the School of Oriental and African Studies*, 38/1 (1975), pp. 32–39.

Wagemakers, Joas. "Between Purity and Pragmatism? Abu Basir al-Tartusi's Nuanced Radicalism," in Rüdiger Lohlker and Tamara Abu-Hamdeh (eds.), *Jihadi Thought and Ideology*. Berlin: Logos, 2014, pp. 16–36.

"Contesting Religious Authority in Jordanian Salafi Networks," in Marko Milosevic and Kacper Rekawek (eds.), *Perseverance of Terrorism: Focus on Leaders*. Amsterdam: IOS Press, 2014, pp. 111–125.

*A Quietist Jihadi: The Ideology and Influence of Abu Muhammad al-Maqdisi*. New York: Cambridge University Press, 2012.

*Salafism in Jordan: Political Islam in a Quietist Community*. New York: Cambridge University Press, 2016.

"'Seceders' and 'Postponers'? An Analysis of the 'Khawarij' and 'Murji'a' Labels in Polemical Debates between Quietist and Jihadi-Salafis," in Jeevan Deol and Zaheer Kazmi (eds.), *Contextualising Jihadi Thought*. London: Hurst, 2012, pp. 145–164.

Wansbrough, John. *The Sectarian Milieu: Content and Composition of Islamic Salvation History*. Oxford: Oxford University Press, 1978.

Watt, W. Montgomery. *Islamic Philosophy and Theology: An Extended Survey*, 2nd ed. Edinburgh: Edinburgh University Press, 1985.

Wickham, Carrie Rosefsky. *Mobilizing Islam: Religion, Activism, and Political Change in Egypt*. New York: Columbia University Press, 2002.

Wiktorowicz, Quintan. "Anatomy of the Salafi Movement," *Studies in Conflict and Terrorism* 29/3 (April–May 2006), pp. 207–239.

Williams, Wesley. "Aspects of the Creed of Ahmad Ibn Hanbal: A Study of Anthropomorphism in Early Islamic Discourse," *International Journal of Middle East Studies* 34 (2002), pp. 441–463.

"A Body unlike Bodies: Transcendent Anthropomorphism in Ancient Semitic Tradition and Early Islam," *Journal of the American Oriental Society* 129/1 (2009), pp. 19–44.

Winter, Tim (ed.). *The Cambridge Companion to Classical Islamic Theology*. Cambridge: Cambridge University Press, 2008.

Wisnovsky, Robert. *Avicenna's Metaphysics in Context*. Ithaca: Cornell University Press, 2003.

Wolfson, Harry Austryn. *Philo: Foundations of Religious Philosophy in Judaism Christianity and Islam*. 2 vols. Cambridge, MA: Harvard University Press, 1947.

al-Yamānī, Abū Dharr al-Samharī. *Maʿālim al-wathaniyya fī al-dawla al-yamaniyya*. 1431[/2010]. www.ilmway.com/site/maqdis/MS_813 (link no longer active).

al-Zabīdī, Murtaḍā. *Tāj al-ʿarūs fī jawāhir al-qāmūs*. Beirut: Dār al-Fikr, 1414/1994.

Zaman, Muhammad Qasim. "The Sovereignty of God in Modern Islamic Thought," *Journal of the Royal Asiatic Society* 25/3 (July 2015), pp. 389–418.

al-Ẓawāhirī, Ayman. *al-Ṣubḥ wa-l-qindīl: risāla ḥawla zaʿm islāmiyyat dustūr bākistān*. N.d. www.ilmway.com/site/maqdis/MS_16441 (link no longer active).

Ziegler, Yael. *Promises to Keep: The Oath in Biblical Narrative*. Leiden: Brill, 2008.

Zīnū, Muḥammad b. Jamīl. *Kayfa ihtadaytu ilā al-tawḥīd wa-l-ṣirāṭ al-mustaqīm*. Riyadh: Dār al-Ṣumayʿī, 1415[/1994–1995].

Zollner, Barbara. *The Muslim Brotherhood: Hasan al-Hudaybi and Ideology*. New York: Routledge, 2009.

"Prison Talk: The Muslim Brotherhood's Internal Struggle during Gamal Abdel Nasser's Persecution, 1954 to 1971," *International Journal of Middle East Studies* 39 (2007), pp. 411–433.

Zysow, Aron. *The Economy of Certainty: An Introduction to the Typology of Islamic Legal Theory*. Atlanta: Lockwood, 2013.

# Index


1965 Organization, 214, 229, 245
ʿAbbāsids, 265, 325
ʿAbd al-Raḥmān ʿAbd al-Khāliq, 263, 287, 313
ʿAbd al-Raḥmān b. Ḥasan Āl al-Shaykh, 141, 270, 280
ʿAbdallāh b. Muḥammad b. ʿAbd al-Laṭīf, 114, 141–143
ʿAbdallāh b. Zayd Āl Maḥmūd, 270
ʿAbduh, Muḥammad, 174
Abū ʿAbdallāh b. Khuwayz Mandād al-Mālikī, 158–159
Abū al-Bakhtarī (Saʿīd b. Fayrūz al-Ṭāʾī), 131–132
Abū Bakr, 118, 134, 139–140, 277
Abū Hammām Bakr b. ʿAbd al-ʿAzīz al-Atharī. *See* al-Binʿalī, Turkī
Abū Ḥanīfa, 114, 147, 150, 155, 162, 211–212, 319. *See also* Ḥanafīs
Abū al-Ḥusayn al-Baṣrī, 60
Abū Muṣʿab al-Sūrī, 275, 291–293, 316
Abū Qatāda al-Filasṭīnī, 245, 276, 289–293
Abu Rabiʿ, Ibrahim, 229
Abū Yaḥyā al-Lībī, 2–4, 12, 306
Abū Yūsuf, 134
ʿAdī b. Ḥātim, 129–132, 135–136, 141, 143–144, 146–150, 161, 163, 179–180, 183, 185, 191, 193, 197, 208–209, 211, 227–228, 243, 253–260, 269, 271, 279, 283–284, 303
Afghanistan, 265, 292, 294, 296, 314
*ahl al-ḥadīth*, 6, 31, 59, 105, 128–129, 137, 153–154, 156, 159–162, 289, 319
*ahl al-raʾy*, 153–154, 156, 159–161
Ahl-i Ḥadīth, 31, 129, 140, 147, 149, 151, 168, 173, 209–211, 280, 319
Aḥmad b. Ḥanbal, 46, 59, 80, 112, 128, 142, 154–156, 277. *See also* Ḥanbalīs
al-Albānī, Muḥammad Nāṣir al-Dīn, 33, 263, 268, 284–287, 314
Āl Bū Ṭāmī, Aḥmad b. Ḥajar, 300
Algeria, 243, 245, 281, 290–293
ʿAlī b. Abī Ṭālib, 147, 277
Aligarh Anglo-Oriental College, 166
All-India Muslim League, 169, 202
al-Ālūsī, Maḥmūd, 303
Amir, Yehoshua, 8, 14, 21, 25–26, 28, 63, 71, 320
Amritsarī, Thanāʾ Allāh, 173, 210
Ancient Near East (ANE), 10–19, 52, 188, 234, 320
Anjum, Ovamir, 6, 39
Anṣār al-Sunna al-Muḥammadiyya, 300
anthropomorphism, 22, 25–27, 74
Arab Spring, 1, 3, 282
Aristobulos, 25
Aristotle, 22, 46, 55, 76
  on causation, 87
  *De Interpretatione*, 8
  *Posterior Analytics*, 43
  "*Theology of Aristotle*," 51
al-Ashʿarī, Abū al-Ḥasan, 65, 90, 109
Ashʿarīs, 14, 30, 56–57, 60, 76, 81, 106, 109, 114, 125, 142, 181, 243, 249, 297, 318
al-Ashqar, ʿUmar Sulaymān, 263–273, 280–281, 286–287, 309, 313
Assmann, Jan, 5, 7, 11, 18, 22, 76, 125, 234–235, 321, 324
Assyria, 18–19
Ataturk, 167, 277
autonomy, vii, 7, 9, 163, 170, 174, 196, 212, 234, 239, 285–286, 306, 320, 322, 326
Avicenna. *See* Ibn Sīnā
ʿAwda, ʿAbd al-Qādir, 237–239
Axial theory, 10–13, 18, 20–21, 23, 26, 28, 37, 50, 63, 66, 95, 202, 233–234, 320–321, 326. *See also* Jaspers, Karl
al-Azhar, 148, 237, 259, 267, 282, 300
Al-Azmeh, Aziz, 6, 42
ʿAzzām, ʿAbdallāh, 274, 314

Bacon, Francis, 233
al-Bahnasāwī, Sālim, 273
Bahrain, 1
Bakr Abū Zayd, 281
al-Bannā, Ḥasan, 209, 272–273
basileomorphism, 19, 22–23, 74
Baʿth/Baʿthism, 218, 264, 274, 285
al-Bayḍāwī, 283
al-Bayhaqī, Abū Bakr, 31, 133–136, 140, 147, 160
Belḥāj, ʿAlī, 292
Bellah, Robert N., 12
Bible, 172, 222
Bible, Hebrew, 5, 12, 18–20, 23–29, 63, 71, 74, 125, 230, 234, 322
*bidʿa*, 6, 97, 104, 116–117, 147, 309, 319
al-Binʿalī, Turkī, 1, 5
Bin ʿAlī, Zayn al-ʿĀbidīn, 2–3
Bin Lādin, Usāma, 296
Bodin, Jean, 308, 321
Brague, Rémi, 7
Brown, Nathan, 236–237, 239
Buber, Martin, 8, 18, 230
al-Bukhārī, 114, 131, 141
  *Khalq afʿāl al-ʿibād*, 81
Bunzel, Cole, 78, 96, 104

Calvert, John, 229
Castoriadis, Cornelius, 36–37
causation
  in Aristotle, 87
  of contingent existents (Ibn Sīnā), 56–57
  in human history, 35–37
  and Ibn Taymiyya's doctrine of *tawḥīd*, 87–93
  in Mawdūdī, 177–178, 190, 192–193, 198
  and meaning of *ḥikma* in Ibn Taymiyya, 106
Chinggis Khān, 207
Chittick, William, 53
Christian Reconstructionism, 5
Christians/Christianity, 10, 14–15, 60, 62, 72, 122, 129–132, 135, 139, 143, 146, 148, 150–151, 180, 185, 190–191, 227–228, 254, 257, 259–260, 282, 299
Clastres, Pierre, 13
Congress Party (India), 166–167
constitutions, 2–4, 237, 244, 272, 296, 309, 316–317, 326
  Egyptian, 284, 306
  Libyan Interim Constitutional Declaration, 2–3
Cook, Michael, 6, 101, 104, 108, 222
cosmogony, 16–18, 22–23, 52
creation, vii, 57, 61
  al-Ashqar on, 267
  in the Hebrew Bible, 23, 25
  human, 37
  of human acts, 85, 176
  Ibn ʿAbd al-Wahhāb on, 106, 109–110, 115
  Ibn Bāz on, 270
  Ibn Taymiyya on, 56, 58, 62–63, 66, 70–71, 75, 90–91
  Jawda on, 279
  *kalām* proofs of, 58, 61, 89, 304
  Mawdūdī on, 182–183
  and power, 19, 22–23, 52, 56, 69, 182–183
  in al-Qūnawī's doctrine, 53
  in the Qurʾān, 46
  Quṭb on, 219
  relation to Allāh, 42, 46, 52, 54, 62–64, 66, 72–75, 77, 297–298
  Sayyid Imām on, 295, 297–298, 302, 304–305
  Ṣūfī monists on, 62
  telos of, 70–71, 106, 270, 297
cult of saints, Muslim, 5, 30, 96–98, 100, 104, 109, 116, 122, 125, 179, 240, 314, 318, 320

*daʿwa*, 309, 314
  ʿAbd al-Raḥmān ʿAbd al-Khāliq on, 313
  Ḥasan al-Bannā on, 272
  Ibn Bāz on, 311
  Quṭb on, 224
  Sayyid Imām on, 313
al-Daʿwa al-Salafiyya, 282
Dāwūd b. ʿAlī al-Ẓāhirī, 154–156, 162
Déclaration des droits de l'homme et du citoyen, 308
DeLong-Bas, Natana J., 7, 103
democracy, viii, 1, 6, 32, 34, 38, 240, 242, 244–245, 273, 275–276, 281–282, 285–286, 291–292, 294, 296, 307–310, 312–314, 316–317, 320, 322
Deobandis, 166, 205, 210
al-Dhahabī, 80, 142, 212
Diffelen, Roelof Willem van, 98–99, 102–103, 105
al-Dijwī, Yūsuf, 78
Durayd b. al-Ṣimma, 151

Egypt, 3, 31, 36, 74, 84, 213, 218, 227, 229, 237–239, 241, 245–246, 258–259, 262, 264, 266–267, 272, 282, 284, 300–301, 306, 312, 316, 326
  ancient, 1, 18, 22, 24, 80, 185, 189–190

elections, 32, 244
  FIS participation in, 290
  Ibn Bāz on, 286
  Islamist participation in, 245
  Jabhat al-Nuṣra on, 316
  al-Maqdisī on, 288
  Mawdūdī on participation in, 272, 309
  Muḥammad Surūr on participation in, 282, 287
  quietist salafīs against participation in, 285
  salafī jihādīs on, 286
  Sayyid Imām on, 307, 309–310, 313, 315
Enlightenment, 13, 47, 170, 231, 233–234, 323–324

faith. *See īmān*, nature of
Fakhry, Majid, 40
Faraj, ʿAbd al-Salām, 326
fascism, 244, 322, 324
Fighting Vanguard, Syrian, 273–276, 280, 289–291, 293
Fiqī, Muḥammad Ḥāmid, 280
Firʿawn/Pharaoh, 1–2, 12, 18, 79–80, 114, 185, 189–190, 197, 222, 279
FIS (Front islamique du salut), 281–282, 286, 290–292
*fitna*, 93, 107, 128, 203, 209
*fiṭra*, 42
  in Ibn Taymiyya's writings, 43, 46, 48, 252
  in Quṭb's writings, 219–220
  in Sayyid Imām's writings, 302
FLN (Algeria), 281
Frankel, Joseph, 308
Free Officers (Egypt), 267
Friedmann, Yohanan, 172

Gauchet, Marcel, 12–13, 233
al-Ghazālī, Abū Ḥāmid, 6, 45, 247, 299–300, 311
al-Ghubāshī, Sayyid, 282–285, 288, 312
GIA (Groupe islamique armé), 243, 245, 290–291
Gideon (Biblical figure), 230, 234
Goitein, S. D., 24
Goldziher, Ignaz, 6, 30, 96–97, 102, 116, 319
Greece, ancient, 10–11, 14–20, 320

Ḥadīd, Marwān, 274, 276
al-Ḥajjāj, 132
al-Ḥajjāwī, 112, 142
*ḥākimiyya/ḥākimiyyat*, 31–32, 165–166, 205, 209, 232, 234–235, 239–240, 243, 245, 258–259, 262, 267, 269, 281, 288, 306, 319
  calque from English 'sovereignty,' 165, 230
  in the doctrine of the Fighting Vanguard, 276, 278–279
  in the doctrine of Jabhat al-Nuṣra, 315–316
  al-Huḍaybī on, 246–248, 250, 255, 258, 261
  in Mawdūdī's writings, 182–183, 189, 195–196, 199–200, 211–212
  in Quṭb's writings, 213–217, 222–229
  and *tawḥīd al-ulūhiyya*, 242, 315–316
  ʿUmar ʿAbd al-Raḥmān on, 260–261
al-Ḥalabī, ʿAlī b. Ḥasan, 33
Halbertal, Moshe, 9, 26, 28, 63, 74, 105
Hallaq, Wael, 31, 128, 152–156, 158–159, 162–163, 319
Ḥamās, 263–264
Hammurabi, 264
Ḥanafīs, 112, 114, 126, 149–150, 154–156, 159, 176, 209, 211–212, 236. *See also* Abū Ḥanīfa
Ḥanbalīs, 6, 31, 42, 59, 93, 100, 126, 128–129, 154–156, 161, 319. *See also* Aḥmad b. Ḥanbal
al-Harawī, al-Anṣārī, 65–66
Harrās, Khalīl, 300
Hartmann, Richard, 97, 102
Hartung, Jan-Peter, 169–172, 174–175, 207, 231
al-Ḥawālī, Safar, 269, 308, 312
Hawting, Gerald, 4–5, 133
al-Haytamī, Ibn Ḥajar, 142–143
Hegel, 10, 173
Hesiod, 25, 27
*ḥikma*, 88, 106, 297
Hindus/Hinduism, 166–168, 197, 201, 232
Hobbes, Thomas, 323–324
Homer, 22, 25, 27
  *Iliad*, 22
Hoover, Jon, 62, 78, 87
al-Huḍaybī, Ḥasan, 32, 245–259, 261, 268–269, 271, 311
  on Qurʾān 9:31, 256–258
  on the *shahāda*, 249–251, 258

Iblīs/Satan, 45, 71, 82–84, 114, 288–289
Ibn ʿAbbās, 79–80, 139, 268–269
Ibn ʿAbd al-Barr, 31, 133, 136, 140, 145, 147, 158–159, 161–162
Ibn ʿAbd al-Wahhāb, Muḥammad, 5, 7, 30–31, 96–125, 127, 159, 164, 172, 175, 178, 181, 183–184, 186, 188,

205–206, 221, 241, 250–253, 263, 269–270, 277–280, 297, 299–300, 304–306, 310, 319. *See also* Wahhābīs
on faith and acts, 115–116
*Kitāb al-tawḥīd*, 98, 103, 105–106, 108, 141, 270, 297, 300
on the meaning of *ilāh*, 108–110, 176–177
on the *shahāda*, 110–116, 179
on *taqlīd*, 117–119, 141–143
Ibn ʿAbd al-Wahhāb, Sulaymān, 112, 119
Ibn Abī Laylā, 132
Ibn al-Amīr. *See* al-Ṣanʿānī, Muḥammad b. Ismāʿīl
Ibn ʿAqīl, 154
Ibn al-ʿArabī, Muḥyī al-Dīn, 53, 55, 62–63, 65, 117
Ibn al-Ashʿath, 132–133
Ibn Bāz, ʿAbd al-ʿAzīz, 263, 270–271, 273, 286–287, 296, 309–312
Ibn Ḥazm, 2, 133, 155–160, 212, 255
Ibn Kathīr, 81, 142, 247, 254, 265, 269–270, 280
Ibn Masʿūd, 135, 155, 162
Ibn Muʿammar (ʿUmar b. Nāṣir b. ʿUthmān), 143
Ibn Qayyim al-Jawziyya, 31, 33, 99, 104, 108, 142–143, 158–159, 270, 277, 280, 307
*Iʿlām al-muwaqqiʿīn ʿan rabb al-ʿālamīn*, 140, 143, 158, 160, 325
*Madārij al-sālikīn*, 65
on *qiyās*, 160
*al-Ṣawāʿiq al-mursala ʿalā al-jahmiyya wa-l-muʿaṭṭila*, 59
on *ṭāghūt*, 248
on *taqlīd*, 140
Ibn Rajab, 142
Ibn Rushd, 42
Ibn Sīnā, 55–58, 231, 247
on efficient and final causation, 87–88, 90–91
on necessary and contingent being, 48, 51–52
*al-Risāla al-aḍḥawiyya fī al-maʿād*, 26, 76–78
on universals, 46
Ibn Suḥaym, Sulaymān b. Muḥammad, 111–112
Ibn Taymiyya, viii, 6–7, 9–10, 14–15, 26, 29–34, 38–95, 105, 113, 116–117, 127, 136–140, 142–143, 153–154, 164, 178–179, 181, 183–184, 186, 192, 194, 212, 221, 225, 230–231, 240–242, 251–252, 265–266, 269–271, 277–280, 288–289, 294–300, 304–307, 312, 315, 318–322
*al-ʿAqīda al-wāsiṭiyya*, 97, 103, 115, 300
*Bayān talbīs al-jahmiyya*, 44, 60
*Darʾ taʿāruḍ al-ʿaql wa-l-naql*, 46, 76, 247
on faith and acts, 114–116, 249, 258
*Faṣl fī al-tawḥīd*, 88–93
*Fī al-jamʿ bayna ʿulūw al-rabb ʿazza wa-jalla wa-bayna qurbihi min dāʿīhi wa-ʿābidīhi*, 64–69, 298
influence on al-Ṣanʿānī, 120–124
the *kawnī/sharʿī* distinction, 82–84, 86, 99, 188, 295
*Kitāb al-īmān*, 230, 257
on the meaning of *ʿibāda*, 196
on the meaning of *ilāh*/the *shahāda*, 107–110, 112, 177, 250, 294, 303
*Minhāj al-sunna al-nabawiyya*, 315
Mongol fatwās, 326
*Mukhtaṣar naṣīḥat ahl al-īmān*, 43, 46, 48
and the origins of Wahhābism, 96–100, 102–104
possible influence on Mawdūdī, 205–207
possible influence on Sayyid Quṭb, 229
on *qānūn waḍʿī*, 247
*Rafʿ al-malām ʿan al-aʾimma al-aʿlām*, 138
*al-Risāla al-tadmuriyya*, 283
*Risālat al-ʿubūdiyya*, 83, 229
*Sharḥ futūḥ al-ghayb*, 86
on *taqlīd*, 129, 136–140, 269
on universals, 43–45, 53–55, 58, 92
Ibn ʿUmar, 139
Ibrāhīm/Abraham, 92, 157, 191
his disputation with Namrūd, 188–190, 220, 223, 234
ʿĪd, Sayyid, 287
Imām al-Sharīf, Sayyid, 245, 293–317, 326
definition of *ilāh*, 294
definition of *tawḥīd al-rubūbiyya*, 297–298, 302–303
definition of *tawḥīd al-ulūhiyya*, 298, 303–304
on democracy, 307–309
on the Egyptian constitution, 306
*al-Jāmiʿ fī ṭalab al-ʿilm al-sharīf*, 244, 295–296
on Ibn Bāz, 286, 309–312
on the *manhaj* of jihād, 312–315
on Mawdūdī, 309
on the meaning of the *shahāda*, 299–300
and modern salafism, 300–301
on monolatry as the telos of creation, 297
on Qurʾān 9:31, 303
and Quṭb, 294, 306

Imām al-Sharīf, Sayyid (cont.)
on relation between *tawḥīd* and jihād, 294–295
on relation between *tawḥīd al-rubūbiyya* and *tawḥīd al-ulūhiyya*, 298–299, 304–305
on Safar al-Ḥawālī, 312
*Taḥqīq al-tawḥīd bi-taḥkīm sharī'at rabb al-'ālamīn*, 295
on theonomy and the *shahāda*, 305–306
on theonomy and *tawḥīd al-rubūbiyya*, 303
on theonomy and *tawḥīd al-ulūhiyya*, 305
*al-'Umda fī i'dād al-'udda*, 292–294
*īmān*, nature of, 79, 257
al-Huḍaybī on, 249–250
Ibn 'Abd al-Wahhāb on, 114–115, 142
Ibn Taymiyya on, 81–82, 84
Iraq, 265–266, 325
IS. *See* Islamic State (organization)
'Īsā/Jesus, 10, 62, 72, 122, 129–130, 139, 191, 198, 252, 254–255, 257
al-Iṣfahānī, al-Rāghib, 184
Isḥāq b. Rāwayhi, 155
ISIS. *See* Islamic State (organization)
Iṣlāḥ Party (Yemen), 281, 285, 287
Islamic State (organization), 2–3, 243, 325–326
Islamic University of Medina, 263, 270
Ismā'īl Pasha, 267
Israel, ancient, 8, 11, 14, 16, 18–21, 28, 230, 320
Israelites, 1, 79, 101, 197
*istiḥsān*, 134, 161–162, 283

Jabhat al-Nuṣra (Syria), 315–316
*jāhiliyya*, 2–4, 72, 99, 105, 109, 119, 123, 127, 145, 151, 171, 175, 177–179, 195–196, 199, 207, 214, 221–222, 224–225, 245, 247, 251–253, 260, 276, 282, 303, 306–307
*jahl* (exculpatory ignorance), 254, 285
Jahm b. Ṣafwān, 51, 59, 80
Jahmites (*jahmiyya*), 46, 60, 64–66, 80–81
al-Jamā'a al-Islāmiyya (Egyptian), 148, 259
al-Jamā'a al-Salafiyya al-Muḥtasiba, 287
Jamā'at al-Muslimīn (aka al-Takfīr wa-l-Hijra), 246, 266
Jamā'at-i Islāmī, 31, 167, 209, 309
Jameelah, Maryam, 229
Jam'iyyat 'Ulamā'-i Hind, 166–167
Jaspers, Karl, 10–11. *See also* Axial theory
Jawda, 'Abd al-Nāṣir, 265, 273, 275–281, 289
Jews/Judaism, 8, 10, 14–15, 21, 24–25, 129–132, 135, 143, 146, 148, 151, 185, 190–191, 227–228, 255, 257, 259–260, 299
jihād
'Abd al-Qādir 'Awda on, 238
in Afghanistan, 291–292
in Algeria, 290
al-Ashqar on, 265
Ibn al-Ash'ath's revolt, 132
Ibn Taymiyya on, 93
al-Maqdisī on, 288
Mawdūdī on, 204
against the Mongols, 207
in Qur'ān 9:24, 233
Quṭb on, 227
in salafī jihādī doctrine, 32, 240, 242, 245, 288, 292, 312–315, 317
Sayyid Imām on, 294–297, 304, 312–315
Jihād Organization (Egyptian), 243, 245, 293, 301, 326
al-Jīlānī, 'Abd al-Qādir, 86
Jordan, 33, 241, 264, 266, 271, 274
Jubayr b. Muṭ'im, 48
Junayd, 66

*kalām*, 14–15, 39, 42, 59–61, 63–64, 71, 83, 88–91, 93–94, 125, 169, 176, 288, 300, 304
apophatism, 59, 61
epistemology, 49
ontology, 55
proofs of Allāh's existence, 40–41, 48–49, 57–58, 60–61
Kant, Immanuel, 7, 323
Kelsen, Hans, 324
Kenite hypothesis, 24
Khārijites, 66, 81, 277, 290
Khilāfat movement, 166
kingship, sacral, 12, 16, 18–19, 27, 320, 324
Krabbe, Hugo, 324
Kubrā, Najm al-Dīn, 49
Kūfa, 130–132, 162
Kuwait, 261, 263–264, 268, 271, 281, 287–288, 316

Lacroix, Stéphane, 262–263
Laoust, Henri, 97–98, 100
Libya, 1–3, 316
Libyan Islamic Fighting Group, 1
Locke, John, 308, 323
Luther, Martin, 172

al-Madkhalī, Rabī', 281
Mālik b. Anas, 138, 155, 161. *See also* Mālikīs

Mālikīs, 112, 126, 133, 136, 139, 154–156, 158–159, 252, 267. *See also* Mālik b. Anas
Mamlūks, 207, 236, 266
al-Maqdisī, Abū Muḥammad, 38, 242, 287–289, 293, 313–314
March, Andrew F., 200, 215
Margalit, Avishai, 9, 26, 28, 63, 105
Marxism, 171, 231
Mashʿal, Khālid, 263
*maṣlaḥa*, 267, 312, 320
Massignon, Louis, 83, 97
Māturīdīs, 14, 81
Mawdūdī, Abū al-Aʿlā, vii–viii, 31–33, 163, 165–212, 214–216, 220–225, 227, 242–244, 264, 267, 272–273, 278–280, 287–288, 315, 317, 319. *See also ḥākimiyya/ḥākimiyyat*
  and the Ahl-i Ḥadīth, 209–211
  al-Huḍaybī's critique of, 246, 250–253, 257, 261
  on Ibn Taymiyya, 206–208, 266
  influence on Sayyid Quṭb, 220, 227–229, 238–239
  on jihād, 204, 208
  on the meaning of *ilāh*, 177–184
  on the meaning of the *shahāda*, 176, 206–208, 266
  and modernity, 167–174, 230–235
  on nationalism, 166, 202, 232
  on Qurʾān 9:31, 179–180, 183, 185, 191, 193, 197, 208, 259
  on *taqlīd*, 180, 193, 197, 208–211
  Sayyid Imām's critique of, 296, 309–310
Medina, 99, 101, 104, 107, 138, 213
Melchert, Christopher, 128, 156
Mitchell, Richard P., 238–239
Mongols, 207, 247, 265–266, 269, 326
monism, 51–53, 55–56, 62–63, 65, 69, 75
Muʿādh b. Jabal, 134, 160, 163, 299
Mubārak, Ḥusnī, 2–3
al-Muhallab b. Abī Ṣufra, 133
Muḥammad b. Ibrāhīm Āl al-Shaykh, 268–270, 301
Mujāhid b. Jabr, 81
Murjiʾa, 65, 81, 114–116, 286
Mursī, Muḥammad, 3
Mūsā/Moses, 1, 21, 190, 197, 223
Muslim Brotherhood, 3, 6, 31–32, 209, 213, 218, 225, 229, 237–238, 240–241, 243, 245–246, 261–264, 268, 271–273, 282, 289–293, 312–313. *See also* Fighting Vanguard, Syrian; Muslim Brotherhood, Syrian; Ṣaḥwa
Muslim Brotherhood, Syrian, 274–276, 280–281, 291
Muṣṭafā, Shukrī, 246, 266
*mutʿa*, 139
Muʿtazila, 14, 29, 40, 47, 56, 59–60, 69
al-Muzanī, 162

Nadhīr Ḥusayn Dihlawī, 147–151
Nadwī, ʿAlī, 229, 231
Najjāriyya, 65
Namrūd/Nimrod, 188–189, 223–224, 234
Napoleonic Code, 267
al-Nasafī, Najm al-Dīn, 176
Naṣr, Muḥammad Mūsā, 284
Nasr, Seyyed Hossein, 169, 230
Nasr, Seyyed Vali Reza, 167–170, 174, 209, 212, 230, 232
National Alliance for the Liberation of Syria, 275, 293
nationalism
  Arab, 213, 244
  Egyptian, 213
  Mawdūdī on, 167, 202, 212, 232
  Quṭb on, 233
Neoplatonism, 23, 26, 43, 46, 51, 53, 59, 87–88, 90–91, 231
al-Nīsabūrī, al-Ḥasan b. Muḥammad, 148
*niyya*
  al-Huḍaybī on, 254, 256–257
  Ibn Bāz on, 310
  Sayyid Imām on, 311–312
Nūḥ/Noah, 62–63, 187–188, 191
Nuʿmānī, Muḥammad Manẓūr, 205–208
Nūr Party (Egypt), 282

Otto, Rudolf, 47–48, 50
Ottomans, 166, 235–236, 266, 277

Pakistan, 167, 169, 202, 267, 296, 309, 317
Pānīpattī, Qāḍī Thanāʾ Allāh, 150–151
Parmenides, 18, 20–23, 55
Parsons, Talcott, 36
Pathankot, 204–206
Peshawar, 292–293, 296
Peskes, Esther, 102–103, 115
Peters, Rudolph, 128
Pharaoh. *See* Firʿawn/Pharaoh
philosophy, 169. *See also* Aristotle; Greece, ancient; Hegel; Ibn Rushd; Ibn Sīnā; Kant, Immanuel; Neoplatonism; Parmenides; Plato; Plotinus; pre-Socratics; Socrates; Xenophanes
  Greek, 13, 17, 20–22
  Ibn Taymiyya on, 42, 59
  Islamic, 79

philosophy (cont.)
  Late Antique, 29
  Mawdūdī and, 174
  medieval Abrahamic, 14
  modern Western, 174
  positivistic reaction against, 36
  and *tawḥīd al-ulūhiyya*, 93–94, 231
Plato, 23, 27, 43, 51
Plotinus, 22, 51
predetermination, 85, 183, 297, 300
pre-Socratics, 18, 20–22
Proof from Mutual Obstruction (*dalīl al-tamānu'*), 88–90
Punjābī, Muḥammad Shāh, 147

al-Qadhdhāfī, Muʿammar, 1–3
al-Qadhdhāfi, Sayf al-Islām, 2
al-Qā'ida, 1–4, 243, 275, 294–295, 306, 315
Qatāda b. Di'āma, 81
Qatar, 270, 300
*qiyās* (analogy)
  in jurisprudence, 128, 134, 153–156, 159–162, 211–212
  in logic, 43, 50
  in theology, 42, 44–46, 58
al-Qūnawī, Ṣadr al-Dīn, 53–55
Qur'ān
  2:258, 188–189, 220, 223
  5:44, 127, 268–269
  9:31, 5, 126–127, 129–136, 139–141, 143–144, 146–152, 156, 163, 179–180, 183, 185, 191, 193, 197, 208–209, 211, 227–229, 243, 253–256, 258–260, 269, 271, 279, 283–285, 290, 303
  21:22, 88–89, 91, 93
  43:84, 80–81, 226, 294
  51:56, 91, 105–107, 277, 297, 302
Quraysh, 4, 288–289
al-Qurṭubī, 283
Quṭb, Muḥammad, 262, 269
Quṭb, Sayyid, vii, 31–33, 165–166, 200, 212–235, 238–239, 242–244, 248, 259, 264, 266–267, 269, 272–273, 277–278, 281, 294, 306, 309, 312, 315, 317, 319. *See also ḥākimiyya/ḥākimiyyat*
  and the '1965 Organization,' 214, 229, 245
  debt to Mawdūdī, 31, 165, 214–215, 220, 227–229
  al-Huḍaybī's critique of, 245–247, 250–253, 255, 257–259, 261
  influence on the Fighting Vanguard, 274, 276, 279–280
  influence on the FIS, 282
  influence on salafī jihadism, 287–288
  influence on 'Umar 'Abd al-Raḥmān, 259–261
  later disapproval of his early writings, 225
  on the meaning of *ilāh*, 224–226
  and modernity, 230–235
  possible influence of Ibn Taymiyya, 229–230
  quietist salafī views on, 281
  Quṭb-salafī fusion, 32, 261–263
  on the *shahāda*, 216–217, 219, 224–225
  on the vanguard, 214, 217–218

Ra's al-Khayma, 300
*ra'y*, 76, 128, 134, 145, 151–152, 160–162, 211–212, 325
  contrasted with *riwāya*, 158–159
al-Rāzī, Fakhr al-Dīn, 49, 60, 148, 151, 247, 259
Rentz, George, 100–101
Rib'ī b. 'Āmir, 234
Riexinger, Martin, 150, 168, 173–174, 231
Rousseau, Jean-Jacques, 308
Ruthven, Malise, 170, 231

al-Sādāt, Anwar, 266, 301, 326
Ṣaḥwa, 261–263, 269, 281, 286–288, 308, 312
salvation, 50, 70, 113, 301
Salvatore, Armando, 232
al-Ṣanʿānī, Muḥammad b. Ismāʿīl, 30, 104, 119–124, 241
al-Sanhūrī, 'Abd al-Razzāq, 267
Sanhūrī Code, 264, 267–268
Saudi Arabia, 96, 240–241, 261–263, 268–270, 281, 287, 316
Sayyid Aḥmad Khān, 173–174
Schacht, Joseph, 128, 131, 152–153, 162
Schleiermacher, Friedrich, 47–48, 50
Schmitt, Carl, 233, 321–325
secularization, viii, 32, 34–35, 174, 199, 233–235, 239, 319–323, 326
al-Shāfiʿī, 130, 134–135, 139, 142, 155–156, 162. *See also* Shāfiʿīs
Shāfiʿīs, 81, 112, 126, 133, 141–142, 154–156, 160. *See also* al-Shāfiʿī
Shāh 'Abd al-'Azīz, 149
*shahāda*
  al-Huḍaybī on, 250, 258
  Ibn 'Abd al-Wahhāb on, 110–116
  Ibn Bāz on, 271
  Ibn Taymiyya on, 70–71, 75, 84, 115
  Mawdūdī on, 206–207, 266
  Muḥammad b. Ibrāhīm on, 269

Quṭb on, 216–217, 225
al-Ṣan'ānī on, 121, 123–124
Sayyid Imām on, 297, 299–301, 305, 326
Shāh Ismā'īl, 147, 149–150, 172
al-Shahrastānī, Abū al-Fatḥ, 76
Shākir, Aḥmad Muḥammad, 265, 269–270, 280, 284
Shākir, Maḥmūd Muḥammad, 269, 280
al-Shawkānī, Muḥammad, 31, 129, 144–147, 151, 154, 158–159, 255, 280, 319
al-Shaykh al-Mufīd, 60
Shepard, William, 213, 225, 229
Shī'īs, 72
*bāṭinīs*, 69
Ismā'īlīs, 51
Qarmaṭīs, 56
Zaydīs, 146–147
al-Shinqīṭī, Abū al-Mundhir, 3
al-Shinqīṭī, Muḥammad al-Amīn, 270, 278–280, 283, 303
*shūrā*, 282, 307
Ṣiddīq Ḥasan Khān, Muḥammad, 151, 259–260, 280
al-Sindī, Muḥammad Ḥayāt, 99–101
*siyāsa* jurisdiction, 236, 265
Socrates, 21, 27
state
'Abd al-Qādir 'Awda on, 237
archaic, 11–13, 16
Carl Schmitt on, 321–325
Islamic, 169, 271, 277, 315, 326
Jawda on, 278
Mawdūdī's conception of, 173, 203, 212, 278–279
modern nation-state, viii, 12, 32, 212, 236, 238–239, 244, 322–324, 326
the Muslim Brotherhood and, 218
Nasserist, 218
Plato's *Republic*, 27
salafī jihādī conception of, 325–326
Sayyid Imām on, 315
'society against the state,' 13
theonomic, 234
Sudan, 296
Ṣūfism, 30, 125
antinomian, 72, 318
Chistī, 166
cultic practices, 73
and eighteenth-century revivalism, 102
epistemology, 49
Ḥanbalī, 65–66, 86, 94
heterodox, 50
Ibn 'Abd al-Wahhāb on, 109–110
Jabhat al-Nuṣra on, 315
Jawda on, 277
Mawdūdī on, 197, 202
monist, 51–53, 55–56, 62, 65, 69, 75
Naqshbandī, 99
and *tawḥīd al-ulūhiyya*, 79, 82–86, 230, 304
Sufyān al-Thawrī, 128
Sufyān b. 'Uyayna, 161
Surūr, Muḥammad, 281–282, 286–287
Syria, 2, 218, 243, 262, 264–266, 272–276, 280–281, 289–291, 293, 315, 325

al-Ṭabarī, 80, 131, 269
*ṭāghūt*, 106–107, 127, 248, 279–280, 284–285, 289, 292, 295, 310, 324
al-Ṭaḥāwī, 113
*takfīr*, 317
Abū Muṣ'ab al-Sūrī on, 293
'Adnān 'Uqla's against the Syrian Muslim Brotherhood, 275–277, 280, 293
al-Ashqar on, 268
al-Huḍaybī on, 254, 258
Ibn 'Abd al-Wahhāb on, 107, 111, 114, 116
Ibn Taymiyya on, 70, 112
al-Madkhalī on, 281
Muḥammad Surūr on, 287
of rulers, 254, 258, 266, 268
salafī jihādī, 242, 286
al-Ṣan'ānī on, 120
slaughter to not-Allāh as grounds for, 111–112
Sulaymān b. 'Abd al-Wahhāb on, 112
Wahhābī, 98
al-Takfīr wa-l-Hijra. *See* Jamā'at al-Muslimīn
al-Tamīmī, Ismā'īl, 252–253
al-Ṭarṭūsī, Abū Baṣīr, 314, 316
al-Ṭūfī, Najm al-Dīn, 130
Tunisia, 316

*'ubūdiyya*, 233
in Ibn Bāz's writings, 271
in Ibn Taymiyya's writings, 68, 70
possible influence of Ibn Taymiyya on Quṭb, 230
in Quṭb's writings, 213, 215–221, 227–228, 239
in al-Ṣan'ānī's writings, 123
'Umar 'Abd al-Raḥmān, 148, 259–261
'Umar b. al-Khaṭṭāb, 118, 134–135, 139, 155, 161
Umayyads, 130, 132–133
universals, 43, 45–46, 53–54, 92

Unmoved Mover, 22, 25, 87
ʿUqla, ʿAdnān, 274–276, 281, 293
al-ʿUtaybī, Juhaymān, 287
ʿUzayr/Ezra, 191, 257

Vasalou, Sophia, 39
Vernant, Jean-Pierre, 16–18
Voll, John, 99–104
al-Wādiʿī, Muqbil b. Hādī, 285, 287

Wagemakers, Joas, 242, 316
*waḥdat al-wujūd*. *See* monism
Wahhābīs, viii, 5–6, 9, 30, 78, 95–105, 116, 119–120, 124–125, 140, 143, 196, 240–241, 262, 269, 279, 300, 311–312, 314, 318. *See also* Ibn ʿAbd al-Wahhāb, Muḥammad
Walī Allāh, Shāh, 101, 143–145, 147–150, 210
Wiktorowicz, Quintan, 242
Wolfson, Harry Austryn, 14

Xenophanes, 20, 25

*yāsaq/yāsā*, 247, 265, 269
Yemen, 119, 129, 134, 146–147, 160, 245, 281, 285, 299, 316

Ẓāhirīs, 133, 154–155, 157, 160–161, 212
Zaman, Muhammad Qasim, 165
al-Ẓawāhirī, Ayman, 293, 296, 317
Zeus, 16, 22
al-Zindānī, ʿAbd al-Majīd, 285
Zīnū, Muḥammad b. Jamīl, 301
Zoroastrians, 69

For EU product safety concerns, contact us at Calle de José Abascal, 56–1°,
28003 Madrid, Spain or eugpsr@cambridge.org.

www.ingramcontent.com/pod-product-compliance
Ingram Content Group UK Ltd.
Pitfield, Milton Keynes, MK11 3LW, UK
UKHW020435250925
463284UK00026B/1140
*9781108817493*